# A Review
# of
# Wildlife
# Management

**James M. Peek**

*College of Forestry, Wildlife and Range Sciences*
*University of Idaho*

Prentice-Hall, Englewood Cliffs, New Jersey 07632

*Library of Congress Cataloging-in-Publication Data*

Peek, James M. (James Merrell)
    A review of wildlife management.

    Bibliography.
    Includes index.
        1. Wildlife management—North America.
I. Title.
SK361.P45 1986        639.9        85-19125
ISBN 0-13-780552-7

Editorial/production supervision and
    interior design: Fay Ahuja
Cover design: Ben Santora
Manufacturing buyer: John Hall

Printed in the United States of America

10   9   8   7   6   5   4   3   2   1

ISBN 0-13-780552-7   01

Prentice-Hall International (UK) Limited, *London*
Prentice-Hall of Australia Pty. Limited, *Sydney*
Prentice-Hall of Canada Inc., *Toronto*
Prentice-Hall Hispanoamericana, S.A., *Mexico*
Prentice-Hall of India Private Limited, *New Delhi*
Prentice-Hall of Japan, Inc., *Tokyo*
Prentice-Hall of Southeast Asia Pte. Ltd., *Singapore*
Editora Prentice-Hall do Brasil, Ltda., *Rio de Janeiro*
Whitehall Books Limited, *Wellington, New Zealand*

# Contents

# Preface

Several decades ago I learned that if there were any scientific merit in conservation, it should be found in the written record. The written record of wildlife conservation is found primarily in bulletins, reports, journals, and other easily misplaced publications, rather than in books. The record is extensive, difficult to locate, and often in publications long out-of-print and not readily available to the practicing biologist and the student. Although it is impossible to cover this diverse field adequately in one volume, it *is* possible to review major aspects. I therefore offer this volume as a starting point to the student who aspires to acquire a knowledge of this field. I also believe that this book may be useful to the professional who wishes to review an area with which he or she has lost contact.

Consequently, this volume breaks old rather than new ground, but it will not substitute for the original written record of which serious students will avail themselves. I have included actual data whenever possible so that the reader can appraise its value as well as my assessment. I have also provided a list of people who have contributed prominently to various subjects by using one or more of their publications. It is important to know who the contributors are.

Although early wildlife biologists contributed much to the fundamental theoretical basis of wildlife conservation, there is now an extensive literature provided by ecologists who do not consider themselves wildlife biologists. This literature is often ignored by the practicing wildlife biologist who may think it has little use in management. Nevertheless, the theoretical basis is beginning to find a useful niche, as the person who attempts to manage predator—prey relationships or is involved in management of waterfowl harvests can well appreciate. Theory in habitat relationships may seem less useful at this time, but there is still a need to consider it. I have included a section on theoretical considerations in many of the chapters, which should at least serve as a reminder to the reader that there is a framework or model upon which conservation can rest if we endeavor to find it. This model is important because it lends rigor and objectivity to the conservation effort.

The field of wildlife management is infested with "experts" who espouse pat, simple answers to complex problems. I believe there is a lack of appreciation of the written record, a tendency to continue to use long outdated practices, and a tendency to underestimate the general level of understanding of the interested public of what constitutes sound conservation practice. It is my hope that this volume will interest informed nonprofessionals, who might use it to urge more efficient management, or to understand better what is being done.

The reader will rapidly discover that not all species or species groups are covered. In some cases I have omitted their consideration because there was insufficient or no information available, while in others, the issue could be addressed adequately by consideration of another species. Although I have tried to give coverage to all North American regions, it should be evident that my experience in the Northwest and upper Midwest colors the material.

The only group considered separately is waterfowl. This group deserves special attention because their management is unique. Also, waterfowl management sets the pace for much of the rest of wildlife management. Conversely, nongame species, upland birds, and big game are deliberately not addressed separately but are treated under subject areas as appropriate. We tend to categorize ourselves as one type of biologist (nongame, big game, endangered species, etc.) but many of the fundamental relationships apply across these rather artificial designations. For instance, the biologist dealing with nongame forest birds may well develop expertise in management of old-growth coniferous forests, which has application in big game management as well.

I could not have written a volume such as this without acquiring a deep appreciation for all the people who have pursued wildlife conservation activities through to the publication of their efforts. Many of these publications are a result of individual initiative rather than as a requirement of the job in this field. Also, I wish to thank many colleagues who provided insights and encouragement. I take no credit for producing much that is new—only for assembling the efforts of others. I believe that those of us who deal with the conservation of wild, free-ranging creatures advance our understanding incrementally, slowly building upon the experience of our predecessors in an effort to do better on behalf of wild creatures. If you believe as I do that the way we treat other living things is a measure of our humanity, then you must realize that wildlife conservation is a social issue of ultimate importance.

I thank the following colleagues for providing comments on portions of this volume: P. D. Dalke, J. E. Applegate, E. G. Bizeau, L. L. Eberhardt, E. D. Garton, G. E. Gruell, R. J. Gutierrez, M. G. Hornocker, L. L. Irwin, L. J. Nelson, L. F. Neuenschwander, S. R. Peterson, K. P. Reese, W. B. Sidle, M. R. Vaughan, and

F. H. Wagner. R. D. Taber provided a solid, critical review of this manuscript, and I remain eternally grateful for his efforts. This volume benefited from comments of my students, and their insights serve as a reminder that each new generation is infinitely better prepared than I. Carmen Savage typed many drafts of this manuscript, and I am eternally grateful. I greatly appreciate the skill, patience, and craftsmanship of Fay Ahuja and Elaine Luthy, whose editing skills are unmatched in my experience.

As with many who were educated at Montana State University, Donald C. Quimby had a profound influence upon my attitudes about the profession of wildlife management. It was through him that I grew to appreciate the value of the written word, and I have retained a desire to convey that value to others in the twenty-five years since I left his formal guidance.

*J. M. P.*

# 1

# What Is Wildlife Management?

## THE DEFINITION

Over half a century ago Aldo Leopold (1933) provided a classic definition of *game management* as "The art of making the land produce sustained annual crops of wild game for recreational use." Let us begin by examining this definition to see how appropriate it is in the current situation. This time-tried definition has six major concepts that must be considered: game, art, land, sustained crops, wild, and recreational use.

*Game*, the first concept, typically connotes the hunted and trapped species, including the upland birds, waterfowl, small game mammals, and larger mammals that are within the purview of management. To these, we may add the furbearers that are trapped. However, we are now concerned also with endangered and threatened species, which certainly are not subject to exploitation but for which management is needed. We also have directed our attention to nongame species, such as raptors and passerines, that are subject to the nonexploitative, appreciative forms of recreational use. It appears, therefore, that the term *game* has become too restrictive a term for the many kinds of species under management today. Consequently, the term *wildlife* has come to the fore. Indeed, while the North American Wildlife Policy (D. L. Allen 1973) defines *wildlife* to mean, most commonly, free-living animals of major significance to humans, we now direct attention to very insignificant forms as well.

Perhaps the Endangered Species Act of 1969 provides the broadest and most useful definition of wildlife: any free-living species from invertebrate to vertebrate. While this may seem to many to be far too generous a definition, it does recognize

1

that we are in fact spending attention on virtually all species, from the "nonre-sources" of Ehrenfeld (1976), to the common mallard and white-tailed deer. In-deed, Aldo Leopold himself directed his attention to the variety of forms regardless of whether they were classical game or not, in his famous *Sand County Almanac* (1949).

*Art*, the second concept to be examined, is defined in *Webster's New Collegiate Dictionary* of 1976 as "the conscious use of skill and creative imagination in the production of esthetic objects." Wildlife management is obviously an art, although some would prefer that it be considered as a composite, applied science. Since we have broadened our definition of wildlife, we must certainly admit to the ultimate esthetic value of this resource. Art implies that the whole of wildlife management encompasses not just the basic biology, nor just the ecology of the species, but also a sociological aspect as well. The practice of management contains as an inherent element an understanding of and interaction with humans. And it is in this arena that the greatest challenges to our skill, creativity, and imagination exist. However, this is not to ignore the need to apply these attributes also to understanding the biology and ecology of wildlife—rather, the current conditions have set a priority for us.

*Land*, the third concept, implies habitat, and habitat indeed is the underpin-ning requirement of all fauna. Without habitat we will not have wildlife, and the inclusion of land in the definition is mandatory. While the term *land* may be con-sidered too broad again, the rest of the definition refines the statement.

*Sustained crops*, the fourth concept, may suggest harvest, but in fact implies viable, reproducing populations. This means retention of genetic diversity, as well. However, there are now situations that come under the broad purview of manage-ment where single species are not the subject of management, but rather entire faunal ecosystems. In such situations, successional trends in species are recognized and any given species may wax and wane according to changing habitats. Then, too, the whole area of animal damage control is involved. This implies alleviating damage but still retaining the wildlife. Therefore, the sustained annual yield concept, as it applies to individual species, appears to exclude some current practices in wildlife management.

Considering the fifth concept, *wild*, it is clear that wild fauna are certainly the objects of management, although we sometimes investigate constrained and other-wise confined populations. However, if we subscribe to the previously advanced idea that the esthetic values of wildlife are paramount, and that habitat is a funda-mental prerequisite, then the term *wild* has to be included in the definition. Although A. Leopold (1933) recognized that all wildlife were in some way artificialized be-cause of the overriding and all-pervasive influences and capabilities of humans, a measure of our success in wildlife management is the degree to which we succeed in keeping wild things wild.

The sixth concept, *recreational use*, implies that there has to be a human value that is readily recognized, whether it be exploitative or nonconsumptive, before we practice wildlife management. As a matter of well-recognized fact, however, we have been providing and manipulating habitats for a variety of nonvalued species in the course of providing for highly desired forms like elk and geese. As our awareness of the interrelatedness of species grows, it seems clear that, rather than permitting such incidental results to stem from our focus on other species, we need to practice knowledgeable management directed at the whole complex.

The primary objection to including recreational use in a viable definition of wildlife management stems from ethical considerations. Must human beings always be self-centered when they become involved with other living forms? The broad concept of stewardship is involved in this issue. It is very likely that one very explicit measure of our humanity is how we treat other living forms of seemingly little value, or perhaps even of negative value, to us. This is particularly true when extinction of a species results not simply from ignorance of the consequences of our actions, but from our purposeful greed and selfishness. So it seems best to omit the seemingly innocuous phrase, *recreational use*, from our definition so that we will not be tempted to exclude any form of wildlife from our management activities. And, for the more pragmatic reason, that no one knows which species we may find valuable next, anyway.

Thus, an up-to-date definition resolves to this: wildlife management is the art of making the land produce wildlife. And we don't have to have a reason for this because we have the obligation.

## THE PRACTICE

Wildlife management in many areas is equated with such mundane chores as raising or lowering water levels, planting food patches, tending checking stations, and mollifying the local sportsmen's group.

Wildlife management indeed includes these activities, but they are only the most superficial manifestations of a far larger task. Management, in fact, requires far-sighted and innovative people who can recognize the basic problems that exist for each population and who can devise means of obtaining information that is directly applicable to solving these problems. This requires wildlife managers who are familiar with the literature and history, and who have the basic technical competence to acquire information and to explain to administrators and the concerned public what is occurring and what is planned for each population.

The trend these days is for people who are not interested in research to be relegated to the task of "management" when, in fact, the task of wildlife management includes research, its application, and its articulation to the public. The complete wildlife manager should not only be an experienced field biologist who maintains an inquiring attitude, but should also be adept in the field of public relations. The manager should be able to recognize where the application of research findings is most appropriate. This is a very difficult and complicated task at which not many of us are truly adept.

It is probably a truism that most people who enter the wildlife field tend to be those who are not interested in human relations, but would rather be associated with the solitude and the peace and quiet they may find in the field. There is a rude awakening for those who enter the field and are not aware that they will be dealing as much or probably more with people than they will with wildlife. The task of wildlife management is therefore much greater, much more pressing, and much more important than just the task of the wildlife researcher. The conservation of wildlife resources is the issue at stake.

As the administrative structures of wildlife management become more intricate and complex, wildlife managers often find themselves caught in a dilemma between the policy their agency follows and what they feel may be most beneficial to the resources in question. On the one hand, we have individuals who essentially subjugate themselves to "agency policy" and follow it blindly without regard to the basic question of whether it is good for a population or not. At the other extreme, we have individuals who are willing to quit their agency and strike out on their own for the cause of what they feel to be correct management for a population. It has been argued that since the public most often pays for our jobs, we should do the public's bidding, whatever that may be, as regards the management of a resource. It has also been argued that we should take the bull by the horns and provide the effective leadership, whatever the consequences, in order to effect proper management for a population. Very frequently, wildlife management is conducted in a highly emotional setting where cool heads are few and far between.

Errington's (1947) fallacy of misplaced concreteness very often enters the picture and we are forced to look at side issues rather than basic questions. (We attribute cause and effect where such is not the case, as in predator-prey relationships.) Very often, an action program is forced upon us before we have information to justify its implementation. It is likely that the major share of the conservation dollar is placed in action programs, whether they be in more intensive law enforcement, restocking, or season changes, more because of external pressures than because a documented reason exists. In many instances, game managers are forced to live with such pressures, and the implications can be serious to them personally. Rationalizations of one sort or another very often are the only way out.

However, wildlife management is not done in a vacuum devoid of data analysis and recommendation from the basis of information. It is well to view wildlife management as a long-term task and to recognize that people are not infallible and that most have the interest of the resource at heart. With this in mind, one can view successes and failures as part of a continuum in the process toward more effective management and one can survive with personal honor in the comfort, however small, that there will be another chance to attack the problem in the future with the added insight that has grown out of experience.

## OUR OBLIGATIONS

It should go without saying that a wildlife biologist's primary obligation is to the resource rather than to the agency or to the people who pay his or her salary. This should always be kept in mind when resource decisions are being formulated. However, this does not mean that agency policy and public acceptance will not be considered and, in fact, human beings and their agencies being what they are, are always subject to change. It should also be remembered that what we feel to be in the best interest of the resource is based on current information, which always needs to be updated and which, in fact, may be inadequate or misleading. Still, the common denominator for successful wildlife management is information—pertinent information about the population and its habitat that is salable to administrators and to the public.

Romesburg (1981), writing in the *Journal of Wildlife Management*, suggested that wildlife science may be headed in the direction of a major upheaval because of the reliance on unreliable knowledge. Unreliable knowledge is defined as a set of false ideas that are mistaken for actual knowledge. Wildlife management is fraught with a heavy load of "common knowledge," bound in tradition and either unverified or unverifiable. The end result is that facts are often not distinguished from nonfacts, and management proceeds on an unsubstantiated basis.

Another obligation of the wildlife biologists is to strive for a defensible management program that rests on a solid data base. Given the lack of time and personnel to do the job, this appears at first to be an ideal rather than an attainable goal. However, if we are to consider ourselves scientists, we have to develop a data base that withstands the scrutiny of the most critical eye, and that can be verified. Romesburg's (1981) argument—that skill in use of scientific method will include formulation of useful hypotheses, designing efficient experiments, and verification—needs to be heeded. This argument applies to managers as well as researchers.

A wildlife biologist is an educator as well. Inevitably people will seek the biologist out when unknowns concerning wildlife arise. In many instances, simple answers to simple questions are all that is needed, but there are frequently times when controversial issues require a more complex response. In case of controversy, the role of the biologist is primarily to provide information. If biologists are to be advocates, then the best way is to conduct themselves in as professional a manner as possible. One may reason that as an advocate for wildlife, one has to be sure that the best knowledge concerning wildlife is made available to the public. Our obligation is to be as unbiased and professional in serving the resource as we can, and this is not an easy task.

It is a drastic mistake to think that generalizations that may be applicable only in the broadest sense will suffice for a highly critical and concerned group of lay people. Wildlife managers can do more harm than good when they speak in generalities that do not fit the specific audience they are addressing. When one is standing in front of a group of people who are well aware that one's information is lacking, there is no crime in saying "I don't know."

The basis for a successful wildlife management program starts fundamentally with information from the field, initially about habitat condition, trend, and plans for the future, and secondly about population performance within the context of habitats. To be able to recognize potential management opportunities based on such information, and to articulate successfully and persuasively a proposed management alternative to administrators and the lay public are among the obligations of the wildlife manager.

The basic human values of patience, technical competence, an inquiring mind, a reasonable degree of gregariousness, and, most of all, goodwill are special prerequisites for a successful wildlife manager.

## MANAGEMENT WITHIN THE CONTEXT OF HABITAT

Leopold pointed out that habitat management is probably the highest level of wildlife management. That is, when wildlife management had evolved beyond hunting restrictions, predator control, establishment of refuges, and artificial stocking aspects to a consideration of habitat and associated issues, this represented the most intensive form of wildlife management.

Some wildlife populations occupy apparently secure habitats, such as national forests, where wildlife populations by law have to be considered in any land management activity or change in practice. Even in such instances, however, wildlife populations are still subject to adverse habitat manipulation that favors other interests, and to external influences such as pesticides, acid rain, and other pollutants. Still, if we understand the specific habitat requirements of the species that are using these lands, plus the effects of artificially produced and natural trends in habitat change, we may view such situations as relatively secure.

In such instances, the ongoing monitoring of a population that is being exploited in one fashion or another, most likely through hunting, becomes the biggest task of the wildlife manager, and habitat considerations may be relegated to a secondary role. The cropping of a population may then be adjusted to account for variations in survival of young, or to accommodate other uses that may modify the time-honored concept of sustained yield from a reasonably stable breeding stock, for example, by requiring lower exploitation in order to provide better opportunities to observe wildlife. As more and more diverse interests are brought to bear on wildlife resources and conflicts increase, this particular task of the game manager becomes more complex and requires such modifications as closing roads or adjusting hunting seasons or adjusting hunting unit boundaries from the traditional or established patterns.

The sociological implications will, as our population expands and interest in wildlife resources intensifies, inevitably dictate even more than now the nature of wildlife management in the future. Nevertheless, the time-tried concepts and ideas that are associated with habitat retention and manipulation will be the basic underpinning for all wildlife management programs. Within this context, however, the intensive uses, both exploitative and nonconsumptive, constitute the major problem that the wildlife manager faces.

## WILDLIFE AS A PART OF OTHER LAND USES

It is axiomatic that if we do not have the habitats that wildlife need we will not have the wildlife, and therefore none of the uses will prevail, whether they be exploitative or nonconsumptive. Our public and private wildlands are subject to intensive management, exploitation, and modification, and wildlife managers must be prepared to integrate their specific task of maintaining wildlife populations into other land-use practices. This may be the greatest challenge to wildlife managers in the future. In order to effectively integrate management of any given population into management of other resources on a given land unit, wildlife managers will first of all have to acquire and maintain the cooperation of other resource managers, which means they will need to understand the problems of those managers as well as their own. Specific definitions of the habitat requirements for a population will be needed, as well as knowledge of the adaptability of species to changes that may occur in their habitats.

The wildlife manager will need more than ever public understanding of the special problems in each area in order to minimize misunderstandings among interested lay people as to his or her own problems and management objectives. It is in this area that wildlife management has been notably least successful.

However, wildlife managers have also been notoriously unsuccessful at integrating wildlife management programs into other land management activities. Although we have recognized that intensive agriculture, while initially benefiting certain species, ultimately will drastically reduce populations, and we have made many efforts to acquaint the public, the farmer, and the appropriate authorities about this, that which we predicted would happen did in fact happen. Economics of the agricultural industry have indeed dictated the pattern.

In forest management, we have been somewhat more successful in some areas, notably the Southeast, in integrating wildlife management into intensive timber management practices, but we still require more specific definitions of habitat requirements and relationships to cutting systems if we are to be most effective.

## ON GENERALIZATIONS IN WILDLIFE MANAGEMENT

Oliver Wendell Holmes once said, "The chief end of man is to frame general propositions and no general proposition is worth a damn" (Flesch 1966:132). The wildlife manager often finds her- or himself in a similar predicament. Each wildlife population exists within a set of unique circumstances, yet we try too often to apply generalities to its management. Where management is not intensive and hunter harvest or other uses are not too much in conflict, we can live with the generalization. However, as demands upon a given population increase, we then need to know its specific habitat requirements, its population performance, and how it differs from the one over the hill.

As long as wildlife managers are few and far between, there is no question that they will have to rely upon information obtained from one population to manage a multitude of others as well. The other alternative is to rely on minimal information that can be obtained from each population of interest as time and money allow. However, we must recognize the basically local nature of wildlife management, both in space and time, if each population is to be effectively managed.

The consequences of relying on minimum information, or using one population to guide management for a multitude of others, are that trends and their causes will not be identified as rapidly as needed. Thus, "management by hindsight" is a not uncommon situation. Such a situation often causes problems in public relations, and opens the door to pressures to initiate ill-conceived programs of, for instance, predator control or reintroductions. While, once again, this can be a reflection of our inadequacies in bringing our cause most effectively to the public, it may also be a reflection of the lack of attention many wildlife managers place on being familiar with literature and management from other areas, and of the inadequacy of the data base for the population in question.

As with many other disciplines, wildlife management goes through fads. Thus, we see a whole region relying primarily on browse or grass utilization for which condition survey information is used as the basic underpinning of a management program, and a technique developed for one type of plant community is broadly applied to many others where it subsequently is proven to be unsuitable. Or, a land management practice such as sagebrush spraying begins to receive intensive interest, and other factors limiting to wildlife tend to receive less attention as a result, even though in many populations other factors are much more important.

It was not uncommon to hear a wildlife manager state that pesticides were probably the cause for decline in a given population when in fact there was no real evidence that such was the case. The clear-cutting controversies of the recent past have also been used as fallbacks when we were not certain of what was happening to a wildlife population, but we suspected that it was declining. And intensive grazing by livestock is always a useful fallback when we have no specific information at hand to help us judge the trend in a population. These circumstances are brought out mainly to illustrate that we do need specific information for each population if we are to adequately manage it, and we cannot rely on judgment calls from the desk no matter how popular the answer given may be in the context of the contemporary situation.

In other words, a wildlife manager should not be overwhelmed by the pressures of the human surroundings, but should be able to retain an inquiring attitude. All too often, readily observed problems have deep-seated and complex roots, both in the ecological and sociological context. An ability to distinguish between supported statements and fiction, and among traditions, fads, and reality, is a special problem of wildlife management.

## HISTORICAL ASPECTS OF WILDLIFE MANAGEMENT

George Santayana once said, "Those who cannot remember the past are condemned to repeat it," and in wildlife management, it is abundantly clear that this is indeed the case. Not only do we all too often ignore the historical record, written and otherwise, but we also frequently are unaware of the activities of our counterparts in other areas. This situation causes us to fall into the syndrome of duplicating often inefficient management, and it tends to stifle initiative and imagination, which could lead to more rapid progress in important areas. The results then attest to the venerable cliché, that history tends to repeat itself.

Of course, wildlife managers are probably no more prone to this fault than any other group whose management is conducted within a highly complex social arena where tradition plays an important role. However, we need to keep in mind that the nature of our work often requires us to pursue avenues of investigation and management alternatives that haven't been tried locally and for which traditions may be lacking. It is axiomatic that each local situation does present unique circumstances which, although duplicated in generality over and over, also are singularly unique in detail. Still, there is no question that a broader understanding of the historical record of the management situation in a given area, and of the issue in its broad context, is an often neglected aspect of wildlife management

This entire book may be considered a partial historical record of the progress in wildlife management, primarily in North America. It is one statement of progress in wildlife conservation.

### Leopold's Sequence

Aldo Leopold (1933) documents a long-term history of wildlife management, dating back to ancient China where culture of fish occurred (and where, it is interesting to note from Marco Polo's records, Kublai Khan developed policies regarding harvest, protection of game, and provision of food and cover for birds in the thirteenth century A.D.). The sequence described by Leopold (1933), which seems to be generally valid is as follows:

1. Restriction of hunting
2. Predator control
3. Reservation of game lands
4. Artificial replenishment
5. Environmental controls

An interesting history that illustrates a variant of this sequence involves the timber wolf of northeastern Minnesota. Efforts to establish a reservation in the form of the Superior Forest Reserve preceded restrictions on the take, but subsequently did restrict exploitation by restriction of access. In the case of predator management, restriction of hunting and predator control became one and the same, as humans are the predators. The wolf was classified as a threatened species because of drastic reduction of its range in the United States under the provisions of the Endangered Species Act of 1969. This in turn led to attempts to reintroduce populations into northern Michigan in 1974 (W. L. Robinson and Smith 1977). Most recently, declines in deer populations in northern Minnesota have been recognized as a danger to the wolf, and thus interest in habitat improvement for white-tailed deer has been motivated out of concern for the wolf (Mech 1973). Efforts to reintroduce the wolf into suitable habitats are also underway. Thus, Leopold's sequence, with some modification, appears to be present even today.

### Hickey's Phases

Hickey (1974) recognized three phases in wildlife conservation: awareness, action, and an ethical phase he calls "the rise of ecology." The *awareness phase* involves recognition of real or imagined catastrophes involving wildlife, then identification of the causes or culprits. The catastrophes could be extermination, as in the case of the passenger pigeon; near extermination, as in the case of the bison; or drastic reduction, as in the case of the peregrine falcon. The culprits often include market hunters, predators, pesticides, pollution, clean-farming, and exploitative logging practices. In recent years, the culprits have been technological processes more frequently than individuals, as in the past.

The *action phase* involves nine readily discernible steps, which expand Leopold's famous sequence: prohibition, atonement, monasticism, education, control, subsidy, public ownership, free enterprise, and science and research.

The *prohibition* step involves restrictions on the take, but extends to other areas such as prohibiting importation of endangered species, prohibiting harassment of wildlife by outdoor recreation vehicles, and banning certain chemicals such as monosodium fluoroacetate (compound 1080) in predator control.

*Atonement* involves reservation of game lands, artificial replenishment, and artificial feeding. Often, especially in the area of artificial replenishment, we have extended our efforts beyond a rational ecological basis, such as introducing exotics. However, we also insist on artificial replenishment of stocks in areas where a breeding population exists, a practice that can be described as, at best, an alternative to proper management (elk) and, at worst, a subsidization of the hunter at great expense (pheasants).

Artificial feeding as an atonement for replacing lost habitat has merits under some circumstances as in the case of the elk herd at Yakima, Washington, which was cut off from winter range by agricultural and highway development. But more often artificial feeding reflects a deeper problem involving habitat and serves only to defray attention to correcting the problem.

Nevertheless, atonement reflects human efforts to account for our transgressions and serves to focus interest and attention on problems we create for wildlife.

*Monasticism,* as used by Hickey (1974), covers Leopold's third step, reservation of game lands. The implication of this step is that we are going to set aside lands strictly for wildlife, thereby depriving ourselves of the opportunity to use them for other purposes. In actuality, we find such lands used for a variety of other purposes, but at least wildlife achieves a high priority on them.

*Education* is a step not listed by Leopold. It is responsible for increasing levels of understanding about wildlife. Hickey points out that the movement centered originally on efforts to recognize species as exemplified by the field guides. The field guide approach has been successful mostly for wild birds and to a lesser extent for wildflowers. Education may be extended to include the broad fields of public relations and conservation education today.

The fifth step involves *control*, whether it be of predators, vermin, fires, or insects. The area of control brings perhaps the greatest conflict between perceived human needs, both for ourselves and for wildlife, and the resources themselves. For every case where benefits accrue, one may cite a failure, and suffice it to say that this overall effort to influence nature will continue to be a source of concern into the foreseeable future.

*Subsidies*, the sixth step, include bounties. Bounties have long been recognized as an ineffectual tool. While we used to bounty everything that ate desirable species from ground squirrels (they eat grass and dig holes that can break the legs of unwitting livestock) to golden eagles and wolves, we are now doing away with this once-popular practice.

The seventh step, *public ownership*, is related to Leopold's reservation of game lands. Acquisition of lands has been notably successful in waterfowl management, and in retaining winter ranges for big game.

The eighth stage, *free enterprise*, involves commercial shooting preserves, private wildlife sanctuaries, and wildlife tours. One special aspect involves hunting by nontribal individuals on Indian reservations. All activities are on the increase, and can generally be considered to bode well for the wildlife resource, since these activities require that healthy populations be maintained.

The ninth and final step involves *science and research*. Hickey (1974) points out that the idea that research on wildlife pays did not emerge until the 1920s, but it may be added that there is still considerable skepticism. However, the need to acquire relevant information that can be used to evaluate and modify management of wildlife is generally recognized as an essential ingredient in management. In the broad context, management involves preservation as well as use or modification, but this area is certainly imperfectly understood.

Hickey's third phase is entitled the "rise of ecology." The theme that undergirds this phase stems back to the concept of our role as steward over the earth's resources. It also means an evolution from thinking of wildlife management simply as a discipline oriented toward manipulating nature for human benefit to understanding its broader role in the natural mechanisms involved in ecosystems, and the effect of humans on them, and therefore on the wildlife resource. While some wildlife biologists are among a minority of people who may have matured to this level, one does not have to experience the ongoing problems of wildlife management for very long to realize that this phase is just beginning. We are still, by and large, in the awareness and action levels.

However, there are some outstanding examples of progress to this third phase. The programs to conserve endangered species, concern for nongame species and predators, and even the discussions of "nonresources" that are of no discernible human value, attest to this. And it is worthwhile to point out that the third phase can include aspects of the preceding phases. Habitat manipulation will obviously be necessary in management of endangered species, and in restoration and reclamation of habitat. But the *context* in which this tool and others are practiced will become more important as more of us mature into the broader thinking involved in the "rise of ecology."

### The North American Wildlife Policy and the American Game Policy

Progress in wildlife management in North America can be seen by comparing the American Game Policy of 1930 with the North American Wildlife Policy of 1973. These policies were initiated by the American Game Protective Association and the Wildlife Management Institute. Many of the laws, policies, and organizations that have guided wildlife management over the last half-century were recommended in the original American Game Policy. Aldo Leopold was the chairman of ✗ this committee, which presented its report at the seventeenth American Game Conference in 1930. This report was being formulated at a time when wildlife management was just becoming recognized as a profession in its own right in the United States. Leopold (1930) recognized that the need to increase production of game was paramount, and that the Game Policy had to deal with the wheres, hows, and whoms.

The American Game Policy dealt with seven fundamental suggestions which ✗ have over the ensuing decades been implemented to some degree.

The first suggested action was to extend public ownership and management of game lands as far as land prices and available funds permit. The committee recognized wildlife as a "thin crop" that often might best be conserved if land acquisitions for uses such as forestry and recreation were integral to the acquisition for wildlife. This recommendation has been carried out extensively in the form of the National Wildlife Refuge System, and in state-owned and leased wildlife management areas. Additionally, the Wilderness Preservation System may be considered beneficial to wildlife, as the 1973 policy recognized. D. L. Allen (1973:16) reaffirmed the need to retain public property in public ownership, concluding that it is "the estate of many generations, to which value will steadily accrue." Attempts to transfer publicly owned lands into private owenrship occur at irregular intervals, as in the 1940s (DeVoto 1947), and again in the 1980s (Leroy and Eiguren 1980).

The first basic action that A. Leopold (1930) brought forth indeed recognizes the need to retain and increase the land base upon which wildlife may reside. The kinds and amounts of wildlife, and the values and uses that we place upon them, must receive a different and lower priority than the fundamental need for habitat.

The second basic action was to recognize the landowner as custodian of public game on all privately owned land. The original committee was simply recognizing that regardless of who owns the wildlife, ultimate control rests with the landowner who manages the habitat. A. Leopold (1930) urged that economic incentives be provided to encourage the private landowner to practice wildlife management. This alternative to posting land has not proven very successful in the current trend of big business agriculture, which includes such practices as draining, cover removal, pesticide applications, and vast expanses of crop monocultures. Since the most productive land is generally privately owned, the need to coordinate wildlife habitat management with agriculture becomes more and more urgent as the available private land base dwindles. Inadequate wildlife management on private lands is the most pervasive failure that continues, exacerbated by the outright loss of land for all resource management purposes. The basic lack of incentive for the private landowner to practice some form of habitat management is the root of the issue, recognized over 50 years ago in the original policy. The 1973 policy reaffirmed this situation and recommended that trespass control be more effective, that economic and other kinds of incentives for managing wildlife be formulated, that better integration of habitat development in soil and watershed conservation programs be encouraged, and that damage by wildlife to crops be recognized as a legitimate concern and be accommodated.

The third basic action advocated was simply termed *experiment*, to encourage people to practice game management. The three parties identified, landowner, sportsman, and public, all needed to be brought into the management practice if it was to be fully effective. The recognition of the social context in which game management was practiced in 1930 is still in need of clarification. More international cooperation in migratory bird management, and better cooperation between states was advocated. While today a framework for cooperation in virtually all aspects of wildlife management is in place in the form of organizations, agreements, committees, councils, workshops, symposia, and other ways too numerous to mention, the degree to which each accomplishes something tangible on the ground is still at issue.

The fourth basic action suggested in 1930 was to train people for the profession of wildlife management, and to make "game" a profession like forestry, agriculture, and other aspects of applied biology. Initially, wildlife management was taught as forest zoology or economic zoology in the early 1900s at Cornell University, the University of Michigan, and elsewhere. However, Aldo Leopold was appointed to teach wildlife management at the University of Wisconsin in 1933 (Errington 1948). The Cooperative Wildlife Research Units were established in 1935 to educate wildlife biologists and conduct research. Certification of wildlife biologists, implemented by the Wildlife Society in 1978, is a further effort to professionalize wildlife management. Most certainly, training of wildlife biologists has been implemented adequately in the United States.

The fifth basic action that A. Leopold (1930) suggested was *find facts*. This basically meant that information was needed to determine ways to practice the new profession of game management. Enactment of the Federal Aid to Wildlife Restoration Act of 1937 was legal recognition that research into problems of wildlife management was needed, as well as habitat acquisition. However, the way in which this act was funded has had a great deal to do with the direction and progress of wildlife management. Funded through hunter expenses, the act provided the states and the federal government with monies to manage and study game species, those the hunters had vested interest in.

It is to be emphatically emphasized that both policies recognized the highest values of wildlife were the nonconsumptive values. Even if the early report was couched primarily in terms of hunted game, the assumption that other wildlife would benefit from sound management was implicit. However, over the years funding has dictated that game rather than wildlife be given priority. Not until the 1970s was nongame management sufficiently identified as an integral part of the entire wildlife management program to be funded. The incentive for funding of nongame management came again from the federal government through the National Forest Practices Act of 1976, Federal Land Management and Policy Act of 1976, and the National Environmental Policy Act of 1969. These acts required that all wildlife species be considered in land management. The Threatened and Endangered Species Acts further served to focus on nonhunted species. While some states, most notably those in the East and Southwest where the public has expressed strong interest, have long been concerned with nongame, the national concern was best expressed in the 1970s with these laws. However, game species still receive most attention.

The urging of the original committee to find facts has evolved, most frequently, to the monitoring of populations, harvests, and habitat conditions. Over the years, dramatic changes in thinking and philosophy of wildlife biologists have occurred that have affected management. Initially food habit studies occupied the time of many, since predation, depredation, and habitat relationships were involved. Since big game populations, especially deer, experienced large increases in the 1940s and 1950s, and since the consequently heavy browsing of forage supplies commonly resulted in spectacular die-offs, attempts to find out what was eaten and to reduce populations to a level compatible with the available forage were the primary management concern. Upland birds were discovered to fluctuate independently of hunter harvest, so efforts to increase hunting opportunities were in vogue, even though sportsmen often resisted. The "deer wars" of the 1940–1950 era represent a classic example of how the public, conditioned to accepting a more conservative approach, was not adequately informed. Efforts to shoot does were stoutly resisted by hunters who advocated retention of the buck law. These "wars" may well be the major stimulus for establishing information and education offices within the wildlife agencies. These "wars" also illustrate the propensity for professional biologists to urge change at a more rapid rate than the public will accept.

However, the suggestion to find facts, as issued by the original committee, and its elaboration in the Federal Aid to Wildlife Restoration Act, is a source of extensive confusion about what constitutes wildlife research and wildlife management. In many cases, routine population and habitat monitoring is considered research. So the mandate of the act to conduct research into problems of wildlife management has become, through the 45 years of its existence, a problem in itself. The need to monitor wildlife exists and is an ongoing program that receives high priority, while fundamental research into improving the tools of wildlife management, including census, harvest control, and habitat manipulation, is not as well funded. As a result, much of the data accumulated through the monitoring programs are of questionable accuracy and frequently no attempt is made to ascertain their validity. However, this situation is increasingly changing as conflicts over resource uses increase and the data become more intensively scrutinized.

The 1973 policy recognized that much has been learned about wildlife management since the 1930s, and many programs and agencies have been established to provide information. However, its framers hastened to add that more can be done.

A sixth basic action recommended in 1930 was to recognize the nonshooting protectionist and the scientist as sharing with sportsmen and landowners the responsibility for wildlife as a whole. Over the ensuing years, this action has not been well implemented. Only recently has legislation been enacted that substantially funds programs involving nongame wildlife. The proliferation of antihunting groups, which have advocated protectionist legislation such as the Wild Horse and Burro Act and the Marine Mammals Act, is mute attestation to the fact that sportsmen and protectionists continue to be polarized. The 1973 policy recognized that antihunting sentiment was a by-product of our increasing urbanization, and a continuing public relations problem for agencies administering hunting and fishing. Wildlife agencies that pursue policies that either ignore or disregard the desires of a strong interest group risk being constrained by legislation.

Specific mention of the miscreant individual whose ethics and conduct while hunting are to be deplored is made in the 1973 policy. This problem of the few who spoil the sport for many is very common today as it has always been.

The seventh recommended action was to provide funds. The 1930 report urged that sportsmen be prepared to pay for management of game, and that the general public be taxed to manage wildlife as a whole. As has been noted, this recommendation, along with several others, has indeed been influential. However, the need to fund wildlife management as a whole has never been adequately addressed.

The 1930 policy classified game in relation to land management into four categories which the 1973 policy reaffirmed as still having use. *Class I game* was farm game, the nonmigratory species suitable for production on farms as a by-product of farming. Perhaps the management of class I game signifies the greatest challenge, in terms of landowner-sportsman relations and practices on private lands.

*Class II game* were defined to include forest and range species suitable for production as a by-product of managed forests and ranges. The deer species are the most commonly thought of class II game, and they admirably lend themselves to management in this context. However, the by-product concept used in the 1930s may well have changed because of public policy and legislation. On many lands, class II game are managed as an integrative system including livestock and trees. On many lands, game receive priority in management when key and critical habitats are involved. On still other lands, including the vast majority of public lands managed for forage and timber, wildlife values are not managed coequally with the other resources that have ready economic value. However, an effort to manage wildlife coequally with forage and timber is detectable.

*Class III game*, the wilderness game, were defined as those species that inhabit cheap land not suitable for farming or other economic uses. This class includes species harmful to or harmed by economic uses and therefore suitable for preservation only in special reservations and wilderness areas. In view of the evolution of legislative wilderness as distinguished from de facto wilderness, and the all-pervasive influence of modern society, one wonders what constitutes wilderness game. Are grizzly bears always harmful to or harmed by economic uses? Can caribou withstand pipelines and oil wells? Do bighorn sheep respond to habitat management? Can the timber wolf coexist with human activity? We have come to realize that much depends on the kind, amount, and timing of human activity as to whether the traditional wilderness game will coexist. Because of this, there is danger these days in relegating wildlife to the wilderness. Timber wolves and grizzly bears do coexist with forest management and less well with livestock. Caribou will have to coexist with oil wells and pipelines, and we must find ways to allow them to do so. Bighorn sheep have evolved with ever-changing habitats, and there is no reason that certain forms of habitat manipulation cannot benefit them. In a time when wilderness is restricted to a much smaller area than 50 years ago, a very different management approach is required than was originally envisioned. The elk may have been considered wilderness game in 1930, but now are certainly best considered a forest and range game species. There are opportunities to restore and retain most, if not all, species of wildlife in areas where some form of human activity and habitat change occurs. Nevertheless, the use of the term *wilderness game* as originally intended still has value in that it connotes species who generally thrive best where human activity is least. Certainly efforts to enhance and retain wilderness on behalf of these species are still needed.

*Class IV game* were defined to include the migratory species that cross political boundaries and therefore require regional, federal, and international cooperation in management. The first priority was establishment of a continental refuge system, which has since been partially implemented. Other priorities included state cooperation, international cooperation and more fact finding. An extensive effort at cooperation through establishment of councils for each waterfowl flyway has proven successful. Ducks Unlimited, which acquires and manages important waterfowl habitats in Canada, is an example of a private organization active in this area. Waterfowl research centers such as those at Patuxent, Maryland; Delta, Manitoba; and Jamestown, North Dakota, plus work by state agencies and universities continue to provide extensive information on waterfowl.

The 1973 policy recommended more acquisition of waters and wetlands, attention to alleviating pollution, and urged the remaining streams not be altered by dams that simply flood precious bottomlands and accumulate silt loads that will ultimately have to be considered.

The 1930 policy pointed out that law enforcement, which was the original and sole function of game officials, was rapidly being replaced by the broader function of providing public leadership in all aspects of wildlife management. The policy recommended a reorganization of state conservation departments to minimize political influence and provide for more continuity in policy and activities; more coordination between game, forestry, and agriculture; better qualified staff; and retention of public input in policy. The most common approach to carrying out this suggestion has been the unpaid commission, appointed to staggered terms by the governor, that serves as a policy-making body, and to which the wildlife agency is responsible. The director of the wildlife agency, appointed by the governor or the commission, was conceived to be, ideally, a technically trained person with administrative ability. The commission was to be vested with all regulatory powers, but should not "meddle in administrative detail." Adequate salaries were judged important if highly qualified people were to be retained by the state agency.

While much of this has indeed been achieved, a trend for state conservation organizations to serve as places to gain experience for people who subsequently seek employment elsewhere reflects the discrepancy in salaries between states and organizations. This has been alleviated somewhat in recent years, and is further modified by the nature of the job. Very often the state agency provides a broader, more flexible job than federal agencies do. Also, both the degree of political influence in management of personnel and the resources available vary considerably from issue to issue and between agencies and will continue to do so.

Above all, the two policies emphasize the need for a better land ethic and the integral value of such an ethic to both wildlife and humans. Large-scale habitat loss, whether it be due to a reservoir, monoculture farming, or increased urbanization, will have an ultimately adverse effect on the human environment as well as on wildlife. Recognition of a tie between a suitable environment for wildlife and humanity, is perhaps the most significant historical achievement that North American wildlife conservationists have brought forth.

The record of progress in wildlife management can be readily perceived as being slow. There is no denying that the fundamental problems of habitat loss and adverse human influence have become even more critical since 1930. D. L. Allen (1973) considered wildlife management to be largely a "holding pattern," an attempt to minimize losses of species, populations, and communities. But if one judges the record of progress in terms of change in public awareness of the issues, legislation and policies that affect the resources, organizations involved in wildlife conservation, the store of information available, and the level of habitat and population management over the 1930–1980 period, then there is indeed room for optimism. Short-term economics and political setbacks do not detract from a slow but steady record of improvement. The level of understanding of the basic worth of the wildlife resource to society has steadily increased. Today, wildlife management remains very much a social issue, one recognized by more and more people. So a "holding pattern" it is, but also a cause that is being more effectively pursued than ever. It is worth recognizing, however, that much of this gain in acceptance has developed outside of the traditional wildlife profession and without the influence of wildlifers.

## THREE CASE HISTORIES

That humans, directly through exploitation and indirectly through habitat alteration, have been the all-pervasive influence on wildlife resources is clearly indicated in the written record. This is evident in the classic study of deer and Dauerwald in Germany, based on data extending back to 1000 A.D. (A. Leopold 1936), and in studies of red deer in Scandinavia (Ahlen 1965), and in Scotland (Lowe 1961).

In 1000 A.D., the original untrammeled German forests were predominantly hardwoods of oak and beech, with conifers dominating the higher elevations and least fertile soils (Figure 1.1). This mixed open forest supported large numbers of big game, which were exploited only superficially by humans using spear, snare, and bow and arrow. The feudal forests of 1100–1400 A.D. were deliberately preserved by the lords and barons who held sway over the land. Hunting, initially highly exploitative, gradually evolved to a more regulated sport. The forests were protected for the combined benefit of domestic swine and game. A general downward trend

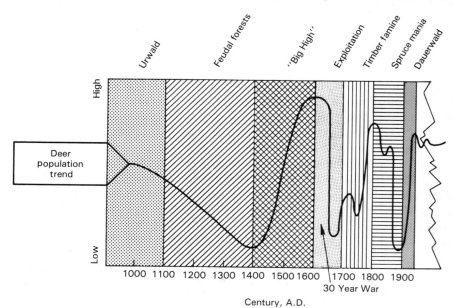

Figure 1.1   General trend of red and roe deer populations as related to forest condition in Germany, 1000–1900 A.D. After Leopold 1936.

of game populations occurred due to the exploitation and spread of agriculture. By 1400 A.D., the feudal kings instigated treaties that resulted in protection of the deer, the first attempt at management. The professional game manager, called a forester, patrolled against poachers and predators, while clergy and nobility voluntarily restricted their kill.

If the forests retained their original composition during early feudal times, by 1500 the deer populations had exploded to unprecedented highs, as a result of the cutting and burning, which created favorable habitat. The Thirty Years War of 1618-1648 brought about extremes in exploitation of both forests and deer, creating a scarcity of both trees and game. Following this war, many people who fled the cities to eke out a living off the land continued the exploitation. A "timber famine" during the 1700s resulted in increasing deer populations at the expense of tree regeneration. Forests consisted primarily of low brush stages, and were often heavily browsed by the dense deer populations. The 1800s, in contrast, were characterized by the extensive planting of spruce that ultimately contributed to declines in deer populations as forage supplies decreased. Deer damage to forest reproduction continued to be critical. As the second and third rotations of spruce failed to grow as rapidly as the initial plantings, due to compaction of clay soils, insect epidemics, and windfall, a return to naturally established forests of mixed conifers and hardwoods occurred after World War I. Deer populations again increased and the problem of reconciling forest growth with the presence of deer has continued.

Currently, 80,000 square miles of West Germany's 96,000 square miles are huntable (Gottschalk 1972). However, the hunting opportunity is very costly. Rental of a revier (hunting district) may cost upward of $5,000, with about 27 percent of the hunters owning a revier and the rest hunting as guests. The local *forstmeister* (forester), who is usually also the local *jaegermeister* (wildlifer), has the responsibility for regulating harvest. Hunting licenses are available to those who pass a rigorous 100-hour course of which 37 percent failed in 1967. Hunters constitute 0.4 percent (220,000) of the population, which is similar to the percentage in 1936. Wildlife are maintained at extremely high expense. Fencing of forest plantations to prevent damage is commonly practiced. Artificial feeding in winter is also a common endeavor. The situation provides large populations, especially of roe deer, but in a much more artificial state than exists in North America.

Ahlen (1965) records the history of red deer in Scandinavia. Early decreases have been attributed to lawless hunting and lack of legislative protection. Recent increases have been attributed to stricter control of the kill to be sure, but Ahlen emphasizes that the increases are also intimately correlated with human land use. In centuries past, when small villages were the rule and livestock were limited in number by winter food, efforts to increase pasture and hay lands resulted in burning and cutting of the forests. Heavy grazing in the forests by domestic livestock resulted in overexploited woodlands to coincide with inadequate control on game harvest. The reduction in suitable habitat due to the grazing practices is thought to have reduced native herbivores to small relict populations in areas such as large estate forests or crown forests where the competition for forage between domestic livestock and big game was negligible. Today, livestock are kept in pastures out of the forests, and the latter are rejuvenating to habitats that, over the last century, have been conducive to increases in game. While the extermination of wolves may be implicated in allowing better survival of deer in marginal habitats, the fact that habitat change and human exploitation run together as fundamental factors affecting population trends cannot be ignored.

Lowe (1961) produced a poignant description of the Scottish red deer population by stating that the current situation is a result of the cumulative effects of two actions of humans, namely, progressive deforestation in the interests of timber exploitation and increased grazing for livestock, and predator reduction in the interests of farming and game preservation. It is of significance to note that the moors of Scotland, so much a part of Scottish culture and tradition today, were once afforested (Lowe 1961; Dubos 1973).

As humans increased their agricultural activities during the Bronze Age of 2000 B.C., land was cleared for tillage and grazing. This process of forest reduction greatly accelerated during the Iron Age when timber provided fuel for smelters. As deer were gradually restricted to areas where feed was of poor quality, a concomitant progressive reduction in size resulted. Lowe (1961) attributed this size decrease to deteriorating habitat quality, related to human exploitation of the forests, and secondarily to a cooling climate, the Little Ice Age of 1550–1850. A prehistoric red deer stag, whose skeleton was uncovered from a peat bog, was fully one-fourth larger than the twentieth-century red deer. The prehistoric stag stood 137 cm high and was 239 cm long from nose to tail, while a royal 12-pointer of current stock measured 104 cm at shoulder and 170 cm from nose to tail.

During the first 1200 years A.D., with climatic conditions improving but forests continuing to be extensively exploited, large-scale appearance of heath moor and disappearance of forests along with a decrease in deer size and numbers resulted. Forests continued to be exploited virtually to elimination by the 1800s, and the deer forests were forests in name only, actually consisting of moorland and open hill.

Closed seasons on red deer were initiated in the 1400s, after market hunting for hides to export onto the continent was eliminated. Deer were protected well through the 1600s, when sheep grazing resulted in restriction of populations from the lowlands. The conflict between sheep and deer continues to the present. Deer forests were established in reaction to this problem by many of the larger landowners in the 1800s. Deer have since been a rather common subject of debate in the Scottish House of Commons, where people interested in the deer have contended with the grazing interests and poaching problems. Current problems center on regulation of herds, to prevent excessive forage use, through culling of individuals; contending with the recreational interests of tourists, skiers, and hikers who disturb the herds; and dealing with habitat deterioration due to disturbance, flooding, and fencing. Recently, hydroelectric developments have further reduced deer habitats as modern civilization advances. An extensive research project on Scottish deer and their habitat has provided information that will enhance conservation of the species in Scotland.

The history of the American wildlife resource is familiar to most of us, and suffice it to say that similarities between ours and the European situation abound. Condense Leopold's 1000 years into 200 and the German history applies to North American forest wildlife. Examine Lowe's statements about impoundments affecting Scottish red deer habitat, and you are unpleasantly reminded of the impacts on wildlife of dams in Idaho, British Columbia, South Dakota, and virtually every state and province.

The disturbing question is raised again: do we ever learn from the experiences of others? Or more importantly, do enough of us care to, out of concern for other living creatures? The issues are profound, for they ultimately involve the question of our own future, our ability to regulate our numbers and our activities in consideration of others not of our own kind. C. S. Elton (1958:50) put it this way: "This means looking for some wise principles of co-existence between man and nature, even if it has to be a modified kind of man and a modified kind of nature." It is obvious that we certainly have a modified kind of nature: now, are we willing to turn our thoughts and actions from just ourselves in order to show concern for wild creatures?

### Public versus Private Ownership

The issue of public ownership of wildlife is very important to understand in all its ramifications. The theory that wildlife are the collective property of the whole citizenry, rather than of the landowner upon whose land wildlife exist, is established in common law, which was brought by William the Conqueror from France to England during the Norman invasion of 1066, modified in the Magna Carta, and adapted in post-Revolutionary America to provide for ownership by individual states in lieu of ownership by the crown.

The individual states have vigorously fought to retain this right of ownership over the years, but it has been modified. The Lacey Act of 1900 authorized the federal government to prohibit interstate transport of illegally taken game. Migratory wildlife, including waterfowl and nongame birds, are essentially regulated by the federal government, first through the Migratory Bird Treaty with Great Britain signed in 1916, and subsequently through a treaty with Mexico signed in 1936. Obviously, management of migratory game that reside in several states and countries during the course of a year needs broader coordination than that afforded by individual states acting alone.

Endangered species also come under the purview of the federal government by virtue of the Endangered and Threatened Species Act of 1969. While some states have actively participated in efforts to conserve endangered species, the legal authority is now clearly federal, with the U.S. Fish and Wildlife Service administering the act.

In addition, legislation concerning wild horses and burros (Public law 94-579, Federal Land Policy and Management Act of 1976) may have tended to erode the traditional right of ownership of nonmigratory wildlife by the states. However, there is abundant federal legislation that verifies this right (Spellman 1963), which continues to be recognized within the federal government (Kleppe 1976). This legislation stems from the *Geer* vs. *Connecticut* opinion in 1896, wherein the defendant was prohibited from transporting lawfully taken game herds outside of the state because this was illegal in Connecticut at that time. The opinion was rendered by the U.S. Supreme Court (Bean 1977).

The biggest conflict involves the fact that wildlife habitats are owned and controlled by the individual landowner, whether that be public or private. So while populations are owned by the citizens of a state in most cases, the ultimate control rests with the individual landowner who has control of the habitat. The fact that the U.S. Forest Service, for instance, has the right to protect national forest lands from damage by wildlife is established by law dating from the famous Kaibab deer irruption in Arizona (Rasmussen 1941).

In states like Idaho where there exist extensive federal landholdings, a close working relationship is needed between the wildlife biologist working for the state and the forest ranger or district manager working for the federal government to ensure consideration for wildlife in land use. In states like Texas where private ownership of lands is pervasive, the state wildlife biologist must cooperate extensively with the landowner if a measure of influence on wildlife management is to be retained. But in either case, it is well for wildlife managers to remember the context in which they manage the wildlife resource, because the pressure to adversely modify habitats for economic, often short-term, reasons is great.

And herein lies the basic dilemma, the very crux of the issue: very often the rights of individuals to do with their land as they wish are at odds with the rights of the state's citizens to conserve the wildlife resource. The rights of the individual versus the rights of the state or public very often conflict in natural resource conservation. When Theodore Roosevelt set aside over 43 million acres of undeeded western lands as forest reserves by Executive Order in 1907, he was recognizing the long-term benefits to society in doing so. When John Wesley Powell was able to establish the principle of federal assistance in the form of subsidizing irrigation of the western region in the 1890s, he was acknowledging that the local citizen could benefit by federal assistance. But these precedents have also meant that the public interest should be protected, and not infrequently those who administer the public interest have found themselves at odds with the local individual who sees them as transgressions upon his or her individual rights. This dilemma frequently occurs when wildlife considerations are at odds with the wishes of the local citizenry.

Classic examples frequently occur on federal rangelands in the West, where big game and livestock jointly graze the forage. Local grazers who often have traditional, long-established use of the land by permit to graze domestic stock, may well resent efforts to enhance wildlife populations that alter their tradition of use. Often, this resentment is founded on economic grounds and is expressed in the context of individual rights. Within the last 20 years, the interested public has expanded to virtually a nationwide group, and local citizens who perceive conflict with their interests view themselves as a small minority, lined up against people who have no economic interest in the issue and whose livelihoods are not affected. This phenomenon exists in many areas where communities are dependent on the timber or grazing resources of federal lands, and nonlocal pressures are brought to bring about changes in management for other resources.

We have also witnessed such conflicts strictly within the wildlife management area. Thus, the efforts of the U.S. National Park Service to bring the northern Yellowstone elk herd into balance with its winter range through direct reduction by Park Service personnel were supported through national conservation organizations but not by local agencies or groups (U.S. Senate 1967). Local groups were comprised of individuals used to seeing and hunting these elk who feared their interest in the elk was being jeopardized.

Thus, wildlife management can become involved in political issues that fundamentally center on the rights of the individual versus the general social welfare. Indeed, conservation has been linked to welfare ever since Franklin D. Roosevelt formed the Civilian Conservation Corps during the Depression of the 1930s to provide people with work in conservation-oriented areas. But the fact cannot be ignored that all too frequently wildlife management efforts find less support among rural groups economically tied to the use of other natural resources than among those who are further removed from the resource base. This is at once a tragedy and a dilemma for the wildlife manager to face, for often the people who are most familiar with the land and its wildlife view the agencies who administer the resources as a threat to their life-style. Cooperation and understanding therefore become difficult to achieve. However, one can rest assured that regardless of our views on uses of the resource, we all tend to be highly sympathetic to perpetuating the wildlife populations, even if this sympathy does not transfer to those who are charged with the task professionally. And this common ground can be used effectively as a basis for communication between the skilled and sensitive biologist and the resource user.

The concepts of long-term public welfare and individual rights are a fundamental source of conflict over wildlife resources that will continue to exist into the future. The extent to which these two concepts are balanced by those involved in management will serve as another measure of our success in perpetuating the resource.


## SUMMARY

Wildlife management has elaborated itself extensively since the 1930s, yet the fundamental practices of guiding populations and habitats plus effective interaction with the public are still the roots of the profession. While we involve ourselves in a variety of environmental issues that were less important a half-century ago, such as pesticides and pollution problems, these are fundamentally habitat-related issues.

The practice of population management, which includes predator and problem wildlife control as well as efforts to manage hunting and trapping, has necessarily intensified, yet the age-old patterns are apparent. Regulation of the hunter harvest is still the major activity in population management.

Our fundamental obligation towards the wildlife resource will never change. This transcends any obligations to the agency we work for. The historical record also shows that the factors that influence wildlife recur again and again through time and space, namely, land-use practices and population exploitation. A comparison of the 1930 American Game Policy with the 1973 North American Wildlife Policy illustrates that change in wildlife management is relatively slow, perhaps best correlated with the degree of general understanding of the public of the important issues, and with a general willingness to make changes that benefit the resource even when such changes are in conflict with some human interests.

# 2

# Characteristics
# of Conservationists

## WHO IS A CONSERVATIONIST?

One of the most chronic problems in wildlife management is the lack of public support for many sound programs. Perhaps one of the major reasons for this has been a basic inability of professional biologists to articulate their stands effectively. When The Wildlife Society (Evenden 1969) polled wildlife administrators about strengths and weaknesses of the new graduate in wildlife, their responses indicated the major weakness was in the communications and public relations areas. It is doubtful, considering the overall reception that wildlife management programs receive, that this criticism should be reserved only for the new graduates in wildlife.

One approach to the problem of communication is to define the various groups of people who are interested in wildlife. Although a variety of ill-defined terms are often used to characterize the various groups, virtually all such persons can be considered *conservationists*. Harry, Gale, and Hendee (1969) further define two major groups of conservationists: those with a *conservation-utilization* emphasis, and those with a *conservation-preservation* emphasis. Both groups are concerned with perpetuation of natural resources and thereby both are conservationists. However, those people with a utilization emphasis are oriented toward the goal of proper resource exploitation, such as hunting or timber harvest, which aims at producing sustained yields by cropping "biological surpluses." This philosophy dates back through Aldo Leopold (remember the original definition of *game management*), Gifford Pinchot of "wise use" forestry fame, and Theodore Roosevelt, to the German forestry concepts brought to North America by Carl Shurz, Bernard Fernow, and others in the late 1800s. "Wise use" is a fundamental doctrine upon which most wildlife management agencies and natural resource management agencies base their management.

Up until the early 1970s, virtually all agencies and organized conservationists had a common ground or frame of reference to work from in the principle of "wise use". Every little town had its sportsmen's, or "rod and gun," club which served as a major communication between a state wildlife agency and the public it served. National sportsmen's organizations such as The National Wildlife Federation also understood this fundamental concept of "wise use."

Conservationists-preservationists, by contrast, are not oriented towards "wise use," but rather espouse an appreciative interest in the resource, preferably in its "natural state" (Harry et al. 1969). It is important to note that this viewpoint had not been effectively represented within most land management agencies, with the possible exception of the U.S. National Park Service. Even state wildlife agencies have been considered to be primarily "wise use"–oriented because so much attention has been paid to the hunting public (Frome 1975), although this has varied considerably between states.

The conservationist-preservationist movement greatly increased in influence in the early 1970s, and is now a major part of the biopolitical scene. These people are largely responsible for broadening activities of wildlife and land management agencies in nongame management, and their influence will undoubtedly become greater, for reasons to be discussed later.

The movement has recently evolved further, into what is termed *environmentalism. Environmentalist* appears to be the accepted terminology for the preservationist of former days. But, while environmentalism may be construed by many to mean only nonconsumptive use, it encompasses the movements to eliminate pollution and abuse of the entire natural and artificial world. As such, environmentalism espouses proper use of the resources, which gets us back to "wise use," or the multiple use concept. While multiple use, or wise use, has been popularized as standing for resource exploitation for commodity production, as distinguished from nonuse, in reality the multiple use–sustained yield concept, when properly applied, is something that binds all conservationists together. In this sense, as we strive to more properly manage resources and obtain a broader understanding of how to do this without deterioration of any one resource, the definitions become less distinct.

Nevertheless, environmentalists were perceived to be an economic threat in the United States by over a third of the general public that Kellert (1980) surveyed. The level of concern decreased as level of education increased and, presumably as a result of education, as understanding of the environmental issue increased. However, over 80 percent of all livestock growers viewed environmentalists as a threat. Undoubtedly the increased regulation and liquidation that affects the livestock industry is responsible, but this should serve as a reminder that the environmental movement has acquired strong opposition from certain traditional interest groups concerned with use of wild lands.

Of course, professionally trained people in all aspects of resource management constitute another identifiable group. One finds all degrees of emphasis among professionals, depending upon the resource they manage. The professional biologist interested primarily in nongame species is quite likely, but not necessarily, to have a philosophy different from that of the waterfowl biologist who further specializes in population dynamics, for instance.

But we all fall under the broad classification of conservationist. The rancher concerned with perpetuation of a grassland pasture can justifiably be called a conservationist. Even the oilman who is primarily concerned with exploration and "production" of oil, but who hires a biologist to ensure minimum damage to the environment, has been known to call himself a conservationist! And hardly anyone can be classified neatly and completely as one type of conservationist or the other.

## CONSERVATIONIST-PRESERVATIONISTS

Wilderness users, bird watchers, backpackers, cross-country skiers, and those expressly opposed to hunting are among those often considered preservationists. Harry et al. (1969) points out that these people are often urban-based. Urban-based occupations are usually many steps removed from the natural resources on which all people ultimately depend. Another important characteristic is that many of these people have a high level of education and as a result are or will be in upper middle class occupations. Such people, therefore, tend to be articulate and generally well informed about their interest in resources. While organized conservationist-preservationists tend to be older than 40, it is doubtful that this group can be characterized by age. A personal commitment to the goal of preserving the resources, and a willingness to spend time and money to do so, also appears to be inherent, although as the movement expands this can be expected to decrease.

The suggestion that organized conservationist-preservationists seem to be unwilling to compromise would receive hearty support from many natural resource administrators who have found themselves at odds with them. The "missionary zeal" that Harry et al. (1969) reported finding in these people seems to complement the attribute. But there is also an overwhelming history that many conservationist-preservationists are abundantly aware of, which undoubtedly enhances this unwillingness to compromise. The history of excessive resource exploitation is a fact we live with, a part of the pioneering of North America. The damming of the Hetch-Hetchy Valley to provide San Francisco with water, the prevention of a dam in Echo Canyon, the removal of Alaskan North Slope oil, and the controversial harvesting of timber in the Boundary Waters Canoe Area (Heinselman 1973) are just a few of many examples, all of which serve as reminders of our historical exploitative orientation and of the continuing pressures. Even *My Weekly Reader Eye* (1975) pounds home to the grade school student the excesses against the grizzly bear, even if the facts are not exactly correct! A glance once again at A. Leopold's *Sand County Almanac* (1949) only serves to verify that conservation-preservation has been a built-in component of the wildlife scene for many years.

One very important conclusion about the nonhunting wildlife enthusiast that

W. R. Shaw and King (1980) reported was that their concerns and activities were not supported by government wildlife management activities. The study involved people who visited bird-watching sites in southeastern Arizona in 1977. While the potential exists for wildlife agencies and the nonconsumptive wildlife enthusiast to cooperate on conservation issues of mutual interest (Witter and Shaw 1979), this potential remained unused. The bird watchers as a result were neither supportive of nor antagonistic toward state wildlife agencies. The obvious reason was that the state agencies were not perceived as interested in incorporating nongame management activities into ongoing management programs. This is now being alleviated through a variety of taxation schemes in many states. Witter and Shaw (1979) concluded that until the nonconsumptive wildlife enthusiast perceives the wildlife management agencies as giving significant attention to their interests, they will continue to finance private wildlife programs and be unsupportive of the public agencies. This significant attention is beginning to occur as broad-based financial support for nongame and endangered species at the state level attests.

### CONSERVATIONIST-UTILIZATIONISTS

Hendee and Potter (1976) summarized research findings as regards a very important conservationist-utilizationist: the hunter. Hunters in the 1970s tended to be more middle-aged than the U.S. population. This worries some hunting groups because there appears to be a lower number of young people entering the hunting fraternity (and a fraternity it is, for women are not nearly as likely to be involved as men). Minimum age restrictions and the lack of opportunities for a high percentage of young people from urban areas in the East to participate, are two reasons that young people don't hunt. The level of education for the hunter tends to parallel that of the U.S. population, as does their income level. Most hunters are not members of organized sportsmen's groups (only about 17 to 36 percent are, depending on which of nine studies one consults). In geographical terms, the Mountain states, with the least urbanization and best opportunities to hunt a variety of species over the longest period, have the highest percentage of hunters. Alaska and Hawaii were excluded from the analysis.

The percentage of hunters in the total U.S. population ranged from 9.1 to 11.2 percent over the 1955–1980 period with no apparent trend, although the actual numbers have increased, as the population has increased (U.S. Dept. of the Interior 1980). While this appears to bode well from the standpoint of perpetuating the sport, it does pose a major problem for the wildlife manager who is often faced with problems associated with congestion, which ultimately results in more regulation and, frequently, restriction of the hunting opportunity.

Again, research by Potter, Hendee, and Clark (1973) demonstrates the complexities of conservationists and the difficulties of categorizing us. When 5540 people in Washington State, a 2 percent sample of the hunting population, were asked why they hunted, a "multiple satisfaction" conclusion was reached. Contact with nature, escape from the daily routine, and companionship were important reasons. Shooting was important to waterfowl and upland bird hunters, but less critical to big game hunters. Skill in woodsmanship and marksmanship were more important to big game hunters and waterfowlers than to upland bird hunters. The key demographic variables of age, income, education, sex, and place of residence were not associated with these criteria. Such items as vicariousness, trophy display, equipment, and amount of game bagged rated down the list of "multiple satisfactions."

Plummer (1971) provided insight into life-styles of hunters who were defined as those buying $11 or more of shotgun shells per year. While much of this work may be applicable only to a segment of the hunting group, the fact that many hunters were oriented towards individualism, or considered themselves self-reliant, with a "pioneer attitude," may be more broadly applicable. Also, the hunter tended to be oriented primarily toward local issues rather than toward broad ecological issues, which often have an influence locally. And the fact that the neophyte hunter was more amenable than the experienced hunter to seeing more research and management efforts may tell professional biologists something about the fruitfulness of their public relations efforts!

## PROFESSIONALS

Very little attention has been given the attitudes of the professional biologist and resource manager. However, information gleaned about wilderness managers by Hendee and Harris (1970) may provide some interesting insight and stimulate some thought. An inflexible, rigid attitude on some important issues in wilderness management was suggested from the questionnaire response of 56 wilderness managers. This attitude appeared to be a result of each individual's own experiences and exposures to the vocal interest groups. If such is the case with wildlife managers, then the views of the more vocal public, often the dissatisfied hunter groups, may weigh heavily on their judgments as to what the public wants.

Also, wilderness managers viewed users as clearly opinionated when in fact a high proportion of users were neutral in responses to questions about wilderness management. If this is the case with wildlife managers as well, the implication is that management may well be less progressive, keyed to the more vocal dissenting individuals who may not represent the population well, and who espouse antiquated management practices.

Foresters tend to view timber management in terms of productivity (Bultena and Hendee 1972), and this undoubtedly holds true for the way the wildlife biologist views wildlife management as well. Also, the views of their immediate superiors were considered legitimate by all foresters questioned. That foresters were not opposed to increased recreational use of forests as long as timber harvest was not restricted, probably equates well with the observed intolerance of some wildlife managers to bird watchers interfering with the hunter. As long as the bird watchers don't interfere, they are tolerated, but often hunting is considered the priority activity. Whether one agrees that the attributes reported by Bultena and Hendee (1972) are typical of foresters, and that such attitudes may also be typical of many wildlife managers as well, the fact that bias in outlook of professionals towards their tasks as regards the people they serve is very probably a critical problem that needs attention. Bultena and Hendee (1972) suggest that such biases result from professionals associating and socializing with other professionals with similar outlooks (a not unhuman condition), the nature and structure of the organizations they work for, and the organizational structure of the working environment. The need for broader academic training, continuing education, more variety of interaction with the various public groups, and occasional relocation, were among recommendations made to combat such biases.

While the professional conservationist may equate good management with high productivity, the studies of Witter and Shaw (1979) suggest that nonconsumptive values, such as the biological role of wildlife and the availability of subjects for study and enjoyment are the highest-ranking values for wildlife as viewed by professionals. This suggests that the educational process, agency goals and practices, and associated peer pressures interact with the professional's personal values. It should be apparent that high productivity may not be strictly compatible with the nonconsumptive values. Wildlife management programs that are traditionally oriented at producing large numbers of individuals for the hunt are not necessarily the equivalent of programs emphasizing nonconsumptive values.

In essence, the professional resource manager, whether forester, biologist, or range conservationist, is ultimately a human being influenced by the local environment. The studies indicate that being objective professionally is not easy, but requires a constant and considerable effort. Ideally, a professional conservationist is neither utilization- nor preservation-oriented, but retains an objectivity and flexibility to see the needs of the resource regardless of the use or nonuse to which it is put. In this day of conflict and confrontation, complexity and difficulty, the problems of conducting an objective and effective job of resource management are not to be assumed lightly. In short, the person dealing with a resource management problem, collecting the information, meeting the public, and making the recommendations deserves the support and recognition that many researchers and teachers often forget to provide.

## HUNTERS AND ANTIHUNTERS

Attitudes of the general public toward hunting are increasingly important in wildlife management. Hunting for meat, subsistence, or for the combination of recreation and meat are generally approved by the public that Kellert (1980) surveyed. However, hunting for recreation alone, and most especially for trophies, received much less approval. Apparently people tend to approve of hunting when a utilitarian connotation is involved but not when pure sport is the goal. People living in rural settings (small towns of under 500 population) were more likely to favor hunting than people living in highly urbanized areas.

As our society becomes more and more urbanized, the antihunting groups, and those who are apathetic to the sport, will probably increase and make themselves heard more frequently within the wildlife management arena (Kennedy 1973). The controversy is ages old, and there is no readily foreseeable means to resolve it because it ultimately stems from two very different if equally valid fundamental philosophies, one with roots in religion, and one with roots in biology.

Perhaps Albert Schweitzer (1923:240) articulated the antikilling case effectively when he stated:

> A man is really ethical only when he obeys the constraint laid on him to help all life which he is able to succour, and when he goes out of his way to avoid injury to anything living. He does not ask how far this or that life deserves sympathy as valuable in itself, nor how far it is capable of feeling. To him, life as such is sacred. He shatters no ice crystal which sparkles in the sun, tears no leaf from its tree, breaks off no flower, and is careful not to crush any insect as he walks. He works by lamplight on a summer evening, he prefers to keep the window shut and breathe stifling air rather than see insect after insect fall on his table with singed and sinking wings.

The "right-to-life" movement indeed spills over to wildlife! True to the Hippocratic Oath of his profession, Schweitzer was pleading for the value of the individual regardless of species, a tradition going back at least to St. Francis of Assissi in our Western culture (White 1967). From the viewpoint of the veterinarian or the medical doctor, who is constantly concerned with treating individuals, the value of the individual is high. This attribution of value can readily be extended to all species and individuals and very often is. The logger who sees a white-tailed deer feeding on the foliage of fallen tree tops cannot help but feel an affinity for that individual. A chipmunk that frequents a campsite is a source of pleasure for many individuals whose experience is enhanced by its presence. The birder learns to recognize individuals by their behavior and coloration at her feeder, an experience that enhances her pleasure and reinforces her expertise. And the wildlife biologist who follows a radio-marked animal and learns of its home range and habitats has forever thereafter developed a personal connection to the beast!

In direct contrast, a fundamental premise associated with hunting is that the "biological surplus" exists, and the welfare of the population takes precedence over the welfare of the individual. If this is a less personal viewpoint, it nevertheless is biologically valid, and modern sport hunting has very definitely enhanced many wildlife populations. The hunter has been willing to abide by the rules and regulations well enough to maintain the populations being hunted, a common justification for hunting.

Traditional justifications for hunting (D. R. Klein 1973) are centered on the following arguments:

1. It is generally more humane to kill outright than to allow death by starvation or at the hands of predators.
2. Man has evolved as a hunter and thus modern sport hunting reenacts the traditional drama.
3. Hunting keeps populations "healthy," generally replacing other mortality.
4. Hunting does not endanger populations.
5. Hunted species are among the most abundant.
6. Hunters tend to be in close touch with "environmental realities."

It is debatable whether modern-day hunting serves to reenact the original hunter-gatherer life-styles, when one considers the extensively equipped hunter of today who hardly needs the game to survive. And it may be more "humane" to kill outright than to allow nature to take its course, but the superimposition of human values and judgments upon naturally evolved processes is a highly debatable action, also. The arguments that hunting replaces other mortality, does not endanger populations, and generally occurs on the most abundant species are rationalizations that do not face the ultimate issue, which is taking a life in the name of sport.

The argument that hunting can be judged only in the context of how it affects humans, rather than other species, is again anthropocentric and contrary to the main orientation of wildlife management, towards species conservation.

The esthetics of the sport, articulated so well by Clarke (1958), Errington (1947), A. Leopold (1933), and others, should however be recognized as legitimate. There is no question that hunting in the total sense can be an exhilarating, stimulating, emotional experience, one that encompasses far more than the killing act. However, hunting and wildlife management have been equated in the minds of many people as being inextricably intertwined, when in fact they are not. A position statement of The Wildlife Society (1982) recognizes that sport hunting is *one* legitimate and desirable use of wildlife resources, among many others.

How do we rationalize this polarization between the regard for the individual versus a regard for the population? It is probably well to begin by recognizing that both viewpoints are ingrained within the various human psyches involved, and that there is a personal commitment that can be well defended on either side. While Albert Schweitzer can be criticized, what value is gained in doing so? A. Leopold can be criticized for his initial articulation of the basis for game management, as well.

The issue of the individual versus the population transcends the wildlife management arena to the human population as well. Do we sacrifice individual humans to disease and starvation in the interests of the general welfare of society? Should the United States quit supplying foreign aid to Third World underdeveloped countries where there is no apparent hope of raising the standard of living or bringing about self-sufficiency? Why do we continue to practice forms of agriculture and forestry that are, in the short-term, economically justified, but that are, in the long-term, ultimately detrimental to the basic soil and water resources and to humans? The hunting-antihunting ethic is one more form of such conundrums that we will live with into the long-distant future. Perhaps LeResche (1974) provides the best rationalization: we have a common ground, that of conserving the wildlife resources, which we should recognize, even if we can't agree about its uses.

## ATTITUDES TOWARD ANIMALS

Kellert (1976) described nine basic attitudes towards animals that further define conservationists and separate them from those not interested. The *naturalistic* attitude, as attributed to those with an attraction to animals and the outdoors, is general. These people may be contrasted with the *humanists*, who have strong personal affection for individuals, often as pets, rather than for wildlife. *Moralists* are distinguished primarily as those concerned for the welfare of wild and domesticated animals, an apparent intergrade between naturalists and humanists. Those with *aesthetic* and *scientific* attitudes tend to incorporate rather detached views of wildlife, the former group viewing them as objects of beauty or as symbols, and the latter group viewing them as objects for study. The *ecologistic* approach, closely related to the former two, encompasses those with detached views of wildlife as part of a natural system that should be protected for the sake of society. These last three attitudes were the least common. *Utilitarians* perceive wildlife as having natural benefits to humans, as being useful. The utilitarian is distinguished from the person with a *dominionistic* atittude by the latter's emphasis on controlling and dominating animals, as an expression of skill. Trophy hunters, dog and horse obedience trainers, and rodeo participants fit the dominionistic attitude. *Negativistic* attitudes towards wildlife involve indifference and the desire to avoid contact with animals. The humanistic, utilitarian, and negativistic or indifference attitudes were most prevalent in the survey, which sampled the entire United States.

The attitude concept that Kellert (1976) used involved distinguishing patterns in related ideas, feelings, and beliefs of people. As such it provides useful insights into understanding the framework of reference that an individual or a group uses in relating to wildlife. Education and sex were the most consistent social predictors of an individual's view. Women were more inclined to be moralistic than men, while naturalistic, utilitarian, dominionistic, scientific, and ecologistic attitudes were more characteristic of men than women. People who were least educated displayed a high degree of negativistic attitude and disinterest in animals, and were more dominionistic and utilitarian in their attitudes than those with higher levels of education. College-educated groups were more naturalistic and ecologistic. However, financial income was relatively unimportant in differentiating these attitudes. Figure 2.1 illustrates the socio-demographic findings.

The exhaustive surveys done by Kellert (1980) provide insight into attitudes of the general public toward wildlife. A major finding, that a majority of Americans

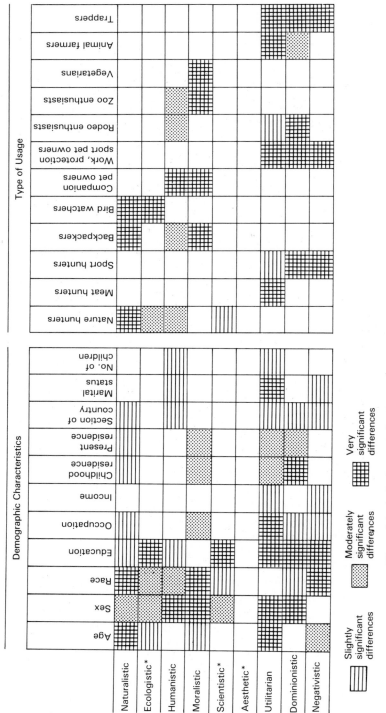

**Figure 2.1** Attitudes toward animals related to demographic characteristics and type of usage. (Asterisk indicates scale and item indices were fair to poor in national study.) After Kellert 1976.

were willing to limit human activity in order to protect and retain wildlife, would appear to bode well for the future. However, many individuals will favor wildlife in general but not necessarily if it means impinging on personal endeavors. Also, Kellert (1980) found that the positive attitude toward wildlife was restricted to species with utilitarian, cultural, or historical value, or that exhibited a biological closeness to humans. Thus, unknown plants, snakes, and spiders that were designated as endangered were less likely to receive public support for protection than eagles, mountain lions, grizzly bears, and other well-known species. The cost of protection, and reason for endangerment, also influenced the general desire to help wildlife. Direct exploitation was viewed as a more compelling reason to help a species than habitat loss.

Another major finding was that the support among the general public for wildlife is primarily emotional in nature rather than based on knowledge. Killing baby seals and using steel leghold traps were issues more people were aware of than were not. However, issues such as the Endangered Species Act, depredations by coyotes on livestock, and steel versus lead shot were understood by a low percentage of individuals in Kellert's surveys. Thus, issues of contemporary concern to wildlife professionals were not necessarily even perceived as issues by a significant number of people outside the profession. On the other hand, illegal killing of wildlife was perceived as a very critical issue, a perception that translates into support for conservation law enforcement. Use of poison to control coyotes and other species that prey on livestock was strongly opposed by the general public. The general public was willing to support efforts by the government to inform and educate people about wildlife, indicating that there is a significant interest in learning more about wildlife.

Kellert (1980) concluded that wildlife management agencies have a considerably expanded constituency, including people motivated by esthetic and nonconsumptive values of wildlife. Wildlife professionals must recognize that they answer to a much larger interest group today than when the traditional hunting and trapping constituency prevailed. This constituency in essence is a large proportion of the American public. Wildlife management that provides responsible stewardship and provides benefits to people as well, two fundamental objectives, will more and more be the hallmarks by which the profession is judged.

## SUMMARY

It is to be emphasized that there are many degrees of each kind of conservationist. The research thus far is sparse, especially about the professional and the preservationist. But, the major conclusion is that we must articulate resource management to more people much better than we have in the past. The professional should learn to know himself or herself better as a prerequisite, as he or she is part of the problem. In fact, we are all "part of the problem," and this basic human condition of variety in attitudes and influences is what will continue into the future to keep the process of wildlife management an art.

# 3

# Laws and Treaties
# in Wildlife Management

Useful references to federal wildlife law are Bean (1977) and House Committee on Merchant Marine and Fisheries (1973).

## MAJOR FEDERAL WILDLIFE LEGISLATION

### Federal Aid to Wildlife Restoration Act

The Federal Aid to Wildlife Restoration Act, also known as the Pittman-Robertson Act, was passed in 1937. This law authorizes the U.S. Department of the Interior to cooperate with states in wildlife restoration in (1) selection and restoration of areas adaptable as feeding, resting, or breeding places for wildlife; and (2) research into problems of wildlife management.

States, in order to participate, must have passed laws for the conservation of wildlife that include agreement that license fees paid by hunters will not be diverted from agency administration of wildlife. The law excludes law enforcement and public relations activities, and game farms and associated stocking activities from funding. Funding is made on a 75:25 federal-state matching basis.

Allocation of funds to states is accomplished as follows:

1. One-half of funds are allocated based on the ratio of the area of the state to total U.S. area.
2. One-half of funds are allocated based on the state to total U.S. ratio of number of paid hunting license holders of each state in the second fiscal year preceding fiscal year of apportionment.

3. No state will receive less than 0.5 percent or more than 5 percent of the total allowable.
4. Eight percent of funds are allocated for administration of this law and the Migratory Bird Conservation Act by the U.S. Department of the Interior.

The funding source (in IRS code, Title IV, Revenue Act of 1932) is an 11-percent excise tax on sporting arms and ammunition and a 12-percent tax on pistols, revolvers, and bows and arrows.

### Fish Restoration and Management Act

The Fish Restoration and Management Act, also known as the Dingell-Johnson Act, was passed in 1950. This law authorizes the U.S. Department of the Interior to cooperate with the states on fish restoration and management provided that the state (1) enacts a law governing conservation of fish; (2) prohibits diversion of license fees from state fish and game departments; and (3) agrees to all terms of the law.

This law provides for research in fish management and culture, with marine and freshwater allocations as follows:

1. Eight percent of funds are allocated to the Secretary of the Interior for administration of this law and the management of migratory fishes.
2. Forty percent of the remaining funds are allocated based on the ratio of total water in the state to total U.S. water.
3. Sixty percent of the remaining funds are allocated based on the state to total U.S. ratio of number of license holders.

The funding source is a tax on reels, creels, rods, lures, baits, and flies. Each state must develop a comprehensive fish and wildlife plan in order to participate.

### Migratory Birds and Insectivorous Birds:
### Treaties and Laws

**Migratory Bird Treaties.**    The Migratory Bird Treaties of 1916 between the United States and Great Britain, and of 1936 between the United States and Mexico prohibit the export and taking of birds (Canada) and of birds and game mammals (Mexico) except legally. These treaties became law in 1918 and 1937, respectively.

**Migratory Bird Conservation Act.**    The Migratory Bird Conservation Act of 1929 provides for the following:

1. Establishment of a Migratory Bird Conservation Commission
2. Acquisition, rental, and acceptance of gifts in the form of lands

3. Establishment of a National Wildlife Refuge System
4. Imposition of a hunting stamp tax, originally $1, then $2, $3, $5
5. Enforcement authority in the U.S. Department of the Interior in cooperation with the states

**Lacey Act.**   The Lacey Act of 1900 provides for enforcement of the Migratory Bird Treaty, and prohibits transport of illegal game between states and countries.

### Fish and Wildlife Coordination Act

The Fish and Wildlife Coordination Act of 1956 established the U.S. Fish and Wildlife Service. Its history dates back to the establishment in 1888 of the Bureau of Fisheries in the U.S. Department of Commerce, and the Bureau of Biological Survey in the U.S. Department of Agriculture. In 1939 both agencies were transferred back to the U.S. Department of Interior, and the following year became the Fish and Wildlife Service.

In spelling out the policy underlying the 1956 act, Congress declared that fish, shellfish, and wildlife make a material contribution to the economy and to the food supply, health, recreation, and well-being of citizens; that resources are a renewable form of national wealth capable of being enhanced with proper management; and that free enterprise in development, protection, and maintenance is encouraged, and federal assistance is needed.

The functions of the law are to provide for cooperation with the U.S. State Department, including representation at international meetings and consultations on fish and wildlife matters, to ensure that each state's prerogatives in management of "resident" game are not infringed upon; to prohibit airborne hunting, excluding depredations and threats to humans as authorized by permit; and to provide for Cooperative Fish and Wildlife training programs.

### Fish and Wildlife Conservation Act

The Fish and Wildlife Conservation Act of 1980, also known as the Forsythe-Chaffee Act, authorizes the federal government to provide financial and technical assistance to enable states to develop and revise conservation plans for fish and wildlife, specifically nongame fish and wildlife. The law calls for a conservation plan to be developed by each state, which identifies the species, its range, the problems involved, and a plan of action to conserve the species and its habitat. The law provides for monitoring on a regular basis. Nongame fish and wildlife are defined as those species not ordinarily taken for food, fur, or sport; that are not listed as endangered or threatened, and that are not marine mammals.

## MAJOR FEDERAL LAND LAWS

### National Forest Management Act

The National Forest Management Act of 1976 essentially replaced the original organic act establishing the U.S. Forest Service in 1897. The motivating purpose was to correct language in the original act that restricted timber harvest to "dead, matured or large growth," an ambiguous restriction. Among the provisions of the act are the following:

1. To develop and prepare a national renewable resource program that is periodically reviewed and updated, and is based on a comprehensive assessment of present and anticipated uses, demand, and supply of renewable resources from the nation's *public* and *private forests and rangelands.*
2. To provide for the federal government to act as a catalyst to encourage and assist other owners in the efficient long-term use and improvement of renewable resources consistent with the principles of sustained yield and multiple use.
3. To recognize the fundamental need to protect and, where appropriate, improve the quality of soil, water, and air resources.
4. To provide for an interdisciplinary approach to managing the multiple resources, and for public input into management decisions and planning.
5. To ensure consideration of economic and environmental aspects of various systems of renewable resources management, including the related systems of silviculture and protection of forest resources, to provide for outdoor recreation (including wilderness), range, timber, watershed, wildlife, and fish.
6. To ensure timber will be harvested only when soil, slope, and watershed conditions will not be irreversibly damaged, where lands can be adequately restocked within five years after harvest.
7. To ensure that timber harvest will be carried out so soil, watershed, fish, wildlife, recreation and esthetic resources, and regeneration of timber resource will be maintained.
8. To provide for road closures within ten years following termination of a logging contract unless the road is needed for the National Forest Transportation System.

### Federal Land Policy and Management Act

The Federal Land Policy and Management Act, passed in 1976, essentially provides the Bureau of Land Management (BLM), Department of the Interior, with a fundamental organic act. It authorizes most public lands to be managed on the basis of sustained yield and multiple use. Lands will be managed in such a manner that will protect the quality of scientific, scenic, historical, ecological, environmental, air and atmospheric, water resource, and archeological values. Provisions to provide food and habitat for fish, wildlife, and domestic animals are included. The act includes but supersedes the Taylor Grazing Act of 1934, which authorized the U.S. Department of the Interior to establish grazing districts on public domain. While the value of the range resource in livestock production is recognized, the act does provide the BLM with a multiple-use charge that should aid in considering the other resources on the public lands.

### Multiple-Use Sustained Yield Act

The Multiple-Use Sustained Yield Act, passed in 1960, provides for national forest administration for outdoor recreation, range, timber, watershed, and wildlife and fish purposes. (Note order listed.) It authorizes the U.S. Forest Service to establish wildernesses consistent with the purposes of this act.

*Multiple use* is defined in this act as follows:

> the management of all the various renewable surface resources of the national forests so they are best utilized in the combination that will best meet the needs of the American people; making the most judicious use of the land for some or all of these resources or related services over areas large enough to provide sufficient latitude for periodic adjustments in use to conform with changing needs and conditions; that some land will be used for less than all of the resources; and harmonious and coordinated management of the various resources, each with the other without impairment of the productivity of the land, with consideration being given to the relative values of the various resources, and not necessarily the combination of uses that will give the greatest dollar return or the greatest unit output.

Multiple use may be achieved by concurrent use of several resources on the same area, alternating use of resources on the same area through time, geographical separation but inclusion of all uses on a larger land area, or combinations of all these options.

### Wilderness Act

The Wilderness Act of 1964 provides for the establishment of a National Wilderness Preservation System. *Wilderness* is defined in this act as follows:

> an area where the earth and its community of life are untrammeled by man, where man himself is a visitor who does not remain. An area of undeveloped federal land retaining its primeval character and influence, without permanent improvement or human habitation, which is protected and managed so as to preserve its natural conditions and which (1) generally appears to have been

affected primarily by the forces of nature with the imprint of man's work substantially unnoticeable; (2) has outstanding opportunities for solitude or a primitive and unconfined type of recreation; (3) 5000 acres or more in size; (4) *may* also contain ecological, geological, or other features of scientific, educational, scenic, or historical value.

### Wild and Scenic Rivers Act

The Wild and Scenic Rivers Act of 1968 provides for preservation of some rivers with outstandingly remarkable scenic, recreational, geologic, fish and wildlife, historic, cultural, or other similar values in free-flowing condition. *Wild rivers* are defined in this act as those that are free of impoundments and inaccessible except by trail, whose watersheds and shorelines are essentially primitive, and whose waters are unpolluted. *Scenic rivers* are similar to wild rivers, except that they are accessible in places by roads, yet "still *largely* primitive." *Recreational rivers* are those that are readily accessible, that have undergone some development, and that may have undergone impoundment and diversion in the past.

## OTHER IMPORTANT FEDERAL LAWS

### Bald Eagle Protection Act of 1972

The Bald Eagle Protection Act of 1972 revised the original act passed in 1940. It prohibits the taking of eagles (bald and golden) except under permit. In cases of violation it provides for the cancellation of the violator's grazing agreement clause, and the imposition of a $5000 fine. Taking for scientific, depredation, exhibition, and religious (Indian) purposes is allowed.

### Endangered Species Conservation Act
### of Fish and Wildlife

The Endangered Species Act of 1969 provides for conservation, restoration, propagation, and protection of selected species of fish and wildlife, including migratory birds, that are threatened with extinction.

The secretary of the Interior carries out the program, but the U.S. Departments of Agriculture and Defense are also charged with conserving affected species. A review of all programs is provided for in order to use those that could further the purpose of the act. Cooperation with states is provided for by means of requiring their consultation. Funding is through the Land and Water Conservation Fund, and Fish and Wildlife Service appropriations. There is also a provision for encouraging similar programs in foreign countries.

*Fish and wildlife* are defined in the act as any wild mammal, fish, wild bird, amphibian, reptile, mollusk, or crustacean. An *endangered species* is defined as any species that is in danger of extinction throughout all or a significant portion of its range. Any species that is likely to become an endangered species within the foreseeable future throughout all or a significant portion of its range is defined as a *threatened species*. The threatened category was distinguished from the endangered category to provide for protection of a species before it became endangered, and also to provide a reduced level of protection for a previously endangered species that was in the process of recovering. Protective measures include no taking, importation, or possession of these species by U.S. citizens, and no habitat deterioration. A provision to delineate critical habitat and for the secretary of the Interior to review all federal programs to see that no deterioration or destruction occurs is included.

### Protection of Wild Horses and Burros Act

"Unbranded and unclaimed" horses and burros on public lands are the objects of the Protection of Wild Horses and Burros Act, passed in 1971. It provides for management of these mammals in a manner designed to achieve and maintain a "natural ecological balance." Adjustments of forage allocations shall consider needs of other wildlife species. The act provides for humane destruction by U.S. Department of the Interior federal marshals only if there is no other practical means to remove excess animals.

### Marine Mammal Protection Act

The Marine Mammal Protection Act, passed in 1972, provides for a moratorium on taking and importing marine mammals and marine mammal products. Exemptions are allowed for scientific research and public display, Alaska Aleuts, Eskimos, and Indians. The act also allows for waiving requirements to allow taking if in "accord with principles of sound resource protection." *Marine mammals* are defined to include Syrenia (dugong), Pinnipedia, Cetacea, polar bear, and sea otter. The act prohibits states from adopting any law involving marine mammals unless the secretary of the U.S. Department of the Interior determines such laws are consistent with this act.

### Land and Water Conservation Fund Act

The Land and Water Conservation Fund Act, passed in 1965, provides for funds to plan, acquire, and develop land and water areas, plus facilities for recreational purposes. Revenues are obtained from surplus property sales, a motorboat fuels tax, and "enhance and administer" fees for national parks and national recreation areas.

The fund is distributed to states as matching monies on a 50-50 basis, with 40 percent going to each state equally, and 60 percent on a "basis of need."

Each state must develop a comprehensive outdoor recreation plan in order to be eligible to participate. The law only allocates; Congress has to appropriate monies.

### National Environmental Policy Act

The purpose of the National Environmental Policy Act, passed in 1969, is to declare a national policy that will encourage productive and enjoyable harmony between man and his environment; to promote efforts that will prevent or eliminate damage to environment; to enrich understanding of ecological systems and natural resources; and to establish a Council on Environmental Quality.

The act established a Cabinet Committee on the Environment that includes the vice-president of the United States and the secretaries of the Agriculture; Commerce; Health, Education and Welfare; Housing and Urban Development; Interior, and Transportation Departments, any of whom may designate alternative members. The functions of the committee are as follows:

1. To recommend measures that ensure that federal policies take into account environmental effects
2. To review the adequacy of the existing system
3. To foster cooperation of federal, state, and local levels
4. To seek advancement of scientific knowledge of changes in the environment and encourage development of technology to minimize adverse effects
5. To stimulate public and private participation in the "war on pollution"
6. To encourage timely public disclosure by all levels of government and by private parties of plans that would affect environment
7. To review plans and actions of federal agencies that affect outdoor recreation and natural beauty

This act also established a Citizens' Advisory Committee to advise the president and the Cabinet Committee. It also established an Environmental Protection Agency, incorporating several other agencies, and the National Oceanic and Atmospheric Administration (NOAA) in the Department of Commerce.

The act provides for an environmental impact statement on federal actions significantly affecting the quality of the human environment, to include the following:

1. Environmental impact of proposed action
2. Adverse effects that are unavoidable
3. Alternatives
4. Relation of short-term uses and long-term productivity
5. Irreversible, irretrievable commitments of resource involved

## SUMMARY

The earlier federal statutes were primarily directed at regulating exploitation of wildlife and acquiring habitat, while more recent legislation emphasizes coordination between federal and state government in the use of previously developed regulatory tools (Bean 1977). The more recent statutes address a broader range of wildlife species, extending the definition of wildlife to include all free-ranging vertebrates. Further, recent legislation covering wildlife management activities by federal land management agencies has thrust consideration of wildlife values into more management activities than previously. As these statutes require consideration of the wildlife resource in virtually all land-use management, attempts to revise the statutes to reduce their effect have been made by interest groups who feel they are adversely affected. Also, older legislation such as the Pittman-Robertson Act has come under scrutiny by antihunting groups. The legislation of the 1960s and 1970s that promoted more rigorous consideration of the wildlife resource will undoubtedly remain controversial for a considerable period into the future.

Federal agencies must of necessity establish guidelines and regulations for implementing legislation that applies to their activities. Thus, an interpretation of the intent of the legislation is required. These interpretations may be altered as new information or different attitudes prevail. Additionally, the ability of administrators to conduct activities under authority of the legislation is subject to level of funding. Finally, other legislation involving land use may well be in conflict with wildlife-oriented legislation, as the wetland drainage program illustrates. The variety of federal legislation that affects wildlife and the diversity of ways in which each law may be addressed by those responsible needs to be understood by the wildlife biologist.

# 4

# Food Habits

## HISTORY AND SIGNIFICANCE

Forage use patterns are a fundamental component of the relationship between an animal and its habitat. Abundance and quality of forage may serve to limit a population, may influence its distribution patterns and selection of specific habitats, and may serve as a focal point in interspecific competition. This is not to imply that populations always increase until the available food is exhausted, nor that forage supplies can be deteriorated through utilization by wildlife. However, it does imply that the abundance and quality of food is likely to influence the general density of a population, as Lack (1954) maintained.

Game food habit studies were among the first to be produced by wildlife biologists. The work of A. C. Martin, Zim, and Nelson (1951) is one culmination of the early food habits surveys. These surveys were instigated for economic reasons by the Bureau of Biological Survey, the predecessor of the Fish and Wildlife Service, in an effort to determine which species were involved in depredations to agricultural crops and commercial timber, and to quantify the extent of the damage attributable to each (McAtee 1918). Many university wildlife departments originated to address aspects of economic zoology, of which crop and tree depredations were important areas of research. The Patuxent and Denver Wildlife Research Centers were the foci for food habits studies, employing specialists in identification of plant parts, hairs, insects, and bone fragments collected from crops, stomachs, and feces of various wildlife species across North America. Reports on grouse crop analysis were written as early as 1880 by the predecessor agency of the U.S. Fish and Wildlife Service.

Since the earlier work, which consisted of long listings of items and their relative amounts in the observed diet, the more recent food habit investigations have
become more elaborate. Objectives are numerous, ranging from questions of physiological responses to those involving mechanisms of population regulation. Efforts to
determine carrying capacity of a habitat for a certain species will inevitably include
one form of a forage relationship analysis or another. Questions involving foraging
theory will be included in the broad context of investigations into food relationships, as well as investigations into niche overlap and competition. Nutritive and
energy values and relative digestibilities of forage items are often included in investigations into forage relationships.

The practical management significance of a food investigation rests in understanding which items in the habitat may become limiting to a population during
times of stress and should, thus, be favored when habitat management is contemplated. This applies to predators as well as to herbivores. A knowledge of major
items in the diet provides an index to which forage species should be favored for
the wildlife species in question when retention or enhancement of a population is
contemplated. In order for these objectives to be adequately addressed, forage use
patterns must be considered one aspect of habitat use patterns and population characteristics. Use of food habits information alone, for directing habitat management,
will be risky.


## FEEDING STRATEGIES: DEFINITIONS

A number of terms are used to clarify different feeding strategies. *Generalists* are
those species that feed on a variety of foods, as distinguished from *specialists*,
which are more selective feeders. These definitions are relative one to the other, but
bears are obviously generalists, being omnivores. North temperate zone ungulates
may be classified as generalists as a group, since a wide range of items are taken by
each species. The sage grouse might be considered a specialist since it relies on the
various sagebrushes for the bulk of its diet.

A species may appear to switch from a generalist to a specialist strategy as
abundance of forages fluctuate. Where forage is not especially abundant and many
species occur, the generalist strategy should be emphasized. However, where one
forage item becomes especially abundant and easy to find or capture, specialization
on that food item may be expected. Conversely, when forage availability becomes
especially low and fewer items are available, then specialization may literally be
forced upon the animal.

*Time minimizers*, as contrasted with *energy maximizers*, provide a further
dichotomy in feeding strategies that illustrate different approaches to survival.
Species with fixed litter or clutch sizes, are likely to be time minimizers. The adaptation is based on the concept that species that exhibit restricted foraging times in
order to pursue other activities are generally less fecund than those that spend more

time foraging. Males must devote energy to acquiring and retaining mates, and hence are likely to pursue the time minimization strategy. Time minimizers follow the strategy of minimizing foraging time which maximizes fitness by providing more time for other activities, such as territorial defense and courtship. Conversely, the energy maximizer is apt to have indeterminate clutch or litter sizes and spend more time feeding. Hummingbirds are good examples of energy maximizers, while the large mammalian carnivores, which spend relatively less time eating than others, are time minimizers. Hixon (1982) considered that there is insufficient data to categorize most species at this time, and that the terms are relative to each other and hence ill-defined. The main difference is that a time minimizer would be predicted to stop feeding after obtaining some level of nutrient requirements, while an energy maximizer would forage continually during the same time period.

Jarman (1974) reported five feeding styles among African antelopes that relate to their body size and habitat selection. This classification is useful for the behavioral, habitat, and physical attributes that food habits are tied to. *Style A* species include those that are highly selective of plant species and plant parts. They feed predominantly upon the flowers, twig tops, fruits, and seedpods of shrubs. A wide variety of shrubs may be used, all generally of high nutritive content. The smallest antelopes, including the duikers and dik-diks are included in this category. *Style B* species include slightly larger species that are also selective feeders but use a variety of grasses and browse, varying seasonally but high in nutritional quality. The reedbuck, bushbuck, and gerenuk fall within this classification.

*Style C* species are the gazelles and impalas, using a variety of grasses and browse with seasonal variation. The variation occurs as habitat use patterns change, and flexibility is apparent. *Style D* species, which feed on a variety of grasses but are selective for growth state and part of plant, include the migratory plains game such as the wildebeest. This style is the least diverse of all and includes items lower in nutritive value than the preceeding styles. Finally, *Style E* species include unselective feeders such as buffalo and eland that utilize a highly diverse diet of generally low nutritive value, and are the largest bovids.

These feeding styles illustrate a general rule: as body size increases, the need for larger quantities of food also increases and the nutritive content per unit ingested may decrease. The highly selective feeders are thus the smaller species while larger species will usually be more generalist in foraging strategy. Deer, for example, will generally be more selective of plant parts than elk. The metabolic demands of deer require a diet higher in nutritional content than that required by elk. Deer are more capable than elk of selecting smaller items, because elk have a larger mouth, which militates against close selection of parts, and a larger body size, which means a need for more forage. Schwartz and Ellis (1981) show that these relationships generally hold for bison, cattle, pronghorn, and domestic sheep.

All of these classifications are relative and should be used comparatively. It is well to remember that environmental conditions can alter feeding behavior dramatically in species that are flexible, as most are.

## THEORIES INVOLVING FEEDING STRATEGIES

Theory in foraging strategy has developed based on the concept that food choice is related to maximization of energy intake for minimum expenditure of energy, which derives from the premise of MacArthur and Pianka (1966) that natural selection will tend to balance time and energy expenditures with benefits derived. Four key aspects of feeding strategies were put forth by Schoener (1971):

1. The optimal diet (quantity and quality)
2. The optimal foraging space
3. The optimal foraging period
4. The optimal foraging group size

When natural selection is considered, the ultimate measures of feeding strategy should relate back to individual fitness. Cost in energy and time (including that amount lost to other activities) required to detect, pursue, capture, and prepare the forage are involved. Nutritional value is an important part of the equation. Switching from a specialist diet to a generalist diet is related to density of forage and ease of obtaining it. As one item or group of items of similar nutritive value increases in abundance, the animal should tend to limit its selection more to those species and omit the less valuable items from its diet. Thus, a generalist forager, using a variety of items, will become more selective as forage abundance increases. Also, if forage is reduced through drought or other forms of habitat deterioration, a generalist forager may become more specialized simply because forage choices are limited. This is not predicted by the properties of the optional diet as defined by Pyke, Pulliam, and Charnov (1977), but is rather to be considered a special constraint that has significance in habitat management.

While the model presented in Figure 4.1 deals only with energy and omits other nutrients, a number of models now consider this issue (Pullian 1974; Westoby 1974). Reichman (1977) suggested that the diet of desert rodents is based primarily

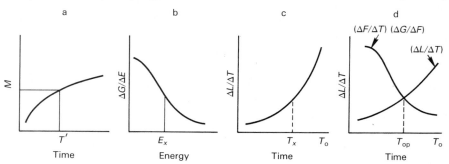

**Figure 4.1** Optimal feeding strategy theory following Schoener 1971. See text for explanation. (Used with permission.)

on considerations involving energy, but that energy intake is not maximized. The reason put forth was that nutritional values other than energy were involved. Also, the fact that some species of seeds found in the cheek pouches of the rodents that were collected did not occur in stomach contents suggests that other behavior is involved in choice of foods than just energy and nutritional value.

Schoener's (1971) general model of feeding strategy may be applied to a herbivore or a predator. The herbivore can be visualized as a predator on vegetation.

Three functions are defined. The first one, $F$, relates total energy obtained, $E$, to time, $T$, spent feeding during time interval $T_o$. $E = F(T)$, and is illustrated in Figure 4.1 (a). $M$ is that amount of energy acquired by an optimal feeder in $T'$ time. MacArthur (1972) categorizes the gathering of food into four phases: deciding when to search, the actual search, location of the food item and the decision whether to pursue it, and the pursuit and possible capture and eating of the prey. Generally, herbivores may expend more energy searching for food than pursuing and capturing it, while carnivores may divide their time more equally between search and pursuit.

A second function, $G(E)$, relates gain in reproductive fitness, the expected future reproduction output, to energy acquired during feeding, $E$, without relating this to time. It must be specified that energy will have to be acquired to maintain reproductive fitness. $E_x$ represents the optimal amount of energy acquired in relation to reproductive fitness.

A third function, $L(T)$, relates the loss in fitness that occurs because the animal spends time feeding rather than in other activities, such as nest building, defending a territory, resting, or breeding.

Figure 4.1 (b) shows the relationship between change in fitness per unit energy acquired feeding. This essentially shows that as more and more energy is acquired, the rate of increase of fitness decreases since $E$ is related to $T$ and again the time spent feeding must be subtracted from time in other activities. This is a highly variable issue especially with seasonal breeders, which may spend great amounts of time feeding during the nonbreeding season and much less time during breeding. And this may be expected to vary between the sexes since males of many species often spend large amounts of energy in displays and other activities associated with breeding while the females do not.

Figure 4.1 (c) relates change in loss of fitness, $\Delta L$, through change in time, $\Delta T$, to time spent obtaining energy, $T_x$. Decrease in fitness as defined will occur as more time is spent acquiring energy.

Figure 4.1 (d) provides the theoretical optimum foraging time $T_{op}$. The curve representing $(\Delta F/\Delta T)(\Delta G/\Delta F)$ will be a decreasing curve since there is a decreasing ability to convert energy into growth of offspring as more time is spent feeding. The optimum foraging time is where the $\Delta G/\Delta T$ and $\Delta L/\Delta T$ curves cross.

Let us go back to MacArthur's (1972) breakdown on the mechanics of food gathering to show a theory explaining forage selection. First we have to assume that the food items are all equal in quality, which obviously is a tenuous assumption in the case of herbivores, but may be appropriate for insectivorous birds, and illustrates a general concept. Search time, $S$, and pursuit time, $P$, are the variables that determine when a new species will be added to the diet (Figure 4.2). Prey item 1 will be included in the diet because, while search time is high, pursuit time is low. The same holds true for item 2, assuming equal quality. Essentially, this means that the predator is spending more time searching for the appropriate feeding habitat, in which pursuit and capture of prey is easiest. The diet will include those items for which mean search time and mean pursuit time is minimized, and where it is likely to capture only better items. Since availability of all items is equal, an additional prey item will be included in the diet only if pursuit time is less than the average of $P$ and $S$ for the previous diet. Change in search time will always be negative since the more variety of items of equal availability that are included in the diet, the less time will be required searching. Ranking of the prey item always proceeds from those where pursuit and capture is easiest to where it is most difficult. Availability in this model is related to $P$, which is in turn a measure of the adaptation of the species for the items in the diet. When the slope of the $\Delta S$ curve is increased, as may occur in a habitat highly productive of the preferred food item, then the number of items in the diet will decrease. The lower the absolute abundance of food, the greater the range of foods that will be eaten. This may be influenced by drought, snow, and competition.

The models illustrated in Figures 4.1 and 4.2 emphasize that the economics of foraging are related to nutrient and energy intake per unit of energy expended, and are part of the life equation which ultimately is judged by reproductive fitness. The tie from food habits to populations is thus well demonstrated. The models can provide insights into understanding habitat condition and competition, both key areas in wildlife management.

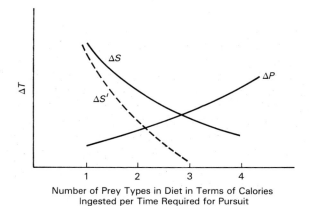

**Figure 4.2** Optimal diet relating change in pursuit $\Delta P$ and search time $\Delta S$ to numbers of prey in diet. From MacArthur and Pianka 1966. (Used with permission.)

## FACTORS INFLUENCING PALATABILITY
## AND PREFERENCES

*Preference* indicates a selective response for one food item over another. It implies that, given a variety of forage items of similar abundance and palatability, an animal may select certain items in lieu of others. Drickhamer (1976) presented evidence that food preferences of *Peromyscus leucopus* and *P. maniculatus* may be inherited. Laboratory-bred individuals showed definite preferences for food in their native habitats. In addition, food preferences of mice could be altered through "food-cue conditioning," or providing different odors to foods, thereby suggesting that prior olfactory experience affected preference (Drickhamer 1972). Food odors from particles adhering to conspecifics, pelage, or through feces, may cause a rat to incorporate a new food with that odor into its diet (Posados-Andrews and Roper 1983). Olfaction has been suggested as the primary sense used to identify palatable foods by domestic sheep (Krueger, Laycock, and Price 1974). Longhurst et al. (1968) identified the olfactory sense as being initially responsible for food item selection while sight is used thereafter in deer. That a "tradition of use" can be highly important is evidenced by the field feeding behavior of waterfowl acquired after agriculture modified their habitats (Bossenmaier and Marshall 1958). D. Q. Thompson (1965) demonstrated individual differences in forage preferences for *Microtus ochrogaster.*

*Palatability* involves physiological features of forage such as its nutritive content and digestibility. Palatability of plants is generally connected with high protein and carbohydrate content and low lignin cellulose content. Here it is important to note that a preferred food item may be no more digestible than a less preferred item and still be consumed in higher quantities. Such a phenomenon is indicated by Urness, Neff, and Watkins (1975) for Gambel oak and Fendler's ceanothus, mule deer forages of which the former is preferred over the latter. Red osier dogwood is known to be lower in protein than willows, yet it appears to be preferred by moose (I. M. Cowan, Hoar, and Hatter 1950). Thus, preference may supersede palatability in the choice of a food item.

Forage choice of young ducklings appears to be related to their need for a high protein source that the immature bird can readily obtain. The mallard duckling diet switches from terrestrial insects to aquatic insects and finally to vegetation characteristic of the adult diet as the ducklings move from the nest to water and learn to submerge their heads and develop the "tip-up" feeding behavior (Chura 1961; Figure 4.3). Some forage species simply are not accessible until more mature feeding behavior patterns are developed.

Allelomimetic (socially facilitated) behavior may also be involved. When groups of two and four ducks are exposed to an *ad libitum* diet, the larger groups ate more and gained more weight (Penney and Bailey 1970). This may suggest that forage choice can be altered by the number of conspecifics in the feeding group, at least among some species.

Displacement behavior that substitutes feeding for aggression during rutting

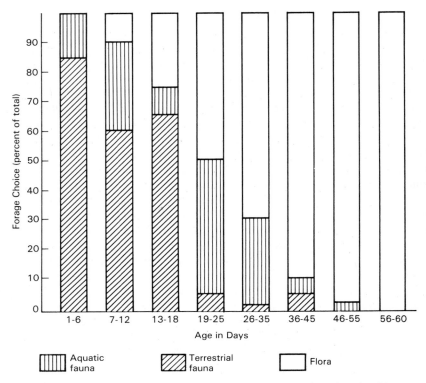

**Figure 4.3** Mallard duckling food habits related to age in days since hatching. Ages up to 18 days represent downy young, 19–55 days, partially feathered, 56–60 days, age when first flying. (From Chura, 1961. Used with permission.)

activities may cause otherwise little-used species to receive attention. Peek, Urich, and Mackie (1976) noted use of alders by moose in the fall, especially in areas where other signs such as antler rubbing, trampling, and rutting pits suggested intensive rutting activity. Since alder was not used much at any other time, it was suggested that feeding on this species, which was most common on the rutting sites, could be a form of displacement behavior.

Bioenergetics of the individual species, and its digestive physiology and anatomy also can be related to forage use. Bell (1971) reported an annual succession of grazing species on the Serengeti Plain of Kenya that could be correlated to the above factors. Gazelles, the smallest antelope species with the highest metabolic rate, were the first to graze an area, using the most succulent forbs and grasses. Next came the larger wildebeest, which grazed the taller grasses. Finally, the zebras came through, grazing on the coarser silicaceous grass stems left after the intensive previous grazing. Zebras, without the four-partitioned stomach of the ruminant, can exist on large quantities of the coarser forage.

### Plant-Related Factors

The more succulent plants with higher moisture content tend to be preferred, although variation on this occurs as noted above. Herbivores are also noted to graze and browse the tips of twigs, seed heads, and leaves where protein tends to be concentrated (Blair and Epps 1967). The current year's growth of beaked hazel and willow contains higher protein levels than the previous year's growth and is the preferred moose browse (I. M. Cowan et al. 1950).

While the relationship between protein content and preference is generally valid, differences do exist that obscure the relationships (Table 4.1). For instance, bacteriostatic chemicals in sagebrush, juniper, and some conifers tend to inhibit rumen function and thus restrict intake by ungulates (J. G. Nagy, Steinhoff and Ward 1964). The amount of monoterpene hydrocarbons in Douglas fir affects their palatability to black-tailed deer (Radwan and Ellis 1975). Farentinas et al. (1981) reported ponderosa pine trees with low amounts of monoterpene were fed upon by Abert's squirrels while trees with high amounts were not. Thus, these species can be preferred items in the diet but are most often used in conjunction with other species that facilitate rumen function and digestibility. Chemical defense in sagebrush may not limit its use by sage grouse, however. Also, Douglas fir and subalpine fir are preferred items in the diet of blue grouse, as are lodgepole and jackpine for spruce grouse, which suggests that tetranoids are capable of assimilating these bacteriostatic chemicals and also that these chemicals are not a selective influence of consequence on these forage species.

Snowshoe hares are known to prefer willows in northern boreal forests (Wolff 1980). Experimental work, preceded by field observation, revealed that willow sprouts less than one year old (*juvenile plants*) contain high levels of tannins, which inhibit digestion and thus act as a chemical defense mechanism (Bryant, Chapen, and Klein 1983). As plants age and can tolerate browsing more readily, tannin content diminishes.

Cates and Orians (1975) demonstrated that plants characteristic of early suc-

**TABLE 4.1    Comparisons of Winter Protein Levels of Some Preferred
White-Tailed Deer and Moose Forage Species with
Some Relatively Unpalatable Species**

| Species | Preference | Crude Protein (percent) | Reference |
|---------|------------|-------------------------|-----------|
| Jackpine | Not preferred | 3.8 | Ullrey et al. 1967 |
| White cedar | Preferred by deer | 2.7 | Ullrey et al. 1964 |
| Willow | Preferred by moose | 5.9 | I. M. Cowan, Hoar, and Hatter 1950 |
| Green alder | Not preferred | 9.9 | I. M. Cowan, Hoar, and Hatter 1950 |

cessional stages, with a lesser commitment to defense against herbivores than plants characteristic of later succession and climax, were more palatable to the slugs *Ariolimax columbianus* and *Arion ater*. Early successional annuals were also more palatable than early successional perennials. Secondary substances produced by plants that are defense strategies against herbivores are implicated in the choice of foods. Plant species that have evolved such adaptive strategies are generally those characteristic of longer-lived successional or climax vegetation and would be more vulnerable over longer periods to herbivores. On the other hand, high reproductive rates of the plants characteristic of early successional stages may obviate the need for such strategies and may be a strategy in itself to protect against herbivory.

Other species, characteristic of climax or late-successional communities, have the capability of withstanding heavy use without damage. Mountain mahogany, a highly preferred forage of mule deer, when consistently browsed over a period of years, assumes a clubbed appearance wherein some leaves become unavailable and thus ensure retention of phytosynthetic tissue. The dead stems that protect such leaves serve much the same role as the spines of cactus and rose, which are another well-known mechanical deterrent to grazing.

Scotch pine needles on young trees are pointed and unpalatable to herbivores, while the needles of older trees are rounded and highly preferred by moose (Ahlen 1968). By the time Scotch pine becomes palatable, a portion of the plant may be unavailable, simply because it has outgrown the browsing range of the moose. Cedars and aspens are also highly palatable tree species and withstand browsing of lower branches without significant damage if upper portions are out of reach.

Production of estrogens by desert annuals, which are preferred valley quail forage, may serve to limit quail populations in dry years (A. S. Leopold et al. 1976). When phytoestrogen levels were elevated, reproductive capabilities of valley quail were impaired, and thus phytoestrogens may serve as a limiting factor to quail population size.

On the other hand, some plant species concentrate certain nutrients that may make them preferred forage items. Sodium is concentrated in aquatics such as pondweeds, which may facilitate their palatability and importance to moose (Botkin et al. 1973). Calcium is concentrated in aspens and hazels, important forage species for a number of wildlife (Gerloff et al. 1966).

Svoboda and Gullion (1972) reported that male aspen buds were preferred ruffed grouse winter forage in northern Minnesota. There were two reasons that these were preferred over female buds and those of birch, juneberry, and other species. First, because male buds are large and very high in calorie content in winter, the amount of energy they provide is more equivalent to energy expended in a cold climate than if other items were sought in preference. Secondly, the aspen branches are stout and provide good support for a perching bird the size of a grouse in comparison to birch or juneberry. The mechanical advantage in perching plus the bioenergetic relationships were both involved in determining preference for male aspen by ruffed grouse in winter.

It is thus apparent that a number of factors influence forage preference and palatability. That each herbivorous species has adapted to certain forages through a combined evolution of behavior, physiology, and morphology, and that there are numerous strategies evolved by plants that counteract herbivory, both attest to the intricate nature of the relationship. An understanding of the basic nature of the relationship is important when wildlife habitat management results are evaluated, and again, no generalizations are warranted.

## UTILIZATION VERSUS AVAILABILITY

Earlier workers generally assumed that availability was the major influence on choice of forage items (McAtee 1918) and indeed this is the case. However, A. Leopold (1933) reported that kinds of food eaten were related to:

1. What was present during the season in question
2. What was available or accessible without undue work or exposure
3. What was palatable in kind and condition
4. What was needed for current physiological processes
5. What the individual was accustomed to eating and skilled in finding

Items 1 and 2 are definitely related to availability, but item 3 is related to palatability, item 4 to physiology and adaptation, and item 5 to preference.

Availability obviously is the fundamental prerequisite to determining whether an item will be eaten, but Glading (1940), working with quail, recognized that preference and palatability had to be considered. The most abundant species are not necessarily the most preferred. A forage species may be used in proportion to, less than, or more than its relative abundance, and it is intuitively logical to assign a ranking to a forage item based on this concept (B. Glading, Biswell and Smith 1940; Bellrose and Anderson 1943; Hungerford 1957).

However, forage use indices do not necessarily reflect the value of a food item. Items low in preference and availability may have rankings similar to those of items high in preference and availability. Also, items common in the diet and of relatively high abundance could be ranked lower than items less common in the diet and even less available.

Forage use patterns may not be indicative of the level within the habitat occupied by a population at which selection occurs. In the case of the waterfowl studied by Bellrose and Anderson (1943), aquatic forages occurred as virtually monotypic stands within a marsh, so the level of selection may have been for the food "patch" rather than the individual item. Animals may choose habitats that have high abundance of forage species, such as when a grizzly bear feeds in a stand of huckleberries or at a salmon spawning site. This means that selection may be at the habitat level rather than for individual food items (Jarman 1974; D. H. Johnson 1980). Patch type rather than food type, as referenced by Pyke et al. (1977), may be more critical in these cases.

Finally, *availability* is merely a term describing the relative or absolute abundance of a food item. Availability of vegetation may not be simply a matter of estimating abundance, since secondary metabolites such as phenols and tannins may inhibit digestion of some plants, making abundance estimates an overestimate of the availability of edible material. In measuring availability of animal matter, one has to consider not only density, volume, or weight but also vulnerability. Hence, while prime adult moose were most numerous on Isle Royale, they constituted a minimal part of the wolf diet, while calves and old-age moose were major items at the time Mech (1966) investigated this system.

The food habits study, as traditionally conceived and carried out, thus has limitations for use in wildlife management. A knowledge of habitat use patterns and population condition is needed to aid in interpreting a food habits study. Individual foods selected must be keyed to the habitat on which they were taken if a full understanding of the significance of the item in the diet is to be obtained. This is because certain habitats and forages will provide food and cover at critical periods such as during severe storms or prolonged drought and, therefore, are more important to survival than other habitats and forages (Gullion 1966). At the same time, forage times that are common in the diet through a given period, in habitats that receive extensive use, must be identified. The degree to which alternate forage items may be substituted within a diet and still maintain the individual is not well understood. Moen (1973) recognized that taxonomic differentiation of forage items may not be valid from a nutritional standpoint if an animal is able to digest and assimilate two different species equally well.

It is safe to assume that the food habits study will continue to be an important endeavor when interspecific competition, regulation of numbers, habitat manipulation to favor preferred items, and an understanding of the overall ecology and behavior of a species are at issue. But assignment of items into forage classes, such as insects, shrubs, grasses, or moose, will no longer suffice. Simple listing of items in the diet, even with a frequency of occurrence or other ranking are not going to be very useful. Investigations into forage use patterns have greatly expanded in recent years, as theoretical considerations and nutritional relationships have received attention. Our understanding of the relationships between the animal and its habitat has been enhanced as the old-style forage study has given way to more complex investigations.

The question of whether or not availability influences forage choice, except at extreme levels of abundance, has been raised by proponents of optimal diet theory. Pyke et al. (1977) specify that inclusion of a food item in the diet should be independent of the abundance of that food type, but related to the abundance of food types more frequently taken than the food in question. The animal should not specialize on a less preferred forage when more preferred forage is available. Westoby (1980) concluded that intake of a forage item by a generalist herbivore should not be affected by its availability except when availability is reduced to very low levels. However, it is apparent that shifts in forage choice do occur, relative to changes in habitat use (Jarman 1974), seasonal changes in forage quality, and presence of competitors (Schwartz and Ellis 1981), irrespective of change in availability.

How does one measure preference? The problem of determining what is available to an animal virtually always requires a subjective judgment in field studies. Owen-Smith and Novellie (1982) specified that the effective path width scanned by herbivores included all the forage that was available to it. This could be a 1-meter-wide belt along a feeding trail. But if the animal has a free choice of paths along which to feed, then this belt becomes a minimum estimate of availability. D. H. Johnson (1980) suggested use of a ranking method that tends to minimize the effect of including items that are questionable as to availability. A measure of availability is needed in order to measure preference, and that measure must be carefully spelled out to avoid misunderstanding.

## EXAMPLES OF FOOD HABITS STUDIES

### Native Ungulates

Food habits studies of North American big game are rife with examples of faulty research and misguided criticism. On the one hand, as Gullion (1966) pointed out, mere listing of items in the diet without supporting evidence to indicate critical items used at critical times can be quite useless from a management standpoint. No indications are obtained of what items may ultimately serve to carry a population through severe periods, and hence of what items to favor in habitat management. On the other hand, portraying food habits studies as inadequate efforts to understand nutritional relationships does not take into account the intent of using the data to direct habitat mangement and predict foraging behavior under critical conditions. The nutritionist, interested in physiological responses and digestibility of certain items, provides insight into functional responses that field studies cannot provide and that help explain why observed forage use patterns occur.

The idea that a food habits study will never be replicable through time is also misleading. While the techniques used in the field are imprecise, virtually all will reveal major items in the diet. When these data are examined in relation to the habitat in which they were used, the weather pattern, and the population data that indicates survivability during the period, the real value of the food habits study then becomes apparent. Items in the diet cannot be interpreted without supporting information, in a management context. There have been innumerable food habits investigations that have not been conducted in this context and, thus, are not very useful. However, if sampling is adequate, a forage use pattern should be predictable when similar circumstances prevail.

An example of how availability affects forage preference in big game is provided by Wetzel (1972) for white-tailed deer in northeastern Minnesota. Availability of forage along a trail made by a feeding deer was determined by twig counts in 4-m$^2$ plots placed at 50-m intervals along the trail, a sampling method that should account for the nonrandom distribution of shrubs (Mueller-Dombois and Ellenberg 1974:38). Since snow depths increased during the sampling period and deer shifted habitat use patterns, the abundance values were not absolute but relative to the depth of snow. As winter progressed, the diet shifted from dogwood, maples, and juneberries, which were used in a 3:1 ratio of use to availability, to a diet dominated by beaked hazel, which was used in a ratio of almost 2:1 (Figure 4.4). Since the most critical winter period is January through March, one might conclude that beaked hazel was a very critical browse species in this area, if food habits data alone were considered. However, at a time when beaked hazel was used, deer had reduced their feeding activity and moved into conifer cover. As R. A. Hoffman and Robinson

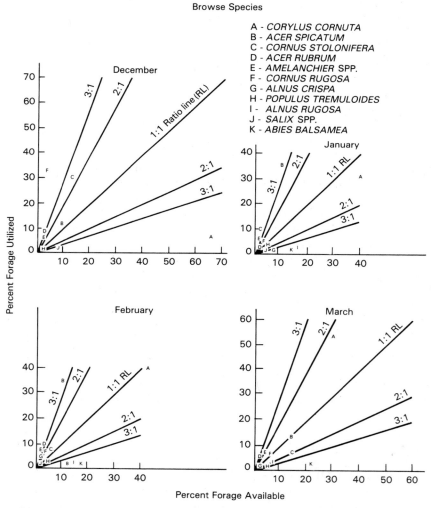

Browse Species

A - *CORYLUS CORNUTA*
B - *ACER SPICATUM*
C - *CORNUS STOLONIFERA*
D - *ACER RUBRUM*
E - *AMELANCHIER* SPP.
F - *CORNUS RUGOSA*
G - *ALNUS CRISPA*
H - *POPULUS TREMULOIDES*
I - *ALNUS RUGOSA*
J - *SALIX* SPP.
K - *ABIES BALSAMEA*

**Figure 4.4** Utilization to availability ratios for 11 browse species used by white-tailed deer in winter, northeastern Minnesota. From Wetzel 1972. (Used with permission.)

(1966), Silver et al. (1969), and other investigators have discovered subsequently through a variety of approaches, whitetails in midwinter revert from an active energy-demanding pattern to a much-reduced activity level that expends much less energy. This is a response to the naturally deteriorated nutritional quality of their forage and its reduced accessibility during the severe winter period. Thus, although beaked hazel becomes a "preferred" food item, it is a major constituent in the diet when other forages are not as readily available and when the deer are using heavy cover and are relatively inactive. The forage species that should receive attention are those used when deer are more actively feeding in cover types more productive of these items.

This work illustrates also that some items will be highly preferred but will be of limited availability and, therefore, presumably of lesser importance than less-preferred items that are more generally abundant. Also, this work demonstrates the need to use food habits information *in context* with a knowledge of habitat use patterns and population information.

Another example illustrating the need to use food habits data as supporting information lies in the studies of Roosevelt elk in the Hoh River Valley of Olympic National Park by Leslie, Starkey, and Vavra (1984). The diet was determined to be low in digestible energy, although generally adequate in crude protein. This may be taken at face value to indicate that habitat management such as logging or burning could benefit the elk population, and to provide additional leverage to reduce the size of the park. However, other information shows this herd to be at high density, using a wide variety of habitats including the famous old-growth forest but not restricted to it. It then becomes obvious that a large elk population may be sustained on a forage base that is relatively less digestible than comparison forages. The means by which this elk population sustains itself under the prevailing conditions cannot be determined with only a food habits study, no matter how comprehensive, to use as evidence. On the other hand, without the food habits analysis, the habitat relationships of this population, and the means by which it has been adapted to the coastal rain forests, will not be understood.

Cushwa et al. (1970) reported that habitat management emphasizing woody browse for white-tailed deer in many parts of the Southeast was based on the faulty assumption that shrubs were important winter food. Their analysis of 489 rumen samples revealed that acorns, grasses, mushrooms, fruits, and leaves of evergreen shrubs were most important and that woody twigs were not a significant part of the diet. The work demonstrates the need to include food habits analyses in habitat management programs and to rely on local information rather than data from other areas.

Efforts to portray moose and caribou as food generalists perhaps best illustrates the means by which management significance of ecological data may be misinterpreted. In the case of caribou, ground or arboreal lichens have been considered important winter forage for this species in northern Canada (Scotter 1964) and mountainous British Columbia (Edwards and Ritcey 1960). However, Bergerud (1974) considered caribou to be food generalists because the harsh environments they occupy dictate the need to be highly mobile and capable of using whatever forage may be available. Indeed sedges and grasses may predominate in the diet in some areas. However, D. R. Klein (1982) points out that lichens are very high in energy but low in protein and serve as a major part, but not the entire part, of the winter diet for a population that is in balance with its habitat. Caribou apparently evolved in relation to lichens as a part of their winter diet because lichens are a highly digestible energy source for the species.

Moose are considered to be obligate browsers, yet LeResche and Davis (1973) reported high occurrences of nonbrowse foods from moose rumens on the Kenai Peninsula of Alaska. Subsequent work by Oldemeyer et al. (1977) suggested that this area provided poor winter range for moose because of the lack of diversity of woody browse. The area is now dominated by paper birch where once birch, aspen, and willlows occurred. The change in species composition attributed to plant succession and heavy browsing has contributed to a decline in the moose population itself. The work illustrates why food habits studies must be used as supporting information to be most useful.

North American ungulates do not fit Jarman's (1974) feeding style classification for African antelopes well. The North American species vary in feeding style between areas. Elk are probably the true generalists, and most adaptable, ranging from migratory in behavior to nonmigratory, subsisting on grasses or browse during the dormant period. Hobbs et al. (1981) concluded that browse (higher in protein) and grasses (higher in energy) complemented each other in the elk diets in Colorado and were thus both important in maintaining elk.

Even white-tailed deer, the smallest of the native Cervidae, can select a widely diverse mix of forage to compensate for rapidly changing forage quality conditions. Van Gilder, Torgerson, and Porath (1982) reported that forage ranked low in digestibility may have high levels of other nutrients and thus be important items in the diet. Management for forage diversity in whitetail habitats is important.

Diet quality was found to be generally higher for pronghorn antelope than bison by Schwartz and Ellis (1981). Pronghorn consumed a wider variety of plant species than did bison, apparently an adaptation toward maintaining the higher-quality diet needed to sustain the higher metabolic rates of the smaller species. Larger species will tend to rely more on highly abundant forages that may be of lower quality, while smaller species may be more selective of forage that will be of higher quality. This implies that management to retain forage diversity and high quality in smaller units will benefit the smaller species, and management to maintain productivity of the most abundant forages in larger units may benefit the larger species.

Forage use patterns for one species can be expected to vary seasonally, between areas, and in one area through time (Nellis and Ross 1969). Provisions to ensure the availability of forages that are used during crisis periods of drought or deep snow conditions are important. A knowledge of the predominant items in the diet for each season, the most preferred items, and the successional status of each within the plant community is needed to properly manage forage for big game.

### Bears

Bears represent the classic case of the opportunistic foraging strategy and thus warrant specific attention. A superficial assumption holds that, since these species are omnivorous and, with the exception of the polar bear, feed on a wide variety of foods such as grass, salmon, mast, and berries that are seasonally extraordinarily abundant, forage will not ordinarily be a limiting factor. However, more critical analyses lend credence to the argument that food is indeed a limiting mechanism in bear populations.

The long-term investigations of the northeastern Minnesota black bear populations by Rogers (1976) showed that nutritional status as indicated by live weight correlated well with cub production and survival. Annual fluctuations in food supply were concluded to be responsible for fluctuations in the adult population level as well. The critical foods were beaked hazel nuts, blueberries, dogwood, fruits, chokecherries, and raspberries, all of which mature in late summer. Garshelis and Pelton (1981) reported that social intolerance among black bears in the Great Smoky Mountain National Park was likely greater during years of poor acorn production. Subadult males appeared to be forced out of fall home ranges by adult males. Beeman and Pelton (1980) reported that food scarcity in late summer and fall was likely the cause of increased bear movements outside this park. The availability of fall mast crops thus appeared to be important in regulating population size.

While mast and berries are apparently the most critical items in the fall diet of black bears, they are not high in protein content (Beeman and Pelton 1980). Animal matter, including insects and mammals, constitutes high-protein foods and comprised only 11 percent of the overall diet in their study. Landers et al. (1979) point out that high-protein foods used in spring are associated with recovery from inanition during denning while the period of use of high-energy foods is associated with the breeding period and the predenning period.

While black bears may be seeking out a diet high in protein in spring in parts of Washington, they feed heavily on sapwood high in sugars at this time of year (Radwan 1969). Feeding on Douglas fir, western hemlock, western red cedar, and red alder (listed in order of descending preference) is a significant source of damage to these valuable species. However, Radwan (1969) reported that in some areas where sugar content in trees was similar, bears did not feed on these species, and therefore a chemical analysis alone did not suffice to explain bear depredations on trees. Undoubtedly this relationship is complex, related in part to availability and palatability of alternative forage sources, bear population density, and variations in bear feeding behavior evolving from tradition.

Craighead, Sumner, and Scaggs (1982) consider the grizzly to be basically a carnivore, but this species is a functional herbivore over most of its range (A. M. Pearson 1975). Previous experience is very important in actual foraging of the highly adaptable species. Immediately after emergence from denning, the grizzly may feed on grasses, sedges, roots of forbs such as *Hedysarum alpinum*, willow catkins, or aspen leaves. Carrion may be important in early spring to bears in Yellowstone National Park (Cole 1972) and Glacier National Park (Martinka 1972). Summer diets tend to be vegetative, although wasps, ants, and ground squirrels are taken as they are encountered.

Craighead et al. (1982) categorized vegetative foods of the grizzly into four energy categories: grasses and sedges, forbs, berries, and nuts. Sites that contained an abundance of these items were considered most critical to the welfare of the bear. Seepage areas where forbs and rushes were most lush, habitats containing heavy understories of blueberry, semivegetated talus where forbs were present, and stands of white bark pine were among the more critical areas for grizzlies in northwestern Montana.

This pattern of switching forages as one group becomes less abundant and another more abundant is apparent with the coastal brown bear as well. Brown bears feed heavily on sedges and grasses, but they concentrate on salmon runs as they develop, and then switch to highly preferred berry crops on Kodiak Island (Berns and Hensel 1970).

The bear is closely attuned to the phenology of its forage sources (Craighead et al. 1982). When forage is abundant they are voracious feeders, but when forage resources decline their metabolic processes begin to change toward the hibernation state. When key forage sources do not become available, as when plant development is delayed, or berry, nut, and mast crop failures occur, then reproduction and survival is lowered. Thus, the population performance of these species is tied closely to the forage base.

### Upland Birds

Referring once again to Gullion (1966), it is well to remember that while a variety of forage species are used by the gallinaceous birds, the important species are those used during critical periods that appear to limit the distribution of populations to rather specific habitats (Table 4.2). These critical periods may be associated with winter conditions or drought, depending upon the area. While in some instances a single species may provide the bulk of the diet during a critical period, as for spruce and sage grouse, often several forage species combine to form the critical diet.

Animal matter in the form of invertebrates, mostly insects, commonly constitutes the bulk of the diet for broods of all species. Stiven (1961) showed that blue grouse chicks using a seven-year-old-burn on Vancouver Island were provided an abundant high-energy food source by the invertebrate fauna. An example of the sequence of change in diet from hatching to adult sage grouse is provided in Table 4.3, using J. G. Peterson's (1970) data from central Montana. The percent of animal matter continuously drops as chicks mature, to below that occurring in the adult diet of August.

TABLE 4.2    Some Forage Species Used During Critical Periods
by Gallinaceous Game Birds

| Bird Species | Forage Species | Location | Reference |
|---|---|---|---|
| Ruffed grouse | Aspens | N.E. Minnesota | Gullion 1966 |
| Ruffed grouse | Serviceberry | Idaho | Marshall 1946 |
| Blue grouse | Douglas fir | Idaho, Washington | Beer 1943; Marshall 1946 |
| Sage grouse | Sagebrush | Idaho | Dalke et al. 1963 |
| Spruce grouse | Spruce | Alaska | L. N. Ellison 1966 |
| Spruce grouse | Jackpine | Ontario | Crichton 1963 |
| White-tailed ptarmigan | Willows | Montana | Choate 1963 |
| Sharptail | White birch, aspen | Wisconsin | Grange 1949 |
| Merriam's turkey | Ponderosa pine, acorns | Eastern Colorado | Hoffman 1962 |
| Merriam's turkey | Snowberry, rose, bearberry | Eastern Montana | Jonas 1966 |
| Hungarian partridge | Barley, wheat | Eastern Montana | Weigand 1980 |
| Chukar partridge | Cheatgrass | Nevada | Christenson 1970 |
| Pheasant | Corn, wheat | Michigan | Dalke 1935, 1937 |

TABLE 4.3    Changes in Diet of Juvenile Sage Grouse in Central Montana

| | Age in Weeks | | | | |
|---|---|---|---|---|---|
| Diet | 1–4 | 5–8 | 9–12 | 13–16+ | Adult (August) |
| Percent animal matter | 30 | 24 | 17 | 3 | 19 |
| Percent vegetable | 70 | 76 | 83 | 97 | 81 |
| *Taraxacum officinale*[a] | 63/33 | 59/23 | 43/19 | 67/30 | 70/33 |
| *Tragopogon dubius*[a] | 46/9 | 83/30 | 60/5 | 41/6 | 60/10 |
| *Artemesia frigida*[a] | 6/tr[b] | 35/3 | 50/19 | 26/3 | 63/11 |
| *Artemesia tridentata*[a] | 6/tr[b] | 2/tr[b] | 41/3 | 27/2 | 37/5 |
| Number of Samples | 26 | 47 | 54 | 24 | 18 |

*Source:* Peterson 1970. (Used with permission.)

*Note:* Data are based on crop and gizzard analysis.

[a]Amounts are percent frequency/volume of all samples for time period.

[b]Tr = trace.

## Waterfowl

Food preferences of mallard ducklings were previously illustrated in Figure 4.3, using Chura's (1961) data. Tables 4.4 to 4.6 summarize results of several studies that indicate differences between species, area, and season. Generally, diving

TABLE 4.4    Preferential Rating of Duck Foods in the Illinois River Valley

| Excellent Duck Foods[a] | Good Duck Foods | Fair Duck Foods | Poor Duck Foods |
|---|---|---|---|
| Rice cutgrass | Giant burreed | Buttonbush | River bulrush |
| Walter's millet | Coontail | Spike rushes | American lotus |
| Wild millets | Teal grass | Water hemp | Pickerelweed |
| Moist soil smartweeds | Duck potato | Marsh cordgrass | Marsh mallow |
| Nut grasses | Marsh smartweed | Sago pondweed | Southern naiad |
| | Longleaf pondweed | Waterlily | Wildrice |
| | | | Small pondweed |

*Source:* Bellrose and Anderson 1943. (Used with permission.)
*Note:* Preference rating based on use/abundance.
[a]Corn omitted; seeds used.

TABLE 4.5    Major Food Plants of 410 Ducks on Winter Range
in Southeastern Texas

| Food Plant[a] | Times Used | Percent of Total Volume |
|---|---|---|
| Rice *(Oryza sativa)* | 159 | 39.99 |
| Dwarf spike rush | 117 | 8.32 |
| Wild millet | 46 | 7.84 |
| Widgeon grass | 86 | 4.29 |
| Smartweed | 54 | 3.98 |
| Square-stem spikerush | 116 | 3.27 |
| Pondweed | 52 | 2.86 |
| Duckmeat | 51 | 2.08 |
| Sawgrass | 73 | 1.89 |
| Sedge *(Cyperus)* | 124 | 1.83 |
| Primrose willow | 38 | 1.55 |
| Spike rush | 141 | 1.44 |
| Sedge *(Cyperaceae)* | 20 | 1.23 |
| Jungle rice *(Echinochloa)* | 25 | 1.14 |

*Source:* Singleton 1951. (Used with permission.)
[a]The item used in each case was *seeds.*

ducks utilize a higher proportion of animal matter than do dabblers. Winter diets of all species in the major Texas winter ranges use increasing amounts of seeds. Bellrose (1976) has summarized forage preferences for all North American waterfowl. Variation between areas is related to available foods.

Of special interest is the field-feeding preference of ducks and geese. This can be an economic problem for grain farmers who live in areas where waterfowl concentrate, such as the Horicon Marsh in Wisconsin. It can also be an economic asset if the fields are leased to hunters. Bossenmaier and Marshall (1958) examined field-feeding behavior of waterfowl in southern Manitoba (Table 4.7). Fields that were

TABLE 4.6   **Food Habits of North American Diving Ducks**
**(item volume as percent of total volume)**

| Food Item | Species[a] | | | | | |
| --- | --- | --- | --- | --- | --- | --- |
| | Redhead | Ringneck | Canvasback | G. scaup | L. scaup | Ruddy |
| Plant foods[b] | 89.6 | 81.5 | 80.6 | 46.5 | 59.5 | 72.4 |
| Animal foods | 10.3 | 18.5 | 19.4 | 53.5 | 40.4 | 27.4 |
| Insects | 5.9 | 10.8 | 8.1 | 7.1 | 12.1 | 21.9 |
| Crustaceans | 0.4 | 0.1 | 0.1 | 6.8 | 1.3 | 2.5 |
| Mollusks | 3.9 | 6.0 | 6.0 | 39.1 | 24.9 | 2.8 |

*Source:* Cottam 1939. (Used with permission.)
[a]Goldeneyes, buffleheads, oldsquads, harlequin, eiders, and scoters are predominantly animal feeders (75% of diet).
[b]Includes muskgrass, pondweeds, wild celery, wild rice, sedges, smartweeds, and waterlilies.

TABLE 4.7   **Summary of Duck and Goose Field-Feeding Preferences**

| Crop Type | Order of Preference for Ducks | | | Order of Preference for Geese | |
| --- | --- | --- | --- | --- | --- |
| | Field Condition | | | Field Condition | |
| | Burn | Dry, Cut | Dry, Stubble | Dry, Cut | Stubble |
| Durum wheat | 1 | 1 | 1 | 2 | 2 |
| Hard wheat | 2 | 3 | 2 | 1 | 1 |
| Barley | 3 | 2 | 3 | 2 | 2 |
| Oats | 4 | 4 | 4 | — | — |
| Flax | — | 6 | 6 | — | — |
| Fall rye | — | 5 | 5 | — | — |

| Field Type | Dry | Flooded | Dry | Flooded[a] |
| --- | --- | --- | --- | --- |
| Burned | 2 | 3 | 2 | — |
| Stubble | 3 | 4 | 3 | — |
| Standing | — | 2 | — | — |
| Swathed | 1 | 1 | — | — |
| Surface tilled | 4 | 5 | — | — |
| Plowed | — | — | — | — |
| Summer fallow | — | — | — | — |
| Disced | — | — | 1 | — |

*Source:* Bossemaier and Marshall 1958. (Used with permission.)
[a]No data available.

flooded, even if in stubble or surface-tilled, were preferred over dry fields. Field types appeared to be distinguishable to the birds from the air, while the crop was identified while they were on the ground. Fall depredations are most serious, and inclement weather that delays harvest and migration maximizes opportunities for depredation. Waterfowl visited fields in all weather except at midday with high temperatures, light winds, and clear skies. Fields closest to lakes used for resting were most vulnerable. The probabilty of crop depredations occurring depends on the following factors:

1. Vulnerability of fields present
2. Relative abundance of vulnerable and nonvulnerable fields
3. Preference rating of vulnerable fields
4. Size of the field-feeding population

## FOOD GUILDS OF NONGAME BIRDS

The guild concept is a useful means of considering food habits among the wide variety of nongame species. Root (1967) defined the *guild* as a group of species that exploit the same class of environmentally related niches without regard to their taxonomic affinities. Root (1967) also used the concept to apply to nonfood items, such as nest site selection (i.e., a hole-nesting guild). In essence, the guild is a step higher than the niche in a hierarchy that attempts to place species in ecologically related groups. Root (1967) considered the guild concept to be useful in the study of communities since species in a guild can be more readily studied than the entire community complex. Also, the guild focuses attention on all sympatric species involved in a potentially competitive relationship regardless of their taxonomic relationships.

Investigations of food guilds have helped to elaborate differences between closely related species. The foliage-gleaning guild in the oak savannah of central California contains five species (Root 1967). These species feed primarily on arthropods that exist on or near tree canopies. A partial description of how the five species partition the food resource in the habitat is presented in Table 4.8. An inspection of this table shows how the five species tend to partition the arthropod resource by varying size and composition in the diet, and by choosing different habitats. Also, some species are more generalist in strategy, like the Hutton's vireo. Others, like the warbling vireo, employ a more specialized strategy of foraging and habitat choice within this guild. The guild concept brings into sharp focus the overlap and inter-relatedness of the theories involving predation, competition, and habitat selection.

A large variety of foraging guilds can occur when the entire avian complex is considered. Thus far, the breeding nongame bird complex, primarily the passeriformes and piciformes, have been treated, with raptors and less common species omitted. Twenty-two species of passerines breeding on the Hubbard Brook Forest, New Hampshire, have been classified into four guilds by Holmes, Bonney, and Pacala (1979): ground foragers, bark foragers, outer-branch foragers, and among-foliage foragers. Willson (1974) categorized guilds by primary food habits, most common feeding stratum, and usual foraging behavior (Table 4.9). Examination of

**TABLE 4.8  Forage Characteristics of Five Species
in the Oak Foliage Gleaning Guild near Monterey County, California**

| Forage Characteristics | Blue-Grey Gnat Catcher | Warbling Vireo | Hutton's Vireo | Orange-Crowned Warbler | Plain Titmouse |
|---|---|---|---|---|---|
| Microhabitat[a] | | | | | |
| Tree foliage | 90 | 90 | 65 | 85 | 49 |
| Subcanopy foliage | 9 | 10 | 33 | 10 | 41 |
| Herb layer | 1 | 0 | 2 | 5 | 10 |
| Mean prey length (mm) | 5.8 | 14.7 | 10.6 | 10.7 | 5.9 |
| % Diet Composition of (arthropods)[b] | | | | | |
| Hemiptera | 36 | 10 | 12 | 48 | 13 |
| Coleoptera | 32 | 15 | 30 | 7 | 55 |
| Lepidoptera | 7 | 62 | 25 | 37 | 7 |
| Hymenoptera | 14 | 7 | 22 | 4 | 10 |
| Other | 11 | 6 | 11 | 4 | 15 |

*Source:* Root 1967. (Used with permission.)

[a]Numbers represent the percent of total forage time spent in each habitat.

[b]Percent of total volume represented by each arthropod.


**TABLE 4.9  A Characterization of Guilds for Breeding Passerines**

A. Primary Food Habits
    1. Seed eater
    2. Insectivore
    3. Omnivore
B. Stratum Most Commonly Used for Foraging
    1. Bark
    2. Ground
    3. Low canopy
    4. Middle canopy
    5. High canopy
C. Usual Foraging Behavior
    1. Bark drill
    2. Bark glean
    3. Ground glean
    4. Foliage glean
    5. Sally

*Source:* After Willson 1974. (Used with permission.)

*Note:* A total of 75 different guilds are possible using this system. A guild can be identified by number, for example, 211 (insectivorous bird feeding on bark by drilling, a woodpecker).

this table shows that the number of guilds that can be identified is very high. Accordingly, a food guild needs to be identified and described with precision, and with a rationale that is justified.

Guild classifications have been quite variable thus far. Diem and Zeveloff (1980) reported 49 different guilds in ponderosa pine forests, based on nesting habitat, feeding behavior, feeding habitat, and food choices.

Conversely, Balda and Masters (1980) reported only five foraging guilds based on location of feeding in pinyon-juniper woodland: ground, foliage, aerial, bark, and flower feeders. Differences in numbers of guilds are related to habitat diversity, which for nongame birds essentially means variety in vegetative structure. L. S. Thompson (1978) concluded that additions of layers of vegetation will increase the number of guilds, while diversity of plant species within each layer will affect numbers of bird species within each guild.


## NUTRITIVE VALUES

Nutritional values have been alluded to throughout the discussions of forage relationships, and warrant special consideration. As our knowledge of kinds of foods eaten has increased and as we have attempted to integrate this information into the overall ecological situation, it has become even more apparent that we need to determine what a population may be deriving in terms of nutrients and energy from the forage base, and how this fits into the regulation of numbers, into behavior and population dynamics, and finally into proper management programs.

Among the earliest work on nutritive values of wildlife forage species, Hellmers's (1940) evaluation of Pennsylvania deer browse stands out. Changes in protein, carbohydrate, fat, crude fiber, and moisture were elaborated for the dormant period, November through April. Concentration of effort by wildlife-oriented researchers on dormant season values was logical since this period appeared most critical to survival of wildlife.

On the other hand, A. Gordon and Sampson (1939), looking at range forage quality for livestock, examined levels of protein, fiber, phosphorus, and calcium during different growing stages through to dormancy. In both the browse and grasses examined during these studies, chemical values varied through time.

Some of the early work in western North America on nutritive values of wildlife forage species was initiated by A. S. Einarson (1946a, b), on the famous Tillamook Burn in Oregon, by A. S. Leopold et al. (1951) on the Jawbone Deer Herd in California, and by I. M. Cowan et al. (1950) on British Columbia moose ranges.

Einarson's evaluations of black-tailed deer forage were in relation to understanding why die-offs occurred among these deer even though their rumens were full of the usual winter foods. Comparisons of protein content of forages in June and December revealed definite decreases for winter, suggesting that the quality of the food had greatly decreased and may have been responsible for the die-offs, which occurred following persistent heavy rains continuing beyond February. On the burned or cutover areas, where forages had higher protein levels, general deer losses did not occur. While the investigation did not distinguish between increases in quantity and quality of browse related to forest succession, the analysis of protein content did reveal differences.

The Jawbone Herd studies of A. S. Leopold et al. (1951) arose from a checkered history of deer-human interactions that included an abortive, if still informative, attempt to slaughter the population to eradicate hoof-and-mouth disease. Highly palatable species were consistently higher in protein content than unpalatable species in this area. When the protein level dropped below 7 to 8 percent (Einarson (1946a) felt it was 5 to 6 percent) then winter losses of deer appeared imminent.

I. M. Cowan et al. (1950) elaborated differences in nutritive values of important moose forage in relation to successional status of the habitats. In the burned-over areas, protein levels were higher than in mature forests, but carotene (vitamin A) was highest in balsam fir, which was not found on the burns.

Since the earlier work, studies of nutritive values of forage species have evolved to a comprehensive effort from several different original frames of reference. As reported earlier, unpalatable species have been shown to have high nutritive values, so evaluations into their relative digestibility using *in vivo* and *in vitro* techniques have been conducted. Additionally, the physiology of the rumen, blood, and other tissues has been investigated and correlated with nutritive values of forages. Where once the habitat-oriented biologist and the population-oriented biologist found minimal ground for mutual involvement in research except through gross correlation of population performance with habitat conditions, a comprehensive tie-in is now possible, as D. R. Klein (1965) conclusively demonstrated.

This section will describe some trends in nutritive values of forages, factors influencing them, and results of digestibility studies. Later sections will tie these relationships to the population and the individual.

### Seasonal Trends in Crude Protein of Shrubs and Grasses

Trends in crude protein provide an index to the amount of the most important nutrient for wildlife that is available in a plant. The natural cycle in the common, palatable shrub, serviceberry, is shown in Figure 4.5. The data are only for stems; leaves contain higher quantities of protein than stems in spring and summer: 18.5 percent in spring, 12.3 percent in summer, and 6.2 percent in fall (Dietz, Udall, and Yaeger 1962). Crude protein includes both protein and nonprotein nitrogen, which is significantly correlated with the digestible protein available to wildlife (Dietz 1970). Notice that, for the Black Hills, South Dakota, data, crude protein of serviceberry twigs drops to the usually accepted minimum level satisfactory for maintenance of ungulates in winter: leaves would be taken more frequently in summer, but different forage, including forbs, would be more preferred. Acid-detergent lignin is included in Figure 4.5 because lignin is generally considered to be indigestible, and therefore serves as an index to digestibility of a species. Moss et al. (1974)

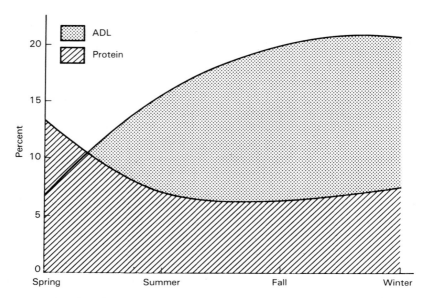

**Figure 4.5** Seasonal variation in crude protein and acid-detergent lignin (ADL) of serviceberry twigs in the Black Hills, North Dakota. ADL is inversely correlated with digestibility. From Dietz et al. 1970. (Used with permission.)

showed that crude fiber was highly and negatively correlated with digestibility of forage by ptarmigan in Iceland.

Variations between shrub species in protein levels are to be expected. Short, Dietz, and Remmenga (1966) showed variations from 8 percent in juniper to 15 percent in willow and 17 percent in aspen in spring on a Colorado mule deer range. However, the season pattern of protein variation in twigs fits Louisiana browse species (Blair and Epps 1969) as well, indicating that the trends presented have a general application in temperate zones with similar phenological patterns of development in shrubs.

Trends in an important range plant, bluebunch wheatgrass, for the Dubois, Idaho, area are shown in Figure 4.6 (Blaisdell, Wiese, and Hodgson 1952). Crude protein levels of this grass were higher in spring than for bitterbrush (15.9 percent) or threetip sagebrush (16.3 percent), but dropped below levels for the two shrubs in fall. Bitterbrush was 9.6 percent on October 27, 1940, and three-tip sagebrush was 7.0 percent on November 1, 1937, while the wheatgrass level was 3.5 percent. These data support the contention of Stoddart, Smith, and Box (1975) that shrubs tend to retain higher protein levels during dormancy than do grasses because they store food reserves in stems rather than in roots as do grasses. Trends in balsam root at Dubois were similar to those for bluebunch wheatgrass.

Bluebunch wheatgrass, Idaho fescue, junegrass, Sandberg bluegrass, and Co-

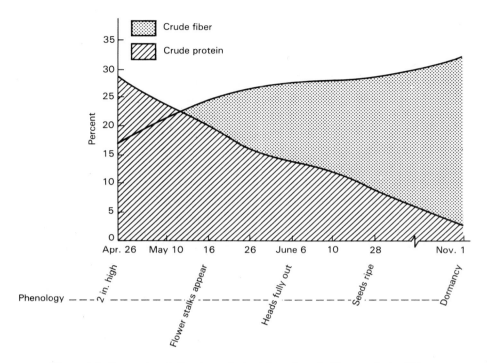

**Figure 4.6** Seasonal variation in crude protein and crude fiber content of blue-bunch wheatgrass at Dubois, Idaho. From Blaisdell, Wiese, and Hodgson 1952). (Used with permission.)

lumbian bluegrass collected on bighorn sheep winter range in British Columbia in August, November, and March show decreasing trends in crude protein to lows ranging from 1.77 percent to 2.83 percent in March (Demarchi 1968). Bluebunch wheatgrass had the highest percent protein content and was the most important bighorn forage. Columbia needlegrass was lowest in protein and was unimportant in the diet. Crude fiber includes lignins, cellulose, and hemicellulose, of which 50 percent, at least, is digestible (Dietz 1970).

Many grasses initiate regrowth in fall when precipitation again starts and temperatures cool from the late summer highs. The introduced annual cheatgrass can be an important late winter forage for deer (Dietz et al. 1962). Protein levels in late winter on their Colorado range were 23.8 to 25.6 percent for this species, which may provide some indication of the values found in regrowth over winter. These values were higher than those reported by C. W. Cook and Harris (1952) for May on Utah ranges (15.4 percent in early May), when cheatgrass was in the boot stage and growing rapidly. Nevertheless, the ingestion of regrowth of grasses would no doubt raise the intake of crude protein.

### Factors Affecting Levels of Crude Protein in Vegetation

**Precipation.**    Laycock and Price (1970) report that heavy precipitation tends to leach protein, phosphorus, ash, and carotene from plants. Such a phenomenon can substantially decrease forage values in areas of high rainfall, such as along the Pacific Coast, and have a somewhat similar effect as deep snows in restricting the availability of nutrients to wildlife.

**Overstory canopy closure.**    Shaded areas tend to retard plant development, decrease herbage production, and may have higher or lower levels of protein in understory forage species when compared to open areas. McEwen and Dietz (1965) showed that Kentucky bluegrass was higher in crude protein and crude fiber growing under ponderosa pine in the Black Hills than in the open. I. M. Cowan et al. (1950) showed little change in protein levels attributable to successional stages of boreal forests in British Columbia. However, Halls and Epps (1969) reported lower crude protein levels in browse plants growing under pine than in those growing in the open in Louisiana. Obviously, variables other than just degree of canopy closure affect protein levels in understory plants.

**Soil moisture.**    Plants growing on soils with higher moisture content appear to have higher levels of crude protein than those growing on soils that are drier. Peek et al. (1976) demonstrated the relationship for two forbs and three shrubs on northeastern Minnesota moose range. Correlations between nutrient levels and overstory canopy closure were insignificant, because of the interaction with soil moisture.

**Soil nutrients.**    While there is obviously a relationship between nutrient levels in soils and the nutritional content of forage species, there are so many other interacting factors that the attempts to quantify the relationship have been difficult. Hundley (1959) concluded that it was not feasible to rate one soil over another for providing browse of higher quality, although in some instances nutrient levels were correlated with soil of a given quality. However, nutrient variations, including mineral excesses and deficiencies, are thought to be caused by soil imbalances (Larcher 1975). Soil pH definitely affects availability of nutrients for plant growth. Also, various plant species accumulate nutrients, including nitrogen, at different levels. Generally, trees and shrubs contain more nitrogen than potassium, while the opposite occurs in herbaceous species.

**Grazing.**    Grazing tends to alter phenological development and productivity of forage species and can, in turn, affect protein levels. Jameson (1963) points out that forage value may be more important than gross dry matter yield of forage, although this can only be true up to a certain limit. However, grazing generally causes an increase in percent crude protein, if it is not heavy or frequent enough to have a severe effect on production. It is well known that moderate grazing can serve to stimulate productivity (Stoddart et al. 1975), and the combination of increasing yield and nutritive values serves as a useful reminder that herbivores and their forage species have evolved together, and that forage condition can actually benefit from judicious use.

**Burning.**    A number of studies on a wide variety of forage species indicate that burning will increase protein levels in forage. Controlled burns of seral shrub range in Idaho increased protein levels over unburned sites for at least two years (Leege 1968). DeWitt and Derby (1955) reported that "hot" burns in Maryland produced greater increases in protein than "cooler" burns. H. A. Pearson, Davis, and Schubert (1972) showed similar responses following a burn on northern Arizona rangeland, but the effects lasted for one growing season only. Scottish heather, a preferred red grouse food, produced higher protein levels following burning for four years after the fire (Moss, Miller, and Allen 1972). The wide area and variation in species from which these investigations come indicate that nutrient levels increase following burning but the duration varies.

**Location on twigs and herbs.**    The terminal ends of the current year's growth are higher in protein than those portions successively closer to the previous year's growth. Blair and Epps (1967) and R. L. Cowan et al. (1970) demonstrate this for twigs (Table 4.10). It is commonly observed that lightly browsed ranges or ranges on which browsing has just begun will show mainly twig ends receiving use, indicating that animals are taking the most nutritious forage first. This nutrient distribution reflects differential storage within a twig during dormancy.

Crude protein distribution within grasses and forbs is similarly variable through the growing season and phenological development. C. W. Cook and Harris (1952) show that grass stems and leaves contain higher levels in July than in August and September, with leaves being higher in protein than stems. Seed heads on the Utah ranges have higher concentrations of protein in August than in July. Forbs on these ranges have the greatest concentration of protein in leaves, with a decline occurring through the growing season. Stems of forbs were low in protein and showed no trends through the growing season.

Fertilization of soils with nitrogen resulted in increases in protein levels in

TABLE 4.10    **Distribution of Crude Protein in Current Year's Twig Growth of Several Woody Browse Species**

| Twig Section (inches from bud) | Percent Crude Protein | | |
|---|---|---|---|
| | Black Cherry | Red Maple | Rusty Blackhaw |
| Bud | 19.69 | 10.31 | — |
| 0–1 | 13.44 | 7.81 | 10.2 |
| 1–2 | 10.81 | 6.94 | 7.2 |
| 2–3 | 10.00 | 6.44 | 6.0 |
| 3–6 | 7.69 | 5.81 | — |
| 6–9 | 6.31 | 5.06 | — |

*Sources:* After Cowan et al. 1970; Blair and Epps 1967. (Used with permission.)

Japanese honeysuckle (Segelquist and Rogers 1975). Bayoumi and Smith (1976) were also able to increase protein in range grasses, bitterbrush, and sagebrush through applications of nitrogen to the soil. Such intensive practices in habitat improvement may be warranted on occasion, but results should be evaluated.

One concludes that the relationship between soil nutrient and plant nutrient levels is extremely complex, and is affected by many interactions between nutrients, differences in plant species physiology, and associated vegetation. Use and understanding of this relationship in wildlife habitat management is in its infancy.

### Forage Digestibility

As stated earlier, while there are good positive correlations between protein levels and digestibility, and negative correlations between lignin and crude fiber and the digestibility of a forage to wildlife, the need to directly measure the actual digestibility is recognized. Investigators of domestic livestock nutrition have long conducted digestion trials in order to define more precisely the value of a particular ration. Wildlife are able to select forages of higher quality than randomly occurs in a stand (Swift 1948; Moss 1967; Miller 1968), which also complicates interpretations of nutrient analysis. Also, microorganisms within the caecum of gallinaceous birds and the rumen of ungulates actually do much of the actual digesting of forage that is eaten—the animal digests the products of microbial digestion. Thus, selection of higher-quality forage must involve interaction with the microbes and a feedback mechanism wherein the physiological well-being of the individual is enhanced.

Digestibility trials for wild ungulates use *in vivo* and *in vitro* techniques. *In vivo* techniques include suspension of a food in the rumen of a fistulated animal and determination of the nutrient content of the residual after a specified time. Often two to three weeks are required for these trials (Short 1970). Another procedure is to place an animal in a metabolism cage, supply a known ration, and measure the excreta (gas, liquid, and solid) that results.

*In vitro* techniques involve extracting rumen fluid from a constrained or a freshly killed animal adding the fluid (liquor) to a forage of known content, allowing the mixture to incubate for a specified time, and measuring the remaining contents. Tilley and Terry (1963) report a two-stage technique for *in vitro* measurement of forage digestibilty and Dietz et al. (1962) describe their experiments in detail.

The question as to whether *in vitro* measurements are comparable to the more widely used *in vivo* techniques has arisen, and Ruggiero and Whelan (1976) suggest that *in vitro* analyses are useful and comparable with *in vivo* data as long as fresh rumen liquor is used and carefully controlled laboratory procedures are practiced. However, Robbins (1983) reported that *in vitro* dry matter digestibilities overestimated *in vivo* values of forages consumed by deer. Some examples of digestion studies follow.

Table 4.11 lists results of digestibility studies for 22 species. The investigations of Ullrey et al. (1964, 1967) using penned deer show that even if aspen and jackpine contained higher percentages of crude protein than white cedar, there was a tendency, although not statistically significant, for cedar to be more digestible.

**TABLE 4.11  Results of Some Evaluations of Forage Digestibility**

| Species | Location | Season | Percent Crude Protein | Percent Digestibility Crude Protein | Percent Digestibility Dry Matter | Reference |
|---|---|---|---|---|---|---|
| White cedar | Michigan | Winter | 2.9 | 12 | 37 | Ulrey et al. 1967 |
| Jackpine | Michigan | Winter | 3.8 | −17 | 45 | Ulrey et al. 1967 |
| Aspen | Michigan | Winter | 5.0 | −305 | −104 | Ulrey et al. 1964 |
| Mountain mahogany | Colorado | Winter | 7.7 | 52.5 | 59 | Dietz, Udall, and Yaeger 1962 |
| Big sagebrush | Colorado | Winter | 10.1 | 52.5 | 59 | Dietz, Udall, and Yaeger 1962 |
| Bitterbrush | Colorado | Winter | 8.7 | 30.6 | 53 | Dietz, Udall, and Yaeger 1962 |
| Heather | Scotland | — | 7.0 | — | 21–30 | Moss and Parkinson 1972 |
| Willow | Iceland | Summer | 19.0 | — | 55 | Gardarsson and Moss 1970 |
| Dandelion | Iceland | Spring | 30.0 | — | 71 | Gardarsson and Moss 1970 |
| Chokecherry | S. Dakota | Fall | — | — | 26 | Uresk, Dietz, and Messner 1975 |
| Kinnickinnick | S. Dakota | Fall | — | — | 46 | Uresk, Dietz, and Messner 1975 |
| (Rumen contents) | Texas | Winter | — | — | 64 | Short 1975 |
|  | Texas | Spring | — | — | 77 | Short 1975 |
|  | Texas | Summer | — | — | 80 | Short 1975 |
|  | Texas | Fall | — | — | 66 | Short 1975 |
| Cheatgrass | Montana | Summer | 7.52 | — | 54 | McCall, Clark, and Patton 1943 |
| Crested wheatgrass | Montana | Summer | 13.58 | — | 57 | McCall, Clark, and Patton 1943 |
| Dandelion | Arizona | Spring | 22 | — | 59 | Urness, Neff, and Watkins 1975 |
| Dandelion | Arizona | Summer | 11 | — | 42 | Urness, Neff, and Watkins 1975 |
| Dandelion | Arizona | Fall | 12 | — | 54 | Urness, Neff, and Watkins 1975 |
| Ragweed | Missouri | Summer | — | — | 56 | Torgerson and Pfander 1971 |
| Aster | Missouri | Summer | 19.5 | — | 77 | Torgerson and Pfander 1971 |

Negative digestibility figures resulted from greater quantities of dry matter in feces than in foods offered, but the mean values did not differ significantly from zero.

Dietz et al. (1962) used digestibility cages to determine digestibility of big sagebrush, mountain mahogany, and bitterbrush by mule deer. Digestible protein was highest in big sage and lowest in bitterbrush, although deer preferred bitterbrush to the other two species and gained weight on it. Sagebrush was unpalatable when fed alone to the experimental deer.

Digestibility trials have been conducted on red grouse by Moss and Parkinson (1972). Between 21 and 30 percent of dry matter of heather, a preferred forage, was digested, equating to 88–112 kcal per day for a 600-gram bird. Lignin appeared to be variably digestible between birds, ranging from 2 to 20 percent. Because lignin had previously been considered indigestible, it was suggested that fiber digestion is initiated when intake falls below a certain level.

Cellulose digestion by ruffed grouse, chukar, and bobwhite was evaluated by Inman (1973). High cellulose content of 15.4 percent appeared to inhibit digestion of other nutrients in all three species, but bobwhites appeared to digest more cellulose on the high diet than the other two species. Since bobwhites digested 65 percent of the cellulose in the caecum and the other two species digested 90 percent, it was suggested that bobwhites digested more in the noncaecal gut or passed more cellulose through the caecum per unit time.

The evergreen kinnickinnick appears to be more digestible than chokecherry twigs in fall (Uresk, Dietz, and Messner 1975). Again, this illustrates the value of low-growing species, which may retain green matter, to wildlife during dormant periods.

Trends in dry matter digestibilities appear to follow seasonal trends in protein content of forage (Short 1975). Digestibility of rumen contents of white-tailed deer is highest during growing season and lowest in winter.

Cheatgrass and crested wheatgrass digestibility in summer is comparable to that of a palatable forb, dandelion (McCall, Clark, and Patton 1943; Urness et al. 1975). And ragweed, an unpalatable species, is as digestible as dandelion (Torgerson and Pfander 1971). Properties of common ragweed which repel deer were not identified.

While trends in digestibilities of forage species generally parallel the trends in crude protein and forage preference, these studies suggest that caution and understanding must be exercised in interpreting both values. Variation in digestibility results may be attributable to feeds, variation among studies and between experimental animals (Dietz et al. 1962). This intricate subject requires more investigation and review to elucidate the interactions and variables involved.

### Minerals

The value of minerals to wildlife is a relatively new area of investigation, despite early work on the value of salt licks to big game and on calcium as a factor limiting pheasant reproduction. The concern over calcium deficiencies was brought about when crop analysis of pheasants revealed insufficient calcium to sustain reproduction (Dale 1955; Greeley 1962). Greeley (1962) was able to cause reduction in egg production, eggshell thickness, egg size, and bone weight of pheasants by reducing levels of calcium in the diet, but found no deficiencies in wild birds. Harper and Labisky (1964) discovered that the grit consumed by Illinois pheasants accounted for a large proportion of the calcium in the diet, and therefore did not limit populations (some other factor was involved). Big game are known to make extensive use of naturally occurring mineral licks, as well as artificially established ones, especially in spring (Dalke et al. 1965). In the Idaho studies, sodium appeared to be the sought-after element, but no difference in rates of migration away from areas with licks as compared to areas without licks onto summer ranges was noticed. Knight and Mudge (1967) reported that sodium bicarbonate and sodium sulphate were the only compounds that occurred in much greater quantities in lick waters than in rocks and waters not related to licks. The "taste" acquired for sodium is well known, and only recently has work been directed towards the role of this element as a limiting factor. While sodium occurs in very limited amounts in most terrestrial forages, the element is accumulated by aquatic plants, rushes, and salt-bushes (Larcher 1975), which may be one reason why such species are eagerly sought by herbivores.

A major thrust of investigations into the effects of environmental modification through pollution with heavy metals and pesticides relates back to the basic metabolism of various elements. Heavy metals (lead, zinc, and copper) are known to accumulate in waterfowl using the Coeur d'Alene River Valley below Kellogg, Idaho (Chupp and Dalke 1964), which occasionally causes losses. Retention of lead shot by waterfowl on heavily hunted areas has been implicated as an important mortality factor (Coburn, Metzler, and Treichler 1951). The knowledge that DDT blocks calcium metabolism, which in turn causes eggshell thinning (Hickey and Anderson 1968), and that pesticides containing methyl mercury can accumulate to lethal levels in wildlife (Borg et al. 1969), also shows that a basic knowledge of mineral levels in forages and their nutritional role can have high significance in wildlife conservation.

Examples illustrating that mineral content varies through time and between plants are given in Table 4.12. Calcium concentrates in leaves and bark, serving to

**TABLE 4.12**  **Percentage of Calcium in Four Forage Plants at Different Seasons**

| | Forage Plant | | | |
|---|---|---|---|---|
| Season | Snowberry | Aspen | Bluebunch Wheatgrass | Balsam Root |
| Spring | 0.90 | 0.90 | 0.45 | 1.21 |
| Summer | 1.17 | 1.29 | 0.58 | 2.21 |
| Fall | 1.31 | 1.28 | 0.39 | 2.04 |
| Winter | 1.27 | 1.25 | – | – |

*Sources:* For snowberry and aspen data, Dietz 1972; for bluebunch wheatgrass and balsam root data, Blaisdell, Wiese, and Hodgson 1952. (Used with permission.)

regulate hydration and activate plant enzymes (Larcher 1975). High calcium to phosphorus ratios in forage are known to block phosphorus metabolism in livestock (Church 1971), but this may not be the case in free-ranging wildlife because of high variation in forage selection and capabilities in retention of elements for future assimilation.

Table 4.12 shows high calcium values for balsam root. Kubota, Rieger, and Lazar (1970) reported higher values of calcium in horsetail, fireweed, and lupine than in sedges, grasses, or twigs in Alaska. The seasonal trend shown in Table 4.12 tends to follow that reported for browse species in Louisiana by Blair and Epps (1969) except that highest values in the southern study were clearly evident for winter.

## SUMMARY

Foraging theory provides a fundamental basis for understanding choice of foods, and thus has management significance. The earlier descriptive work, which provided long listings of items in the diet, has largely been superseded by studies that report availablity of forage as well as its occurrence in the diet. This provides a means of assessing relative preference of a food item, which in turn is an index to its value.

Forage items that are used during the critical periods when a population is stressed are in need of identification so they may be favored in management. This means that a knowledge of forage use patterns is one important aspect of habitat use, but not the only aspect, needed for management.

A number of factors influence forage choice, including prior experience, odor, and allelomimetic behavior. Plant protein content, energy content, moisture content, and presence of digestion-inhibiting compounds also affect forage choice. Age of plant, and its phenological stage also are involved. Phytoestrogen levels in desert annuals may affect productivity of species feeding on those plants.

The numerous investigations of food habits for the big game and upland birds reveal a wide variation in forage choice between areas, which has management significance because it is related in part to availability and in part to preference and palatability. Habitat management must deal with plants that are available to the animal in the area. However, management for forage diversity as well as for forages used during critical periods is indicated.

The food guild concept is a highly useful means of aggregating groups of non-game birds with similar foraging behavior and forage choice for management purposes. Habitat management that provides for each group of food niches thus ensures habitat for each species included within the guild.

An extensive body of work on forage quality has shown the trends that can be expected in protein and energy levels, and more recently, in the relative digestibilities of forage items. This work will indicate the degree to which one forage may be substituted for another, assuming both occur in an area. We are steadily acquiring a more comprehensive understanding of the relationship of food quality to an individual's energy and protein requirements, especially with the white-tailed deer. A number of factors affect levels of crude protein in vegetation, including precipitation, overstory canopy closure, soil moisture, grazing, and burning. Work on mineral nutrition and content in wildlife foods is relatively new, but sodium and calcium have been postulated to be limiting in some situations.

Food habits studies, which now include the more comprehensive investigations into digestibility and energy relationships, will continue to be an important aspect of wildlife management in the future. We are progressively making the tie between habitat condition and population condition clearer through these investigations.

# 5

# Habitat Relationships

## INTRODUCTION

The relationships of a population to its environment, along with direct human exploitation, constitute the two most important factors involving wildlife management. Understanding these relationships presents a difficult challenge to the manager who wishes to manipulate the habitat for the purpose intended. Habitat relationships involve food habits, competition with other populations, predation, and other issues that are addressed elsewhere. However, in many ways, from the theoretical base to the management strategy, habitat relationships unify the entire spectrum of wildlife management. There is no potential limiting factor, whether it be a pesticide, a hunter, or a predator, where the relationship of the population to its environment does not modify the interaction and effect. It is important that students of wildlife biology train and condition themselves to consider the population in question in the context of its environment. Whether the subject is a predator that is several trophic levels removed from its habitat, or a herbivore that feeds on its habitat and interacts more directly, the land is ultimately the fundamental basis for its existence.

Habitat relationships inevitably involve the question of what regulates a population. The most basic components of the habitat, climate and substrate, are ultimately involved. These components essentially dictate the availability of nutrients and their expression in the biota that depends on them. Further, the nutrient supply or forage base that sustains a population and that evolves according to the climate and substrate is an ultimate check on population size (Lack 1954).

Within this ultimate check, however, other mechanisms either alone or in concert may serve to regulate numbers at some level below the forage base. Territorial behavior that tends to space individuals within a population at some level below the number that could exist if forage were the only limiting factor is obviously very important in some species. Availability of nesting sites (colonial species, hole nesters, bank nesters) may serve to restrict a breeding population below the level dictated by food. Predation, disease, genetic feedback mechanisms, quality of cover, and climatic and weather conditions may all lower populations to levels below that dictated by the forage base.

However, there is a general correlation between population size and the food base. Soil fertility and fecundity of cottontail rabbits are related in Missouri (C. E. Williams and Caskey 1965) and Alabama (Hill 1972), possibly through the interaction of soil pH and calcium on nutrient content in plants. Illinois mourning doves living on the most fertile soils where corn was an important food item were heavier than those living on sandy, less fertile soils where noxious weeds and native plants were important food items (Hanson and Kossack 1957). Cougar populations tend to be concentrated on ungulate winter ranges where the density of prey is greater, even as they space themselves according to a land-tenure system (Seidensticker et al. 1973). Wolf densities in northern Minnesota were greatest in the deer yards along the north shore of Lake Superior (Van Ballenberghe, Erickson, and Bynam 1975). Elk occupying seral shrub ranges of north Idaho were most abundant during the most developed stages of the shrub communities that provided food (Leege 1968). Seagull colonies off the coast of Maine appeared to have higher reproductive success where food was artificially elevated by the presence of garbage dumps (G. L. Hunt 1972).

Another fundamental principle underlying the habitat relationship has to do with plant *succession*. Habitats are dynamic; they change regardless of whether humans are involved. Any natural alteration, such as those due to wildfire, hurricanes, drought, flooding, or volcanic activity, will modify habitats; artificially induced alterations, those made by humans, may be directly or indirectly caused.

Direct causes include prescribed fire, logging, bulldozing (this encompasses subdivisions, dams, roads, etc.), and herbicides. Indirect causes include grazing of domestic stock, lowering or raising of water tables, fertilization, and exploitation of other resources (other forage or competitors).

Plant succession is not unidirectional; rather, it is reversible, and the rate may also vary with seral stage and at climax. Horn (1974) points out that the more diverse and complex communities and the climax communities are inherently the most fragile. Wildlife species characteristic of these situations likewise pose highly challenging problems in habitat management, especially when the communities are commercially valuable, as with old-growth forest.

## DEFINITIONS: HABITAT SELECTION, PREFERENCE, USE, AND REQUIREMENTS

Whittaker, Levin, and Root (1973) defined *habitat* as the complex of physical variables on the range in which the species exists, a definition that may be used at the individual population level as well. *Habitat selection* implies choice among those available: an individual may search for certain habitats to breed, feed, and rest in. *Habitat preference* implies choice of one habitat over another without regard to whether one may be available or not. The preference exists, even though the preferred habitat is not available. *Habitat use* implies occupation of a given habitat without any connotation of preference.

It is to be emphasized that preference for one habitat over another is extremely difficult to ascertain without experimentation. In field studies, use is observed, and selection can be inferred by examining use and comparing it with availability. It is also possible to infer preference by examining population characteristics, such as breeding success and other reproductive parameters, or survival, and relating them to habitat use. Presumably, the habitats in which reproductive success, or survival, is greatest will be the habitats that are selected or chosen.

However, there are dangers in this approach, since very often high-density populations, through a variable combination of intrinsic or extrinsic factors, "spill out" into less optimal habitats (Fretwell and Lucas 1970; Figure 5.1). Also, high survival and high reproductive success may not occur in the same habitats. A species

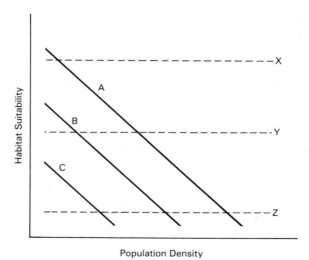

Population Density

**Figure 5.1** The effect of population density on habitat suitability. Symbols are as follows: A = habitat of highest suitability; B = habitat of intermediate suitability; C = habitat of lowest suitability; Z = largest population; Y = next largest population; X = smallest population. From Fretwell and Lucas 1970. (Used with permission.)

may exhibit longer life expectancies in situations that emphasize security of the individual, while other habitats that maximize the nutritional levels of the breeding population may enhance reproductive success at the expense of long life expectancy. Much of the habitat selection process may depend upon factors limiting the populations, and this can change through time as limiting factors change.

There is also a distinction to be made between *habitat requirement* and *habitat preference. Requirement* implies that the habitat attribute is needed for the species to survive, while *preference* is a qualitative term that implies choice among habitats that may well all fulfill the fundamental requirement. As with the determination of preference, the actual habitat requirement involves experimentation and cannot be determined with certainty from the usual observational field study.

D. H. Johnson (1980) identified a natural ordering of selection processes, which is useful in organizing field observations. In this schema, *first-order selection* is the physical or geographical range of a species. *Second-order selection* determines the home range of an individual or social group within the geographical range. *Third-order selection* determines the usage of various habitat components within the home range. Finally, selection of food items within a habitat component could be considered *fourth-order selection.* Actual nesting sites, bedding or roosting areas, and other specific sites that are used for a specific purpose could also be included in fourth-order selection.

## HABITAT SELECTION: FACTORS INVOLVED

Lack (1949) formulated the basic view of factors involved in habitat selection: specific choice of habitat is based upon its characteristics, which are identified by selection mechanisms, which in turn are adaptations induced through interspecific competition favoring detection of the most favorable environments. Two facets of habitat selection include *ultimate factors* (those conferring survival value or having adaptive significance) and *proximate factors* (the mechanisms involved, often the immediate cause or stimuli). Individuals respond in choice of habitat to the summation of these factors.

Ultimate factors usually include food, cover or shelter from enemies and adverse weather, nesting or denning sites, and interspecific competition (Hilden 1965). Proximate factors may include stimuli of landscape, terrain, and competitors. The general landscape features of aspect, slope, and vegetative characteristics are included in an innate habitat response. Hilden (1965) pointed to the principle of stimulus summation to explain why every habitat occupied by a species need not possess all features of an undefined optimum habitat; occupation implies only that the combined effects of individual stimuli suffices, or exceeds the threshold required to occupy a site. Also, a key stimulus, such as a suitable hole for nesting or the presence of water, may be sufficient for a species to occupy an otherwise highly suboptimal habitat. The psychic factor thus plays an important role in habitat selection.

Douglass (1976) demonstrated that interspecific competition between sympatric voles, *Microtus montanus* and *Microtus pennsylvanicus*, influenced habitat selection in south central Montana. *Microtus montanus* actually had larger home ranges when *M. pennsylvanicus* was present than when it was absent. Also, spacing between *M. montanus* individuals was closer when *M. pennsylvanicus* was absent. *M. montanus* demonstrated a broader habitat preference, occurring within a greater range of vegetative cover than *M. pennsylvanicus*.

However, Lack (1966) recognized that direct evidence for competition is scanty because it may have occurred in the past, which would result in different species avoiding competition by selecting slightly different habitats. Thus, the role of tradition in habitat selection becomes important, and we may be observing preferences that are consequences of past adaptations and selective influences that are hard to determine. This becomes even more difficult when we are dealing with species with broad habitat requirements that seemingly overlap. Nevertheless, competition plays an important, perhaps dominant, role in the dynamic process of habitat selection as MacArthur's (1972) analysis of species distribution patterns indicates.

Habitat selection is partially innate, as Wecker's (1964) experiments with the deer mice *Peromyscus maniculatus bairdii* and *P. m. gracilis* suggest. The woodland subspecies, *gracilis*, when born and raised in a laboratory environment and thus with no prior exposure, tended to select and be most active in woodlands rather than prairie habitats (Figure 5.2). The reverse was true for the prairie deer mouse subspecies, *bairdii*. Similar experiments with birds have produced similar results (Partridge 1978).

Imprinting, a learned behavior resulting from experience acquired during a brief period in early life (Hess 1966), also influences the habitat selection process in some species. While this phenomenon has been most frequently associated with the tendency for young birds to follow a moving object after hatching, as originally investigated by Lorenz (1937), Hilden (1965) presents evidence from European studies that this applies in habitat selection as well. Hochbaum (1955) suggests that imprinting upon habitats probably occurs in wild ducklings, but points out that the traditional use of the term, as indicated above, may foster confusion. Also, he felt that a clear distinction between imprinting and ordinary conditioning was virtually impossible.

Variation relative to habitat specificity is tremendous among species. On the one hand, MacArthur (1958) demonstrated that five closely related species of warblers occupying the homogenous, mature spruce forests in Maine, had quite specific preferences. Cape May warblers tended to feed on the uppermost and outermost branches of spruce trees, taking frequent long foraging flights. Myrtle warblers had the most variable feeding habits, appearing least specific in habitat choice, and occurring generally at constant, low densities. The black-throated green warbler exhibited highly restricted feeding habitats centered on the dense parts of branches at midelevations in the tree, and was the dominant species. The bay-breasted warbler feeds high in trees, but moves more deliberately away from the ends of tree

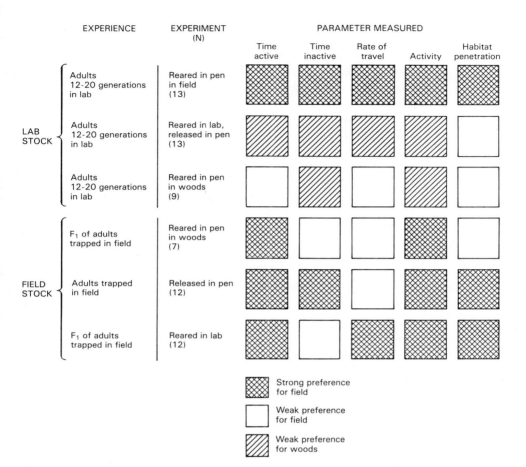

**Figure 5.2** Summary of S. C. Wecker's (1964) experiments on habitat selection of *Peromyscus manicutas bairdii*, which illustrates that hereditary and learned aspects are involved in this behavior.

limbs and does not fly frequently. This species appears to have the most restricted feeding habits of the five warblers. The Blackburnian warbler appears to occupy an intermediate position between the bay-breasted warbler and the black-throated green warbler. It feeds high in trees but moves out from the base to the tip of branches, with occasional flights.

That such behavior and habitat selection can have adaptive significance is evidenced by the evolution of finches that Lack (1953) described as having occurred on the Galapagos Islands. Here, a common finch ancestor had apparently evolved a wide variety of beak sizes and shapes from a thin warbler form typical of insect feeders, to a thick-billed seed-eating form.

In contrast to such specific habitat selection behaviors, that of North American ungulates is rather broad, which can be readily expected, given their wide distribution and limited number of species. On the other hand, the large variety of African ungulates, with a long evolutionary period dating back to the Tertiary within which to adapt, show more specific habitat use patterns (Estes 1974) and adaptations to the habitat occupied.

Learning may be very important in ungulates and carnivores in North America. The experience and knowledge of the habitat accumulated in adults and passed on to young through the duration of their association with adults may serve to retain a tradition of use of an area. This mechanism may be transferred through certain segments, such as the mature ram in the case of bighorn (Geist 1971b), or the matriarch in the case of elk (Darling 1937).

Finally, the physiognomic characteristics of an area dictate habitat use. Water-holes may serve to focus activities in arid regions. Low passes may guide movement from one area to another in mountain country. "Patchy" habitats with restricted cover, as in heavily agriculturalized areas, may be used regardless of traditions or their lack.

In general, many of the larger mammals probably retain habitat use patterns from one generation to the next through learning mechanisms and traditions that become established. Many of the more specialist species, including many of the birds and rodents, probably inherit a larger measure of their habitat use patterns genetically.

## HABITAT SELECTION: THE NICHE CONCEPT

The theoretical bases for habitat selection have been further elaborated in terms of foraging strategies (Pyke, Pulliam, and Charnov 1977; Schoener 1971), competition (MacArthur and Levins 1964), and the niche. The first two concepts are treated in separate chapters and the niche is considered here.

Whittaker et al. (1973) recommended that the term *niche* be applied exclusively to the intracommunity role of the species. This is the functional role, or occupation, definition and distinguishes niche from *habitat*, the latter being defined as the complex of physical variables on the range in which the species exist. The niche, plus the habitat, describes the ecotope of the species.

The definition of the niche has been extensively considered, and is not easily arrived at. For instance, Hutchinson's (1958) view of the *fundamental niche* as an $n$-dimensional hypervolume is logical from a conceptual standpoint, but is difficult to deal with in practice because of the infinite numbers of dimensions involved, and because reproductive fitness is the measure. Pianka's (1976) review indicated that the ecological niche has come to be identified with resource utilization spectra, which can be studied more readily in the field than reproductive fitness. However reproductive fitness is still the ultimate measure of the niche (Rosenzweig 1974). The niche concept is complex and involves interactions with the other concepts of competition and foraging strategies. Hutchinson's (1958) *realized niche* is the

hypervolume in which a species actually exists after competition and other interactions reduced the fundamental niche to a smaller size in space.

Colwell and Futuyma (1971) presented methods of niche analysis that help
to illustrate the approach to measurement involving resources. *Niche breadth* was
simply defined as the distance through a niche along some particular line in space,
one of the dimensions in the *n*-dimensional hypervolume. *Niche overlap* was
defined as the joint use of a resource by two or more species, or the region in niche
space shared by two or more contiguous niches. Niche breadth will be considered
here. Consider a resource matrix in which species are rows and kinds of resources
are columns:

r = number of resource states
S = number of species
Y = total number of individuals of species i
X = total number of individuals of all species combined
    for resource state j
Z = total number of individuals in matrix

Resource States

$$N_{11} \cdots N_{1j} \cdots N_{1r} \cdots Y_1$$

$$N_{il} \cdots N_{ij} \cdots N_{ir} \cdots Y_i$$

$$\frac{N_{sl} \cdots N_{sj} \cdots N_{sr} \cdots Y_s}{X_l \cdots X_j \cdots X_r \cdots Z}$$

(Species, at left along the matrix)

Niche breadth, **B**, for the *i*th species is

$$B_i = \frac{1}{\sum\limits_j P_{ij}^2} = \frac{(\sum\limits_j N_{ij}^2)}{\sum\limits_j N_{ij}^2} = \frac{Y_i^2}{\sum\limits_j N_{ij}^2}$$

where

$$P_{ij} = \frac{N_{ij}}{Y_i}$$

Colwell and Futuyma (1971) point out that when an equal number of individuals of species *i* are associated with each resource state, $B_i$ is maximized, and has
the broadest possible niche associated with the resources. This condition indicates a
generalist, as compared to a specialist species that is associated with only one resource state.

Problems with these measurements include defining the range of measurement, determining the spacing between the resource states, and taking into account the fact that the range may be nonlinear, all of which are considered further by Colwell and Futuyma (1971).

These concepts and their measurements are important in wildlife habitat management. If an understanding is to be attained of what factors within the environment serve to limit population size, then a definition of the niche the population occupies is useful. Identification of factors that reduce the fundamental niche to the realized niche for the population can guide management efforts. These identifications are commonly made in practice, implicitly assuming the limiting factors are defined. Often investigation of the assumptions on a local basis will help refine and make management more efficient.

In many instances, population response to habitat management cannot be directly measured. This is especially critical when long-lived species are involved whose reproductive success varies for numerous reasons besides habitat conditions. Accordingly, the definition of the niche in terms of resource utilization spectra is quite useful. Such an approach can be useful in understanding ecological relationships of important forage and cover species that are to be favored, as well as the wildlife population itself.

## WILDLIFE AND FORESTRY

While integration of wildlife management and timber management is in rudimentary stages in the Northwest, it has a long history of successful efforts elsewhere in the United States. Perhaps the outstanding example is in the southeastern states where longleaf pine is grown on a 60-year rotation. This species occurs as a "grass" stage which is highly resistant to damage by fire, for as long as ten years. Herbert L. Stoddard, working in the 1920s, recognized the value of burning to provide a high-quality quail habitat. "Cool," slow-creeping ground fires, which did not injure the pine, but reduced shrubby species and increased legumes and other species important to the bobwhites, were started at one- to three-year intervals. Upwards of 30 coveys of quail per square mile could be produced using fire in these pinelands, and fire hazard and disease was reduced in the pine (Stoddard 1935).

A committee of the New England Section of the Society of American Foresters was at work in the early 1930s on management plans for forest wildlife in that region (N. W. Hosley, Chairman, 1934; Hosley and Ziebarth 1935). This group recognized that facilitation of maximum wood production from every forest was not productive for wildlife, and that providing so-called "forest weeds" in certain parts of a forest was needed to foster wildlife populations. It was recognized that silviculture in the form of thinnings, partial cuttings, and group and strip cuttings could be used to favor food production. Also, the need for adequate cover for ruffed grouse and deer was recognized. The committee recognized that foresters have the means to enhance or hinder wildlife populations.

It is of interest to note that this committee recognized not only the need for more information, but also that a start towards doing something was needed, and that this in itself could help fill gaps in knowledge. Even today, where forest management is contemplated and efforts to enhance wildlife habitat are considered, we still are faced with the need to go ahead with the best available judgments, which are often not supported by adequate data. In fact, J. W. Thomas et al. (1976) have argued that the lack of knowledge is not the biggest problem, but rather that the lack of a conceptual framework—one that allows for consideration of all species in planning, for retention of the ability to emphasize management of particular species, and for identification of specific habitats requiring special attention in land alteration schemes—is most critical.

Hosley and Ziebarth (1935) provided recommendations for habitat improvement for deer through forestry practices applicable in central Massachusetts that included planting coniferous cover, weeding hardwoods to maintain them at suitable feeding heights, and sowing clover on fire lines and roadsides. These recommendations arose from a winter field investigation of deer food habits and habitat use, serving as an early model of means to apply ecological data to practical habitat management.

Cahalane (1939) recognized that the silviculturist has unlimited opportunities to provide wildlife habitat in the Central states region (Ohio, Michigan, Wisconsin, Minnesota, Iowa, Missouri, and Kentucky). Reforestation practices that produced monocultures of pure coniferous stands could be diversified in composition by planting hardwoods. Selection cutting systems were thought to be best for wildlife, with the idea that breaks in the forest canopy helped to provide abundant ground cover. Slash disposal was recommended, and clear-cutting in small blocks or narrow strips was considered the next best practice to selection cuts.

In the coniferous forests of the Lake states, early work included that by Aldous (1941) on integrating management of white cedar and white-tailed deer. This highly palatable tree also provides winter cover, and the practice of supplemental feeding by cutting branches and culling trees in winter concentration areas was recommended. However, the problem of regenerating cedar stands in deer areas was paramount, and deer-proof fences and herd reduction were two recommended measures. Krefting (1962) and Verme (1965) subsequently elaborated silvicultural-wildlife realtionships in the region. These will be addressed later.

In the Northwest, integration of wildlife and forest management is a relatively new endeavor. The extensive and diverse nature of the coniferous forests, the abundance of game in the 1950s and early 1960s, and the minimal area being logged, all tended to focus attention on other problems. It was not until the late 1960s that logging became extensive enough to warrant concern. It then became readily apparent that a large proportion of the old-growth forest was rapidly being cut. Attributes of old-growth coniferous forest are (1) large, live trees, (2) large snags, (3) large logs on land, and (4) large logs in streams (J. F. Franklin et al. 1981). A wide variety of tree sizes exists, and understory variability is also high. Old-growth Douglas fir typically has an irregular, large, coarse branch system and a long crown. Franklin et al. (1981) concluded that gross productivity is high in most old-growth stands, and merchantable timber volume remains high for several centuries. Approximately 200 years are required to develop old-growth forests in the Coast and Cascade ranges, depending on site quality; the prime example of old growth in these areas is 350- to 750-year-old Douglas fir—western hemlock. Old growth is not necessarily the climax forest, although, because of its longevity, it may approach climax. The controversy between timber and wildlife interests has focused in large measure on the old-growth forests in this region. Concern in the Pacific Northwest was for species like the Northern spotted owl, which requires Douglas fir forests much older than the 40- to 70-year-rotations that are anticipated in the future (Bandy and Taber 1972). These writers reiterated the views of many when they stated that forest management as currently practiced and wildlife values conflict.

The lack of planning for wildlife values was nowhere more obvious than in the Bitterroot Valley of Montana, where large clearcuts in prime summer-fall elk habitat virtually precluded use of some drainages by that species. This conflict received national attention when a large number of citizens became highly critical of the logging practices from a variety of standpoints, including adverse effects on wildlife (Popovich 1975). This situation has stimulated more attentiveness to other resources in planning and conducting timber management activities in the region, but the conflicts continue as more land is cut.

The root of the problem is that demand for all forest resources threatens to outrun supply (Ripley 1973). If the forests had not been progressively logged so extensively, the conflicts with other resources and those interested in them would have been less critical. Ripley (1973) also pointed out that typical planning and budgeting systems of the recent past, and all too often, the present, have fostered the conflict, since integrated planning for all resources was ignored. Each resource was provided for through separate budgeting and planning, often designed to maximize the resource in question on every possible acre. People given responsibility for maximizing one product, be it electricity, irrigation water, recreation, wood fiber, red meat or wildlife, will obviously try to do just that. The integrated planning programs for all resources arose from recognition of such conflicts and will become more widespread in the future. Wildlife biologists must recognize, in such planning, that their obligation is to ensure retention of adequate high-quality habitat, but within the context of other land uses, which means compromise and coordination.

There is no sense in condemning any one silvicultural practice for its detrimental effects on wildlife. Pengelly (1972) listed a variety of adverse effects, among them the following:

1. Slash and debris poses obstacles to travel.
2. Slash prevents reestablishment of new vegetation.
3. Logging roads displace game and increase access.
4. Herbiciding of competing shrubs for "release" of young conifers destroys forage.

5. Large clearcuts receive little use.
6. Current forestry tends toward monocultures of commercially valuable species.
7. Scarification to prepare seedbeds and planting sites eliminates shrubs valuable as forage.

Yet, one can show benefits to wildlife from each practice. Slash piles provide cover for small game. Logging roads help spread out the harvest. Herbiciding of shrubs often stimulates resprouting and is in itself a useful tool for rehabilitating vigor of some shrubs. Large clearcuts are used on the peripheries by big game and the centers are left to restock without damage. Many natural conifer stands are essentially monocultures themselves, and logging can diversify such stands. And scarification produces seedbeds for desirable forage species as well as conifers.

The point is that judgment is needed if timber and wildlife management are to be practiced together. Judicious application of virtually any silvicultural practice can benefit a particular wildlife species, if done with that goal in mind. The problem resolves down to deciding which species to favor, how to go about it, and working effectively with the forester (who often has a personal interest in wildlife) and others to get the job done. As our forests become more intensively managed, and the resources therein become more valuable, the need to work together becomes greater. And this task poses one of the great challenges for wildlife biologists now and in the future.

### Response of Habitat to Logging

Silvicultural treatments affect the response of understory vegetation. Prescribed fire is often an important treatment, and is considered in Chapter 6. While the clearcut is often castigated for its appearance immediately after logging, numerous studies indicate that it is the best producer of forage among those logging techniques commonly used. Selective cuts of several kinds were not as productive of wildlife forage as clearcuts in Oregon (Figure 5.3) and Idaho (Figure 5.4). Murphy and Ehrenreich (1965) reported that timber stand improvement practices in Missouri oak forests did not appreciably increase production of understory forage (Table 5.1). Krefting and Phillips (1970) reported similar results in northern Michigan (Table 5.2). However, Behrend and Patric (1969) reported that deer browse did respond to removal of either high or low shade in hardwood and mixed growth stands in New York. Removal of low cover simulates a timber stand improvement practice in this area.

In many cases, retention or improvement of wildlife habitat is not restricted to improvement of understory forage. This is especially true where hole-nesting or other species require mature forest. In some cases as with mast-producing trees and trees that harbor arboreal lichens, mature trees are the food producers. Very often in these cases the wildlife biologist would prefer that a stand not be logged because of its high wildlife values. Equally often, the decision to log has been made and the wildlife biologist is faced with saving as much habitat as possible.

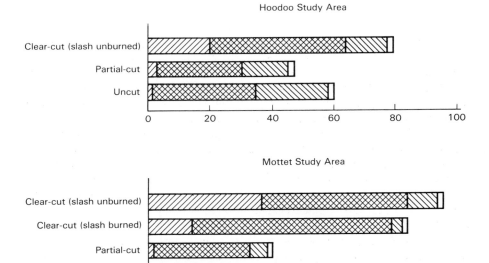

**Figure 5.3** Foliage cover five growing seasons after logging in clear-cut, partial-cut, and uncut mixed conifer stands, Hoodoo and Mottet timber sales, northeastern Oregon. After Edgerton 1972. (Used with permission.)

In the cases where mature timber is the habitat to be retained, several options are available. Some species, such as the oaks and ponderosa pine, lend themselves to partial or selective cutting systems. In these cases, mast-producing and den trees may be left. Alternatively, small blocks of clearcuts, the group-selection cuts, can be used, thereby leaving other blocks uncut. Other species, such as spruces, often wind-throw if partially cut so retention of mature forest in logged areas essentially requires a group-selection system.

While there are a number of options available to forest and wildlife managers to integrate the management of the two resources, much depends on the amount of available land and the nature of the forest. An average stand, highly susceptible to fire, disease, and insect infestations, is often prime wildlife habitat because of its great diversity. At the same time, it is often a very fragile stand, difficult if not impossible to maintain through long time spans. While efforts to retain old-growth stands are commendable in the short term, efforts to identify the components of the old-growth forest that are needed by each species and to actively recreate and

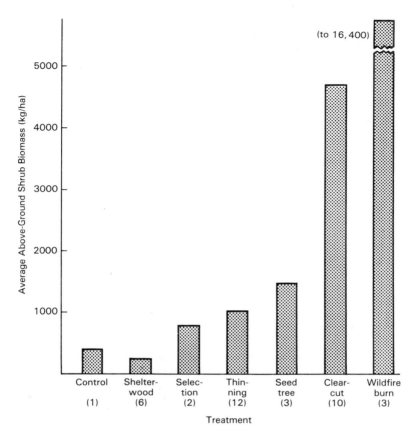

**Figure 5.4** Predicted total shrub biomass in grand fir-cedar-hemlock habitat types according to silvicultural treatment. Number of stands sampled is in parentheses. From Irwin 1976. (Used with permission.)

manage for them is the challenge for the future. Specific actions tailored to the species in question, as reviewed in the rest of this chapter, illustrate a wide variety of ways to address this long-term challenge.

### Responses of Nongame Birds to Timber Management

Avifauna are known to undergo dramatic changes in species composition and densities following logging. Of special concern are effects on endangered and threatened species and those species with unique habitat requirements, such as the hole nesters or some of the raptors. Because of the variety of species, diversity indices have been a common means of evaluating change. An example is McLay's (1974) evaluations of diversity following modification of the New Zealand beech forests.

**TABLE 5.1  Production of Preferred Deer and Turkey Foods Following Logging, Timber Stand Improvements in Missouri White Oak Type, Selection Cut System.**

| Time since Disturbance | Pounds Per Acre | |
|---|---|---|
| | Preferred Deer Foods | Preferred Turkey Foods |
| No disturbance | | |
| Grass | – | 14 |
| Forbs | 24 | 17 |
| Browse | 26 | – |
| Total | 50 | 31 |
| 0–3 years | | |
| Grass | – | 11 |
| Forbs | 16 | 11 |
| Browse | 26 | – |
| Total | 42 | 22 |
| 6–10 years | | |
| Grass | – | 19 |
| Forbs | 38 | 29 |
| Browse | 38 | – |
| Total | 76 | 48 |

*Source:* Murphy and Ehrenreich 1965. (Used with permission.)

**TABLE 5.2  Summary of Experimental Cutting on Browse Production and Deer Use, Upper Peninsula Experimental Forest in Michigan**

| Treatment | Number of Stems per Acre | | Pounds of Browse per Acre | | Number of Pellet Groups per Acre | |
|---|---|---|---|---|---|---|
| | 1960 | 1966 | 1960 | 1966 | 1960 | 1966 |
| Diameter-Limit | 12,163 | – | 72.7 | 34.3 | 64 | 26 |
| Selection | 9,824 | – | 21.8 | 26.7 | 60 | 26 |
| Shelterwood | 12,376 | – | 97.2 | 28.9 | 94 | 54 |
| 0.4 Acre clear-cut | 11,188 | – | 63.4 | 40.1 | 18 | 8 |
| 75' X 400' strip clear-cut | 15,886 | – | 82.3 | 56.7 | 38 (102)[a] | 16 (88)[a] |
| Uncut control | 6,300 | – | 9.6 | 9.6 | 30 | 14 |

*Source:* Krefting and Phillips 1970. (Used with permission.)
*Note:* Areas were cut in 1952–1953 or 1953–1954.
[a]Adjacent uncut strip in parentheses.

Bird density increased as forests were changed from the virgin state to modified forests (cut, regenerating naturally), to conifer plantations, to suburban bush and garden habitats. However, the number and diversity of native bird species declined as forests were most extensively altered, even if total density remained constant.

Avifauna diversity is related in turn to plant species diversity and foliage height diversity, measures of the complexity of the relevant portions of the habitat (MacArthur and MacArthur 1961). In forested habitats, the avifauna composition will follow a successional sequence that coincides with the vegetational successional sequence following cutting. Meslow and Wight (1975) describe the changes in avifauna following clear-cutting in coastal Dougals fir in Oregon (Table 5.3). Here, shrub-sapling stages had the highest number of species present, but older second-growth and mature old-growth forests had more nesting species, particularly the habitat-specific hole-nesting birds.

**TABLE 5.3   Changes in Avifauna in Coastal Douglas Fir Related to Cutting and Subsequent Succession**

| Seral Stage | Age (years) | Number of Species | Number Nesting | Number of Hole Nesters |
|---|---|---|---|---|
| Grass-forb | 1–7 | 38 | 6 | 0 |
| Shrub-sapling | 8–15 | 72 | 39 | 4 |
| Second growth | 16–40 | 59 | 31 | 6 |
| Older second growth | 41–120 | 64 | 51 | 14 |
| Mature forest | 120+ | 58 | 46 | 14 |
| Total species | | 84 | | |

*Source:* Meslow and Wight 1975. (Used with permission.)

Franzreb (1977) listed species of birds that were beneficially or adversely affected by logging mixed conifer forests in Arizona. Coues's flycatcher, purple martins, and western bluebirds were restricted to harvested sites, which contained snags and considerable slash. Ten species were beneficially affected by the logging. Twelve species were adversely affected, and overall numbers were higher on the unlogged area. Snags were of similar density in both areas. Population size was related to foliage volume, nest site availability, degree of predation, microclimate, and food abundance. Tall trees, especially Douglas fir, white fir, and Engelmann spruce were preferred over ponderosa pine, white pine, and subalpine fir.

In Virginia, mixed oak stands that are cut illustrate another pattern in succession of both vegetation and birds (Conner and Adkisson 1975). Greatest diversity and numbers occur in younger forests in this area (Table 5.4).

Webb, Behrend, and Saisorn (1977) reported responses of 26 New York bird species to four different levels of logging in hardwoods. Eleven species were not affected, 8 increased with logging, and 7 decreased. The Blackburnian warbler decreased under all logging treatments from heaviest to lightest crown removal. The black-throated warbler and rose-breasted grosbeak did not respond to light logging but responded negatively and positively, respectively, to heavy logging. The American redstart increased progressively with increased logging intensity and the ovenbird decreased progressively as logging intensity increased. The heaviest overstory removal left all trees below 14 inches diameter at breast height (dbh), or 40–50 square feet per acre of basal area remaining. Trees took two to five years to respond to the harvest, and at the tenth year of the study most populations showed evi-

**TABLE 5.4   Changes in Bird Species Composition Following Clear-Cut Logging in Mixed Oak Stands in Virginia**

| Seral Stage | Number of Birds | Number of Species | Breeding Bird Diversity | Common Species |
|---|---|---|---|---|
| 1-year clearcut | 39 | 8 | 1.9 | Bluebird, indigo bunting, prairie warbler, rufous-sided towhee |
| 3-year clearcut | 162 | 19 | 2.66 | Indigo bunting, rufous-sided towhee |
| 7-year clearcut | 154 | 21 | 2.68 | Indigo bunting, rufous-sided towhee, hooded warbler |
| 12-year clearcut | 143 | 20 | 2.52 | Towhee, yellow-breasted chat, blue-gray gnatcatcher |
| Pole | 44 | 11 | 2.26 | Ovenbird, tufted titmouse |
| Mature oak | 93 | 16 | 2.51 | Wood pewee, ovenbird, wood thrush |

*Source:* Conner and Adkisson 1975. (Used with permission.)

dence of returning to levels characteristic of the uncut forest. Thus, postlogging responses of the breeding bird fauna were relatively short-lived in comparison to the long intervals between logging in this forest type.

Trends in bird species composition and numbers are directly related to availability of suitable habitats. Thus, in forests that are least uniform, with greatest diversity in habitats, one will find the greatest variety of species. The question arises as to how to define quality habitats—on a basis of numbers of birds or on a basis of numbers of species? Variety of species is probably all-important in most situations. Numbers of individual species, if they are threatened, are unique in some way to an area, or are hunted, may be critical. However, large numbers of one species may also reflect an environment of narrow diversity that may not be suitable for many others.

Threatened species deserve special consideration and habitat management. Kirtland's warbler is a fine example. Its nesting range is a 60-by100-mile area in the northern lower peninsula of Michigan (Schneegas 1975). Optional habitat is composed of jackpine, 5 to 18 feet tall on sandy soils, originally created by wildfire. Currently, tree removal and planting coupled with controlled burning is occurring on 11,000 acres to maintain habitat.

The California condor illustrates another means of providing for an endangered species. Less than 50 birds remain on the Los Padres National Forest of California and the vicinity. Two sanctuaries have been established that contain 90 percent of the nesting sites, as well as roosting and wintering areas, and both are closed to entry by the public. No timber management is indicated for the species, as yet.

Northern spotted owls nest in old-growth Douglas fir with broken tops in the

Pacific Northwest, a unique habitat requirement. Currently, no cutting within a 30-chain radius of each nest site is allowed. Newton (1972) points out that the species has been a source of confrontation between wildlife biologists who advocate no cutting of old-growth forests inhabited by the owl, and forest industry representatives who observe that if this occurs, there will be enough timber left standing to cause economic disruption. Alternatives of no cutting or short-rotation, even-age management are both unacceptable, and Newton proposes longer rotations of 120–140 years as a possible solution. Franklin and De Bell (1973) point out that there is no ecological necessity to clear-cut Douglas fir in the region, and that shelterwood or strip cuts may be appropriate. The point is, if we look hard enough, use our intellect and ingenuity, and retain good will towards our counterparts in forestry as well as towards the bird, we are likely to arrive at an accommodation.

Cavity nesters pose a unique habitat problem. Primary hole nesters, the wood-peckers, excavate their own nest sites from dead snags or decaying trees, usually each spring. The red-cockaded woodpecker is an exception, each pair nesting in the same hole for several years (Scott et al. 1977). Secondary hole nesters are those species that are incapable of excavating their own hole, such as the bluebirds and owls. At least 85 species of birds are known to use tree cavities (Table 5.5).

Red-cockaded woodpeckers prefer to nest in trees over 60 years old (Hooper, Robinson, and Jackson 1980). Further, a heart-rot fungus, which infects pines in the Southeast and softens the heartwood, often facilitates excavation of the nesting cavity by the woodpecker, and may be a prerequisite to nest site selection. Mature, parklike stands of pine with few hardwood trees, 5 to 10 acres in size, is prime nesting habitat for colonies of this species. Foraging areas are needed adjacent to colony sites, and consist of pole (4–9 inches dbh) or preferably mature trees over 9 inches dbh, which can include more hardwoods. The territory for individual colonies ranges from 100 acres in mature pines to several hundred where habitat is of lower quality. Rotations of 100 years in longleaf pine, and 80 years in other pine species on areas of 10 to 30 acres are recommended. Attention to preventing isolation of the colony site from feeding areas, preventing hardwood invasion of habitat, through prescribed burning, and deferment of harvesting colony sites are other habitat management recommendations.

McClelland et al. (1979) provide a list of tree sizes used by hole-nesting species in a northwestern Montana forest (Table 5.6). A direct correlation generally exists between size of bird and size of tree required. Pileated woodpecker requirements for trees that are 23 inches dbh for nesting coincides with the requirement reported by Bull and Meslow (1977) for northeastern Oregon. Management for hole-nesters involves managing for the most sensitive species, which in the Northern Rockies is the pileated woodpecker. This species requires the largest snags, which are in shortest supply. Feeding territory for pileated woodpecker is usually between 500 and 1000 acres in northwestern Montana and between 320 and 600 acres in northeastern Oregon. Bull and Meslow (1977) recommended 90 snags plus replacement snags over 20 inches dbh for each square mile of pileated woodpecker habitat

TABLE 5.5   North American Cavity Nesting Birds

| | |
|---|---|
| Black-bellied whistling duck | White-headed woodpecker |
| Wood duck | Black-backed three-toed |
| Common goldeneye | woodpecker |
| Barrow's goldeneye | Northern three-toed woodpecker |
| Bufflehead | Ivory-billed woodpecker |
| Hooded merganser | Sulphur-bellied flycatcher |
| Common merganser | Great-crested flycatcher |
| Turkey vulture | Wied's crested flycatcher |
| Black vulture | Ash-throated flycatcher |
| Peregrine falcon | Olivaceous flycatcher |
| Merlin | Western flycatcher |
| American kestrel | Violet-green swallow |
| Barn owl | Tree swallow |
| Screech owl | Purple martin |
| Whistered owl | Black-capped chickadee |
| Flammulated owl | Carolina chickadee |
| Hawk owl | Mexican chickadee |
| Pygmy owl | Mountain chickadee |
| Ferruginous owl | Gray-headed chickadee |
| Elf owl | Boreal chickadee |
| Barred owl | Chestnut-backed chickadee |
| Spotted owl | Tufted titmouse |
| Boreal Owl | Plain titmouse |
| Saw-whet owl | Bridled titmouse |
| Chimney swift | White-breasted nuthatch |
| Vaux's swift | Red-breasted nuthatch |
| Coppery-tailed trogon | Brown-headed nuthatch |
| Common flicker | Pygmy nuthatch |
| Pileated woodpecker | Brown creeper |
| Red-bellied woodpecker | House wren |
| Golden-fronted woodpecker | Brown-throated wren |
| Gila woodpecker | Winter wren |
| Red-headed woodpecker | Bewick's wren |
| Acorn woodpecker | Carolina wren |
| Lewis's woodpecker | Eastern bluebird |
| Yellow-bellied sapsucker | Western bluebird |
| Williamson's sapsucker | Mountain bluebird |
| Hairy woodpecker | Starling |
| Downy woodpecker | Crested myna |
| Ladder-backed woodpecker | Prothonotary warbler |
| Nuttall's woodpecker | Lucy's warbler |
| Arizona woodpecker | House sparrow |
| Red-cockaded woodpecker | European tree sparrow |

*Source:* Scott et al. 1977. (Used with permission.)
*Note:* Eighty-five species are known to use cavities in trees.

TABLE 5.6  Measurements of Trees Used for Nesting
by 16 Bird Species in Northwestern Montana

| Bird Species | Number of Nest Trees | Diameter at Breast Height (inches) | |
| --- | --- | --- | --- |
| | | Average | Range |
| Pileated woodpecker | 22 | 32 | 23–41 |
| Goldeneye | 2 | 30 | 21–39 |
| American kestrel | 5 | 27 | 22–33 |
| Williamson's sapsucker | 4 | 26 | 17–37 |
| Mountain chickadee | 35 | 25 | 7–49 |
| Yellow-bellied sapsucker | 111 | 23 | 9–47 |
| Mountain bluebird | 4 | 23 | 19–29 |
| Common flicker | 28 | 21 | 10–51 |
| Red-breasted nuthatch | 31 | 21 | 4–35 |
| Brown creeper | 3 | 20 | 14–29 |
| Tree swallow | 20 | 16 | 9–39 |
| Hairy woodpecker | 10 | 14 | 9–29 |
| Downy woodpecker | 3 | 10 | 7–14 |
| Black-backed three-toed woodpecker | 2 | 10 | 8–12 |
| Northern three-toed woodpecker | 4 | 10 | 7–11 |
| Black-capped chickadee | 10 | 8 | 4–12 |
| Total | 308 | 22.2 | 4–51 |

*Source:* McClelland et al. 1979. (Used with permission.)

following silvicultural treatment. McClelland et al. (1979) recommended the following:

1. Within each 1000 acres of areas where hole nesters are to be retained, 50–100 acres of old growth should be retained for feeding areas.
2. Old growth should be scattered rather than grouped, with travel routes between stands consisting of old growth.
3. Old growth should be roughly square but linear strips 300 feet wide along streams are suitable.
4. Old growth can often be retained in areas without roads, water influence zones, travel zones, campgrounds, or critical scenic areas.
5. Feeding substrate of logs, snags, and culls should be provided in the rest of each 1000-acre unit.
6. Firewood cutting should be limited to trees less than 15 inches dbh, and use of larch, ponderosa pine, and black cottonwood should be discouraged.
7. Closure of logging roads to save high value snags may be necessary.

Snags with broken tops are highly preferred nesting areas, with western larch, ponderosa pine, black cottonwood, aspen, and paper birch being most commonly used (McClelland et al. 1979).

Scott (1978) reported that ponderosa pine snags over 75 feet tall, over 15 inches dbh, and over 40 percent bark cover that had been dead for six or more years were preferred nesting habitat in Arizona. Recommendations by Szaro and Balda (1979) for managing birds in ponderosa pine forests in this area were as follows:

1. Total basal area of a given stand can be reduced 15–50 percent, but removal should be in strips or blocks. A thinning operation should remove 30 percent of total basal area.

2. Remove no more than 45 percent of those trees over 9 inches dbh and leave at least 32 trees per acre.

3. Remove no more than 75 percent of those trees between 6 and 9 inches dbh and leave at least 17 trees per acre.

4. Remove 80 percent of trees with dbh between 3 and 6 inches and leave about 25 trees per acre.

5. Remove no gambel oak if possible, but no more than 25 percent.

6. Leave several overmature trees per acre to allow for snag recruitment.

7. Leave at least 2.6 snags per acre.

These several recommendations and others, such as those of Benson (1979), all provide for the total avifauna complex. The avid birder is usually more concerned with variety than great numbers of one species, and monocultures of pole stands are to be avoided, while habitat diversity is to be emphasized. The need to manage for the most sensitive species or an indicator species is also critical.

### Wild Turkeys

Wild turkey populations have increased dramatically as plant succession to more mature deciduous forest, more intensive habitat management, and better regulation of the legal and illegal take have occurred. Mosby (1949) emphasized that control of the legal and illegal harvest was a high priority if turkey populations were to respond to habitat management. Destruction of habitat, most particularly the mature mast-producing deciduous timber, was a major problem, while excessive livestock grazing and adverse agricultural practices were frequently implicated as well.

High-quality turkey habitat varies across the range, but mature, open forests of mixed species that produce mast, berries, or nuts are very important (Markley 1967). Hardwood forests of oaks, beech, cherry, and ash are important in the northeastern portions of the range (Bailey and Rinell 1967; Donohoe and McKibben 1970; Gill et al. 1975). Stoddard (1963) reported that mixed terrain of fields and woodlands were important habitat on the southern Georgia coastal plain. The woodlands should consist of large timber, both in creek valleys where hardwood would predominate, and on uplands where pines dominate. Greatest turkey concentrations occurred near ideal roosting areas, such as gum or cypress growing over water or groups of large pines or hardwoods. Dickson, Adams, and Hanley (1978) demonstrated the adaptability of turkeys to a variety of Louisiana habitats, where poaching pressure was the most significant effect on distribution. Highest turkey populations were in batture hardwoods of mature hackberry, elm, ash, and sweet pecan. In Louisiana, a variety of forages may substitute for oak mast in winter for turkeys.

Size of area suitable to be managed for turkeys has been a source of concern. Early workers in Virginia recommended at least 50,000-acre blocks of mature timber interspersed with openings for successful turkey habitat management if public hunting was to be exercised (Mosby and Handley 1943). Stoddard (1963) felt that turkeys would be hard to establish on areas of less than 20,000 acres in the southern coastal plain. Kozicky and Metz (1948) recommended 10,000- to 15,000-acre management units as a minimum in Pennsylvania. These recommendations were based upon the need to minimize effects of relatively uncontrolled hunting and poaching on turkey populations as well as annual habitat requirements. However, in Ohio areas of 5000 acres have been successfully restocked (Donohoe and McKibben 1970). While retention of as much turkey habitat as possible is always in order, opportunities to establish turkey populations in smaller areas should not be overlooked.

Average annual range for gobblers was 750 acres (475- to 1088-acre range for four birds) and for hens was 2050 acres (two birds) in Missouri (Ellis and Lewis 1967). While the size of the home range will likely vary inversely with quality of habitat, the Missouri studies led Ellis and Lewis (1967) to believe that, if supplemental food patches like corn were provided during winter when turkeys may otherwise have to wander extensively, the size of the areas to be managed could be less. Near Lake Springs, Missouri, turkeys were thriving on 7600 acres where oak-hickory forest constituted 49 percent, old fields 21 percent, pastures 18 percent, and cultivated land 12 percent of the area.

Good eastern turkey habitat consists of mature hardwood forests of mixed species that produce reliable winter forage, roosting sites, and cover during the hunting season. Clearings provide green forage in spring, brood range and insects for broods, plus loafing, nesting, strutting, and dusting areas (Bailey, Uhlig, and Breiding 1951). Donohoe and McKibben (1970) provide specific habitat management guidelines that would benefit turkeys on two areas, one 4300 acres and the other 15,000 acres in size:

1. Water should be available on every 160 acres.
2. No more than 5 percent of the area should be maintained in openings, which should be about 2 acres in size and located on ridgetops and in valleys.
3. At least 25 percent of the timber should be oak, with 60 percent of the area in mast-producing sawtimber and pole stands.
4. Clear-cuttings should be distributed through the area to increase opening numbers.
5. Human disturbance (timber harvest, recreational development, etc.) should be minimized in April, May, and early June during nesting.
6. Valuable forage sources, including shrubs, vines, orchards, and berry thickets, should be preserved.

In West Virginia, selective cuttings that retained mature forest but created travel lanes and opened canopies sufficiently to allow understory development to occur were recommended over clear-cuttings (Bailey et al. 1951). Where timbering is to occur, trees that are inherently high producers of acorns (or other mast) should be retained (Goodrum, Reid, and Boyd 1971).

In the Georgia-Florida coastal plain where pines predominate, Stoddard (1963) recommended long-rotation forestry, which produces sawtimber. Selective cutting that retains well-stocked stands was recommended. Again a variety of pine species should be retained to account for the annual variations in seed crop production for any one species. Stoddard (1963) recommended that understories be burned to remove litter and to stimulate legumes and other plants and insects that serve as turkey food.

Jonas (1966), D. M. Hoffman (1968), and Boeker and Scott (1969) all recommend retention of tall, mature ponderosa pine for roosting Merriam's wild turkeys. Overmature trees with sparse crowns are preferred and should be retained when logging is planned.

### Pine Marten

The pine marten is often used as a species representing wildlife that require mature forest, when forest management plans are being devised. In central Idaho, martens prefer high-elevation basins dominated by spruce-fir and mountain hemlock (Koehler, Moore, and Taylor 1975). If marten habitat is to be maintained, clearcuts should be small since martens rarely cross openings more than 300 feet wide. Clearings that provide green forage cut so as to retain over 30 percent canopy cover can be maintained but old growth on mesic sites should be left, especially where upland areas are open. In Maine, Soutiere (1979) reported that partially harvested spruce-fir forest where fir trees less than 15 cm dbh and spruce and hardwood trees less than 40 cm dbh were left, had similar densities of marten as uncut forest. A commercial clearcut, which left only isolated nonmerchantable trees, retained lowest marten densities. A residual population of marten could be retained in this area if a minimum of 25 percent of trees was left in undisturbed pole and mature spruce fir. A nucleus population could be supported where watercourses and nonoperable stands were left. Partial cutting methods appear to be most suitable for retaining pine marten, where logging is to occur.

### Responses of Small Mammals to Timber Management

Small mammals commonly include rats, voles, mice, shrews, chipmunks, and squirrels. The group occupies a wide diversity of microhabitats within a forest, and also exhibits a wide variety of forage preferences. Deer mice, chipmunks, and tree squirrels consume larger amounts of seeds, while voles and ground squirrels tend towards leaves, flowers, and stalks. Shrews are generally insectivorous. Deer mice are known to consume large quantities of conifer seeds (Ahlgren 1966) and foresters have been concerned with the potential impact in regenerating desired species.

Responses of each species to silvicultural treatment varies greatly, according to habitat requirements.

As would be expected, clear-cutting eliminated red squirrels from an interior Alaskan forest (Wolff and Zazada 1975). A shelterwood cut that altered the original white spruce forest from 472 to 81 trees per hectare reduced the squirrel population from one per 0.69 ha to one per 2.0 ha. Gashwiler (1970) showed similar results for both red squirrels and flying squirrels in an Oregon Douglas fir forest that was clear-cut. "Commercial clear-cut" logging of a New York mixed hardwood-coniferous forest, however, had no real detrimental effect on red squirrels, although populations were reduced (Krull 1970). A "commercial clearcut" in this area involved removing all hardwood trees over 14 inches dbh, and all softwoods over 12 inches dbh, leaving a significant number of trees.

Chipmunks appeared to decrease following clear-cut logging in Oregon and northwestern California, and then to increase to higher levels as woody species reinvaded the site (Gashwiler 1970; Trevis 1956b). Hooven and Black (1976) also reported that chipmunks were initially reduced after a clearcut of coastal Douglas fir in Oregon, but appeared to be increasing as woody species appeared.

Chipmunk populations in a northern Minnesota jackpine forest were low and showed no significant response to logging and subsequent burning (Ahlgren 1966). The New York "commercial clearcut" had no effect on chipmunk populations (Krull 1970). Deer mice usually incease in numbers following logging and/or burning (Ahlgren 1966; Gashwiler 1970; Hooven and Black 1976). These seed eaters find a profusion of flowering forbs and grasses in clearcuts and burns, which appears to benefit them. Similar responses by voles of the genus *Microtus* have been noted. However, the red-backed vole can be expected to decrease from numbers observed in the uncut forest, probably because of a decrease in their food supplies (Ahlgren 1966). Figure 5.5 shows trends in deer mice and chipmunk populations from Gashwiler's (1970) long-term Oregon studies.

Ground squirrels are commonly observed in clearcuts containing primarily herbaceous vegetation. Colonization of these sites may be rapid even though colonies may not be near a cut, apparently because they are highly mobile and capable of rapidly dispersing to suitable habitats. Gashwiler (1970) reported that ground squirrels in a logged and burned site increased one year after the burn. Populations may be expected to decrease concomitant to reestablishment of woody vegetation and conifers. Occasionally, ground squirrels can cause significant damage to regenerating stands.

Shrews show variable responses to logging. Hooven and Black (1976) reported that logging adversely affected shrews, and Gashwiler (1970) suggested that an initial decrease following logging would occur, followed by an increase. Shrews did not appear to be adversely affected in the Minnesota jackpine logging investigations of Ahlgren (1966).

The research into small mammal response to logging is related to the effect these species have on attempts to regenerate the forest. Sullivan (1979) points out that very few individual deer mice are needed to cause heavy destruction of seed

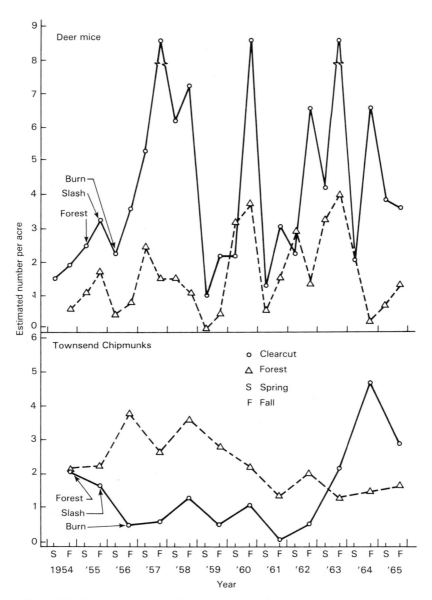

**Figure 5.5**  Trends in numbers of deer mice and chipmunks in uncut and clear-cut Oregon Douglas fir forests. After Gashwiler 1970. (Used with permission.)

sources used to regenerate the stand. Deer mice can rapidly reinvade a site after it has been poisoned, and a small population can cause significant damage. Alternatives to poisoning, such as use of partial cutting systems that do not favor small mammal increases, alternative conifer species, alternative forages, repellants, and, as a last resort, use of patience in awaiting regeneration, are in order. Logging activities can be expected to influence composition and numbers of species.

### Ruffed Grouse

Integration of ruffed grouse habitat management into forest management in northern Minnesota has developed beyond evaluating responses of the birds to planning for creation of habitat. The recommendations for habitat management are provided by Gullion (1972). The basic biological requirements of the species and a knowledge of aspen management were integrated to formulate the guidelines. Grouse in this area are known to survive longest and occur in highest density in aspen stands (Gullion and Marshall 1968).

Aspen provides high-quality winter forage, brooding, breeding, and nesting cover, but at different stages of development. This species is seral in boreal forests, highly intolerant of shading (H. L. Hansen and Kurmis 1972), and thus lends itself to clear-cutting. It suckers readily, and grows in even-aged stands. The goal to retain grouse habitat involves aspen of three age classes. Stands of suckers less than 10 years old provide brood cover. The sapling and pole stands 10 to 25 years of age are used in winter and as breeding cover. Older aspen stands provide food and wintering and nesting cover. Each grouse will have a home range of 6 to 10 acres, which dictates the size of the cutting unit.

Recommendations are to clear-cut aspen on a 40- to 60-year rotation, with maximum size of any cut being limited to 10 acres. Debris on the ground will provide cover for predators and, thus, should be burned or removed. Drumming logs, which may be boulders, stumps, and dirt mounds as well as logs, are necessary and should be 12 to 14 inches above ground, with unobstructed surveillance for 50 to 60 feet in all directions. Figure 5.6 provides one scheme that illustrates how a unit of land could be managed for grouse, using the criteria. Cutting occurs at 10-year intervals in this scheme. These recommendations culminate a period of research into ruffed grouse covering over 20 years, and are an outstanding example of integrated wildlife and forest management.

### Elk

Elk habitat relationships studies have increased in the last decade in response to increased timber harvest and road-building activities in elk range. This species is highly adaptable to a wide variety of habitat conditions, but coordination between land managers and wildlife managers is critical to retaining habitat that is best suited for elk in each local situation. This species usually has a large home range and is highly mobile. Thus, it will respond readily to activities within one area by shifting habitat use patterns to areas away from the activity. While behavior of this kind need not imply that population size is affected, hunting opportunity and general use patterns in an area can well be. The elk is perhaps the best example illustrating that behavioral responses, rather than density change, must be measured. It is a long-lived species, highly adaptable and mobile, and shifts in movement patterns

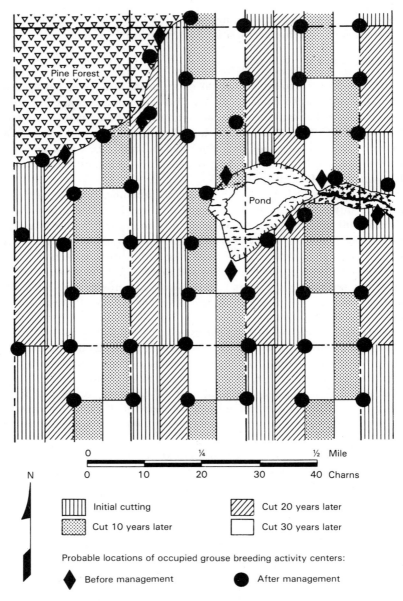

**Figure 5.6**  Diagram suggesting how fairly extensive commercial timber harvesting could be done in aspen or hardwood forests in a manner that should substantially benefit ruffed grouse and other forest wildlife species. Each of these rectangular strips consists of 10 acres, and 160 acres could be cut from a square mile in each operation, spaced at ten-year intervals. On the other hand, cuttings could be at five-year intervals, cutting half as much each time. (From Gullion 1972. Used with permission.)

and habitat use will ordinarily precede a change in population size. However, isolation of effects of logging or road-building activities on elk behavior can be readily confounded by variations in weather, snow conditions, summer drought, hunting season changes, and a variety of other factors to which elk can be expected to respond. Lyon (1979) concluded after eight years of study that annual variations in snowfall and summer drought influenced elk distribution more than logging activity in a western Montana study area.

**Roads and elk.**    One of the major sources of concern involves the increased access resulting from construction of logging roads. When the traditional logging methods are used, road densities may be above 5 linear miles of road per square mile. When this occurs, access is dramatically increased and hunting success can be dramatically, although temporarily, increased as well (Thiessen 1976). So while a logging operation may in fact be coordinated to leave a satisfactory elk habitat, the associated road system may well preclude use of the area by elk if human activity is not controlled. This points to the need for close cooperation between land managers, engineers, and wildlifers when activity in elk habitat is being planned. Changes in hunting regulations, restrictions on road use, timing of logging and road-building activity, and locations of roads and logging areas, all must be considered.

While emphasis on regulation of human activity along roads is needed because this appears to be the main source of distruption to elk, a commonsense approach to road construction is also needed so that fills, cuts, and debris do not restrict access by wildlife across a road. Actual habitat loss through roads has not been considered critical in most cases, especially since summer ranges are most often affected, and an abundance of summer range is assumed to be present. Vegetation alteration along rights-of-way can either be beneficial or detrimental, usually depending on whether foraging areas can be provided and whether cover is removed.

In general, restriction of use of roads by vehicles during hunting will improve the quailty of the hunt in the more open habitats (Basile and Lonner 1979, Marcum 1976; A. L. Ward 1976; Perry and Overly 1976; Rost and Bailey 1979). Basile and Lonner (1979) found that travel restrictions in open areas may reduce the movement of elk to less accessible areas during the hunting season in more heavily forested areas where suitable cover constitutes at least two-thirds of the total area and is well dispersed. A prediction of loss of elk habitat relative to road density and the crown canopy (Figure 5.7), shows that dramatic differences in loss of effective elk habitat occur when roads are developed dependent upon amount of tree cover. Lyon (1979) cautioned that amount of habitat used in occupied elk range probably cannot be reduced below 10–15 percent by roads alone. At these low levels, topography, cover distribution, and behavior patterns of elk may override the cover-traffic effect.

Elk often cross roads where dense cover, saddles, seeps, drainages, and springs occur (Black, Scherzinger, and Thomas 1976). These traditional travel routes should receive special consideration when road-building and logging activities are planned.

In general, managing vehicle access is largely a matter of informing and edu-

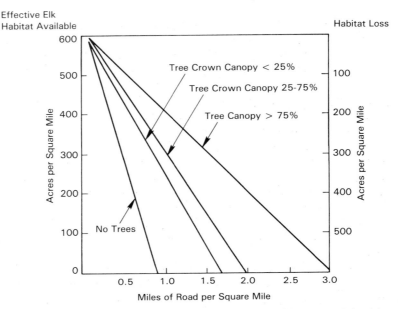

**Figure 5.7** Predicted levels of effective elk habitat with different road densities and tree cover. After Lyon 1979. (Used with permission.)

cating the user of the road. Rational explanations of the reasons why a road is restricted of use are paramount in importance. Enforcement is critical and may have to change through time, with warnings and intensive patrol initially, then less intensive patrol and citations later. Use of a road may be restricted to times when animals are not using an area, or over a short period if use has to occur. While elk in national parks and other areas that aren't subject to hunting will become conditioned to vehicles, those in the hunted areas must be given consideration when vehicle access is planned.

**Logging and elk.** Harper (1971) was among the first to recognize that use of cut-over lands by elk (and other wildlife as well) was related to a number of factors, all of which could be important. In western Oregon areas, use of clearcuts was dependent upon amount of soil disturbance, aspect, position on slope, cover type that was cut, and past logging treatments. Elk use was highest five to eight years after logging on areas when soils were disturbed enough to produce large amounts of herbaceous forage. Rhododendron–Oregon grape communities on ridgetops and south slopes that were logged and burned were preferred feeding areas.

Models developed by Lyon and Jensen (1980) predicting elk use of clearcuts based on pellet group density provided real insight into factors affecting elk use in Montana forests. Size of clearcut and average depth of slash in the cut, depth of dead and down timber in the adjacent forest, and height of vegetation influenced elk use in areas where forests were dense. In more open areas, cover amount of adjacent forest was the important variable. In all areas, vehicle access was the single

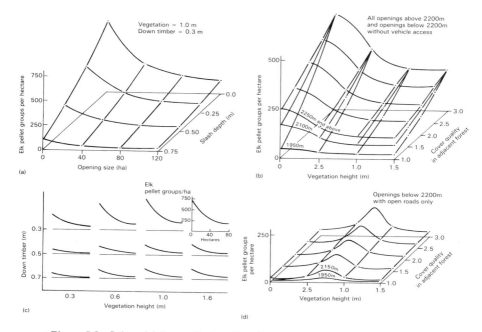

**Figure 5.8**  Submodel for predicting elk pellet–group densities in clearcuts, Montana. (a) and (d) relative to size of clear-cut. (b) and (c) relative to vegetation height. From Lyon and Jensen 1980. (Used with permission.)

most important influence, illustrating the need for security by elk. A preference for clearcuts with cover in the opening, which still provided significant amounts of forage, was indicated (Figure 5.8).

Partial cutting systems, which do not affect the character of a forest as much as clear-cutting, produce a mixed response in elk use. If cover values are destroyed and forage values are not appreciably changed, then elk use may be expected to decrease (Edgerton 1972). In cases where partial cutting systems do open up stands to produce more forage, and adjacent cover is suitable, then elk use will be retained or increased (Patton 1974, 1976; H. G. Reynolds 1966a).

In habitats where forest growth is rapid, seral stages 30 to 40 years old may provide adequate cover, or forage, and a mixture of age classes from new clearcut through mature timber to old growth can provide excellent elk habitat (Irwin and Peek 1983). Vegetation structure is the criterion affecting elk habitat use, and a knowledge of succession and its relationship to vegetation height and density are critical (Figure 5.9).

On winter range where forage abundance is important, the value of adequate cover still has to be considered. Elk often bed on north-facing slopes where snows are soft and deep and the vegetation tall and dense. Beall (1976) reported that beds of elk in the Bitterroot Valley in winter were often associated with trees of 8–14 inches dbh, with the bed less than 1 foot from the tree. Such large trees reflect and

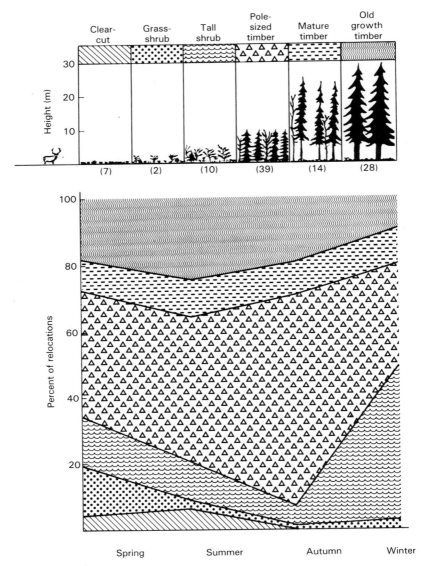

**Figure 5.9** Percentages of radiolocations of elk within successional stages in the cedar-hemlock zone of northern Idaho. Numbers in parentheses indicate percentage of study area occupied by each successional stage. After Irwin and Peek 1983. (Used with permission.)

emit more energy than smaller trees, and elk may seek this energy source, plus the security a large tree provides. Aspect of the bed location was related to temperature: higher temperatures tended to cause elk to bed on north aspects during the day and south aspects at night. Obviously, the microclimate associated with the actual bed site is a factor in cover selection, as Ozoga (1968) discovered in relation to white-tailed deer yards in Michigan.

The large number of investigations has produced an extensive amount of information about habitat selection patterns of elk in a variety of habitats. Some generalities can be deduced, but the fact remains that, with a few exceptions, we are a distance from being able to predict with certainty what will happen to a population under any given plan. Close study of the existing data base, coupled with consultation with others experienced in the specific area in question, and monitoring of results of any planned habitat alteration are still warranted. If Bunnell (1976) can dispell the "myth of the omniscient forester," versed in all aspects of land management, wildlife biologists should also beware of the limitations of their own knowledge and be prepared to witness unexpected results from recommendations.

### Mule Deer

As has been the case with many other species, investigations of mule deer and forest management initially centered on depredations of the deer on conifer reproduction. The Oregon Game Commission investigations of Columbian black-tailed deer on the Tillamook Burn were initiated in 1958 to determine impacts of browsing on survival and growth of Douglas fir plantations (Hines 1973). Investigations of the same subspecies inhabiting redwood–Douglas fir forests in California also were directed at this problem, and indicated that deer numbers needed to be controlled in reforestation areas (Browning and Lauppe 1964). More recently, efforts to provide deer habitat through proper forest management practices have been made in conjunction with consideration of conifer damage problems (D. L. Campbell and Evans 1975). In Colorado and Arizona, efforts to improve deer habitat have received emphasis rather than efforts to minimize conifer damage, as Regelin et al. (1974) and Patton (1976) indicate. Relationships of mule deer to forest management practices have received less attention than elk relationships, but there is enough data to indicate some trends to be expected.

Edgerton's (1972) work in the Blue Mountains of Oregon showed that timber harvest in that area had less influence on mule deer than on elk. While similar trends in habitat use existed for both species, the differences in use were small for deer. Openings in the forest seemed to be less attractive to mule deer than to elk. H. G. Reynolds (1966a) reported similar findings in northern Arizona spruce–fir forests. Preference as indicated by pellet groups for edges of openings was shown, with most use occurring within 200 feet of the border between forest and opening. Openings created by logging were preferred to natural ones, probably because forbs, the preferred summer deer forage, were more abundant in logged areas. Openings smaller than 20 acres received heaviest use. Ponderosa pine forests in Arizona used in summer by deer had different use patterns in relation to openings (H. G. Reynolds 1966b). Deer droppings were distributed similarly out to 600 feet from forest borders into openings, after which a decrease occurred. Openings less than 46 acres (1600 feet across) received greatest deer use. Lyon (1976) reported that deer preferred openings in the 60-acre size class (range of 40 to 80 acres), dependent upon the amount of vegetation and slash in the opening and down timber in the adjacent forests in western Montana. Where dead and down timber exceeds 2 feet in height, access to cuts was precluded, and slash in excess of 2 feet in height in an opening will reduce deer use by at least 50 percent. These investigations suggest that cover type and interspersion of openings has an effect on use of various sized cuts. The clearcuts studied by Edgerton (1972) were 20 and 39 acres in size.

Patton (1969, 1974) further elaborated mule deer use of Arizona ponderosa pine forests subject to timber harvest (Table 5.7). Deer use these watersheds primarily in spring and fall, on their way to and from summer range. After logging, deer use increased for three years and then stabilized, probably because animals were attracted to the area from adjacent habitats. The increased use was attributable to increased forage production following logging of almost 100 percent over the uncut stand. The study indicated that well-stocked ponderosa pine forests in the area can be cut in various sizes from 2 to 32 acres to benefit deer and elk. Total acreage cut, however, may not be as important as the width of the cut, which should be less than 1600 feet across. Similar results in mixed conifer forests (spruce, fir, pine, aspen) were noted in the same general area, which were selectively cut in small blocks, with removal of trees over 10 inches dbh, and salvaging of defective trees (Patton 1976).

Delayed responses to habitat change by mule deer using the Kaibab summer range was noted by Hungerford (1970). Approximately 10 percent of the total summer range on national forest land has been modified through fire, logging, and blowdown, then revegetated with mixtures of forbs, grasses, and shrubs. Although responses have been influenced by hunter harvest, yearlings appeared to colonize newly created openings and use planted forage first. Thus, deer populations with high reproduction and survival rates and high proportions of yearlings may be more responsive to habitat change than are less productive populations. Change in home

**TABLE 5.7    Deer- and Elk-Days Use for Uncut and a Cutover Watershed in Ponderosa Pine Forests of East Central Arizona**

| | Days Use per Acre | | | |
| | Logged Drainage (900 acres) | | Unlogged Drainage (1163 acres) | |
| Year | Deer | Elk | Deer | Elk |
| --- | --- | --- | --- | --- |
| 1967 | 1.6 | 0.3 | 0.7 | 0.2 |
| 1968 | 3.2 | 1.9 | 0.7 | 0.7 |
| 1969 | 4.2 | 3.6 | 0.7 | 0.7 |
| 1970 | 2.0 | 1.9 | 0.5 | 0.1 |
| 1971 | 2.6 | 2.6 | 0.6 | 0.5 |
| 1972 | 3.2 | 1.4 | 0.3 | 0.2 |

*Source:* Patton 1969, 1974. (Used with permission.)

*Note:* Forests were cut between October 1966 and August 1967. One-sixth of the logged drainage (150 acres) was clear-cut and 12 patches of 2 to 32 acres were selectively cut to reduce trees from 45 to 12 per acre.

range areas and condition of animals were the two major effects of the habitat change.

Wallmo (1969) showed that clear-cutting lodgepole pine and spruce fir forests in strips from 1 to 6 chains wide with alternating uncut strips of similar widths doubled mule deer use of an area 10 years after logging in central Colorado. While 15 years following logging, nutritive values and digestibility of forage in logged and unlogged areas were similar, greater species diversity and productivity of forage in logged areas still attracted deer (Regelin et al. 1974). Logging summer range did not appear to be necessary to produce larger deer populations in this area, but the treatment did stimulate beneficial habitat changes, which continued to receive high use (Wallmo, Regelin, and Reichert 1972).

Mature pinyon pine–juniper woodlands in the southwest are manipulated to produce forage rather than wood products (Short, Evans, and Boeker 1977). Extensive clearings benefit livestock, but elk and mule deer use decreases. Smaller clearings in the range of 30 m to 200 m wide (length is less critical) interspersed with unlogged woodland is recommended.

Thus far, investigations suggest that partial cuts and clearcuts will increase mule deer use of an area, depending on the size or width of the cut, the amount of slash in the cuts, the amount of down timber adjacent to the cut, and the composition of understory vegetation in the cut. All investigations have been conducted using pellet group frequency distribution data.

### White-Tailed Deer and Forestry

As with mule deer, initial work on white-tailed deer and forestry was centered on damage to merchantable conifer and hardwood species. Similar trends towards integration of white-tailed deer habitat management with forestry have subsequently occurred, but J. S. Jordan (1970) stated that a satisfactory definition of deer habitat management was lacking, and an ability to solve habitat problems has been consistently overestimated.

Initial conflicts between forest management and white-tailed deer were severe (Krefting 1975; Neils, Adams, and Blair 1955). Forest fires and unregulated logging created excellent habitat in many areas in the 1930s and 1940s. Subsequent efforts to establish conifer plantations on deer range often failed because of the browsing. Recommendations to plant older stock (three years old) and less palatable species, such as spruce, which are more tolerant of browsing have helped (Krefting and Stoeckler 1953), but the problem continues to exist.

The effects of this heavy browsing on subsequent stand composition are of concern. In a mixed coniferous-deciduous forest of northern Minnesota, Ross, Bray, and Marshall (1970) reported that seedling and sapling density was much lower outside a deer exclosure established in 1937 and that white pine, red maple, red oak, and balsam fir densities were greatly reduced with the less palatable red pine and white birch dominating the sapling stage of the forest. Hard maple has been adversely affected in New York forests (Tierson, Patric, and Behrend 1966) and basswood, hemlock, and yellow birch have been virtually eliminated from some

Michigan forests (Graham 1958). Pimlott (1963) reported that balsam fir and white birch had been reduced and white spruce and quaking aspen had been favored in boreal forests of Anticosti Island in eastern Canada. Neils et al. (1955) reported severe damage to ponderosa pine regeneration in western Montana, which often coincided with the best pine-producing lands. Reductions in the deer population, change in emphasis from timber production to deer management on winter range, limited fencing, and planting of less palatable trees have all been suggested as means to alleviate the rangewide problem.

Verme (1965) provided a deer habitat management plan for swamp conifer deer yards in northern Michigan that accommodated the need for forage and cover for the deer, and for northern white cedar regeneration. White cedar swamps provide excellent winter browse at 20–40 years after cutting, and excellent shelter when the trees reach 40 feet in height (Figure 5.10). Even-aged stands over 70 years old, with closed even canopies were demonstrated by Ozoga (1968) to have higher relative humidities, lower accumulative wind flow, narrowest temperature ranges, and shallowest and hardest snows of six cover types typical of this region, which describes preferred deer cover (Table 5.8). A system of strip clear-cutting 1 chain wide, which accommodates the open microhabitat needed for cedar to reseed, was recommended (Figure 5.11). After regeneration was established, the remaining strips were cut.

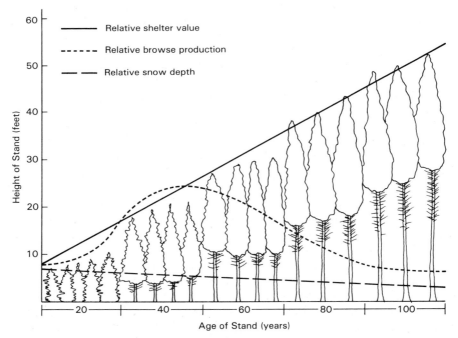

**Figure 5.10** Value of white cedar as deer browse and cover, related to stand age, height, and snow depth. From Verme 1965. (Used with permission.)

**TABLE 5.8 Microclimate Data for Six Cover Types in Northern Michigan**

| Microclimate | Upland Openings | Northern Hardwoods | Mixed Hardwood Conifers | Even-Aged Swamp Conifers | | |
|---|---|---|---|---|---|---|
| | | | | Saplings | Poles | Mature |
| Temperature (°F) | | | | | | |
| Maximum | 30.9 | 29.1 | 29.2 | 30.6 | 38.0 | 29.1 |
| Minimum | 8.4 | 8.9 | 8.8 | 8.1 | 8.2 | 10.1 |
| Range | −8 to +45 | −9 to +44 | −8 to +43 | −8 to +43 | −8 to +42 | −8 to +43 |
| Total miles wind for 52 days until March | 4542.5 | — | 630.8 | 372.8 | 118.4 | 22.3 |
| February relative humidity | | | | | | |
| Maximum | 90+ | — | — | — | — | 88 |
| Minimum | 60 | — | — | — | — | 75 |
| Mean | 78 | — | — | — | — | 82 |
| Average snow depth Jan.-Mar. (feet) | 1.71 | 1.52 | 1.79 | 2.42 | 1.1 | 1.33 |
| Depth of 3-lb weight into snow (feet) | 0.59 | 0.67 | 0.60 | 0.82 | 0.60 | 0.46 |

*Source:* Ozoga 1968. (Used with permission.)

*Note:* The mature swamp conifer type is preferred white-tailed deer winter cover. Data for February 1966 are given.

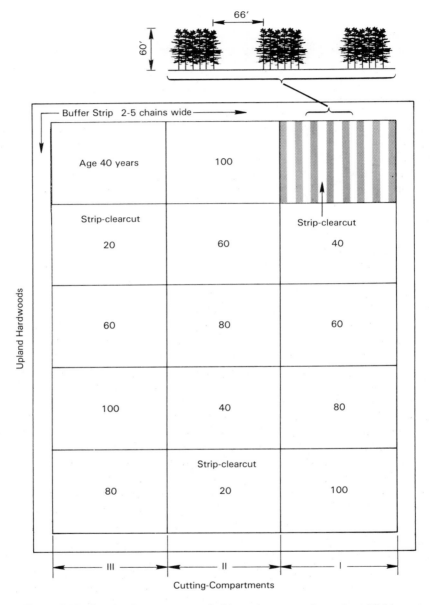

**Figure 5.11** Suggested management of white cedar swamps in northern Michigan deer yards. The cutting units are cut in alternate 1-chain strips to allow for reseeding of cedar before the remainder of the clearcut is completed. From Verme 1965. (Used with permission.)

Each cutting unit must be large enough (at least 40 to 160 acres in size) to exclude deer from a clearcut until regeneration is established. Five age classes of trees were recommended to be created, with age differences of 15 to 20 years between each class. An 80- to 100-year rotation for each stand was suggested. The procedure was not considered suitable for stands less than 200 acres in size because individual units would be too small to prevent deer browsing on the regeneration. In the smaller yards, one practical method was to clear-cut the entire stand at 60- to 80-year intervals.

Krefting (1962) stated that pulpwood cuttings in the Lake states provided better deer habitats than those done for dimension lumber. Pulpwood was cut on a shorter rotation and the resultant shrub stages made up a greater proportion of a rotation. Again, the recommendation was made that clearcuts should not exceed 75 feet, or about 1 chain in width, and that cover to provide travel lanes to browse when snow was deep was important for access. Table 5.2 shows results of investigations in mixed conifer-hardwood types in Michigan by Krefting and Phillips (1970), which confirms the earlier recommendation. However, the shelterwood cut, which reduced basal area by three-fourths on two sites, received high use also, and all cutting treatments received higher use than the uncut control.

Crawford et al. (1975) pointed out that while clearcuts provided more palatable forage than selective cuts in Virginia oak-pine stands, the advantage may be negated because of the length of time between clear-cuttings was greater than between selective cuts.

Wetzel, Wambaugh, and Peek (1975) investigated an intensively logged forest in northeastern Minnesota, where white-tailed deer populations were not responding in numbers as might be expected if the experimental work was applicable. While a large portion of this area was logged, the location of the logging relative to deer wintering areas was not well correlated. Deer habitat improvement in this area of deep snows and severe winter weather should be directed at providing fall and early winter forage sources near wintering areas. Upland mixed conifer-hardwoods and aspen types, which produce large quantities of browse and were preferred fall–early winter habitats, were given priority for habitat improvement. Again, clear-cutting in 50-yard strips on mesic sites where most palatable forage species occurred was indicated. Since aspen was not found to be as important in the deer diet as some associated shrubs, recommendations were made to cut in summer to minimize aspen resprouting and to maximize development of other species. Use of cutover areas in summer in a similar area suggested highest preference in late July and late August (Kohn and Mooty 1971). Least dense stands, with trees 11 to 30 feet tall, also received highest use, suggesting that the combination of cover and forage was adequate to those sites.

Sizes of clearcuts in loblolly–shortleaf pine forests of the Southeast should be between 20 and 100 acres in size (Halls 1973). The smaller cuts may be overbrowsed by deer, while larger ones do not receive as much use, and may create a serious lack of food immediately after harvest. The sizes coincide well with Verme's recommendations.

Creation of permanent openings in forests has received extensive attention in Wisconsin, where large unbroken stands are known to be less suitable than those with greater diversity (McCaffrey and Creed 1969). The permanent opening created by plowing, disking, and planting to grasses and legumes is also a recommended habitat improvement practice in loblolly–shortleaf pine stands in the Southeast (Halls 1973) as well as elsewhere. Holbrook (1974) recommended cultural treatments to enhance oak mast production, and planting of evergreens and honeysuckles to enhance whitetail habitat on southern forests.

Whitetails apparently exhibit dramatic changes in winter habitat selection between areas and between winters of different severity in Idaho and Montana. In northern Idaho, H. G. Shaw (1962) reported highest pellet group densities during a mild winter in more open areas, especially in shrub stages of the cedar-pachistima habitat types and intolerant tree stages in Douglas fir–ninebark habitat types. Conversely, during a severe winter on the North Fork of the Flathead River, whitetails preferred dense, mature spruce stands, and other areas where overstory cover was most dense (Singer 1979). In the Snowy Mountains of central Montana, 85 percent of all whitetails observed were in agricultural areas adjacent to ponderosa pine stands, which were used for rest and escape cover (Kamps 1969). Aspen and shrub types were most heavily used during the 1965-1966 winter in the Bear Paw Mountains of north central Montana (Martinka 1968).

The need for closed-canopy, mature forests, which provide good cover during severe winters, or where snow depths exceed 46 cm in the region, is apparently critical. Whitetails can develop trail systems similar to those of the "yards" typical of the Lake states region, which allows them access to forage adjacent to the premium winter cover.

Singer (1979) indicated that whitetails on the Flathead River area would be unable to substantially exploit new habitats created by crown fires unless fires were small and located near suitable cover, but that surface fires, typical in ponderosa pine, could create highly preferred forage that was accessible. Hildebrand (1971) reported deer in the Swan Valley of Montana were confined to unlogged areas and made only light use of clearcuts in winter. Clearcuts and larger burns may provide important forage at other times of year, especially if plants also provide some concealment. Thus, logging and fire may significantly alter, either favorably or unfavorably, the use of an area by whitetails in this region. If cutting or burning of mature forests that provide winter cover occurs, a shift in use to adjacent areas will have to take place during the severe parts of the winter, but the new vegetation may be used as a fall or spring foraging area. Size, location, and interspersion of cuts and burns is thus critical, and more definitive investigations are needed to ensure that proper habitat management coincides with timber management practices. Pengelly (1963) indicated that most white-tailed deer winter range in north Idaho was on privately owned cutover lands, and that this factor must be considered in habitat management. Much of this discussion applies across the northern whitetail range, as Drolet (1978) shows similar response for the maritime provinces in Canada.

Habitat management in central Florida is primarily oriented at providing a continuous supply of nutritional forage for whitetails (Harlow et al. 1980). In sand pine–scrub oak types, clearcuts 1 to 7 years old provided the greatest amount of forage. Natural thinning of 60-year-old stands, which allowed sunlight to penetrate to the forest floor, increased mast and forage production over that in younger closed-canopy stands. Younger stands can be thinned to create more forage. Frequent cutting of shrubs is necessary to stimulate fresh growth and ensure production of quality forage in this area. Prescribed fires at 3-year intervals or less was recommended for forage conditioning in longleaf pine stands.

Bennett et al. (1980) point out, from a comprehensive evaluation of the economics, hunter success, hunter participation, forage production and deer population response to several cutting treatments, that an area where improvement in deer habitat, as determined by population response, is greatest may not be where the greatest hunting pressure or hunter success occurs. Areas in Michigan that received a 25 percent or 50 percent harvest of timber showed the greatest deer population response five years later, but the areas where 75 percent of the timber was removed had higher deer harvests. Total recreational benefits, including hunting other species, snowmobiling, hiking, and other activities increased most in a 50-percent timber harvest treatment. When large-scale deer habitat improvement through forest management is contemplated, studies such as this one help indicate the range of management options available to the land and wildlife manager, and help to integrate resource management. The study also illustrates that alterations of habitat through forest cutting practices that are less than optimal in terms of maximum population response may be quite adequate in terms of hunter satisfaction or some other measure.

### Moose

Moose occupy boreal forest and montane forest habitats that are subject to logging. Most boreal forest habitats occupied by moose evolved in the presence of wildfire, and the moose is eminently adapted to rapidly colonize resultant burns where suitable forage is available (Peek 1974a). Areas in British Columbia and Ontario, which were unoccupied by moose in the late 1800s, have subsequently been colonized after fires and logging created suitable habitat (R. L. Peterson 1955). Thus far, moose populations have fluctuated in logged areas without any appreciable consideration having been given to their conservation and management. Peek, Urich, and Mackie (1976) demonstrated increases in moose populations following logging in northeastern Minnesota that were inadvertent and unplanned. LeResche, Bishop, and Coady (1974) reported a moose population in southeast Alaska that was dependent upon secondary succession following clear-cutting of timber. Conversely, Telfer (1974) has reported that extensive clear-cut logging in eastern Canada has reduced moose use by reducing the needed diversity of cover and forage. And, as with other species, moose have proliferated in some areas following logging to levels that have caused damage to conifer regeneration (Bergerud and Manuel 1968).

Opportunities to create or enhance moose habitat by manipulating forests are great, but as with other big game, specific recommendations must be formulated on each area. Aspen stands within Shiras moose range in Montana are important habitat and can be regenerated through prescribed burning (F. A. Gordon 1976). Tractors with shearing blades and choppers have been used on the Kenai National Moose Range to replace white spruce stands with palatable browse (Spencer and Hakala 1964; Hakala et al. 1971). Such mechanical habitat improvement is expensive but can be justified where intensive habitat management is warranted. Prescribed burning is a tool of high potential value, also, applicable to more area because of its economy. However, logging will be the major means of improving habitat over most of the moose range.

Moose habitat in northeastern Minnesota is a mosaic of coniferous and deciduous forests of different ages (Figure 5.12). Aspen-birch stands and aquatic areas are preferred summer habitats, while the cutover areas are used during September and again in fall and early winter. Spruce-fir stands over 40 years old are important

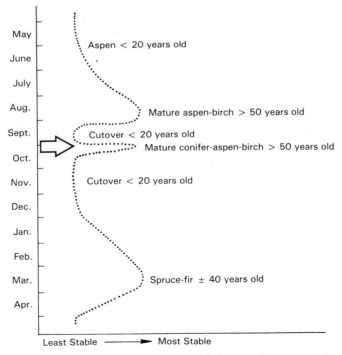

**Figure 5.12**  Habitat utilization by moose in northeastern Minnesota. After Peek 1974b. (Used with permission.)

winter habitats. On a basis of habitat stability, provision of younger stands, which produce the most forage, should be given priority in habitat management for this region. Cutovers in the size range of 177 acres, interspersed with mature timber were prime moose habitats. Peek et al. (1976) recommended township-size blocks be managed with moose habitat being considered. Composition for these blocks was given in Table 5.9.

A reason for such broad recommendations was that sufficient flexibility should be given the land manager to accommodate moose habitat recommendations into other land uses. The valuable pine stands in this region were not found to be preferred moose habitat. It was urged that intensive management for timber should be practiced for pine stands on the most productive sites, and emphasis for moose should be placed on aspen and other species elsewhere, without conversion to pine. The topography of the area essentially dictates acreage and shape of cutting units, and slopes were not considered critical in habitat management.

Telfer (1974) reported that winter moose ranges in Nova Scotia were composed of mixtures of species of all ages in patches 0.4–0.8 ha in size. Bergerud and Manuel (1968) found 240-acre (97.0 ha) cuts with some residual stands of poles and adjacent uncut conifer stands constituted high-density moose range in Newfoundland. Pimlott (1953) suggested that clearcuts of 0.5 square miles could be tolerated by moose. That cuttings of various sizes and kinds have favored moose across its range can be seen from Kistchinski's (1974) report on northeastern Siberia habitats and Markgren's (1974) review of the Fennoscandian moose history. However, the more intensive forest management currently practiced in Sweden, including increasingly larger clearcuts concomitant with use of mechanical equipment, may be detrimental (Markgren 1974). Similarly, intensive forest management, including herbiciding and planting, has a potential adverse effect on Minnesota moose habitat (Peek et al. 1976). However, the results of these practices were so variable that until more efficiency occurred, they were not considered to affect much of the range.

Some Shiras moose populations of the northwestern United States occupy

**TABLE 5.9  Recommendations for Moose Habitat Improvement
in Northeastern Minnesota**

| | | |
|---|---|---|
| 1. *Township-size* blocks of habitat are minimum units, stands distributed as follows: | | |
|    a. Cutover <20 years old | 40–50% | |
|    b. Spruce fir | 5–15% | |
|    c. Aspen-birch >20 years old | 55–35% | |
| 2. Clearcuts to 200 acres in aspen-birch type will be used in this area *in fall*. | | |
| 3. Pine-dominated areas of low priority, aspen-birch of high cutting priority. | | |
| 4. Specific sites, size of clearcuts, shapes, etc., to be left to forester to determine on basis of topography, stand sizes, etc., from on-site inspection. | | |
| 5. Forty- to fifty-acre patches of spruce fir over 30 years old will provide cover for small groups of moose and should be distributed through areas. | | |

*Source:* Peek et al., 1976. (Used with permission.)

high-elevation coniferous forests in early winter or throughout the entire winter period (Peek 1974b). Even on the commonly used willow bottom ranges, the adjacent forest cover provides bedding and escape habitat. Logging winter moose range in this area poses a special problem in that the conifers (Douglas fir, subalpine fir) are important winter forage and are also important cover. High-elevation winter range usually has very deep snow, which restricts moose movement and increases the importance of mature conifer cover where snows are less deep, over areas where snow characteristics are less severe. Similar situations occur in the Revelstoke area of British Columbia and in eastern Canada, where deep snows restrict movement. In such areas, large clearcuts may produce forage that can be used in fall and spring, but the negative effect in reducing midwinter cover values may be sufficient to adversely affect a population. Fortunately, most high-elevation spruce-fir is not especially productive of merchantable timber. In some areas, moose winter in merchantable old-growth spruce-fir that is subject to logging. Absence of information on the amount of mature conifer cover needed to retain the population, and on how much spring–fall forage can substitute for winter cover by increasing the health and condition of individual moose prior to and after the winter period are critical in assessing the impacts of timber harvest in these areas. In lieu of adequate information, a conservative approach is indicated to assure retention of adequate cover.

### Black Bears

If black bear populations are to be retained in areas where logging activity occurs, retention of the key forage groups used during spring, summer, and fall, plus denning habitat must be considered. This assumes that hunter harvest and other human activity is controlled at levels that do not adversely alter bear densities and habitat use patterns.

The practice of converting longleaf pine and scrub oak stands to slash pine through clear-cutting and replanting will likely decrease bear densities on the Atlantic Coastal Plain areas in the southeast (Landers et al. 1979). Reduction of mast crops and increased access would be the cause of this loss. Hardwood swamps 525 ha in size, densely vegetated and with poor access were critical areas of escape cover during the hunt in this area.

Other areas where some kinds of intensive forestry appear less compatible with bears include central Honshu, Japan (Furubayoshe et al. 1980), and northern California (Kelleyhouse 1980). As in the case of stand conversions in the Southeast, conversion of natural vegetation to plantations is at issue. In Japan, bear damage to forest plantations is most extensive where these stands and clearcuts are more prevalent. In northern California, conversion of manzanita brush types to plantations reduces the abundance of the important manzanita berry crop without providing a substitute.

Clear-cutting practices on the west coast of Washington and Oregon produced high-quality bear foraging areas as long as herbiciding the resulting shrub stands was not an adverse effect and sufficient timber was left (Lindzey and Meslow 1977). If control of access roads was practiced, and the intensity of logging and subsequent stand management was not too great, bears could benefit from logging since food availability was increased in that region.

Tree dens are frequently used by black bears in the east (Pelton, Beeman, and Eager 1980). As is the case in other areas, the trees that are so valuable to wildlife are considered overmature or cull trees by the forester interested primarily in wood production. Trees used by black bears to den in are large and have cavity entrances at least 38 cm wide, with inside dimensions of at least 60 cm (Pelton et al. 1980). In Alberta, black bears commonly excavate dens under rootmasses of fallen trees (Tietje and Ruff 1980), while in Montana, Jonkel and Cowan (1971) reported that hollow trees were most often used. Pelton et al. (1980) concluded that tree cavities were the most preferred sites, and that these trees should be considered of prime importance in maintaining high-quality bear habitat. Landers et al. (1979) reported that denning habitats on their coastal plain study area were dense Carolina bay thickets (shallow, poorly drained depressions, densely vegetated with evergreen woody plants). Denning bears in this area were vulnerable to disturbance, and the preferred tree cavities were largely removed through extensive logging.

As is the case with other species that have large home ranges or exhibit flexibility in habitat use patterns, the effects of habitat alteration on populations will be slow and difficult to document and to isolate from other factors. Nevertheless, security during the denning season from weather and humans, plus retention of forage groups critical to the bears at all nondenning periods, must be considered when planning for bears in managed forests.

## THE QUESTION OF SINGLE-SPECIES HABITAT MANAGEMENT

A majority of investigations are oriented at providing habitats for single species through forestry practices. The question inevitably arises as to the effects on other species, as well. This problem may be especially critical when recommendations for one species conflict with those that might be effective for others. The waterfowl refuge system, however, provides an outstanding example of what sound waterfowl habitat management can do for the associated water and shorebirds, as any avid birder will say. *Featured species* plans developed for southern forests take into account the presence of other wildlife (Holbrook 1974). Habitat-specific species, such as the red-cockaded woodpecker, can be provided for in management for white-tailed deer, turkeys, and quail simply by leaving some trees with red heartrot, which serve as nesting sites. Schemes to retain bald eagle nesting trees often serve a dual role for other species requiring mature conifer cover. The very specific recommendations for ruffed grouse habitat provided by Gullion (1972) would create a highly diverse aspen forest, which will be used by a variety of associated species.

Siderits (1974) provides an example of integration of forestry and wildlife managment that stresses habitat diversity. The variables that are controlled are age classes, species composition, and spatial distribution of vegetation types. The initial concern is not for species management, but for maintenance or improvement of the vegetation. Land capabilities, the inherent productivity of the site which ultimately dictates what can be produced, have to be identified, and are basically physiographic units of similar soil types. Comparisons of existing vegetation characteristics for an area with the desired characteristics, recommendation for stand modification to attain the goals, and a critical evaluation of the area to be treated are then made. Such a system is one effort to accommodate all wildlife by emphasizing diversity of habitats.

Another system involves guidelines for maintaining wildlife habitat, developed by J. W. Thomas et al. (1976) for the Blue Mountains in Oregon and Washington. This approach addresses the fundamental problem of what to do when there is inadequate knowledge of habitat requirements for individual species, and when forest management will continue in spite of this. Lack of knowledge was not considered to be the biggest problem; at issue, rather, were lack of a conceptual framework to consider all vertebrates in planning, retention of sufficient flexibility to emphasize management of any particular species, and identification of specific habitats requiring specific attention in land alteration schemes. Guidelines are designed to enable foresters to predict consequences of their land management activities. The woodpeckers are among those that require specific habitats, that is, trees to excavate holes for nesting and for feeding. In addition, the holes are used by a variety of other species that may be provided for if the woodpeckers are considered. Four levels of information concerning any species are provided to planners: life-form (Table 5.10); use of habitats for feeding and reproduction (Figure 5.13), summari-

TABLE 5.10 **Description of Vertebrate Life-Forms**
**Occurring in the Blue Mountains**

| Life-Form Number | Reproduces | Feeds |
|---|---|---|
| 1 | In water | In water |
| 2 | In water | On ground, in bushes and/or trees |
| 3 | On ground around water | In water, on ground, in bushes and trees |
| 4 | In cliffs, caves, rims, and/or talus | On ground or in air |
| 5 | On ground without specific water, cliff, rim, or talus association | On ground |
| 6 | On ground | In bushes, trees, or air |
| 7 | In bushes | On ground, in water or air |
| 8 | In bushes | In bushes, trees, or air |
| 9 | Primarily in deciduous trees | In bushes, trees, or air |
| 10 | Primarily in conifers | In bushes, trees, or air |
| 11 | In trees | On ground, in bushes, trees, or air |
| 12 | On very thick branches | On ground or in water |
| 13 | Excavates own hole in a tree | On ground, in bushes, trees, or air |
| 14 | In a hole made by another species or naturally occurring | On ground, in water or air |
| 15 | In underground burrow | On or under ground |
| 16 | In underground burrow | In water or air |

*Source:* After J. W. Thomas et al. 1976. (Used with permission.)

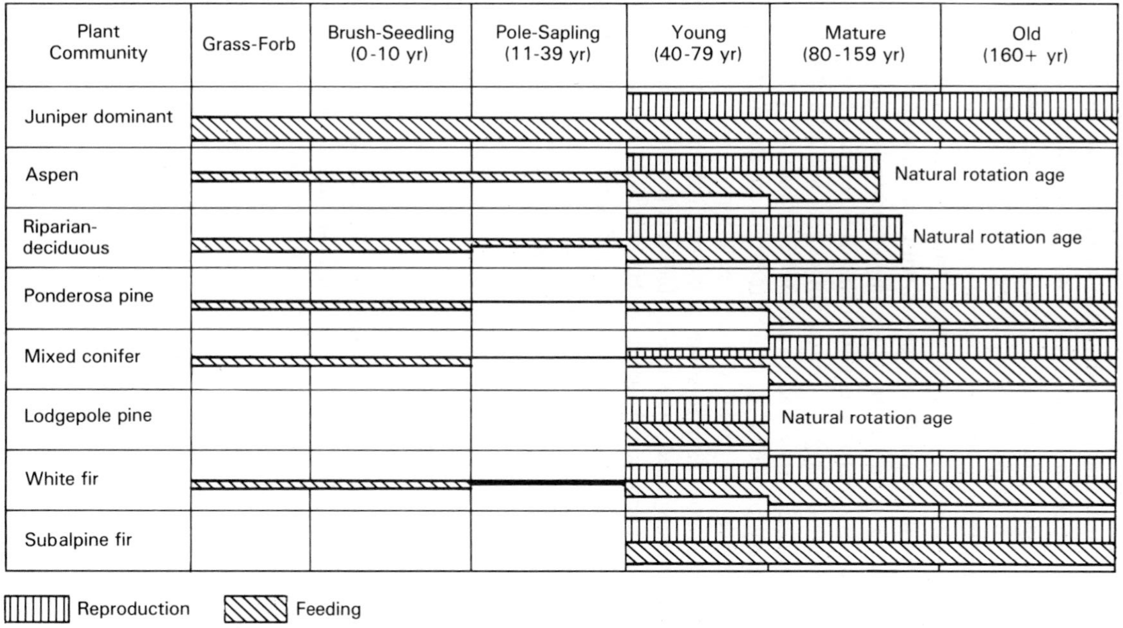

| Plant Community | Grass-Forb | Brush-Seedling (0-10 yr) | Pole-Sapling (11-39 yr) | Young (40-79 yr) | Mature (80-159 yr) | Old (160+ yr) |
|---|---|---|---|---|---|---|
| Juniper dominant | | | | | | |
| Aspen | | | | | Natural rotation age | |
| Riparian-deciduous | | | | | | Natural rotation age |
| Ponderosa pine | | | | | | |
| Mixed conifer | | | | | | |
| Lodgepole pine | | | | | Natural rotation age | |
| White fir | | | | | | |
| Subalpine fir | | | | | | |

▨ Reproduction     ▨ Feeding

**Figure 5.13** Use of successional stages of life-form 13 (excavates own hole, feeds in bushes, trees, or air) in eight different vegetation communities in the Blue Mountains. Relative use of each sere is indicated by bar width. After J. W. Thomas et al. 1976. (Used with permission.)

zation of detailed biological data for each species; and finally literature sources for each species.

These investigators point out that there is sufficient information to predict consequences of forest management decisions for most vertebrates from the information available. This is an important step forward in integrating wildlife and forest management, for two reasons. First, it serves as a basis to judge the accuracy of the predictions, and second, it helps to show where insufficient information exists. Accommodation of a variety of species can be met using this approach.

The habitat management recommendations for big game species should also be compatible for other wildlife, if those species with special requirements such as the hole-nesting birds are accounted for. These large mammals require such a variety of habitats that effective management for other forms seems assured as long as they are  actively considered. Big game winter ranges that are acquired for that primary purpose often develop into excellent upland bird habitat. Of course, if the prey species are adequately provided for, their predators are also accommodated as long as there is enough space to maintain viable populations.

In essence, this issue goes back to some of the original tenets of wildlife management. Aldo Leopold recognized the value of habitats for all species, and recommendations provided for family-sized farms by Herbert L. Stoddard, Sr. (1956), one of the original promoters of sound forestry-wildlife practices, take into account the complexity of the wildlife resource. It appears that most wildlife habitat management efforts are not in danger of promoting "monocultures" of single species.

## SUMMARY

Habitat use studies must be tied to a knowledge of population density and characteristics, since many species occupy diverse habitats. The assumption that the best habitats will be occupied by those individuals of highest rank implies that an understanding of behavior patterns of a species is also important. Habitat selection is partially inherited, partly learned, and related to availability of different habitats as well. Other factors influencing habitat selection are dispersion of food and cover, weather, predators, and competitors. Often these other factors are ultimately responsible for habitat choice while landscape features such as aspect, slope, or vegetative characteristics serve as proximate stimuli to choice of habitat. The niche concept provides a useful theoretical basis for understanding habitat selection.

Forest management has received extensive attention by wildlifers because it is such an all-pervasive influence on habitats. Evaluations of different silvicultural practices on habitats of many species reveals a number of options in forest management that can be selected to ensure accommodation of wildlife. The need, however, to retain old-growth forest with its component of snags and understories is apparent for many species. It is nevertheless important to recognize that a silvicultural practice that may benefit one group of species may adversely affect another group. Also, no one silvicultural practice will likely be uniformly satisfactory to manage one species across its range. Timber management activities may be viewed as alternatives in habitat manipulation and any one practice may either benefit or adversely affect a species, depending on its application.

Habitat management must include consideration of its effect on accessibility of an area to humans. When areas are opened to unregulated ready access, the oft-resulting increase in human activity may well alter wildlife distributions. Road or access management programs are important to incorporate into habitat management programs if full realization of benefits to wildlife are to occur.

The recent efforts to provide habitat management guidelines for wildlife in some regions are a positive way of integrating wildlife habitat considerations into other land-use practices. These guildelines, when used with care and coupled with an understanding of their application to the local situation, need to be implemented and evaluated as a means of learning more about providing for wildlife effectively.

# 6

# Fire and Wildlife

## INTRODUCTION

Before the Smokey Bear era, humans regularly used fire with little hestitation, and the following were common reasons (C. F. Cooper 1961):

1. To promote flowering of seed-producing species
2. To eliminate harvest residues
3. To fertilize fields
4. To improve grazing
5. To improve hunting or aid in the conduct of the hunt
6. To eliminate weeds
7. To locate acorns
8. As a means of communication
9. To control insects and plant diseases
10. To reduce the threat and intensity of uncontrolled fires
11. To clear land

The improvement of hunting could be direct, by influencing movements to facilitate harvest, or indirect, by modifying habitats to influence longer-term patterns or perhaps by increasing population size.

The use of fire in resource management is an area where efforts are in progress to demonstate and implement uses for what once was a readily used tool. Thus, we demonstrate that grazing can be intensified, production and nutrient content of forage can be increased, and wildlife habitats can be favored as if all this hadn't been general knowledge, literally for centuries. Of course, much work is now a critical, intensive effort to use fire in the best manner for specific objectives, and the need to demonstrate the obvious is in fact necessary. Just as Peter and the Wolf, and Bambi continue to influence wildlife conservation, so does Smokey Bear. And as with predator control, hunting, and in fact all of the tools of wildlife management, the tool of fire can be misused unless judgment and sensitivity to the local situation are also practiced.

The holocaustic fires of the past, such as the Tillamook Fire in Oregon in 1933, which devastated a 270,000-acre area in 30 hours and burned 311,000 acres before it ended (R. E. Martin, Robinson, and Schaeffer 1976), or the Peshtigo Fire in Wisconsin in 1871, which burned over a 1,280,000-acre area and caused 1300 human deaths (Wells 1968), are responsible for our concern over forest fire. These devastating burns, and many more common but less well remembered abuses of the land involving fire serve as an impetus to suppress all fires.

[Nevertheless, wildfires have played a part in the history of wildlife management even as suppression activities were the single predominating factor. The holocaustic fires of 1910, 1919, and 1928 in the northern Idaho–western Montana area created habitats that supported high elk populations. The Clearwater area in Idaho supported large herds (V. A. Young and Robinette 1939) that increased after the fires. Similarly, the Flathead elk herds proliferated (Gaffney 1941). In both instances, the elk populations served as a major argument for wilderness status for the Bob Marshall and Selway-Bitterroot wildernesses.]

The Tillamook Burn ultimately supported high populations of black-tailed deer (Einarsen 1946b). The proliferation of moose on Isle Royale (Krefting 1951) and the Kenai Peninsula of Alaska (Spencer and Hakala 1964) following large fires were also well known. All of these populations were the ultimate result of large fires and were an inadvertent, unplanned response.

In contrast, in the southeastern United States especially, prescribed burning was being used to improve wildlife habitat. The outstanding success in using fire to improve quail habitat and increase populations in pinelands of the Southeast is one of the major success stories in wildlife management. Herbert L. Stoddard and subsequently Edwin V. Komarek, directors of the Cooperative Quail Study Association and now the Tall Timbers Fire Research Station, have researched, promoted, and evangelized the role of fire as a useful tool in wildlife management. Through the use of light, easily controlled fires, burning only understory in midwinter to late April, populations of one quail per 10 acres have been achieved. This means that a hunter with good dogs may expect to see 15 to 20 or more covies in a six-hour day. The missionary zeal with which these men have dramatized their success has extended far beyond quail and the Southeast; investigations of fire ants, earthworms, and vegetative responses have been among the many studies they promoted.

Wisconsin was another area where prescribed fire was used successfully early in the history of wildlife management. The southeastern work was recognized and applied to Wisconsin conditions by Aldo Leopold and Wallace Grange (Vogl 1967).

Succession from oak savannah–tallgrass prairie to jackpine and red oak with fire protection decreased sharptail, prairie chicken, and white-tailed deer populations. Prescribed fire on such areas as Crex Meadows Wildlife Management Area has restored the prairie savannah communities (Curtis 1956).

A variety of forces have recently been brought to the attention of conservationists that have given impetus to using fire and attempting to understand its role in the environment. Costs of fighting fire have increased, which provides impetus to weigh the benefits of allowing a fire to burn against the disadvantages and then exercise suppressive action where it is most needed. Fires in areas where no potential harm occurs, or where resultant vegetation modification is likely to be an improvement over the current condition, are more apt to be allowed to burn.

Also, high fuel accumulations that result in some habitats from prolonged protection from fire can, if burned, produce more severe and damaging results. Thus, judicious use of prescribed burns to reduce fuel accumulations is practiced in order to prevent larger fires.

Along with the economic aspects has come the growing realization that in many ecosystems flora and fauna are well adapted to and dependent on fire (H. E. Wright 1974). Actual fire frequencies in some areas are short, occurring every five years or so. Under such conditions, fire can maintain vegetation pattern in a manner that would not occur in its absence, as the tallgrass prairie–oak savannah borders in the Midwest were maintained (Curtis 1956). Heinselman (1973) argued that a large-scale experiment is inadvertently being conducted when fire is excluded in boreal forest, with implications for retention of certain species of wildlife dependent upon fire-created seral communities, including the wolf. And, there is evidence in the record of charcoal from corings of sediments from peat bogs that fire has been a component of many systems since glacial times (Swain 1973).

Such arguments have caused land managment agencies, most notably the U.S. Forest Service and the U.S. National Park Service, to develop guidelines for restoring fire to a more natural role in national parks and wilderness areas. The extensive work in California initiated by Harold Biswell and his colleagues in the 1940s extends to fire management plans for Sequoia and Kings Canyon National Park (Kilgore 1973). Efforts to reestablish wildfire in Yellowstone, Grand Teton, Rocky Mountain, Glacier, Isle Royale, and other national parks have subsequently been made.

The White Cap Fire Management Plan in the Selway-Bitterroot Wilderness was the first U.S. Forest Service plan to allow wildfire to burn in wilderness (D. F. Aldrich and Mutch 1973). Subsequently, wildfires in much of this wilderness and others are being allowed to burn under conditions that safeguard humans and resources outside the fire zones as much as possible. Plans for allowing fires to burn outside of wilderness areas and national parks under certain conditions will undoubtedly be implemented as more experience and knowledge of fire behavior is gained. Stankey (1976) found that while most wilderness users favored suppression, as an understanding of the role of fire increased, support for a more natural role for fire also increased. Thus the need for public education was once again demonstrated.

Fire is thus currently being considered in two different but related ways, both of which have implications to wildlife management: retention of the natural role of fire in ecosystems that are known to be fire-dependent, and deliberate habitat modification through controlled burning to retain desirable conditions for wildlife or other natural resources.

Restoration of the natural role of fire in national parks and wilderness areas is an attempt to restore the natural ecosystem and not to improve wildlife habitat; in these cases wildlife populations would be expected to ebb and flow in the natural sequence of habitat change where fire is the dominant force influencing pattern and structure of the vegetation. As a practical matter, wildlife populations should benefit from this, and knowledge gained from studies in these areas may well lead to improved management elsewhere, using fire as a tool.

The use of fire in habitat management means that planning and knowledge of population responses is needed. In some cases, research has been directed primarily at understanding habitat responses. In other cases, population responses are directly monitored. In all cases, the ultimate gauge of the success or failure of a burning program will be the response in numbers of the wildlife population in question.

## INFLUENCE OF FIRE ON WILDLIFE HABITAT

Wildlife habitat can be influenced by burning cover and forage, which in turn may be beneficial, detrimental, or have short-term responses that are different from long-term responses. Among the factors that are involved, cover types, species composition, fire intensity, size, and frequency are important. Growing conditions as influenced by precipitation and temperature will also affect productivity of postburn vegetation just as it does in the absence of fire.

### Fire Frequency

A partial listing of investigations into fire frequency for various vegetative types in North America illustrates the extreme variations that can be encountered (Table 6.1). Generally fires are most frequent in grasslands that are highly productive and subject to annual drought periods such as tallgrass prairie in the Midwest. Fire frequencies decrease as moisture regimes increase as in spruce-fire and cedar-hemlock forests. There is much variation between areas as the sage-grassland data from Yellowstone and Idaho in Table 6.1 suggests. The larger, holocaustic fires apparently require a three- to eight-month period of extremely low precipitation prior to ignition, with above-normal temperatures involved to a lesser extent (Haines and Sando 1969). There is evidence that some plants have evolved survival mechanisms and flammable properties that perpetuate their presence in fire-dependent plant communities (Mutch 1970), which further emphasizes the pervasiveness of fire in many ecosystems. Obviously, wildlife inhabiting areas with high fire frequencies are similarly adapted, as will be discussed later.

**TABLE 6.1  Some Fire Frequencies for Various Vegetative Types and Areas**

| Vegetative Type | Area | Fire Frequency (years) | Reference |
|---|---|---|---|
| Boreal forest | Northeastern Minnesota | 60–70 | Swain 1973 |
| Ponderosa pine | Western Montana | 6–11 | Arno 1976 |
| Ponderosa pine | Arizona | 6–7 | Weaver 1951 |
| Mixed conifer-hardwood | Itasca State Park, Minnesota | 22 | Frissell 1973 |
| Boreal forest | Sweden | 80 | Zackrisson 1977 |
| Lodgepole pine | Jasper Park, Alberta | 27 | Tande 1979 |
| Douglas fir | Jasper Park, Alberta | 18 | Tande 1979 |
| Grassland-savannah | Jasper Park, Alberta | 21 | Tande 1979 |
| Subalpine forest | Jasper Park, Alberta | 74 | Tande 1979 |
| Sagebrush-grassland | Yellowstone National Park | 20–25 | Houston 1973 |
| Sagebrush-grassland | Upper Snake River, Idaho | 50 | Wright, Neuenschwander, and Britton 1979 |
| Sequoia | California | 7–9 | Kilgore 1973 |
| White spruce | Fairbanks, Alaska | 40–200 | Quirk and Sykes 1971 |
| Western hemlock | Pacific Northwest | >150 | Martin et al. 1976 |

**Vegetative Type**

Fire intensity and timing in relation to phenological stage of each plant species, and subsequent precipitation patterns will affect species composition of postfire vegetation. However, many species associated with fire-adapted plant communities tolerate burning well, and thus the species present before and after burning will be the same. Prime examples are pine communities in the West (H. E. Wright 1974) and Southeast (Komarek 1974) that burned relatively often. If the southeastern pine communities are not burned, woody shrubs will dominate and a successional sequence that will favor woody species other than pine will be initiated.

Similarly, prairie-savannah vegetation areas in the Midwest that are burned will consist of tallgrasses such as big bluestem and Indian grass while presence of woody species is greatly reduced. If fire is not present, the woody complex invades. In essence, these types of grasslands are maintained by periodic fire and are in a constant successional stage, dependent upon fluctuating climatic conditions and fire (Vogl 1974). Many marsh areas such as those in the Everglades (Kuklas 1973) and Okefenokee Swamp (Cypert 1973) are similarly maintained by fire. Broad schlerophyll brushlands throughout the world, of which the California chaparral is a prime example, are also maintained by fire (Biswell 1974). Pinyon-juniper woodland may also be maintained in a perennial grass-forb stage through judicious use of fire (Barney and Frischknecht 1974). Burkhardt and Tisdale (1976) demonstrated that fire was the major factor preventing invasion of western juniper onto sagebrush grasslands in southwestern Idaho.

Aspens are fire-tolerant and resprout extensively after burning (Graham, Harrison, and Westell 1963). In the absence of burning, succession to other communities in which aspen is absent or of minimal significance will occur. Deterioration of aspen stands in the Yellowstone–Grand Teton region, while in part due to heavy browsing by elk, is also a result of eliminating fire from the region (Gruell and Loope 1974).

Annual grassland in California is little affected by burning (Heady 1973). Similarly, species composition in the snowberry union that exists under Ponderosa pine or Douglas fir will be little affected because virtually all associated species resprout. The bluebunch wheatgrass union appears to withstand burning well unless fires are very hot (Weaver 1968). Thus a number of vegetative types that do not necessarily succeed to other vegetation tolerate burning well.

Hot fires in bunchgrass communities may stimulate cheatgrass production at the expense of perennial grasses (Klemmedson and Smith 1964). Bunchgrass seedling establishment may be hindered when cheatgrass seeds are present (J. A. Young and Evans 1978). This indicates that indiscriminate burning of deteriorated bunchgrass ranges may well hasten the conversion to annual grasses.

Some types of boreal forest, eastern deciduous forest, and mountain coniferous forest dominated by Douglas fir, true firs, hemlock, or cedar produce long-lived shrub seral stages following burning. These seral stages may consist of species poorly represented or absent in the preburn stand or mature forest, such as redstem and

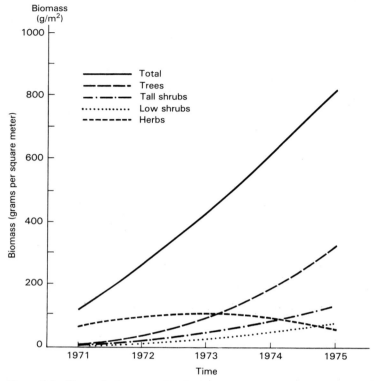

**Figure 6.1** Change in biomass of individual strata and total vegetation following the Little Sioux Fire in northeastern Minnesota. Herb data fitted to a quadratic function, all other data fitted to linearized power function. From Ohmann and Grigal 1979. (Used with permission.)

shiny-leaf ceanothus, or those that also occur in the mature forest such as beaked hazel and pincherry. The longevity of these shrub stages varies from less than 10 years to over 50 years depending on habitat type and site (Ohmann and Grigal 1979; Lyon 1971; Wittinger et al. 1977). This seral stage is gradually replaced by trees, as the data from Ohmann and Grigal (1979) indicate (Figure 6.1).

Thus fire can maintain some vegetative types that would succeed to other vegetation in its absence, produce long-lived woody stages consisting of species different from those in the climax forest, or have no essential effect on vegetation, depending on vegetative type involved.

### Fire Intensity

The severity of the fire can extend from the cool spring ground fires used so successfully in the southeastern United States to burn off litter, to the extremely hot crown fires that leave blackened soil subject to erosion, to the deep peat fires in dry marshes that can reduce vegetation such as sawgrass to a different, relatively

**TABLE 6.2    Year-Old Aspen Root Sucker and Stump and Collar Sprouts**
**Following Light and Moderate Burns in Ontario.**

| Measurement | Root Suckers | | Stump and Collar Sprouts | |
|---|---|---|---|---|
| | Light Burn | Moderate Burn | Light Burn | Moderate Burn |
| Number of milliacre quadrats stocked to 1+ stems | 92 | 97 | 32 | 26 |
| Total stems per 100 milliacre quadrat | 800[a] | 1323 | 229 | 189 |
| Average stem height (feet) | 2.8[a] | 3.3 | 2.6 | 2.4 |

*Source:* Horton and Hopkins 1965. (Used with permission.)
[a]Significant difference between light and moderate burn at $\alpha = 0.05$.

permanent condition. The intensity of a burn affects production, density, and nutrient accumulation in the postburn vegetation.

Horton and Hopkins (1965) compared density of collar and stump sprouts
and suckers in aspen following a light and moderate burn. More root suckers and
fewer stump and collar sprouts occurred on the moderately burned area (Table 6.2).
Owens (1982) reported heavier weights of current annual growth of four species
when over 50 percent of the preburn canopy was killed than when lesser percentages were killed (Figure 6.2). DeWitt and Derby (1955) reported that protein levels

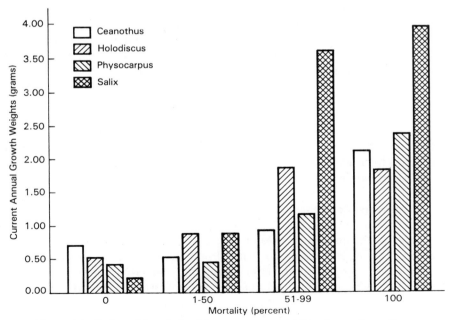

**Figure 6.2**  Twig weight relationships to canopy mortality classes. From Owens
1982. (Used with permission.)

in shrubs resprouting after a high-intensity burn were elevated for two years, while for a low-intensity burn the effects lasted for one year. It thus appears that, up to a point, more severe burns will stimulate resprouting and increase production and protein levels more than lighter burns.

## Fire Size

Wildlife habitat has a dimension to it that is often overlooked when using fire. The size of a burn is a major factor in determining wildlife response. The fact that Bendell (1974) could find little information on size of fire relative to population density illustrates the inattention to the problem. In addition, the diversity of post-fire vegetation within the burn perimeter affects wildlife use. The burn that might be prescribed for bobwhite quail will have to be of a different size than that pre-scribed for deer, if a population response is intended for each species. While this may sound rudimentary, a tendency to burn too little area is apparent. Often, fi-nancial and personnel constraints are involved (Biswell and Gillman 1961), and a program of treatment that covers a period of years must be developed to counteract these problems. The programs that have produced most notable results are large enough and sufficiently sustained through time to show results. While the argument can be made when initiating a program that virtually any size of burn that generates experience for local personnel is better than none, eventually results in terms of population response must be shown or enthusiasm is difficult to sustain.

The size of burn that will produce benefits will obviously vary by area as well as by species. Much the same arguments that apply to size of logging areas apply to size of fires. Gullion (1972) illustrates an approach to determining what size may be indicated for an area and species, using the ruffed grouse as the example. The year-long home range size and habitat requirement (food and cover) for the grouse was determined. With these estimates, the various habitats can be created, with fire as one tool where appropriate.

In most instances, habitats for a specific use such as nesting might be usefully created by fire. Here knowledge of tolerance of individuals to crowding during this activity and the effect of altering habitat on predator-prey relationships are among the factors to be addressed.

Size of burn is a factor that needs further consideration.

## Forage and Cover Production

One of the major objectives of using prescribed fire in wildlife habitat man-agement is to increase the productivity of important forage and cover species. In-creased cover may be important for upland birds, waterfowl, and some nongame birds, while increased forage may be critical for native ungulates as well as other species. In both cases, forage and cover increases can be measured in terms of vege-tative biomass.

**Herbaceous species.**    Daubenmire (1968) and Vogl (1974) have reviewed the available record on response of grasses to fire. Generally production increases are found, but exceptions occur if burning is too frequent, too severe, or at the wrong time. Increases in production following burning are usually short-lived, varying from three to six years on tallgrass prairies (Vogl 1974). Productivity of some tall-grass prairies in Illinois, Iowa, and Missouri can be doubled by annual burning. Alternate-year burning produced less, and reductions in productivity resulting from annual burning of these grasslands further west can occur (Daubenmire 1968).

Desert grass–shrub ranges have been dramatically changed from predominately grassland to predominately woody plants through heavy grazing and fire prevention. J. G. Reynolds and Bohning (1956) reported burning could decrease production of perennial grasses but increase annual grasses on a southern Arizona range (Table 6.3). While fire may have been instrumental in maintaining the original desert grassland that was dominated by *Bouteloa, Hilaria,* and *Aristida,* Humphrey (1974) con-cluded that current conditions of heavy woody plant cover and sparse grass density would have a major effect on the response of grasses to fire. This implies that plant vigor is a factor affecting response to fire.

Table 6.3 presents some comparisons of production on burned and unburned grasslands that illustrate the extreme variation in responses. Precipitation following burning has a profound effect on vegetation response to burning as the tobosa grass example illustrates. Site moisture also affects response as the tallgrass prairie data from central Wisconsin indicates. Time of burn in relation to plant phenology is critical, demonstrated by Louisiana tallgrass responses. South Florida grassland will produce well over a ton of forage per acre two years after burning, while Texas coastal prairies produce almost a ton within a year after burning. Midgrass prairies respond well, although production is not as high as tallgrass.

Fire intensity is also a factor, as the Ponderosa pine–grassland information from northern Arizona shows. The unthinned stand had a hot crown fire pass through it, while the thinned stand had a cooler ground fire. Idaho fescue data from southeastern Idaho illustrates the effects of different burns, and shows the sensi-tivity of this species to fire.

Timing of peak production after fire can be expected to vary according to a variety of factors, including precipitation, site, condition of vegetation prior to burning, and time of fire. The variation in response of bluebunch wheatgrass be-tween the central Washington and central Idaho burns shows the differences to be expected. Peak production of the entire complex of a sage-grassland in Idaho was three years after burning. Also, not all species will benefit, as the central Washing-ton and Idaho fescue data show. Undoubtedly competition between species sur-viving the fire is also involved in this relationship. Wright, Neuenschwander, and Britton (1979), Vogl (1974), and Daubenmire (1968) discuss individual species' responses in more detail. When fires are prescribed to enhance habitat of specific wildlife species, a knowledge of these species' food preferences and of how the forage species respond to burning will be needed.

TABLE 6.3  Comparison of Burned and Unburned Grassland Productivities

| Type of Vegetation | Location | Species | Productivity | | Year of Peak Productivity after Burning | Reference | Remarks |
|---|---|---|---|---|---|---|---|
| | | | Burned | Unburned | | | |
| Desert grass–shrub | Arizona | Perennial grasses | 400 lb/acre | 425 | 3rd | J. G. Reynolds and Bohning 1956 | |
| Tobosa grassland | Texas | Tobosa grass | 2813 lb/acre | 1128 | <1 | Wright 1973 | Wet year |
| Tobosa grassland | Texas | Tobosa grass | 844 lb/acre | 954 | 1st | Wright 1973 | Dry year |
| Tallgrass prairie | Wisconsin | Little bluestem dominated | 300± g/m² | 220± | 1st | Zedler and Loucks 1969 | Prairie depression |
| Tallgrass prairie | Wisconsin | Little bluestem dominated | 90± g/m² | 90± | 1st | Zedler and Loucks 1969 | Prairie upland |
| Rangeland | South Florida | Pineland three awn | 2730 lb/acre | – | 2nd | Hughes 1975 | May burn |
| Longleaf pine–tallgrass | Louisiana | Pinehill bluestem | 2289 lb/acre | 2230 | 2nd | Grelen 1975 | March burn |
| Longleaf pine–tallgrass | Louisiana | Pinehill bluestem | 1954 lb/acre | 2230 | 2nd | Grelen 1975 | May burn |
| Coastal prairie | Texas | Indian grass | 1900 lb/acre | 1800 | <1 | Chamrad and Dodd 1973 | Fall burn, mid-spring production |
| Midgrass prairie | North Dakota | Little bluestem | 431 g/m² | 335 | <1 | Hadley 1970 | Spring burn, late summer production |

| Ponderosa pine | Arizona | Native perennial grasses | 148 lb/acre | 59 | 2nd | H. A. Pearson, Davis, and Schubert 1972 | Unthinned pine |
| Ponderosa pine | Arizona | Native perennial grasses | 594 lb/acre | 443 | 1st | H. A. Pearson, Davis, and Schubert 1972 | Thinned pine |
| Sage-grassland | Idaho | Idaho fescue | 18.6 lb/acre | 22.3 | 12th | Blaisdell 1953 | Light burn |
| Sage-grassland | Idaho | Idaho fescue | 18.2 lb/acre | 22.3 | 12th | Blaisdell 1953 | Moderate burn |
| Sage-grassland | Idaho | Idaho fescue | 9.3 lb/acre | 22.3 | 12th | Blaisdell 1953 | Heavy burn |
| Sage-grassland | Idaho | Bluebunch wheatgrass | 21 g/m² | 13 | 2nd | Peek, Riggs, and Lauer 1979 | Suppression 1st year |
| Sage-grassland | Idaho | 14 species | 482 lb/acre | 294 | 3rd | Mueggler and Blaisdell 1958 | |
| Palouse prairie | Washington | Bluebunch wheatgrass | 80.7 g/m² | 34.3 | 2nd | Uresk, Rickard and Clint 1980 | 61.1 burned, 46.1 unburned 1st year |
| Palouse prairie | Washington | Cusick's bluegrass | 2.4 g/m² | 4.3 | 1st | Uresk, Rickard and Clint 1980 | |
| Palouse prairie | Washington | Thurber needlegrass | 0.9 g/m² | 2.3 | 2nd | Uresk, Rickard, and Clint 1980 | Little difference 1st and 2nd years |

Scotter (1964) reported a successional sequence of lichens in taiga communities in northern Canada that has significance for caribou forage (Table 6.4). The most palatable lichens were most productive in 76- to 120-year-old stands of spruce. Scotter (1964) noted that forest fire was very prevalent in the taiga of North America. Subsequent work by D. R. Miller (1976) indicated that although short-term deterioration of lichen forage by fire occurred, rejuvenation of unproductive stands that were very old was a benefit of fire. Caribou dependent upon arboreal lichen forage will be adversely affected when fires burn their habitat (Edwards 1954).

**TABLE 6.4   Arboreal Lichen Production in Taiga in Northern Canada**
**(pounds per acre)**

| Value of Lichens | Age of Forest (years) | | | | | |
|---|---|---|---|---|---|---|
| | 1-10 | 11-20 | 31-50 | 51-75 | 76-120 | 120+ |
| High value | 1 | 12 | 61 | 66 | 205 | 164 |
| Medium value | 2 | 16 | 88 | 183 | 125 | 179 |
| Low value | 2 | 47 | 44 | 34 | 25 | 39 |
| Total | 5 | 75 | 193 | 283 | 355 | 482 |

*Source:* Scotter 1964. (Used with permission.)

**Woody species.**    Nonsprouting species such as big sagebrush will be killed by burning, which leads to the erroneous assumption that fire should not be used on ranges where the species is important for wildlife. The fallacy in this reasoning is that sagebrush stands, as is the universal case, become decadent and unproductive through time, and rejuvenation needs to be considered. Sagebrush occupies a dominant position in the climax plant associations in many mountain and shrub-desert types; thus it will eventually reinvade burned areas (Harniss and Murray 1973). The rate at which this species will reestablish is highly variable (Wright et al. 1979), so efforts to rejuvenate sagebrush must be tailored to the rate of reinvasion of each stand. This is especially important since burning may favor associated species, such as rabbit brush, that may be less desirable as forage. Other sagebrush species, such as three-tip sage and silver sage, do resprout following burning (Wright et al. 1979).

Burning of habitats comprised of sprouting woody species may be done for two reasons. In areas where plant succession has advanced to conditions favoring other species such as conifer, burning can kill the overstory and stimulate resprouting and seeding of shrubs. Work in northern Idaho by T. A. Leege and his colleagues exemplifies this practice. In other areas, such as chaparral in California, bitterbrush-saskatoon stands in southeastern British Columbia, and climax stands dominated by bitterbrush, Stansbury cliffrose, or true mountain mahogany in the Great Basin and surrounding regions, fire can be used to rejuvenate stands that are deteriorated from heavy browsing or are out of reach as food for wildlife. The long-term investigation of the Tehama deer winter range in California by Biswell and Gilman (1961) is a prime example of this objective. Burning of weak-sprouting species such as bitterbrush should be done in spring or fall when soils are wet and fires will be cool and do minimal damage to root collars. Burning for seedling establishment of bitter-brush and mountain mahogany has not been adequately investigated.

Lay (1967) described the effects of fire on production of shrubs in southern pinelands (Table 6.5). Slight increases in forage production are apparent, with a higher proportion of the production used by deer. The trend of increased production following fire was apparent three years after burning. Lay concluded that, in this area, a reduction in browse and increase in herbaceous forage existed for two years following burning. Also, benefits to deer browse supply may not be worth the loss of habitat to turkeys, squirrels, and quail in the area, or even to the loss of other foods for deer. Important items in the deer diet included fruits, which cannot be maintained with frequent fire. Prescribed fire in Tennessee oak–pine woodlands produced more woody browse for five years with no significant change in nutrient content (Dills 1970).

**TABLE 6.5    Response of Longleaf Pinelands in Texas to Prescribed Burning**

| | Annual Availability and Utilization of Browse before and after Burn on Burned and Unburned Parts of a Deer Pen (Pounds per acre green weight) | | | | | |
|---|---|---|---|---|---|---|
| | Unburned | | | Burned | | |
| Year | Available | Used | Percent | Available | Used | Percent |
| Before fire | | | | | | |
| 1958 | 272 | 81 | 30 | 264 | 66 | 25 |
| After fire | | | | | | |
| 1959 | 296 | 56 | 19 | 270 | 109 | 40 |
| 1960 | 306 | 40 | 13 | 332 | 90 | 27 |
| 1961 | 286 | 11 | 4 | 349 | 31 | 9 |

| Changes in Species Production after Burning, and Value to Deer | | | |
|---|---|---|---|
| Increased Production | | Decreased Production | |
| Species | Palatability | Species | Palatability |
| *Ilex vomitoria* | High | *Ilex opaca* | Low |
| *Symplocos tivetoria* | Low | *Vaccinnium* | Moderate |
| *Callicarpa americana* | Low | *Cornus floridana* | High |
| *Cyrilla racemiflora* | High | *Viburnum molle* | High |

*Source:* Lay 1967. (Used with permission.)

Leege (1968) reported that fall burns did not stimulate as much resprouting as spring burns in the Clearwater region of Idaho. However, fall burns stimulated more redstem ceanothus seed germination. The problem of when to burn in this region is a critical issue. While spring burns are safest and least expensive to conduct, the amount of time that vegetation will burn is generally minimal in spring. Conversely, fall burns are more risky to conduct, since the chance of burning adjacent timber is higher. However, different vegetation types such as shrubfields on south-facing slopes and conifer on north-facing slopes are known to have different capabilities for conducting fire under the range of moisture, wind, temperature, and humidity regimes that exist, and prescriptions for fall burning of shrubfields have been developed successfully in the region when the knowledge is applied. Willows, maples, and serviceberry are prolific sprouters in the cedar-hemlock zones of this region (Leege 1969). Individual willow sprouts may grow as high as 10 feet in one year after fire, thus rapidly becoming out of reach to elk. Firecherry and redstem are less prolific resprouters.

Productivity of six shrub species in xeric ridgetops and south-facing slopes in the upper Selway River of Idaho showed the variable responses related to site and species (Merrill, Mayland, and Peek 1982). Production of these snowberry-dominated sites did not change following a fall burn, but differences between species were noted (Table 6.6). Snowberry and spiraea increased in production the year following the fire and remained higher over a four-year period. Ninebark, a taller shrub that was growing on marginal sites for the species, did not show similarly high production on burned sites as did the former two species. Redstem was scarce on burned sites for a year, and then occurred as seedlings. Serviceberry and rose showed increasing trends in productivity over the four-year period.

**TABLE 6.6    Production of Shrubs Following Burning, Upper Selway**
**(grams per square meter)**

| Shrub | Unburned Mean | Year After Burning | | | |
|---|---|---|---|---|---|
| | | 1st | 2nd | 3rd | 4th |
| Serviceberry | 0.2 | 0.4 | 0.5 | 0.7 | 0.7 |
| Redstem | 3.6 | 0.01 | 0.1 | 0.1 | 0.1 |
| Ninebark | 1.9 | 1.2 | 0.8 | 0.9 | 1.2 |
| Rose | 0.6 | 0.5 | 0.8 | 0.9 | 1.1 |
| Spirea | 0.3 | 2.1 | 1.1 | 1.1 | 1.0 |
| Snowberry | 2.8 | 8.1 | 5.0 | 5.9 | 7.1 |
| Total | 9.5 | 12.0 | 8.2 | 9.6 | 11.0 |

*Source:* Merrill, Mayland, and Peek 1982. (Used with permission.)

Huckleberries are important foods for bear and other wildlife, and are known to resprout following burning. An analysis of factors affecting density of blue huckleberry stems after burning showed that prior stem density had the greatest influence on density after burning (M. Miller 1977). More rhizomes were killed by fall fires than by spring fires when soil moisture content was higher. Numbers of stems were always greater following spring burning. The most beneficial fire treatment would be one that removes senescent stems and causes minimal rhizome damage.

Figure 6.1 illustrates changes in shrub production following the Little Sioux

Fire in Minnesota (Ohmann and Grigal 1979). A jackpine–balsam fir stand showed a change in tall shrub biomass from 10.3 g/m² the first year after burning to 312.6 g/m² by the fifth year. Tall shrubs included juneberry, willows, and beaked hazel. Low shrubs, including blueberries, raspberries, sweetfern, and wintergreen, increased in biomass during the first two years after fire, then levelled off or fluctuated in weight thereafter. Thus, dramatic changes in biomass of taller shrubs following burning can be anticipated over the first five years.

### Nutritive Values

Fire intensity has a major effect on nutritive content of vegetation following burning as previously indicated. Also, the effect of increased biomass on nutrient content is a consideration. Nutritive value per unit of vegetation may not change, but if production increases following burning, the result is a higher nutrient content per unit area. So nutrient content per unit of vegetation and per unit area are both involved in assessing fire effects. As a result, a fire that reduces or has no effect on production of vegetation may still influence nutrient levels, while a fire that does not affect nutrient content but does increase vegetative production may result in overall improvement in forage quality.

Daubenmire (1968), reviewing the effects of burning grasslands on nutrient content, concluded that nutrient content generally increases. However, variability in responses is attributed to soil fertility, fire intensity, competition from underground senescent organs not affected by burning, and stimulation of root activity by burning. Responses in grasses may well be short-lived when responses do occur (H. A. Pearson et al. 1972).

Similarly, nutrient responses in shrubs following fire are generally short-lived. Moss, Miller, and Allen (1972) reported nitrogen and phosphorus content in heather was highest the year following burning, returning to preburn levels by the fifth year. DeWitt and Derby (1955) found increased protein levels in burned plants to last one year on low-intensity burns and over two years on high-intensity burns. Leege (1969) also showed differences in protein levels extended over a two-year period (Table 6.7). Ohmann and Grigal (1979) show decreasing percentages of nitrogen following burning over a five-year period for most shrub and tree species, but responses for P, K, Ca, and Mg were different. Phosphorus increased for two years after the burn, while Ca, Mg, and K levels were variable in response between years and species.

Nutrient changes not related to increased productivity thus have fewer long-lasting effects on forage than do changes in vegetation production as related to burning. The short-term natural flush is likely to be important in attracting animals to burned sites, which may occur through dispersal or shifting of range use patterns. Species that have high reproductive rates would be expected to respond in numbers and density more to nutrient increases than species that have lower reproductive rates, and likely respond more to the longer-lived increases in production.

TABLE 6.7    Nutrient Analysis of Browse in Northern Idaho
Following Spring and Fall Burning Compared with a Control

| Species | Treatment | Percent Protein in Twig Ends |
|---------|-----------|------------------------------|
| Redstem | Control | 9.2 |
| | Fall burn | 9.5 |
| | Spring burn | 9.9 |
| Juneberry | Control | 8.0 |
| | Fall burn | 9.9 |
| | Spring burn | 10.2 |
| Ninebark | Control | 6.9 |
| | Fall burn | 9.0 |
| | Spring burn | 7.9 |

*Source:* Leege 1969. (Used with permission.)
*Note:* Data were collected in February, two years after the burns.

## INFLUENCE OF FIRE ON WILDLIFE

Reviews of fire-wildlife relationships are now available (Bendell 1974; Kelsall, Telfer, and Wright 1977; Lyon et al. 1978). Generalizations are risky since response of wildlife to burning varies greatly just as with flora. However, the conclusion of Lyon et al. (1978) that fire is a dynamic and important force in the life histories of many species is important, and reflects the general presence of fire in the natural ecosystem.

### Small Mammals

Fires can cause high mortality among small mammals (Chew, Butterworth, and Grechman 1959) but recolonization of burned areas can be very rapid (Tevis 1956a). Recolonization of vacant land by dispersing individuals where intraspecific competition is low is a possible reason for this rapid invasion. Also, small islands of unburned habitat provide refuges where individuals can survive (Table 6.8). The longer-term population response is related to vegetative change and is variable (Table 6.9). Changes in species composition in chaparral is well correlated with habitat change (Figure 6.3). Arboreal species such as flying squirrels and tree squirrels will obviously decrease when crown fires reduce or eliminate tree canopies.

The major information centers on deer mice and red-backed voles (Table 6.9). Red-backed voles have generally decreased after fires, as have voles of the genus *Microtus*. Conversely, deer mice have generally increased. The decrease of voles is related to decrease in cover, while the increase in deer mice is related to increase in seed production of forage species. Increased predation due to cover reductions is also involved (Crowner and Barrett 1979; Lawrence 1966; Figure 6.3).

Keith and Surrendi (1971) reported different responses of snowshoe hares to

TABLE 6.8    Habitats that Provide Maximum Survival Conditions During Burning

| Exposed Habitat Sites | Protected Habitat Sites |
|---|---|
| 1. Southwest-facing slopes with dry vegetation, low soil moisture, and exposure to winds | 1. Northeast-facing slopes that are shaded, moist, and protected from prevailing winds |
| 2. Upper surfaces of granite outcroppings surrounded by chaparral | 2. Deep crevices in granite outcroppings surrounded by little inflammable material |
| 3. Within hollow logs on the ground or standing, with much exposed wood unprotected by living bark | 3. Under logs or tree trunks insulated by living bark |
| 4. Shallow burrows less than 5 inches in depth and lacking cross ventilation | 4. Burrow systems well below the 5-inch depth with several surface openings |
| 5. Lower branches of the woody trees that are above dense dry grass or dry chaparral | 5. Lower branches of woody trees that touch the ground and have no inflammable material below |
| 6. Underground nesting areas that are poorly insulated | 6. Underground nesting sites insulated by dry mineral soil |

*Source:* Lawrence 1966. (Used with permission.)
*Note:* Site information was developed for California chaparral.

areas of different fire intensities in Alberta. Severely burned habitat was not reoccupied for a full year after a spring fire, while moderately burned habitats were reoccupied. Reoccupation was related to cover changes. No hare carcasses were found on the 640-acre burned area sampled, and egress of juvenile hares from the burn was indicated for a two-month period after the burn. Adult hare densities increased threefold on occupied habitat after the fire, but the overall population for the entire area did not change. Short-term responses such as these will be different from the longer-term response where major hare foods and favorable cover proliferate after the burn.

### Nongame Birds

Emlen (1970) investigated the hypothesis that bird habitat selection is determined by gross visual aspects of the vegetative physiognomy, as proposed by Hilden (1965), by examining bird species composition and population studies in burned and unburned slash pine stands in Florida. Bird counts in the burned and unburned stands for five months after burning were not different, indicating no major response to the fire. Individual attachments to home ranges and foraging areas may have outweighed species-specific habitat selection. Fire frequency in this area is high, with no important changes in the tree stratum resulting from this fire. The major change in understory was a strong increase in bare ground exposure. The high fire frequency implies that adaptation to fire by the avian species complex may have played an important role in minimizing species change in this community.

Bock and Lynch (1970) illustrate the effects of a crown fire on numbers of

TABLE 6.9  Summary of Several Small Mammal Species Responses to Fire in Different Habitats

| Species | Preburn Habitat | Response to Burning | Reference | Remarks |
|---|---|---|---|---|
| *Clethrionomys californicus* | Coastal Douglas fir | Decrease | Gashwiler 1959 | 2-year response |
| *Clethrionomys gapperi* | Subboreal conifer–hardwood | Decrease | Krefting and Ahlgren 1974 | 12-year response |
| *Clethrionomys gapperi* | Brush prairie–savannah | Decrease | Beck and Vogl 1972 | Long-term response |
| *Eutamias townsendi* | Coastal Douglas fir | Decrease | Gashwiler 1959 | |
| *Microtus californicus* | Shrub–grassland | Decrease | S. F. Cook 1959 | 2-year response |
| *Microtus pennsylvanicus* | Tallgrass prairie | Decrease | Tester and Marshall 1962 | 5-year response |
| *Perognathus californicus* | Chaparral | Increase | Lawrence 1966 | 3-year response |
| *Peromyscus californicus* | Chaparral | Decrease | Lawrence 1966 | |
| *Peromyscus leucopus* | Brush prairie–savannah | Decrease | Beck and Vogl 1972 | |
| *Peromyscus maniculatus* | Brush prairie–savannah | Increase | Beck and Vogl 1972 | |
| *Peromyscus maniculatus* | Subboreal conifer–hardwood | Increase | Krefting and Ahlgren 1974 | |
| *Peromyscus maniculatus* | Coastal Douglas fir | Increase | Gashwiler 1959 | |
| *Peromyscus truei* | Chaparral | Increase | Lawrence 1966 | |
| *Reithrodontomys megalotis* | Shrub–grassland | Increase | S. F. Cook 1959 | |
| *Reithrodontomys megalotis* | Chaparral | Increase | Lawrence 1966 | |
| *Sorex cinereus* | Tallgrass prairie | No change | Tester and Marshall 1962 | |
| *Spermophilus tridceemlineatus* | Brush prairie–savannah | Increase | Beck and Vogl 1972 | |

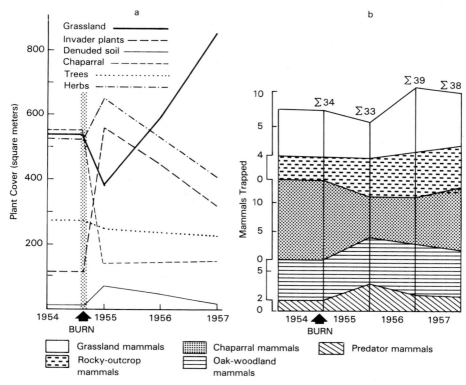

**Figure 6.3** Changes in (a) vegetation and (b) mammal populations following burning of chaparral in California. (a) Vegetational change is correlated with chaparral burning with the coverage of the major plant associations shown for each of the four years of the transect sampling period. (b) Grassland increases were associated with increases in mammals associated with grassland and rocky outcrops including *Perognathus californicus, Peromyscus maniculatus, Reithrodontomys megalotis*, and *Neotoma fuscipes*. From Lawrence 1966. (Used with permission.)

breeding birds according to foraging type (Figure 6.4). Species that forage in needles and twigs of conifers were reduced on the burn, which was dominated by low brush and open ground feeders five years after the fire. Woodpeckers were more common on the burn, reflecting the infestation of deadwood by wood-boring insects, a common observation (Blackford 1955). The effect of change in height and composition of vegetation was pronounced on the bird community. Of 32 regularly breeding species in the area, 28 percent were unique to the burn and 19 percent unique to the nearby mature forest. The higher percentage on the burn may have included species using small unburned pockets within the burn perimeter. Bird biomass on the burn was greater, consisting of heavy-bodied species like the flicker, mountain bluebird, and robin. Much of the food on unburned sites consisted of insects living on foliage of live conifers. Chickadees and kinglets, small in body size, were common on the unburned area.

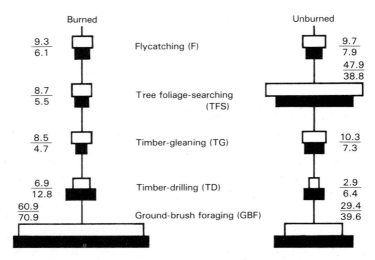

**Figure 6.4**  Percentage distribution of breeding birds according to foraging type in burned and unburned areas. Solid bars indicate distribution by consuming biomass; shaded bars indicate numbers of individuals. Numbers are actual percentages. From Bock and Lynch 1970. (Used with permission.)

Major reductions in incense cedar and white fir, and increases in gooseberry and ceanothus following burning under giant sequoia produced decreases in ground-feeding and nesting birds (Kilgore 1971). Western wood pewees and robins increased, while rufous-sided towhees, Nashville warblers, hermit thrushes, and mountain quail were the most noticeable decreasers. Again, only a small percentage of the 30 species found on the study areas noticeably responded to burning treatment over the three years of study which included one year after burning.

Lawrence (1966) reported increases in raptors and the common raven following a burn in chaparral. Exposure of prey on burned habitat was considered responsible for the influx of avian predators. Similarly, surface insects became more vulnerable to birds following fire.

Bendell (1974) indicated, from a survey that included these investigations, that fire results in an avifauna slightly richer in larger birds, but that 80 percent of the avifauna showed no response to fire. Greatest positive response to burning was among grassland and shrub-inhabiting species. Bendell (1974) considered this population stability within a rapidly fluctuating environment as indicating that many birds are able to control their populations independently of fire disturbances.

### Upland Birds

The upland bird complex has generally proven to be exceptionally responsive to burning of habitats, with the inevitable exceptions. Manipulation of bobwhite quail habitat with fire in the southeastern United States, as previously mentioned, is the classic example.

Stoddard (1931) did caution about burning quail habitat in the proper manner. He recognized the need to retain thickets for escape cover by not allowing annual burning. At the same time, unbroken areas of decadent broomsedge and wiregrass are poor quail habitat and require winter burning to stimulate legumes, critical quail food. Spring burning after plant growth is initiated will reduce quail food. Fire was considered a convenient tool for occasional use in cover control. On areas where quail food production was desired, burning alternate years in winter was recommended. Stoddard (1931) emphasized that responsible, judicious use of fire was needed to ensure that goals for quail habitat were met, and he condemned indiscriminate use of fire. Rosene (1969) pointed out that the best quail nesting habitat was comprised of last year's dead grasses, which were used for cover and nest construction. Rosene (1969) recommended backfires into a 5- to 8-mile-per-hour wind be used to maintain quail habitat. Headfires could be used to reclaim quail habitat in brushy areas. Dimmick (1971) reported that the hatching dates of nests in burned habitat were later than those in unburned areas in Tennessee (Figure 6.5). Thus, different kinds and frequencies of fire are involved in quail habitat management, depending upon the kind of habitat.

On the opposite extreme in response to fire, spring breeding density of spruce grouse was reduced by 60 percent after a fire in spruce forest in south central Alaska (L. N. Ellison 1975). However, a certain low frequency of fire in this type of forest that retards permafrost development and retains white spruce in the forest is needed. Such low fire frequencies may be useful in maintaining productive sage-brush habitat for sage grouse as well. These species, which are characteristic of late stages of plant succession or climax vegetative communities, may benefit from a low frequency of fire that maintains productivity of critical plant species.

Red grouse populations exhibit a delayed response to burning of their major forage and cover plant, heather (Moss, Miller, and Allen 1972). The density of

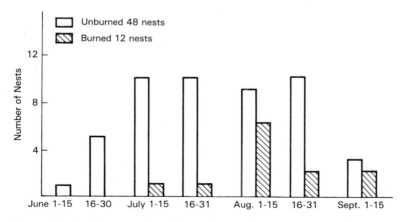

**Figure 6.5**   Hatching dates for 60 bobwhite nests in burned and unburned habitat, Ames Plantation, 1967–1971. From Dimmick 1971. (Used with permission.)

grouse increases one year after the fire, even though protein levels have begun to decrease (Figure 6.6). The lag in response is related to structure and height of the heather. Red grouse prefer to feed on heather that is 20–25 cm tall, and this requires several growing seasons following burning. The population increase lasts through year 4 following the burn.

Implicit in much of the use of fire to benefit wildlife is the assumption that nutritive values and production of forage will result in population increases. This food-limiting hypothesis for the natural regulation of numbers (Lack 1954) may seem obvious, but when the effort is made to demonstrate it, the generality very often gives way to more intricate relationships. J. F. Bendell and his co-workers F. C. Zwickel and J. A. Redfield recognized this in the long-term investigations of blue grouse on Vancouver Island. While a generalized curve for population growth of these grouse related to years since logging or burning mature forest could be drawn (Figure 6.7), Redfield, Zwickel, and Bendell (1970) concluded that (1) high densities of blue grouse in the early 1950s were not related to a large lowland burn of 1938, being as high on areas that were logged and slash-burned; (2) a large wildfire in 1951 did not prevent a decline in grouse; (3) a wildfire in 1961 was followed by a period of stability in grouse populations; and (4) areas that were logged and burned did not support any more grouse than areas that were merely logged.

Bendell (1974) reported that size of burn may be important in grouse re-

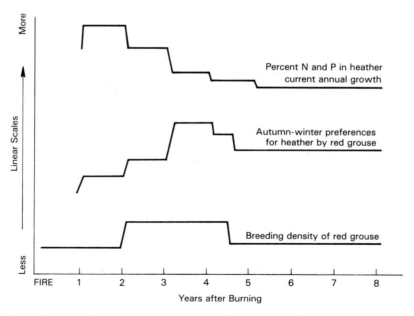

**Figure 6.6**  Relationships of red grouse breeding population following burning to nitrogen and phosphorus content in heather and preference for heather. From Moss, Miller, and Allen 1972. (Used with permission.)

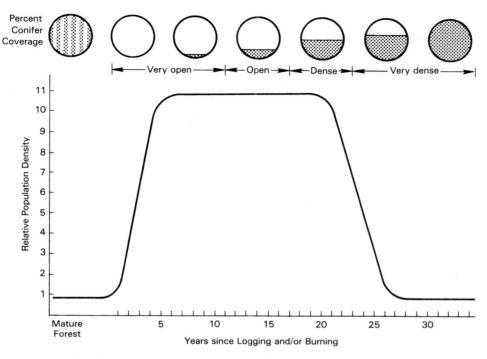

**Figure 6.7**  Blue grouse response to burning and/or logging of mature forest, Vancouver Island. Population density is low in the mature forest but rapidly builds to
a stable density. The terms *very open, open, dense* and *very dense* refer to structure of the vegetation. After Redfield, Zwickel, and Bendell 1970. (Used with
permission.)

sponse, and that male breeding territories were smaller when burn size was larger.
A systematic examination of extrinisic factors that might relate to population density included soil analysis, weather, predation, and disease. Several investigations
indicated that intrinsic factors were operating to limit population size and confound the food-limiting generality. Redfield (1974) reported that blue grouse yearlings colonizing newly logged areas were genetically different from yearlings that
remained in established populations. However, Zwickel, Redfield, and Kristensen
(1977) could not demonstrate consistent differences in reproduction and survival
among birds colonizing vacant habitat and an established population. Behavioral
differences (hooting, clucks) were interpreted as being related to age and social
status rather than heritability. Bergerud and Hemus (1975) released blue grouse
from three different populations onto islands and found that males from low-
density populations were more aggressive, dispersed more from release sites, had
larger territories, and were spaced further apart than males from high-density populations. This supported the idea that intrinsic factors, rather than factors in the
habitat, were limiting the populations.

In terms of practical wildlife management, the findings that populations may

be self-limited do not preclude attempts to increase density through habitat population, including burning. However, this knowledge can serve to explain why population responses are variable, depending upon the nature of the colonizing individuals.
If knowledge of the population from which colonizers are likely to come is available, their response to a fire may be more predictable. Most certainly, efforts to
improve habitats in the vicinity of populations that are least likely to respond rapidly will be least fruitful, and very often the game manager will have no way of
determining this prior to the manipulation.

Ruffed grouse require habitats maintained by fire (Gullion 1970; Rusch and
Keith 1971b), most especially aspen. Gullion (1970) reported periods of greatest
grouse abundance in northern Minnesota came at intervals of 2–4 and 10–12 years
after peak fire seasons. However, prime ruffed grouse habitat includes a variety of
vegetation heights and densities (Gullion 1970). Doerr, Keith and Rusch (1970)
reported decreased use by drumming males of a 510-acre burn within a 4-square-
mile study area in Alberta two years after a fire. However, grouse distributions, and
overall mortality on the study area were not affected by the fire. One advantage of
burning habitats when aspens will be favored, is that reduction in conifer cover may
also reduce predation on grouse in some areas (Gullion 1970, Rusch and Keith
1971). Use of fire in ruffed grouse habitat management must take into account the
overall habitat needs of the population, which was discussed earlier.

Quite similarly to ruffed grouse, the sharptail existed originally in a fire-
frequent environment. Kirsch and Kruse (1973) point out that complete nonuse or
annual grazing and haying of North Dakota prairie will not provide the habitat
required for grouse that occur on the prairie. The increases in plant variety and seed
production following burning, which are not as apparent from protection and annual grazing, make better grouse habitat. Sharptails use buds from woody plants in
winter, such as birch, aspen, willow, and chokeberry, and they use riparian zones
and other brushy areas as cover in winter (K. E. Evans 1968). Northern sharp-tailed
grouse that occupy bogs, marshes, and burned uplands benefit from fire that per-
petuates shrubland in boreal forest. Fires that enhance vegetation diversity and
provide nesting and brood cover can benefit sharptails, as long as the shrub complex
is retained for winter food and cover.

The prairie chicken requires large expanses of grassland habitat. Kirsch (1974)
specified the following management for greater prairie chicken nest-brood habitat
in the Dakotas:

1. A minimum of 2 square miles, contained within no more than 8 square miles,
   with minimum blocks of 100 acres and minimum width of ½ mile should
   constitute a management unit.
2. When vegetation is high-quality grassland, rotational burning at three- to five-
   year intervals is best. Rotation mowing which leaves ⅔–¾ acre unmowed each
   year may be used if burning is not possible, with unmowed blocks being at
   least ½ mile wide.

3. If nest-brood habitat is to be established, a mixture of grasses and legumes may be planted (timothy, brome, alfalfa, sweet clover) with maintenance as in (2).

Such high-quality nest-brood cover will suffice for winter cover as well, and efforts to provide winter food on breeding range seem a low priority (Kirsch 1974).

Chamrad and Dodd (1973) report medium-dense stands of tallgrasses and midgrass with admixtures of forbs for nesting and brood cover for Attwater prairie chickens can be maintained by fall-winter-spring burns. Sufficient regrowth will be available for nesting in coastal Texas prairie the second season after burning. Burns will be used the first year for booming, feeding, loafing, and roosting areas. Grazing may be a suitable alternative to burning in this habitat. Robel, Henderson, and Jackson (1972) reported increased use of burned claypan range sites by the lesser prairie chicken, apparently attracted to the abundant green forb and grass growth.

While fire kills sagebrush and can thereby destroy sage grouse habitat Klebenow (1972) points out that the diversity of cover created by prescribed burning is a means of restoring rangeland to more productive sage grouse habitat. This is likely true for the more productive habitats that have an inherently high diversity. Higher vegetative diversity in understories that contain sage grouse foods is one benefit from burning. Repeated burning, or larger, hot fires that remove extensive amounts of cover can be detrimental to sage grouse, just as they will be for ruffed grouse or sharptails. The key to appropriate use of fire is to know the habitat requirements of the species involved, and have specific objectives for burning in mind. Fires seldom burn uniformly or completely, but attention to creating diversity of vegetation in the burn area is always in order.

### Waterfowl

Fire can be used to reduce or rejuvenate vegetative growth in dried potholes and marshes, prevent invasion of woody species into nesting cover, and restore grazing areas for geese (P. Ward 1968; Perkins 1968). Kelsall et al. (1977) point out that deliberate burning of marshes to rid them of dead grass, sedges, and shrubs has a long history in North America. Tester and Marshall (1962) recommended spring burning to retain nesting habitat for ducks, even though nesting cover the year following burning would be reduced. Pintails may nest on recently burned sites but prefer taller vegetation (Keith 1961), and the other species of ducks generally prefer to nest either in last year's growth or when current growth is tall enough to provide concealment. The value of burning for waterfowl nesting cover will generally be delayed, which makes it no less important. Fire can prevent deposition of plant debris into marshes and potholes (P. Ward 1968). In the famous Delta Marsh of Manitoba, plant deposition in unburned marsh can rapidly convert sloughs and marshes of open water to vegetation-choked areas of lower value to waterfowl. The eventual effect of this deposition is to convert marshes to prairie. Thus, fires have undoubtedly contributed to retention of the pothole region in the north central

United States and south central Canada that is so critical for waterfowl. Tester and Marshall (1962) concluded that repeated burning was an important component of the environment in which prairie waterfowl evolved through time.

### Big Game

Ungulates have been assumed to benefit from modification of their habitat by fire, but the relationship has largely been based on general correlative observations and minimal documentation. Bendell (1974) pointed out that the relationship of moose to fires on the Kenai peninsula of Alaska was not simple, being affected by conditions on burned and other ranges and by moose movements. The responses to fires in this region by moose have ranged from long delays, to immediate response, to no response. The fires of 1910, 1919, and 1934 in northern Idaho and Montana are widely considered to be the cause of major increases in elk. However, populations in the Upper Selway reached highs some 40 years after a fire. In contrast to such long delays, Peek (1974) and Irwin (1975) reported a fivefold increase in moose on a 5920-ha burn in northeastern Minnesota within two years after the fire. The initial increase was related to immigration, while calf production subsequently increased (Table 6.10). Local shifts in distribution to burned sites has also been documented for elk and deer (Kruse 1973), and bighorn sheep (Peek, Riggs, and Lauer 1979).

**TABLE 6.10   Numbers and Sex-Age Composition of Moose on the Little Sioux Burn, Minnesota**

|  | 1960–1969 | 1971 | 1972 | 1973 |
|---|---|---|---|---|
| Moose per km² | 0.16 | 0.31 | 0.90 | 1.03 |
| Sex-age composition (%) |  |  |  |  |
| Adult bulls | – | 26 | 24 | 30 |
| Yearling bulls | – | 18 | 10 | 17 |
| Cows | – | 38 | 46 | 34 |
| Calves | – | 18 | 19 | 19 |
| Twins (% of births) | – | 0 | 0 | 42 |
| Total seen | – | 77 | 78 | 112 |
| Cow:calf ratio | – | 48 | 42 | 53 |

*Source:* Peek, 1974 and Irwin, 1975. (Used with permission.)
*Note:* Fire occurred in spring 1971.

Increases in black-tailed deer after burning California chaparral are almost immediate (Table 6.11). Burning produces an abundance of seedlings and crown sprouts, which attract deer, so local shifts in distribution cause the initial increase in populations. The actual density of deer is related to size of burn since movement to the area is the mode of initial increase. Subsequent population densities are also a reflection of higher fawn production (Taber and Dasmann 1957).

In contrast to the rapid fluctuation in deer densities on chaparral, Vogl and

TABLE 6.11  Comparisons of Deer Densities in Burned and Unburned Chaparral
in California

| | April–June | | July–August | | November–December | |
|---|---|---|---|---|---|---|
| Season | Average | Range | Average | Range | Average | Range |
| Unburned[a] | 20 | (13–28) | 30 | — | 29 | (26–30) |
| First year after burn | — | | 120 | | 86 | |
| Second year | 75 | | 106 | | 56 | |
| Third year | 48 | | 52 | | 50 | |
| Fourth year | 32 | | 44 | | 32 | |

*Source:* Taber and Dasmann 1957. (Used with permission.)
[a]Average for 1949, 1950, and 1951.

Beck (1970) reported high white-tailed deer use of an area burned eight years previously in northwestern Wisconsin. But Irwin (1975) could see no important response by whitetails to the Little Sioux fire of 1971 in northern Minnesota.

Caribou have traditionally been assumed to be harmed by fires in their habitat. Edwards (1956) felt fire was responsible for the decline of the Wells Gray, British Columbia, population, as did Scotter (1964) for the declines in barren ground caribou in northern Canada. However, D. R. Miller (1976) reported that fires create a diversity of cover that benefits caribou using taiga winter range. The potential for improving conditions for terrestrial lichen growth by burning muskeg and for removing needles under old conifers, which then allows growth of caribou food, were aspects of improvement.

Thus a wide variety of responses to fire by ungulates have been reported. Size of burn, nature of postfire vegetative response, characteristics of the wildlife population, and weather and snow conditions will all be involved in the kind of response to be expected. White-tailed deer will probably respond best to smaller fires adjacent to heavy cover (Singer 1979), while moose can use larger burns. Sparse populations with low reproductive potential cannot be expected to stock new habitat as rapidly as denser, more productive populations. The potential of mule deer to colonize burns that have cover values lower than those of the unburned areas appears to be greater than that of whitetails in Idaho (Keay and Peek 1980), suggesting that habitat preferences are also involved.

Responses of ungulates to postfire habitat have been indirectly appraised by examining differences in foraging patterns. Forage species that ordinarily receive light use can become more palatable following burning. Leege (1969) and Keay and Peek (1980) reported that the usually unpalatable ninebark was readily used by deer and elk after burning. Also, decadent or unproductive plants that are rejuvenated by burning have been shown to be more palatable (Peek, Riggs, and Lauer 1979).

### Carnivores

Response of predators to fire involves the effect on prey and prey habitat. Stenlund (1955) noted that wolves and deer occurred more frequently in cutover and burned areas than in unmodified areas in northeastern Minnesota, as an early example of the obvious. Less obvious, however, are the relationships of arboreal predators such as martens to fire. While earlier investigations cited fire as being detrimental to martens, Koehler and Hornocker (1977) reported that the mosaic of vegetation created after burning in the Selway-Bitterroot Wilderness supported a diversity of cover and foods favorable to marten. Items in the marten diet included voles and other small mammals that occur on meadows and burns, and were important in summer and fall. Winter habitat was mature closed-canopy spruce-fir forest, but the more open habitats were used at other times of the year.

### SUMMARY

A major aspect of wildlife management involves protection of habitat for wildlife from the many and various transgressions by humans. In the case of fire, the outright attempts in the past to eliminate it from the enviroment must count as one of these transgressions. Proper use of fire can be extremely important in retaining and restoring habitat for almost all species. Even those species that seemingly thrive in the oldest forest, furthest removed from fire, should be considered. The simple facts that nothing lives forever, and that fire is nature's tool for rejuvenation, must be recognized. With some exceptions in the tundra, the coastal forest, and the desert, wildlife habitat consists of some combination of vegetation that quite likely is adapted to fire. Our task is to use fire in a prudent and judicious manner where possible, in an effort to retain and restore productive wildlife habitats. As the land base diminishes in the face of other uses, the need to enhance the productivity of the remaining wildlands becomes more critical.

# 7

# Snow and Wildlife

## ADAPTATIONS TO SNOW

North temperate and arctic wildlife spend a good share of their lives in a snowy environment and the adaptations to exist in this medium vary greatly. Obvious adaptations include migration to more temperate climes when snows render habitats undesirable or unusable. Hibernation is another means of avoiding the rigorous snowy environment. But a large number of species have evolved physiological, morphological, and behavioral adaptations that enable them to exist in snow. A threefold classification of species has been used to identify the relative proclivity for existing in snow (Pruitt 1960). *Chionophiles*, the "snow lovers," have evolved morphological or behavioral adaptations to snow that enable them to live in snowy regions and in effect limit their distribution to such areas. *Chionophores* are species that are able to exist in snowy areas, but that do not have special adaptations to do so. The *chionophobes* are species that are unable to adapt to snow environments.

Snow-wildlife relationships have received casual attention by North American biologists for a considerable length of time. Generally, this has been in the form of relating snow depths to winter severity. Severinghaus (1947) exemplifies this attention by referring to the rule of thumb that depths over 18 inches for 60 days impose serious difficulties for whitetails, and depths over 36 inches restrict moose movements. However, the Russian biologist, A. N. Formosov (1946), reported extensive observations of snow relationships to a variety of species, and Nasimovich (1955) continued the Russian investigations. Canadian investigations were stimulated when translations of the Russian work became available, and interest in the United States followed soon after. As might be anticipated, the northern natives of both continents who have existed by hunting in the extensive snow cover of the arctic, have an extensive vocabulary describing the nuances of snow (Table 7.1). Types of skis and snowshoes developed by these people reflect the nature of the

#### TABLE 7.1   A Partial Glossary of Snow Terminology

*Barchan*   A crescent-shaped drift of snow, convex upwind, with gentle windward and steep leeward slopes.[a]

*Chionophore*   An animal that is able to exist in snowy regions but does not have special morphological or behavioral adaptations to snow.[a]

*Chionophile*   An animal that possesses definite morphological or behavioral adaptations enabling it to live in snowy regions, and that is limited in its distribution to snowy regions.[a]

*Chionophobe*   An animal that, because of morphological or behavioral specializations, is unable to adapt itself to snow conditions.[a]

*Glaze*   An ice formation on solid objects formed by freezing of water droplets; surface is smoother than that of *rime*.[b]

*Gololeditsa*   An icy crust formed by snow wetted by freezing rain.[c]

*Graupel*   A snow crystal thickly coated with *rime*.[b]

*Hoar*   Crystals formed by sublimation of water vapor onto any fixed object.[b]

*Khivus*   Large fluffy flakes falling with a strong wind.[c]

*Kid*   Heavy snowfall.[c]

*Kukhta*   Snow that accumulates on trees;[c] Also called *qali*,[a] *naves, navis*.[c]

*Kurritsya*   Blowing snow; Also called *vyuga, myatel*.[c]

*Nast*   A thickened crust on the surface of a mature snow cover; Also called *charym, chyr*.[c]

*Nival*   An adjective referred to snow;[a] Also called *chionic*.[c]

*Pad*   Large fluffy flakes falling on an already light snow cover.[c]

*Perenova*   Fresh snowfall; Also called *porosha, perenoga*.[c]

*Pukak*   The fragile latticelike structure of snow grains formed at the base of a snow cover by redistribution of water molecules by sublimation;[a] Also called *depth hoar*.[b]

*Qanimiq*   A bowl-shaped depression in the snow cover under coniferous trees.[a]

*Rime*   An ice coating on solid objects formed by freezing of very small water droplets immediately upon deposition.[b]

*Ryamda*   Dense wet snow of warm weather.[c]

*Skovoroda*   A thin icy snow crust that breaks noisily.[c]

*Snow*   Solid precipitation formed in the atmosphere by sublimation of water vapor onto minute solid nuclei.[b]

*Snow crystal*   A single crystal of snow.[b]

*Snow flake*   A cluster of snow crystals that have become stuck together while falling to earth.[b]

*Sun crust*   The crust that forms on the surface of a snow cover in the spring when the sun is high enough to cause slight melting of the topmost layer during the day, which refreezes at night.[a]

*Uboy*   Snow strongly compacted by wind.[c]

*Ubrod*   Deep soft snow. Also called *khlupniet*.[c]

*Vyduv*   Places cleaned of snow by the wind.[c]

*Zastrugi*   Aeolian sculpturings such as cornices on lee sides of ridgetops.[c]

*Zoboys*   An accumulation of windswept snow.[c]

---

[a]Eskimo and English terms from Pruitt 1959.

[b]English terms from G. J. Klein, Pearce, and Gold 1950.

[c]Russian terms from Formosov 1946.

snow they contend with. And those French, Swiss, and German physicists concerned with avalanche problems and the U.S. Army researchers concerned about moving heavy equipment over snowy terrain, have provided much information about snows that has value in ecology (Bader et al. 1954).

## CHARACTERISTICS OF SNOW

### Regional Differences

Formosov (1946) recognized that snows differed among regions. *Tundra snows* tend to be of the *uboy* type, strongly compacted by wind, not very deep, and not subject to melting during the winter. *Taiga snows* are deep, soft, and unaffected by wind. These factors effectively deny access to taiga by certain life-forms, including most wildcats, musk deer, and foxes. *Steppe snows* are characterized by their inconsistency, lack of depth, and generally short duration. Species characteristic of steppe regions tend to be sensitive to unusually deep snows. *Mountain snows* are characterized by their variability, but usually remain for long periods through the winter. Species such as moose that are found in both mountain and taiga exhibit differences in habitat use patterns that can be related to snow characteristics. Bilello (1969) showed that densities in northern Alaska averaged 0.31 g/cc in tundra, 0.27 g/cc in taiga, and 0.24 g/cc in mountains.

### Metamorphosis

Snows undergo a metamorphosis or maturation process through time after they fall. Generally, snows that fall first are light and fluffy, and low in hardness and density. They become denser and harder as the winter continues. This aging process, or *firnification*, changes the characteristics of a snowpack in several ways. Grains of snow grow together, or bond, and greatly increase the strength of the pack (G. L. Klein, Pearce, and Gold 1950). Snow density also increases as the winter progresses. The meteorological environment of wind, precipitation, temperature, and sunlight, plus the substrate upon which it rests, further alters the snow. Layering in a snowpack develops. Depth hoar, or *pukak*, develops at the base of the snowpack as a result of redistribution of water molecules by sublimation or through melting.

Sommerfeld and LaChapelle (1970) have classified snow on a basis of the major physical processes involved in its metamorphism, which illustrates the process:

1. Unmetamorphosed
   a. No wind action: many fragile snow crystal forms easily distinguishable; little difference from snow in the air.
   b. Windblown: shards and splinters of original snow crystals; parts of original forms recognizable, but whole forms very uncommon.
   c. Surface hoar.

2. Equitemperature metamorphism
   a. Decreasing grain size—beginning: original crystal shapes recognizable, but corners show rounding and fine structure has disappeared; advanced: very few distinct plates or fragments recognizable, grains show distinct rounding.
   b. Increasing grain size—beginning: original crystal shapes unrecognizable, grains show a distinct equidimensional tendency, indistinct facets may be visible; advanced: larger equidimensional grains present, strong tendency toward uniform grain size, faceting absent.
3. Temperature-gradient metamorphism
   a. Early: result of strong thermal gradient on new-fallen snow, associated with the first snowfalls of the season.
   b. Late: result of strong thermal gradient acting on snow in later stages of metamorphism.
4. Firnification
   a. Melt-freeze metamorphism to densities of 0.6–0.7 g/cc.
   b. Pressure metamorphism to densities of 0.7–0.8 g/cc.

**Ecologically Significant Characteristics**

Generally, four characteristics of snow appear to have ecological significance: temperature, density, hardness, and depth. Temperatures in a snowpack vary through its profile, approaching air temperature nearest the surface (Bader et al. 1954). Gullion (1970) reported snow temperatures of 10° to 20° F 8 inches below a northern Minnesota snow surface in early February 1970, while ambient temperatures ranged from −40° to +40° F, showing the insulating qualities and relative stability of snow temperatures during great changes in air temperatures (Figure 7.1). Ruffed grouse burrow into soft snows to roost, a definite energy conservation measure during cold weather. A moose bedded in deep, soft snow may also be considered to be seeking its insulative qualities. Des Meules (1964) stated that preferred snow condition for bedding purposes was a layer of snow 20 to 24 inches deep, into which a moose will sink 15 inches. In fact, bedding cover for moose may be so important that when all the suitable bedding sites are used, a moose may leave the area even though plenty of browse is still available (Des Meules 1964). A bed, once used, becomes hard enough to support the weight of a human and is not used again. Formosov (1946) also reported that small mammals survive well under protective mid-winter snow cover, but when snows are less favorable or sporadic, they are subject to high predation rates.

Density provides an index to the compaction of individual snow crystals within a snowpack (Maykut 1969). Density increases during metamorphosis, from densities as low as 0.004 g/cc to as high as 0.3 g/cc, averaging 0.1 g/cc, depending upon air temperature, crystal form, wind speed, and rate of deposition. Figure 7.2 shows trends in snow densities in northeastern Minnesota illustrating the increase in both open areas and closed-canopy habitats (Peek 1971). Similar findings in

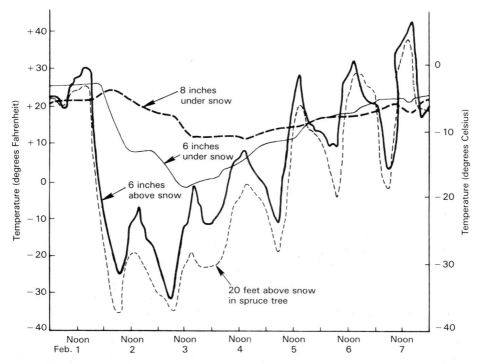

**Figure 7.1** Relationship of snow temperatures to snow depth and ambient temperatures in northern Minnesota. After Gullion 1970. (Used with permission.)

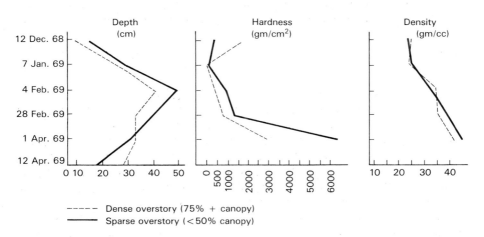

**Figure 7.2** Relationship of snow depth, hardness, and density to cover characteristics in northern Minnesota. From Peek 1971. (Used with permission.)

eastern Canadian moose and white-tailed deer winter ranges were reported by Kelsall and Prescott (1971).

Hardness or load reflects the degree of bonding between snow crystals and, along with density, is a measure of strength of a snowpack, or its ability to support weight. Maykut (1969) reported a definite relationship between the specific volume (cc/g) of a snow and its hardness (g/cm$^2$). Snow load measured at the surface provides an index to the hardness of the crust. Figure 7.2 shows how this index varies between open and closed-canopy forests. Essentially, the hardness in open areas increases greatly as a sun crust develops.

Snow depth is the most common parameter measured, although it is not necessarily the most significant. Edwards (1956) was able to correlate ungulate declines with winters of deep snows in British Columbia. The concentration of mule deer and moose on small areas during winters of deep snows caused overuse of forage and subsequent die-offs. A number of workers have reported that snows of a certain depth caused big game to concentrate activity in smaller locales. Leege and Hickey (1977) reported that snows in excess of 1.5–2.0 feet caused elk to shift to lower elevations and southerly exposed slopes where access was least restrictive in Idaho. The maximum snow depth tolerated by moose was considered to be 40 inches by Des Meules (1964), while Kelsall (1969) reported that depths of 70–99 cm (28–40 inches) severely restricted this species. White-tailed deer winter in over 3 feet of snow in the upper peninsula of Michigan by yarding for as much as five months of the year in close-canopied conifer swamps where they restrict movements to well-used trails (Verme and Ozoga 1971). However, in the absence of trails, 20 inches of snow or less will probably restrict deer movements. This is the height of chest above ground (Kelsall 1969). D. L. Gilbert, Wallmo, and Gill (1970) show how less than 12 inches of snow concentrated mule deer use to less than 10 percent of the original range that was available in Colorado (Figure 7.3). Bison in Yellowstone National Park commonly winter in 40–45 inches of snow, and may be regulated on a basis of fluctuating snow levels (Meagher 1973). And dzhiggetais are greatly impeded by 20–25 cm of soft snow (Nasimovich 1955).

Snow depth nevertheless often receives singular attention at the expense of the parameters of hardness and density. Formosov (1946) and Nasimovich (1955) recognized that the depth to which an ungulate sinks into the snow was the significant criterion and this reflects a combination of depth, hardness, and density. These workers made extensive use of weight-load-on-track data for different species in order to assess the relative adaptability of each to a snowy environment. The weight-load-on-track is determined by weighing a specimen and calculating the supporting area of the hooves. Average values of ungulates were 100–970 g/cm$^2$ of supporting area (Nasimovich 1955). A wolf has a weight-load-on-track similar to that of a reindeer (140–180 g/cm$^2$). Table 7.2 lists weight loadings for several Eurasian species, and for moose and white-tailed deer. While Kelsall (1969) points out that an animal can adjust its weight loading by varying its speed of movement, its use of dewclaws and lower legs, and shifting its weight, these figures probably reflect in part adaptation to the multiple snow parameters for each species. The moose, due its longer

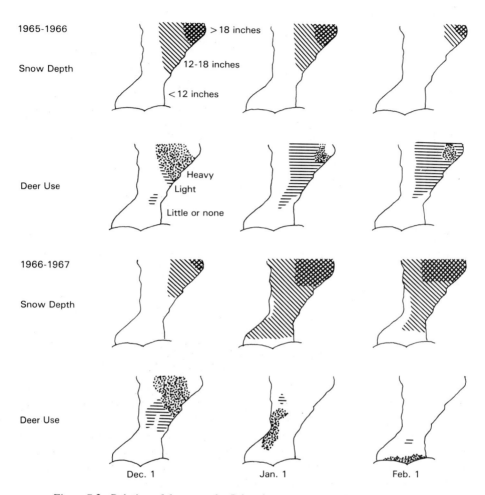

1965-1966

Snow Depth

> 18 inches

12-18 inches

< 12 inches

Deer Use

Heavy

Light

Little or none

1966-1967

Snow Depth

Deer Use

Dec. 1                     Jan. 1                     Feb. 1

**Figure 7.3**    Relation of deer use of a Colorado range to snow depth. From Gilbert, Wallmo, and Gill 1970. (Used with permission.)

legs, is obviously more adapted to the more severe conditions of boreal forest snows than the white-tailed deer, while the weight-load-on-track data are similar to that of the deer (Kelsall 1969). Wolves and reindeer (caribou as well) are similarly adapted accordingly to the weight loading. Mech, Frenzel, and Karns (1971) indicate how delicate the balance between the whitetail and the wolf is in northern Minnesota (Figure 7.4). When snows are shallow, and the depth to which the deer sinks is shallow, predation on deer is much less effective than in the softer, deeper snows. Nasimovich (1955) suggests that Crimean red deer have heavier weight-load-on-track than the Altai deer, the latter being adapted to the deeper and softer snows of their native habitat. Edwards (1954) reported that mountain caribou used high-elevation winter range when snows have hardened sufficiently to allow access.

TABLE 7.2    Weight-Loadings-on-Track for Several Eurasian Species,
and for Moose and Deer

| Species | Sex | Age (years) | Weight-Load-on-Track (g/cm²) |
|---------|-----|-------------|------------------------------|
| Reindeer | — | — | 140–180 |
| Chamois | ♂ | 1.5 | 200 |
| Roe deer | ♀ | — | 320 |
| Red deer | ♂ | — | 300–400 (East Altai Mtns.) |
| Red deer | ♂ | — | 594–720 (Crimea) |
| Mustelidae | — | — | 6–50 |
| Red fox | — | — | 40–50 |
| Wolf | — | — | 140–180 |
| "A Siberian skier" | — | — | 10–25 |
| White-tailed deer | ♀ | 0.5 | 430–508 |
| White-tailed deer | ♀ | 1.5 | 483–567 |
| White-tailed deer | ♀ | 4.5 | 525–805 |
| White-tailed deer | ♂ | 0.5 | 456–605 |
| White-tailed deer | ♂ | 1.5 | 488–753 |
| White-tailed deer | ♂ | 4.5 | 530–1124 |
| Moose | ♂ | 0.5 | 512 |
| Moose | ♂ | 1.5 | 368–894 |
| Moose | ♂ | 4.5 | 701–1204 |

*Sources:* Data for Eurasian species are from Nasimovich 1955; moose and deer data are from Kelsall 1969. (Used with permission.)

Table 7.3 shows how snow depth, hardness, and density relate to caribou, elk, and moose population densities. Pruitt's (1959) classic study provided the impetus in North America to examine the complex of three snow characteristics in relation to ungulate ecology. Caribou were most common in areas where density and hardness of snow was least great, while depth was less well correlated. Elk in southwestern Montana mountain ranges contend with much harder snows, but shift to feed on exposed south slopes and ridgetops when forage elsewhere is unavailable because of snow. Peek (1971) demonstrated that moose shifted to dense conifer cover when snow depths in openings were only 18 inches, but hardnesses were significantly less in the denser cover.

### Qali and Qanamiq

Two other snow characteristics need to be mentioned. *Qali*, or *kukhta*, the snow intercepted on tree crowns, has significance in further insulating the forest floor below, and affects movement by arboreal species. While Satterlund and Haupt (1970) report that over 80 percent of this snow ultimately reaches the ground in northern Idaho forests, it definitely compacts the snow surface when it falls and causes an uneven, but harder and denser snowpack. Formosov (1946) noted that *kukhta* helps reduce wind flow and noise in the forest, which may make the floor

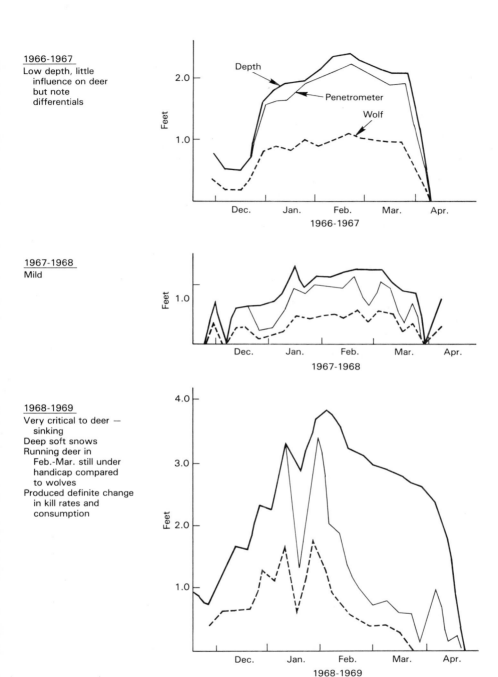

**1966-1967**
Low depth, little
  influence on deer
  but note
  differentials

**1967-1968**
Mild

**1968-1969**
Very critical to deer —
  sinking
Deep soft snows
Running deer in
  Feb.-Mar. still under
  handicap compared
  to wolves
Produced definite change
  in kill rates and
  consumption

**Figure 7.4** Snow depths and compaction related to deer and wolf movements in northern Minnesota. Penetrometer depths reflect deer penetration in the snow. The 1968–1969 critical period for deer increased predation by wolves. From Mech, Frenzel and Karns 1971. (Used with permission.)

**TABLE 7.3  Comparison of Elk, Caribou, and Moose Distribution in Relation to Depth, Density, and Hardness of Snow**

| Species | Location | General Density of Animals | | | | | | | | | Reference |
| | | None | | | Occasional | | | Common | | | |
| | | Snow Depth (cm) | Snow Density (g/cc) | Snow Hardness (g/cm$^2$) | Snow Depth (cm) | Snow Density (g/cc) | Snow Hardness (g/cm$^2$) | Snow Depth (cm) | Snow Density (g/cc) | Snow Hardness (g/cm$^2$) | |
|---|---|---|---|---|---|---|---|---|---|---|---|
| Caribou[a] | Northern Saskatchewan | 56 | 0.31 | 993 | 45 | 0.25 | 469 | 45 | 0.17 | 34 | Pruitt 1959 |
| Elk[b] | Southern Montana | 69 | 0.50 | 60,000 | 53 | 0.42 | 4000 | 6 | 0.27 | 12 | Peek 1967 |
| Moose[c] | Northeastern Minnesota | 116 | 0.44 | 1500 | 108 | 0.39 | 1170 | 87 | 0.33 | 570 | Peek 1971 |

[a]Forest snows.
[b]March 15, 1967; north-facing slope, bottom, and south-facing slope locations.
[c]February 28, 1969.

more habitable for ungulates (Ozoga 1968), but which also retards movements of arboreal species. Martens and squirrels are known to spend more time on the ground when *kukhta* blocks access in the forest above.

Pruitt (1958) reported that *qali* affects succession in boreal forests. Snow accumulation on trees can break down weaker-stemmed specimens, thereby creating openings in a conifer forest. Succession in these openings then include seral deciduous shrubs and trees. The typical boreal forest mosaic may be related in part to this phenomenon.

*Qanamiq*, the "tree well" that occurs beneath trees as a result of the interception of snow above, also has significance. Such areas may provide access to forage for some species during critical winter periods. Access in dense forests may be enhanced if sufficient *qanamiqs* exist, and moose can exist in high-elevation mountain habitats in forests by feeding in these areas. *Qanamiqs* are best developed underneath conifers such as the firs that have wide, spreading branches extending low to the ground. Moen (1968) demonstrated that infrared radiation underneath a spruce tree was slightly higher than underneath a birch tree, illustrating another value of *qanamiqs* in winter survival of wildlife.

### Measuring Instruments and Techniques

The classic instrument for testing snow load is the German *ramsonde*, which is an adaptation of the cone-penetrometer for soil. Load can be measured with special gauges such as those developed by the National Research Council of Canada (G. L. Klein et al. 1950), or a railroad push-pull gauge to which discs of various sizes are attached.

Snow densities can be measured by slicing a known amount of snow from a snow profile and weighing it. Instruments developed by G. L. Klein et al. (1950) can be duplicated at little cost.

Verme (1968) developed a snow compaction gauge that estimates the depth to which a deer will sink in a snowpack. This gauge in effect measures both hardness and density. It consists of a 2-foot length of 1-inch (inside diameter) copper tubing into which sufficient lead is poured to make it weigh an even 3 pounds. The cross-section area of the base of the gauge is about 1 square inch. The gauge is held just above the snow surface and dropped. The distance traveled into the snow represents the support factor, from a vertical force of 3 pounds per square inch.

Two winter severity indices, which take into account snow conditions, have been developed. Verme's (1968) index involves assessment of air chill and snow hazard. Air chill is a measure of the number of kilowatt hours required to maintain 10 pounds of distilled water at 39° F. A snow hazard rating is the sum of mean values for total depth and support, as determined by the compaction gauge, recorded during a week. Picton and Knight (1971) provide a winter index that is computed using daily maximum temperatures and snow depths. The daily maximum temperature is subtracted from 32° F, and is multiplied by snow depth for each day, then summed for the winter to provide a cumulative winter index.

Chionophiles and chionophores have other adaptations to cold, snowy environments that cannot be related to snow characteristics alone. Coloration, size, feeding habits, fat deposition, and other factors are integrated into the equation that equals survival in the north. However, an understanding of snow relationships has provided insight of management significance, if for no other reason than the cover requirement for wildlife in winter has been more extensively defined. And the fact that research across the holarctic region has been recognized and integrated extensively into the current literature and work suggests the importance and interest in the single ecological factor of snow.

## SUMMARY

Snow is an extremely important part of the north temperate and arctic environment. Chionophiles have evolved morphological and behavioral adaptations to snow that limit their distribution to snowy regions. Chionophores are capable of existing in snowy regions but do not have special adaptations to do so. Chionophobes are intolerant of snow.

Snows undergo a metamorphosis or firnification, increasing in hardness and density as time since snowfall increases. Four characteristics of snow have ecological significance: depth, temperature, hardness, and density. Hardness is the degree of bonding between snow crystals, or the "crust." Density is the degree of compaction between crystals. Snow acts as an insulator since midwinter temperatures within a snowpack do not drop as low as ambient temperatures.

Snow depth affects mobility of prey and predator but often in different ways since hardness and density are also involved. A wolf has a lighter weight-load-on-track than a moose, so it will not sink as far into a snowpack as the larger prey. Nevertheless, light, fluffy snows that are deep may favor the moose. The differentials in snow depth, hardness, and density between open and closed cover types appear to influence habitat use patterns greatly.

Winter severity indices that include measurements of snow characteristics have been developed to help assess the degree to which deer and other species will be influenced in winter.

# 8

# Competition

## DEFINITIONS

Competition between wildlife species and between wildlife and livestock poses one of the more complex management issues. Not only is it difficult to evaluate, but it is often fraught with biopolitical overtones where vested interests assume opposite positions and contribute to the problem. Birch (1957) considered competition to exist in two types of situation:

1. When a number of organisms utilize common resources that are in short supply
2. When the organisms seeking a resource that is not in short supply harm each other in the process

In either situation the competition may be *intraspecific* (within a species) or *interspecific* (among species).

   Poole (1974:129) defined competition as "The effect of the population density of one species on the rate of increase of a second, except if one species serves as food for the other." Cole (1958) defined competition, in practical terms related to forage and range use by big game and livestock, as involving four criteria, all of which must be met:

1. Species must use the same range, although not necessarily at the same time. Often, spring cattle range is big game winter range.

2. Forage species must be used by both species. This implies that only competition for forage is to be considered. It must be recognized that livestock forage may be nesting or brood cover for birds and thus competition may be actually in terms of different uses of the same vegetation.

3. Forage species must be important to at least one of the species involved. Food habits must overlap, and at least one forage species must be a major item in the diet for one of the animal species involved. This criteria requires a judgment as to when a species is considered a major item in the diet.

4. Forage species must show deterioration as a result of the dual use. This is the key criterion in determining competition. Obviously, if there is sufficient forage and no deterioration in productivity of individual species, or change in vegetation composition, then competition cannot be established.

Competition for space, such as for nesting sites, is also among the factors to be considered. In such cases, different criteria for assessment must be established. Breeding densities, degree of habitat use compared to that in areas where species do not overlap, reduced survival or productivity, behavior differences such as activity patterns, and territory size can be used to evaluate competition when forage is not involved.

One difficulty in assessing competition is that it may be a result of historical factors that influenced habitat use and population patterns in the past, but that now exist to a lesser degree. Thus, a species that may have filled a certain ecological niche may well have adjusted its activities slightly to accommodate the competition from a closely associated species. It can be seen that competitive exclusion is a transient phenomenon lasting as long as the dominant species fills its habitat.

Competition may not exist continuously, but rather may occur only at certain critical times. Migration patterns of big game in mountainous regions are variable according to weather or snow conditions. During a critical winter, when animals are restricted to the lowest parts of their ranges, they may be significantly competitive with livestock, while during a more open winter they may not be. Competition for breeding territories will occur only during that period when territories are established or occupied.

## COMPETITION THEORY

Insight into the significance of competition may be provided by an examination of the *competitive displacement principle*. The crux of this principle, which is defined by Hardin (1960) to mean that "complete competitors cannot coexist," is that competition plays a major role in evolution and is a continuing process that precipitates adjustments in the role of ecological niche of an organism that confer survival value. DeBach (1966:184) defines *competitive displacement* more precisely as a condition in which "different species having identical ecological niches cannot coexist for long in the same habitat." Implicit in this definition is that all species differ to some degree, no matter how closely related, or else they are in fact the same species. Ecological homologues will eventually demonstrate different adaptation to any given habitat, which will demonstrate different fitness. The *fundamental niche*, that which occurs in the absence of competition, will adjust to the *realized niche* (Hutchinson 1958) when competition occurs. A logical means of determining whether competitive displacement has occurred is to examine niche breadth for two species in allopatric and sympatric situations. If niche breadth is smaller in the sympatric situation, then competitive displacement can be inferred, even if it cannot be proved. Hardin (1960) has pointed out that the principle can be theoretically proven, but it can only be supported or not supported by empirical data.

Human-induced competition, as where livestock are introduced into a rangeland system, should be recognized as a special aspect of competitive displacement, but the implications of this artificially induced competition to the adaptations of native species are of major importance in their conservation.

DeBach (1966) defines a *coexistence principle* as a corollary to the competitive displacement principle: different species that coexist indefinitely in the same habitat must have different ecological niches. He emphasizes that closely analogous species may coexist in the same habitat as long as resources allow. This condition may exist if population densities are low relative to the available resources, if limiting factors for each species are different, if the advantage of one species over another is continually reversed, and if the superior ability of one to utilize a common resource is affected by the superior ability of the other to discover unutilized sources. Huffaker and Laing (1972) believe that competitive exclusion cannot exist if there is no shortage of resources, and the theoretical controversy continues.

### The Lotka-Volterra Equations

The logistic model of population growth can be modified to express growth of a population in the presence of a competing population. The deterministic model presented here is overly simplistic because it does not take into account random events that occur external to the fixed conditions set up in the model. The more complex stochastic models, such as the Leslie-Gower model, account for chance occurrences and provide an estimate of the probability associated with an event. However, the deterministic model may be used to examine the effects of competition on a population with specified, fixed constraints without concern for unpredictable external events. This allows demonstration of several important ideas relevant to competition that may have management significance. The examples are deer versus cattle, and elk versus cattle, artificialized systems that are common in the western rangeland. Actual results of field investigations will be presented later in this section. For more detailed discussions of the various models, refer to Krebs (1978), Poole (1974), and Wilson and Bossert (1971).

In the absence of competition, population growth is expressed as:

$$\frac{\Delta N_1}{\Delta t} = r_m N_1 \; \frac{K_1 - N_1}{K_1}$$

where

$\Delta N_1 / \Delta t$ is the change in numbers/change in time

$r_m$ is innate capacity for increase

$K$ is the carrying capacity

$N_1$ is number of individuals of species $N$

$(K_1 - N_1)/K_1$ is unused opportunity for population growth.

The value of $r_m$ will be calculated in the yield section, but will be arbitrarily provided for present purposes.

In the presence of one competing species, population growth of species $N_1$ is expressed as:

$$\frac{\Delta N_1}{\Delta t} = r_m N_1 \; \frac{K_1 - N_1 - VN_2}{K_1}$$

where

$V$ is a conversion for expressing species $N_2$ as an equivalent of species $N_1$

$N_2$ is the number of individuals of species $N_2$.

The first example involves competition between mule deer and cattle. The number of cattle, $N_2$, is fixed at 100, simulating a grazing permit involving a specified number on a federal rangeland. The rangeland is also deer winter range, where the predominant browse species is bitterbrush. The number of deer, $N_1$, is varied at levels from carrying capacity, $K_1$, which is defined in terms of the allowable use on bitterbrush, or 50 percent of current year's growth, to lower levels. The yield, or change in numbers per unit time, is estimated from the equations. Assume (1) a pasture that winters a variable number of mule deer, but where $r_m$ is constant at 0.50; (2) population of deer is at $K_1$ when utilization of the current year's growth of bitterbrush is at the level where further use causes deterioration of plants; (3) this population level has been shown through experience to be somewhere in the area of 100 deer ($K_1 = 100$); (4) we wish to graze 50 to 100 cattle on this pasture for a specified period. Cattle are equated with deer in terms of the proportion of bitterbrush in the diet of each species. The proportion of bitterbrush in the cattle diet is 10 percent that of deer, so $\alpha = 0.10$. Cattle graze the area in summer, then deer graze the same growth the following winter.

| N, Deer | Yield of Deer | | |
| --- | --- | --- | --- |
| | In Absence of Cattle | In Presence of 50 Cattle | In Presence of 100 Cattle |
| 100 ($K_1$) | 0.0 | −2.5 | −5.0 |
| 90 | 4.5 | 2.25 | 0 |
| 80 | 8.0 | 6.0 | 4.0 |
| 70 | 10.5 | 8.75 | 7.0 |
| 60 | 12.5 | 10.50 | 9.0 |
| 50 | 13.0 | 11.25 | 10.0 |
| 40 | 12.0 | 11.0 | 10.0 |
| 30 | 10.5 | 9.75 | 9.0 |
| 20 | 8.0 | 7.50 | 7.0 |
| 10 | 4.5 | 4.25 | 4.0 |
| 0 | 0 | 0 | 0 |

The model shows that a deer population at 0.5 $K_1$ (50 individuals, in this case) will yield 13 individuals in the absence of cattle and 11.25 individuals in the presence of 50 cattle. At $K_1$ the yield is 0 in the absence of cattle, implying no population change, and a negative 2.5 in the presence of 50 cattle. Actually, the negative figure represents the number of deer that must be removed to compensate for the presence of cattle, if $K_1$ is fixed at 100. In reality, $K_1$ is a fluctuating figure because utilization cannot be regulated closely, but rather becomes an average based on a number of winters of varying snow depths and weather patterns that will influence deer densities. We may infer from this example, however, that on a basis of $\alpha = 0.10$ and $K_1 = 100$, the yield of deer will be reduced if cattle are allowed to graze the bitterbrush. It may be seen that this competition does not materially affect the deer population at any level. While bitterbrush may be a significant part of the deer diet, it is undoubtedly a minor item in the cattle diet, with grasses constituting the bulk of the cattle use. No effect of cattle grazing on the associated species is considered in the model, and the extent to which competing vegetation is altered and its subsequent effect on bitterbrush and the condition of the rangeland vegetative complex is also not considered. All other factors being constant, however, the model suggests that a light level of use of bitterbrush by cattle would not significantly affect the deer population.

Consider now the competition between elk and cattle for a forage species that constitutes a major share of the diet for both species: Assume (1) a pasture that winters a variable number of elk, but where $r_m$ is a constant at 0.35; (2) the population of elk is at $K_1$ when utilization of current growth of bluebunch wheatgrass is at the level where further use causes deterioration, or 50 percent of current year's growth; (3) this population level is somewhere near 100 (assume $K_1$ is 100), and when it is above this level, production drops off and dispersal becomes important, both of which are to be avoided; (4) the forage requirement of elk is half that of a cow, $\alpha$ is fixed at 0.50, based on this criterion. Using the same arguments as before, the yield of elk will be as follows:

| $N_1$ Elk | Yield of Elk | | |
| --- | --- | --- | --- |
| | In Absence of Cattle | In Presence of 50 Cattle | In Presence of 100 Cattle |
| 100 ($K_1$) | 0 | −8.75 | |
| 90 | 3.15 | −4.72 | |
| 80 | 5.60 | −1.40 | |
| 70 | 7.35 | 1.23 | |
| 60 | 8.40 | 3.15 | |
| 50 | 8.76 | 4.38 | 0 |
| 40 | 8.40 | 4.90 | 1.40 |
| 30 | 7.35 | 4.73 | 2.10 |
| 20 | 5.60 | 3.85 | 2.10 |
| 10 | 3.15 | 2.28 | 1.40 |
| 0 | 0 | 0 | 0 |

The competition for forage between cattle and elk is much more severe than between deer and cattle in the previous example. All other criteria being equal, yields of elk will be reduced greatly at population levels of 0.4 $K_1$ or greater in the presence of 50 cattle, and even more if 100 cattle coexist on the same range. Actual management practices on federal lands give this implicit recognition by allocating forage use between elk and cattle, for example by allocating 50 percent of the allowable use to cattle and adjusting the levels of elk to allow for an average of 50 percent of the allowable use on the key forage species by both grazing species. The point of this is that proper forage allocation and regulation of use will allow for domestic livestock and competing wildlife species to coexist on the same range without adverse effects to either, or to the range itself. If no consideration of the competitive aspects of coexisting species is made, then wildlife, the range, and ulti- mately the livestock will be affected.

Once again, it is to be emphasized that these examples are very rough approx- imations of actual conditions, and are valid only for the assumptions that were made. However, they serve to illustrate critical points about competition between wildlife and livestock and are useful for this purpose.

MacArthur and Levins (1964) expand on this basic competition model by considering two habitats, one with a distribution of units of resource $a$, and another in which units of resource $b$ are distributed. A species or individual that utilizes both resources in proportion to their occurrence is termed fine-grained, while a species that selects only one of the two resources is termed coarse-grained. Both cases involve species that are specialists in terms of resource use. The resources are distributed in uniform units, or grains.

The process of competition between species $x$ and $y$ for resources $a$ and $b$ becomes competitive exclusion when one species reduces the level of resource which both depend on to where the other species cannot maintain itself. The process is defined as:

$$\frac{\Delta x}{\Delta_t} = [i_1 (a_1 - c_1) + i_2 (b_2 - c_2)] \; x$$

$$\frac{\Delta y}{\Delta_t} = [j_1 (a_1 - d_1) + j_2 (b_2 - d_2)] \; y$$

where

$x$ and $y$ are fine-grained species

$a_1$ and $b_2$ are resource populations

$c$ and $d$ are threshold densities of resources below which species $x$ or $y$ have a net energy loss

$t$ is time

$i$ and $j$ are the effectiveness of species $x$ or $y$ to utilize the resources to reproduce.

For coarse-grained species $V$ that specializes on resource $a_1$ and $W$ that specializes on $b_2$, the equations are

$$\frac{\Delta V}{\Delta_t} = [a(a_1 - m)] \; V$$

$$\frac{\Delta W}{\Delta_t} = [b(b_2 - n)] \; W$$

A plot of the quantity of resources a and b on a graph can determine a point which describes a habitat (Figure 8.1). Isoclines that describe species $x$, $y$, and $z$ at equilibrium can be drawn from the plot of each species' habitat back to the ordinate and abscissa on the graph. Species $z$ will then come into equilibrium with species $x$ at resource level P, which is at a lower level for both than when one or the other was absent. This is attributable to a reduction in resources available to both, as a result of the dual use of the resources. However, species $y$ can invade because it can increase with resources at level $P$. Thus, species $y$ replaces $z$ at equilibrium $Q$ since level $P$ is larger than level $Q$, and level $Q$ excludes species $z$.

Figure 8.2 illustrates how one species $z$ withstands attempts at colonization by species $x$ and 7 by being able to use resources $a_1$ and $b_2$ at a lower level (either $S$ or $T$) than the two colonizing species. In Figure 8.2, species $z$ can be considered a generalist while species $y$ and $x$ are specialists.

MacArthur and Levins (1964) concluded that pursuing species such as weasels and accipiters can specialize and individual species (predators) will be separated by coarse-grained (i.e., prey species) differences. Grazing mammals and small birds that spend more time searching for food will be generalists, with fine-grained differences separating species, all of which will show marked habitat selection.

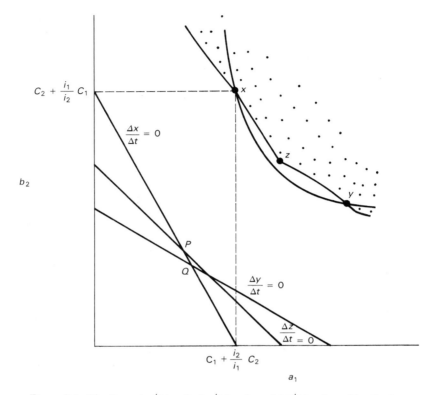

**Figure 8.1**  The lines, $\Delta x/\Delta t = 0$, $\Delta y/\Delta t = 0$, and $\Delta z/\Delta t = 0$ marking the inner boundaries of the areas in which species $x$, $y$, and $z$ can increase. $a_1$ and $b_2$ are the quantities of resource $a$ and resource $b$, respectively. Point $x$, with coordinates $(C_1 + i_2 C_2/i_1,\ C_2 + i_1 C_1/i_2)$, and points $y$ and $z$, with coordinates similarly defined by the intercepts of the respective lines, then determine the isoclines $\Delta x/\Delta t = 0$, $\Delta y/\Delta t = 0$, and $\Delta z/\Delta t = 0$, completely. Other possible species might lie at other points in the stippled region. The curve intersecting the stippled area at $x$ and $y$ is an equilateral hyperbola for reference purposes. From MacArthur and Levins 1964. (Used with permission.)

When a pertinent resource for which three species compete is continuously distributed, MacArthur and Levins (1967) show that as niche breadths are broadened, species diversity is lowered by excluding the intermediate species rather than one of the extremes. Thus, measurements of niche breadth are needed to determine competition (Pianka 1976).

Fretwell (1978) recognized that these models suggest that two separate resources are more likely to be used by a single species than is one continuously varying resource. His field tests of the two models, using woodpecker and sparrow communities, supported their implications. Regions that were rich in ground-feeding sparrow species tend to have more middle-sized species in areas of high species diversity than in areas of fewer species.

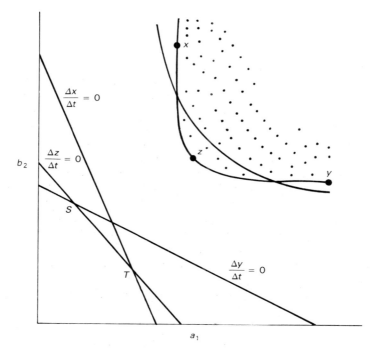

**Figure 8.2** The meaning of the lines and stippled area is as in Figure 8.1. The stippled area is more convex than an equilateral hyperbola, and species z can effectively invade the community consisting of x and y which comes to equilibrium at point 0. From MacArthur and Levins 1964. (Used with permission.)

Pianka (1976) points out that competition is exceedingly difficult to investigate in the field because native species reduce or avoid competition whenever possible. Competition is likely to be an intermittent process that will not always be in evidence (Wiens 1977). Thus, the existing evidence for competition is largely circumstantial. These conditions have high practical significance where livestock and wildlife compete for forage and space since the typical short-term study may not uncover evidence for competition, or may cover a situation when overlaps in resource use are more severe than usual.

### Field Investigations of Competitive Development

Sheppard (1971) demonstrated factors involved in competition between two chipmunk species occupying Alberta mountains. *Eutamias amoenus luteiventris* is commonly found in rocks, logs, or brush in open forests, while *E. minimus oreocetes* usually occurs at higher elevations with some overlap with the former species in open coniferous forest at treeline. Thus, both species may occupy similar habitats, and competitive displacement appears to exist. When both species were introduced into unfamiliar environments, *E. amoenus* was clearly dominant over *E. minimus* in

33 of 68 aggressive encounters, with the latter dominating in only one instance. *E. amoenus*, the larger of the two species, was also most active in terms of being first to emerge from nest boxes, and total activity period (2185 minutes vs. 993 minutes of 3000 total minutes of observation). *E. amoenus* successfully defended established home ranges in familiar environments from *E. minimus* more frequently than vice versa.

The fundamental niche of both species was estimated to be similar and equivalent in all habitats occupied by each including alpine, deciduous forest, coniferous forest, and semidesert. In the presence of one another, the realized niches were both smaller than fundamental niches, but the limiting effect of *E. minimus* on *E. amoenus* was not determined. One mechanism for competitive exclusion appeared to be aggressive behavior, and the evidence suggested strongly that the principle was in operation. Heller (1971) presented similar evidence for three species of Sierra Nevada chipmunks.

J. H. Brown (1971) investigated two other chipmunk species and found habitat relationships a critical factor in competitive exclusion. Again, aggressive behavior of one species, *E. dorsalis*, when trees were widely spaced, was the mechanism for exclusion of *E. umbrinus*. But when trees were dense and large, the less aggressive species, being arboreal, readily escaped the fruitless, energy-wasting chases and appeared to have a competitive edge.

Territorial behavior is thus recognized as a mechanism in competitive exclusion in numerous birds and to a lesser extent in mammals. Conspecifics show the greatest degree of competition for limited resources, but interspecific territoriality also occurs. Two species of shrews, *Sorex vagrans* and *S. obscurus* defended territories irrespective of sex or species during the nonbreeding period (Hawes 1977). Competitive success is determined by habitat in southwestern British Columbia. *S. obscurus* maintained territories against *S. vagrans* in western hemlock habitats, while *S. vagrans* outcompeted *S. obscurus* in western red cedar habitats. Red cedar forests support a greater number of insects and microarthropods than the more acidic soils under hemlock. The more durable teeth of *S. obscurus*, plus possible differences in hunting techniques, may provide a greater advantage in utilizing the smaller-bodied microarthropods of the acidic soils, while the superior reproductive effort of *S. vagrans* may confer advantage in red cedar. Such subtle differences in adaptation to microhabitats probably reflect evolutionary change from less specific habitat preferences in the presence of competition.

These examples of competition illustrate the *compression hypothesis* of interspecific competition (Wilson 1975:277). Where two or more species that utilize common resources exist sympatrically, the resources are partitioned further and the realized niche for each species may be expected to decrease from the niche that is occupied in the absence of the competition. This has adaptive significance, in that efforts to minimize competition should also reduce loss of genetic fitness and promote variation within a population.

Competition between two species may be affected by the presence of other organisms, also. The nematode parasite, *Parelaphostrongylus tenuis* produces cerebrospinal nematodiasis in moose (R. C. Anderson 1965). This parasite is endemic to white-tailed deer and is tolerated without severe pathological responses in this species. Upwards of 40 percent of some white-tailed deer populations may be infected by the parasite (Karns 1967). Conversely, moose do not tolerate this parasite and infection usually results in paralysis and death. Telfer (1967) has demonstrated that moose populations in Nova Scotia do not proliferate in areas of high deer concentrations, wintering at higher elevations in deep snows where deer are absent. Since forage use patterns are similar between the two species, the presence of the parasite may confer a competitive advantage to the whitetail over the larger, seemingly more competitive moose on sympatric range where habitats are suitable for both species. It is to be noted that Irwin (1975) reported major increases in moose populations in northern Minnesota following a fire, in the presence of deer known to carry this parasite, which suggested that habitat conditions can modify the relationship if they confer a benefit to moose over deer.

Another mechanism for competitive exclusion involves convergence of behavior patterns among competing sympatric species. *Character convergency* means that different species develop common traits because of selection pressures, which is a form of *convergent evolution*. Convergent evolution is generally reserved for species of entirely distinct ancestry that evolve similarities, but character convergency may involve closely related species. Cody (1969) proposed to restrict the term to situations that promote dispersion through aggression. Again, territorial behavior between different species is involved. The hypothesis developed by Cody (1969) specifies that convergence of characters used in territorial defense, including appearance and voice, would allow two species to divide the available space as if they were a single species. Males involved in territorial defense would not distinguish species if voice and/or appearance were the same.

An example of similar-appearing species occupying similar habitats in northern Mexico is provided by Cody and Brown (1970). *Pipelo erythrophthalmus* and *P. ocai* are known to hybridize in brushy forest ecotones except where a third species, the brush finch *Atlapetes brunneinucha*, occurs. The latter two species are interspecifically territorial and extremely similar in appearance, while the two towhee species do not look as similar. It was concluded that character convergence between *Atlapetes* and *P. ocai* was a powerful selective force that acted against hybridization of the two towhees. Hybridization would counteract the character convergency and thus select against *P. ocai* when *Atlapetes* was present. However, *P. ocai* and *P. erythrophthalmus* are also interspecifically territorial and have similar songs. This means that *Atlapetes* and *P. ocai*, and *P. ocai* and *P. erythrophthalmus* have nonoverlapping territories, but that *P. erythrophthalmus* and *Atlapetes* territories should overlap. In cases where territories do overlap, they are larger presumably to compensate for the reduced food available to each bird. The wildlife habitat manager needs to be aware that manipulations intended to benefit one species may be confounded simply by the presence of another.

## GRAZING: A FACTOR AFFECTING COMPETITIVE RELATIONSHIPS AMONG PLANTS

The interaction of selective grazing pressure upon vegetation composition as mediated through competition has had profound effects on wildlife. Increases in species that were less palatable to domestic livestock but that were more palatable to deer, such as sagebrush, bitterbrush, and forbs, undoubtedly created large areas of winter range that were subsequently a predisposing reason for deer population irruptions. This phenomenon produced a "storage effect" as described by A. Leopold, Sowls, and Spencer (1947), wherein a large forage source was "stored," and was responsible for major population increases. The fortuitous set of circumstances of past heavy livestock grazing; subsequent vegetation change favoring more palatable forage species; reduced predation due to extensive control campaigns directed at alleviating livestock problems; a world war or two, which reduced poaching and other human activity on the game ranges; and conservative hunting seasons or closures contributed to the high deer populations of the 1950s and early 1960s. Now livestock grazing is much better managed over most of the range, and changes in vegetation management generally favor increases of grasses at the expense of shrubs. As a result, deer populations should not be expected to increase to the high densities of two decades ago, although this may occur locally if habitat conditions and factors affecting immediate survival of deer combine again. The effect of such a combination on sage grouse populations has not been considered, but may be similar to that on deer. On the other hand, species such as elk and bighorn sheep that are benefited by improved grasslands should prosper if competition for forage from livestock is not an overriding factor.

Competition is readily apparent in plants as well as animals, and may exist for water, nutrients, light, heat, carbon dioxide, oxygen, or space. Cheatgrass outcompetes bluebunch wheatgrass seedlings by more rapid root growth in winter and by maturing four to six weeks earlier, thereby reducing soil moisture available to the native wheatgrass seedlings (A. Harris 1967). Competition is an important aspect of plant succession as it affects the abilities of each species to occupy a site in the presence of other species.

Intraspecific competition may affect succession as well. Farmer (1962) demonstrated that apical dominance of older aspen stems inhibited root-suckering in aspen clones. This chemical inhibition process could adversely affect regeneration of aspen and promote succession to coniferous species. Apical buds are known to inhibit growth of lateral shoots of numerous species by production of indole-3-acetic acid, an auxin compound. Removal of apical buds through browsing thus stimulates growth of lateral shoots and serves to retain a plant in vigorous condition.

Activities of herbivorous species also affect competitive relationships among plant species, with important implications in wildlife management. Western rangelands have been exposed to extensive grazing by livestock in the past, as well as by big game. The selective grazing on some plants has profoundly altered vegetation composition by reducing the competitive advantage of the grazed species. L. Ellison

(1960) perhaps stated the problem best when he said that assessing the influence of grazing on plant communities is difficult and most studies have been confined to the extremes that are most easily documented.

Hull and Hull (1974) reported that the original vegetation in the Cache Valley of Idaho and Utah was predominantly grassland dominated by bluebunch wheatgrass, arrowleaf balsam root, and other perennial forbs, with small amounts of big sagebrush. Heavy livestock grazing, which started in the 1860s, altered this original complex to a condition dominated by big sagebrush. Fire suppression may also be implicated. Within the intermountain sagebrush-grassland region, including the Wyoming plains, the Snake River Valley in Idaho, and the Great Basin of Oregon, Nevada, and Utah, early writing suggests a pristine vegetation dominated by shrubs (Vale 1975). Stands of grass were confined to wet valley bottoms, moist canyons, and mountain slopes. However, impacts of grazing in these areas undoubtedly accentuated the dominance of sagebrushes and other shrubs. The exclusion of fire from this area has also contributed to invasion or expansion of shrubby species and trees such as western juniper on intermountain rangelands (Burkhardt and Tisdale 1976).

These trends are often not readily noticeable because they occur over long periods. Evanko and Peterson (1955) compared mountain rangeland vegetation that was protected for 15 to 18 years with heavily grazed adjacent vegetation (Table 8.1). While generalizations about species groups (shrubs, grasses, forbs) can be made from these data, it is apparent that individual species respond differently to the grazing pressure, which ranged from heavy to light. Sandberg bluegrass was more abundant on grazed than ungrazed sites, which reflects its ability to withstand summer use, after it has seeded. Bluebunch wheatgrass responded negatively to the grazing, but variations in Idaho fescue between sites were thought to be related to

**TABLE 8.1   Vegetative Cover on Five Sites Grazed by Cattle and Five Sites Ungrazed for 15-18 Years in Southwestern Montana**

| | Amount of Cover ($cm^2$/0.1-m plot) | | | |
| | Grazed Sites | | Protected Sites | |
| Species | Average | Range | Average | Range |
| --- | --- | --- | --- | --- |
| Grasses and sedges | 97.5 | 54.9-154.7 | 117.1 | 63.7-175.8 |
| *Agropyron spicatum* | 2.7 | 0.9-3.8 | 4.6 | 1.1-12.8 |
| *Festuca idahoensis* | 58.2 | 5.1-110.1 | 84.7 | 9.4-156.1 |
| *Poa sandbergii* | 22.2 | 3.7-36.9 | 14.6 | 1.1-32.1 |
| Forbs | 45.6 | 16.3-82.6 | 38.3 | 13.1-66.3 |
| *Erigeron trifidis* | 3.7 | 0.2-7.4 | 6.7 | 0.3-18.7 |
| *Phlox hoodii* | 11.9 | 2.9-25.7 | 10.2 | 1.5-30.1 |
| Shrubs | 10.8 | 2.7-34.6 | 5.6 | 1.7-14.9 |
| *Artemisia frigida* | 2.9 | 0.3-11.9 | 1.3 | 0.1-4.3 |
| *Chrysothamnus viscidiflorus* | 2.2 | 0.6-5.5 | 1.9 | 0.5-5.2 |

*Source:* Evanko and Peterson 1955. (Used with permission.)

normal compositional variation associated with the range type involved. Forbs appeared to decrease overall with the grazing, but in no case were the variations significant. *Erigeron trifidus* did significantly decrease on one site, and suggestions that other species responded variably to the grazing are illustrated by the data for *Phlox hoodii*. Shrubs generally were less prevalent on ungrazed sites. Trends reported from this study included increases in unpalatable forbs and shrubs on grazed ranges over ungrazed range. Cover changes were small, but differences were consistent, and when soils and vegetative cover are not disrupted, changes in species composition are likely to be very slow.

McLean and Tisdale (1972) concluded that 20 to 40 years were required for overgrazed ranges in rough fescue and ponderosa pine zones to recover to excellent range conditions when grazing is totally excluded. Mueggler (1975) reported that Idaho fescue and bluebunch wheatgrass required 3 and 6 years respectively to fully recover vigor after one heavy clipping. Again, the slowness of change is emphasized. Range and wildlife managers are constantly faced with the problem, that once a rangeland has lost its productivity and species composition has been altered, even complete rest is not going to lead to speedy recovery, and usually complete rest is not possible, anyway. This is why grazing management programs such as the rest-rotation system developed by Hormay and Talbot (1961) are being implemented.

Efforts to balance grazing pressure on rangeland species with what each species can physiologically withstand were early initiatives to prevent rangeland deterioration. Grazing management programs could theoretically then be designed around the "proper use" factor for the "key species," or a major forage species on the site. Table 8.2 summarizes results of such studies for a variety of woody species important as wildlife forage. The "rule of thumb," graze half and leave half of the current growth, will underutilize some species such as mountain maple and the willows, but will result in overuse of red maple, white cedar and mountain ash, if continued over a period of years. However, these studies do not account for the competition factor that interacts to alter the single species clipping study in the real world.

Mueggler (1970) evaluated the effect of clipping Idaho fescue in the presence and absence of native competing vegetation (Table 8.3). The study illustrates that the effect of competing vegetation on production of Idaho fescue compounds the adverse effect on the individual plant.

Competition may also be responsible for the deterioration of key species that is usually blamed on grazing. Hubbard and Sanderson (1961) demonstrated that competition for soil moisture between grasses and bitterbrush reduced growth and production of the latter, a palatable deer forage. Weeding out competing vegetation produced significant increases in leader lengths and numbers of leaders of bitterbrush. Such responses suggest that planned grazing programs involving two or more species of grazer, which promote removal of competing forage species, may serve to enhance rangeland conditions, as well as make more efficient use of the forage.

Another variation of this theme was discovered by Peek, Johnson, and Pence

**TABLE 8.2  Some Estimates of Proper Utilization of Woody Species During the Nongrowing Season**

| Species | Estimated Allowable Utilization of Annual Growth (percent weight removed) | Reference |
|---|---|---|
| Red maple, *Acer rubrum* | 20–25 | Schilling 1938 |
| Mountain maple, *Acer spicatum* | 80+ | Krefting, Hansen, and Stenlund 1956 |
| White birch, *Betula papyrifera* | 50 | Aldous 1952 |
| Beaked hazel, *Corylus cornuta* | 50–75 | Aldous 1952 |
| Fire cherry, *Prunus pennsylvanica* | 50–75 | Aldous 1952 |
| Willow, *Salix* spp. | 75+ | Aldous 1952 |
| Black ash, *Fraxinus nigra* | 50–75 | Aldous 1952 |
| Mountain ash, *Sorbus americana, S. decora* | 25 | Aldous 1952 |
| Greenbriar, *Smilax* spp. | 50–60 | Schilling 1938 |
| Red osier, *Cornus stolonifera* | 25–50 | Aldous 1952 |
| Red elder, *Sambucus pubens* | 25 | Aldous 1952 |
| Bitterbrush, *Purshia tridentata* | 60–65 | Garrison 1953 |
| Mountain mahogany, *Cercocarpus ledifolia* | 50–60 | Garrison 1953 |
| Rabbitbrush, *Chrysothamnus nauseosus* | 50 | Garrison 1953 |
| Big sagebrush, *Artemisia tridentata* | <50 | C. W. Cook and Stoddart 1959 |
| Utah honeysuckle, *Lonicera utahensis* | 60–65 | Young and Payne 1948 |
| Evergreen ceanothus, *Ceanothus velutinus* | 35–40 | Garrison 1953 |
| Quaking aspen, *Populus tremuloides* | 65–70 | Julander 1937 |
| Serviceberry, *Amelanchier alnifolia* | 60–65 | V. A. Young and Payne 1948 |
| Rose, *Rosa* spp. | 60–65 | V. A. Young and Payne 1948 |
| White cedar, *Thuja occidentalis* | 15–20 | Aldous 1952 |
| Balsam fir, *Abies balsamea* | ±50 | Bergerud and Manuel 1968 |
| Jack pine, *Pinus banksiana*<br>Red pine, *Pinus resinosa*<br>White pine, *Pinus strobus* | red pine least resistant<br>jack pine most resistant | Krefting and Stoeckler 1953<br>Marshall, Shantz-Hansen, and Winsness 1955 |
| Red-stemmed ceanothus, *Ceanothus sanguineus* | 60 | V. A. Young and Payne 1948 |

*Note:* Allowable utilization varies according to site, age of plant, time of year, past use, etc.; hence these figures should serve only as relative guides for comparison.

**TABLE 8.3** Effects of Clipping Idaho Fescue at Three Levels
in the Presence of Native Competing Vegetation

| Parameter Measured | Treatment[a] | Degree of Competition | | |
| --- | --- | --- | --- | --- |
| | | None | Partial[b] | Full |
| Herbage volume (cc) | None | 698 | 352 | 251 |
| | Heavy | 570 | 319 | 174 |
| | Extreme | 370 | 117 | 41 |
| Flower stalks per plant | None | 43.2 | 37.3 | 10.4 |
| | Heavy | 36.4 | 12.1 | 0.3 |
| | Extreme | 11.4 | 0.1 | 0.0 |
| Flower stalk length (cm) | None | 57 | 63 | 58 |
| | Heavy | 60 | 56 | 48 |
| | Extreme | 50 | 39 | – |

*Source:* Mueggler 1970. (Used with permission.)

[a]Heavy treatment was 75-percent clip of fescue herbage volume at flowering stage. Extreme treatment was 100-percent clip to 1 cm height.

[b]"Partial" competition was created by clipping all vegetation within a 60 cm radius to ground level around treated plants.

(1978) in a ponderosa pine–bitterbrush community in Idaho. Consistent annual use of bitterbrush by mule deer and elk at about 50 percent of current year's growth retained productivity and vigor of this species. The site was shown to be a Douglas fir–snowberry habitat type, with the current community resulting from past fire and livestock grazing. The palatable species, such as kinnickinnik and snowberry, which are part of the climax for the site, were undoubtedly being browsed extensively enough to preclude advancement of the succession. In this instance, the combined use of all species was retaining the productivity of a seral, long-lived stage.

## WILDLIFE-LIVESTOCK COMPETITION

### Grazing Systems

A variety of livestock grazing systems are available for use on rangelands that provide resource managers with great opportunities and flexibility to properly integrate wildlife use of an area with livestock grazing. Acquisition of key winter ranges for big game, or nesting grounds for waterfowl, upland birds, and other species often meets resistance by ranchers because livestock grazing is anticipated to be removed or greatly restricted. While in some cases removal of livestock may be indicated because of extremely deteriorated range conditions or other overriding needs that take priority, often this is not necessary. In fact, as A. Leopold (1933) has indicated, the "cow" can be used to restore wildlife populations, and livestock grazing to improve wildlife habitat should be recognized as a highly useful tool.

Often, biopolitical considerations are involved. Ranchers may be opposed to acquisition of wildlife habitat because of fears that grazing will be stopped. Attempts to consider wildlife on multiple-use lands are often feared because of this. On the other hand, many people concerned primarily with wildlife are inclined to visualize livestock as a major detriment. The wildlife manager must often work between these two opposing views and finds that accommodation of the wildlife resource with livestock is extremely difficult.

We cannot acquire every important wildlife area and eliminate livestock, nor should this be a goal. Further, if wildlife management is restricted to only those units that are acquired specifically for wildlife, or to areas such as wilderness where human activities are minimal, we will be restricting our efforts to a fraction of the area upon which wildlife exist. It is imperative that we work with land managers and ranchers to arrive at accommodations that will benefit wildlife, even if the accommodations are not immediately optimal. Thus, a knowledge of range management and grazing systems, plus a willingness to work with others, are attributes of the complete wildlife manager. There are 1.2 billion acres of range lands in the conterminous United States (U.S. Forest Service 1972).

Planned grazing systems include deferred, rotation, deferred-rotation, and rest-rotation systems (Stoddart, Smith, and Box 1975). These may be distinguished from the continuous grazing system wherein no manipulation of livestock grazing patterns is made, the traditional system. Planned systems were established when it was recognized that continuous grazing often resulted in excessive use of some areas within a range, and reduction in livestock numbers was not a practical means to rapidly improve range condition. In some cases, where no alternatives to continuous grazing have been available on public lands, recommendations to reduce livestock numbers to levels compatible with the available forage have resulted in ranchers' terminating grazing and occasionally their entire operation, because of the importance of the area to the year-long livestock operation and lack of alternative areas to graze. The dilemma of the range manager is thus twofold: how to restore or retain adequate range condition, and how to accommodate the livestock concurrently. The wildlife manager is most concerned with the first part of the dilemma but should recognize the latter aspect as well.

*Deferred grazing* is essentially a delaying action. This system can be implemented in cases where grazing can be timed to start after the important forage plants have matured and produced seed.

*Rotation grazing* means that a range unit is subdivided and the subsequent pastures are grazed in a succession. This system is intended to make more uniform use of all forage by concentrating livestock and denying them a choice. This theoretically prevents grazing from providing a competitive advantage to less palatable species. The duration of grazing on any given pasture is also reduced, which allows for plants to regrow or complete more of their annual growth cycle before grazing is initiated.

*Deferred-rotation grazing* combines the previous two systems, and can be used on two or more pastures. Deferment may be altered between pastures from one year to the next or may be applied to one pasture for several years before switching to another pasture. This may be useful where one pasture is in better condition than others.

The *rest-rotation grazing* system is being widely implemented on federal rangeland. It is essentially a modification of the deferred-rotation system to include complete rest of one pasture. First applied on California ranges (Hormay and Talbot 1961), it has been used successfully on mountain rangelands as a means of improving range condition without decreasing livestock numbers. Figure 8.3 outlines a five-treatment grazing system following Hormay (1970). The sequence of grazing for one unit is as follows: continuous the first year, rest the second, graze after seed-set the third, rest the fourth, and graze after flowering the fifth year. Modifications on this are numerous, but usually a rest period follows grazing after the flowering period.

Rest-rotation grazing has been quantitatively evaluated as a tool to restore range condition. Ratliff and Reppert (1974) found that vigor of Idaho fescue was higher on a rest-rotation system 16 years after its establishment than on a pasture that was moderately but continuously grazed. However, the continuous grazing was not reducing vigor of Idaho fescue in that area. Hormay and Talbot (1961) had concluded earlier that selective grazing of most palatable species in a continuous grazing system could not be avoided and harmful effects of this selection could be conteracted through rest-rotation grazing. While the subsequent work found this to be so, it should be noted that the moderately and continuously grazed system was maintaining itself. Planned grazing systems are useful tools to restore range condition, but may not necessarily be indicated for ranges in good condition where livestock grazing is moderate.

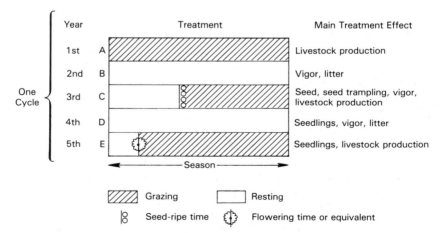

**Figure 8.3** Diagram of a five-pasture (five-treatment) rest-rotation grazing system. From Hormay 1970. (Used with permission.)

These grazing systems must have a built-in flexibility to accommodate drought, or unusually wet springs, and other contingencies that affect grazing management. The range manager may wish to defer grazing on the spring pasture if grasses have not matured as rapidly as expected. If drought is prolonged enough to greatly decrease forage production, a system may have to be temporarily broken in order to provide enough grazing for the livestock. The wildlife manager must recognize these contingencies and provide relevant advice so wildlife are accommodated.

Although one purpose of these systems is to decrease selective grazing by livestock, this does not mean that complete utilization of a pasture has to be accomplished. Where wildlife are to be accommodated, utilization may have to be adjusted to a lower level. Wildlife managers have voiced concerns about implementation of these grazing systems on areas critical to wildlife, because the grazed pastures can be bereft of forage or nesting cover afterwards. Additionally, systems designed to increase production and vigor of grasses may adversely affect species that require browse if succession greatly decreases woody species at the expense of grass. Cooperation between range and wildlife managers can usually prevent such occurrences, but there are instances, as with bighorn sheep and domestic sheep, where combined grazing is not indicated.

### Big Game-Livestock Competition

Competition between antlered or horned game and livestock is usually evaluated in terms of forage use patterns, habitat overlap, and effects on the range used in common. A few investigations have evaluated the presence of livestock on use of an area by game. Stevens (1966) reported that elk did not use mountain meadows after sheep arrived, even though elk remained in the general vicinity and presumably could have made use of the areas. On the other hand, Ward (1973) reported that elk and cattle appeared to be socially compatible since both species grazed the same areas at the same time. Pronghorn and domestic sheep were observed by Severson, May, and Hepworth (1968) feeding, resting, and watering together. Skovlin, Edgerton, and Harris (1968) reported that pastures heavily grazed by cattle received less elk and deer use than pastures less heavily grazed (Figure 8.4). Compatibility among wildlife and livestock is probably related to conditioning of individuals to the presence of livestock, the intensity of livestock grazing, and associated human activities. The presence of a herder with dogs may well decrease wildlife use in an area. Such displacements must be considered temporary, and as long as alternative, suitable habitats are available for game to use the problem should not be great. When displacements due to heavy grazing occur, the results may be longer-lasting and efforts to accommodate game use through alteration of livestock management practices may be indicated. The potential for competition to affect big game will likely be greatest on ranges used by wildlife in winter and spring, which are more restricted than other seasonal ranges.

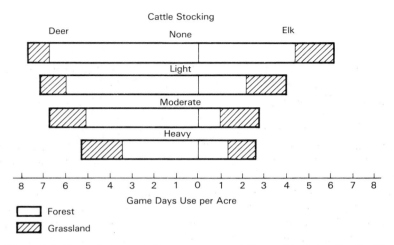

**Figure 8.4** Days of deer and elk use per acre as influenced by intensity of cattle stocking on a northeastern Oregon range. After Skovlin, Edgerton, and Harris 1968. (Used with permission.)

**Livestock food habits.** Competitive studies must incorporate forage use patterns of both livestock and wildlife as a fundamental component of the evaluations. McMahan (1964) in Texas and Stevens (1966) in Montana demonstrated that forage use by livestock changes according to intensity of use of a range (Table 8.4). The Texas data show that grass predominated in the cattle diet in all pastures, but that forbs constituted a significant proportion of the diet in lightly grazed areas. Stevens (1966), Mackie (1970), Blood (1966), and Julander (1955) have also reported that grasses predominated in the summer diet of range cattle, but that forbs constitute

TABLE 8.4 Change in Use of Forage by Sheep and Cattle
Related to Intensity of Use of a Range

| Species | Intensity of Range Use | Forage Use (Percent) | | |
|---|---|---|---|---|
| | | Browse | Grass | Forbs |
| Cattle (Texas) | Heavy | 0 | 100 | 0 |
| | Moderate | 0 | 89 | 11 |
| | Light | 1 | 84 | 15 |
| Sheep (Texas) | Heavy | 13 | 83 | 4 |
| | Moderate | 31 | 61 | 8 |
| | Light | 33 | 60 | 7 |
| Sheep (Montana) | 1st time on site | 1 | 10 | 89 |
| | 2nd time on site | 0 | 30 | 70 |
| | 3rd time on site | 1 | 47 | 52 |

*Sources:* Texas data is from McMahan 1964. Montana data is from Stevens 1966. (Used with permission.)

*Note:* Only summer data are presented.

a significant proportion and browse is not important. The individual species preferred varies, of course, between areas.

The domestic sheep diet varied extensively between the Montana and Texas study areas, and according to prior degree of range use. On the Texas area, browse decreased in the sheep diet as range use increased. Browse was not important in the sheep diet on the Montana study area, while grasses increased and forbs decreased in the diet as sheep were herded over the same site two more times. J. G. Smith and Julander (1953) reported nearly equal amounts of browse, grass, and forbs in the sheep diet on a Utah range, but the proportions varied among vegetative types.

These data emphasize that the potential for competition may increase as intensity of use of a range increases. While the examples illustrate changes in diet of livestock or prior range utilization changes, the same applies to wildlife.

**Deer and domestic sheep.** Deer and domestic sheep forage use is often quite similar, and the potential for competition between these two species is great. J. G. Smith and Julander (1953) found that six of ten species most prominent in the summer site of mule deer and sheep were prominent in both diets: aspen, chokeberry, snowberry, clover, dandelion, and Letterman needlegrass. McMahan (1964) reported that competition between white-tailed deer and sheep, goats, and cattle for browse and between sheep and deer for forbs was high in a Texas area. "The similarity of deer and sheep diets is sure to cause conflict wherever the supply of preferred species is inadequate to satisfy the requirements of both animals" (J. G. Smith and Julander 1953:112). At the same time, deer were able to graze virtually their whole study area, while sheep used only 80 percent of it because of insufficient or undesirable forage or unfavorable terrain.

Sheep grazing may occur on winter deer ranges as well as summer range. J. G. Smith and Julander (1953) reported that the sheep diet on a winter range included oak, bitterbrush, and mountain mahogany, all prime mule deer forages. Because sheep were wintered at lower elevations than foothill winter deer range, little potential for competition existed. However, spring grazing by domestic sheep on a mule deer winter range in Utah caused deer to use more herbaceous material and less shrubs than on an adjacent site ungrazed by sheep, although shrubs remained the dominant item in the diet of the deer (M. A. Smith, Malechek, and Fulgham 1979). Sheep grazing reduced standing dead herbaceous material, which apparently promoted earlier greenup of herbs, thus causing the deer to switch to the herbs earlier. The intensity of sheep grazing was 150 days of sheep use per hectare over a 20-day period in May and early June, resulting in about 70-percent utilization of current forage crops, indicating that mule deer would depend on regrowth after grazing for winter forage the subsequent year. Jensen, Smith, and Scotter (1972) concluded that range management practices geared to maintaining high productivity would include use of sheep grazing during periods when use of shrubs was low and use of herbaceous species was high so that shrub growth would be favored. Such grazing would take place in early spring before shrubs began to grow rapidly.

Since sheep grazing can be closely regulated by the herder, who usually

accompanies a band, opportunities to reduce the potential for competition are high
if sufficient knowledge of deer distributions, satisfactory range conditions, and a
willingness to accommodate deer in a grazing plan exist.

**Deer and cattle.**    Deer and cattle habitat use patterns and forage preferences
are generally different enough to make combined use of a range complementary
rather than competitive. This again is predicated upon range condition and intensity
of use. Mueggler (1965b) found a high negative correlation between cattle use and
distance up hillsides from a bottom. On mountain rangelands that were moderately
stocked at 2 to 4 acres per cow-month, Mueggler (1965b) predicted 75 percent of
the cattle use on a 10-percent slope will occur within 810 yards of the foot of a
slope. On a 60-percent slope, 75 percent of the use will occur within 35 yards of
the bottom. Julander and Jeffrey (1964) reported similar findings (Table 8.5), that
cattle use decreased sharply on slopes over 30 percent, and most use was on 0- to
10-percent slopes. Mackie (1970) found that slopes over 25° received minor use by
cattle. Additionally, most use occurred within ¾ mile from a water source. Thus,
cattle distribution is concentrated on bottoms and gentle slopes, close to water.

Mule deer in Utah preferred slopes of 30 to 40 percent or greater (Julander
and Jeffrey 1964). Mackie (1970) reported greatest use of slopes between 19 percent and 100 percent, and within ¾ mile of a water source in central Montana.
Mackie concluded that water distribution was not a significant factor in mule deer
distribution in that area because water sources were located on the habitat type
that received high use. Furthermore, during drier seasons, mule deer locations near
water decreased. Julander (1958) also reported that deer grazed further from water
than did cattle. A separation in habitat use based upon slope and possibly distance
to water thus occurs between cattle and mule deer, which tends to minimize competition further. On a mule deer winter range in Utah, however, Julander (1955)
reported that cattle and mule deer overlap in range occupied was one-third of the
range. Such data would serve to specify the area where forage use patterns could be
evaluated to see if competition for any particular species exists.

Grass use by deer is highest in spring, indicating that the greatest potential for
competition with cattle would be at that time. However, Willms et al. (1979) reported that mule deer preferred Sandberg's bluegrass while cattle preferred wheatgrass on a British Columbia spring range. However, availability of wheatgrass to deer
was related to the degree of prior fall grazing by cattle, and availability of Sandberg's bluegrass was related to the amount of early spring moisture. Thus, when dry
springs follow years of heavy grazing of wheatgrass by cattle, competition for
wheatgrass by mule deer and cattle is likely.

While grasses constitute the bulk of their diet, cattle may graze shrubs, which
constitute most of the diet of the mule deer in some cases (Julander 1955). This is
accentuated after grasses have been heavily grazed, when cattle may begin to use
more browse or forbs. McMahan (1964) reported heavy cattle use of live oak shoots
and acorns, preferred white-tailed deer forage in winter. Browse species constitute
a substantial forage source for white-tailed deer and cattle in northern Idaho

**TABLE 8.5  Use of Topographic Position in Order of Preference by Deer, Elk, and Cattle**

| | Deer[a] | | Elk[b] | | Cattle[a] | |
|---|---|---|---|---|---|---|
| Preference | Topographic Position | Days Use per Acre | Topographic Position | Days Use per Acre | Topographic Position | Days Use per Acre |
| First | Upper slopes | 8.0 | Upper slopes | 4.1 | Lower finger ridges | 13.1 |
| Second | Ridgetops | 3.6 | Middle slopes | 2.5 | Lower slopes | 12.7 |
| Third | Middle slopes | 3.2 | Ridgetops | 2.3 | Middle slopes | 11.9 |
| Fourth | Upper finger ridges | 2.3 | Upper finger ridges | 2.2 | Upper slopes | 6.4 |
| Fifth | Lower slopes | 1.6 | Lower slopes | 1.8 | Upper finger ridges | 5.1 |
| Last | Lower finger ridges | 1.3 | Lower finger ridges | 1.2 | Major ridgetops | 3.5 |

*Source*: Julander and Jeffrey 1964. (Used with permission.)

*Note*: Total grazing use was indicated by fecal counts. Days use per acre was determined by counting droppings of each species and converting counts to days use by dividing by average defecation rates per day for each species.

[a]Differences in animal-days use significant at the 1-percent level.
[b]Differences in animal-days use nonsignificant at the 20-percent level.

(Thilenius and Hungerford 1967). Where moderate densities of both species occur, and no sign of inadequate forage supplies were apparent, competition would be relatively unimportant. However, where heavy cattle grazing decreases shrub density and height, decreased use of an area by whitetails may be expected because of the decreased cover as well as forage. In many areas, separation in use by slope or distance from water will not occur because the terrain is not steep enough to affect cattle distribution. Proper utilization of a range is imperative if competition between cattle and deer is to be minimized.

A variety of grazing systems are available for the rancher, some of which allow intensive short-duration grazing by cattle, sheep, and goats coupled with deferment. Reardon, Merrill, and Taylor (1978) concluded that highest deer densities existed under the grazing systems that were best for livestock, including a seven-pasture, short-duration system, and a four-pasture, 12-month grazing-4-month rest system. The seven-pasture system, which is grazed six to nine weeks per year, maintained highest deer densities, as well as the highest concentrations of livestock. Continuously grazed pastures had the lowest deer densities. Thus, grazing systems that included large periods of deferment were considered best for the whitetails in the Edwards Plateau region of Texas.

Two studies suggest that social interaction between mule deer and cattle is minor (Julander 1955; Kramer 1973).

**Elk and sheep.**    Elk forage preferences are wide-ranging and may overlap with virtually all other wild and domestic grazers. For instance, Stevens (1966) reported that both elk and sheep made extensive use of pale agoseris and sedges on a Montana summer range, and a severe degree of competition was possible even though areas of common use were used for only a short time by elk. When elk were using the mountain parks used by sheep, their diet was shifted towards grasses, even though elsewhere the summer diet was chiefly forbs, illustrating how competition may modify forage availability.

**Elk and cattle.**    The major share of livestock-wildlife competition evaluations have been directed at elk and cattle because cattle are the most widely distributed livestock species on western rangelands, their apparent conflict with elk has been perceived as being potentially high, and elk have generally received substantial attention and interest of ranchers, sportsmen, and resource managers. Studies have been done across the elk range from Canada to Arizona.

Blood (1966) concluded that elk and cattle in Riding Mountain National Park, Manitoba, used largely different forage classes, used a very limited area in common, and the few species that were used in common were present in excess of the demands of the animals. This conclusion was made in spite of the fact that cattle grazing had appreciably changed vegetative composition in many areas. The rough fescue prairie was replaced by a seral bluegrass-dandelion association, which in turn can be altered to an annual weed association under further grazing. Both species were palatable to elk in this area, so the change in composition due to cattle use was not necessarily detrimental to elk.

Mitchell and Cormack (1960) described deterioration of rough fescue rangelands in mountainous Alberta that was a result of combined elk and cattle use. Heavy past grazing had reduced the fescue association to a club moss and pasture sage community on some sites. Rough fescue is especially sensitive to heavy grazing, and efforts to properly manage ranges on which this highly productive and palatable species occurs must consider its sensitivity. In this case, reductions in grazing by both cattle and elk were recommended in order to begin restoration of the rangelands.

Stevens (1966) considered competition possible in the spruce-fir zone comprising elk and cattle summer range in Montana. However, the cattle diet in this area was 71 percent grasses and the elk diet was 72 percent forbs. Bluegrass, dandelion, and clover formed significant portions of the diet for both species, so if competition occurred, it was probably for these species.

Mackie (1970) reported extensive habitat overlap between cattle and elk for spring and fall in central Montana. Grass, especially western wheatgrass, comprised the major portion of the diets during dry summers and in winter of both species. In winter, elk restricted their occupation of areas to those that were not used much by cattle. Elk generally occurred from ¼ to ¾ mile from a water source.

Julander and Jeffrey (1964) reported that elk use patterns were least influenced by topography, although they preferred upper slopes, middle slopes, and major ridgetops, while cattle were located primarily on the lower slopes. Elk used steeper slopes more frequently than cattle. Habitat preference was less well defined in this Utah area than for deer or cattle (Table 8.6), and changed through the season. Elk were less specific in habitat selection than either mule deer or cattle, illustrating their high flexibility in coping with changing conditions.

Skovlin et al. (1968) demonstrated, using pellet group distribution data, that use of spring–fall ranges by elk, like that of mule deer, decreased as the stocking rate of cattle increased in northeastern Oregon (Figure 8.4). Differences in use patterns between years were related to weather, which dictated the length of time deer and elk remained on the adjacent winter ranges, but not the changes in plant production and composition. Cattle grazed these ranges in summer when elk were elsewhere.

This study also evaluated the use of a deferred-rotation grazing system by deer and elk. When cattle stocking rates were high, elk preferred the deferred pastures, but when utilization of the season-long pasture by cattle was light, elk preferred that area over the deferred-rotation system.

Grazing of a summer rangeland by both elk and cattle, if done properly, can provide for more efficient use of a rangeland. If stocking of both species is kept at a practical level, food habits of the two species will probably be different enough to

**TABLE 8.6** Use of Vegetation Types in Order of Preference by Deer, Elk, and Cattle

| Preference | Deer[a] | | Elk[b] | | Cattle[c] | |
|---|---|---|---|---|---|---|
| | Vegetation Type | Days Use per Acre | Vegetation Type | Days Use per Acre | Vegetation Type | Days Use per Acre |
| First | Mixed shrub | 6.4 | Mixed shrub | 3.9 | Grass–forb | 16.2 |
| Second | Oak | 5.3 | Aspen | 2.8 | Mixed shrub | 10.3 |
| Third | Aspen | 4.2 | Oak | 1.8 | Aspen | 7.7 |
| Fourth | Conifer–shrub | 3.7 | Grass–forb | 1.8 | Aspen–conifer | 4.9 |
| Fifth | Aspen–conifer | 2.1 | Aspen–conifer | 1.7 | Oak | 3.0 |
| Last | Grass–forb | 0.7 | Conifer–shrub | 1.7 | Conifer–shrub | 1.3 |

*Source:* Julander and Jeffrey 1964. (Used with permission.)

*Note:* Total grazing use was indicated by fecal counts. Days use per acre was determined by counting droppings of each species and converting counts to days use by dividing by average defecation rates per day for each species.

[a]Differences in animal-days use significant at the 10 percent level.

[b]Differences in animal-days use significant at the 1 percent level.

[c]Differences in animal-days use nonsignificant at the 20 percent level.

be complementary. A. D. Smith and Doell (1968) specify that a grazing plan that is designed to provide forage for wildlife and livestock must fulfill several requirements, which are generalized below:

1. The utilization of wildlife forage by livestock must be kept at a low level. This is especially applicable to species that are not major items of the livestock diet, and will generally include browse and forbs.

2. Herbaceous forage grazed primarily by livestock should be grazed at the season and intensity that will maintain it but not permit it to increase at the expense of wildlife forage. This implies that successional patterns must be understood, and that judicious grazing can be used to maintain or alter vegetation composition and production to benefit specific wildlife populations.

3. Specific areas may need to be grazed at different times over a period of years to balance out the effects of grazing on the vegetative complex. Livestock grazing can be regulated much more easily than wildlife grazing, the latter being a function of weather conditions and population levels. This does not mean that wildlife populations can be left without management of their numbers: in fact, it is equally imperative that numbers be made compatible with the whole system.

E. W. Anderson and Scherzinger (1975) provide further insight into the potential for combining use of a range by wildlife and livestock. The Bridge Creek Wildlife Management Area in Oregon has a history not atypical of many elk winter ranges acquired by wildlife agencies to secure the wintering grounds for this species. Upon its acquisition in 1961, cattle were excluded in an effort to improve range conditions. Range conditions did improve over the next three years, and the elk herd increased from approximately 120 to about 320. Range inspections showed that a large proportion of the area was not being grazed much by elk, and much grass forage appeared to be left unused. The initial increase in elk was attributed to the increased volume of available forage resulting from the removal of the cattle. The lack of use by elk of much of the area was related to a decrease in forage quality resulting from the leaching of nutrients from the rank growth. This postulated reason for decreased use of what appeared superficially to be a high-quality forage base was then used as a rational for reintroducing cattle.

Following a three-year lag in response of elk to the modification of forage from the cattle grazing due to snowmobile activity that prevented elk use of the entire range, elk did increase use of the area, and have subsequently increased to near 1200 animals. Moreover, cattle grazing was increased from 340 to 900 animal unit months (aum) under a grazing system where two herds are grazed simultaneously from May through mid-June, after elk have left and Idaho fescue and bluebunch wheatgrass has matured to the "boot" stage. Grazing was just heavy enough to set back the growth cycle of the bunchgrasses but still allow for regrowth of the grazed plants (Figure 8.5). The theory is that this level of grazing will retard grass growth to where the cycle is retarded and nutrients normally translocated to roots

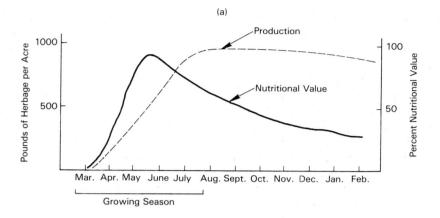

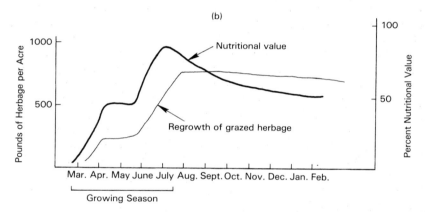

**Figure 8.5** (a) Relationship between nutritional value and forage production of ungrazed grass. (b) Hypothetical effect of using livestock grazing to interrupt and postpone plant physiological functions to improve nutritional value of regrowth following grazing. After E. W. Anderson and Scherzinger 1975. (Used with permission.)

are fixed in the aerial portions of the regrowth during the summer senescence and are therefore available to elk during the subsequent winter. Since plant reserves are reduced through this treatment, the cattle grazing is rotated among several pastures so that no one area is treated more than once every two or three years—a rest-rotation system. Elk have responded to this system by extending their grazing period and by using the treated areas. Range conditions have improved concurrently with the instigation of this system, which must be considered an outstanding example of coordinated-intensive livestock and wildlife habitat management. Control of elk numbers at a level near 1200 is anticipated. Deer have not responded to this system, which emphasizes grass management, but mountain bluebirds, western bluebirds, and blue grouse have benefited.

Grazing systems such as this can be modified to accommodate wildlife populations that graze browse and forbs as well as grass. The principle of stimulating productivity of browse through light grazing at the proper time by livestock was recognized by A. D. Smith and Doell (1968), and management plans can be tailored to the specific area and the wildlife species under consideration. Knowledge of forage preferences, and close regulation of cattle grazing are prerequisites to successful management.

**Pronghorn and livestock.**    The same problem involving range condition is the overriding factor determining whether pronghorn will be in competition with domestic livestock. Buechner (1950) reported that prolonged overgrazing by cattle greatly reduced highly palatable species on a Texas rangeland, but increased other species that continued to supply pronghorn with an adequate diet. Heavy sheep grazing tended to reduce forbs on Texas rangelands to the detriment of pronghorn.

Severson et al. (1968) found the competition for food, measured in percent overlap in use of each species, was 8.2 percent on a yearly basis for pronghorn and sheep on Wyoming Red Desert. Carrying capacity of one 120-acre range unit was 8 antelope or 7.2 sheep for one year where only one species grazed, or 6.0 antelope and 6.2 sheep for one year when both species grazed the area. Sheep were grazing primarily grasses on this range while pronghorn preferred shrubs, and 5.67 sheep consumed as much  browse as 1 pronghorn, while 43.5 pronghorn consumed as much grass as 1 sheep.

One of the most critical, if artificial aspects of pronghorn-livestock competition involves the fence. Pronghorn can jump a fence, but prefer to crawl underneath the lowest wire, and may well be impeded by woven-wire fences if too high. Rouse (1954) recommended that fencing of public lands should be kept to a minimum, with four-section pastures being recommended on Red Desert sheep ranges. Where woven-wire fences were needed, 3-rod gaps spaced not more than 1½ miles apart should be opened when pastures are not used by sheep to permit the passage of pronghorn. Woven wire 26 inches high, with barbed wire 4 and 16 inches above the top of the woven wire was suggested. The Interstate Antelope Conference approved in 1962 a height above ground of 16–18 inches to the lowest strand of barbed wire on all-barbed wire fences, which has been widely implemented.

**Other big game species.**    Mountain goats and moose are also found on rangelands grazed by domestic livestock, but the potential for competition has not been evaluated extensively. Because mountain goat habitat is generally unsuitable for livestock grazing, potential competition is minimal. Moose may receive competition from cattle for willow under certain circumstances. When early fall snows occur while cattle are still on open range, extensive use of willow may occur locally for a relatively short period. Such a situation may have an effect if enough willow is browsed to subsequently limit its availability to moose, but these conditions are not common. Moose appear to be unaffected by the presence of cattle, and it is not uncommon for ranchers to be temporarily delayed in feeding their livestock by the presence of a pugnacious bull moose at the haystack.

Mountain sheep pose a special problem, in that many diseases associated with their population fluctuations are transmissible through their domestic cousins. Buechner (1960), and many other workers have reported the lungworm-pneumonia complex as being a critical mortality factor in bighorn. As a result, domestic sheep grazing should be restricted in areas where bighorn occur. In addition, the potential for competition with cattle and especially elk is great because of the similarity of dietary preferences. Bighorn should be given priority whenever possible because of their low numbers, reduced distribution over former times, and apparent sensitivity to competition.

### Waterfowl, Upland Birds, and Livestock

Major influences upon waterfowl by livestock grazing activities are variable from detrimental (associated with heavy grazing), to neutral (proper grazing), to decidedly positive. The positive side has to do with development of stock-watering impoundments on arid regions of the West. R. H. Smith (1953) has reported that 12 species of waterfowl have been observed on these impoundments in eastern Montana, including mallard, gadwall, American wigeon, pintail, green-winged teal, blue-winged teal, shovelor, redhead, lesser scaup, bufflehead, ruddy, and coot. Pied-billed grebes, eared grebes, and American mergansers were also observed occasionally. The three most abundant species were mallard, pintail, and blue-winged teal, and only dabbling duck (mallard, pintail, blue-winged teal, American wigeon, shovelor, green-winged teal, and gadwall) broods were seen on these reservoirs. Reservoirs were apparently not suitable breeding areas for diving species, although they did use these areas during migration. Essentially, areas that lacked water in the past had been developed and were providing substantial waterfowl habitat. Canada geese have subsequently established breeding populations on some large reservoirs in the region.

Grazing around stock-water impoundments and natural potholes is of substantial concern. Dabbling ducks typically nest in dried grasses of the previous year's growth, and heavy grazing that depletes the cover will also decrease waterfowl nesting habitat (Kirsch 1969). Bue, Blankenship, and Marshall (1952) and Kaiser, Berlinger, and Frederickson (1979) showed that the highest and densest grassland cover was preferred waterfowl nesting nabitat, and that water areas where shorelines were grazed and trampled too much received little use by waterfowl. They recommended fencing of shorelines or else reduction in livestock grazing on mud shores to improve waterfowl habitat. Pintails will nest in shorter cover than other species, so different degrees of grazing can alter composition of the nesting population.

Even the smaller ponds will provide security for waterfowl if vegetation exists on the shorelines and as emergents in the ponds. Young broods will frequently use the small shallow ponds. As more and more artificial impoundments are established, and grazing practices become more in balance with range condition, waterfowl will benefit.

Cattle graze emergent vegetation such as cattail and soft-stem bulrush (Keith 1961). Cattail invasion of ponds can eliminate or reduce other species that are palatable to waterfowl. Heavy grazing of cattail seedlings by cattle in midsummer can be a method of reducing its abundance and retaining some open water in ponds, but once cattail is established and vegetative reproduction begins, cattle grazing has little effect. Also, other emergents such as soft-stem bulrush are more palatable to cattle, so opportunities to control cattail by cattle grazing are limited.

In southeastern Alberta, cattle grazing at a level of 1.2 acres per head per month from July to November did not seriously affect duck nesting cover, because much of the cover was comprised of unpalatable species (Keith 1961). However, rest-rotation systems will often preclude selective grazing pressure, and can therefore reduce nesting cover for waterfowl. Such appeared to be the case in a central Montana area, where grazing during summer and fall resulted in decreased brood production the following spring (Gjersing 1975). However, the general increase in vegetation provided by the grazing system was providing increased nesting cover. The pastures that were given complete rest or that were grazed only in the previous spring or summer were the preferred duck nesting areas. Thus, grazing management practices can be used to benefit waterfowl if properly applied.

Upland and nongame birds respond variably to grazing intensity, depending upon the specific habitat requirements of the species. Wiens (1973) reported that heavy grazing slightly reduced species diversity but responses of individual species were variable (Table 8.7). Horned larks, characteristic of shortgrass habitats, were more prevalent on grazed plots, including heavily grazed plots, than on ungrazed sites. Western meadowlarks and Brewer's sparrows were more abundant on a moderately grazed shortgrass prairie in Colorado than on ungrazed prairie. Because Brewer's sparrows nest in arid-land shrubs such as sagebrush and saltbush, if grazing alters a grassland and favors proliferation of these shrubs, this species may benefit. Western meadowlarks and grasshopper sparrows were more prevalent on ungrazed sites in the area. Tester and Marshall (1962) reported that bobolinks, savannah spar-

TABLE 8.7 Effects of Grazing Intensity on Populations of Nongame Birds on a Colorado Shortgrass Prairie (ungrazed:grazed ratios)

| | Grazing Intensity | |
| --- | --- | --- |
| | Heavy | Light |
| Number of species | 1.33:1.00 | 0.80:1.00 |
| Species diversity | 1.32:1.00 | 0.96:1.00 |
| Total density | 0.81:1.00 | 0.81:1.00 |
| Horned lark density | 0.60:1.00 | 0.93:1.00 |
| Western meadowlark density | 0:1.00 | 1.09:1.00 |
| Lark bunting density | 0:1.00 | 1.67:1.00 |

*Source:* Wiens 1973. (Used with permission.)

rows, and LeConte's sparrows were adversely affected by heavy grazing on a tallgrass Minnesota prairie, with LeConte's sparrows being less sensitive.

The species composition and density of nongame birds may be one of the more sensitive indicators of rangeland condition. Generally, the more diversity of vegetation that occurs, the greater the diversity of the avifauna to be expected. Sites that have but a few species, even though they may be very numerous, are probably characteristic of least vegetative diversity. It must be recognized that grasslands of very low vegetative diversity may be in virtually pristine condition, however, and grazing of such sites, which may increase the variety of vegetation, can enhance the variety of an avifauna population. Thus, opportunities to manage avifauna complexes by manipulation of grazing practices appear to exist, and the few investigations bear this out.

Crested wheatgrass (*Agropyron cristatum*) seedings are a major means of restoring depleted rangelands in some parts of the western rangelands. These seedings are usually intended to increase production of spring forage for livestock on areas that have been increasingly dominated by sagebrushes and where native grasses have been seriously reduced in productivity and density. The need to restore such rangelands to more productive status is well recognized, but the effects on wildlife of establishing crested wheatgrass stands have to be given consideration. Concern occurs when crested wheatgrass is planted in monotypic stands. L. C. Stoddart and Anderson (1972) reported jackrabbit densities ranged from 2.6 to 3.0 per hectare on sagebrush types and from 0. to 1.0 per hectare on crested wheatgrass types. Significant decreases in relative density of birds, mammals, and reptiles have accompanied conversion of sagebrush-grasslands to crested wheatgrass monocultures in southeastern Idaho (T. D. Reynolds and Trost 1979), illustrating the serious changes that may occur. While the planting of mixtures including legumes and several grass species can alleviate this problem, recommendations to graze these plantings to a 2-inch stubble height to maximize livestock weight gains (Currie 1975) will offset any benefits to wildlife. Crested wheatgrass stands will maintain high productivity indefinitely on Wyoming big sagebrush types in northern Idaho (Hull and Klomp 1966). This species withstands heavy grazing, fire, and environmental extremes, and spreads into adjacent areas.

Black-tailed jackrabbits are known to damage crested wheatgrass seedings (Westoby and Wagner 1973) but also are an important prey species for raptors, including ferruginous hawks (R. P. Howard and Wolfe 1976). Grazing pressures in crested wheatgrass pastures by jackrabbits can be substantial and may prevent successful seedling establishment. However, Westoby and Wagner (1973) reported less than 10 percent of forage was removed from one pasture by a population that was at the ten-year high in its cycle. Most grazing occurred within a 300-m band around the pasture perimeter.

Range improvement practices that alter habitats for lagomorphs and smaller mammals can affect the predator-prey relationship. Many raptors, for example, nest in trees. Reductions in juniper through chaining or burning should be planned so nesting trees are left undisturbed. At the same time, juniper control that increases

**TABLE 8.8   Changes in Small Mammal Populations
on the Benmore Experimental Range in Utah, Following Juniper Removal**

| Species | Experimental Condition | Number Caught in Traplines Set for Three Nights[a] | | | |
|---|---|---|---|---|---|
| | | 1967 | 1968 | 1969 | 1970 |
| Deer mice | Untreated | 9 | 89 | 30 | 27 |
| | Treated | 6.7 | 112 | 19 | 28 |
| Pocket mice | Untreated | 1 | 6 | 0 | 5 |
| | Treated | 1 | 11 | 7 | 2.6 |
| Other species[b] | Untreated | 1 | 1 | 1.7 | 0.67 |
| | Treated | 0 | 2 | 2 | 0 |

*Source:* M. F. Baker and Frishknecht 1966. (Used with permission.)

[a]Means for chained-seeded-chained, chained-windowed-seeded (traps along windows), and chained-windowed-seeded (traps between two windows).

[b]Longtailed voles, jackrabbits, cottontails, and ten other small mammal species.

herbaceous composition can increase the diversity and abundance of the prey base (Table 8.8). On the Benmore Experimental Range, increases in deer mice (*Peromyscus maniculatus*) were most benefited by the increase in cover following the treatments, especially around piled trees. Individual species preferences for different habitats were thus apparent. Ferruginous hawks can change diet to accommodate the change in prey composition, but appear to produce more young during years of jackrabbit abundance (Table 8.9). When jackrabbits are more easily taken, nesting success was greater, and territories were larger.

Benson (1979) recommended that seedings and other sagebrush treatments be planned to create alternating areas of treated and untreated vegetation, increasing the edge and diversity of food supply, and retaining adequate cover. This will benefit prey species and thus raptors. Other recommendations involve retaining habitat diversity and minimizing human disturbance of raptors during nesting.

**TABLE 8.9   Density of Occupied Ferruginous Hawk Territories and Successful Nests
Related to Changes in Jackrabbit Density in Southern Idaho**

| Rabbit Density | Hawk Breeding Pairs | Successful Nests | Hawk Density | |
|---|---|---|---|---|
| | | | In Occupied Territory (per m²) | Per Successful Nest |
| High | 43 | 31 | 45.8 | 63.5 |
| Low | 54 | 26 | 33.8 | 82.5 |

*Source:* R. P. Howard and Wolfe 1976. (Used with permission.)

*Note:* Jackrabbits constituted 89 and 79 percent of the biomass in diet for the two periods, respectively, while the jackrabbit population decreased by 79 percent.

The upland game birds associated with rangeland ecosystems vary in responses. Sage grouse populations may well have benefited in some areas by increases in sagebrush after heavy grazing, especially where cover is needed, but this is not necessarily the case. Sagebrush control through herbiciding will be treated in detail later, but even this practice shows variable affects on this species.

Zwickel (1972) and Mussehl (1963) have emphasized the importance of leaving adequate cover, after grazing of the previous year's growth or of current growth, for blue grouse brooding habits. On a heavily grazed range in Washington, the number of breeding male grouse was not different from that on an adjacent ungrazed range, but hooting activity of males was much greater on the ungrazed area. Also, broodless hens were found primarily in thickets on the grazed area. A higher proportion of breeding success was suggested for the ungrazed area (Zwickel 1972). Herbaceous brood cover in Montana included a high degree of vegetative canopy coverage, an effective vegetation height of approximately 8 inches to conceal broods especially during the first six weeks of brood life (June–early August) and dominance of native bunchgrasses and herbs such as balsamroot. Brood activity was very infrequently observed on heavily grazed sites in the Montana study areas (Mussehl 1963).

Lek species (sage grouse, sharp-tailed grouse, prairie chickens) require areas of very short vegetation for mating (A. E. Anderson 1969). Presumably grazing could be used to create or retain such conditions, but the facts that most nesting will occur adjacent to the leks and that taller cover is needed for broods generally preclude this opportunity. Residual grass cover (previous year's growth) can be important to sharptails during inclement weather or when predators are about (R. L. Brown 1966). Alternatively dead grass and litter may block travel lanes or access to bare areas used for sunning, and act as a barrier to feeding for prairie chickens (Tester and Marshall 1962). Sharptail distributions change annually in response to changes in residual cover, with new dancing grounds being established when cover improves, either through increased precipitation or reduction in grazing pressure (R. L. Brown 1966). K. E. Evans (1968) reported that sharptail habitat should consist of at least 50 percent preferred cover that was not heavily grazed or mowed. Openings nevertheless are important brood cover. Hamerstrom (1963) reported 80 percent of all brood observations on a Wisconsin area occurred in grasslands. Prairie chicken habitat was rated by K. E. Evans and Gilbert (1969) as indicated in Table 8.10, for Colorado range.

It seems valid to conclude that a level of grazing compatible with maintenance of prairie grouse populations is one that reduces litter cover, stimulates or at least does not reduce herbaceous production, does not reduce the height of brood cover below the critical limit, and provides sufficient residual cover. However, these criteria are not necessarily applicable to all grazing situations, since they imply very light grazing at levels below that which a grazer may be able to sustain if just rangeland vegetation condition were to be considered. Prairie chicken habitat has been drastically reduced, primarily through change to agricultural cropland; and the need to acquire habitats specifically for this species is well recognized. In some cases, the

TABLE 8.10   Ground Cover Composition on Three Areas in Colorado
Illustrating Habitat Requirements of Prairie Chickens for the Region

| | Abundance of Prairie Chickens | | |
| | Present | Rare | Absent |
| Ground Cover | Percent of Ground Cover | | |
| --- | --- | --- | --- |
| Tall grasses (protection) | 14.01 | 9.35 | 9.37[a] |
| Shrubs | 9.48 | 4.08 | 3.53[a] |
| Bare ground | 50.42 | 57.53 | 65.70[a] |
| Cereal grain (winter food) | 5.00 | 5.00 | 0.00[a] |
| Short grasses | 12.64 | 12.13 | 12.18 |
| Forbs | 3.37 | 3.33 | 4.52 |
| Litter | 6.18 | 5.32 | 6.95 |
| Unidentified grasses, forbs, sedges | 3.90 | 3.26 | 1.75 |

*Source:* Evans and Gilbert, 1969. (Used with permission.)
[a]Significant differences between study areas at $P<0.05$.

same applies to sharp-tailed grouse. Habitat retention is thus an overriding need at present, and invariably grazing tends to be restricted or eliminated on wildlife management areas that are intended for these species. At the same time, judicious grazing as a means to enhance some habitats should be accepted as a useful tool. In addition, many of the public rangelands where prairie grouse must coexist with domestic livestock can be productive of both if the needs of both are considered. Game managers must not wash their hands of the grazed rangelands as a habitat for prairie grouse, but instead should consider them as a challenge and an opportunity for effective, integrated resource management.

## CONCLUSIONS

As with other human activities that affect wildlife habitat, grazing by domestic livestock cannot be categorized as detrimental or beneficial. To the extent that domestic grazing serves to replace in kind grazing by the original fauna, it must be considered a form of competition with which wildlife species have evolved. There is probably no clear stage at which livestock grazing becomes severe enough that it precludes replacement of the effects of the original grazing pattern. Buffalo wallows were a form of range deterioration, and concentration  areas of other ungulates must have altered vegetation composition in manners similar to those identified through current investigations.

Perhaps the major problem is attributable to the all-pervasive nature of grazing practices of the recent past (and sometimes the present), coupled with other more permanent forms of encroachment upon the rangelands by humans. Livestock grazing must be considered, first, a permanent fixture on the western rangeland and second, a practice that can, if abused, cause serious vegetation deterioration and wildlife habitat destruction. But it is also subject to correction, and can, as we have seen, be a useful tool in wildlife habitat management. Examples of any of these conditions are readily found. The challenge for the rangeland wildlife manager is to promote proper grazing on wildlife areas of all kinds and to work with the ranchers and the range conservationists to enhance wildlife habitats.

# 9

# Pesticides and Herbicides

Pesticides including rodenticides, fungicides, piscidides, insecticides, and herbicides, are products that most would rather not use. They add to the cost of crop and live-stock production, or to tree production. As with so many other resource issues, their use represents first a symptom of an underlying problem, after which they be-come another problem in themselves. If high-intensity, high-yield agriculture was not mandated by the economics of the farmer's world and the need to feed an ever-burgeoning human population, we could better tolerate pests and the resultant decreases in yields. If intensive silviculture was successfully replacing the over-mature forests with a productive and diverse regeneration there might be more tolerance to forest insect outbreaks in the overmature forests we need to retain. It is probable that management favoring monocultures rather than more diverse forests, either in terms of age or species composition, serves to compound the pesticide problem. Monocultures are generally more susceptible to damage than stands com-posed of mixtures of several species. As we move towards more effective manage-ment, one may anticipate a reduction in the need for pesticides, but we must address ourselves to the current situation. As Mrak (1969) states, the need for pesticides will continue to increase for the forseeable future. Pesticides are a part of the man-agement toolbag, and we must use them efficiently and with minimal impact on nontarget organisms. Mrak (1969) estimated that active pesticide chemicals totalled 900, with 60,000 different formulations, and the number continues to increase.

Pesticides may be defined as those chemicals used to cause the death of non-human organisms considered by humans to be inimical to their interests. Included in this definition are commonly known chemicals such as DDT and target-specific chemicals such as sodium monoflouroacetate (compound 1080), which is used in coyote control. The herbicides 2, 4-D and 2, 4, 5-T also fall under the general classi-fication of pesticides. Pesticides that are specific to target organisms, such as lampricide (used to control ammocoete larvae) and squoxin (squawfish), are cer-tainly more ecologically tolerable than the nonspecific chemicals such as DDT.

## INSECTICIDES

Two major attributes of an insecticide that have ecological significance are its rela-tive degree of persistence in the environment and the degree to which it is specific to the target organisms. Both relate to the ecological magnification of pesticide con-centrations in higher trophic levels of a food chain.

Chlorinated hydrocarbons such as DDT and dieldrin are much more persis-tent than organophosphates (parathion, malathion, diazinon) or carbamates (car-baryl). Persistence of DDT and dieldrin in light is 105 and 45 days, respectively, while the other groups deteriorate in less than 10 days. This higher persistence is what makes the chlorinated hydrocarbon both a more effective insecticide, and a greater cause of environmental damage. DDT came into use shortly after World War II as a means of controlling malarial mosquitoes, and was a major reason for decreases in the disease in tropical areas. It has been generally banned for use in the United States but is still being produced in this country for use by foreign countries and by the United Nations for malaria control. While the less persistent chemicals are now used extensively, especially the organophosphates, insects are known to build up resistance to these compounds rapidly, thereby diminishing their effective-ness as control agents.

Another key chlorinated hydrocarbon is methoxychlor, which was used for fly control on cattle, dutch elm disease, and home use. Aldrin is a soil insecticide used in cornfields, and for ant control. Dieldrin has been used for termite control, and soil corn insects. Endrin, chlordane, and heptachlor were also used for similar purposes.

The nonpersistent pesticides, of which malathion and carbaryl are examples, are used for stock and crop insects where it is essential that nonpersistence occurs because of the danger of contamination of foods or livestock. Zectran is a possible replacement for DDT in control of forest insect pests. Virtually all major insecti-cides are nonspecific, and therefore can be expected to "control" nontarget or-ganisms as well as the specific pest.

Modes of contamination of the environment are through all media—air, soil, and water—with air being the most common (Figure 9.1). Air is the most common means of applying pesticides in large-scale operations typical of agricultural and forest programs. Dispersal of particles is thus dependent upon wind and thermal conditions at the application site. The best time to apply pesticides is in early morning when air is heaviest, and wind is least. In morning, the ground is colder and the surface temperature is coolest, which also tends to minimize movement away from the area of application.

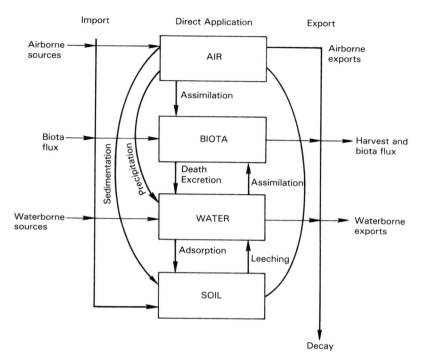

**Figure 9.1**  Movement of pesticides in the environment. From Mrak 1969.

Figure 9.1 illustrates pathways involved in cycling a pesticide through an ecosystem. Woodwell (1967) pointed out that radioactive substances or persistent pesticides may enter meteorological or ecological cycles, which in turn distribute and concentrate them in higher trophic levels or in substrates. Concentration of DDT residues in a Long Island estuary is presented in Table 9.1. Concentrations of 0.00005 ppm in water to 75.5 ppm in the ring-billed gull at the top of the food chain have been recorded.

There are several important differences between natural cycles and these artificial cycles involving pesticides or radioactive substances. First, because there is no natural source of pesticides, they can be eventually reduced or eliminated if we cease to introduce them. Second, the cycle is incomplete since a pesticide will break down in time to other substances. Total DDT in the biosphere has been esti- mated at around 2 million metric tons, with about 100,000 metric tons being pro- duced annually (Mrak 1969). However, there is evidence that as more careful application or outright elimination of use occurs, levels of pesticides do decrease in animal tissue (Linn and Stanley 1969; Enderson and Wrege 1973), and the amount of DDT in the environment has decreased since this estimate was made.

Forest insect outbreaks that cause extensive timber damage may still be con- trolled through mass application of DDT. Tussock moths were controlled in the Pacific Northwest in 1974, resulting in accumulations of DDT levels in cattle that

TABLE 9.1    DDT Residues in an Estuary on Long Island, New York

| Sample | DDT Residues (ppm) |
|---|---|
| $H_2O$ | 0.00005 |
| Zooplankton | 0.04 |
| Crickets | 0.23 |
| Cordgrass shoots | 0.33 |
| Hard-shelled clam | 0.42 |
| Chain pickerel | 1.33 |
| Cordgrass roots | 2.80 |
| Common tern | 3.15 |
| Herring gull brain | 4.56 |
| Herring gull, immature | 5.43 |
| Double-crested cormorant | 26.4 |
| Ring-billed gull | 75.5 |

*Source:* Woodwell, Wurster, and Isaacson 1967. (Used with permission.)

*Note:* Residue data include DDD and DDE. The DDT was applied by aerial spraying for mosquitoes, directly on water. DDT and its metabolites have a half-life of 15 years. They are insoluble in water, but highly soluble in fats and oils, and thus are stored there. As these data indicate, local monitoring in songbirds and herbivores is only a partial monitoring, and does not cover species most apt to be affected.

were three times the allowable limit. Strickler (1975) showed that lambs grazing these sprayed forests rapidly accumulated DDT residues for a 2-week period. Removal of the lambs to uncontaminated areas brought about declines in DDT levels in fat after 14 to 22 weeks.

High levels of residues can also be expected in wildlife species following DDT application. These levels may be considerably above the levels set for domestic livestock that are intended for meat consumption. While such sublethal pesticide residue accumulations appear to be the rule, there are still examples of mortality of nontarget species due to misapplication of pesticides. An outstanding example is the loss of 157 lesser snow geese attributable to dieldrin poisoning. The dieldrin was ingested on southeastern Texas winter range, but the mortality was noticed in Missouri (Babcock and Flickinger 1977).

Mrak (1969) summarized the effects of persistent insecticides on nontarget organisms. Phytoplankton significantly reduce photosynthetic activity when exposed to a few parts per billion of DDT. Controlled experiments wherein phytoplankton were exposed to 1.0 ppm of aldrin, chlordane, DDT, dieldrin, heptachlor, methoxychlor, or toxaphene showed productivity was reduced by 70 to 94 percent. Thus minute concentrations of chlorinated hydrocarbons in water have the capability of altering oxygen production by the most important producers.

Beneficial insects are more severely reduced than target herbivorous species, due both to the direct effects of the pesticide and its indirect effects through the food base. Spectacular increases in target organisms that were intended to be controlled by insecticides but that were less susceptible than the predatory species have been recorded. Bees are especially susceptible to carbaryl.

Concern in wildlife management has centered primarily on birds, especially the raptors and other predators at the top of the food chains. DDT is known to have caused decreased reproduction and survival in peregrine falcons, an endangered species. Hickey and Anderson (1968) demonstrated that weight changes in peregrine eggshells of up to 26 percent had occurred since DDT became widespread in the environment, by comparing museum specimens with more recent collections (Table 9.2). Enderson and Wrege (1973) reported the relationship of eggshell thickness was directly correlated to ppm DDE, a metabolite of DDT (Figure 9.2). DDT appears to interfere with calcium metabolism, which is critical in eggshell production. Eggshell thinning has been reported in brown pelicans, herring gulls, western gulls, murres, ashy petrels, white pelicans, and mallards. Gallinaceous species generally accumulate less DDT because they feed on plants and herbivorous insects that are lower on the food chains and contain lesser amounts of chemicals than those species higher on the food chain.

Other sublethal effects caused by DDT ingestion include delay in attainment of migratory condition in sparrows (Mahoney 1975) plus a variety of other physiological, reproductive, and behavioral responses (Pimental 1971). Sublethal effects are likely much more prevalent in wildlife than mortality attributable directly to pesticides.

PCB, polychlorinated biphenyl, is a common plastic pollutant that can be mistaken for DDT in some analytical techniques. Risebrough and Anderson (1975) produced evidence that PCB and DDE, the DDT metabolite, can interact to influence reproductive success in mallards. While PCB does not induce eggshell thinning, it can impair reproduction in birds and mammals (Conney and Burns 1972). However, Zepp and Kirkpatrick (1976) reported no effect on body weight or reproduction of cottontails when fed *ad libitum* 10 ppm PCB. Stendell et al. (1977) reported PCB was found in canvasbacks from across the species range in central Canada, but at levels below those known to affect reproduction or survival. The significance, however, is that it was found in 96 of 97 eggs analyzed, indicating how widespread the chemical is in the environment of the canvasback.

**TABLE 9.2   Weights of Peregrine Eggshells in Museum and Private Collections**

| Location | Date | Number of Eggshells | Average Weight (g) | Percent Change | Population Trend |
|---|---|---|---|---|---|
| British Columbia | 1915–1937 | 29 | 4.24 | | |
| | 1947–1953 | 15 | 4.18 | −14 | Stationary |
| California | 1895–1939 | 235 | 4.20 | | |
| | 1940–1946 | 49 | 4.07 | −3.1 | No data |
| | 1947–1952 | 31 | 3.41 | −18.8 | Declining |
| New England | 1888–1932 | 56 | 4.38 | | |
| Vermont | 1946 | 3 | 4.30 | −1.8 | Stationary |
| Massachusetts | 1947 | 3 | 3.47 | −20.8 | Extirpated |
| New Jersey | 1950 | 3 | 3.24 | −26.0 | Extirpated |

*Source:* After Hickey and Anderson 1968. (Used with permission.)

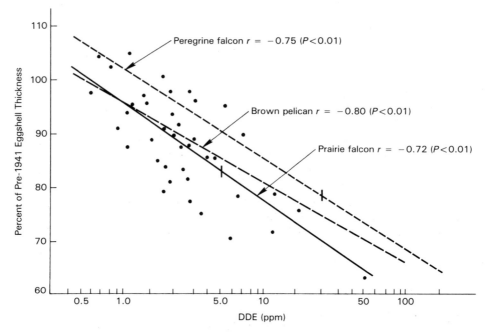

**Figure 9.2** Relationship of DDE residues in 40 prairie falcon eggs from Colorado with percent of pre-1941 eggshell thickness (data points included). Comparative data for brown pelican eggs (based on pre-1946 eggshell data) is from Blus et al. 1972. The peregrine falcon values (based on pre-1947 eggshell data) are calculated from Cade et al. 1971. Vertical dashes are DDE means. From Enderson and Wrege 1973. (Used with permission.)

Similarly, application of mercury for seed protection also can result in accumulations of this heavy metal in wildlife. Mullins, Bizeau, and Benson (1977) reported that pheasant hens treated with 20 mg of phenyl mercury showed significant decreases in egg hatchability, eggshell thickness, and chick weight and survival. However, hens fed wheat treated with phenyl mercury fungicide at normal field rate showed no adverse effects. As with PCBs, game birds commonly acquire levels of mercury, but at sublethal levels. These levels may frequently rise above Food and Drug Administration tolerances for domestic meat and poultry, and thus should be considered as possible health hazards. When levels in game birds increase beyond the maximum allowable, news releases and signs warning hunters have been used (Figure 9.3).

Organochlorine components such as DDT are also used occasionally in controlling noxious birds and mammals. Bat colonies that are judged to harbor rabid individuals can be the subject of intensive control efforts. Kunz, Anthony, and Rumage (1977) reported that, contrary to expectations, a bat colony that was exposed three times to DDT and chlordane applications was undergoing mortality

# ATTENTION! PHEASANT HUNTERS!!

**IDAHO PUBLIC HEALTH OFFICIALS RECOMMEND THE FOLLOWING RULES IN CONSUMPTION OF CHINESE RINGNECK PHEASANTS KILLED IN HUNTING SEASONS THIS FALL:**

- **DO NOT EAT MORE THAN ONE MEAL A WEEK OF PHEASANT**
- **THROW AWAY THE BACK (OR KIDNEYS) AND ALL GIBLETS**
- **PREGNANT WOMEN SHOULD AVOID EATING FOODS WITH KNOWN OR SUSPECTED MERCURY CONTENT**

**FARMERS ARE ALSO ADVISED TO CLEAN UP ANY TREATED GRAIN THAT MAY BE SPILLED, AND TO USE PHENYL MERCURY INSTEAD OF ETHYL OR METHYL MERCURY TREATED SEEDS**

**By Courtesy of
IDAHO FISH & GAME DEPARTMENT
John R. Woodworth, Director**

Figure 9.3   Warning issued to pheasant hunters in 1970. (Used with permission.)

four years after the last application. The implication was that such situations increased health hazards to humans, pets, and other wildlife, since moribund bats falling to the ground were then likely to be found. The authors suggest that permits to apply DDT or other organochlorine compounds to bat colonies only be allowed when documented evidence of a serious public health hazard exists.

Since 1971, when chlorinated hydrocarbons were placed under more restrictive regulation through the Federal Environmental Pesticide Control Act, monitoring of some wildlife populations has provided clues to how long reproduction and survival of young may remain impaired after wide-scale application of contaminants ceases. Henry et al. (1977) reported that osprey populations in Virginia and Delaware increased from 1970 to 1975, but continued to decline from 1958 through 1975 in New Jersey. DDT was widely and intensively applied to control mosquitoes in New Jersey from 1946 to 1966, while elsewhere it was applied in much lower amounts.

Herring gulls along the Great Lakes have recently suffered reproductive failure and decreases in colony size (Gillman et al. 1977). Seven contaminants, ranging from insecticides (DDT, dieldrin) to industrial pollutants (PCB), were identified in varying amounts within the five lakes.

Similar evidence is reported from Britain by B. N. K. Davis (1974). Although peregrine falcons, kestrels, and golden eagles have increased in areas where dieldrin and aldrin have been less widely used, white herons have continued to decrease and some peregrine populations have declined due to introduction of other pollutants into the food chains. This indicates that some species and populations are more vulnerable than others, given similar exposure to pollutants.

We must conclude that pesticides are a common component of the environment. Generally, their presence in animal tissue is at sublethal levels, and usually below levels at which physiological or behavioral response is evinced. However, numerous exceptions have been documented, and are common enough to warrant concern. Some populations appear to be recovering in recent years, while other populations remain heavily affected. The battle to clean the environment will continue, aided by federal legislation to clear up the air and the water.

## HERBICIDES

Herbicides are used extensively on forest and rangelands to control broad-leaved vegetation that competes with conifers and grass. The two major chemicals are chlorophenoxy acetic acids, 2,4,5-T and 2,4-D, which are plant growth regulators. Like DDT, these compounds became widely used after World War II in weed control applications, and in range improvement and forestry in the late 1940s. As with insecticides, there is a long list of unplanned-for, adverse consequences involving use of these herbicides.

### Direct Effects on Wildlife

Table 9.3 compares the $LD_{50}$ (dose lethal to 50 percent of animals tested) of each of the two herbicides with DDT, indicating a lower level of toxicity for the herbicides to various birds and mammals. These data are taken by orally administering dosages to confined animals. However, unlike the chlorinated hydrocarbons, the phenoxy acetics do not persist long within the environment and do not accumulate in body tissues (Zielinski and Fishbein 1967). Low temperature and low soil moisture tends to retain activity of 2,4-D for longer periods than otherwise, with persistance up to 147 days in greenhouse tests (DeRose and Newman 1974), and up to one month in field tests (C. I. Harris and Sheets 1965). Soil retention of 2,4,5-T appears to be longer than that of 2,4-D. Also, 2,4,5-T is generally more toxic. If no rain occurs, herbicide residues may remain on grasses for as long as eight weeks in concentrations over 1 ppm (Morton, Robison, and Meyer 1967).

Because of the possibility that herbicides deposited in soils can leach into adjacent streams, considerable field study of the problem has been done. The chloro-

TABLE 9.3    Comparison of $LD_{50}$s of 2,4-D, 2,4,5-T, and DDT

| Species | $LD_{50}$ (mg/kg body weight) | | |
| | 2,4-D[a,c] | 2,4,5-T[b,c] | DDT[d] |
| --- | --- | --- | --- |
| Rat | 375 | 500 | 100–800 |
| Mouse | 375 | 389 | 150–400 |
| Chicken | 541 | 310 | >1300 |
| Dog | 100 | 100 | – |

*Sources:* Rowe and Hymas 1954, Hill and Carlisle 1947, and Negherbon 1959. (Used with permission.)

*Note:* $LD_{50}$ is the dose lethal to 50 percent of animals tested. These data are taken by orally administering the dosages indicated to confined animals. While they demonstrate that the common herbicides used in range and forest lands are almost as lethal as DDT, it is emphasized that the herbicides are non-persistent in the environment (i.e., do not remain in soil or on vegetation and break down rapidly to harmless substances) and are rapidly excreted if they are ingested rather than accumulated in tissues as is DDT and other chlorinated hydrocarbons.

[a]2,4-D = 2,4-dichlorophenoxy acetic acid.

[b]2,4,5-T = 2,4,5-trichlorophenoxy acetic acid.

[c]These $LD_{50}$s are for the acid derivatives. Typically, from 0.5 to 3 pounds acid equivalent per acre mixed in diesel fuel are sprayed on sagebrush or on pine during "release" projects.

[d]Variations are due to substance with which dose is administered. The average $LD_{50}$ of DDT for all animals is 250 mg/kg.

phenoxy compounds are readily leached from soils, especially light sandy types. Norris and Moore (1971) stated that concentrations of 2,4-D and 2,4,5-T exceeding 0.1 ppm will seldom be encountered in streams adjacent to well-managed forest spray operations and concentrations exceeding 1.0 ppm have never been observed. Herbicides do appear in streams that flow through treated areas, generally a result of direct application to the water (Montgomery and Norris 1970). Such "accidents" often appear in large-scale poorly controlled treatments. Adverse effects on flora and fauna appear unlikely if spray concentrations and techniques for application are carried out with care.

Kutches, Church, and Duryee (1970) reported that high concentrations of 2,4,5-T (100 mg/ml) in the rumen will affect microbial processes, but at 250 ppm there was no effect. Also, 2,4-D is known to improve the palatability of pigweed and ragweed for cattle. These plants contain potassium nitrate, which changes to nitrite through rumen microorganism function, and deaths have been reported by Frank and Grigsby (1957). However, their tests suggested that day-to-day variations in nitrogen content were often great and were often of greater significance than variations due to herbicidal treatment. Berg and McElroy (1953) reported that application of 2,4-D did not affect nitrate content in oats, bromegrass, timothy, alfalfa, or clover, but may have in a number of weeds, including dandelion. Milk from cows grazing treated pastures (2 lb of 2,4-D per acre) contained from 0.01 to 0.09 ppm 2,4-D for two days after spraying (Klingman et al. 1966).

The Mrak Report (1969) discussed teratogenicity of herbicides, based on laboratory experiments with 2,4-D on rats. Cleft palate and cystic kidneys were significantly more prevalent in animals administered 113 mg/kg of body weight of 2,4-D. Rats given oral dosages of 4.6 to 46.4 mg/kg on days 10 to 15 of gestation showed excessive fetal mortality, with high incidence of kidney anomalies. Subsequently, Dow Chemical Corporation reported that a by-product, dioxin, associated with the manufacture of 2,4,5-T was responsible for the teratogenicity. The studies were conducted with dosages much higher than would be likely to occur with field application, but they did result in cautions being issued and, at least temporarily, in curtailment of 2,4,5-T usage on federal lands (B. Nelson 1969).

The conclusion to be derived from the abundant work on the effects of phenoxyacetic compounds is that direct adverse effects on wildlife are unlikely. Unusually high dosages can be expected to cause adverse consequences and can occur if cautions in use and application are not followed. Therefore, use of herbicides in areas where wildlife values are high should be monitored and planned for with wildlife given full consideration.

### Indirect Effects on Wildlife

If direct effects are to be largely discounted, the indirect effects of herbicide application on habitats can be profound. Way (1974) points out that herbicides can cause shifts in plant communities in unfavorable as well as favorable directions, and because of the ease of their application, they can produce wide-scale effects on vegetation. He concludes that we should remember that herbicides are very poisonous to plants and very few plants are weeds. Quimby (1966) recognized that the "target" species such as sagebrush were often important components of the wildlife habitat, and the importance of associated species that were susceptible to herbiciding was often ignored.

There is no question that on ranges where grasses are present and are being suppressed through competition with sagebrush, grass production can be initially and dramatically increased through sagebrush control. Hull and Vaughn (1951) found that after a spray operation in their study area, the grass understory increased its production sixfold. Hyder and Sneva (1956) found 650 pounds more forage per acre was produced following spraying, although yields were found to drop slightly thereafter. Mueggler and Blaisdell (1958) compared forage production on untreated and sprayed areas three years after spraying. The untreated control area produced 900 pounds of forage, air dry weight, per acre. Of this, sagebrush produced 500 pounds per acre; forbs, 100 pounds; and grass, 300 pounds. The sprayed area produced 875 pounds of forage per acre distributed among forage classes in this manner: sagebrush, 150 pounds; browse, 25 pounds; forbs, 150 pounds; and grass, 550 pounds. Grass production had increased 250 pounds per acre and sage production had decreased 350 pounds per acre on the spray areas, as compared with the control. Mueggler and Blaisdell (1958) discuss the decrease in total production after spraying and note that similar decreases have been observed after a burning project. Some browse species such as sage may be better able than associated grasses to take advantage of deeper ground water. It is possible more forage production can be expected from shrub-grass communities available in the form of palatable species on the shrub-grass community. These authors also found grasses increased most the third year after spraying. It was thought that 2,4-D indirectly stimulated growth of grasses by "releasing" them from sage competition, reducing evapotranspiration from the site, and retaining snow accumulations among dead standing sagebrush.

The studies reviewed have indicated that a cautious approach should be taken to spraying sagebrush in view of the possible effects on other species, namely desirable shrubs and forbs. For instance, Cornelius and Graham (1958) state that if burning is feasible on a sagebrush range, that method is preferred to spraying. Mohlberg (1960) cautions about use of herbicides because of unknown effects, and effects on nontarget species. Blaisdell and Mueggler (1956) state that indiscriminate spraying may entirely destroy associated species and allow replacement by inferior plants or undesirable annuals. They state total forage production may be impaired for a number of years, especially on sheep and game ranges. They conclude that the range manager should be aware that spraying may produce deleterious effects on desirable species and should balance this against the benefits. Mueggler and Blaisdell (1958) state that spraying may be highly undesirable on sheep ranges. A 39-percent loss of forbs occurred in their study area.

Bohmont (1954) states that as many as 75 percent of susceptible plants may be removed from a sprayed range. He pointed out that sage helps to hold snow, and is a valuable winter forage in some areas. He further stated that the long-term ecological significance of vegetative changes resulting from spraying has yet to be determined.

However, more specific studies of the effects of spraying a sagebrush community give conflicting findings. Hurd (1955) lists *Agoseris glauca, Antennaria rosea, Arnica fulgens, Castilleja lutea, Frasera speciosa,* and *Potentilla* spp. as being susceptible to 2,4-D. *Achillea lanulosa, Arenaria* spp., *Galium boreale,* and *Polygonum bistortoides* were found to be resistant. Cornelius and Graham (1951) point out that desirable forbs and browse are susceptible to 2,4-D but do not list any species. Hull and Vaughn (1951) state that in their study area, *Phlox* spp. were completely killed back to ground level for one year. *Chrysothamnus nauseosus* was killed back to ground level but *Tetradymia canescens* and other plants were unaffected. Mueggler and Blaisdell (1958) found that spraying using a water carrier reduced forb production 39 percent, mainly *Lupinus* spp. and *Erigeron* spp. Other species were little affected. They found that *Purshia tridentata* and *Tetradymia canescens* benefited by spraying, but a pronounced reduction of other shrub species occurred. Schiue, Brown, and Reese (1958) report using 2,4,5-T to kill aspen before cutting for timber. McIlvain and Savage (1949) found that lupines were severely affected in a Texas study area, but other weedy species were not. Alley and Bohmont (1958) found a 50-percent decrease in forbs over a four-year period after spraying. *Lupinus serecious, Agoseris purpurescens,* and *Arnica fulgens* were completely removed. *Taraxacum officinale* and *Cerastium arvense* increased. Blaisdell and Mueggler (1956) present more extensive data on spray effects on forbs and shrubs associated with big sage. They found 13 of 38 forb species were moderately (34–66%) to heavily (67–100%) damaged, in terms of density before and after spraying. Four of 15 shrubs and trees were similarly affected. Table 9.4, taken from their data, indicates the relative effects on various species resulting from the spray operation.

**TABLE 9.4    Effect of 2,4-D on Forbs and Shrubs Associated with Big Sage**

| Genera Reduced 67–100% in Density | Genera Reduced 34–66% in Density | Genera Reduced <33% in Density | Genera Not Affected |
|---|---|---|---|
| *Astragalus* | *Agoseris* | *Agastache* | *Achillea* |
| *Balsamorrhiza* | *Lithospermum* | *Antennaria* | *Aplopappus* |
| *Castilleja* | *Lupinus* | *Arnica* | *Astragalus* |
| *Helianthella* | *Artemesia cana* | *Comandra* | *Calochortus* |
| *Lupinus* | | *Erigeron* | *Crepis* |
| *Mertensia* | | *Eriogonum* | *Delphinium* |
| *Pentstemon* | | *Pentstemon* | *Geranium* |
| *Potentilla* | | *Phlox* | *Linum* |
| *Geum* | | *Senecio* | *Rumex* |
| *Zygadenas* | | *Viola* | *Solidago* |
| *Amelanchier*[a] | | *Chrysothamnus* | *Perideridia* |
| | | *Pinus* | *Ceanothus*[a] |
| | | *Populus* | *Opuntia* |
| | | *Prunus* | *Potentilla* |
| | | *Salix* | *Pseudotsuga* |
| | | *Symphoricarpos*[a] | *Purshia* |
| | | | *Tetradymia* |

*Source:* Modified from Blaisdell and Mueggler 1956. (Used with permission.)

*Note:* The researchers concluded that vegetal composition, class of animals, and seasons of use are factors that must be considered in planning a sagebrush operation.

[a]Aerial portions severely damaged.

It will be noted that spraying affects some very desirable forage species such as balsamroot, as well as undesirable species such as cactus, under the conditions that sage is sprayed. On the other hand, some other desirable species, such as sticky geranium, appear unaffected. These effects may be expected to vary with the area. Further improvement in selectivity of the herbicide used will alleviate this to a large extent.

The life expectancy of sagebrush spray projects has been evaluated in Wyoming and Montana. On a Wyoming area that was sprayed in 1949, W. M. Johnson (1958) reported the number of sagebrush plants per square foot increased from 0 in 1949 to 6.0 in 1966 on a sprayed area, as compared to 8 plants per square foot on an un-sprayed area. Desirable grass production declined to 280 pounds per acre on sprayed plots as compared to 403 pounds per acre on unsprayed areas. The Montana studies (J. R. Johnson and Payne 1968) suggested that site characteristics influenced sage-brush reinvasion. Adjacent sagebrush seed sources were not influential, but sage-brush surviving treatment was critical. Nonsage vegetation, slope, erosion, soil texture, and precipitation did not influence reinvasion, but exposure was critical. Grazing appeared to enhance sagebrush reinvasion in both instances.

The condition of the range prior to sagebrush spraying is also critical in determining whether the project will increase grass production and ground cover. If sage and associated species are the major plants on a site, herbiciding may cause sufficient exposure of soil to induce accelerated erosion. Thus Pechanec et al. (1965) recommend that sagebrush should be controlled under the following conditions:

1. Where sagebrush stands are dense and tall, indicative of fertile soils and sufficient moisture to promote a response in grasses.
2. Where sagebrush constitutes over one-half of the plant cover, indicating that reduction in forage is occurring.
3. Where other undesirable plants are not important parts of the plant cover or will be controlled. If plants such as cheatgrass are present, spraying may favor their increase on a site.
4. When proper grazing management will be provided. There is no sense in spending money on costly range improvement practices if grazing pressure is not to be managed.
5. Where seeding can be done promptly, if needed. If a satisfactory grass stand cannot be provided, then the initial step, herbiciding, should not be undertaken.
6. Where soils will not erode easily.
7. Where sagebrush is not needed as forage for livestock or wildlife habitat.

The wildlife biologist should be familiar with all of these criteria in order to effectively advise on or implement rangeland-wildlife habitat alterations.

### Sagebrush Spraying and Sage Grouse Responses

A number of investigations are available concerning the responses of wildlife to rangeland herbiciding with the major concern being for sage grouse. First of all, the herbiciding of sagebrush and consequences for sage grouse became a source of concern in the late 1950s, after it became apparent that large amounts of rangeland were going to be treated. However, land managers, charged with the task of restoring rangelands to a more productive condition, saw herbiciding as a means of rapidly increasing productivity of grasses. To be sure, some of the pressure to improve rangelands came from wildlife interests who were concerned about the existing situation, as well as from ranchers and others who were aware of the condition of the rangeland. Sagebrush spraying caused such spectacular increases in grass production on some areas that it was readily accepted as a useful tool by both land managers and ranchers. As a result, many programs to bring about proper use of a range included sagebrush control coupled with temporary deferment of grazing as agreed upon by the rancher, and, subsequently, range improvements such as water development and most important, more refined guides for grazing that would retain the condition and productivity of the range. Herbiciding was often a key to securing the cooperation of the rancher.

The overriding concern to improve range condition and secure better control of the grazing often meant that the land manager did not adequately consider sage grouse or other species of wildlife in the planning process. But, when faced with the need to retain sage grouse habitat where populations existed, the land manager needed a definition of the habitat requirements of the bird, and specific information was lacking. In fact, over 20 years passed from the time the problem was recognized until Braun, Britt, and Wallestad (1977) published guidelines for maintaining sage grouse habitat. This does not mean that efforts and knowledge did not accrue before 1977, as will be seen, but it does indicate that we have not been as immediately responsive as we might have been to a land management problem of major proportion. The reasons for this can be long debated, and involve many agencies with limited funds and diverse personalities, but the problem has not exactly been attacked with timeliness and vigor.

Montana investigations of sage grouse habitat requirements with specific reference to the herbiciding problem were initially addressed by N. S. Martin (1970). A 90-square mile study area contained 1710 acres of herbicided rangeland, with three unsprayed strips 5 chains by 1.25 miles long interspersed within the spray project. Over three summers of observation, only 4 percent of the sage grouse were observed on sprayed areas. Examination of sites that were used by broods or adults revealed a frequency of occurrence of big sage of 64 and 78 percent, respectively. Average number of big sage plants per acre was 4700 and 5900 at brood and adult grouse locations. Crown coverage of big sage was 19 and 25 percent at sites used by broods and adults, respectively. Nest sites were located under big sage plants averaging 12 inches tall. Klebenow (1969) reported similar findings, with broods preferring more open sagebrush areas, and nests occurring often under three-tip sage averaging 17 inches tall in adjacent Idaho. Wallestad and Pyrah (1974) reported that 68 percent of 22 nests were located within 1.5 miles of a strutting ground, but only one nest was nearer than 0.5 miles. Successful nests were located in sagebrush stands with significantly higher sagebrush cover than unsuccessful nests, averaging 27 percent canopy coverage and 16 inches tall.

Male sage grouse preferred sagebrush habitats where canopy coverage of sage averaged 32 percent (Wallestad and Schladweiler 1974). During breeding season, radio-marked grouse were located commonly within 0.8 mile of the strutting ground. Sagebrush again was important cover, and recommendations to protect areas within a radius of no less than 1.5 miles from the strutting ground resulted from this study. Wallestad (1975) subsequently documented a 50-percent decline in cocks using a strutting ground where 24 percent of the adjacent suitable habitat had been herbicided the previous year. However, the population had recovered to pretreatment levels three years later, and an adjacent strutting ground where 11 percent of the habitat was sprayed showed no change in the male population. However, a 31-percent loss of habitat adjacent to a third ground did result in a 63-percent decrease in cocks for two years after treatment.

Eng and Schladweiler (1972) identified winter sage grouse habitat as the more dense sagebrush stands, where sage constituted over 20 percent of canopy coverage. All roosting areas were on flat ground. The association with dense sagebrush begins in late August or early September and ends in spring. Table 9.5 summarizes findings from these studies.

TABLE 9.5    Sagebrush Requirements of Sage Grouse

| Season | Sagebrush Characteristics | | | Reference[b] |
|---|---|---|---|---|
| | Canopy Coverage (percent) | Density (per 100 ft²) | Height (inches) | |
| Nesting cover | 27 | 34.5 | 15.6 | Wallestad and Pyrah 1974 |
| Brood cover | 85[a] | 18.1 | – | Klebenow 1969 |
| Breeding season (males) | 20–50 | – | – | Wallestad and Schladweiler 1974 |
| Winter | >20 | – | 10 | Eng and Schladweiler 1972 |
| Summer | <25 | – | 7–25 | N. S. Martin 1970 |

[a]Total shrub cover including bitterbrush was less than 31% for areas where 95 of 98 broods were observed.

[b](Used with permission.)

Guidelines for maintenance of sage grouse habitats and a review of the effects of sagebrush control were developed by Braun et al. (1977: 103): The recommended guidelines were as follows:

1. The state wildlife agency should be notified of each specific proposal to control vegetation a minimum of 2 years in advance of treatment by means of an "Environmental Assessment." In such situations where it is not possible to provide such notice (i.e., private lands), the state wildlife agency should be notified as soon as the project is proposed. An adequate amount of lead time is necessary to properly evaluate control projects during all seasons of the year.
   a. The public land-management agency will provide the state wildlife agency with detailed maps on which the proposed areas to be treated are located and defined along with detailed plans as to the type of treatment and expected results.
   b. The state wildlife agency will plot sage grouse use areas on the maps furnished them: (1) leks, (2) nesting areas, (3) wintering sites, and (4) meadows and summer range or brooding areas.
   c. Representatives of the cooperating agencies will meet on the proposed project area for an on-the-ground inspection following completion of the maps.
   d. No sagebrush will be treated or removed until a comprehensive multiple-use management plan has been formulated for the area.

 e. Project plans for sagebrush control will include provisions for long-term quantitative measurement of vegetation before and after control to acquire data on the effects on wildlife habitat, and to ascertain whether the objectives of project were accomplished. The land-management agency involved should bear the responsibility for evaluation of the project as it relates to habitat, while the state wildlife agency should assume the responsibility of measuring the effects of the project on the sage grouse resource.

2. No control work will be considered where live sagebrush cover is less than 20 percent, or on steep (20 percent or more gradient) upper slopes with skeletal soils where big sagebrush (*A. tridentata*) is 30 cm or less in height.

3. The breeding complex (leks and nesting areas) will be considered as all lands within a 3 km radius of an occupied lek (in some situations, depending on the quality of the nesting habitat, this radius may well exceed 3 km). Control of vegetation within the breeding complex will not be undertaken within 3 km of leks, or on nesting and brood areas. On-site investigations by land management and state wildlife agency personnel will be essential to determine inviolate areas. Areas to be protected from treatment will be clearly defined on the maps in 1-b above.

4. There will be no control attempted in any area known to have supported important wintering concentrations of sage grouse within the past 10 years (delineated in 1-b).

5. No control will be attempted along streams, meadows or secondary drainages (dry and intermittent). A 100-m strip (minimum) of living sage will be retained on each edge of meadows and drainages. On-site inspections by land management and wildlife agency personnel will be made to assess the desirability of increasing or decreasing the width of untreated strips in specific areas.

6. When sagebrush control is found to be unavoidable in sage grouse range, all treatment measures should be applied in irregular patterns using topography and other ecological considerations to minimize adverse effects to the sage grouse resource. Widths of treated and untreated areas can vary for the convenience of application technique; except, treated areas will not be wider than 30 m and untreated areas will be at least as wide as treated areas. The untreated areas will not be treated until food and cover plants in the treated areas attain comparable composition to that of the untreated areas.

7. Where possible, spraying will be done with a helicopter or ground equipment. No spraying will be done when wind velocity exceeds 10 km per hour.

8. Whenever possible, complete kill or removal of sagebrush in treated areas should be avoided. Partial kill or removal of sagebrush may enhance the area for livestock, prevent loss of all snow cover in winter and allow for some use of the disturbed area by sage grouse.

Braun et al. (1977) prudently advise that each individual situation should be investigated and that recommendations should be tempered with judgment. There is probably enough information now to integrate sage grouse habitat management into other land management activities. Nevertheless there has to be an awareness that the birds deserve consideration, a willingness to consider them, and a spirit of cooperation and willingness to consider the needs of all concerned before the guidelines or the data will be considered. As usual, someone will still have to stand up and be counted on behalf of the birds every time their habitat is proposed to be changed.

### Other Birds

Braun et al. (1977) point out that guidelines for sage grouse habitat retention should not preclude providing for other wildlife species. Sagebrush-grassland habitats provide cover for Brewer's sparrows, sage sparrows, vesper sparrows and sage thrashers, among other species. These species nest either in the sagebrush or on the ground beneath sagebrush.

Spraying will cause up to 100-percent mortality of sagebrush, and most often over 90 percent, but the dead shrubs remain standing. Thus, Best (1972) reported Brewer's sparrows nesting in the thicker branches of larger shrubs that were killed. Both Brewer's sparrows and vesper sparrows, which are ground nesters, appeared to adapt to the abruptly changed conditions to some extent by selecting sites where additional grass cover provided substitutive concealment. Best concluded that available cover determined nest site selection and that whether sagebrush was living was not an influential factor.

Food habits of the two species reflected in part the changes in vegetation after spraying. Dominant foods used by each species were similar on sprayed and unsprayed areas, with differences expressed in amounts rather than variety. On untreated areas, a greater variety of insects was apparent in the diet of both species. Vesper sparrows utilized a greater variety of plant foods on the sprayed areas.

Brewer's sparrows declined by 54 percent on the sprayed areas one year after spraying, while vesper sparrow breeding populations fluctuated without any relation to spraying. Schroeder and Sturgis (1975) reported 67- and 99-percent reductions in use of tested sagebrush by Brewer's sparrows one and two years after spraying (Table 9.6). As dead sagebrush breaks down following treatment, nesting habitat

**TABLE 9.6  Results of Herbiciding Sagebrush on Breeding Populations of Brewer's Sparrows on Montana and Wyoming Study Areas**

| Area | Number of Breeding Pairs per 100 Acres | | |
|---|---|---|---|
| | Prespray | 1st Year Postspray | 2nd Year Postspray |
| Montana | | | |
|   Unsprayed sites | 45–50 | 45 | — |
|   Partial kill (53%) | 40 | 40 | — |
|   Total kill | 32.5 | 15 | — |
| Wyoming | 30–44 | 0 | 0 |

*Sources:* After Best 1972 and Schroeder and Sturgis 1975. (Used with permission.)

for Brewer's sparrows will decline accordingly. The trend in populations would thus be related to deterioration of dead standing sagebrush and reinvasion of woody species at a later date. Table 9.6 summarizes population trends of Brewer's sparrows as related to sagebrush eradication on the Montana and Wyoming areas.

Beaver (1976) did not find significant differences in bird populations comprised of nine species on sprayed and unsprayed plots in a California brushfield. Very little change in shrub cover was noted, and the herbicides did not cause leaf drop in the two major species after application. Thus, even if mortality occurred, stand structure was relatively unaffected. Subsequent resprouting of the shrubs would further render any shifts in bird populations generally of a temporary nature.

### Big Game

The use of herbicides as a wildlife habitat improvement tool has not received much attention. Herbiciding sagebrush winter range, with the attendant decreases in herbaceous and woody vegetation, is of course verboten although there are instances where this has occurred with the inevitable decreased use of areas by mule deer (A. E. Anderson 1969). Antelope and mule deer winter ranges are not places where herbicides should be used, and we need not investigate the obvious any further.

Possibilities to increase grass production and elk use of sagebrush areas through applications of herbicides were demonstrated to exist by Wilbert (1963). Borreco, Black, and Hooven (1972) reported higher use during the growing season, of herbicide-treated areas in western Oregon by black-tailed deer, which suggested that herbiciding could improve habitat for these deer. Krefting and Hansen (1969) reported similar findings following herbicide treatment of Minnesota brush ranges where the herbiciding stimulated resprouting of high-preference deer browse such as mountain maple. Krefting, Hansen, and Stenlund (1956) reported that spraying this species when it was in early bud-burst, with 2 pounds of 2,4-D per acre, would stimulate resprouting and hence rejuvenation of taller, unproductive plants in terms of deer browse. In contrast, Mueggler (1966) could not find any one time when northern Idaho shrub ranges could be herbicided to benefit all palatable species, and redstem ceanothus was adversely affected at all times (Table 9.7).

The judicious use of herbicides to stimulate resprouting of palatable woody

**TABLE 9.7  Effects of Herbiciding Big Game Winter Range in Northern Idaho**

| Species | Time Herbiciding Stimulates Most Resprouting | Time Herbiciding Kills Most Plants | Recommended for Use on This Range |
|---|---|---|---|
| Mountain maple | June | October | Yes |
| Scouler willow | August | September | Yes |
| Oceanspray | — | June | Yes |
| Ninebark | — | June, September | Yes |
| Redstem | — | All dates | No |

*Source:* Mueggler 1966. (Used with permission.)

forage species and to increase production of grasses through reducing competition from sagebrush does have some potential application as a wildlife habitat management tool. This may be especially applicable when times between treatments will be great, where use of more ecologically sound tools such as fire may not be practicable, where size of area is restricted, and when other values of the area to be treated have been adequately considered. However, use of these chemicals in wildlife habitat management does constitute a highly artificialized practice with possible unanticipated adverse consequences not in keeping with the traditional patterns of using more natural tools. Certainly, evaluation of the effects of herbicide application as to whether or not the objectives were obtained must be part of every management plan.

## SUMMARY

Pesticides, including rodenticides, fungicides, piscicides, insecticides, and herbicides, have direct and indirect effects on wildlife. Direct effects include alteration of behavior, reproductive performance, or survival. Indirect effects include, most commonly, habitat alteration. The persistence of a chemical in the environment greatly influences its ability to interact with wildlife. The chlorinated hydrocarbons such as DDT are highly persistent, while most herbicides and organophosphate insecticides usually break down rapidly into harmless compounds when applied in the field. Persistent pesticides progressively accumulate to higher levels as they enter food chains, so raptors, pelicans, and other predators may acquire lethal or near-lethal doses even if the individuals they prey on have lower levels.

While pesticide use is strictly regulated, there is difficulty in enforcing these regulations. Guidelines for use of herbicides on public lands where upland birds, big game, and nongame species need to be considered provide for monitoring of the application and the posttreatment situation. It is important that these suggestions be followed.

# 10

# Predation

## INTRODUCTION: HISTORICAL PERSPECTIVE

Werner O. Nagel (1956) defined a predator as "any creature that has beaten you to another creature you wanted for yourself." The definition "doesn't include animals that eat creatures you don't care about." We may wish to define a predator in a more objective manner, but as a matter of practicality, Nagel's definition is quite applicable for those interested in wildlife management. In historical times the creatures that predators beat us to included other human beings as well as those non-humans we domesticated; in some instances, as in the wilder parts of Africa, this may still apply. Currently, predators mostly beat us to a variety of creatures. But our personalized view of predators can be traced to the Bible and beyond, and it is an ingrained attribute that we have to contend with. Perhaps it is because we have competed with predators throughout our own history as a species.

The closer to the land you are, the more likely you are to view predators as a threat. They ate the deer that fed all winter on the tops of the trees that you cut, and which you developed a feeling for. They ate the sheep that you depended on for a source of income. They destroyed the nest of the pheasant hen (perhaps before you destroyed it with a hay-mower). And you saw more predator tracks than deer tracks last hunting season. They got into your tent and ate all of your food while you were fishing. Name any case imaginable, and Nagel's definition applies.

Predators are often blamed for things that we ourselves are ultimately responsible for. It is much easier to investigate, place the blame, and control the fox in order to save the pheasant than it is to solve the ultimate problem of habitat loss. We can control the wolf and coyote with much less hassle and conflict than we can control our own exploitation of the caribou or deer. It is much easier to blame the bear for the plight of an elk herd than it is to bring about adequate habitat restoration. In short, predators vote only by proxy. Nowhere in wildlife management is the practice of using "scapegoats" more prevalent than in issues involving predators. Probably nowhere in wildlife management has more of the precious conservation dollar been wasted than on predator problems. When one realizes that we have spent more on efforts to control predators, including research into predator control, than we have on understanding basic biology and ecology of the predators themselves, it is no wonder that we are accused of putting the cart before the horse.

One has to wonder why professional wildlife biologists have been willing to spend money on superficial aspects of predation problems. After all, our basic proclivity probably centers around more precise and well-grounded efforts that consider conservation of predators as well as their prey. The answer lies in the complexity of the wildlife management arena itself: we ultimately have to respond to perceived wishes of the people who own the wildlife and its habitat, we have not been able to effectively and consistently articulate an alternative set of actions that could substitute for the prevailing attitude of predator control as the palliative for all problems, and we have often been categorized as "predator lovers" by those we attempted to work with. "So you're one of those guys who believes that wolves don't eat deer, eh?"

Perhaps Errington's (1946:235-236) summary of his extensive review of predation best illustrates the basic framework of reference that wildlife biologists have used to approach the predator-prey issue:

> An attempt has been made to appraise the population effects of predation upon vertebrates, particularly through the consideration of automatic adjustments or intercompensatory trends in rates of gain or loss in prey populations.
>
> After distinguishing between the more or less inexorable factors underlying the vulnerability of a population to predation and the responsiveness of predators that may be symptomatic of vulnerability, we may see that a great deal of predation is without truly depressive influence. In the sense that victims of one agency simply miss becoming victims of another, many types of loss—including loss from predation—are at least partly intercompensatory in net population effect.
>
> Regardless of the countless individuals or the large percentages of populations that may annually be killed by predators, predation looks ineffective as a limiting factor to the extent that intraspecific self-limiting mechanisms basically determine the population levels mantained by the prey. A certain degree of correlation indeed seems to exist between territoriality (or intolerance, in one form or another) and lack of effectiveness of sub-human predation as a population check. In considering the classes of vertebrates, we may find far better examples of relatively complete intercompensations shown by highly territorial (or intolerant) mammals and birds than in the less territorial fishes, and more evidence of significant population effect of predation upon the fishes.

Among the mammals and birds, the numbers of those tolerant of crowding (such as some of the ungulates and waterfowl) appear most influenced by predation, but there are too many special cases presented by insular species and forms unable to cope with exotic predators, etc., to allow easy generalizations. Unanswered questions also remain as to what proportions of the habitats that are marginal for various prey species might accommodate greater populations were it not for interspecific predation. Then, too, so large a proportion of the known depressions of populations of mammals and birds through predation is linked with exploits of the dog family and of man that the consequences described might very possibly have been due to the rather unique pressures that these astute and often selective predators are capable of exerting.

On the whole, in view of the usual human tendencies to overestimate the population effects of conspicuous or demonstrably heavy predation, something of a scaling down of emphasis should well be in order, notably in appraising the role of direct predation in the population mechanics of higher vertebrates. Thresholds of security and their associated inverse relationships between the numbers of adults resident and the numbers of young produced or tolerated are frequently suggested by the published data, and these in turn quite evidently operate in conjunction with characteristics of habitat and with "cyclic" and other depression phases; but the patterns revealed may look remarkably little influenced by variations in kinds and numbers of predators. Even in equations depicting predator-prey interactions in lower vertebrates, loss types may substitute naturally for each other instead of pyramiding, and compensatory reproduction should not be ignored when a resilient instead of a rigid fecundity is indicated.

This summary was an indicator of a developing attitude among biologists: a "scaling-down" of emphasis on the importance of predation as a regulating mechanism in wildlife definitely followed World War II when the advent of modern-day wildlife management training in universities blossomed. The biologist educated in the 1950s, 1960s, and early 1970s very often was left with the impression that predation was overemphasized, that consideration of it as a possible adverse influence of consequence on any wildlife population was an attribute of the uneducated or unsophisticated. We in the profession all knew, of course, that populations compensated for natural losses, including those from predation, by increasing productivity and/or survival. We all learned of "thresholds of security" in the habitat that dictated the vulnerability of the "biological surplus" to the predator. We learned of ultimate factors that predisposed prey to the proximate mortality cause of predation. We also were aware from Leopold's sequence that predator control was a primitive phase of game management that preceded the most sophisticated phase, habitat management. Then too, there were examples, notably in the southern pinelands, where proper management of food and cover to favor a prey species served as a more ecologically amenable method of coping with predators than direct control.

We tended to ignore the implications of the oft-repeated idea that predators could compete in situations where populations were being intensively harvested by humans, especially on habitats that were deteriorated. The combined effects of multiple mortality causes could theoretically serve to reduce a population below the carrying capacity of the habitat. The work of those who suggested that predation could serve to regulate numbers at a level below that which food or cover availability would allow, such as that of Craighead and Craighead (1956), was largely ignored because of sampling problems (Hamerstrom 1958) even though the implications were great. The extensive studies of predator-prey relationships among invertebrates were cast off as inapplicable in wildlife management. Conversely, a reason commonly advanced for ungulate irruptions such as that of the Kaibab mule deer was the intensive predator control campaigns that often preceded the spectacular increases of deer. We listened to what we wanted to hear, ignored the implications of what we did not want to hear, and failed to think through the consequences of "truisms" or the dogma of game management to which we were exposed and with which we felt comfortable. If wildlife biologists considered their approach to predation to be a sophisticated cut above the generally accepted approach, they simply demonstrated some basic human attributes in doing so: the security of our peer group of wildlife biologists was implicit, and we "knew" that predation was compensated for by increased production and survival.

The late 1960s and early 1970s brought forth attitudes and actions that have subsequently opened up the predation issue to more examination. From the standpoint of predation on domestic livestock, the Cain Report (Report to the Council on Environmental Quality and The Department of Interior by the Advisory Committee on Predator Control) of January 1972 stimulated presidential actions of significant consequences. Removal of all toxic chemicals from use in control, including compound 1080, was perhaps the most important action. While this will be discussed later, suffice it to say that subsequently the controversy among sheep ranchers and conservationists increased in vigor and intensity. Whether or not the removal of poisons from the western rangeland simply caused less efficient methods to be used and increased livestock losses was immaterial: ranchers used to using poisons saw this action as one more ill-conceived governmental intervention blocking their already depressed sheep industry from regaining its health, with conservationists as the influential pressure group.

This controversy has stimulated efforts to understand the predator-livestock interaction more fully and with a broader perspective, efforts that continue at this writing. Even wildlife biologists who once disdained the issue are now willing to recognize that the livestock owner has a legitimate problem that needs attention.

Controversies inevitably seem to imply that someone is to blame, and the predation issue is fraught with projections of blame on those who are "responsible." We may argue that sheep ranchers who lamb on open ground near cover deserve the coyotes they attract. We may argue that conservationists who worry about the poisoning of nontarget species are willing to place the life of a magpie ahead of the welfare of a rancher, with all the moral implications of that! The process of placing blame, while perhaps serving as an initial form of communication, is ultimately of little value. All too often the most ardent champions of the predator are frustrated agriculturists, yearning for a connection to the pastoral aspects of their past. All too often the most avid, rabid predator haters have a deep knowledge of the predators in contention and are compelled to assume a radical position by their opponents who feed on and encourage their statements. But we are in this together, predator advocate and opponent, not to mention predators and prey as well. The task of the future lies in accommodation of the opposing interests with the goal of retaining the wildlife populations involved and alleviating the conflicts. Flexibility, sensitivity, objectivity, and a full view of the ultimate obligation that the wildlife biologist assumes toward wildlife are among the more important tools to be used for this task. That more of us are willing to rise to this challenge probably is in part attributable to the Cain Report and the objective review of the data by those seven biologists on the Cain committee (Table 10.18) who set an example and perhaps made such activities "professionally acceptable" to others.

The issue of predation on domestic livestock received attention in the early 1970s that was of benefit in reestablishing interest, but it was preceded by even more broadly important work affecting predator conservation. The Craighead brothers initiated grizzly bear research in the late 1950s using the new methodology of radiotelemetry. The work focused international attention on one of the most enigmatic predators (remember Nagel's definition), most importantly from the standpoint of their preservation.

Preservation of African carnivora, most especially the lion, became an issue of concern even for European aristocracy, largely through the efforts of Bernhard Grzimek and the researcher George Schaller. Grzimek, who founded the Serengeti Research Institute and solicited support for much of the research and conservation efforts on East African wildlife, was a master at securing funding for African conservation causes among the European benefactors (Hayes 1975). Schaller's research on the lion, and the very effective presentation of its results in a wide variety of media, was an enormous contribution to the cause of lion preservation and that of predators in general.

In North America, several studies subsequently augmented the Craigheads' bear research. The Isle Royale wolf population came under long-term, continuing observation by Durward Allen and co-workers from Purdue University. The initial conclusions of this investigation, that wolf predation took approximately the equivalent of the annual increment produced by the moose population, provided a fresh viewpoint in contrast to the more commonly accepted one that predation had no influence on numbers. But this was emphasized as being beneficial to the moose, keeping them from adversely altering their habitat as had occurred in the 1940s prior to the arrival of the wolf on Isle Royale. Thus the wolf was portrayed as beneficial in an objective fashion by people with credibility. While subsequent research has proven the moose-wolf interaction to be much more complex, the basic goodwill that the early work created for the wolf has done much to assure its preservation on Isle Royale and elsewhere. Work that L. David Mech subsequently continued on the Minnesota wolf populations has augmented the Isle Royale investigations in achieving public support for this species.

In 1964, a solitary carnivore, the cougar, came under intensive investigation by Maurice Hornocker in the central Idaho wilderness. This project captured the imagination of many more lay people who were in basic sympathy with the cougar and were intrigued with the use of hounds, the cooperation of an expert trapper, and radiotelemetry to capture and study these cats. Initial work revealed that the cougar did not regulate the numbers of its prey, but rather influenced prey behavior in ways that served to retain the "wildness" of the prey (a desirable attribute from many points of view) and that minimized habitat damage. Establishment of the cougar as a game animal rather than as a predator in Idaho and elsewhere was one measure of the effectiveness of this research in reaching a difficult western public with a history of vested interests and long-term anticougar traditions. But this work, like the wolf studies, provided additional perspectives on the role of predation in the context of ecosystems that wildlife biologists, among others, could relate to regardless of their proclivity.

One of the interesting aspects of these studies of *predation* is that they subsequently evolved to studies of *predators*. As is the case with so much research, often the initial results raise more questions than they answer. Thus Hornocker's initial monograph (1970) reported a predation study, while the subsequent work (Seidensticker et al. 1976) detailed the spacing of the cougar population and the reasons. The original Minnesota wolf studies centered on predation (Mech and Frenzel 1971), while subsequent work focused more broadly on wolf biology, including communication (Peters and Mech 1975) and spacing and population trends (Mech 1977). Implicit in this progression of research from predation to predator was the recognition that little was known about the predator itself. As in the past, this progression was due to the nature of the funding base, which initially related to predation, but the merits of investigating the biology of the predator for its own sake as a matter of more effective conservation seemed readily apparent.

Although these were not the only important studies during the period, they all share two things in common that single them out: they dealt with the largest mammals, and they were highly publicized in the lay press. Wolves, cougars, grizzly bears, and lions capture the human imagination much more than does the praying mantis or the mink, especially when skillful portrayal of their life-styles and the research efforts conveys the proper stimulation.

A variety of studies have since revealed different slants on the effect of predators on prey. It is safe to conclude from the recent history that we have a better understanding of the predator and that a much deeper base of public support for effective management and conservation of these species has developed. The issue of predator control is in better perspective as a wildlife management tool. This is all convincing evidence that the value of information derived from research, properly presented to the lay public, is the best kind of public relations effort in wildlife conservation.

As a matter of fact, one might conclude that a good measure of our ethical and moral growth would be how we learn to treat those creatures that might beat us to other creatures we wanted for ourselves. The wildlife biologist has a stake in this measure.

## THEORY

### The Initial Theory

Mathematical theory of predator-prey relationships developed from the Lotka-Volterra equations of the mid-1920s. Two equations exist, one describing predator population growth and the other describing prey population growth in terms of birth and death rates and population sizes.

$$\text{Predator population growth } \frac{\Delta N_1}{\Delta t} = B_1 N_1 N_2 - D_1 N_1$$

$$\text{Prey population growth } \frac{\Delta N_2}{\Delta t} = B_2 N_2 - D_2 N_1 N_2$$

where

$N_1$ = predator population size

$N_2$ = prey population size

$B_1$ = birth rate of individual predator

$B_2$ = birth rate of individual prey assuming no predators

$D_1$ = individual death rate of the predator

$D_2$ = individual death rate of the prey

$t$   = time

One assumption is that the individual birth rate of the predator is directly related to prey density. Another is that the prey death rate is directly proportional to predator abundance. Both assumptions imply that the predator population is regulated directly by the prey base, and vice versa, a closed system without other interacting factors. In many vertebrate predator populations, densities are regulated by territorial behavior of one form or another, at a level below the forage supply, while prey populations may be regulated at levels dictated by the forage base and by intraspecific and interspecific competition, as well as by predation. Thus, the original models are oversimplifications of actuality.

This does not diminish their importance in providing some basic insights into predator-prey relationships, and as a fundamental starting point from which further work developed. For instance, the equations predict that the product, $N_1 N_2$, affects the birth rate of predator and death rate of prey. If both predator and prey populations are proportionally reduced, the birth rate of predator and death rate of prey will be reduced. Accordingly, the predator population will subsequently decrease while the prey population will increase, assuming a single proportional reduction in both populations (as through a pesticide application). This is Volterra's principle, one important application of the original equations (Wilson and Bossert 1971).

Another implication of these equations is that the predator-prey relationship takes the form of a cycle, wherein prey populations peak ahead of predator populations, as the famous lynx-hare cycle appears to indicate. Thus predator and prey theoretically can coexist in some state of equilibrium. Keith (1963), however, points out that these oscillations are not intrinsic to the predator-prey system but are influenced externally. Watt (1968) considered weather to trigger at least some fluctuations. There are, of course, many predator-prey systems where cyclic population fluctuations have not been demonstrated, but it is also to be noted that, except in the case of exotic introductions into simple or highly altered systems without refugia for the prey and without the presence of alternative prey species, no cases of prey extinction through predation are known.

### Components of Predation

The components of predation form a basis from which predator-prey relationships can be quantitatively investigated (Table 10.1). Of the many variables that affect predation, prey and predator population density are always the two basic components (Holling 1966). Most theory is built upon analyses of predator-prey relationships wherein only one species of each is included, although the abundance of *buffers*, or alternative food sources for the predator, is important with respect to most vertebrate predation situations. The *optimal diet* models of MacArthur and

**TABLE 10.1**  Components of Predation and Possible Components of Functional Responses to Prey and Predator Density

| Components of Predation | | Components of Functional Responses in Prey and Predator Density |
|---|---|---|
| Leopold | Holling | |
| 1. Density of prey | 1. Density of prey | 1. Rate of successful search for prey by predator |
| 2. Density of predator | 2. Density of predator | 2. Time prey exposed to predator |
| 3. Predator food preference | 3. Characteristic of prey | 3. Handling time |
| 4. Physical condition of prey | 4. Density and quality of alternate foods available for the predator | 4. Hunger |
| 5. Abundance of buffers | 5. Characteristic of the predator | 5. Learning by predator |
| | | 6. Inhibition of prey |
| | | 7. Exploitation |
| | | 8. Interference between predators |
| | | 9. Social facilitation |
| | | 10. Avoidance learning by prey |

*Sources:* Components of predation from A. Leopold 1933 and Holling 1959; components of functional responses from Holling 1966. (Used with permission.)

Pianka (1966) are attempts to evaluate the inclusion of additional prey items in the diet with respect to energetics involved and are generalized situations that can apply to a herbivorous "predator" as well as the carnivorous predators. Holling's (1959) evaluation of predation by a small mammal complex on one species of insect is another exception.

The physical condition of the prey can be expanded to include behavioral attributes as well. This includes responses to predators, defense mechanisms such as the "broken wing" activity of a female ruffed grouse with a brood when confronted by an enemy. Included also is the territorial behavior of certain prey species, such as the muskrat, wherein individuals of lower rank are forced to occupy habitats that predispose them to greater rates of predation. Larger aggregations of prey, such as pronghorn antelope, that occupy open cover are probably a response to the presence of predators, wherein the group takes the place of cover as a source of security. These factors affect the rate of successful search for prey by the predator, the time prey is exposed to the predator, and the amount of area a predator covers in searching for prey. In addition, they relate to prey density as behavior such as territoriality is altered through density-dependent effects. When prey densities are low in relation to security cover, the effects of territorial behavior that predisposes individuals to predation will be less evident.

The characteristics of the predator population also change with predator density. As predator density rises, the exploitation component increases because of competition for the same resource. However, the chance that any individual predator will discover any individual prey decreases. In addition, interference between individual predators competing for the same prey increases as contacts between individuals increase (Holling 1966). As predator density increases, social facilitation due to contact with conspecifics may stimulate the individual to eat more, or search more rapidly, or capture prey more readily and thereby possibly increase the vulnerability of the prey population. At the same time the prey population may acquire more effective means of avoiding predators as frequency of nonlethal contact with predators increases.

Solomon (1949) identified functional and numerical responses to predation. The numerical response is simply the change in predator population density, the outcome of the effects of preying on predator reproduction, survival, and immigration and emigration. The functional response relates to prey consumption, or prey population change. Components of the functional response (Holling 1966) include (1) rate of successful search for prey, (2) time prey is exposed, (3) handling time, (4) hunger, (5) learning by predator, (6) inhibition by prey, (7) exploitation, (8) interference between predators, (9) social facilitation, and (10) avoidance learning by prey. The first three components are related to prey density, and the third component assumes that killing even after satiation is related in some manner to hunger. Learning is especially important among raptors and larger mammals but is considered a subsidiary component.

Components 6–10 are related to predator density. Exploitation is included because predators compete for the same resource: as the density of predators increases, the chance that any individual predator will discover an unattacked prey decreases. The interference component relates to agonistic behavior among predators, which increases as density increases. Social facilitation is included because some degree of association with conspecifics may stimulate prey consumption, especially among the more social predators. The final component of avoidance of predators is the converse of component 5 since prey can learn to avoid predators as much as predators may learn to selectively search for certain prey.

The available models of functional responses do not encompass all ten components (Holling 1966). All models appear to be restrictive, applicable to only a limited number of predator-prey systems, and are based on assumptions that have not been tested. Holling's work is among the most comprehensive, leading to sophisticated, detailed models for vertebrate and invertebrate responses (Holling 1965, 1966). The initial equation (Holling 1965) is illustrative of the approach, expressing the effects of prey density on number attacked:

$$N_a = a(T_T N_O)/(1 + a T_H N_O)$$

where

$N_a$ = number of prey attacked

$a$ = rate of successful search

$T_T$ = time the prey are exposed to the predator

$N_O$ = Prey density

$T_H$ = time spent handling each prey (time to pursue, capture, kill and eat)

Holling (1966) considered this a generalized statement in which $a$, $T_T$ and $T_H$ were components with unspecified values. The equation states that at any given prey density, the number attacked by one predator depends upon the rate of successful search, $a$, the time prey are exposed to predators, $T_T$, and the handling time for each prey item, $T_H$. Subsidiary components are then considered to exert their effect through any or all of the three principal components, and hunger may affect all of the components, for example. Holling (1966) presents detailed analyses of the functional responses of invertebrate predators to prey density using this format as the starting point.

### Types of Predation

Errington (1946) distinguished two types of predation, compensatory and noncompensatory. *Compensatory predation* is related to the security threshold of the cover for the prey. As the prey population increases to a certain level, then predation increases as the vulnerability of the prey increases. This is a density-dependent relationship wherein the density of the prey relative to the ability of the cover occupied to provide security from predation determines the degree of predation on the prey population. Conversely, *noncompensatory predation* is linearly related to prey population density and does not increase when a prey population exceeds a security threshold of its habitat.

Holling (1959) reported four types of predation, using functional, numerical and total responses as the medium (Figure 10.1). Three possible numerical responses exist: a direct response, no response, and an inverse response. The numerical responses are theoretically possible for all four types of functional responses. *Type I* functional response assumes that the number of prey consumed per predator is directly proportional to prey density, hence the straight line. In *type II* predation, the functional response rises at a continually decreasing rate. These first two types are considered applicable to invertebrate systems, while the subsequent two are applicable to vertebrates. *Type III* is the standard sigmoid curve, and was found by Holling (1959) to be applicable to an experimental situation involving small mammals preying on insect larvae. These three types of responses are considered basic patterns, since changes in other components are not included. *Type IV* is one modi-

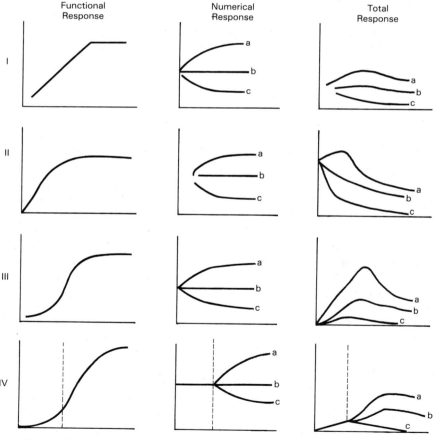

**Figure 10.1**  Four types of predation. From Holling 1959. (Used with permission.)

fication wherein compensatory predation occurs. The functional response curve is identical to type III, but numerical responses are related to the security threshold, wherein there is no numerical response until that threshold is reached.

Total responses of both predator and prey populations reflect the possibility that predation can control numbers of prey, and this is one important conclusion from Holling's (1959, 1965) investigations into vertebrate predation. The peaked curves suggest that control of the prey population may occur, while the declining curves represent cases where control is not possible. Holling (1959) points out that these curves are oversimplifications, since predator density is portrayed as being directly related to prey density, and predator populations do not respond immediately to changes in the functional response. The delay in numerical response will be more apparent when alternative prey sources are available, when density-dependent factors are operating within the predator population, and when reproduction, mortality, and immigration or emigration are slow.

### Stability of Predator-Prey Systems

The question arises as to how stable a predator-prey system might be, and a number of models have been developed to consider this aspect of predation. Frequently one hears that a predator is wreaking havoc on a prey population, with the implication being that the prey numbers are being reduced to extremely low levels.

Several models are available that mimic warm-blooded predator-prey systems and provide insight into the dynamics of these systems, including those of Smith and Slatkin (1973), Rosenzweig (1973), and Tanner (1975). The Smith and Slatkin model, envisioned for a small mammalian predator such as the weasel, which preys on mice (life expectancy one year or less), indicates that if a stable coexistence between a single predator and a single prey species exists, it will be at a prey density not much below that which would occur in the absence of predators. The stable coexistence is made more likely if differences in vulnerability of prey to individual predators occur, as might be attributed to age or social status of the predator. If the prey is provided with cover, which allows a portion of the population to escape predation, coexistence may be less likely because the predator can become extinct without the prey population doing so too. Predation may cause an otherwise non-fluctuating prey population to fluctuate, as well.

Rosenzweig (1973) has presented models that further serve to demonstrate that predator and prey can coevolve without the extinction of either. One can imagine a predator evolving, through natural selection, more efficient means of capturing prey that would cause excessive exploitation of the prey. Without counterbalances, the end result of such selective processes is extinction of prey and predator. This is termed evolution in an exploitative ecosystem.

On the other hand, the "prudent" predator does not cause extinction of its prey, and given a reasonable degree of stability within the ecosystem in which the species involved occur, the interaction between predator and prey should continue indefinitely. Figure 10.2 diagrams the relationship in stable and unstable systems.

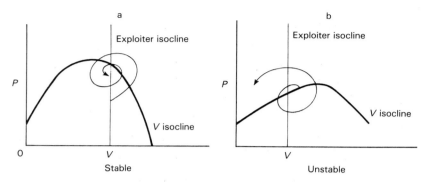

**Figure 10.2** Two exploitation systems. System (a) is stable where predator and prey coexist indefinitely and system (b) is unstable where extinction occurs. $P$ is the predator density; $V$ is the prey density. After Rosenzweig 1973. (Used with permission.)

The prey isocline in the figure is hump-shaped, while the predator isocline is a straight vertical line because competition between individual predators causes depletion of each other's resources. If the predator isocline occurs to the right of the peak of the prey incline, the toleration equilibrium is stable.

Tanner (1975) presented two-species models of predator-prey systems that included examples from field studies to assess stability of the systems. Assumptions in these models include the following: (1) the two populations inhabit the same area so densities are directly proportional to numbers; (2) there is no time lag in the responses of either population to changes; (3) the prey's food supply may be limited by some models but is never so exploited as to reduce food production; (4) the prey is the sole food of the predator; and (5) the mortality rate of the predator from causes other than starvation is constant.

The growth of the prey population in the presence of predators is

$$\frac{\Delta H}{\Delta t} = rH\,(1 - HK^{-1}) - wHP\,(D + H)^{-1}$$

where

$H$ = prey (herbivore) numbers

$t$ = time

$r$ = intrinsic rate of population growth

$K$ = maximum number of herbivores (carrying capacity)

$w$ = maximum predation rate

$P$ = predator numbers

$D$ = a constant specifying how fast the predation rate increases at low prey densities

The predation rate $Y$ is:

$$Y = wH (D + H)^{-1}$$

The growth rate of predators is assumed to be a function of the ratio of predators to herbivores or prey:

$$\frac{\Delta P}{\Delta t} = sP (1 - PJH^{-1})$$

where $J$ is the number of herbivores required to support one predator at equilibrium, or when $P = H/J$, and $s$ is the intrinsic rate of increase of the predator population. If $P > H/J$, the predator population will decline. This logistic model implies that intraspecific competition among the predators occurs at high levels of $P$.

Six properties of populations affect the stability of the predator-prey system. First, the presence and strength of a self-regulation or density-dependent control on prey population growth, involves factors other than predation. This affects $K$ in Tanner's prey population growth equation. If $K$ is slightly larger than $H$, the limitation is strong, but if it is much larger than $H$, the limitation is weak, meaning that the closer a population exists to $K$, the greater the self-limiting properties are effective in regulating, while if $H$ is much below $K$, predation may be serving to depress the population to some limited extent by replacing the self-limiting mechanisms.

Second, the relative length of the predator's searching time is involved. This is related to $D$, wherein the larger $D$ becomes, the longer the searching period (Figure 10.3).

Third, the presence of self-limitation mechanisms in predator population growth other than food is involved. This is found to be the case in some instances with the larger carnivora such as wolves and cougars.

Fourth, the presence or absence of intraspecific competition for food among predators affects the stability of the system. Tanner (1975) states that this is present if the predator's limit is a function of $P/H$, or if prey numbers are related to predator numbers.

Fifth, the ratio of $s/r$, the intrinsic rates of prey and predator population growth, is also included. Many predators have equal or higher intrinsic rates of population growth than their prey, although this does not mean that predator populations exceed prey populations in size. Also, if there is no intraspecific competition for food among predators, $s/r$ has no effect on system stability in the models presented by Tanner (1975).

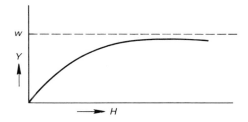

**Figure 10.3** Prey killed per predator per time, $Y$, as a function of prey density, $H$, where $w$ is the maximum predation rate. After Tanner 1975. (Used with permission.)

Sixth, the occupation of one or two habitats by the prey, with one habitat providing more security from predation than the other, is important. This may be related to variable drought or snow conditions as they affect cover and ability of prey to escape the predator.

Properties that most affect the stability of the system are prey self-limitation, and searching time. Self-limitation or long searching time will produce a stable system regardless of other properties. Next in importance is the combination of intraspecific competition for food among predators in a system where $s/r$ is large.

Two examples to illustrate stable predator-prey systems are provided by Tanner (1975). The muskrat populations studied by Errington (1963) appeared to be limited by habitat suitability, which varies with drought conditions, and this determines the number of territories that are secure from predators, especially the mink. Predators work primarily upon the surplus that occupies the more vulnerable habitats. Figure 10.4 illustrates a model to describe this condition.

Native ungulates have poorly developed self-limiting mechanisms and can cause deterioration of their food sources. Mech (1970) provided examples where wolves have suppressed ungulate populations through predation. Figure 10.5 provides a graphic description of this system, where $s/r$ is large and competition among predators for prey exists. While Tanner (1975) reported that it is unclear how this competition operates, Van Ballenberghe, Erickson, and Bynam (1975) show that

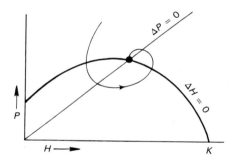

**Figure 10.4** A phase-space diagram describing a muskrat-mink predator-prey system when $K$ is small, and the system is stable for all values of $s/r$. Two habitats exist, one more secure than the other, but predator occurs in both since the equilibrium density is less than $K$. After Tanner 1975. (Used with permission.)

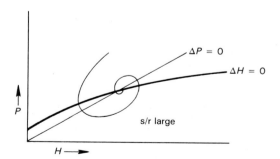

**Figure 10.5** A phase-space diagram illustrating a stable ungulate-predator system where $K$ is large and $s/r$ is large. Tanner 1975. (Used with permission.)

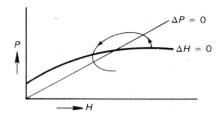

**Figure 10.6** A phase-space diagram illustrating a snowshoe hare–lynx cycle where $s/r$ is small. Tanner 1975. (Used with permission.)

wolf densities and territory size appear related to prey density, and smaller territories occur where prey are most dense.

Stable limit cycles, as shown in Figure 10.6, can explain the cyclical nature of some predator-prey systems such as that of the snowshoe hare and lynx in northern boreal forest. Competition among hares for food is weak, but is probably strong among lynx. The habitat is considered uniform in this case.

These models illustrate situations where populations of both prey and predator can coexist, either in cyclic or stable fashion, assuming no outside perturbations of the system occur. Perturbations, such as plant succession, that progressively change habitat from a more favorable to a less favorable one for the prey, may upset the system. Time-lag responses in predator populations that are self-limited to changes in prey density can also be expected. Prey have altered natural food sources in many instances, and there is as much reason to assume that mortality rates from causes other than starvation are compensatory as that they are constant. However, the models serve to describe how predator-prey systems can be stable, and are valuable for the insights they provide toward this end. They also illustrate what population parameters are involved and what conditions must be met to achieve stability. Undoubtedly, other conditions and assumptions can be included, as field work or further computer analyses reveal them.

## FIELD INVESTIGATIONS OF THE EFFECTS OF PREDATION ON OTHER WILDLIFE

A major issue is the extent to which predation compensates other forms of mortality. This compensation may be direct and immediate, where other mortality causes are reduced at the time that predation is occurring. Compensation may also be delayed, wherein mortality that would come later is lessened because predation occurred prior to the time. In either case, predation is one of a number of mortality factors acting upon a population, and any one cause of mortality becomes less important than the totality. One cause is substitutive for another.

### Two Early, Important Case Histories

Errington's (1943) field investigations of the mink-muskrat relationships are illustrative of one form of compensatory mortality. Mink predation on Round Lake, Iowa, from 1933 to 1939 was related to muskrat density (Table 10.2). High-

**TABLE 10.2  Muskrat Population Densities, Mink Population Status, and Degree of Mink Predation on Muskrat at Round Lake, Iowa, 1933–1939**

| Period | Muskrats | | | | Minks | |
|---|---|---|---|---|---|---|
| | Resident Breeding in Summer | Young Produced by Winter | Relative Status of population | Status of Population | Incidence of Muskrat Remains in Mink Feces | Comments |
| June–Aug. 1933 | 80 | 640 | Low | Moderate | 2% (2 of 126 mink scats) | |
| June–July 1934 | 180 | 1140 | High | Moderate | Substantial (no exact figures) | |
| Sept. 1934 | – | – | – | – | 5% (2 of 37) | Overpopulation phenomena noticed earlier in summer but little post-breeding mortality noted in muskrats. |
| May–June 1935 | 260 | 1450 | Very high | High | 52% (25 of 48) | |
| July 1935 | – | – | – | – | 25% (15 of 59) | |
| Aug. 1935 | – | – | – | – | 14% (1 of 7) | |
| May–June 1936 | 80 | 330 | Low | Moderate | 31% (adults only, 42 of 137) | Diseased later litters in muskrats. |
| June–July 1936 | – | – | – | – | 19% (36 of 194) | Drought. |
| Aug.–Sept. 1936 | – | – | – | – | 0% (0 of 76) | Period of local vulnerability of muskrats because of drought passed by midsummer. |

| Date | | | | | | |
|---|---|---|---|---|---|---|
| Oct. 1936 | — | — | — | — | 19% (4 of 21) | Influx of drought evicted muskrats from other marshes bearing most of mink predation. |
| May–Aug. 1937 | 86 | 544 | Low | Moderate | 0% (0 of 86) | |
| Fall 1937 | — | — | — | — | 0% (0 of 81) | Victims were young from groups of muskrats living near shore. |
| June 1938 | 64 | 515 | Low | Low | 7% (8 of 110) | |
| July 1938 | — | — | — | — | 0% (0 of 50) | |
| Aug. 1938 | — | — | — | — | 6% (5 of 89) | Victims were half-grown muskrats from shore-frequenting family groups, same as in June 1938. |
| Sept.–Oct. 1938 | — | — | — | — | 11% (4 of 35) | |
| June–July 1939 | 200 | 1079 | High | Low | 3% (4 of 150) | Mortality of drought exposed adult muskrats (wanderers and residents of peripheral ranges) from numerous causes was severe but more or less independent of mink predators. |
| Sept. 1939 | — | — | — | — | 0% (0 of 92) | |

*Source:* Errington 1943. (Used with permission).

est predation, as indicated by presence of muskrat remains in mink scats, occurred when both muskrats and mink were at high population levels. Predation on adults was related to their physical condition, wherein 6 of 31 carcasses complete enough to necropsy showed evidence of wounds attributable to intraspecific strife. Transient muskrats that lived in dry land holes and on other sites where vulnerability to mink was high were either killed by mink or found dead on highways or along lakeshores. These transients usually had intraspecific strife wounds. In July 1936, summer drought exposed back burrows above water and was correlated with increased predation on the inhabitants. In contrast, a regularly used lodge, which was a retreat for mink on one side and for muskrats on the other, apparently provided satisfactory security for the adults, even if the young did not last long. Thus predation was interpreted as being directed at the doomed surplus, the amount of which was related to security levels of the habitat. Muskrats that were confined to less secure habitats as a result of intraspecific strife were those most likely to be preyed upon. Errington's studies involved detailed descriptions of environmental conditions as well as condition of predation and prey populations. They reflect the skills of the individual in being able to interpret sign and details in the field in order to understand what was happening and why.

Predation becomes noncompensatory when it is additive to other mortality forms, and reduces the population level below that which would exist in its absence. The investigations of predation by a raptor complex on a prey base in Michigan and Wyoming by Craighead and Craighead (1956) serve to illustrate how this may occur. Food habits analysis, correlated with prey density estimates, suggested that predation by the raptor population was roughly proportional to relative prey densities (Table 10.3). Although evaluations of "prey risk factors" or security factors including protective cover, prey movements, dispersion, activity and habits, age of prey, and predator activity modified the raptor-prey density relation, prey density was still the major factor determining what the raptors fed upon. In winter, meadow mice were the major food item of the raptor population. Calculations indicated that 26 percent of the total meadow mouse population was taken by raptors in winter. By maintaining continual pressure on the winter prey (when they are

**TABLE 10.3**   Proportion of Prey Items in Collective Diets of a Raptor Population Relative to Number of Prey; 1942 and 1948 Winters, on a Michigan Study Area

| Prey Item | Percent of Raptor Diet | | Number of Prey | |
|---|---|---|---|---|
| | 1942 | 1948 | 1942 | 1948 |
| Meadow Mice | 87.4 | 54.8 | 303,000 | 75,000 |
| White-footed mice | 8.4 | 35.8 | 33,000 | 27,000 |
| Small birds | 0.9+ | 3.3+ | 23,000 | 23,000 |
| Game birds | 0.3+ | 0.8+ | 1500 | 1100 |
| Rabbits | 0.3 | 2.4 | 300 | 1200 |
| Fox squirrels | 0.02 | 0.16 | 300 | 1000 |

*Source:* Craighead and Craighead 1956. (Used with permission.)

nonbreeding) raptors were considered to reduce the breeding stock, and the meadow mouse population was considered to be limited by predation. No other mortality factors were of the same magnitude as predation. There could still be a delayed compensatory response wherein more young were produced and survived the following year as a result of the decreased winter population levels, as Craighead and Craighead (1956:308) note.

Craighead and Craighead (1956:306) also concluded that "no single force . . . will be controlling at all times." Predation could be effective alone or in combination with other regulatory forces. These researchers disagreed with the conclusion of Errington (1943) that victims of predation were largely doomed regardless of whether predators took them or not. Also, they questioned the argument that the fact that there exists a doomed surplus is important, and emphasized that how the surplus dies and that this removal serves to maintain population levels in balance with the environment is more critical.

Thus we see two different approaches to predator-prey relationships. One stemmed from long-term investigations of a single mammalian predator–single mammalian prey interaction, the other from investigations of a multiavian predator–multiprey system. It is not difficult, in retrospect, to see where conclusions as to the effects of predation might differ. While Errington (1946) suggested a "scaling down in emphasis" concerning the effects of predation, Craighead and Craighead (1956) saw predation as being a very important influence. However, both recognized the role of the predator as important in an ecological and conservation context.

### Predation on Ungulates

The Texas investigations of coyote and bobcat predation on white-tailed deer were initiated to define causes of juvenile mortality, which was considered to be a major determinant of population density. Of a total sample of 81 1- to 12-day-old fawns who were radio-collared and followed over a two-year period, 58 or 72 percent died (Table 10.4). Ninety-three percent of the mortality occurred during the first 32 days of life. The percentage loss of the radio-collared fawns was similar to estimated losses of a sample of 400 marked fawns and just slightly higher than the estimated unmarked fawn loss (66%) for the study area, which suggests that the marking did not elevate the mortality rate, and that the neonatal mortality rate of whitetails is indeed high. Coyote predation did account for the largest loss of fawns, and the conclusion was made that this predator played a major role in maintaining a stable relationship between the deer population and its food supply.

It was recognized that disease could be a predisposing factor to predation and could be more important as a regulatory mechanism in this deer population than was indicated. The deer population was exceedingly high, in excess of 100 per square mile. Knowlton (1976) reported that when coyotes were excluded by fence from a portion of the deer population, fawn survival increased as expected, but gains were negated by mortality later in life. The enclosed population subsequently

**TABLE 10.4   Mortality Causes of 58 Radio-Collared Fawns
at the Welder Wildlife Refuge, Texas**

| Cause of Mortality | Number of Dead Fawns | Percent of Total Fawns that Died |
|---|---|---|
| Nonpredation Losses | | |
| Starvation | 5 | 9 |
| Disease | 4 | 7 |
| Accident | 1 | 2 |
| Total | 10 | 18 |
| Predation Losses | | |
| Coyote | 29 | 50 |
| Bobcat | 2 | 3 |
| Coyote and other factors | 4 | 7 |
| Uncertain (coyote probable) | 13 | 22 |
| Total | 48 | 82 |

*Source:* R. S. Cook et al. 1971. (Used with permission.)

declined to a level approaching that of the population exposed to coyotes. It was concluded that precipitation levels, which affect vegetative growth, which in turn correlates with fawn survival through the nutrition interaction, were ultimately responsible for fawn mortality. Years of good precipitation produced higher fawn survival. Coyotes fed on alternative food sources, namely fruit, during wetter years, and fawns were dropped over a shorter period with coyotes unable to prey on a large proportion of them as occurs during drier years.

Salwasser, Hoel, and Ashcroft (1978) also concluded that the nutritional level of the doe during late gestation and lactation, as influenced by vegetation condition, was ultimately implicated in fawn production and survival of the North King's River deer herd in California, even if coyotes were proximally responsible for the bulk of the postnatal mortality.

These two investigations show the pitfalls and fallacies of considering predation as a single entity as it relates to mortality. The predator may well be the proximate cause of death, while the prey is predisposed to predation by other ultimate factors. Studies that simply document the percent of mortality that is attributable to predators can be very misleading.

Bergerud (1971) demonstrated that the interaction between disease and lynx predation could induce high losses among caribou calves in Newfoundland. This long-term study determined that severe spring weather, which is commonly thought to induce calf losses, was only weakly correlated with caribou calf mortality rates. The nutrition of the parturient female was also weakly correlated, as indexed by comparing the previous winter's severity with calf survival. Eighty-four dead caribou calves were found that carried cervical abscesses, the result of infections by *Pasturella multocida*. Finally, one single calf was located with neck lesions and a spinal fracture. Lynx saliva was cultured and found to contain the same organism. Necropsies of caribou calves confined in pens in which lynx were present to attack them further confirmed that the disease was transmitted to calves via attacks by lynx. Even if the calf was not killed outright by the lynx, the resulting infection would cause death. Finally, experimental removals of lynx from a calving ground substantially increased survival up to breeding age when compared to a calving ground where lynx were not controlled (Table 10.5).

**TABLE 10.5  Effect on Caribou Population of Experimental Removals of Lynx from Calving Grounds in Newfoundland**

|  | Pot Hill (lynx not removed) | | Middle Ridge (lynx removed) | |
|---|---|---|---|---|
|  | N[a] | % | N | % |
| Calf survival, June 1965 | 89 | 49 | 98 | 85 |
| Percent calves in population in October | 299 | 2.7 | 92 | 16.3 |
| Yearlings per 100 does, June 1966 | 190 | 4.7 | 109 | 27.5 |
| 2-year does per 100 adult does, June 1967 | 172 | 2.9 | 167 | 10.2 |

*Source:* Bergerud 1971. (Used with permission.)
[a]N represents number of adult does sampled.

Northeastern Minnesota's white-tailed deer population has severely declined over the 1968–1975 period, and Mech and Karns (1977) have attributed this to a combination of deteriorating habitat and severe winters that have apparently predisposed the population to heavy predation by wolves. Estimates of wintering deer populations decreased by 51–73 percent in three wintering areas from 1968–1974. Wolf numbers were initially high, when fawn production began to decrease markedly. Severe winters apparently continued to depress fawn survival, and wolves continued to take high proportions of older animals and vulnerable fawns. Subsequently deer declined in the wolf's summer diet, while beavers increased. Moose began to increase in the winter wolf diet, indicating a switch to alternative prey species as the deer population continued to decline. Local extirpations of deer, initially in poor habitats, extended to good habitat. Van Ballenberghe et al. (1975) anticipated the ultimate effects of a deer population decline on wolf populations, and Mech (1977) documented the wolf population decline. Deer habitat improvement programs are obviously indicated as a means of restoring both deer and wolves to higher population levels.

The Isle Royale investigations illustrate a sequence of change in the moose-wolf interaction over a 20 year period. The early research by Mech (1966) suggested that a winter moose population of 600 animals was being controlled by a population of about 22 wolves. The calculated moose calf production was 227, while the kill rate of moose was 0.227 adults per day and 0.209 calves per day. Calves and moose over eight years old were the age classes vulnerable to wolf predation. The moose population estimate in 1960 was based on a complete census of the 210–square mile island, which revealed 529 moose, with an upward revision in the estimate to 600 to account for missing individuals, which may have still been an

underestimate. P. A. Jordan, Botkin, and Wolfe (1971) reported a moose population census, based on stratified random sampling of quadrats, of 1000 animals that
was considered to be stable over the 1959–1969 period. Theoretical kill rates by
wolves were 0.339 adults per day and 0.871 calves per day, considerably higher
than the earlier estimates. Wolfe (1977), using pellet group counts and aerial censuses, reported that the population was increasing at a rate of 10 percent per annum
over the 1964–1970 period, with substantial increases from 1964–1967 and stabili-
zation during 1968–1970. These contrasting figures indicate the difficulty of determining moose population trends in boreal forest, as well as actual numbers present.
R. O. Peterson and Allen (1974) reported that in years of deep snow, wolves increased their kill rates of calves and prime-age moose. In snow depths over 76 cm
one- to nine-year-old moose constituted 60 percent of the wolf kill, compared to
53 percent (including all moose over age one) in lesser snow depths. Percentage of
calves increased from 31 to 49 percent of the kill for all age classes when snow
depths exceeded 76 cm. However, Wolfe (1977) reported that incidence of calves in
the winter kill over the 1959–1969 period ranged from 9.1 to 52.6 percent with no
apparent trend. Wolfe (1977) drew a few "speculative" conclusions about the
moose-wolf interaction. The wolf was the major source of mortality and a significant factor in the long-term equilibrium of the island's moose population. However, wolves had not completely controlled their prey within the last decade, and
the mortality attributable to wolves was variable over the years depending upon the
winter severity.

Several investigations have demonstrated that high postnatal mortality in various ungulates can be attributable to predation. Wolf predation on caribou calves
was considered to be a major mortality factor by F. L. Miller and Broughton (1974),
where 18 of 57 deaths were determined to be caused by wolves. Abandonment,
disease and other pathological conditions, plus injuries and malnutrition were also
causes of mortality. A wolf population of 25 preying upon a population of 24,000
parturient caribou producing 19,200 calves at a rate of one calf per day per wolf
would take between 20 to 30 percent of the calves, based on their estimates.

Schlegel (1976) reported that black bears were responsible for 94 percent of
elk calf mortality in a northern Idaho study area over a three-year period, 1973–
1975. Similar to results elsewhere, when bears were removed an increase in survival
of elk calves occured in this area. Subsequently, restrictions in hunter harvest contributed to increases in elk populations in areas where bears were not removed.

LeResche (1968) reported similar high incidence of postnatal mortality among
moose calves in the Knik River drainage of Alaska, where cow to calf ratios declined
from 100:84 in May-June to 100:36 in October. Drowning, entrapment by vegetation, abandonment, injury inflicted by the dam, and predation by brown bears were
causes of calf mortality. Chatelain (1950) suggested high incidence of black bear
predation on moose calves on the Kenai Peninsula, indicating that bears were factors in  moose survival particularly on calving areas.

The high postnatal mortality among infant ungulates is well documented
(Table 10.6). That predation is a major proximate mortality factor has been equally

**TABLE 10.6 Summary of Studies of First-Year Mortality of Ungulates**

| Prey Species | Time Interval | Number of Years Studied | Percent of Loss Attributable to Predation | Predator Species Implicated | References |
|---|---|---|---|---|---|
| Caribou | 60 days | 1 | 20–30 | Wolf | F. L. Miller and Broughton 1974 |
| Mule deer | 45 days | 3 | 55 | Coyote | C. O. Trainer 1975 |
| Mule deer | 30 days | 4 | 70 | Coyote | Salwasser, Hoel, and Ashcroft 1978 |
| Elk | 40 days | 3 | 64 | Black bear, mountain lion | Schlegel 1976 |
| Whitetail deer | 60 days | 2 | 53 | Coyote | R. S. Cook et al. 1971 |
| Caribou | 6 months | 10 | 69 | Lynx | Bergerud 1971 |
| Moose | 1 year | — | 73[a] | Wolf | P. A. Jordon, Botkin, and Wolfe 1971 |

*Sources:* F. L. Miller and Broughton 1974, caribou; C. O. Trainer 1975, mule deer; Salwasser, Hoel and Ashcroft 1978, mule deer; Schlegel 1976, elk; A. S. Cook et al. 1971, whitetail deer; Bergerud 1971, caribou; P. A. Jordon, Botkin and Wolfe 1971, moose. (Used with permission.)

well established. However, simply because this is so does not mean that predators are ultimately responsible for regulating population levels. Morris (1959) has pointed out that mortality factors that cause a relatively constant mortality from year to year contribute little to population variation in comparison to factors that, even if they contribute less mortality, are more variable and correlate better with population change. Further, in order to determine whether prey populations are regulated, accurate estimates of numbers and mortality rates are needed. The Isle Royale studies show the difficulty of obtaining these estimates with native ungulates.

The mountain lion predation studies conducted by Hornocker (1970) reveal yet another variation in the predator-prey relationship. Evidence obtained suggested that the major prey populations, elk and mule deer, were increasing over the four-year period of investigation, while mountain lions remained stable on the study area (Table 10.7). Mature males and young of the year were selected by mountain lions out of proportion to their occurrence in the elk and mule deer populations. There was no evidence that animals in weakened condition were more vulnerable to lion predation than those in good condition. This relates to the mode of hunting by this predator, which relies on stealth, and on opportunistic conditions, that arise when individuals place themselves in situations vulnerable to predation. While Hornocker

**TABLE 10.7    Summary of Findings from Evaluations of Mountain Lion Predation on Big Game in Central Idaho**

| Prey Population Estimates and Trends (1964–1968) | | |
|---|---|---|
| Prey | Estimated Population | Trend |
| Cougar | 13–18 | Stable |
| Elk | 799–1294 | Up |
| Mule deer | 1099–1724 | Up |
| Bighorn | 125 | Stable |

| Predation Findings | |
|---|---|
| Sex composition of kills | Elk and mule deer bulls and bulks taken in greater proportion than occurrence in population. |
| Age composition of kills | Elk and mule deer fawns and calves taken in greater proportion than occurrence in population. |
| Physical conditions of kills | Equivalent numbers of animals judged to be in good or poor condition taken. |
| Frequency of kills | One deer every 10–14 days, longer for elk. |
| Composition of kills | 53 elk, 46 deer, 3 coyotes, 2 bighorn, 1 mountain goat. Kills located over four seasons. |
| | Deer and elk 70% of prey item occurrences in scats, snowshoe hare 5.5%; various small mammals and grass the remainder. |
| Condition-trend of browse forage supplies on ungulate winter range | Originally judged down, subsequently determined to be stable. |

*Source:* After Hornocker 1970. (Used with permission.)

(1970) originally concluded that ungulate winter range conditions were deteriorating, subsequent investigations by Claar (1973) showed that they were in fact stable.

Mountain lions were not regulating their prey populations in this area, in the sense that predation rates were equal to birth rates, but Hornocker (1970) concluded that predation could have a very critical effect on the prey. Deer and elk are kept moving on their winter ranges, which helps to distribute browsing pressure more equitably. Individuals possessing certain behavioral traits, such as preference for habitats frequented by lions, were predisposed to predation. Thus, the kind of individual removed was important.

These long-term investigations strongly imply that predation on ungulates, whether it accrues to the younger age group or is distributed more equitably among age classes, can in fact depress populations for extended periods in some situations. However, weather conditions and habitat conditions strongly influence the interaction between prey and predator. Simple documentations of the numbers of prey eaten do not provide enough evidence to define the ultimate effects of the predation, nor do they provide adequate information by which to predict circumstances under which predation will be more efficient than at other times. Short-term increases in survival of young may be offset by higher mortality later on. We may conclude, as did Pimlott (1967), that native ungulates have very efficient predators, and one of the reasons that self-regulatory mechanisms have not apparently evolved is that ungulate evolution has been directed more at adaptations to coping with mortality factors. The predator is definitely a major mortality factor, if not the most critical one, excluding the artificialized influences of humans. But the relationship, as is invariably the case, varies in time and space and cannot be simplified to accommodate our wishes.

### Predation on Other Species: Three Case Histories

**Predation on snowshoe hares and ruffed grouse.**    Long-term investigations of snowshoe hare populations in central Alberta have been conducted by L. B. Keith and associates (Keith and Windberg 1978). Nellis, Wetmore, and Keith (1972) reported results of a four-year segment of this research. Snowshoe hares comprised 75.7 percent of the winter food biomass of lynxes, with ruffed grouse being the next most prevalent prey item at 9.2 percent on the 57-square mile study area. Censuses of lynx showed a declining population, from 11 in 1964-1965, to 3 in 1966-1967, then increased to 9 in 1967-1968. Lynx predation on hare, in terms of percent of total mortality, did not show clear trends, ranging from 8 to 37.1 percent (Table 10.8). About 20 percent of the total overwinter mortality of ruffed grouse was attributed to lynx. Lynx numbers were directly related to hare population trends, as was survival of lynx young through the first year. However, prey populations were not considered to be regulated by lynx predation alone.

Rusch et al. (1972) reported impacts of great horned owl predation on snowshoe hare and ruffed grouse on the same area during spring. Owls consumed from 0

TABLE 10.8   Impacts of Lynx Predation December–March on Snowshoe Hare
and Ruffed Grouse Populations in a Central Alberta Area

|  | Snowshoe Hare | Ruffed Grouse |
|---|---|---|
| December population estimate[a] | 3437–10,176 | – |
| April population estimate[a] | 2628–9434 | 2360–4073 |
| Estimated loss[a] | 741–4111 | – |
| Number removed by lynx | 118–432 | 37–134 |
| Percent of December population removed by lynx | 2.1–6.4 | 1.4–5.7 |
| Percent of total loss attributed to lynx | 8.0–37.1 | ±20 |

*Source:* After Nellis, Wetmore, and Keith 1972. (Used with permission.)
[a]Range for four years of estimates given. Ruffed grouse were estimated in April only, and no total losses were calculated for the December–April period.

to 5.3 percent of the ruffed grouse population, and from 1.2 to 4.1 percent of the snowshoe hare population during the short period. Shifts in predation from grouse to hares occurred during increases in both populations, illustrating the buffer effect as related to changing prey densities. Owl populations, as with lynx, increased as hare populations increased.

Rusch and Keith (1971a) analyzed ruffed grouse population trends on the same study area. Adults and juvenile females suffered higher mortality rates than males during late summer, which was attributed in part to brood-defense behavior that would increase vulnerabilty of the hen to predation. Males were selectively preyed upon by great horned owls in April–June, which was attributed to the conspicuous drumming behavior of the male. This also was evident in fall, when some drumming occurs. Predation was considered to be, *in toto*, the most important proximal source of grouse mortality, accounting for over 80 percent of the annual loss. In July, the predator complex accounted for 12.4 percent of the grouse population for two years. Dietary shifts by great horned owls from grouse to hares during the hare population increase allowed for greater survival of juvenile grouse. Nutritional relationships were not implicated, because predators did not preferably select grouse of lighter weight over those of heavier weight.

Rusch et al. (1972) pointed out that the entire predator community should be evaluated to obtain meaningful analysis as to the effects of predation upon a prey species. Since the presence of alternate prey in this area appeared to be important, one may add that the "buffers" must also be considered. Windberg and Keith (1976) suggested that hare populations, when at high density, declined through deterioration of winter browse supplies. The hypothesis that winter food shortage initiates the decline, and higher rates of predation follow, was supported by feeding experiments conducted by Vaughan and Keith (1981). Thus, again the interaction between predator, prey, and habitat is to be emphasized.

**Predation on black-tailed jackrabbits.**   Coyotes prey extensively on black-tailed jackrabbits in the northern Utah–southern Idaho area where the relationship was investigated over an eight-year period (Wagner and Stoddart 1972). Three independent lines of evidence indicated that coyote predation was a major mortality factor in the rabbit population. Stoddart (1970) showed that 64 percent of the known mortality accruing to 75 radio-marked rabbits was due to mammalian predators, primarily coyotes. The mortality rates obtained from telemetry data compared very favorably with demographic estimates ranging from 47 to 82 percent mortality with over 50 percent of total mortality attributable to coyotes when the

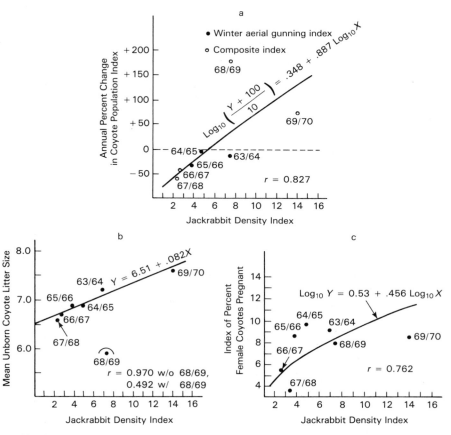

**Figure 10.7** Relationships between the 1963 to 1969 (first date for each point) fall jackrabbit density and three coyote population parameters for Curlew Valley. (a) Relationship to rates of change in the annual coyote population index of the following year (second date) for Curlew Valley. The correlation is significant at the 0.05 probability level. (b) Relationship to mean, annual coyote litter size the following spring (second date). The correlation is significant at the 0.01 probability level without the 65/69 value but not significant with this value included in the test. (c) Relationship to annual index of percentage of female coyotes breeding (second date). The correlation is significant at the 0.05 probability level. Jackrabbit data are from Wagner and Stoddart 1972. After Clark 1972. (Used with permission.)

rabbit population was low. Jackrabbit mortality rates, predicted from a coyote-rabbit index derived from census data, suggested that as the rabbit population decreased in relation to the coyote population, mortality rates increased. This indicates that coyote predation was related to jackrabbit mortality. The conclusion was that changes in coyote predation are a major influence of rabbit population trends. However, the authors surmised that the classic Lotka-Volterra oscillation was unlikely to continue, since the rabbit population can increase at a potentially higher rate than coyotes, causing the rate of coyote predation to decline. Other mortality factors were thought to cause reversal of the rabbit population trend to where coyote predation rates could again increase to become the major mortality factor. Interactions with jackrabbit habitat conditions as influenced by precipitation are likely involved.

On the other hand, Clark (1972) found high correlations between coyote population indices and jackrabbit densities (Figure 10.7). Coyote litter sizes and percentage of females breeding were also positively correlated to jackrabbit densities. Thus the major food item in the coyote diet appeared to determine coyote density.

**Predation on nesting ducks.**   Sargeant (1972) pointed out that predation losses of nesting ducks occur at a time of year when populations are at lowest levels and losses are largely noncompensatory. He also noted that hens predominated in the remains of ducks found at fox dens (Table 10.9). D. H. Johnson and Sargeant (1977) found that mallard hens were especially vulnerable to fox predation, constituting 79.8 percent of the adult mallards found at red fox dens on an eastern North Dakota study area. This may account in part for the observed unbalanced sex ratios favoring males in waterfowl populations. The unbalanced sex ratio was attributable to human-related mortality factors rather than an adaptive strategy. Reduction of nesting habitat concentrates hens into smaller areas than in pristine times. Nest losses promote renesting, which exposes a hen repeatedly to predators. Foxes were probably much less numerous when wolves and coyotes were more prevalent because the food base would be less stable before modern agriculture occurred, thereby creating better habitat for wider-ranging predators than the sedentary fox. Mallard sex ratios were thus judged to more closely approximate parity in pristine times.

### Summary

Errington (1963) points out that it is important to distinguish between the fact of predation and the effect. The investigations covered here clearly demonstrate that predation may be a major mortality factor and influence on population dynamics of prey species. Mortality due to predation may be compensated or noncompensated, but it should be clearly understood that it is difficult to determine the magnitude of effect predation has in field studies. There is evidence that prey population size influences predator populations. And the importance of habitat and

TABLE 10.9  Species and Sex Composition of Adult Ducks Found at Fox Dens in Eastern North Dakota During the Nesting and Brood-Rearing Period of 1969

| Species | Number of Ducks (May 26–June 4) | Species Composition (percent) | Number of Ducks (June 16–July 9) | Species Composition (percent) | Number of Sex-Determined Ducks | Females as Percent of Sex-Determined Ducks |
|---|---|---|---|---|---|---|
| Blue-winged teal | 19 | 26 | 27 | 32 | 39 | 85 |
| Pintail | 28 | 38 | 18 | 21 | 43 | 79 |
| Shoveler | 10 | 13 | 13 | 15 | 11 | 100 |
| Mallard | 9 | 12 | 9 | 11 | 16 | 87 |
| Gadwall | 3 | 4 | 12 | 14 | 13 | 78 |
| Green-winged teal | 2 | 3 | 5 | 6 | 4 | 75 |
| American widgeon | 3 | 4 | 1 | 1 | 3 | 100 |
| Total or Average | 74 | 100 | 85 | 100 | 129 | 84 |

*Source:* After Sergeant 1972. (Used with permission.)

other environmental factors as they influence the predator-prey complex is not to be underestimated. It appears that intercompensations frequently occur. Rabbit, hare, mallard, and grouse populations fluctuate according to other factors as well as to predation. Wildlife habitats, even in the absence of human influence, are subject to change that can precipitate change in the predator-prey relationship. Short-term investigations of the subject are thus probably quite suspect. Thus, Errington's (1963:192) admonishment to students of predation stands:

> On the basis of my own experience as a student of predation, the best advice I have to offer anyone interested in exploring the subject on his own responsibility or to those trying to obtain workable concepts of its mechanisms, is in short: Watch out for the compensations in attempting to distinguish between what does or does not count. When compensations are important in population dynamics they simply cannot be ignored in calculations as to regulation effects of mortality factors, if the truth is to be reached.

## MANAGEMENT OF PREDATOR-PREY RELATIONSHIPS

Predation on upland game birds is at times spectacular and highly visible to the public, but evaluation of control efforts to increase pheasant production in Minnesota provides insight into the economics and ecological aspects of control (Chesness, Nelson, and Longley 1968). Southern Minnesota was once very high quality pheasant habitat, but the clean-farming methods have greatly reduced winter cover. The study involved a 2560-acre area where control of the entire predator complex was attempted over a three-year period, and a 4080-acre area 2 miles away where control was not practiced. About 75 percent of the cropland is fall-plowed and bare of cover during the winter (Table 10.10). Winter cover, consisting of fencerows, ditches, sloughs, farmsteads, and other noncropland constituted about 9 percent of the control area and 6 percent of the uncontrolled area.

TABLE 10.10  Cover Types on Pheasant Predation Study Areas in Minnesota

| Cover Type | Percent |
|---|---|
| Crops (corn, soybeans, oats, alfalfa, etc.) | 77.25 |
| Pasture, retired cropland | 15.05 |
| Strip cover (fencerows, ditches) | 2.70 |
| Other (farmsteads, sloughs, roads, etc.) | 4.87 |
| Total | 99.87 |

*Source:* Chesness, Nelson, and Longley 1968. (Used with permission.)

A total of 434 predators, including skunks, raccoons, ground squirrels, house cats, crows, rats, weasels, foxes, owls, and woodchucks, were removed from the control area over the three-year period, using traps and poisonous-gas cartridges

(Table 10.11). Trapping was done during the nesting season, from 40 to 109 days. Nesting success was related to the quality of the nesting cover on each area (Table 10.12). Hatching success was 29 percent on the trapped area and 19 percent on the untrapped area, with success being greatest in areas of excellent cover on both areas. Pheasant breeding populations on the trapped area were lower in 1960 than on the untrapped area, but decreased less and were at a higher density in 1963 after control efforts were concluded.

TABLE 10.11   Total Predators Removed in 4–Square Mile Study Area in Three Years

| Predator | Number Removed |
|---|---|
| Skunks | 111 |
| Raccoons | 35 |
| Ground squirrels | 142 |
| House cats | 32 |
| Crows | 53 |
| Rats | 17 |
| Other (weasels, foxes, owls, woodchucks) | 44 |
| Total | 434 |

*Source:* Chesness, Nelson, and Longley 1968. (Used with permission.)

TABLE 10.12   Pheasant Nesting Success in Areas Where Predators Were Removed Compared to a Control, in Relation to a Rating of Quality of Nesting Cover

| Nesting Cover Rating | Number of Nests Observed | | | Percent of Nests Destroyed by Predators[a] | | |
|---|---|---|---|---|---|---|
| | Experimental Area | Control Area | Total | Experimental Area | Control Area | Total |
| Excellent | 30 | 25 | 55 | 17 | 48 | 30 |
| Good | 89 | 78 | 167 | 26 | 44 | 34 |
| Fair | 64 | 44 | 108 | 41 | 66 | 51 |
| Poor | 24 | 9 | 33 | 41 | 89 | 55 |

*Source:* Chesness, Nelson, and Longley 1968. (Used with permission.)

[a]Predation destroyed 18.7 percent, while farming pastures destroyed 24.8 percent, and flooding destroyed 1.7 percent on the experimental area. Predators destroyed 30.5 percent, farming pastures 26.6 percent, and flooding 0.2 percent of nests on the control run.

Costs of the control effort amounted to $21 per predator removed and $4.50 per additional pheasant chick produced (Table 10.13). Thus the "saving" of young pheasants from predation was achieved at a relatively high cost. The investigators concluded that the cost-benefit ratio of predator control would improve if control were implemented over a broader area, but it was doubtful if control would be of much benefit in most years. Dispersal of predators into control areas undoubtedly accounted for the continued high numbers removed during the study (85 in 1960, 127 in 1961, 222 in 1962). The control effort did not prevent an overall pheasant population decline during the study period.

**TABLE 10.13 Costs of Removing Predators**

|  | 1960 | 1961 | 1962 |
|---|---|---|---|
| Man-days effort | 64 | 102 | 123 |
| Wages, meals, mileage | $1360 | $2168 | $2614 |
| Cost per Acre per Year[a] | 80¢ | 80¢ | 80¢ |
| Total predators removed | 85 | 127 | 222 |
| Cost per predator[b] | $16.00 | $17.07 | $11.77 |
| Number of chicks per 100 Acres |  |  |  |
|   Experimental area | 33 | 43 | 26 |
|   Control area | 26 | 15 | 8 |
| Change in Breeding population (total birds) from 1960 to 1963[c] |  |  |  |
|   Experimental area | Down from 3.9 to 1.6 | | |
|   Control area | Down from 4.6 to 0.9 | | |

*Source:* Chesness, Nelson, and Longley 1968. (Used with permission.)

[a] For 2560 acres.

[b] Cost figures do not include expenditures for traps, baits, ammunition, and miscellaneous equipment. Average cost was $21.00 per year per predator removed, and $4.50 per additional chick produced.

[c] Numbers based on crowing counts.

A similar investigation conducted in South Dakota by Trautman, Fredrickson, and Carter (1974) revealed that intensive control of foxes only increased pheasant populations an annual average of 19 percent over a five-year period, at a control level that reduced the fox population by 83 percent. Control of foxes, badgers, raccoons, and skunks increased pheasant population size by 338 percent over the pre-control level.

The major impact of predator control was related to improved survival of juveniles and adults rather than to changes in rate of nesting success. Cost of controlling foxes average $30 per square mile, and for all mammals, $41.10. When all mammals were controlled, small rodents increased 18 percent when compared to uncontrolled check areas. These authors concluded the control of small carnivore populations should not be considered as a substitute for habitat improvement, but rather as a tool for enhancing production and carrying-capacity capabilities of existing habitat for pheasants. Predator control should be achieved by the public utilizing the predators for their values as fur and as a recreational resource rather than by agencies where costs are prohibitive.

Deer populations can also benefit in some instances from intensive predator control, as shown by the Texas investigations of Beasom (1974a, b) and Guthery and Beasom (1977). An intensive removal campaign on the King Ranch resulted in a reduction of 188 coyotes and 120 bobcats over a two-year period on two 5400-acre study areas (Table 10.14). Track counts were reduced from 8–10 coyotes and 1–1.5 bobcats on sets of 2-mile transects on each area in January to nearly no tracks in June of each year. Observed fawn to doe ratios were 0.47 fawns per doe

**TABLE 10.14   Predator Removal and Whitetail Deer Response, King Ranch, Texas**

|  | Experimental Area | | Control Area | |
|---|---|---|---|---|
|  | 1971 | 1972 | 1971 | 1972 |
| Predators removed |  |  |  |  |
| Coyotes | 129 | 59 | – | – |
| Bobcats | 66 | 54 | – | – |
| Track counts[a] |  |  |  |  |
| Coyotes | 8–10 | ~0 | 8–10 | 8–10 |
| Bobcats | 1–1.5 | ~0 | 1–1.5 | 1–1.5 |
| Number of deer per 100 acres[b] | 6.29 | 8.04 | 3.25 | 3.17 |
| Deer production (fawns per doe) | 0.47 | 0.82 | 0.12 | 0.32 |

*Source:* Beasom 1974a. (Used with permission.)

*Note:* Removal period ran from February 1, 1971, to June 30, 1972. Methods consisted of traps, M-44s, poison, and shooting. Each area was 5400 acres.

[a]Based on sets of 2-mile transects on each study area. Data under 1971 is actually for January 1972; 1972 data is for June 1972.

[b]Based on helicopter census.

on the experimental area and 0.12 fawns per doe on the uncontrolled area. Helicopter censuses revealed over twice as many deer on the controlled area as on the uncontrolled area.

A cost-benefit evaluation of the predator control operations was related to the intensity of the harvest. If only 10 percent of the surplus of turkeys and deer was taken, then the control effort cost more than the value of the game that was taken (Table 10.15). At 50 percent, a net return of 62¢ per acre was realized; at 100 percent, the net return was $2.59 per acre. Thus, the predator control effort was efficient only if a very high proportion of the surplus population produced by the control efforts was taken.

**TABLE 10.15   Cost-Benefits of Predator Control**

| Surplus Game | Value per Individual | Total Value by Percent of Surplus Harvested | | |
|---|---|---|---|---|
|  |  | 100% | 50% | 10% |
| Male turkeys | $50 | $ 4,350 | $ 2,175 | $435 |
| Male whitetails | $150 | 12,750 | 6,375 | 127 |
| Female whitetails | $50 | 4,200 | 2,100 | 420 |
| Total |  | $21,300 | $10,650 | $982 |
| Less costs[a] |  | −7,315 | −7,315 | −7,315 |
| Total net benefits |  | $13,985 | $3,335 | −$6,333 |
| Net return per acre on 5400 acres |  | $2.59 | $0.62 | −$1.17 |

*Source:* Beasom 1974b. (Used with permission.)

[a]Costs included truck rental, technician, traps, poison, rifle and cartridges, etc.

One of the most important experimental investigations of the effect of predation on waterfowl nesting success was conducted over a six-year period on the Agassiz National Wildlife Refuge in Minnesota (Balser, Dill and Nelson 1968). The investigations were motivated out of concern for a low rate of nesting success, which ran at 33–38 percent of duck nests hatching out after earlier investigations showed averages of 60 percent. The refuge was of course, being intensively managed for waterfowl production, and nest predation appeared to be a major factor in decreasing production (Table 10.16). The basic study plan consisted of removing nest predators from the west half of the refuge for three years with the east half serving as a control, and then reversing the predator removal operation to the east half for the next three years. Removal was directed at the entire predator complex, except snapping turtles and northern pike, through the use of strychnine-poisoned baits, live traps, and steel traps.

Table 10.16 summarizes results of the six-year study. A total of 1342 predators were removed from the treated areas, resulting in an increase in number of successful nests from 28.6 to 58.7 percent. Treated areas produced 1.56 times as many class 1, down-feathered ducklings as did the untreated areas, without any increase in number of breeding pairs. Breeding pairs appeared to fluctuate according

**TABLE 10.16    Predation Studies on Waterfowl**

| Predators Removed over a Six-Year Period by Poisoning and Trapping | |
|---|---|
| Species | Number |
| Raccoon | 444 |
| Skunk | 761 |
| Fox | 137 |
| | 1342 |

| Hatching-Success of Natural Duck Nests on Treated and Control Areas | | |
|---|---|---|
| | Treated Areas | Control Areas |
| Total number of nests | 247 | 112 |
| Percent of nests successful | 58.7 | 28.6 |

| Breeding Pair Counts | | | | | | |
|---|---|---|---|---|---|---|
| Species | 1959 | 1960 | 1961 | 1962[a] | 1963 | 1964[a] |
| Blue-winged teal | 6041 | 5584 | 7684 | 7346 | 5614 | 1673 |
| Mallard | 2504 | 4450 | 4228 | 918 | 1748 | 1195 |
| Gadwall | 1179 | 2217 | 2858 | 1974 | 2488 | 1110 |
| Total | 9724 | 12,251 | 14,770 | 10,238 | 9850 | 3978 |

*Source:* Balser, Dill, and Nelson 1968. (Used with permission.)
[a]Droughts in 1962 and 1964.

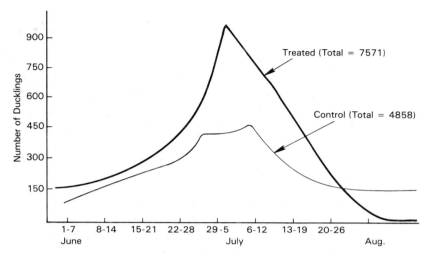

**Figure 10.8** Duckling hatching curves for 1950–1964, based on number of blue-winged teal, mallard, and gadwall ducklings observed on treated and control areas. From Balser, Dill, and Nelson 1968. (Used with permission.)

to water conditions rather than to the predator removal operation, with floods in 1962 and 1964 contributing to decreases.

Ducks are capable of renesting if the initial attempt fails. Theoretically, predation may serve to distribute the hatching period over a longer time span and therefore maintain a high rate of nesting success in the face of such adversities as temporary flooding or storms (Cartwright 1952). However, during this investigation predation was heavy enough to reduce duckling production without much compensatory effect, with the major effect of predator control being a two-week earlier peak of hatching (Figure 10.8).

Balser et al. (1968) presented important conclusions about the use of predator control as a management technique:

1. Measurements of the amount of nest destruction should be made before, during, and after control, to determine whether nest destruction is known to be severe enough to warrant control, whether the control is effective, and whether the costs of the control are justified. The costs of this control effort (1959–1964) were $3000, or 21¢ per additional duckling produced.

2. The entire predator complex should be controlled or compensatory predation by species not affected may occur.

3. No one method of control will suffice over long periods or under all conditions. Raccoons, for example, became shy of strychnine-laced eggs after the first season of control.

4. Special precautions in using poisoned baits are important to observe, with supervision of the control effort being critical.

5. Alternative means of alleviating predator losses should be investigated. Nesting concentrations along dikes and ponds in small islands of suitable habitat, are likely to suffer more serious predation losses than when nests are dispersed.

6. The importance of effecting a comprehensive public relations program is to be emphasized. Efforts to prevent misunderstanding, overoptimism, and accidents, and to explain the reasons for the control operation are needed.

7. General application of results from one investigation to other situations is to be avoided.

The investigators were very cautious about the last item, pointing out that the situation at Agassiz Refuge may have been unique.

This investigation illustrates the effects of predation in a situation where intensive managment of waterfowl and nesting habitat may have concentrated nesting populations and thereby inadvertently predisposed them to predation. This problem reduces itself to one of inadequate habitat, where creation of nesting cover was successful but where no attention to the potential concentrations of predators was given. In addition, it is noted that breeding populations were not increased due to the control efforts, even if duckling production was increased. The fate of these extra ducklings was not determined, and they may have been made available for harvest, a portion of the surplus may have found other breeding habitat, and some may have returned to the refuge to breed. The question of whether the effect of control extended through to augumentation of breeding stock is thus unanswered.

One argument against controlling predators is that their removal may cause increased numbers of prey such as rodents, lagomorphs, and deer, which can in turn increase in numbers to where range damage or competition with livestock becomes a problem. Schnell (1968) concluded, from comparison of cotton rat (*Sigmodon hispidus*) populations introduced on predator-free islands and populations subject to predation by a complex of at least eight different predators (two mammals, six avian species), that a "predator-limited" carrying capacity existed. A model of the annual cycle in population density of this rodent was presented, suggesting that predation could effectively reduce a cotton rat population to a level of 15 per acre in winter. These findings support those of Craighead and Craighead (1956) in that a mobile and highly diverse predator population may well serve to control rodent numbers, and prevent severe oscillations in prey density.

Conversely, Guthery and Beasom (1977) presented evidence from intensive short-term mammalian predator control efforts that little or no effect on density trends of bobwhite quail, scaled quail, rodents, or lagomorphs occurred. The Texas study involved a greater complexity of prey species, but did not consider avian predation. The Georgia study (Schnell 1968) involved evaluations of predation by the entire predator complex on a single prey species.

The theoretical aspects of predation indicate that one may expect to see a variety of responses in prey species to predation, and that predator control will have a highly variable effect on prey numbers, depending upon the local situation. Referring back to Leopold's original criteria, the abundance of prey and predators, plus the presence of buffers, will all weigh in to affect the interaction. For the present, the conclusions of Balser, et al. (1968) are well to heed. The role of predators and the tool of control is a highly complex issue, requiring constant evaluation and monitoring.

Nevertheless, predator control is a legitimate wildlife management tool. There will be circumstances where game populations can be enhanced by control of the predator. When introductions of species such as pronghorn are contemplated, predator control may also be indicated (Arrington and Edwards 1951). When endangered species are involved, predator control may again be justified. Rather than being a primitive phase of game management, predator control thus requires exercise of great discretion and judgment as a means of intensive population management. The inherent values of the predator complex itself must be weighed, as well as the benefits of its suppression. Only in specific instances should its use be considered in wildlife management, but at the same time we may realize that predators have intrinsic capabilities of responding in compensatory fashion, as much as the prey species we intend to benefit. Thus the object is not to cause local extinctions, but rather to manage populations, when indicated, so other species will occur at higher levels.

## MANAGEMENT PROGRAMS FOR LARGE PREDATORS

Bears, wolves, and mountain lions are classified as game species and as such require special management programs that account for their depredations on domestic livestock or other wildlife as well as their trophy value. Management must be flexible to accommodate the local situation and should be based on a knowledge of the biology of the population.

### Mountain Lions

Hornocker (1971) proposed a management plan for the mountain lion in Idaho that serves as a model for development of plans for this species across its range in areas where it may be hunted. Based on the long-term research in the central Idaho wilderness, the biology of the population pertinent to its management was described as follows:

1. The population has remained stable, and maintained a rather rigid social organization comprised of resident adults, juveniles accompanied by their mother, and transient adults.
2. The density was one resident adult per 12–14 square miles in winter which greatly decreased in summer. This density was regarded as a maximum density since the population was unhunted.
3. Resident population was 50 percent adult females, 20 percent adult males, and 30 percent young of the year.

4. Resident females produce young at two-year intervals, averaging 2.5 young per litter.

5. Resident females are essential to maintenance of the populations, but resident males are expendable if adjacent populations provide replacements to the resident population.

Harvests must obviously be held at levels below the total annual increment, implying control by permit and hunt-unit designation. The breeding female segment should be left intact and unexploited if at all possible in order to retain the breeding stock. Female lions will likely not breed unless they are established on a territory. Harvests should be uniform between populations to prevent overharvests in one unit since populations will decline in adjacent units if overharvest occurs. The permit hunt allows a check on the location, age, and sex of each individual taken, if hunters cooperate and provide the necessary information.

The suggested plan, to be successful, requires a knowledge of density and age structure, plus a level of competence among hunters enabling them to identify males from females. The density and biology of the species as identified from the research is probably applicable to other wilderness situations in the Northwest, but in the absence of information specific to an area, management units and quotas to be harvested will have to be established on a trial-and-error basis, then adjusted as more data are made available.

If depredations occur, Cain (1972) suggested removal of the individual offending cougar. Nonconsumptive permits that allow the hunter to chase and tree lions with dogs and to photograph them have been used to increase the recreational opportunities potentially available from the lion population without reducing its size.

The mountain lion is now a game animal in most states where it occurs. Priority for management is to maintain it as a game species, with control usually on a local basis as necessary. Hunters are ordinarily encouraged to take males, although either sex may be taken, accounting for the difficulty in recognition of sex in the field by hunters. Hunting of kittens and females accompanied by kittens is usually prohibited. Control of depredations on livestock is the responsibility of the U.S. Fish and Wildlife Service, in agreement and cooperation with the state wildlife organization, while control of mountain lion damage to wild game is ordinarily the responsibility of the state and is ordinarily accomplished through sport hunting, livetrapping, and translocation.

### Wolves

Wolf management has traditionally consisted of control through hunting, trapping, poisoning, and bounties. Alaska established a wolf bounty at $10 in 1915 (Harper 1970) and Ontario's first bounty was established in 1793 (Clarke 1970). This tradition continued until the late 1950s in Ontario, at which time the bounty was abolished and wolf management plans were initiated. As Clarke (1970) succinctly stated, "whatever else the wolf bounty has done, it never hurt the wolf." Following the abolishment of the bounty, extensive poisoning programs were initiated in Ontario, but these were subsequently replaced by management that provides for protection of wolves in parks and preserves, and hunting and trapping elsewhere. Persons suffering damage from wolves are allowed to kill them by any means on their own property. Occasionally wolves are taken in conjunction with deer habitat improvement projects where deer may concentrate and become subject to severe pressure from wolves if no control is implemented.

Alaska declared the wolf a big game animal in 1963 (Harper 1970). Rough correlations between increases of moose and caribou during the early 1960s, following the wolf control programs of the 1950s, and sharp declines of these species in the early 1970s, following cessation of control, prompted research into the wolf-moose and wolf-caribou relationships in several areas of Alaska by Gasaway et al. (1983). These investigators concluded that wolves can exert substantial control over moose (Table 10.17) and caribou populations that can prevent efforts to maintain high populations of prey. Wolf population levels are now being regulated by direct control by Alaska Department of Fish and Game personnel when moose and caribou populations are found to be low or declining because of low calf survival due to wolf predation. Gasaway et al. (1983) concluded that because populations of caribou and moose must be high enough to meet the needs of wildlife users, periodic removals of wolves are the most practical means of maintaining populations at huntable levels. There are cases in Alaska and other regions where caribou and moose populations cannot withstand human harvest and wolf predation without declining. Since many humans are dependent upon these species for sustenance in the northern regions, efforts to regulate both human harvest and predator numbers are justifiable.

Minnesota's wolf population was hunted and trapped without regulation until 1970, at which time these activities were forbidden on the Superior National Forest in the northeastern part of the state (Mech 1977). The species was declared endangered in 1974, and legal killing was prohibited thereafter, although poaching continued. The species has been reclassified from endangered to threatened and a management program has been implemented that accounts for the need to control depredations and to protect the species. This program was initially developed in 1970, but was not implemented until 1978, a delay that attests to the highly controversial nature of the wolf in this state.

The state now is divided into management zones in which different management strategies will be pursued. In the vicinity of the Boundary Waters Canoe Area, the wolf will be completely protected. Other zones containing significant populations may be subject to control by authorized state and federal employees if individuals commit depredations on lawfully present domestic animals.

Progress in wolf management has increased in recent years as information about the species and its relationships to big game and livestock have increased. Attempts to reestablish a timber wolf population in northern Michigan by transplanting Minnesota stock have not been successful (W. L. Robinson and Smith

**TABLE 10.17 Survival of Moose Calves and Yearlings before and after Wolf Reduction, Tanana Flats and Alaska Foothills Areas, Alaska**

| Area | Period | Calves per 100 Females | | Yearlings per 100 Females | | Wolf Density (km²/wolf) | |
|---|---|---|---|---|---|---|---|
| | | Mean | Standard Error | Mean | Standard Error | Mean | Standard Error |
| Tanana Flats | Before | 25 | | 17 | | 61 | |
| | After | 65 | 4 | 59 | 5 | 229 | 39 |
| Eastern foothills and mountains | Before | 9 | | 7 | | 77 | |
| | After | 45 | 6 | 25 | 10 | 144 | 26 |
| Western foothills and mountains | Before | 0 | | 7 | | 58 | |
| | After | 18 | 7 | 11 | 2 | 93 | 20 |

*Source:* Gasaway et al. 1983. (Used with permission.)

*Note:* Reductions of wolves to densities of less than one-third the original density on the Tanana Flats caused survival of yearlings to improve by over one-third, while reductions of less than half in the western foothills area caused little change because of predation by grizzly bears and greater year-long predation by wolves.

1977) but will be considered again as opportunities allow. There are obvious opportunities to establish wolf populations in the national parks and some wilderness areas of the west that should be taken advantage of.

### Black Bears

Black bears provide significant sport hunting opportunities virtually throughout their range. Both fall and spring hunts exist, and in some areas seasons extend through the entire year. Use of dogs is a tradition particularly in the southern United States. Black bears are being reintroduced into formerly occupied range in Arkansas, which attests to heightened interest in the species as a game animal.

Extensive damage to conifer tree reproduction by black bears has occurred in western Washington, prompting extensive research into the problem of alleviating the damage (Poelker and Hartwell 1973). Extension of hunting season length to year-long hunting with no bag limits did not prevent damage. A system of permits that allowed bears to be controlled by the Washington Forest Protection Association proved to be a solution to the problem. Also, black bears occasionally cause significant depredations on domestic livestock, and control through trapping and shooting by U.S. Fish and Wildlife Service personnel or state fish and game personnel occurs. Similarly, campground depredations are ordinarily controlled through livetrapping and transplanting to areas where campgrounds are not frequented. All such efforts are directed at individual offenders.

Bear management in national parks has evolved from programs designed to entertain visitors, such as establishing opportunities to view bears feeding at dumpgrounds, to policies of reestablishing wild populations that are not dependent on humans for sustenance and are not viewed in artificial settings. Black bear management in Yellowstone National Park involves public information and law enforcement programs that are designed to reduce artificial food sources such as those found at campgrounds and from car passengers who intentionally feed bears. A daily bear monitoring system that identifies locations of bears observed relative to developed areas and visitor activity serves to help warn visitors where they may encounter bear problems, and where they may see bears (Meagher 1977). Problem bears are first trapped and removed to isolated areas of little visitor use. If they return and continue to cause damage, they are retrapped or killed by National Park Service personnel, on a case by case basis that takes into account the nature of the damage. Unfortunately, individual visitors continue to cause problems by feeding bears, leaving ice chests unprotected at campgrounds, and engaging in other illegal or unintentional acts. Thus, the problem of bear management can be resolved to one of public education, and is directly related to the degree of public acceptance of, and cooperation with, the program.

Several evaluations of black bear harvest characteristics have been made. Black bears taken in fall are usually taken by hunters of other big game animals (Lindzey 1976, Willey 1971). Males tend to be more vulnerable to hunters than females (Willey 1971), although Lindzey (1976) and A. W. Erickson, Nellor, and

Petrides (1964) reported that hunters tend to identify female bears as males and found no differential vulnerability related to sex. Lindzey (1976) found that both pelts and meat were taken from 27 percent of bears harvested in Oregon, and that pelts from many bears taken in August were not used because they were not in prime condition.

Wildlife agencies have generally liberalized bear hunting regulations over the past decade in recognition that higher harvests could occur without harm to populations. However, because black bears are known to be vulnerable to hunter harvest under certain circumstances, better control of the take is needed. Hunters with well-trained dogs can exploit the black bear with a high degree of success. Bears that frequent readily accessible openings, such as tide marshes in Alaska in spring (McIlroy 1972), can be heavily harvested. Reduction in age structure of harvested bears and in hunter success are indices that have been used to detect population changes attributable to harvest.

A. W. Erickson (1959) reported that cubs as young as $5\frac{1}{2}$ months and as small as 18 pounds may be self-sufficient and capable of surviving without the presence of the mother, even if injured. This may be expected to vary between populations, and years. Lindzey (1976) reported that increased cub mortality during years of low cub production could be related to predation by adults but status of cubs relative to presence or absence of the mother was not available. Ability to locate food sources and suitable denning sites would also influence cub survival. The fact that cubs can survive at such young age, however, does raise possibilities for coping with problem adults with cubs. Cubs may be captured and released in areas of suitable habitat and low bear densities with hopes of surviving if the mother is killed. In areas where bear densities are high, however, removal of the mother may well reduce the chances of survival of the cubs, a fact that should be given consideration when hunting seasons and control operations are planned.

## PREDATION ON DOMESTIC LIVESTOCK

Predator control for the purposes of reducing or eliminating livestock losses has been an aim of wildlife management for as long as people and their domesticated livestock have lived in proximity to wildlands, and will continue to be. The issue is not whether we will continue to control predators, but rather how much control is necessary, and where it should be undertaken. Since before Massachusetts passed a bounty law in 1630, predators have been an issue in America. A long history of intensive effort has resulted in major reductions of grizzlies, wolves, and cougars from much of their original range and today the coyote is the main predator of concern in the contiguous United States. If W. B. Robinson's (1961) observations—that as the larger predators are reduced the smaller ones take over—apply, then perhaps the elimination of these big predators has served as a stimulus to coyote populations. However, the larger species are still subject to control where they exist in conflict with human activities. Grizzlies still prey on domestic livestock near Yellowstone National Park, just as they did 35 years ago when Murie (1948) discussed the problem. Alberta, as well as other provinces and states, still has problems with cougars, grizzlies, and wolves (Roy and Dorrance 1976).

The forerunner of the U.S. Fish and Wildlife Service, the Bureau of Biological Survey, became concerned with evaluations of predation as early as 1870, and became engaged in predator control activities in 1915 when Congress made the initial appropriation for this purpose (Cain 1972). The various states initiated control programs even earlier, but were most active in the 1930s and 1940s. The federal government has carried major responsibilities for control efforts, however, in cooperation with the states and private interests.

Predator control has been severely criticized by an increasingly large segment of the public, although it has been supported by ranchers, who suffer livestock losses, and those who felt predators were responsible for declines in wildlife populations. The assumptions are that predators do cause extensive livestock damage, and that the federal government has an obligation to protect the livestock owners interests. The livestock interests might be expected to reduce predator populations below that necessary if they assume the task. All of these considerations have weighed heavily in promoting federal action in predator control through the years in the United States. However, the controversy over the effectiveness and desirability of predator control has continued unabated to the present.

Two major investigations, a report to the Secretary of Interior in 1964, the Leopold Report (A. S. Leopold 1964), and one to the Council on Environmental Quality and the Secretary of Interior in 1972, the Cain Report (Cain 1972), have influenced the direction of predator control in recent years. The Leopold Report was highly critical of the old Predator and Rodent Control Division of the U.S. Fish and Wildlife Service, where the control program was administered. Indiscriminant, nonselective control was criticized for its inefficiency, unnecessary killing of individual predators that were not causing damage, and its effects on nontarget species that were inadvertently killed. A greater degree of professionalism among government trappers was suggested, including a public relations aspect to enhance understanding of the complexities and realities of control. Leopold concluded that much more control was being practiced than was necessary.

The Cain Report found similar inadequacies seven years later, with the following statement serving to point out the problem: "As reexamined in 1971, it is clear that the basic machinery of the federal cooperative-supervised program contains a high degree of built-in resistance to change" (Cain 1972:2). Fifteen recommendations were made to improve the program (Table 10.18).

**TABLE 10.18  Recommendations from Report to the Council of Environmental Quality and the Department of Interior by the Advisory Committee on Predator Control**

1. We recommend that federal-state cooperation in predator control be continued, and that all funds in its support come from appropriations by Congress and the legislatures.
2. We recommend that immediate Congressional action be sought to remove all existing toxic chemicals from registration and use for operational predator control. We further recommend that these restrictions extend to those toxicants used in field control of rodents whose action is characterized by the secondary poisoning of scavengers. Pending,

and in addition to, such Congressional action, we recommend that the Secretary of the Interior disallow use of the aforementioned chemicals in the federal operational program of predator and rodent control, and that this ruling be made a standard in cooperative agreements with the states. Moreover, we recommend that the individual states pass legislation to ban the use of toxicants in predator control.

3. We recommend that the field force of the Division of Wildlife Services be professionalized to emphasize employment of qualified wildlife biologists capable of administering and demonstrating a broadly based program of predator management.

4. We recommend that in all states a cooperative trapper-trainer extension program be established as a means of aiding landowners in the minimum necessary control of predators on private land.

5. We recommend that Congress provide some means of alleviating the economic burden of livestock producers who experience heavy losses by predators.

6. We recommend that grazing permits and leases written by federal land management agencies provide for possible suspension or revocation of grazing privileges if regulations governing predator control are violated.

7. We recommend that all methods of predator control be prohibited in statutory Wilderness Areas.

8. We recommend that federal and state legislation be passed that would make the shooting from aircraft of wildlife, including predators and game animals, illegal except under exceptional circumstances and then only by authorized wildlife biologists of the appropriate federal and state agencies.

9. We recommend to the Federal Aviation Authority that a provision be made for suspending or revoking the license of a private pilot and the confiscation of the aircraft when he knowingly carries a passenger whose acts lead to conviction for illegal predator control, such as shooting from the aircraft or distributing poisons.

10. We recommend that action be taken by Congress to rule out the broadcast of toxicants for the control of rodents, rabbits, and other vertebrate pests on federal lands, and that the possibility of correlative action be explored for private lands as well.

11. We recommend a long-term research program based in the Division of Wildlife Research, Bureau of Sport Fisheries and Wildlife, that would cover the gamut of ecological problems associated with predators.

12. We recommend that the Division of Wildlife Research of the Bureau of Sport Fisheries and Wildlife undertake a detailed socio-economic study of cost-benefit ratios of predator control as a means of evaluating the need for and efficacy of the program and its separate parts.

13. We recommend that the Division of Wildlife Research of the Bureau of Sport Fisheries and Wildlife be delegated the responsibility for the study of the epidemiology of rabies in the field by a team of specialists provided with adequate funding.

14. We recommend that Congress give the Secretary of Interior authority to take measures necessary to protect all species of predators that have been placed on the Endangered Species List by the Federal Government.

15. We recommend that the several states take measures to supplement the federal protection of rare and endangered species by enacting laws and taking measures to protect locally rare populations.

---

*Source:* Cain 1972. Committee members were S. A. Cain, J. A. Kadlec, D. L. Allen, R. A. Cooley, M. G. Hornocker, A. S. Leopold, and F. H. Wagner.

One recommendation, that federal-state cooperation be continued and that funding come from appropriations by Congress and the legislatures, illustrates an important concept in wildlife management. First, wildlife species are the concern of everyone, they are public property, vested within each state. While it may seem desirable to allow the individual who is suffering damage to be responsible for control, as McCabe and Kozicky (1972) urge, this may well lead to indiscriminate mortality. Also, predators have other values to people, are an integral part of the wildlife heritage, and deserve equal consideration along with other forms of wildlife. This gives implicit recognition of the tendency of individuals, when faced with damage to their property by predators, to desire more intensive control than is necessary.

Another controversial recommendation, removal of toxicants as a control measure, was subsequently implemented through presidential executive order. Poisoning of nontarget species, and the inhumaneness of poisons, especially strychnine, were at issue. Evidence reviewed by the committee did suggest that the use of sodium monofluoroacetate, compound 1080, did achieve a reduction in coyote numbers after it became widely used in the 1940s (Figure 10.9) and that this reduction was correlated with reduced predation losses of sheep (Figure 10.10). However, these figures were reported to the U.S. Fish and Wildlife Service and the U.S. Forest Service. When data for sheep and lamb losses to all causes reported to the Statistical Reporting Service, U.S. Department of Commerce, are compared with those reported to the U.S. Fish and Wildlife Service and the U.S. Forest Service, no differences in losses pre- and post-1080 introduction are apparent (Figure 10.11). The following explanations have been proposed for the discrepancies between the two sets of data: both sets are biased, the level of predation on sheep is too low to affect total losses; or predatory and nonpredatory losses are compensatory. The Leopold Report (A. S. Leopold 1964) recognized that 1080 was an efficient and humane means of controlling coyotes, and use of selective poisons in a prudent manner is probably a viable tool in control operations. Dorrance and Roy (1976) suggested that sheep losses in Alberta where poison was used were lower than in the United States in 1974, where poisons were banned.

The cooperative trapper-trainer programs recommended by Cain (1972) are efforts to allow individuals who are receiving predator damage to help themselves through supervision and education. These programs often, but not always, emphasize the use of traps, although these can be highly nonselective of the animals taken, and coyotes are notorious for learning to avoid them. W. E. Howard (1974) feared that implementation of this program would increase wildlife losses. A. S. Leopold (1964) pointed out that the current cost of government control exceeded the losses of privately owned livestock, so some modification was definitely in order. The cooperative systems have worked well in midwestern states (Sampson and Nagel 1948; Henderson and Boggess 1977), but may not be as effective on the western public ranges where distances are great, people are fewer, and a different tradition centered on the "Government trapper" exists. Cooperative programs have advantages in that they cost less, involve fewer public employees, have an educational value, and allow the individual suffering the damage to do the actual control, under supervision. Public agencies provide advice, control devices, and supervision that hopefully reduces the opportunity for abuse by taking more wildlife than necessary.

Other recommendations of the Cain Report have also been implemented.

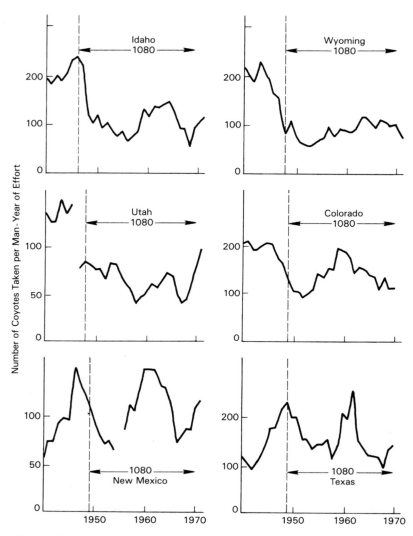

**Figure 10.9** Annual number of coyotes taken per man-year of effort in six western states. From Cain 1972.

Predator control has largely ceased in wilderness areas, although the occasional grizzly is still removed from areas where campsites and campers are being disturbed. Long-term research efforts, including work in Texas, Utah, and Montana to understand the ecology of the coyote as a prerequisite to understanding depredations more fully, have been implemented (Knowlton 1972, Wagner and Stoddart 1972; O'Gara 1982). A number of authorities concerned with predators have recognized

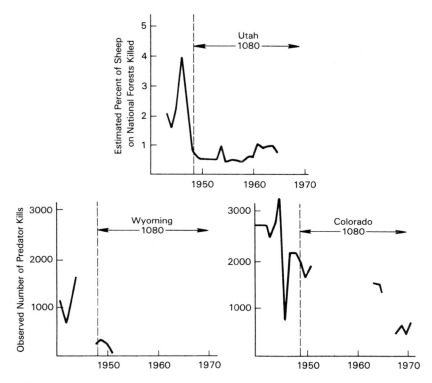

**Figure 10.10** Predation losses of sheep reported by the U.S. Fish and Wildlife Service and U.S. Forest Service. From Cain 1972.

the need to understand the creature being controlled as a prerequisite to effecting proper management (Knowlton 1972, Berryman 1972; Hornocker 1972).

Coyotes do cause substantial losses of sheep that graze on open range (O'Gara 1982). Losses to a herd in Montana despite predator control comprised 30 percent of the lamp crop one year and none the next, illustrating extremes that have been documented (O'Gara 1982). However, investigations of sheep losses in Wyoming by Tigner and Larson (1977) and in Idaho by Nass (1977) revealed less than 3 percent of the populations under study were lost to predation, where predator control was in progress. The Idaho investigations indicated that terrain and vegetation that prevented effective control of coyotes by aerial gunning was responsible for increased predation. Inexperienced and unsupervised herders and poor management of ewes and lambs or lambing grounds were implicated in the Wyoming study. Coyotes have consistently been responsible for the major share of the predation on sheep, but domestic dogs, golden eagles, bears, cougars, and bobcats are also involved. Lambs are more vulnerable to predation than ewes, but physical condition is not an important factor in predation on domestic sheep (Tigner and Larson

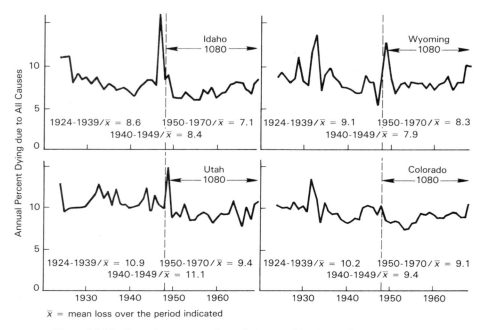

Figure 10.11   Annual percentage loss of sheep and lambs to all causes. $\bar{x}$ = mean loss over the period indicated. From Cain 1972.

1977). It is possible that the more vigorous lambs actually attract the attention of predators.

Balser (1974) reported that while a large number of ranchers sustain sheep losses to coyotes, most ranchers suffer minimal damage (Figure 10.12). This would suggest that certain localities and ranching operations are more susceptible to coyote predation than others. Dorrance and Roy (1976) indicated that predation losses in northern Alberta where forest cover is more prevalent were higher than on the southern Alberta prairies (Table 10.19). Larger bands of sheep were more susceptible to predation than smaller bands. When predation occurred on confined flocks, it tended to be severe. Coyotes accounted for 88 percent of the reported losses to predators, but dogs, wolves, black bears, and cougars were also implicated.

Connelly and Longhurst (1975) provided insight into the effects of different levels of control on coyote populations through the use of a model (Figure 10.13). The primary effects of control are to reduce coyote densities, of course, but control also stimulates density-dependent changes in birth and natural death rates. Immigration to the control area is also stimulated. Assumptions in the model are that 70 percent of the adult females and 10 percent of the yearling females produce litters when uncontrolled, and that 90 and 70 percent of adult and yearling females, respectively, produce litters when the population is artificially reduced to 50 percent of the uncontrolled density. Further, an increase in litter size from 4.5 to 9.0 pups was assumed to occur where the population was controlled, and the natural

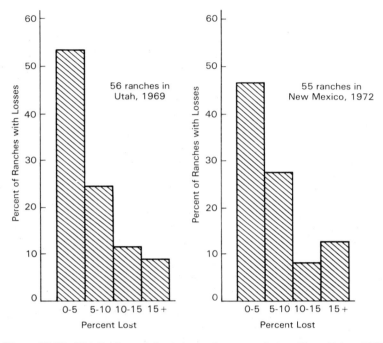

**Figure 10.12**  Distribution of sheep losses due to predation. From Balser 1974. (Used with permission.)

**TABLE 10.19  Sheep Losses to Predators and Other Factors in Alberta (percent of sheep population)**

| Cause of Loss | Northern Parkland | | Prairie | | Provincewide | |
|---|---|---|---|---|---|---|
| | Ewes | Lambs | Ewes | Lambs | Ewes | Lambs |
| Predation | 3.2 | 6.8 | 1.1 | 3.2 | 1.6 | 2.8 |
| Other[a] | 5.9 | 13.7 | 5.8 | 7.7 | 5.0 | 12.9 |
| Total | 9.1 | 20.5 | 6.9 | 10.9 | 6.6 | 15.7 |

*Source:* Dorrance and Roy 1976. (Used with permission.)

[a]"Other" includes lambing, disease, bloat, and poisonous plants.

annual adult mortality rate was reduced from 40 to 10 percent. A population of 100 coyotes would then stabilize at 72 six years after control was instigated (Figure 10.14). Over 75 percent of the population would have to be taken annually to cause its extinction at 50+ years after control efforts were initiated. In addition, populations can rebound to precontrol levels within five years after termination of a 75 percent control effort and within three years after control at a 50 percent level.

This simulation shows how remarkably resilient coyote populations can be to control efforts, assuming that the compensatory responses specified in the model

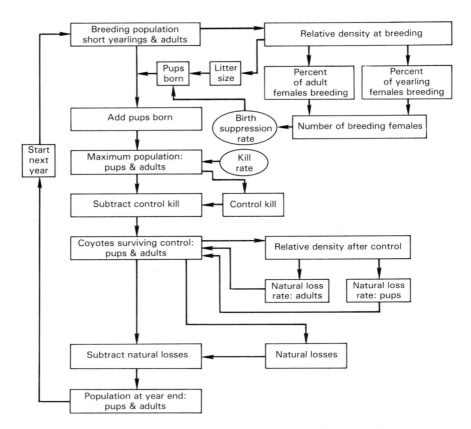

**Figure 10.13** Coyote population dynamics model. From Connelly and Longhurst 1975. (Used with permission.)

occur. Evidence that coyote populations fluctuate dramatically in conjunction with food supplies, even where intensively controlled (Clark 1972), suggests that control efforts will be more effective when coyote numbers are reduced through prey scarcity and compensatory responses are less apt to be operating as effectively. Nevertheless, the compensatory response in reproduction is one reason why efforts to control only the offending animals are advocated. Other reasons center on the loss of efficiency at attempting general, prophylactic control, plus ecological and ethical reasons.

Control of only the offender is important when larger, scarcer carnivora are involved. Control using nonlethal means such as livetrapping and transplanting is definitely preferable except in the most difficult of circumstances. However, Cain (1972) points out that, with reference to coyotes, the correlation between population density and sheep losses may indicate a need to suppress populations rather than just offending individuals of this species, since offenders may constitute a rela-

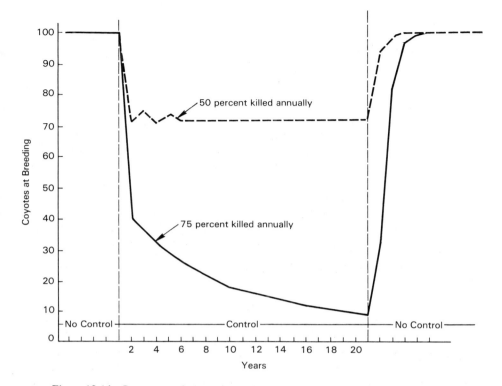

**Figure 10.14**  Coyote population responses to control. From Connelly, and Long-hurst 1975. (Used with permission.)

tively constant proportion of the population. Control efforts will thus vary with the species involved and the specific situation.

Predator control should not be either an objective or a goal, but rather a means to accomplish a broader management objective such as reduction of sheep losses (Berryman 1972). Control should be applied only to the extent necessary to achieve the objective, meaning that evaluations of the effort in terms of the desired result are necessary. Decisions to control should be made in the context of all resource values involved, and with the cooperation of all individuals and agencies concerned. Esthetic, social, economic, ecological, and political considerations must be weighed, and all have a legitimate place in the decision making process.

Knowlton (1972) identified four situations where control is indicated. First, there is the need to suppress populations to avoid epizootics or preclude economic hazards, such as livestock losses, resulting from "sheer numbers of coyotes." A second situation arises when local, short-term depredations occur. A third situation involves areas where coyotes pose consistently high risks and where the only suitable alternative is elimination of the coyote population from the area. This situation leads to a fourth, which is a need to restrict immigration to high-risk areas from adjacent areas.

Whenever general population reduction is desired, as would occur in situations 1 and 3, control efforts should be undertaken after dispersal decreases and prior to whelping, directed at the resident breeding population. Control efforts at other times may be less efficient since much of the population will be reduced naturally anyway, and the effort is supplanting natural mortality. Figure 10.15 illustrates annual coyote population fluctuations in Kansas, showing the larger mortality of pups in May through July. Control efforts during this period would be inefficient except in local situations.

Where short-term reductions are desired, spot control at the time depredations are occurring seems useful. Such control efforts could be initiated shortly before the depredations are anticipated and should be discontinued after the critical period. Control will have to be accomplished annually, since no carryover effect on the coyote population can be anticipated.

Efforts to prevent immigration to chronic high-risk areas probably mean intense population suppression not only in the areas of depredation but in adjacent areas as well. Knowlton (1972) recommended directing the control effort in adjacent areas at the individuals that are likely to disperse, namely, pups and yearlings,

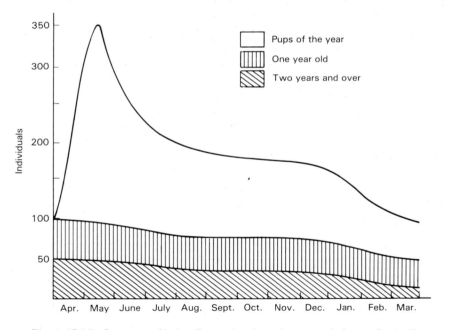

**Figure 10.15**  Coyote population fluctuation throughout a typical year. On April 1, approximately 50 percent of the population is composed of yearlings. Each 100 individuals (50 pairs) will produce an average of 250 young by mid-May. Decrease is rapid through May, June, and July, then stabilizes until the winter hunting season. By the next March, again approximately half of the coyotes are yearlings. From Gier 1968. (Used with permission.)

rather than at breeding adults. Another alternative is the use of antifertility agents (Balser 1964). Field tests of this method have not been very successful, since many coyotes were not exposed to baits, and the agent diethylstilbestrol is effective for only a limited period (Linhart, Brusman, and Balser 1968). Results of field testing diethylstilbestrol on foxes were also only partially effective (Oleyar and McGinnes 1974). The difficulty of implementing control to reduce immigration is that dispersal of coyotes can occur over long distances. Migrant coyotes from Yellowstone Park average 28 miles travelled, with some moving 115 miles from park boundaries (W. B. Robinson and Cummings 1951).

*Aversive conditioning* involves injecting sheep carcasses with chemicals such as lithium chloride that act as emetic agents. Those carcasses are distributed in areas where coyotes prey on sheep, where the carcasses will be scavenged, causing the coyote to vomit and thereby become conditioned against eating sheep (Gustavson et al. 1974). This method, if successful, would allow coyote populations to stabilize in an area with reproduction and survival of pups being lower, and reduce depredations to sheep. Coyotes apparently learn to avoid carcasses laced with lithium chloride and prefer to kill prey than eat dead animals (Conover, Francik, and Miller 1977). Coyotes obviously are capable of learning to avoid adverse agents, a major reason for their continued existence in the face of heavy exploitation.

The crux of the predator control issue is to find means to accommodate the legitimate needs of those suffering losses with the needs of the wildlife resource involved. We should recognize that it is better to manage predator populations, even if this means elimination of some populations from local areas, in order to provide a better attitude and tolerance of the species involved over broader areas. In the case of common predators, this does not pose a difficult problem. However, in the case of the rarer species, whose ranges and populations are already greatly reduced, it may mean that those suffering losses will have to be accommodated in some fashion other than by reducing the predators. While federal or state subsidy in the form of direct economic relief may be indicated, as Cain (1972) suggests, perhaps we may consider that these predators are valuable enough to warrant the reverse— reduction or alteration of human activity in areas where these species exist. Since public lands invariably comprise a large proportion of the remaining grizzly, cougar, and wolf range, such accommodations to serve these species may be entirely acceptable to a large majority of the public. Perhaps Cain (1972:33) summarizes the problem well with the following statements:

> The speciation of living things has taken place over such long time periods that even small tendencies toward selectivity of prey by predators would have evolutionary effects. The inscrutable culling of predation has been a major factor in producing in game animals those qualities of alertness and escape most prized by sportsmen today. There is an implied long-term penalty in the kind of intensive management that would eliminate predation and allocate the annual production of big-game herds, as much as possible, to the gun. This abrogates the primordial selection process and redirects speciation in unpredictable directions.

None of the higher animals of this world survives alone. The continued existence of each is dependent on the ecosystem of which it is a part and in which it plays some functional role. Through a higher degree of ecological understanding, it will be possible to devise land-use and wildlife management programs that will utilize natural constructive processes and the mutual dependencies of species. In terms of both rodent and predator control operations, even the more obvious innovations of policy and program have hardly been tried.

# 11

# Population Exploitation

## INTRODUCTION

Regardless of whether or not we are dealing with wildlife species that are hunted, a knowledge of how a population responds to exploitation is important. We may define *exploitation* as any form of artificially induced mortality, which would include that accruing to a species affected by a pesticide application as well as that attributable to hunting or trapping. Exploitation can thus be distinguished from *natural mortality*, which results from causes such as predation, disease, or starvation. However, the distinction is not clear, since humans so often influence "natural" mortality as well. However, exploitation refers to mortality caused directly by humans, acting upon a population either by plan or inadvertently.

It is important to recognize that the same principles apply to nongame species and game species alike, whether the mortality was caused intentionally or not. However, it is more important to realize that each population responds to exploitation according to its characteristics; to the nature, timing, and duration of the exploitation; and to the effect on other organisms that it interacts with. Thus, application of data from one population to another of the same species that exhibits a different age structure or reproductive rate, and is influenced by environmental factors of a different kind and magnitude is quite inappropriate. We can tolerate such activity as long as exploitation is low relative to the potential, but as exploitation becomes more intensive, information from the population in question becomes necessary.

Populations in general should be considered resilient entities, capable of responding to external influences so as to ameliorate their effects on the general size of the population. The loss of one individual is generally not to be considered a permanent loss to the population, because compensations occur to replace it. Compensation of exploitation in the form of more immigration to a population, less emigration from it, increased natality, and increased survival cannot be ignored. Changes in individual behavior such as reproductive status resulting from the establishment of a breeding territory may serve to compensate mortality. Additionally, one form of mortality may be substituted in part for another—hunter harvest may reduce rates of predation loss, for instance. Still, a population is in fact temporarily reduced when an individual is removed, and this is much more readily observed than are the compensations. Also, the consequences to a population resulting from the removal are delayed, sometimes for a considerable period of time. As a result, attention is often focused on the mortality and its consequences are ignored.

If removal of individuals from a population is not compensated for in some way, the end result will be extinction. Let us recognize that prey have evolved to cope with predation and other natural mortality factors by adjusting natality and survival rates. The assumptions that exploitation may either substitute for some of the natural mortality or that a population can respond in other ways is critical and implicit in wildlife management.

On the other hand, population levels do fluctuate in response to variations in mortality rates. Populations also compensate in different ways and at different rates. The real questions are whether exploitative and natural mortality are compensatory or additive, to what degree the various sources of mortality substitute for each other, and what time intervals are required to achieve the compensation.

In the case of endangered species at low population levels, removal of any one individual can nevertheless be important. Many such species are $K$-selected, indicating life expectancy is great once adulthood is reached but chances of survival to breeding age is low, age to breeding maturity is long-delayed, intervals between breeding are long, and compensations are slow or absent. In such cases, a mature breeder may not be easily replaced, and the nonbreeders themselves become important for their potential contribution to the population. The response to exploitation can in these cases be effectively nil and efforts to stop human-induced mortality are to be supported.

We cannot ignore the fact that exploitation is seldom the only form of mortality, and we must have some knowledge of how exploitation is interacting with other mortality factors impinging on the population. Knowledge about the natural regulation of numbers is not to be considered of only theoretical significance. Rather, it is essential to understand how a population responds to natural mortality factors if we are to judge how a population compensates for exploitation or how exploitation interacts with natural mortality. For most game populations, opportunities to determine what regulates numbers in the absence of human influence are extremely limited, since exploitation is so all-pervasive and the ecosystems in which they exist are modified. However, where exploitation rates are low or nonexistent and ecosystems, including predators, competitors, vegetation, and factors influencing each, are still relatively intact, we do have a chance to understand these issues.

An often forgotten aspect of exploitation is the effect it might have on associated species. We have occasionally directed our attention toward harvests of one species, such as elk, to favor a more desirable species, such as bighorn sheep, but the intended effects on other species as a result of exploiting one species are not well understood. We still pay most attention to the population we are interested in without considering other populations. Holt and Talbot (1978) reported the serious and unanticipated consequences of seining for tuna on associated porpoise populations. One may speculate that the illegal exploitation of some species, such as moose, which are mistaken for elk, has been a significant population depressant.

Exploitation, like so much of wildlife biology, must thus be placed in the ecological contest within which the population exists to be fully understood. The temptation is to focus strictly on the artificially caused mortality without considering other factors affecting the population. When viewed in this context, the issue of understanding how populations fluctuate is indeed complicated, and given the general level of hard data available for any given population, one must once again reflect on the value of good judgment, insight, and intuition, all of which are part and parcel of population management as commonly practiced and continue to make wildlife management an art.

## YIELD THEORY

Assume, for the purposes of illustrating yield theory, that a highly productive white-tailed deer population of 100 exists on high-quality habitat. Assume that this population is growing unchecked, with no mortality, and the age distribution is stable. The doe to fawn ratio in fall is 100:100; and the sex ratio of adults is 50:100 ($\male$:$\female$), with the sex ratio of fawns being equal. Age-specific natality rates are as follows:

Fawns (6 month old): 50 percent breed, each producing one fawn.

Yearlings (18 months old): 100 percent breed, each producing one fawn.

Adults: 100 percent breed, each producing two fawns.

The breeding population consists of 100 deer including 20 males over one year old; 40 females, 10 of which are yearlings; and 40 fawns, 20 of which are males. In terms of numbers of deer produced the next spring, we have

30 adult females × 100% breeding × 2 fawns each = 60 fawns

10 yearling females × 100% breeding × 1 fawn each = 10 fawns

20 female fawns × 50% breeding × 1 fawn each = 10 fawns

total fawn production = 80 fawns

breeding population = 100

next fall breeding population = 180

The formula for unchecked population growth is

$$N_t = N_o e^{rt}$$

where

$N_t$ = population at time $t$

$N_o$ = population at time $o$

$e$ = natural logarithm

$r$ = coefficient of population growth

$t$ = time

In our example,

$$N_o = 100$$
$$N_t = 180$$
$$t = 1 \text{ year}$$

We wish to calculate the finite rate of increase, $\lambda$, which is done using the formula

$$\lambda = \frac{eN_t - eN_o}{t}$$

$$= \frac{e180 - e100}{t}$$

$$= \frac{5.19296 - 4.60517}{1}$$

$$= 0.58779$$

$$= 0.59$$

Assume the carrying capacity $K$ for the habitat in question is 1000 deer. This is arbitrarily specified as the level at which additional deer cause damage to their habitat, which in turn causes a reduction in the population. We may "grow" this population, using the following formula:

$$\frac{\Delta N}{\Delta t} = \lambda \frac{K - N}{K}$$

where

$\Delta N/\Delta t$ = rate of increase of population per unit of time, or yield

$\lambda$ = finite rate of population growth, or $e^r$

$N$ = population size

$K$ = population size at carrying capacity

$K - N/K$ = unutilized opportunity for population growth

The population grows as indicated in Figure 11.1. $K$ is reached at 13 years, and the population growth follows the classic sigmoid curve, with an accelerating, inflection, and decelerating phase.

It is important to recognize that the assumptions of a stable age distribution, and existence of no other mortality do not occur in nature, for all practical purposes. The hypothetical example is thus useful only to illustrate the theory involved and would not be usefully applied to the field situation. First of all, $K$ as defined

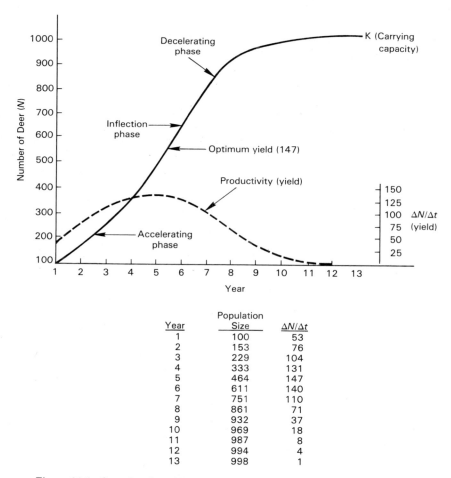

| Year | Population Size | $\Delta N/\Delta t$ |
|------|-----------------|---------------------|
| 1 | 100 | 53 |
| 2 | 153 | 76 |
| 3 | 229 | 104 |
| 4 | 333 | 131 |
| 5 | 464 | 147 |
| 6 | 611 | 140 |
| 7 | 751 | 110 |
| 8 | 861 | 71 |
| 9 | 932 | 37 |
| 10 | 969 | 18 |
| 11 | 987 | 8 |
| 12 | 994 | 4 |
| 13 | 998 | 1 |

**Figure 11.1** Growth of a white-tailed deer population, illustrating the relationship between productivity and carrying capacity.

will vary with such factors as snow depths and precipitation patterns, which affect vegetation growth, which influences $K$. The same factors will affect the coefficient of population growth and the age distribution. The deterministic model predicts an exact outcome given specific conditions and is thus an oversimplified statement of actual population growth.

D. E. Davis (1973) cautions that $r$ is derived as a constant and its calculation from the logistic equation is invalid because assumptions do not hold. The term $\Delta N/\Delta t$ should be used to describe rates of increase rather than $r$. D. E. Davis (1973) provided an example using starling population data from Massachusetts, where $r$ is defined as the rate of increase by subtracting deaths from births, equal to 0.6 in the example. The equation used was

$$\frac{\Delta N}{\Delta t} = bN\frac{K-N}{K} - dN\frac{K-N}{K}$$

where

$b$ = number of births per individual (birth rate)

$d$ = number of deaths per individual (death rate)

The starling population trends follow patterns observed in the hypothetical example, and the principles that were reported still are applicable. Notice that in our example with the white-tailed deer, no mortality was assumed so $b = r$ and $d = 0$, cancelling the last term of the equation.

The delayed logistic model was observed by Caughley (1976:210) to provide a good fit to ungulate populations even though the assumptions involved are "biologically nonsensical." The model was defined by Hutchinson (1948) as

$$\frac{\Delta N(t)}{\Delta t} = rN_t[1 - N(t-T)/K]$$

where

$t$ = time interval

$T$ = the time lag involved in responding to population density change

If $N(t-T)/K$ is considered as an average population size roughly equal to the regeneration time of vegetation following browsing (or any other factor that influences population response to fluctuations influencing $K$), the model becomes more realistic (May 1973). If $T = 0$, as in our hypothetical model, $N = K$ and there is a stable equilibrium population. This means, for instance, that vegetation recovers from browsing within one year after browsing occurs, and the hypothetical population responds as previously shown since the time interval over which the population changes is the same as the lag.

While the logistic model has been criticized, Wagner (1969) stated that it and its implications are sufficiently close to population behavior to be useful conceptual tools and first approximations. Thus the logistic theory is the fundamental basis upon which population exploitation, or harvests, rests (Ricker 1954; Wagner 1969; Gross 1969; Holt and Talbot 1978). It assumes that as a population is reduced below $K$, a surplus of young will be produced beyond the number that is needed to sustain the population at that level.

Silliman and Gutsell (1958) provide the following principles involved in the theory of exploitation:

1. Any exploitation of an animal population reduces its abundance.
2. Below a certain exploitation level, animal populations may be resilient, increasing their survival and/or growth rates and production rates to compensate for the individuals removed.
3. Where populations are regulated primarily through density-dependent processes, exploitation rates (up to the maximum sustained yield) will tend to increase productivity and reduce natural mortality of the remaining individuals.
4. Exploitation rates can reach a point at which extinction of the population will occur if continued.
5. Somewhere between no exploitation and excessive exploitation there lies a level at which the maximum sustained yield can be obtained.
6. The maximum exploitation rate is at least partially a function of the biotic potential or production rate of the species.
7. The age composition and the number of animals remaining after exploitation are key factors in the dynamics of exploited animal populations.

Caughley (1976:227) provided additional principles about yield curves:

1. If a population is stable in numbers [($K$ in our example)] it must be reduced below that density to generate a croppable surplus.
2. For each density to which a population is reduced, there is an appropriate sustained yield.
3. For each sustained yield, there are two density levels from which it can be harvested (i.e., about 73 animals may be harvested from a population of 150 or a population of 870, if $K = 1000$ and all other assumptions hold).
4. There is only one density at which a maximum sustained yield may be harvested (MSY of 147 is taken from the hypothetical population when it is at 464 animals).

Holt and Talbot (1978) provide assumptions in using this model, all of which are very difficult to test in practice:

1. The stock is more or less self-contained.
2. The stock has attained, before exploitation began, a steady state at carrying capacity.

3. There are no significant trends in carrying capacity during the period of exploitation.

4. The nature of the implied density dependence of reproduction, growth and/or natural mortality, and, in particular, any time lags in the response of the stock to exploitation, are not such as to cause fluctuations of large amplitude in the stock.

5. The process of reducing the initial stock by exploitation is reversible.

Holt and Talbot (1978) point out that the effects of exploitation on age composition is often ignored, as is the effect on social organization and behavior. Obviously, if exploitation tends to reduce the age structure of a population where older animals are most fecund, the effect on reproduction and survival of young will not be compensatory. R. M. Laws (1974) demonstrated that the nature of the early cropping systems for African elephants, which concentrated on old or barren cows, served to remove the leaders thereby increasing group sizes, which in turn created more, rather than the intended less, grazing pressure on the habitat. Significant trends in carrying capacity are often related to changes in habitats, which again illustrates the intimate tie between population and environment, and implies that attempts to assess population response to exploitation without assessment of critical habitat factors will often be only partially valid.

## COMPENSATORY VERSUS ADDITIVE HUNTING MORTALITY

The question of whether or not exploitation can be compensated for is in fact a major issue. If hunting is a compensatory form of mortality then populations may be presumed to fluctuate in response to other factors and stocks are little affected by exploitation. However, if hunting is additive to other forms of mortality then it serves as a population depressant. For populations that annually produce large numbers of offspring that are lost before the next reproductive period, exploitation of this biological surplus will not affect the subsequent year's breeding stock. For populations that produce offspring that would be added to the subsequent breeding stock in the absence of exploitation, artificially caused mortality is additive and reduces population density. Additive mortality does not necessarily imply that the population is not capable of withstanding exploitation, since the level of exploitation, if kept at or below the level that replaces the breeding population will not suppress it. Also, in instances where population suppression is desired, exploitation at rates above the replacement level will serve to accomplish that purpose. D. R. Anderson and Burnham (1976) state the hypotheses involved as described below.

**Hypothesis of completely compensatory mortality.**

$$V = V_0 + bH \text{ for } H \leqslant c$$

where

$H$ = annual kill rate

$V$ = natural mortality rate

$V_0$ = annual natural mortality rates when $H = 0$

$b$ = regression coefficient ($-1.0$ if two mortality forces are exactly compensatory)

$c$ = threshold point above which natural and artificial mortality causes a decrease in survival rate. $c \leqslant V_0$

D. R. Anderson and Burnham (1976) illustrate the relationship by plotting $V$ as a function of $H$, using the above relationship (Figure 11.2). If $H$ is lower than $c$, nonhunting and hunting mortality are completely substitutable or compensated for. Figure 11.2(b) illustrates the annual survival rate is not a function of the hunting mortality rate until $H = c$, after which the relationship changes. This illustrates the density-dependent, compensatory relationship of the two distinct types of mortality, with the added proviso that a threshold exists beyond which the relationship no longer applies. The threshold may not be a fixed point, but an area that varies according to variations in carrying capacity of the habitat and the consequent variation in what naturally regulates the population.

In this context, the implication that natural mortality factors may also vary should be recognized. There is danger in assuming that a population is naturally regulated consistently only by one factor, when in fact the mechanism of population regulation may depend upon population size and variations in environmental conditions.

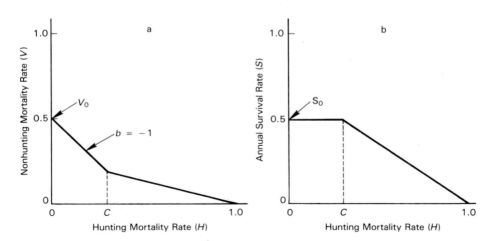

**Figure 11.2** A simple illustration of the hypotheses of completely compensatory forces of mortality: (a) nonhunting mortality as a function of hunting mortality rate, and (b) annual survival rate as a function of hunting mortality rate. After D. R. Anderson and Burnham 1976.

**Hypothesis of additive mortality.**

$$V = V_0 + bH \text{ for } b - 1, \text{ and } b = -\alpha \frac{1 - \overline{S} - \overline{H}}{1 - \alpha \overline{H}}$$

where

$\overline{S}$ = average annual survival rate

$\overline{H}$ = average annual kill rate

$\alpha = 0.95$ ($\alpha = 1.0$ may be used, but 0.95 gives a better approximation to the slope $b$ under the additive hypothesis)

The illustration [Figure 11.3(a)] shows a straight-line relationship between $V$ and $H$ for the additive hypothesis, rather than a concave curve as indicated for the compensation hypothesis in Figure 11.2(a). In addition, there is no threshold $c$ ($c = 0$) so $H$ at any level reduces $S$ [Figure 11.3(b)].

D. R. Anderson and Burnham (1976) recognized that these two hypotheses were extremes, and that the most realistic relationship was probably somewhere in between. Assuming that $V$ is a function of $H$ and that the relationship is linear, $V = V_0 + bH$ can be a satisfactory approximation. The effect of $H$ on $V$ is represented by $b$, and $b$ should lie within the interval

$$-1 \leqslant b \leqslant -\alpha V_0$$

where

$$V_0 = 1 - S_0 = \frac{1 - \overline{S} - \overline{H}}{1 - \alpha \overline{H}}$$

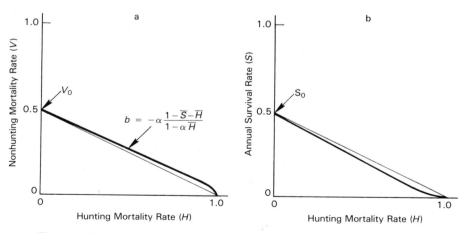

**Figure 11.3** A simple illustration of the hypothesis of completely additive forces of mortality: (a) nonhunting mortality rate as a function of hunting mortality rate; (b) annual survival rate as a function of hunting mortality rate. After D. R. Anderson and Burnham 1976.

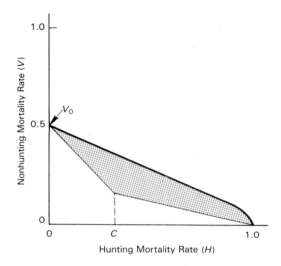

**Figure 11.4** The hypotheses that hunting is an additive form of mortality (top line) or is compensated for by other forms of mortality (bottom line). The shaded area represents a mixture of these two types of mortality process ($V_0$ is arbitrary, for illustration only). After D. R. Anderson and Burnham 1976.

with $\alpha$ being 0.95 as a useful approximation. If a threshold $c$ is specified such that $c < V_0$, hunting mortality additive to natural mortality must occur. Figure 11.4 illustrates the synthesis, wherein the shaded portion of the graph represents that area where additive and compensatory mortality both exist, and was judged to be more realistic than the two extreme hypotheses.

Watt (1968) stressed that optimal exploitation strategies must be based on the situation encountered, which in turn depends upon the previous exploitation decision. The use of an average level of exploitation has disadvantages because in some years populations will be overharvested and in others, underharvested (D. R. Anderson 1975). Thus, a knowledge of population density and survival is mandatory if exploitation is to be kept at the optimal level. Since most game populations are not monitored intensively enough to determine exact population size and survival rates, a conservative level of exploitation is generally indicated. Models of optimal exploitation strategies developed by D. R. Anderson (1975) are dependent upon adequate data collected annually, and use the concept that prior exploitation levels affect current decisions concerning optimal exploitation strategy. This approach is biologically realistic because factors affecting the relationship between exploitative and natural mortality are stochastic or random processes, varying from one year to the next.

Stock-recruitment curves derived from fish populations provide further insight into ways a population may respond to harvest (Ricker 1954). The 45° line ($A$) in Figure 11.5 describes a population that responds to exploitation in a noncompen-

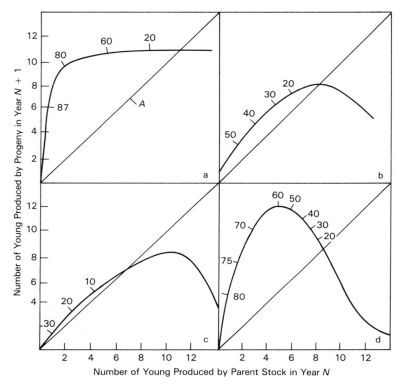

**Figure 11.5** Equilibrium densities of adult population for various rates of exploitations. This applies to populations where adults are of a single age class, and breed once a year, and where exploitation removes only the breeding stock. After Ricker 1954. (Used with permission.)

satory fashion, since the number of young produced is directly proportional to the adult population size. No yield ($\Delta N/\Delta t$) results since the young produced exactly replace the adult stock at any point on the line. The equilibrium density may be described as the carrying capacity, or $K$.

If a population responds in density-dependent, compensatory fashion, then a curve that rises above and to the left of the 45° line and ends below and to the right of it is appropriate. The curves that do this were developed for adult populations of a single age class that breed once a year, and for which exploitation removes only the mature stock prior to breeding, as is the case with salmon. The nature of the curve varies with the reproductive and associated biology of the species. In Figure 11.5(a), (b), and (c), the equilibrium population if exploited is always smaller than the unexploited population. For example, in Figure 11.5(a), the adult population, if unexploited, is of the approximate size 10.5, as is the population at year $N + 1$ (actually year $N + 4$ in the case of salmon). The rate of exploitation, up to approximately 50 percent of the mature stock, does not appreciably decrease the subsequent generation size, and actually only beyond the 80-percent exploitation rate is the subsequent breeding stock reduced. The maximum sustained yield for this population is at about 80 percent.

In Figure 11.5(b) exploitation at any level reduces the subsequent breeding stock, but reproduction decreases as the adult population increases beyond the equilibrium point. Thus, if the population is large (over 8), exploitation can cause an increase in reproduction and subsequent population size. However, if the population is at size 8 or below, then it responds similarly to that population in Figure 11.5(a), except that the rate of exploitation it can sustain is much lower, and there is no abrupt drop in reproduction at a certain age. The maximum sustained yield is at approximately 36 percent of the breeding population, which results in the greatest proportion of young produced in relation to parent stock.

Figure 11.5(c) represents a population that does not replace itself at high densities, and that has an extremely low maximum sustained yield (18%). In order to obtain equal numbers of young, the population must be reduced to about 60 percent of the level that produces maximum absolute numbers of young, and to about 30 percent of that same level to obtain the maximum sustained yield.

Figure 11.5(d) represents a population that, if reduced below equilibrium density, actually produces more young up to a level of exploitation of about 75 percent of the adult breeding stock. The maximum sustained yield is at 65 percent exploitation.

The curves may best be understood if it is recognized that the population, if unexploited, will tend to return to the level that replaces itself, the equilibrium level where the curve crosses the 45° line. Hence if a population at time $N$ is above that curve, and it is of the shape of Figures 11.5(b), (c), or (d) then a subsequent decrease in progeny at time $N + 1$ is to be expected. Of course, environmental conditions as they affect reproductive behavior will produce variations in population response, and oscillations about the equilibrium density will occur. Populations of the kind represented in Figure 11.5(a) are perhaps illustrative of the classic density-dependent response in that exploitation rates can be very high before a decrease in progeny results. Harvest strategies for such populations, however, would have to be carefully devised since the threshold at which the population decreases rapidly is very close to the maximum sustained yield. Populations represented by Figure 11.5(b) are less sensitive to levels of exploitation beyond the level of maximum sustained yield, although the proportion that may be removed if a maximum sustained yield is to be continued will be considerably lower.

Populations represented by Figure 11.5(c) do not afford as much yield, and the maximum sustained yield occurs at about 0.5 $K$, a much higher level than for the two previous examples. The population in Figure 11.5(d) also produces the maximum sustained yield at 0.5 $K$, but the yield is high in relation to $K$.

Ricker (1954) points out that if we are interested in achieving a population reduction, then populations illustrated in Figure 11.5(a) and (b) provide the easiest opportunities, because any reduction of the breeding stock will result in a subsequent decrease in population size. However, if populations are characterized by

Figure 11.5(c) and (d), and the population is above $K$, then exploitation up to a certain level would only dampen an imminent decrease. Also, a population typified by Figure 11.5(d) would actually be increased by any level of exploitation up to 73 percent, indicating that very intensive sustained control efforts would be indicated before a reduction could be anticipated.

Conversely, if maximum breeding stock were desired, as for example where a population is not only harvested for sport but also maintained for nonconsumptive purposes, populations with curves represented by Figure 11.5 (a) and (d) might be most easily managed, while those represented by Figures 11.5 (b) and (c) would have to be managed with compromises between the competing uses.

D. R. Anderson (1975) and D. R. Anderson and Burnham (1976) in their reviews, reported that upland game such as pheasants, quail, and rabbits appeared to be examples where compensatory mortality is common, while deer, marine mammals, and waterfowl were more representative of additive mortality.

## FIELD INVESTIGATIONS

### Upland Birds

**Pheasants.**   The monograph of Wagner, Besadny, and Kabat (1965) provides extensive insight into pheasant responses to exploitation. In Wisconsin, a daily bag limit of two cocks and a possession limit (total in possession) of four were in force from 1932 to 1958. In 1959–1962, the bag and possession limits were reduced to one and two cocks, respectively. Hunting season lengths have varied considerably between 1936 and 1960, ranging from 6 to 44 days. Correlation of season length and percentage of cocks shot shows that changes in season length beyond 25 days had little effect on percentage of cocks shot (Figure 11.6). This finding is similar to the earlier studies of D. L. Allen (1947) at Rose Lake, Michigan, where 70 percent of the kill occurred the first week, 20 percent in the second week, and 10 percent in the last week of the season.

The concept that a higher percentage of cocks will be harvested when populations are at high densities than when they are at low densities (Dale 1952) is illustrated by examinations of winter sex ratios of the Wisconsin pheasants at various population densities (Table 11.1). The average number of hens per cock in winter was twice as high at high density when compared with the low-density estimates. Thus, hunters tend to harvest the available cocks rapidly when populations are low and a threshold, in terms of hens per cock, is reached when proportionately more cocks are present in the population at low density. Pheasant populations at low density tend to retain higher proportions of cocks than higher-density populations. Hunting pressure on cocks appears to be self-regulating in relation to pheasant density.

An average of 73 percent of the Wisconsin cock pheasant population was estimated by Wagner, Besadny and Kabat (1965) to be shot every year, and total

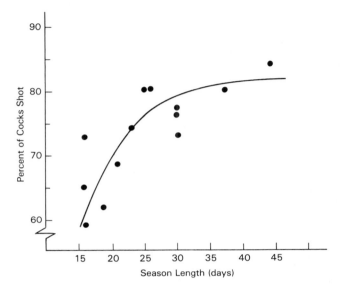

**Figure 11.6** Correlation between pheasant hunting season length and percent of cocks shot. From Wagner, Besadny, and Kabat 1965. (Used with permission.)

kill estimates seemed to roughly represent population trends. However, pheasants are polygamous, one male breeding 12 or more females, and the kill of males would not affect trends. The percentage of young cocks (young of the year) in the Wisconsin bag averaged 91.8 percent from 1946 to 1959.

D. L. Allen (1947) argued that southern Michigan pheasants could also support heavy exploitation of males without affecting breeding populations. The idea that a given area has a carrying capacity for cock pheasants subjected to heavy hunting pressure that is above the level where breeding stocks are affected was evidenced in his Rose Lake, Michigan, studies. Hunters are attracted, in essence, to the areas where they are likely to be most successful, and as success decreases, hunting shifts to other areas. At Rose Lake, Allen (1947) reported that in a season when

**TABLE 11.1  Winter Sex Ratios of Pheasants Related to Population Density in Wisconsin**

| Population Density | Sex Ratio[a] | | Number of Birds Observed | |
|---|---|---|---|---|
| | Mean | Range | Mean | Range |
| Very good | 7.1 | 3.7–11.4 | 2328 | 841–9247 |
| Good | 4.3 | 3.1–6.0 | 1939 | 165–6161 |
| Fair-poor | 3.5 | 1.4–5.4 | 1632 | 55–3644 |

*Source:* Wagner, Besadny, and Kabat 1965. (Used with permission.)

[a]Hens per cock in winter according to pheasant density, 1948–1957.

ten birds are taken per 100 acres, at least 25 percent of the prehunting cock population will not be killed. He concluded that in areas with adequate cover, proper basic regulations, and effective law enforcement, there was little danger of overshooting pheasant populations. On Pelee Island in Lake Erie, the percentage of cocks shot each year, 1947-1950, averaged 85 percent and ranged between 78 and 93 percent, with no effect on reproductive success (Stokes 1952).

Hen pheasants are killed illegally during cock-only seasons, and have been legally taken in other cases. Wagner et al. (1965) reported that of 495 hens killed by cars and examined under a fluoroscope, 36, or 7 percent contained body shot. Using an estimate based on the premise that the number of cocks with shot (33%) divided by the percent of cocks killed (74%) would equal the percent of hens with shot (7%) divided by the percent of hens killed, they reported that 16 percent of the hen population was killed during the hunting season. The Wagner et al. (1965) review of the illegal hen kill indicated variations from 60 percent to 8-10 percent of

TABLE 11.2   Results of Either-Sex Seasons on Pheasant Populations

| Area | Daily Bag Limit | Results |
|---|---|---|
| Wisconsin | 1 hen (1946, 1947) | Wild cock kill declined to 40% below level in cock-only areas; ten years of hen protection were required before return to prior cock-kill levels; 50–60% of hens taken during the either-sex seasons (1946 and 1947, nine counties). |
| Minnesota | 1 hen (1933, 1935–1937, 1941-1943) | Pheasant kill declined every year following hen shooting; hen kill estimated at 33% of population. |
| Indiana | 1 hen (1940, 1941) | Cock kill in 1942 was 60% below 1940 level of hens killed; 28% (1941); 20% (1941); population declines occurred in years when adjacent states were experiencing pheasant increases. |
| Washington | 1 hen (prior to 1941) | Hunting removed 69% of population, 50–60% of hen population; populations increased 370% and 96%, respectively, on two study areas five years after hen seasons terminated. |
| California | Variable: 1–10 hens per season per hunter | Hunting took 10–11% of hen populations in 1955-1957, up to over 50% in some areas; population estimates steady at 10–11% population declined at 35–47% harvest. |
| Pelee Island | ? | Thirty-percent harvest of hens appeared to approximate the maximum sustained yield, when 78–93% of cocks are killed annually. |

*Source:* Wagner, Besadny, and Kabat 1965. (Used with permission.)

the population in different states. Most of the illegal and accidental hen kill occurred during the early parts of the hunting season and in the best pheasant range. The hunter population early in the season is comprised of proportionately more inexperienced hunters who apparently discourage more easily and tend to shoot at hens more often than experienced hunters. Thus the illegal and accidental hen kill can be an important mortality factor.

Hen seasons have been authorized occasionally, which provided comparisons of population response between years of either-sex hunting and cock-only hunting. Wagner et al. (1965) reviewed the results of either-sex seasons from eight states and Pelee Island (Table 11.2). On Pelee Island, excellent pheasant habitat that was relatively free of predators during Stokes (1952) investigations, approximately 30 percent of the hen population could be removed to keep the population from increasing. Without hen shooting, the population could increase at a rate of 70 percent each year (Wagner et al. 1965). Figure 11.7 shows the correlation between percent of hens shot and the change in preseason hen population, after Wagner et al. (1965). On other areas, removals of 20-25 percent will reduce populations, and even the 16 percent illegal hen loss in Wisconsin could effect the subsequent breeding population.

Wagner et al. (1965) concluded that pheasants, while having a high biotic potential (i.e., the potential 70 percent increase on Pelee Island if hens were not hunted), usually attain only a very small portion of that potential. Of the potential production, they estimated that only 20 percent of eggs laid survive as birds to

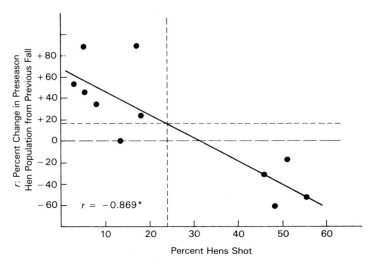

*Significance at .01 level

**Figure 11.7**  Correlation between percent of pheasant hens shot in previous fall and $r$, percentage change in preseason hen population on Pelee Island. From Wagner, Besadny, and Kabat 1965. (Used with permission.)

the fall. A variety of mortality factors interact to cause the reductions, including mowers, weather, predators, and other causes. Some of these are density-dependent, but others, like weather, are density-independent. Thus compensations involving substitutability of hunting mortality for other forms, while they appear to occur, are not great. Further, fall densities are correlated with spring densities (Figure 11.8) indicating no clear population reduction in winter that would produce the biological surplus of Errington (1956). Most of the mortality occurs when food and cover are abundant. Thus, heavy hunting of cocks and no hunting of hens, which sustain illegal losses regardless, does have a biological basis.

**Scaled quail.** Scaled quail (*Callipepla squamata*) are monogamous and lay large clutches (12.7 average, range 5-22; Schemnitz 1961) that usually result in fall populations of considerably larger size than the breeding population. Schemnitz (1961) showed that the high variability in nesting success that occurred in an Oklahoma study area was inversely related to rainfall patterns.

H. Campbell et al. (1973) concluded from comparisons of unhunted and hunted populations in New Mexico that hunting had little effect on quail populations, merely substituting for some part of the inevitable natural mortality. Table 11.3 summarizes some pertinent aspects of their analysis. Daily bag limits ranged from 10 to 20 quail between 1960 and 1968 in the study areas with seasons extending for over a month. The hunted area was subject to very intensive harvest, five

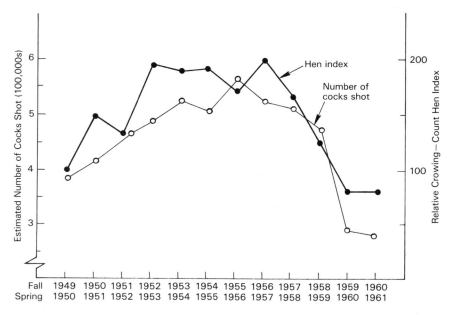

**Figure 11.8** Comparison of spring pheasant population density (crowing count index) with population level of preceding fall (estimated kill) in Wisconsin. From Wagner, Besadny, and Kabat 1965. (Used with permission.)

TABLE 11.3  Some Characteristics of Scaled Quail Populations in New Mexico, 1960–1968, on a Hunted Area and an Unhunted Control Area

| Population Characteristic | Hunted Area | | Control Area | |
|---|---|---|---|---|
| | Mean | Range | Mean | Range |
| Known March population (per square mile) | 21.9 | 8.2–46.8 | 29.2 | 5.5–62.9 |
| Known breeding pairs (per square mile) | 3.4 | 0.7–11.8 | 4.2 | 0.7–13.3 |
| Known population in Oct.–Nov. (per square mile) | 38.6 | 9.4–69.9 | 44.7 | 13.3–88.7 |
| Percent young of year, prior to hunt in fall, in trapped samples | 74.0 | 60.0–89.2 | 72.9 | 48.9–88.4 |
| Percent males in young in fall trap samples | 43.1 | 27.7–52.5 | 44.2 | 23.7–63.6 |
| Percent male adults | 56.3 | 26.9–78.6 | 62.7 | 45.5–73.9 |
| Annual first-year mortality rate of fall-banded young based on trapping return | | | | |
| Both sexes | 95.5 | | 92.6 | |
| Males | 94.6 | | 91.5 | |
| Females | 96.3 | | 93.5 | |
| Annual first-year mortality rate of fall-banded young based on hunter recoveries | | | | |
| Both sexes | 86.0 | | | |
| Males | 82.4 | | | |
| Females | 89.1 | | | |

*Source:* H. Campbell et al. 1973. (Used with permission.)

times greater than the pressure in the most heavily hunted county in New Mexico. The number of quail bagged per square mile averaged 17.1 (range 2.2–50.0) over the 1960–1968 period, with hunter days per square mile averaging 15.7 (range 4–28).

The covey count data for March, when quail populations were at their annual lowest, followed similar trends on both control and hunted areas, although the population on the hunted area was consistently lower than on the control area. This was considered attributable to hunting, but the difference was judged to be unimportant and a trend towards greater densities on the hunted area occurred as populations increased during the study. Breeding pair counts averaged slightly higher on the control area, but not consistently so, as did known minimum fall populations prior to hunting.

Percentages of young quail followed similar trends on both areas, averaging about 73 percent of the fall populations in trapped samples. Percentage of males in young of the year was probably near 50 percent, but the sex ratio was definitely weighted towards males in the adult age group. The differential mortality was attributed to egg-laying and brooding activities, which cause females to be more vulnerable to predation.

Trapping returns following hunting showed slightly higher mortality rates for the hunted population than the unhunted one. First-year returns were judged unrealistically high, and recoveries from hunters indicated that lower mortality rates were probable. Average first-year mortality was approximately 86 percent, and mean annual adult mortality was near 70 percent, with females having higher mortality rates than males of both age groups whether hunted or not.

The conclusion was that such intensive hunting was not harmful to scaled quail, which have a very high natural turnover rate. Hunting was largely compensatory with over-winter mortality factors, although there was, at the intensive levels that occurred during this study, a slight depressing effect. The population appeared to fluctuate according to variation in precipitation patterns, especially spring-summer rainfall, which affects forb production.

**Bobwhite quail.**   A number of investigations into the effects of exploitation of bobwhite quail (*Colinus virginianus*) point out the compensatory nature of hunting with other mortality, as has been documented for scaled quail. Responses of this species to hunting in Oklahoma (Baumgartner 1944), Missouri (A. Leopold 1945; Marsden and Baskett 1958), Texas (Parmelee 1953), and Iowa (Errington and Hamerstrom 1935) adequately demonstrate this conclusion.

Baumgartner's (1944) investigations involved comparisons of census data during breeding season, fall (prior to hunting), and winter (after hunting) for hunted and closed areas (Table 11.4). The hunted area sustained higher quail populations than the unhunted area, probably due to more favorable forage and cover distribution on the former area. The sharp drop in numbers during 1940 on both areas was thought to be caused by unusually severe winter weather, while the decline on the hunted area in spring 1943 was due to a March fire that reduced ground cover. Re-

**TABLE 11.4   Comparison of Bobwhite Quail Counts on a Hunted and an Unhunted Area in Oklahoma (birds per 100 acres)**

| Year | Season | | Hunted Area | Unhunted Area |
|------|--------|--|-------------|---------------|
| 1939 | Apr. 1 | (beginning of breeding) | 11.0 | 9.4 |
|      | Nov. 1 | (prior to hunting) | 25.0 | 12.6 |
|      | Jan. 1 | (after hunting) | 11.0 | 12.0 |
| 1940 | Apr. 1 | | 3.1 | 2.2 |
|      | Nov. 1 | | 9.8 | 8.9 |
|      | Jan. 1 | | 7.1 | 8.4 |
| 1941 | Apr. 1 | | 6.8 | 8.0 |
|      | Nov. 1 | | 21.8 | 13.2 |
|      | Jan. 1 | | 10.9 | 12.3 |
| 1942 | Apr. 1 | | 11.6 | 11.9 |
|      | Nov. 1 | | 24.7 | 14.7 |
|      | Jan. 1 | | 17.4 | 13.9 |
| 1943 | Apr. 1 | | 10.6 | 13.0 |
|      | Nov. 1 | | 18.5 | 15.0 |
|      | Jan. 1 | | 9.4 | 13.9 |

*Source:* Baumgartner 1944. (Used with permission.)

movals of 20 to 55 percent of the birds by hunting did not result in "conspicuous" changes in the subsequent breeding population unless unfavorable environmental conditions were involved. After comparing census trends on the hunted and un-hunted areas, Baumgartner (1944) believed that quail populations on the hunted area would not have changed in the absence of hunting.

Parmelee (1953) investigated the effect of weather on hunting success. The drought years of 1950 and 1951 on his Texas study area created very difficult hunt-ing. Quail coveys ran from dogs or flushed beyond the range of hunters, in the poor ground cover, and single birds that had been flushed were difficult to locate. Hunt-ing was characterized as poor by hunters interviewed, with approximately 6 birds of the allowable daily bag limit of 12 being taken per day. An estimate of 20.8 percent of downed quail were not recovered. The December–mid-January quail season was judged too late because much of the fall surplus was eliminated prior to the season from nonhunting causes.

A. Leopold (1945) reported that young of the year constitute 72 to 83 per-cent of fall quail populations in Missouri, based on examinations of hunter-killed birds. Sex ratios of killed birds are known to favor males (53.1% males to 46.9% females in a sample of 1633 birds, 1939-1943) in this species. However, the sex ratio of immature first-year birds in the bag was equal, since the differential mor-tality accrues to the population after the hunting season. The distortion is greatest in spring and summer (Stoddard 1931), and A. Leopold (1945) and Marsden and Baskett (1958) suggested that hen losses during breeding season were responsible. Thus hunting was not considered responsible for causing the disparate sex ratios in this species, although Bennitt (1951) subsequently showed that young were slightly more vulnerable than adults (Table 11.5).

TABLE 11.5  Sex and Age Ratios of Bobwhite Quail Bagged
in Successive Weeks of the Hunting Season in Missouri

| Weeks | Sex Ratio 1938–1948 (males per 100 females) | Age Ratio 1944–1947 (young as percent of total) |
|---|---|---|
| 1 | 112.51 | 85.25 |
| 1–2 | 111.62 | 83.47 |
| 1–3 | 111.97 | 82.43 |
| 1–4 | 112.41 | 82.51 |
| 1–5 | 112.47 | 82.54 |
| 1–6 | 112.94 | 81.96 |
| 1–7 | 113.01 | 82.24 |
| 1–8 | 113.05 | 81.78 |

*Source:* Bennitt 1951. (Used with permission.)

Records of 1156 banded quail provided Marsden and Baskett (1958) an opportunity to evaluate the effects of exploitation in more detail. Survival rates of young adults in an unhunted population were similar after October 1 indicating that the differential vulnerability by age was not attributable to hunting. This is anticipated by Bennitt's (1951) findings that only a very small rise in sex ratio

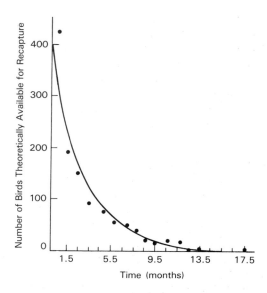

**Figure 11.9** Extinction curve for banded bobwhite quail in Missouri. From Marsden and Baskett 1958. (Used with permission.)

favoring cocks occurred during Missouri hunting seasons (Table 11.5). Percentages of young in this study population suggested that 98.6 percent of the population would disappear annually, 16.6 percent from emigration (Figure 11.9). Thus, the very high annual mortality of this unhunted quail population supports the theory that hunting is merely a substitute for other mortality.

Bennitt (1951) concluded that quail hunters with dogs were more successful than those without dogs. Those with dogs flushed 25 percent more coveys per eight-hour hunting period, bagged 15 percent more birds per gun hour, and lost 34 percent fewer downed birds. An average of 7.7 percent of all downed quail were lost according to hunter reports. About 45 percent of the hunting occurs on weekends and holidays, but the hunting success is lower on those days than during the rest of the season. Inclement weather appeared to slightly increase hunter success.

More recently Roseberry (1979) reported that mortality rates of unhunted and hunted bobwhite populations in Illinois were different. Hunted populations suffered greater mortality before breeding season than unhunted populations, which suffered higher postbreeding (summer) losses. This indicated that population levels would be different in relation to breeding season, with hunted populations being lower even if annual mortality rates were similar. Thus, the compensatory relationship between hunting and nonhunting mortality was incomplete and hunting at an annual harvest rate of 55 percent reduced breeding densities. Recruitment rates tended to rise as fall–spring losses increased because of density independence up to a level of 70 percent fall–spring loss. Heavy harvests followed by severe winters did reduce the subsequent quail population to a level below the preharvest population, which was not entirely compensated for by increased reproduction.

Roseberry (1979) pointed out that bobwhite habitat in Illinois is isolated and patchy, and that hunters concentrate their efforts in the most productive areas.

This tends to increase harvest rates. Recommendations to decrease season lengths by two weeks or by approximately one-third during years when populations are down, and to establish earlier seasons were in order, rather than reducing bag limits.

**Valley quail.** An experiment involving two 720-acre areas, one hunted and one unhunted, was used to assess impacts of hunting on valley quail (*Lophortyx californica*) populations by Glading and Saarni (1944). Hunters removed between 18.6 and 26.5 percent of the estimated quail population on the hunted area (Table 11.6). Total exploitation loss was as high as 40 percent, including crippled and bagged birds. Figure 11.10 shows that although March census data for the hunted area was below that of the check area, populations were similar on both the next fall. The overall population trend on both areas was down, suggesting that factors other than hunting were regulating the trend. No correlation between preseason population level and indices to hunter success (birds per hunter, birds per hunter hour, shells per bird) was found. Banded bird data suggested that immigration to the hunted area from other areas was not an important influence on the size of the fall population on the hunted area.

TABLE 11.6  Summary of Valley Quail Population Data on Hunted and Unhunted Areas in California

| Area | 1938–1939 | 1939–1940 | 1940–1941 | 1941–1942 |
|---|---|---|---|---|
| Hunted Area | | | | |
| Preseason (Nov.) census | 513 | 245 | 278 | 349 |
| Total bag | 136 | 62 | 52 | 84 |
| Unrecovered cripples | 57 | 26 | 14 | 25 |
| Total bagged and crippled | 193 | 88 | 66 | 109 |
| Postseason (Mar.) census | 214 | 141 | 167 | 184 |
| Check Area | | | | |
| Preseason (Nov.) census | 349 | 288 | 256 | 325 |
| Postseason (Mar.) census | 257 | 185 | 216 | 202 |

*Source:* After Glading and Saarni 1944. (Used with permission.)

One may conclude that the quail species are good examples of compensatory mortality, where hunting pressure generally will not serve to influence levels of populations in subsequent years. The very high natural mortality rates inherent in these species suggest that a biological surplus indeed exists, which may as well be harvested as not. The reservation to this is that there are instances where habitat is diminished and patchy, making populations more vulnerable to hunting. Also, circumstances may arise where hunter harvest could be restricted to provide more prey for predators.

**Ruffed grouse.** Comparisons of hunted and unhunted ruffed grouse (*Bonasa umbellus*) populations in Michigan provide information on the effects of exploitation (Palmer and Bennett 1963). Harvest levels averaging 29 percent (range 18–53%) of the hunted population over a seven-year period did not affect the subsequent breeding population (Table 11.7). Populations on both areas declined from 60 to

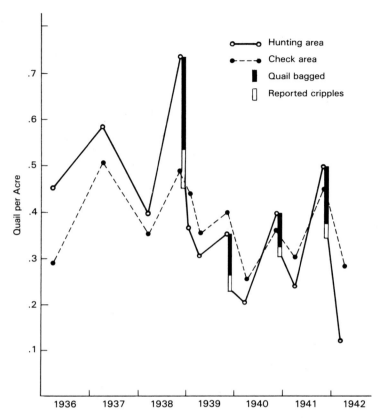

**Figure 11.10** Population trends of valley quail on unhunted and hunted areas in California. After Glading and Saarni 1944. (Used with permission.)

**TABLE 11.7 Comparisons of Ruffed Grouse Population Data on Hunted and Unhunted Areas in Michigan**

| Area | 1950 | 1951 | 1952 | 1953 | 1954 | 1955 | 1956 | Mean |
|---|---|---|---|---|---|---|---|---|
| Hunted Area | | | | | | | | |
| Fall population | 28.1 | 17.5 | 16.2 | 15.7 | 7.5 | 6.5 | 6.4 | 11.6 |
| Spring population[a] | 6.6 | 6.9 | 4.1 | 4.4 | 3.4 | 0.8 | 0.8 | 3.4 |
| Percent decline | 76.5 | 60.6 | 74.7 | 72.0 | 54.7 | 87.7 | 87.5 | 70.7 |
| Percent harvest of fall population | 18 | 22 | 53 | 31 | 27 | 43 | 22 | 29 |
| Unhunted Area | | | | | | | | |
| Fall population | 24.8 | 17.6 | 9.2 | 15.7 | 1.9 | 2.4 | 3.6 | 10.7 |
| Spring population[a] | 6.6 | 5.9 | 8.4 | 3.4 | 3.1 | 1.4 | 0.9 | 4.2 |
| Percent decline | 73.4 | 66.5 | 8.7 | 78.3 | * | 41.7 | 75.0 | 60.7 |

*Source:* Palmer and Bennett 1963. (Used with permission.)
[a]Estimates are birds per 100 acres.

70 percent from fall to spring. Populations on the hunted area were generally higher, as was percent decline fall to spring, when compared with the unhunted area. Palmer and Bennett (1963) felt that 50 percent of the population could safely be harvested annually.

About 75 percent of the ruffed grouse harvest occurred the first 15 days of the season, and 95 percent within the first 30 days. An additional four weeks of hunting in November and early December was estimated to increase percent harvest by 8.7 percent, and an eight-week extension 12.6 percent. Obviously, extended seasons that would provide more sport without materially increasing harvest could be implemented. Palmer and Bennett (1963) report an investigation in New York where professional hunters tried to exterminate a grouse population in a square-mile area through winter and spring in three successive years. After a "few" grouse remained, the hunters could not approach them within gunshot range, and concluded that it would be impossible to exterminate the population through this means.

Gullion and Marshall (1968) were able to compare survival of 188 male ruffed grouse in a Minnesota refuge with that of 117 males in an adjacent hunted population (Figure 11.11). The hunted population existed on readily accessible habitat

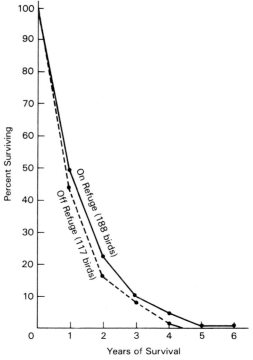

**Figure 11.11** Comparison of mortality rates of banded male ruffed grouse on hunted and protected areas in northern Minnesota. After Gullion and Marshall 1968. (Used with permission.)

that was intensively hunted. The difference in survival of a theoretical population of 100 grouse, based on the banded bird data, would be 6 birds less for a hunted population the first two years than if it were not hunted. These differences were in reality unimportant demographically. Male grouse apparently learn to escape hunters and their vulnerability decreases as more experience accrues.

Habitats selected during hunting season may also confer survival value. Gullion and Marshall (1968) reported that survival of male ruffed grouse that select pure hardwood stands for drumming was higher than that of those that selected habitats containing conifers. While the pure aspen-birch hardwood stands afforded better protection from natural predators such as the goshawk and great horned owl, they may also afford more protection from hunters.

Regardless, the conclusion of Bump et al. (1947:392) concerning the effect of hunting ruffed grouse populations still appears valid: "Fluctuations continue regardless of the protected or unprotected status of the coverts."

**Ptarmigan.** Bergerud's (1970, 1972a) investigations of willow ptarmigan (*Lagopus lagopus*) in Newfoundland suggested that harvest levels of up to 40 percent of the population were not correlated significantly with spring pair densities, August densities, or number of hunting licenses sold (a measure of hunting pressure). Percentage harvest was negatively and significantly correlated with the number of young raised per hen (Figure 11.12). The number of young raised per hen was used as a viability index, since this should reflect number of young surviving to autumn. The data suggested that the vulnerability of the population to hunting changed between years.

In addition, there appeared to be a lag between densities and vulnerability, since when birds first reached peak numbers, harvests were lower than later (Table 11.8). Thus harvest statistics may not precisely reflect changes in densities. Still, numbers of hunters were related to bird densities and hunting success: 51, 24, 10, and 15 percent of the seasonal kill occurred during the first, second, third, and

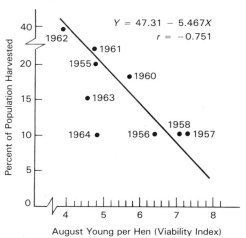

**Figure 11.12** Regression of precentages of harvest of young per hen ptarmigan on the Avalon Peninsula, Newfoundland. After Bergerud 1972. (Used with permission.)

TABLE 11.8    Ptarmigan Population and Harvest Data from Newfoundland

| Year | Density (per square mile) | | Birds Killed per License Report | Licenses Sold (hundreds) | Young per Hen[a] | Number of pairs[b] |
|------|--------|--------|------|------|------|------|
|      | Spring Pairs | August | | | | |
| 1955 | 1.2 | 9 | 1.8 | 99 | 4.8 | 40 |
| 1956 | – | – | 1.2 | 96 | 6.5 | 12 |
| 1957 | – | – | 2.4 | 92 | 7.3 | 130 |
| 1958 | 2.8 | 26 | 3.6 | 126 | 7.1 | 120 |
| 1959 | 3.6 | 36 | 3.2 | 128 | 7.9 | 129 |
| 1960 | 4.0 | 32 | 4.7 | 140 | 5.7 | 27 |
| 1961 | 4.3 | 31 | 4.0 | 151 | 4.8 | 154 |
| 1962 | 3.9 | 24 | 4.3 | 173 | 3.9 | 141 |
| 1963 | 2.8 | 18 | 1.8 | 166 | 4.6 | 78 |
| 1964 | 2.6 | 19 | 2.2 | 174 | 4.8 | 69 |

Source: After Bergerud 1972a. (Used with permission.)
[a]Young per hen = percent of pairs with young × number of young per brood ÷ 100.
[b]Pairs with and without young in sample.

fourth weeks of the season, respectively. Proportionately more birds were removed early in the season when populations were low than when they were high. Hunting pressure early in the season was intense enough to disperse covies.

Although there was no correlation between chronology of the hatching season and size of the harvest (Bergerud 1972), late-hatched young did appear to be more vulnerable to the gun than young hatched earlier (Bergerud 1970a). Early-hatched young and adults appeared to be equally vulnerable to hunting.

McGowan (1975) concluded that neither autumn nor spring removal of 40 percent of a rock ptarmigan population in Alaska depressed breeding stocks the following year. Replacement of breeding stock may occur the same spring as the removal but more commonly will be delayed one year.

Red grouse (*Lagopus lagopus scoticus*) are driven by beaters to shooters hiding in blinds in Scotland (Jenkins, Watson, and Miller 1970). The highest percentage taken of an August population was 45 percent, which was not high enough to depress subsequent population levels to where breeding territories were vacant and no nonterritorial (nonbreeding) birds were left. This long-term investigation suggested that this type of shooting, as intensive as any applied to grouse populations, was unlikely to be too heavy.

**Sharp-tailed grouse.** Investigations of marked sharp-tailed grouse (*Pediocetes phasianellus*) in South Dakota indicated an annual mortality rate of 70 percent with hunters removing 25 percent of the population (Robel, Henderson, and Jackson 1972). These investigations took place in prime sharptail habitat.

Ammann (1963), dealing with small populations on diminishing habitat in Michigan, showed decreases in sharptail populations following 41-day seasons with bag limits of two to three per day (Table 11.9). Following closed seasons, populations

TABLE 11.9   Number of Male Sharp-Tailed Grouse on Dancing Grounds in Spring
Compared to Prior Hunting Season Status, Drummond Island, Michigan

| Year | Number of Males on Spring Dancing Grounds | Hunting Season Status |
|------|-------------------------------------------|------------------------|
| 1956 | 33 | Closed |
| 1957 | 69 | 3 birds per day, 6 in possession,[a] 15 per season, 41 days long |
| 1958 | 71 | 2 birds per day, 4 in possession, 8 per season, 41 days long |
| 1959 | 45 | Closed |
| 1960 | 63 | 3 birds per day, 6 in possession, 15 per season, 41 days long |
| 1961 | 32 | Closed |
| 1962 | 46 | Closed |
| 1963 | 65 | Closed |

*Source:* After Ammann 1963. (Used with permission.)

[a]Possession limits indicate the number of grouse that may be in the possession of a hunter at
any one time.

increased the following spring. Although no information except numbers of cocks
on spring dancing grounds was reported, it appeared that hunter harvest could be
responsible for suppression of numbers of birds.

Over much of the sharptail range, habitats are not limited and hunting is dispersed and concentrated at the opening date. Efforts to increase harvests and promote more recreational use of the populations have been the rule. Prairie grouse
may be taken incidentally during hunts for big game and waterfowl throughout the
seasons, but exploitation rates have not been considered high enough to warrant
serious concern. Efforts to preserve and enhance the habitats have received greatest
attention. In areas where habitats are limited or deteriorating, and where hunting
pressure is likely to be intensive, restriction of hunting may be indicated.

**Turkeys.**   Turkeys (*Meleagris gallopavo*) are perhaps the most difficult birds
to hunt under present regulations, being extremely wary. They are one of the most
sought-after species, and have therefore been extensively reintroduced into formerly
occupied range and introduced into new, suitable habitats. Turkeys are promis-
cuous, produce broods of over eight (McDowell 1956), and may be sexually mature
at age one (Lewis and Brietenbach 1966).

Mosby (1967) surveyed hunting mortality accruing to eastern wild turkeys,
finding that the two major influences on percentage removal were accessibility of
the area, and type of hunting (any turkey or gobbler only). About 8 percent of the
estimated population was removed under gobbler-only seasons. Mosby (1967) felt
that a 10-percent removal under any-turkey seasons was a resonable estimate of the
average hunting mortality. Removals from a West Virginia study area ranging from
13 to 21.5 percent of the population did not bear any relation to population size
(Bailey and Rinell 1965). Markley's (1967) survey of allowable harvest indicated
that 40 to 60 percent of a population could be removed annually in high-quality
Florida habitat, a higher level than Pennsylvania estimates of 40 percent in less

productive habitats. Burget (1957) found that 40 percent of a population could be removed with safety at Devil Creek, Colorado.

Table 11.10 shows a hypothetical life equation of a stable turkey population that Mosby (1967) based on Virginia data. The population was stable when sustaining 60.4 percent total annual mortality and 33.3 percent hunting mortality.

**TABLE 11.10    Life Equation for a Stable Turkey Population Based on Virginia Data**

| Factor Causing Change in Population Numbers | Population |
|---|---|
| Spring breeding population (50:50 sex ratio) | 1000 |
| Number of successful nests (number of females × percent hatching success): 500 × 35.1% = 175.5 | |
| Number of poults hatched (number of successful nests × average clutch size × percent hatchability): 175.5 × 12.3 × 93% = 2000 | |
| Number of poults in fall (number of poults hatched × percent of poults surviving): 2000 × 75.5% = 1490 | |
| Fall adult population (number of adults in spring × percent of adults surviving): 1000 × 99.3% = 993 | |
| Total pre–hunting season population | 2483 |
| Hunting season harvest (pre–hunting season population × percent harvested): 2483 × 33.3% = 827 | |
| Post–hunting season population | 1655 |
| Overwinter loss (26.4% of total annual mortality) | 655 |
| Spring breeding population | 1000 |

*Source:* Mosby 1967. (Used with permission.)

Poaching losses have been estimated to range from negligible to as much as the legal harvest (Markley 1967). Crippling losses are equally variable, ranging from 0 to 30 percent of the reported legal harvest.

Jonas (1966) reported that most hunting (78%) for Montana turkeys occurred the first two days, when most (75%) of the birds were killed. Following introductions of Merriam's turkeys into the Long Pines area of southeastern Montana, birds that were semidomesticated and that inhabited ranch and farmyards were largely eliminated during the initial hunting seasons. Hunter harvest was fairly constant after this occurred, although hunting pressure was quite variable, being related to access as influenced by weather. Hunter success over a six-year period averaged 27 percent, which can be compared with 50 percent in Colorado (Burget 1957), 12 percent in Missouri (Lewis 1967), and 5 percent in Tennessee (Holbrook and Lewis 1967).

A model simulating changes in a hypothetical population of 1000 turkeys was used to estimate the effects of a spring gobbler hunt by Lobdell, Case, and Mosby (1972). Assumptions for using the model were that the population was 40 percent adults and 60 percent immatures, each age group having a 50:50 sex ratio. Total annual mortality was assumed to be 60 percent, ranging between 45 and 75 percent with no differentials between sex or age classes. The ratio of immature to adult females averaged 3.025:1. Fall hunting removed 25 percent of the population (range 10–40%) and was again free of differentials between sex and age classes. Fall mortality due to hunting was considered to be part of total annual mortality. Complete removal of gobblers over two years old in spring resulted in a slight depression of the population. However, complete removal of gobblers in spring is unlikely, and it was concluded that spring hunting could be implemented without adverse effects on the population. If either-sex fall hunting mortality was less than one-half of the total annual mortality and was not additive, then both fall and spring hunting were biologically justified.

**Mourning doves.**   The mourning dove (*Zenaida macroura*) represents another reproductive strategy that differs from the gallinaceous species and the waterfowl. Instead of producing one large clutch per year with renesting if the initial attempt fails, mourning doves produces a small clutch of two (rarely one or three) and nest from two to seven times a year. Doves use a wide variety of nesting sites, from ground to tall trees (McClure 1943). Some young of the year, from early clutches, become sexually mature the same year they hatch in areas where long nesting seasons occur (Irby and Blankenship 1966). Work in California (J. B. Cowan 1952) and Texas (Swank 1955) revealed the highest number of nesting attempts. Nesting is progressively delayed as latitudes increase and suitable nesting weather decreases, so three to four broods are produced per year in Kansas (Schroeder 1970), Iowa (McClure 1943), and southern Minnesota (S. W. Harris, Morse, and Langley 1963). In southern Michigan (Caldwell 1964) and North Dakota (Boldt and Hendrickson 1953) two to three broods are produced per pair each season. Marginal habitat and disease are factors that reduce dove productivity and density in Georgia (Hopkins and Odum 1953). Trichomoniasis and pox infections are known to cause severe losses (Locke, Herman, and King 1960). A summary (Table 11.11) indicated that the average number of young fledged per pair varied from 1.4 to 6.7, related to number of nesting attempts. An average production of 5 young

**TABLE 11.11   Productivity and Nesting Periods of Mourning Doves**

| State | Nesting Period | | Fledglings per Pair |
|-------|------|-------|---------------------|
|       | Peak | Range |                     |
| Georgia | May | Mar.–Sept. | 2.1 |
| Iowa | June | Mar.–Oct. | 5.3 |
| Illinois | May | Apr.–Sept. | 2.4 |
| Kansas | June–July | Apr.–Sept. | — |
| North Dakota | June–Aug. | May–Sept. | 3.2 |
| Texas | May–July | Mar.–Sept. | 6.7 |
| California | July | Mar.–Sept. | 6.2 |
| Idaho | July | May–Sept. | 3.2 |
| Michigan | Apr.–June | Apr.–Sept. | 2.2–2.5 |
| Mississippi | July–Aug. | — | 1.4–1.53 |

*Source:* Summarized by Hanson and Kossack 1963 and U.S. Fish and Wildlife Service 1977. (Used with permission.)

per pair of adults prior to hunting in eastern states was calculated by the U.S. Fish and Wildlife Service (1977b).

Mourning dove populations fluctuate dramatically on an annual basis (Swank 1955), due primarily to variations in weather. High precipitation in June and July of one year, which reduces hatching success, has been correlated with subsequent reduced breeding populations the following year in Iowa (LaPerriere 1972). Nesting success in Minnesota is commonly high later in summer when rains and cold spells are less likely (S. W. Harris et al. 1963). LaPointe (1958) concluded that nesting success was variable even within the same habitat due to variations in weather and degree of production in Illinois. Because of this high annual variation, Swank (1955) recommended annual breeding pair surveys prior to establishment of hunting seasons. Population indices, determined from call-count surveys across the breeding range, are now coordinated annually by U.S. Fish and Wildlife Service and summarized in administrative reports in June. The call-counts are conducted at 20 listening stations for three minutes each, 1 mile apart on lightly travelled roads between May 20 and June 5 (Ruos and Dolton 1977).

The long nesting season, which extends into September, has been a source of concern in regulating timing of harvest. Schroeder (1970) reported that early September hunting seasons discouraged nesting in Kansas, where abandonment of young in the nest and mortality of nesting adults was significant. S. W. Harris et al. (1963) reported that, in Minnesota, as many as 20 percent of all young fledged in September, the inference being that hunting would cause mortality to nestlings. J. B. Cowan's (1952) estimate for a central California study area was that 10 percent of broods raised were still on nests in September. However, Caldwell (1964) reported only 2 of 164 nests examined in his southern Michigan area were active after September 8, and Hanson and Kossack (1963) reported only a small part of the Illinois population nesting in September. Hunters tend to concentrate on large flocks of nonbreeding birds rather than the dispersed breeding populations (*Mourning dove investigations* 1957). An environmental assessment conducted by the U.S. Fish and Wildlife Service (1977b) indicated no effect on nestling survival by September hunting, based on data from 27 states. Less than 10 percent of annual production in the United States was estimated to occur after September 1, with highest proportions occurring in northern states where hunting is least prevalent.

Doves are a highly mobile species except for some nonmigrating populations in southern areas (Aldrich and Duvall 1958). Migration starts in midsummer with juveniles (McClure 1943), and as much as 75 percent of a population as far south as central California may have migrated by the second week of September (J. B. Cowan 1952). Since the Migratory Bird Treaty prohibits hunting prior to September 1, much of the northern populations have already gone south. Conversely, D. J. Nelson (1957) reported that the main dove migration into Georgia occurred after September. Major concentrations of migrant birds occur in Arizona, California, Florida, Georgia, and Texas (Aldrich and Duvall 1958). Approximately 42 percent of the Texas dove harvest is of migrating birds (Dunks 1977). The Florida harvest

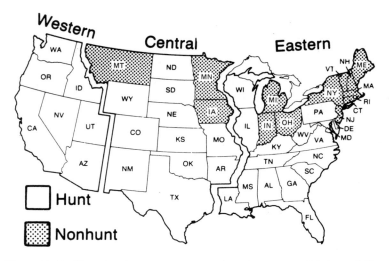

**Figure 11.13**  Mourning dove management units. After Ruos and Dolton 1977.

is comprised of 61 percent migrant immatures and 49 percent migrant adults (Marion, O'Meara, and Harris 1981). Management units (Figure 11.13) based on migration patterns facilitate establishment of hunting regulations (Hanson and Kossack 1963).

Mourning doves constitute a larger harvest than all other migratory birds combined (U.S. Fish and Wildlife Service 1975), and effects of hunting have been evaluated in numerous areas. Season length is not as critical an effect on harvest as is opening date, since most birds are taken early (Hanson and Kossack 1963; Gallizioli 1955). Shooting hours that restrict hunting to a portion of the day may also reduce harvest (U.S. Fish and Wildlife Service 1975:253). Hunting probably does not affect migration patterns but could presumably cause local shifts, if pressure were intense (Schroeder 1970). An increase in bag limit from 12 to 18 birds in eastern states did not affect number of doves harvested or hunter participation (Hayne 1975). Delays in harvest in southern states until the maximum number of migratory birds are present could increase the percentage of migratory birds in the bag (Marion et al. 1981).

Rice and Lovrien (1974) reported that 2.6 young per breeding pair would have to be available at hunting time in order to maintain a stationary population in South Dakota. Their analysis of band recoveries indicated that mortality of young could be no more than 35 percent if 4 fledglings are produced per pair, but that level of mortality prior to hunting was unlikely. Annual mortality of mourning doves in this area was approximately 60 percent, and adult mortality was slightly lower. When hunting seasons were open, annual mortality increased 3–4 percent, and hunting removed less than 10 percent of the population. Reeves (1979) estimated from band analyses that 9 percent of the dove population in the Eastern Management Unit (EMU) was harvested the first season after hunting, and 5 percent of the Central Management Unit (CMU) population was taken during that first time span. Recovery rates for banded doves ranged between 31 and 38 percent for direct (first season) recoveries, and from 44 to 65 percent from indirect (later season) recoveries, for the EMU and CMU. Higher recovery rates in the CMU were attributed to use of reward bands in Mexico and Central America. These recovery rates contrast with the low rates of 1.3 percent that Gallizioli (1955) reported in Arizona, at a time when dove hunting was very popular but hunters were fewer and populations were much less exploited.

No differential vulnerability of immature birds or adult birds to hunting has been found (D. J. Nelson 1957; Rice and Lovrien 1974), but differential migration related to age does affect the proportions of young in the bag (Hanson and Kossack 1963). Caldwell (1964) and Hanson and Kossack (1963) reported 52 percent of the harvest in Illinois was immatures, the low percentage being attributed to early migration of immatures. D. J. Nelson (1957) reported higher percentages of juveniles in the bag in September hunts than in December-January in Georgia, relating this to availability rather than differentials in vulnerability. Overall, juveniles constitute 78 percent of the estimated 49 million doves harvested annually in the United States (U.S. Fish and Wildlife Service 1977b).

High crippling losses of 33 percent occurred when birds fell into dense cover behind hunters who were shooting into fields (D. J. Nelson 1957). Crippling losses averaging 26 percent have occurred in the southeast (Rice and Lovrien 1974).

As with other species, mourning doves appear capable of withstanding extreme hunting pressure without adverse effects on populations. The concern over nestling mortality has led to studies extensive enough to indicate that September hunting has negligible effect on populations. The limiting factors of weather and occasionally disease and predation appear to override the hunting factor. However, as Keeler (1977) recommended, more detailed information on populations is needed as hunter harvest becomes ever more intense on this most popular migratory game bird.

### Big Game

Big game native to North America include all members of the mammalian families Antilocapridae, Bovidae, Cervidae, Tayassuidae, and Ursidae. Additionally jaguars, mountain lions, wolves, and turkeys are sometimes designated as big game but these species are not considered as such in this section and are discussed elsewhere. Wild horses and burros are considered nongame species. Current taxonomic status of the big game species is presented in Table 11.12. Note that elk or wapiti are considered conspecific with European red deer, and the brown bear species complex includes the grizzly, Alaska brown bear, and European brown bear as all conspecific.

The basic reproductive biology of native Antilocapridae, Bovidae and Cervidae is presented in Table 11.13. The information on minimum breeding ages and litter

**TABLE 11.12  Current Taxonomic Status of Native North American Big Game with Subspecific Identifications for Some Currently Important Species**

| Order | Family | Genus and Species | Common Name |
|---|---|---|---|
| Carnivora | Canidae | *Canus lupus* | Gray wolf |
| | Ursidae | *Ursus americanus* | Black bear |
| | | *Ursus arctos middendorfi* | Alaska brown bear |
| | | *Ursus arctos horribilis* | Grizzly bear |
| | | *Ursus maritimus* | Polar bear |
| | Felidae | *Felis onca* | Jaguar |
| | | *Felis concolor* | Mountain lion |
| Artiodactyla | Tayassuidae | *Tayassu tajacu* | Collared peccary |
| | Cervidae | *Cervus elaphus nelsoni* | Rocky Mountain elk |
| | | *Cervus elaphus rooseveltì* | Roosevelt elk |
| | | *Cervus elaphus manitobensis* | Manitoba elk |
| | | *Cervus elaphus nannodes* | Tule elk |
| | | *Odocoileus hemionus hemionus* | Mule deer |
| | | *Odocoileus hemionus columbianus* | Columbian black-tailed deer |
| | | *Odocoileus hemionus sitkensis* | Sitka black-tailed deer |
| | | *Odocoileus hemionus crooki* | Desert mule deer |
| | | *Odocoileus virginianus* | White-tailed deer |
| | | *Odocoileus virginianus couesi* | Coues whitetail |

| Family | Scientific name | Common name |
|---|---|---|
| | *Odocoileus virginianus clavium* | Key whitetail |
| | *Odocoileus virginianus leucurus* | Columbian whitetail |
| | *Alces alces gigas* | Alaskan moose |
| | *Alces alces andersoni & americana* | Canadian moose |
| | *Alces alces shirasi* | Shiras moose |
| | *Rangifer tarandus groenlandicus* | Barren-ground caribou |
| | *Rangifer tarandus granti* | Alaskan barren-ground caribou |
| | *Rangifer tarandus caribou* | Woodland caribou |
| | *Rangifer tarandus pearyi* | Peary's caribou |
| Antilocapridae | *Antilocapra americana* | Pronghorn |
| Bovidae | *Bison bison bison* | Plains bison |
| | *Bison bison athabascae* | Wood bison |
| | *Oreamnos americanus* | Mountain goat |
| | *Ovibos moschatus* | Musk ox |
| | *Ovis canadensis canadensis* | Rocky Mountain bighorn |
| | *Ovis canadensis californiana* | California bighorn |
| | *Ovis canadensis nelsoni, mexicana, texiana, cremnobates, weemsi* | Desert bighorn |
| | *Ovis dalli dalli* | Dall's sheep |
| | *Ovis dalli stonei* | Stone's sheep |

*Source:* Modified from Jones et al. 1982 and Honacki, Kinman, and Koeppl 1982. (Used with permission.)

**TABLE 11.13  Comparative Reproductive Biology of Common Hoofed Big Game Mammals of North America**

| Species | Age at Sexual Maturity (years) | | Breeding Season | Gestation Period (days) | Partuition | Expected Litter Size | Mating Behavior |
|---|---|---|---|---|---|---|---|
| *Odocoileus virginius* (White-tailed deer) | ♂♂ 1½ ♀♀ ½ | | Peak: mid-November (early Oct.–late Jan.) | 202 | Peak: early June (mid-May–mid-July) | First: 1 Later: 1–3 | ♂♂ promiscuous; wanders over home range, pursues selected ♀. |
| *Odocoileus hemionus* (Mule deer) | ♂♂: 1½ ♀♀: 1½ | | Peak: mid-November (early Oct.–late Jan.) | 202 | Peak: early June (mid-May–mid-July) | First: 1 Later: 1–2 | ♂♂ promiscuous; wanders over home range, pursues selected ♀. |
| *Antilocapra americana* (Prong-horned antelope) | ♂♂: 1½ ♀♀:: 1½ | | Peak: mid-September | 252 | Peak: late May (late Feb.–July 1) | First: 1–2 Later: 2 | ♂♂ polygamous; herding of ♀♀ "holds" harem of ♀♀ w/wo fawns. |
| *Cervus elaphus* (Rocky Mountain elk) | ♂♂: 1½ ♀♀: 1½ | | Peak: October 1 (early Sept.–late Nov.) | 247 | Peak: June 1 (early May–July 1) | First: 1 Later: 1 | ♂♂ polygamous; herding of ♀♀ followed by pursuit of one ♀. |
| *Alces alces* (North American moose) | ♂♂: 1½ ♀♀: 1½ | | Peak: October 1 (early Sept.–late Dec.) | 240 | Peak: late May (early May–June 1) | First: 1 Later: 1–2 | ♂♂ promiscuous; wanders over home range, followed by pursuit of one ♀. |

| Species | Sex | Age (yr) | Mating season | Gestation (days) | Birth season | Young | Behavior |
|---|---|---|---|---|---|---|---|
| *Ovis canadensis* (Rocky Mountain bighorn) | ♂♂:<br>♀♀: | 1½<br>1½ | Peak: late November (mid Oct.–late Dec.) | 180 | Peak: early June (late Apr.–June 1) | First: 1<br>Later: 1 | ♂♂ promiscuous; wanders across range; pursues selected ♀. |
| *Oreamnos americanus* (Rocky Mountain goat) | ♂♂:<br>♀♀: | 2½<br>2½ | Peak: late November (late Oct.–late Dec.) | 180 | Peak: early June (mid-May–July 1) | First: 1<br>Later: 1–2 | ♂♂ promiscuous; wanders across range; selects and protects receptive ♀. |
| *Rangifer tarandus* (Barren-ground caribou) | ♂♂:<br>♀♀: | 1½<br>1½ | Peak: late October (late Sept.–early Dec.) | 225 | Peak: early June (late May–July 1) | First: 1<br>Later: 1 | ♂♂ promiscuous within herd; selects and may defend receptive ♀ from aggregation. |
| *Bison bison* (Bison) | ♂♂:<br>♀♀: | 1½<br>1½ | July–October | 270–300 | April–May | First: 1<br>Later: 1 | ♂♂ polygamous. |
| *Ovibus moschatus* (Muskox) | ♂♂:<br>♀♀: | 2½<br>2½ | August–September | 240–270 | April–May | First: 1<br>Later: 1 | ♂♂ polygamous. |
| *Tayassu tajacu* (Collared peccary) | ♀♀: | <1 | November–April (rainy season) | 145 | May–August (rainy season) | First: ?<br>Later: 1–4 | ♂♂ promiscuous within herd; one dominant ♂ mates with most estrous ♀♀. |

sizes (where more than one) is only a guide and is well known to be influenced by social and environmental conditions. Thus female white-tailed deer fawns may be capable of breeding, and may contribute substantially to the productivity of populations in Iowa (Kline 1965), but not in north Idaho (Will 1973) or in northern Michigan (Verme 1961). Alternate-year breeding has been observed in whitetails in northwestern Montana (Mundinger 1981). Columbian black-tailed deer are less fecund and attain maximum fertility later in life than mule deer (D. C. Thomas 1983). Elk in the Blue Mountains of Oregon and Washington may be capable of breeding as 18-month-old yearlings, and add significantly to total production (C. P. Conaway 1952; Buechner and Swanson 1955), but probably contribute very little in western Oregon (Harper 1971) or in the Yellowstone (Greer 1966). While bighorn sheep appear physiologically capable of breeding as yearlings (Buechner 1960) and many produce twins (Spaulding 1966), Geist (1968) considered rams over eight years of age would do most of the breeding and singletons were most common. That our native big game exhibit rather variable productivity that is dependent upon environmental conditions as they affect forage production and quality is well known. The long-term record of mule deer population composition trends in the Missouri River Breaks of Montana described by Mackie (1973) is a good example of this phenomenon, where severe winters or spring-summer drought is critical (Figure 11.14). Teer, Thomas, and Walker (1965) demonstrate the impacts of drought on Texas white-tailed deer populations (Table 11.14).

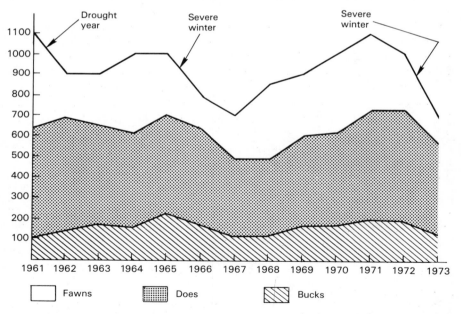

**Figure 11.14** Year-to-year trends and relative proportion of bucks, does, and fawns in early winter populations of mule deer on a 100–square mile study area in the Missouri River Breaks, 1961–1973. From Mackie 1973. (Used with permission.)

**TABLE 11.14  Effects of Severe Drought on White-Tailed Deer Population Density, Productivity, and Mortality in South Central Texas**

| Year | Approximate Rainfall (inches) | Population Density (deer per 100 acres) | Embryos per Female Fawn | Embryos per Adult Female | Percent Fawns in Population | Natural mortality (percent standing crop lost) |
|---|---|---|---|---|---|---|
| 1953 | 20 | – | – | – | 43 | – |
| 1954 | 11 | 18 | – | – | 27 | 52 |
| 1955 | 25 | 8 | – | – | 12 | – |
| 1956 | 10 | 12 | – | – | 34 | 28 |
| 1957 | 35 | 9 | 0.32 | 1.54 | 19 | 8 |
| 1958 | 33 | 14 | 0.11 | 1.26 | 44 | 9 |
| 1959 | 37 | 18 | 0.11 | 1.05 | 38 | 14 |
| 1960 | 30 | 18 | 0.11 | 0.93 | 31 | 4 |
| 1961 | 28 | 19 | – | – | 25 | – |

*Source:* After Teer, Thomas, and Walker 1965. (Used with permission.)

**White-tailed deer.** Michigan white-tailed deer have probably been among the most intensively investigated big game populations. Harvest characteristics were investigated in that state by Eberhardt (1960). Hunting seasons have been predominantly for bucks with antlers over 3 inches long, with some either-sex permit hunts in areas of high density. The hunter is quite obviously the major cause of mortality in bucks with a year class or cohort being virtually removed in four to five years. Estimates of the Michigan population were at about 700,000 animals in fall, with the legal harvest varying between 70,000 and 100,000 deer in the late 1950s.

The proportion of the buck population that was shot each year varied between 40 and 80 percent, being higher in southern Michigan (Table 11.15), with the highest proportion coinciding with the highest reproductive rate. Thus no evidence existed that this level of harvest was adversely affecting reproduction.

TABLE 11.15    Hunting Effort and Percent of White-Tailed Deer Bucks
Harvested in Two Areas of Michigan, 1952-1958

| Area | Hunting Effort[a] | | Percent of Buck Population Harvested | |
|---|---|---|---|---|
| | Average | Range | Average | Range |
| Upper Peninsula (District 2) | 44.1 | 40.2–47.6 | 47.9 | 39.5–53.3 |
| Lower Peninsula (District 8) | 93.6 | 78.5–102.6 | 68.9 | 60.0–80.7 |

*Source:* After Eberhardt 1960. (Used with permission.)
[a]Hunting effort equals number of hunter days per square mile of deer range.

Hunting effort, measured in terms of hunter days per unit area, was roughly related to the proportions of the deer population that was killed (Table 11.15). However, the proportion of the buck population that was vulnerable to hunting decreased during the hunting season (Figure 11.15), and a density of hunters of over 15 per square mile did not result in much increase in the harvest. This suggests that such high levels of hunters cause a decrease in efficiency of the individual and a lessened opportunity to kill a deer.

Minnesota investigations show that weather has a profound influence on hunting success (A. B. Erickson et al. 1961), and presence or absence of snow is the single most important factor. When ideal conditions, 3-4 inches of fresh snow plus a few days of zero temperatures occur, hunter success increases. Seasons that coincide with the rut result in greater buck kills. About 60 percent of the deer kill occurred during the first three days of the season, and 84 percent during the first six days in Minnesota over the years of record.

Yearling bucks are known to be more vulnerable to harvest than older animals (Maguire and Severinghaus 1954), presumably because of their inexperience. Eberhardt (1960) did not find this to appreciably influence the harvest in Michigan because some yearlings had sublegal-sized antlers so that the proportion of yearlings in the harvest, especially in the northern areas where such animals were more common, was lower than the overall proportion of bucks taken. Percentages of year-

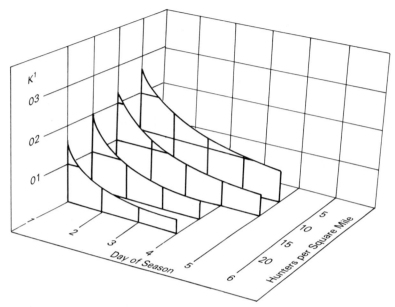

**Figure 11.15** Joint effect of day of season and hunter density on $k'$, the percent of buck population shot per hunter-day. From Eberhardt 1960. (Used with permission.)

ling males in the fall male population ranged from 35.6–69.9 percent and did not vary through the hunting season.

Eberhardt (1960) concluded that since yearling vulnerability did not change through the hunting season, changes in deer behavior including shifts to dense cover were probably responsible for the decline in vulnerability of the buck population to hunting. Maguire and Severinghaus (1954) reported vulnerability of yearling bucks to be higher early in the hunting season than it was later, indicating that wariness developed in this age class as the season progressed. However, for the season as a whole, wariness did not significantly distort the age composition of the kill, except for a buck season one or two days long. No evidence occurred that adult females were more or less vulnerable to hunting through changes in wariness. Adult males may be less wary during the height of the rut in some areas.

Illegal killing of does and fawns during buck-only seasons is known to be substantial. The Michigan surveys of nonlegal mortality (Eberhardt 1960) indicate that over 70 percent of adult buck and doe mortality was hunter-related, while approximately 48 percent of the fawn mortality was due to starvation (Table 11.16). However, the proportion of the buck population that was not legally killed but still died amounted to only 12 percent of the bucks surviving the hunting season. For the entire population, approximately 55 percent of total mortality was nonlegal mortality caused by hunters, 32 percent was caused by malnutrition, and 12 percent by predation, accidents, and other nonhunting causes. Eberhardt (1960)

TABLE 11.16  Results of Deer Mortality Surveys, 1955, 1956, and 1959, in Michigan

| Cause of Mortality | Adult Males | Adult Females | Juveniles | Total[a] |
|---|---|---|---|---|
| Shot[b] | 61 (0–100) | 43 (3–7) | 17 (6–32) | 24 (14–44) |
| Found dead[c] | 14 (0–100) | 33 (15–47) | 25 (17–38) | 31 (19–36) |
| Starved | 0 | 15 (9–18) | 48 (27–61) | 33 (17–40) |
| Dog or predator | 0 | 4 (0–8) | 9 (0–12) | 5 (2–8) |
| Accident | 25 (0–100) | 5 (0–17) | 4 (3–5) | 4 (2–9) |
| Disease | 0 | 0 | 2 (0–5) | 1 (0–3) |
| Unknown | 0 | 0 | 1 (0–3) | 2 (0–5) |
| Mean observed annual loss (number of deer) | 947 (394–1741) | 10,647 (8483–13,930) | 21,298 (17,098–23,772) | 36,023 (32,517–41,646) |

*Source:* Eberhardt 1960. (Used with permission.)

*Note:* Figures represent the mean percentages of total mortality, excluding legal harvest, for each sex-age class for all three years. Ranges (in parentheses) represent the extreme differences between years.

[a]Includes deer whose sex and age were unknown.

[b]Shot but not recovered by hunter.

[c]Undetermined fall–early winter mortality probably attributable to hunting.

felt that limited special seasons, when does and fawns could be taken, could reduce the nonlegal, hunter-related mortality, but that these losses probably must be accepted. Poaching losses were not estimated, and could be of significance locally. Poaching was concentrated in early fall and midwinter. Illegal hunting is often tolerated by residents and can be an important limiting factor in some areas (Decker, Brown, and Sarbello 1981).

Eberhardt (1960) cited an unpublished report by J. J. Hickey that concluded that the illegal kill could be expected to amount to half of the legal harvest during buck-only seasons in the eastern United States. Crippling losses in central Texas were estimated at 15 percent of the legal recovered kill by Teer et al. (1965). Thus, buck-only seasons indeed appear wasteful of white-tailed deer, since substantial mortality to other sex-age classes accrues. Still, bucks-only seasons are useful when populations are low and hunting is to be allowed. These seasons have been seriously criticized for their wastefulness and inability to reduce malnutrition loss and over-browsing of winter range in past years, and rightfully so given the conditions that existed. Nevertheless, they are to be recognized as one legitimate alternative in game management and should be considered on a basis of merit for the situation at hand, rather than on the emotion-laden biopolitical experiences under which they were dictated in the past, and in some cases still are. It can be very difficult for a game manager who has been ordered to implement a season because of bio-political implications to objectively consider that season on its merits, and the "buck-law" is perhaps the outstanding example of this. "Buck-laws" are still in existence, and pose a restriction of flexibility in management which can still be a serious problem.

Archery hunts have become popular, and serve to provide additional sport without contributing much to the harvest. F. R. Martin and Krefting (1953) reported success of archers at Necedah Refuge Wisconsin averaged 2.2 percent in comparison to 21 percent for gun hunters. Archers took a total of 356 (18-129 per year) deer as compared to 3989 (248-1687 per year) by gun hunters over the 1946-1950 period on that area. Minnesota archers were similarly successful over the 1951-1960 period, averaging 250 deer per year, as compared to an average of 71,347 deer per year by gun hunters (A. B. Erickson et al. 1961). Hawn and Ryel (1969) estimated 1930 deer taken by archers and 94,190 by firearms during the 1966 season in Michigan. There are complaints from gun hunters that archers disturb deer and decrease success during the gun season, but these are obviously not substantiated by the figures. Archery hunts are a useful means of increasing the hunting opportunity without appreciably affecting the harvest, but the wounding rate by archery hunters may be higher than that by gun hunters (Stormer, Kirkpatrick, and Hockstra 1979).

The George Reserve deer herd occurs on a 1200-acre enclosure in southern Michigan, and has been intensively studied since 1933 (O'Roke and Hamerstrom 1948; Chase and Jenkins 1962). Populations were censused by driving in early winter, and harvested by experienced personnel, providing a reasonably complete record of population changes. The 1942-1961 period was one in which attempts to

TABLE 11.17  Population Data from the George Reserve Deer Herd in Southern Michigan, 1942–1961

| Year | Prefawning Population | Computed Fawn Crop | Peak Population | Removals by Hunting[a] | | | | Other Removals[a] | | | | Removals by Unknown Causes | Total Removed | Percent of Peak Population Removed |
|---|---|---|---|---|---|---|---|---|---|---|---|---|---|---|
| | | | | Males | | Females | | Males | | Females | | | | |
| | | | | Ad. | Juv. | Ad. | Juv. | Ad. | Juv. | Ad. | Juv. | | | |
| 1942–1943 | 49 | 51 | 100 | 17 | 4 | 17 | 3 | – | – | – | – | 2 | 43 | 43.0 |
| 1943–1944 | 57 | 32 | 89 | 12 | 2 | 14 | 4 | – | 1 | – | – | – | 33 | 37.1 |
| 1944–1945 | 56 | 25 | 81 | 12 | 3 | 9 | 6 | – | – | – | – | – | 30 | 37.0 |
| 1945–1946 | 51 | 26 | 77 | 10 | 2 | 10 | – | – | – | – | – | – | 22 | 28.6 |
| 1946–1947 | 55 | 19 | 74 | 3 | – | 4 | – | 3 | – | – | – | 3 | 13 | 17.6 |
| 1947–1948 | 61 | 65 | 126 | 17 | 7 | 23 | 3 | – | – | 2 | – | – | 52 | 41.3 |
| 1948–1949 | 74 | 25 | 99 | 16 | 2 | 9 | 3 | – | – | – | – | – | 30 | 36.3 |
| 1949–1950 | 69 | 4 | 73 | 12 | – | 6 | 1 | – | – | – | – | – | 19 | 26.0 |
| 1950–1951 | 54 | 51 | 105 | 14 | 4 | 8 | 5 | 2 | – | 1 | – | 1 | 35 | 33.3 |
| 1951–1952 | 70 | 34 | 104 | 17 | 6 | 20 | 7 | – | 2 | – | 1 | 4 | 57 | 54.8 |
| 1952–1953 | 47 | 19 | 66 | 8 | 1 | 1 | 1 | – | – | – | – | 3 | 14 | 21.2 |
| 1953–1954 | 52 | 43 | 95 | 18 | 2 | 13 | 5 | 1 | – | – | – | 2 | 41 | 43.2 |
| 1954–1955 | 54 | 51 | 95 | 14 | 6 | 17 | 5 | 2 | – | 1 | – | – | 45 | 47.4 |
| 1955–1956 | 50 | 43 | 93 | 34 | 1 | – | 1 | – | – | – | – | 2 | 38 | 40.9 |
| 1956–1957 | 55 | 74 | 129 | 15 | 17 | 25 | 10 | 7 | 1 | 6 | – | 2 | 83 | 64.3 |
| 1957–1958 | 46 | 65 | 111 | 25 | 3 | 22 | 5 | 1 | – | 4 | – | – | 60 | 54.1 |
| 1958–1959 | 51 | 26 | 77 | 11 | 2 | 3 | – | – | – | – | – | 3 | 19 | 24.7 |
| 1959–1960 | 58 | 41 | 99 | 21 | 1 | 16 | 6 | 1 | – | 3 | 1 | 1 | 50 | 50.5 |
| 1960–1961 | 49 | 30 | 79 | 16 | 8 | 3 | 3 | 2 | – | – | – | – | 32 | 40.5 |

Source: After Chase and Jenkins 1962.

Note: Average removal was 37.0 percent over the 19-year period, during which harvests approached a sustained yield.

[a]Ad. = adults; Juv. = juveniles.

stabilize the population through hunting occurred (Table 11.17). The average population peak was 93 animals during the period, about 45 deer per square mile. An average of 37.4 deer were removed, or 39 percent of the fall population. The harvest was 44 percent antlered bucks and 56 percent antlerless deer. Nonhunting mortality was always very low, averaging 9 percent of the total mortality. Chase and Jenkins (1962) felt that censusing errors probably attributed to some of the inconsistencies in the data, but the population was still a good example of sustained yield. The percentage removed each year varied from 17.6 to 64.3 percent. The annual harvest rate exhibited in this investigation would not be approached in areas where other mortality factors were more prevalent. The annual harvest rate was higher than O'Roke and Hamerstrom (1948) estimated earlier for the maximum sustained yield for this population.

In Iowa, Kline (1965) estimated that 20 percent of a highly productive deer population was harvested annually between 1954 and 1962, during which time the population increased by an estimated 34.2 percent. Banasiak (1961) reported that approximately 20 percent of the fall deer population in Maine was removed by all causes during the hunting season, 15 percent legally (Table 11.18). Pre-hunting season losses appeared to be about 15 percent of the postfawning population. Winter loss accounted for an average of 10 percent of the post-hunting season population. C. M. Kirkpatrick et al. (1976) reported that 20 to 25 percent of the fall population on an Indiana study area was harvested annually. An additional 15 to 18 percent of the population was lost to causes other than legal hunting in this highly productive population. Teer et al. (1965) estimated that 14 percent of the Llano Basin, Texas, deer herd was harvested annually, or about half of the annual increment. A number of reports suggest that removals of approximately 33 percent of a white-tailed deer population can be sustained (Eberhardt 1960; Teer et al. 1965; Arnold and Verme 1963). However, the amount of this removal that is available for harvest appeared to be quite variable.

The question of whether white-tailed deer population density does have an influence on reproductive rates was investigated by Teer et al. (1965) and Eberhardt (1960). The Texas data suggest that an inverse relationship between density and conception rates of yearlings and adults existed (Figure 11.16). In addition, breeding and ovulation was delayed as density increased. The hypothesis most logical for this inverse relationship was that forage supplies were inadequate to sustain high reproductive effort at high densities. Eberhardt (1960) found reproductive rates of does age two and over to be 67.6 percent (range 50.3–79.1) and of yearlings to be 4.7 percent in the northeastern lower Peninsula of Michigan with 30 deer per square mile. In areas where deer population density was 15 per square mile, the rates were 82.2 percent (range 65.9–89.8) for does and 8.5 percent for yearlings. These data indicate that an inverse relationship occurs between reproductive rate and population density, but differences were not considered great enough to suggest that reductions would be compensated enough to substantially increase yield in actual numbers. The evidence suggests that hunter harvest can induce increases in reproductive performance, if weather and forage conditions do not override the

**TABLE 11.18  Life Equation of the Statewide Deer Herd, 1954–1957, in Maine**

| Season | Fawns | | Adults | | All Ages | | | |
|---|---|---|---|---|---|---|---|---|
| | Male | Female | Male | Female | Male | Female | Total | Percent Males |
| Prehunt population | 156 | 139 | 364 | 341 | 520 | 480 | 1000 | 52.0 |
| Hunting season loss | 28 | 25 | 83 | 63 | 111 | 88 | 199 | 55.9 |
| Posthunt population | 128 | 114 | 281 | 278 | 409 | 392 | 801 | 51.1 |
| Winter loss | 18 | 19 | 20 | 23 | 38 | 42 | 80 | 46.1 |
| Prefawning population | 110 | 95 | 261 | 255 | 371 | 350 | 721 | 51.4 |
| Fawns to adults | 110 → | 95 → | 110 | 95 | | | | |
| Fawning gain | 232 | 198 | | | 232 | 198 | 430 | 53.9 |
| Postfawning population | 232 | 198 | 371 | 350 | 603 | 548 | 1151 | 52.4 |
| Summer loss | 76 | 59 | 7 | 9 | 83 | 68 | 151 | 54.2 |

|  | Losses | Fawning Gains |
|---|---|---|
| Hunting season | −199 | |
| Winter loss | − 80 | |
| Summer loss | −151 | |
| Total | 430 | 430 |

*Source:* After Banasiak 1961. (Used with permission.)

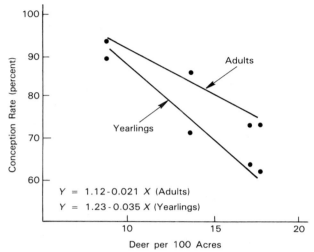

**Figure 11.16** Regression of conception rates of yearling and adult does on density of deer in the Llano Basin from 1957 to 1960. From Teer, Thomas, and Walker 1965. (Used with permission.)

influence. If weather conditions allow, a population reduction through hunter harvest may well be a means of providing more forage for the remaining population. This can improve the nutritional status and thereby increase productivity. However, the more likely significant result may well be to allow forage conditions to improve, and to reduce alternate forms of mortality, especially winter malnutrition loss, vehicle loss, and perhaps predation. Thus more intensive hunter harvest is probably a substitute for other mortality and thus affects survival more significantly than production. Also, intensive hunter harvest may serve to reduce the dramatic fluctuations in a population that are attributable to adverse weather and forage conditions.

White tails existing on areas where weather extremes consistently exert an important control will not likely exhibit the compensatory responses suggested for populations existing in areas where weather exerts less influence. In Manitoba, low temperatures cause low annual increments to whitetail populations in spite of relatively high fertility levels and an adequate forage supply (Ranson 1967). In such cases, hunting mortality becomes additive at a much lower harvest level than where weather is not limiting. The lower survival and production rates observed for whitetails in northern Idaho (Will 1973) and northwestern Montana (Mundinger 1981) indicate that lower harvests and less compensatory response to hunting is likely in these areas.

Finally, the question of accurately estimating deer harvests is a source of concern, and Michigan data provide insight into sampling efforts designed to judge the harvest. Hawn and Ryel (1969) were able to compare a mail questionnaire survey of 1 out of 40 firearm license holders and 1 out of 15 bow and arrow license holders with an attempted survey of all license holders, after the legislature amended the 1967–1968 appropriation to require the canvass of all hunters. The total survey was conducted through the use of report forms from license agents who collected information from license buyers about the previous, 1966, year's hunt. This was compared with the standard sample survey, which includes up to five mailings to individuals who are included in the sample to ensure adequate responses and which was over 90 percent of the people selected from the sample. The sample survey estimated 94,190 deer killed by firearms and 1930 by archers, while the total survey estimated 104,044 deer killed by firearms and 4680 by archers. The total survey estimates were not available until 15 months after the season, compared to 6 months for the sample. There was no way to judge the accuracy of the total survey, while the sample survey was statistically valid and estimates at 95-percent confidence intervals were ±4 percent. In addition, an estimated 67 percent of archers and 74 percent of firearm hunters were contacted through the total survey. Thus, the idea that the sample survey resulted in inflated deer harvest figures was not substantiated by the attempt at a complete enumeration of the harvest. The inability to determine the accuracy of the total harvest estimate supported the use of the sampling technique, whose accuracy could be judged. While this comparison may well have served a purpose in convincing some of the value of sampling, many inveterate critics of the management program no doubt remain unconvinced in keeping with the emotional nature of this issue.

One conclusion from these investigations stands out: the white-tailed deer can sustain very heavy hunting pressure without undue effect on productivity or standing crop in many parts of its range. It is often taken for granted because it is so ubiquitous and adaptable, but its wariness and elusiveness make it a premium game animal.

**Elk.** Elk populations are subject to a wide variety of hunting seasons and resultant harvest intensities that are related to population size; accessibility to hunters; hunting traditions, which include type of hunt and style of hunting; and management objectives. Populations that are readily accessible are hunted under more conservative regulations, such as limited permits or short seasons, than are populations that occupy less accessible backcountry. However, as hunting pressure has increased, and hunters have become better equipped and proportionately more skilled, there has been a trend toward more conservative seasons that more closely regulate the harvest. Colorado hunting seasons typify this trend, wherein liberal either-sex seasons alternating with bulls-only seasons during the 1948–1952 period in the White River area created wide fluctuations in numbers harvested annually. Establishment of a general bull season with limited either-sex permits in 1953 created a steadily increasing harvest through 1965 (Boyd 1970).

The specific kind of hunting season will often depend upon past experience and current management objectives, although data for some populations is now extensive enough to apply computerized models such as those of Walters and Gross (1972) that help to predict results of various hunting season alternatives. Generally, the game manager has sufficient information on results of past seasons, plus population estimates of varying reliability which nevertheless indicate the general trend in numbers, and sex and age ratio information to allow a judgment as to what type of season is most suitable. Thus season setting often involves a combination of data examination and accumulated experience with the elk populations and the hunting citizenry, plus others such as ranchers and outfitters who have an interest in or are influenced by the elk. If a population existing in backcountry and subject to long either-sex seasons is to be increased, then a change to shorter either-sex season coupled with a general bull season, or simply elimination of antlerless hunting may be in order. Restrictions on season length may be useful for migratory populations that become more available to hunters in late fall after snows remain, but variation in number of permits or length of the antlerless harvest are often more suitable for populations that do not migrate and commonly receive most of the harvest early in the season. Elk are very highly sought by hunters, and thus populations can be readily manipulated through hunting season adjustments in most cases.

Hunter success is nevertheless related to weather and snow conditions. In western Oregon and Washington, Roosevelt elk are less vulnerable to hunters if fog and rainy conditions prevail (Harper 1971). Cold weather tends to heighten rutting activity and bugling during daylight hours, which enhances hunter success. Usually, a high harvest may be expected early in the season followed by low numbers taken until snow cover creates better hunting conditions. Daily elk harvest during a January season in the Gallatin River area of Montana was highest on the days following a snowstorm and temperatures at or below 0°F (Peek 1966).

One of the major concerns is the effect that extremely low proportions of bulls in populations may have on subsequent productivity. The White River, Colorado, elk population data demonstrate the problem nicely. Postseason sex ratios among adults ranged between 9:100 and 28:100 during the 1960-1965 period, while preseason sex ratios ranged from 33:100 to 69:100 (Boyd 1970). Preseason cow to calf ratios showed a downward trend during this period from 100:70 to 100:50, the latter of which still exceeds ratios for most elk populations. Boyd (1970) concluded that even though yearling bulls were capable of breeding, a correlation between number of bulls in a herd during breeding season and the resulting number of calves produced the next season did exist. The postseason sex ratio of 9:100 apparently did affect calf production.

Breeding trials conducted in western Oregon indicated that Roosevelt elk yearling bulls did not reach sexual maturity until the breeding season was in progress, resulting in calves being born later (July 1-15) than when older bulls were present (Hines and Lemos 1979). Calf production and survival was also lower when only yearling bulls served as breeders. Prothero, Spillett, and Balph (1979) reported rutting activity of yearling bulls started later, was shorter in duration and less frequent than among older bulls. Additionally, yearling bulls were not as vocal or aggressive during rutting as mature bulls.

Conversely, C. E. Trainer and Lightfoot (1970) found no evidence that calf production of Roosevelt elk in western Oregon was adversely affected where sex ratios were reduced to 7:100 in the posthunting season. Cow to calf ratios averaged 100:37 for the 1954-1960 period (yearling bulls unhunted) and 100:44 for the

1961-1968 period (yearling bulls hunted). The relatively low cow to calf ratios, when compared with those of elk in northeastern Oregon (100:51 average, 1950-1969) were attributed to a lower plane of nutrition for the western Oregon elk (C. E. Trainer 1971).

No significant changes in pregnancy rates of yearling and adult females of the Cache, Utah, herd could be attributed to a change in hunting season where yearling bulls were initially 36 percent of the male harvest and subsequently 75 percent (Kimball and Wolfe 1974). Pregnancy rates varied considerably between years, ranging from 76 to 100 percent in adults and 0 to 17 percent for yearlings between 1970 and 1977 when an open bull season reduced survival rates of males to 21.9 percent from an earlier rate of 58 percent when more restrictive hunting seasons were in use.

Boyd (1970) postulated that yearlings may not be capable of successfully breeding all cows in large harems, or that large numbers of immature cows added to herds with progressively fewer bulls may reduce the cow to calf ratio even though production among breeding cows was not affected. Harem size of elk inhabiting denser forests may be lower than those occupying more open terrain, but Knight (1970) reported that older bulls were associated with larger harems than younger bulls. Also, some harems in the Sun River, Montana, population contained yearling bulls, which suggests they were sexually immature and hence tolerated by the harem bull. Follis (1972) reported that conception dates of cows bred by yearling bulls tended to be later than for cows bred by older bulls. Data concerning effects of severely reduced proportions of bulls in populations on subsequent breeding success are scanty, but imply that factors other than age structure of the bull population are involved. These factors include population density, female age structure, proportion of breeders in the female population, behavior of both sexes during the rut, and perhaps cover density as it may affect harem size. Many male populations are reduced to less than 20 percent of the entire adult population by hunting with no effect on subsequent breeding success.

The Utah data of Follis (1972), which shows cows bred by yearling bulls to have later conception dates than those bred by older bulls, may suggest a delayed but still detrimental effect of allowing age structures in the male segment of the population to drop to levels where yearling bulls do most of the breeding. Calves that are born late and are thus smaller when they enter the winter may be more vulnerable to mortality related to severe winter conditions. The Cache elk population in Utah, wherein yearling bulls comprised progressively higher percentages of the harvest over a nine-year period until 81 percent were yearlings in 1971, still showed high productivity (Kimball and Wolfe 1974). The Utah workers recognized the possible relationships between calf size and survival through winter, and also that a different harvesting regime than unlimited bull harvest would be necessary if trophy production (i.e., more mature bulls) was a goal for the future. Another result of this study was that unlimited bull seasons tended to slow population growth. This was attributed to an increase in hunting activity upon change from permit or restrictive hunts to unlimited bull season with limited either-sex permits for some areas, which raised the associated illegal losses in the population. Hunting activity increased fivefold with the liberalized season.

Batchelor (1968) raised another possibility involving detrimental aspects of sustained heavy exploitation of the conspecific red deer in New Zealand. Concomitant with population declines attributable to year-long hunting, a decline in productivity of the remaining females occurred. This was attributable to shifts in habitat selection to areas more secure from hunters but less productive of forage. While hunting seasons on elk are not long enough to cause such shifts, combinations of other types of human activity on ranges of elk that are hunted and therefore conditioned to fear humans may prevent occupation of traditionally used range and confound management based solely on hunter harvest. Thus, restriction of human activity, especially on winter and spring ranges but also on other ranges, may be in order where productivity is low, and should be monitored.

Evidence that yearling bulls are more vulnerable than older bulls to hunting mortality was provided by Picton (1961). Reasons include the presence of yearling bulls in large cow-calf groups which may occur in more accessible areas where they are more easily located than adult bulls. Also, calves are frequently harvested during either-sex seasons at lower levels than they occur in the population (Boyd 1970). Differential distribution by sex and age of elk within a migratory population (Peek and Lovaas 1968) will be reflected in relative vulnerability of the various age and sex classes to the gun. Thus, analysis of sex and age distributions in the harvest may be as much an analysis of relative vulnerabilities of the sex and age classes as an analysis of age structure of the population. Data on distribution and movements are thus critical to interpreting population changes.

Knight (1970) reported that early season hunters in the Sun River, Montana, area usually took higher proportions of calves than those hunting later. Also, during years of light harvest when weather conditions remained mild, the same phenomenon occurred. Movement data suggested that elk summering in the Sun River Game Preserve, closed to hunting, did not become available to hunters until late in the season after severe weather and these elk had lower cow to calf ratios than those living outside the preserve. Several investigations suggest an inverse relationship between calf production and density of an elk population (Table 11.19). This does not always mean that a density reduction caused by hunting may increase subsequent calf production, however. Leege (1978) reported no increase in cow to calf ratios in the Lochsa River, Idaho, area following a series of heavy harvests that reduced browsing pressures on the winter ranges. Bear predation on elk calves was found to be a significant factor preventing increases in calf survival (Schlegel 1976).

An inverse relationship exists between calf production and survival and density of an elk population relative to the forage (Table 11.19). As harvests become high enough to reduce the population to levels where the survivors have a greater amount of forage and the general nutritional level of the population increases, calf survival can be increased (Buechner and Swanson 1955). This increase is frequently related to increased productivity of yearling cows (Greer 1966; Buechner and Swanson 1955), as well as to subsequent survival of calves produced by all age

TABLE 11.19   Summary of Data Showing an Inverse Relationship between
Elk Population Density and Calf Production

| Area | Evidence for Increased Calf Production Related to Density Change | Reference |
|---|---|---|
| Northern Yellowstone: reduction of herd from ca. 10,000 to ca. 5000, winter 1961–1962 | Pregnancy rate of yearling ♀♀ winter 1961–1962 was 9% (sample 70). Pregnancy rate in 1963–1964 was 28% (sample 32). Pregnancy rates of yearlings in 1962–1963, 1964–1965 and 1965–1966 were 0%, 9% and 4% of 13, 35, and 27 ♀♀ examined. | Greer 1966 |
| Sun River, Montana: elk using game preserve in North Fork more lightly harvested than in other areas | Cow to calf ratios of elk using game preserve, 1957–1965, averaged 100:36 while those not using preserve averaged 100:40 over same period. | Knight 1970 |
| Sun River vs. Judith River, Montana | Population composition included 9% and 13% calves in Sun River and Judith River areas, respectively. Life expectancies of elk at 2 years were 2 (♂) and 4 (♀) for Judith and 4 (♂) and 5 (♀) for Sun River populations. | Picton 1961 |
| White River, Colorado | Decrease from 100:70 in 1961 to 100:59 in 1965, as population increased from over 3200 to over 4800, and sex ratios became more disparate. | Boyd 1970 |
| Blue Mountains, Washington | Yearling pregnancy rates in 1954 were 54% (35 examined) following large reductions through harvest in 1949–1950. Percent of 2½-year-old ♀♀ lactating was 21%, 42%, and 58% of 14, 12, and 19 examined in 1952, 1953, and 1954 respectively. | Buechner and Swanson 1955 |

classes (Boyd 1970). However, Knight (1970) could not correlate lowered calf production and survival in the Sun River Game Preserve with intensity of forage utilization. Nor did harvest reduction of elk to levels below allowable use of winter forage increase calf survival in the Lochsa River, Idaho, area (Leege 1978). Predation (Schlegel 1976) prevented increased calf survival in the Lochsa, while severe winters affected yearling pregnancy rates in the Yellowstone (Greer 1966). The difficulty of attempts to generalize and possibly oversimplify the relationship between density and productivity in this species lies with our inabilities to predict effects of winter severity and predation on elk. Thus, modeling efforts that ask the question, "what if?" are useful. By calculating the effects of altered mortality rates of each age class, as might occur due to weather or predator effects, such models help the game manager to formulate possible hunting seasons given past results, contingent upon the weather and other factors that may subsequently limit the population.

The Leslie projection matrix affords a means of manipulating age-specific fecundity rates, survival rates, and age structure to determine rates of increase and yield. Emlen (1973:246), Poole (1974:21), and others describe the calculations, which involve matrix algebra, and Usher (1972) illustrates its use for a population of red deer. The basic matrix multiplies age specific fecundity and survival rates times a population structure as follows:

$$M_n = \begin{matrix} F_1 & F_2 & F_3 & F_4 & F_{k-1} & F_k \\ S_1 & 0 & 0 & 0 & 0 & 0 \\ 0 & S_2 & 0 & 0 & 0 & 0 \\ 0 & 0 & S_3 & 0 & 0 & 0 \\ 0 & 0 & 0 & S_4 & 0 & 0 \\ 0 & 0 & 0 & 0 & S_{k-1} & S_r \end{matrix} \qquad N_m = \begin{matrix} A_1 \\ A_2 \\ A_3 \\ A_4 \\ A_k \end{matrix}$$

where $N_m$ is the matrix composed of the numbers in each age $A_1 - A_k$ in a population; and $M_n$ is the matrix composed of $S_1 - S_k$ (age specific survival rates) and $F_1 - F_k$ (average number of young born per female alive at start of preceding year).

For the elk population described in Table 11.20, the structures of $N_m$ and $M_n$ are as follows (for females only, since the computations have to be done separately for each sex):

| $N_m$ | $M_n$ | | | | | | | | | |
|---|---|---|---|---|---|---|---|---|---|---|
| 346 | 0.0 | 0.128 | 0.451 | 0.451 | 0.451 | 0.451 | 0.451 | 0.451 | 0.451 | 0.451 |
| 205 | .80 | 0 | 0 | 0 | 0 | 0 | 0 | 0 | 0 | 0 |
| 164 | 0 | .95 | 0 | 0 | 0 | 0 | 0 | 0 | 0 | 0 |
| 148 | 0 | 0 | .95 | 0 | 0 | 0 | 0 | 0 | 0 | 0 |
| 134 | 0 | 0 | 0 | .95 | 0 | 0 | 0 | 0 | 0 | 0 |
| 120 | 0 | 0 | 0 | 0 | .95 | 0 | 0 | 0 | 0 | 0 |
| 108 | 0 | 0 | 0 | 0 | 0 | .95 | 0 | 0 | 0 | 0 |
| 95 | 0 | 0 | 0 | 0 | 0 | 0 | .95 | 0 | 0 | 0 |
| 53 | 0 | 0 | 0 | 0 | 0 | 0 | 0 | .95 | 0 | 0 |
| 25 | 0 | 0 | 0 | 0 | 0 | 0 | 0 | 0 | .95 | 0 |

For purposes of illustrating potential yield for elk populations of different characteristics using this model, the following assumptions are made: (1) fecundity rates do not change; (2) survival rates do not change; (3) population density does not affect the fecundity rate; and (4) sex ratio does not affect fecundity. Caughley (1977:111) has pointed out that fecundity is difficult to calculate from field data, since it is defined as the number of individuals born per females of each age who will be alive in the age group comprising individuals less than one year old. However, this does not apply to the matrix because the births occur at start of the time period and mortality is then built into the survival rate. Fecundity rates as used in the following analyses are actually proportions of females in each age class that bear calves. This parameter may be estimated from slaughters in late winter that allow enumerations of pregnant cows, or by rectal palpation of females trapped or cap-

**TABLE 11.20** Age Structure and Population Changes after Ten Years under Various Harvest Strategies for a Highly Productive Elk Population with High Survival Rates

| | | | | | | | | | | | 75% Bulls, 10% Calves, and 15% Cows Harvested | |
| | Survival Rates (percent) | | Initial Population | | No Harvest | | 75% Bulls | | | | | |
| Age (years) | ♂ | ♀ | ♂ | ♀ | ♂ | ♀ | ♂ | ♀ | ♂ | ♀ | |
|---|---|---|---|---|---|---|---|---|---|---|
| Calf | 80 | 80 | 345 | 346 | 1434 | 1434 | 1434 | 1434 | 349 | 349 |
| 1 | 95 | 95 | 205 | 205 | 995 | 995 | 995 | 995 | 265 | 265 |
| 2 | 95 | 95 | 41 | 164 | 813 | 813 | 203 | 813 | 62 | 211 |
| 3 | 95 | 95 | 9 | 148 | 663 | 663 | 41 | 663 | 15 | 168 |
| 4 | 95 | 95 | 2 | 134 | 543 | 543 | 9 | 543 | 3 | 134 |
| 5 | 95 | 95 | 1 | 120 | 446 | 446 | 2 | 446 | 1 | 108 |
| 6 | 95 | 95 | 1 | 108 | 368 | 368 | 1 | 368 | 1 | 87 |
| 7 | 95 | 95 | 0 | 95 | 304 | 304 | 1 | 304 | 0 | 70 |
| 8 | 95 | 95 | 0 | 53 | 253 | 253 | 0 | 253 | 0 | 57 |
| 9 | 0 | 0 | 0 | 25 | 211 | 211 | 0 | 211 | 0 | 52 |
| 10 | — | — | 0 | 0 | | | | | | |
| Total by sex | | | 604 | 1398 | 6029 | 6029 | 2684 | 6029 | 695 | 1499 |

| | | | | |
|---|---|---|---|---|
| Population Total | 2002 | 12,058 | 8713 | 2194 |
| Bull:cow:calf ratio | 25:100:54 | 100:100:52 | 7:100:52 | 9:100:58 |
| Annual rate of increase | — | 1.158 | 1.158 | 1.008 |
| Percent of population harvested in 10th year | | | 10.8 | 22.2 |

| Number killed in 10th year | | | | |
|---|---|---|---|---|
| Bulls | | | 938 | 259 |
| Cows | | | 0 | 199 |
| Calves | | | 0 | 30 |
| Total | | | 938 | 488 |

*Note:* Fecundity rates for this population were 27 percent for yearlings and 95 percent for adults.

tured. Since mortality can occur before parturition and after the rate is estimated, such methods probably overestimate the fecundity rate. Survival rates may be obtained by aging livetrapped individuals, or by using a sample of the hunter harvest, which probably underestimates the actual age structure (Quick 1958).

Sufficient information, summarized by Follis (1972), is available to indicate the range of adult and yearling pregnancy rates that may exist in elk, even if the sample sizes for any one investigation are low. Pregnancy rates for yearling females in 24 studies reviewed by Follis averaged 24 percent and ranged between 0 and 81 percent. Pregnancy rates of adults over one year old averaged 86 percent and ranged between 43 and 100 percent. Most adult females retain their capability to produce a calf through old age although Greer (1966), Lowe (1969), and Flook (1970) suggest some decrease in pregnancy rates occurs among the oldest age classes.

Age structure and survival rates for a highly productive elk population with a sex ratio of 25:100 and a cow to calf ratio of 100:54 is presented in Table 11.20. Survival rates are purposely set extremely high, which means mortality other than by hunting is very low. The matrix is projected for a ten-year period, for a population starting at 2002. The unbalanced sex ratio and population numbers as distributed are assumed to have resulted from prior harvest manipulations that have been discontinued. Under a no-harvest strategy, a sixfold population increase at ten years occurs, and the stabilized rate of increase, $g$, is 1.158 ($g$ being the finite rate of increase of a population from time $t$ to time $t + 1$; Caughley 1977). No change in cow to calf ratios has occurred, which verifies Caughley's (1974a) conclusion that this index to productivity does not serve as an index to population change. The sex ratio has attained equality after ten years of no harvest.

If the yearling fecundity rate of 27 percent is changed to 50 percent while adult fecundity rate and all survival rates are the same, the population increases 13-fold at ten years with no harvest (Table 11.21). The cow to calf ratio has increased to 100:69, a reflection of the increase in yearling breeding. Yearling fecundity may be quite variable between years, depending upon winter severity, which affects age at attainment of sexual maturity. The comparison of the effect of 27 versus 50 percent yearling fecundity on population performance indicates considerable influence of this age-specific fecundity rate if the fluctuations are of the magnitude indicated. It is pertinent to note here that opportunities to obtain sufficient numbers of yearling females in late winter to determine the fecundity rate with relative confidence are not often found, and require intensive effort.

Harvests of bulls only at the level of 75 percent of all animals over age one does not affect the rate of increase (Tables 11.20 and 11.21). However, the sex ratio drops to 7-8 bulls per 100 cows, and 80 percent of the bull population excluding calves is in the yearling age class. At the tenth year of such intensive male-only harvesting, 11-12 percent of the population has been harvested—938 males of 8713 elk in Table 11.20, and 2258 males of 19,962 elk in Table 11.21. Obviously, this rate of population increase cannot be sustained and density-dependent factors affecting the mortality rate would become apparent. However,

**TABLE 11.21  Changes in Elk Populations Shown in Table 11.20 When Yearling Fecundity Rate is Increased to 50 Percent**

|  | Initial Population | | Population after Ten Years of Strategy | | | | | | | | |
|  |  | | No Hunting | | 75% Bulls Harvested | | 75% Bulls, 20% Cows and Calves Harvested | | 75% Bulls, 25% Cows and Calves Harvested | |
| Age (years) | ♂ | ♀ | ♂ | ♀ | ♂ | ♀ | ♂ | ♀ | ♂ | ♀ |
|---|---|---|---|---|---|---|---|---|---|---|
| Calf | 345 | 346 | 3844 | 3848 | 3844 | 3848 | 563 | 563 | 321 | 321 |
| 1 | 205 | 205 | 2444 | 2445 | 2444 | 2446 | 390 | 390 | 230 | 227 |
| 2 | 41 | 164 | 1842 | 1843 | 460 | 1843 | 89 | 284 | 55 | 164 |
| 3 | 9 | 148 | 1389 | 1391 | 16 | 1391 | 20 | 208 | 13 | 119 |
| 4 | 2 | 134 | 1052 | 1053 | 3 | 1053 | 5 | 152 | 3 | 86 |
| 5 | 1 | 120 | 800 | 800 | 1 | 800 | 1 | 112 | 1 | 63 |
| 6 | 1 | 108 | 611 | 611 | 1 | 611 | 1 | 83 | 1 | 46 |
| 7 | 0 | 95 | 469 | 470 | 0 | 470 | 1 | 61 | 0 | 34 |
| 8 | 0 | 53 | 362 | 363 | 0 | 363 | 0 | 46 | 0 | 25 |
| 9 | 0 | 25 | 282 | 283 | 0 | 283 | 0 | 35 | 0 | 19 |
| 10 | 0 | 0 | 0 | 0 | 0 | 0 | 0 | 0 | 0 | 0 |
| Total by sex | 604 | 1398 | 13,095 | 13,107 | 6855 | 13,107 | 1067 | 1933 | 623 | 1104 |

| | Initial | No Hunting | 75% Bulls | 20% | 25% |
|---|---|---|---|---|---|
| Population total | 2002 | 26,202 | 19,962 | 3000 | 1727 |
| Bull:cow:calf ratios | 25:100:54 | 100:100:69 | 8:100:69 | 12:100:77 | 13:100:79 |
| Annual rate of increase | — | 1.255 | 1.255 | 1.038 | 0.9817 |
| Percent of population harvested in 10th year | | | 11.3 | 25.0 | 28.5 |

Number killed in 10th year

| | 75% Bulls | 20% | 25% |
|---|---|---|---|
| Bulls | 2258 | 378 | 227 |
| Cows | 0 | 274 | 196 |
| Calves | 0 | 99 | 70 |
| Total | 2258 | 751 | 493 |

this level of exploitation is representative of what may happen when elk populations are allowed to grow unchecked except for bull-only harvest.

These populations can be stabilized by a 75-percent bull harvest coupled with harvest rates of 10 percent of calves and 15 percent of cows if yearling fecundity is 27 percent (Table 11.20) or coupled with harvest rates of over 20 percent of cows and calves if yearling fecundity is stable at 50 percent (Table 11.21). Note that cow to calf ratios are higher than when the population is unhunted, and also the sex ratio shows more bulls per 100 cows. For the 27-percent yearling fecundity, the population is essentially stable when 23 percent of it is harvested according to the 75 percent, 15 percent, 10 percent bull:cow:calf distribution in the kill.

A change from 20 to 25 percent of the cows harvested causes a population decline for the most productive population (Table 11.21). This is of significance because the small change in percent harvested required to change the population trend would be extremely difficult to detect in the field. This problem requires that an accurate population estimate is available, and that the harvest is completely monitored. When illegal mortality caused through poaching and crippling is involved, the problem of gauging effects of harvest on population trend becomes even more difficult.

Table 11.22 illustrates effects of harvest strategies on a much less productive population, not too dissimilar to the red deer on the Isle of Rhum in 1957 (Lowe 1969), that may be representative of many lightly harvested populations at or near range carrying capacity. Age-specific fecundity rates are very low, at 60 percent, with no yearling breeding. Middle-aged cows produced 10 percent more female than male calves, as Lowe (1969) reported. A U-shaped mortality curve typical of slightly harvested or unharvested populations (Caughley 1966) is followed, and the age distribution of this population extends to 13 years. This longevity is still an underestimation, since older individuals are known to be present in small numbers up to 20 years and a little beyond.

The population as set up is essentially stable with rate of annual increase at 1.001 at ten years. The cow to calf ratio is low, 100:34, and the sex ratio of three bulls per four cows reflects the known lower survival of bulls than cows in populations of this nature (Flook 1970; Peek, Lovaas, and Rouse 1967).

When 75 percent of the bulls are harvested from this population the population decreases through a five-year period, since the high number of bulls is removed. At year 5, 130 bulls are taken from a population of 1512 at the 75 percent level of harvest. The rate of increase is negative at 0.946 at five years and 488 bulls have been harvested over the five-year period. The population stabilizes at year 5, and proportion harvested remains similar through year 10. The sex ratio has been changed dramatically, but no change in cow to calf ratios has occurred throughout the ten-year simulation. Addition of 1-percent harvest of cows and calves to the 75-percent bull harvest causes a population decline from the original. This harvest included only 9 cows and 3 calves out of a population of 1375 elk at year 10. Obviously, when no compensatory response in fecundity or survival occurs, as is very likely to be the case when a population is limited by forage or other

**TABLE 11.22** Age Structure Changes under Various Harvest Strategies for a Red Deer Population

| Age (years) | Survival Rates (percent) ♂ | ♀ | Initial Population ♂ N | % | ♀ N | % | After Ten Years of No Hunting ♂ N | % | ♀ N | % | After Five Years of 75% Bulls Harvested ♂ N | % | ♀ N | % | After Ten Years of 75% Bulls Harvested ♂ N | % | ♀ N | % | After Ten Years of 75% Bulls, 1% Cows and Calves Harvested ♂ N | % | ♀ N | % |
|---|---|---|---|---|---|---|---|---|---|---|---|---|---|---|---|---|---|---|---|---|---|---|
| Calf | 72 | 80 | 188 | 22 | 208 | 19 | 190 | 22 | 211 | 18 | 189 | 52 | 210 | 18 | 190 | 52 | 210 | 18 | 172 | 52 | 190 | 18 |
| 1 | 85 | 85 | 136 | 16 | 167 | 15 | 136 | 16 | 168 | 15 | 136 | 38 | 168 | 15 | 137 | 37 | 168 | 15 | 124 | 38 | 152 | 15 |
| 2 | 85 | 90 | 115 | 15 | 142 | 13 | 116 | 13 | 143 | 13 | 29 | 8 | 142 | 12 | 30 | 8 | 143 | 12 | 27 | 8 | 129 | 12 |
| 3 | 85 | 90 | 98 | 11 | 128 | 11 | 99 | 11 | 129 | 11 | 6 | 2 | 128 | 11 | 6 | 2 | 128 | 11 | 6 | 2 | 116 | 11 |
| 4 | 85 | 85 | 82 | 9 | 115 | 10 | 84 | 10 | 116 | 10 | 1 | <1 | 114 | 10 | 1 | 1 | 115 | 10 | 1 | <1 | 105 | 10 |
| 5 | 85 | 85 | 70 | 8 | 97 | 9 | 71 | 8 | 98 | 9 | <1 | <1 | 97 | 8 | 0 | | 98 | 8 | <1 | <1 | 89 | 9 |
| 6 | 80 | 80 | 59 | 7 | 82 | 7 | 60 | 7 | 84 | 7 | <1 | <1 | 83 | 7 | 0 | | 83 | 7 | <1 | <1 | 76 | 7 |
| 7 | 70 | 80 | 48 | 6 | 66 | 6 | 49 | 6 | 67 | 6 | 0 | | 67 | 6 | 0 | | 68 | 6 | 0 | | 61 | 6 |
| 8 | 60 | 75 | 33 | 4 | 52 | 5 | 35 | 4 | 53 | 5 | 0 | | 53 | 5 | 0 | | 53 | 5 | 0 | | 48 | 5 |
| 9 | 50 | 65 | 20 | 2 | 39 | 3 | 20 | 2 | 40 | 3 | 0 | | 40 | 3 | 0 | | 41 | 4 | 0 | | 36 | 3 |
| 10 | 40 | 55 | 10 | 1 | 22 | 2 | 10 | 1 | 26 | 2 | 0 | | 26 | 2 | 0 | | 26 | 2 | 0 | | 23 | 2 |
| 11 | 30 | 45 | 8 | <1 | 9 | <1 | 4 | <1 | 14 | <1 | 0 | | 14 | 1 | 0 | | 14 | 1 | 0 | | 13 | 1 |
| 12 | 20 | 35 | 2 | <1 | 3 | <1 | 1 | <1 | 6 | <1 | 0 | | 6 | <1 | 0 | | 6 | <1 | 0 | | 6 | 1 |
| 13 | 20 | 35 | 1 | <1 | 1 | <1 | 1 | <1 | 2 | <1 | 0 | | 2 | <1 | 0 | | 2 | <1 | 0 | | 1 | <1 |
| 14 | 0 | 0 | 0 | 0 | 0 | 0 | 0 | 0 | 0 | 0 | 0 | | 0 | | 0 | | 0 | | 0 | | 0 | |
| Total by Sex | | | 870 | | 1130 | | 875 | | 1156 | | 362 | | 1150 | | 364 | | 1156 | | 330 | | 1045 | |

| | Initial | No Hunting | Five Years 75% Bulls | Ten Years 75% Bulls | Ten Years 75% Bulls, 1% Cows |
|---|---|---|---|---|---|
| Population total | 2000 | 2031 | 1512 | 1520 | 1375 |
| Bull:cow:calf ratios | 74:100:34 | 72:100:34 | 5:100:34 | 5:100:34 | 5:100:34 |
| Annual rate of increase | | 1.001 | .946 | 1.001 | 0.9911 |
| Percent of population harvested in 5th or 10th year | | 0 | 8.6 | 8.6 | 9.5 |
| Number killed in 5th or 10th year | | 0 | 130 | 130 | 130 (3 calves, 118 bulls, 9 cows) |

*Note:* Fecundity and survival rates of this population approximate those of the 1957 population studied by Lowe (1969).

extrinsic factors and when hunting does not alter this limitation, very minor mortality to the female segment will cause a decline.

Data required for these simulations is not easily obtained in the field. Adequate assessment of fecundity and survival of calves requires examining animals at breeding age in late winter and subsequently calves in the fall and winter. In many areas, heavy cover precludes fall assessment of calf survival, and even adequate winter classification. If Quick's (1958) data on the roe deer apply, wherein a representative age structure requires a sample of at least 50 percent of the population, then survival will always be underestimated. The simulations also specify that no changes in fecundity or survival occur during the time period, an obvious departure from actuality.

Nevertheless, simulations of the nature presented serve to show effects of certain harvest strategies on elk populations of differing fecundity and survival rates. A game manager, through a combination of data and experience with a population, can often fit a herd into a simulation using estimates, and by varying the survival and fecundity rates within a range judged likely to include the actual condition, can see what a likely harvest strategy is going to do. The simulations thus serve as a useful aid to interpreting observed population changes and establishing an appropriate harvest strategy, but they do not substitute for direct examination of a population. The simulation should show how insensitive a cow to calf ratio is for detecting change in productivity and survival, from one year to the next. Changes in calf survival through a one-year period can be estimated, however, as long as adult survival is not changed during the period in question.

As more and more populations receive intensive harvest, the need to regulate the kill becomes ever more critical. An accurate assessment of the harvest for each population is also important under intensive harvest conditions. Often, the long-term trend in population size is apparent, but short-term changes, from year to year, are less easily detected. Under these conditions, it is better to err on the conservative side than to harvest above the replacement rate, unless range conditions or damage complaints indicate a population reduction is in order.

It should also be apparent that extralegal loss may be an especially critical factor when populations are intensively exploited. Efforts to minimize crippling loss through hunter awareness and education are useful. In areas where poaching loss is substantial and an accepted part of society, the legal harvest simply has to be lowered to account for it. Extralegal losses are always difficult to estimate and may substantially affect population performance especially if legal harvest is high. Thus, regulation and assessment of exploitation on elk involves a series of difficult problems in sampling and in social values, none of which can be ignored.

**Moose.** Since the moose is holoarctic in distribution, it is to be expected that the species is subject to a wide variety of different hunting traditions. It is an important part of the subsistence life-style in Siberia, Alaska, and Canada where, in some places, seasons essentially never close. It is hunted with dogs in Norway where specific age classes including calves and old-aged individuals are emphasized in the take (Lykke 1974). In the Utah, Montana, Wyoming, and Idaho area, hunting by permit, often only for bulls, is the traditional means of harvest.

Three investigations in the 1950s served to dispel the notion that moose were very unproductive, and served to increase its importance as a game species. Douglas Pimlott (1959a) working on the Newfoundland population, reported that yearling cows (as many as 67 percent in some areas) were breeding and that as many as 41 percent of adult cows produced twins. In addition, Pimlott (1959b) reviewed the Fennoscandian moose hunting data, and found that annual harvests of up to 25 percent of fall population were common over large areas. Simultaneously, R. Yorke Edwards and Ralph Ritcey (1958) reported no yearling female breeding, but high incidence of pregnancy and twinning rates of older cows in a British Columbia population. The Matanuska Valley, Alaska, population studied by Robert A. Rausch (1959) corroborated these findings, illustrating that the Alaska subspecies was capable of breeding as a yearling and adults could commonly produce twins. Variation in yearling breeding and twinning rates between areas was attributed to differences in range quality. Reviews of this history and its impact on moose management have been presented by Pimlott (1961) and Simkin (1974). High fecundity rates for the subspecies *shirasi* in Montana (Schladweiler and Stevens 1973), and the subspecies *alces* in Sweden (Markgren 1969) have supported the earlier work (Table 11.23).

There is confusion in the literature on moose reproduction and productivity that should be recognized. Pimlott (1959a) recognized this and referred to A. Leopold's (1933) definitions. Productivity was defined as the percentage that could be removed yearly without diminishing the population, a harvest connotation. Potential productivity is the theoretical percentage that could be removed if there was no mortality. Gross productivity was the percentage of production which would be attained if all embryos *in utero* at end of the breeding season survived.

Net productivity is the percentage remaining after all nonhunting mortality (prior to the hunt) is deducted from the gross production figure. Pimlott (1959a) used fall classifications of calves ($C$), yearlings ($Y$), and adults ($A$) to measure net productivity, from a formula originally used by Robinette and Olson (1944):

$$\text{Net productivity} = C/(C + Y + A)$$

In this instance calves are considered the measure of net productivity, while yearlings have also been used: $Y/(Y + A)$. The yearling statistic provides a better estimate of recruitment to the breeding population.

Gross productivity was based on embryo counts from December and later reproductive tract collections, with yearling females separated from older females.

These definitions have been used to describe moose productivity in subsequent literature on moose. However, Caughley (1974b) noted that these figures do not estimate the rate of increase nor potential hunting yield from a population. The analyses do not account for nonhunting mortality of the adult population, assuming that hunting is the only mortality factor. An estimate of population size (ideally, relative to carrying capacity), plus age-specific fecundity and mortality rates is

**TABLE 11.23  Moose Reproductive Rates in Six Areas**

| Area | Yearling Pregnancies | | | Adult Pregnancies | | | | Twinning in Adults | | | Reference |
|---|---|---|---|---|---|---|---|---|---|---|---|
| | Number Sampled | Number Pregnant | Percent Pregnant | Number Sampled | Number Pregnant | Percent Pregnant | Number Pregnant | Number Pregnant with Twins | Percent Twin Pregnancies | | |
| Alaska (Matanuska Valley, 1956–1958) | 5 | 1 | 20 | 78 | 73 | 93 | 73 | 19 | 26 | | Rausch 1959 |
| British Columbia (Wells Gray Park, 1952–1956) | 15 | 0 | 0 | 80 | 61 | 76 | 61 | 15 | 25 | | Edwards and Ritcey 1958 |
| Northwestern Ontario (1957–1961) | 12 | 2 | 17 | 87 | 87 | 100 | 87 | 22 | 25 | | Simkin 1965 |
| Newfoundland (1951–1956) | 78 | 36 | 46 | 239 | 194 | 81 | 182 | 25 | 14 | | Pimlott 1959 |
| Southwestern Montana (1965–1971) | 22 | 7 | 32 | 73 | 63 | 86 | 63 | 10 | 16 | | Schladweiler and Stevens 1955:59 |

*Note:* Rates are based on embryo counts taken from cows during gestation periods as compared with earlier investigations reported by Peterson 1955.

needed before the hunting yield can be obtained. The net productivity figures thus overestimate the potential yield from a population. Rate of increase, calculated from $C/(Y + A)$, does not estimate population growth. Caughley (1977) provides methods for calculating rate of increase, yield, and other population measures. The information on moose reproduction derived from corpora lutea, embryo counts, and postpartum field classifications can provide estimates of fecundity rates (corpora lutea, embryos) and a mix of fecundity and survival rates (field classifications), the latter being a difficult statistic to interpret without substantial supporting information.

The Fennoscandian moose populations have received the most intensive harvest management over the longest period of time. Norway and Sweden harvested approximately 40,000 moose, or 36.5 moose per 100 km$^2$ of productive forest in the early 1970's (Lykke 1974). The Finland, Norway, and Sweden moose population was estimated at 200,000 animals on a total land base of 1,110,535 km$^2$ (Markgren 1974); and has apparently increased. Hunting rights in Scandinavia belong to the landowner. Norway harvests moose on an area basis, wherein a minimum area required for taking a moose is established by the Department of Conservation (Lykke 1974). This area usually runs between 200 and 2000 ha of moose habitat. Landowners apply for permission to harvest moose. Sweden harvests moose on a two-season basis consisting of a two- to four-day general season and a longer special season of variable length. The general season has had no bag limit, but is slowly being dropped in favor of the more controlled hunt.

Control of the age and sex distribution in the harvest has been a major concern in Scandinavia. Efforts to maintain a fairly equal sex ratio in the population, to limit the take of mature cows, and to emphasize harvest of calves are made (Lykke 1974). These efforts help ensure retention of the high productivity exemplified by most Scandinavian populations. High percentages of calves in the harvest is intended to harvest the age group with largest death risk in the coming winter and reduce the take of prime-age breeding cows. There is evidence that calves do not survive well over the first winter if the dam is killed during the hunting season (Markgren 1975). Efforts to reduce damage to growing timber by moose and to prevent overbrowsing by the dense populations are implicit in the intensity of the harvest in these countries.

Moose populations in the USSR, as elsewhere across their range, increased markedly during the 1940s and 1950s (Heptner and Nasimowitsch 1967). Legal moose harvest began in the late 1940s, but has not prevented increases in the European part of the USSR (Filonov and Zykov 1974). Of an estimated 1971 population in the Asiatic USSR of 215,610 moose, slightly over 3 percent were taken by licensed hunters, while the estimated kill, which includes native take, is at least three times that percentage (Syroechkovskiy and Rogacheva 1974). Local harvests are more intensive, but the harvest of moose in the USSR is not as proportionately high as in Norway and Scandinavia. However, because of the severe winter conditions of northern Asia, quotas for hunters are considered to be low, no more than 10 percent of the total population, which is also considered to be underestimated.

The intensive bull harvest in the Matanuska Valley and the Kenai Peninsula of Alaska has resulted in fall sex ratios of 10:100 or less (Bishop and Rausch 1974). A wide range in fetus sizes at specific time periods has been noted on the Kenai, indicating that the disparate sex ratio tends to increase the length of breeding season. Also, some populations evidence lowered production concomitant with the low sex ratio, suggesting a correlation. Yearling bulls are capable of breeding (Peek 1962) and probably contribute substantially to the breeding success in populations where sex ratios are greatly reduced.

Bubenik, Timmermann and Saunders (1975) emphasize that the physiological capability to breed may not coincide with actual breeding success since social factors interact. This has been extended to a broader criticism of harvest management that relies solely on age structure without consideration for social factors. Bubenik (1971) classified moose according to social classes: kids or infants (up to 11–15 months for males, 12–17 months for females), teens (up to $3\frac{1}{2}$–$4\frac{1}{2}$ years for males, less than $3\frac{1}{2}$ for females), mature (up to at least 10–11 years), and senior (over 10–11 years). The objective of harvest management should be to maintain an "adapted social balance," in this perspective (Bubenik, Timmermann, and Saunders 1975). This balance is the population structure that has developed in response to regulative pressures in the area. This argument presupposes that moose are to be managed for the benefit of the population as an environmental structure, rather than as a resource to benefit humans (Bubenik 1975). With the possible exception of bighorn sheep, such philosophy is hardly a part of current big game harvest management. R. A. Baker (1975) illustrates that such is a concern among some moose biologists, however.

Another issue on many moose ranges involves access by hunters. Where access is restricted, the harvest tends to be concentrated on those moose that are most accessible and that may not comprise a major segment of the population. Investigations in Ontario (Goddard 1970; Saunders and Williamson 1972) indicate that dispersing moose did not move more frequently into heavily hunted areas than into other areas that received less hunting pressure. However, dispersal could serve to support populations that are subject to heavy harvest. Cumming (1974) reported an area in northern Ontario that was heavily harvested continued to produce the same number of moose, although the adult harvest was comprised of over 40 percent yearlings. The Newfoundland moose harvest was also unevenly distributed with less hunting in the less accessible areas (Mercer and Manuel 1974). Cumming (1974) reported that when snowmobiles became a common means of transport and season lengths were extended, some increase in hunting of remote areas occurred coincidentally with increased public controversy and criticism.

Pimlott (1959a) and Simkin (1965) reported yearling moose were more vulnerable to hunters in Newfoundland and Ontario, respectively. Yearlings were estimated by Simkin (1965) to be shot at 1.26 to 1.76 times their occurrence in Ontario. When vulnerability factors such as these are calculated, this bias can be accounted for in age structures obtained from harvest. Schladweiler and Stevens (1973) could find no differential vulnerability between yearlings and adults in

Montana, where restricted harvests occur. When yearlings are harvested at greater rates than their occurrence in the population, dispersal and recruitment to the adult breeding stock may be reduced. Ritchie (1978) reported that many Idaho moose hunters selected trophy bulls.

Does a population reduction through hunting increase productivity of the moose population? Bergerud, Manuel, and Whelan (1968) could find no evidence that productivity increased following a decrease of a Newfoundland population of about 50 percent. An extremely severe winter following the herd reductions apparently increased calf mortality and controverted the analysis of the population response to hunter harvest. Schladweiler and Stevens (1973) reported increases in ovulation rates of adult cows following population reductions and improved range conditions in southwestern Montana. The question of compensation for reduced population size by increased production and survival is thus tied also to weather and range condition. In areas where wolves exert effective pressure on moose populations, this factor may also be involved if moose densities are low enough to cause the predation rate to increase. Such instances have existed in parts of Alaska in the 1970s and 1980s.

The problems of assessing population change related to harvest were discussed by Addison and Timmermann (1974). An objective of moose management in Ontario was to allow hunting pressure to increase until the age structure, obtained from the hunter harvest, indicated that mortality was in equilibrium with the highest rate of recruitment. However, age structures of the same population varied significantly between years and were judged not indicative of population processes. Mandible collections were small, and biased by differential vulnerability of moose to hunting between years. Analyses of ages were variable according to method used, with wear-class and eye lens methods being less accurate than cementum annulation analysis. Accurate estimation of the yearling vulnerability bias was also difficult. These researchers concluded that population analysis did not provide managers with easy answers, and had to be used cautiously. Further, direct population estimation through aerial census and pellet census was not accurate enough to detect minor changes in size that may still be important (LeResche and Rausch 1974; Franzmann et al. 1976; Novak and Gardner 1975).

Change in sex ratio to progressively favor cows appears to be a useful indicator of heavy harvest of moose (Cumming 1974). A deliberate overharvest of moose in southern Ontario resulted in a change from more bulls in the harvest to more cows with the initiation of this experiment. Change in percentage of calves harvested did not reflect hunting pressure, but indications that percentage of yearlings increased as the harvest intensity increased were evident. Decline in numbers harvested through time was the best indicator of excessive harvest, but this may not be easily distinguished from other factors influencing the harvest (Table 11.24). However, Downing (1981) cautions that sex ratios in the harvest are not reliable indicators of population welfare, so shifts in harvest sex ratios should be used as a signal that further investigation is needed.

Timmerman (1975) illustrated some problems in assessing harvest levels

**TABLE 11.24  Change in Sex and Age Ratios of Moose in Tweed District, Ontario, Relative to Changes in Moose Harvest Levels**

| Year | Number of Licensed Hunters | Number of Moose Harvested | Number of Moose for which Sex and Age was Reported[a] | Sex Ratio (bulls per 100 cows)[a] | Cow:Calf Ratio (calves per 100 cows)[b] |
|---|---|---|---|---|---|
| 1956 | 71 | 30 | 30 | 140 | 60 |
| 1958 | 116 | 41 | 41 | 146 | 69 |
| 1960 | 116 | 52 | 52 | 70 | 22 |
| 1961 | 254 | 62 | 62 | 76 | 72 |
| 1962 | 172 | 33 | 31 | 29 | 53 |
| 1963 | 132 | 10 | 8 | 20 | 40 |
| 1965 | 117 | 28 | 17 | 133 | 33 |
| 1968 | 241 | 21 | 13 | 67 | 33 |
| 1970 | 152 | 33 | 21 | 69 | 10 |
| 1972 | 206 | 42 | 6 | 52 | 0 |

*Source:* After Cumming 1974. (Used with permission.)

[a]Harvest decline after 1961 is generally reflected in lower sex ratio and population decrease.

[b]Changes in cow to calf ratios were not considered reflective of harvest intensity.

where general seasons are used in Ontario. The nonresident moose harvest can be double-checked by comparing export permits (usually to the U.S.) with checking station data. Over a three-year period, where 212 hunters were involved, only 9 percent of the records were identical for both sets of data. Differences in date of kill, number of days hunted, sex and age of moose killed, and location were among the more important discrepancies noted between the two sets of data (Table 11.25).

**TABLE 11.25   Discrepancies in Data Obtained from Nonresident Hunters from Checking Stations and Export Permit Records in Ontario, 1971-1974**

| | | | Discrepancy Rate (percent) | |
|---|---|---|---|---|
| Discrepancy | Number of Hunters | Number of Discrepancies | Average | Range 1971–1974 |
| Number days hunted | 208 | 136 | 68 | 54–82 |
| Kill location | 168 | 70 | 37 | 35–40 |
| Time shot | 50 | 21 | 42 | (one year only) |
| Group structure at time of kill | 212 | 23 | 23 | 10–36 |
| Number in party | 209 | 38 | 22 | 12–26 |
| Kill date | 212 | 43 | 20 | 14–30 |
| Means of hunter access | 157 | 29 | 19 | 12–26 |
| Mailing address | 212 | 20 | 9 | 7–12 |
| Sex | 203 | ? | 6 | 0–14 |
| Relative age | 203 | 7 | 3.4 | 2–4 |
| License number | 212 | 4 | 2 | 0–5 |

*Source:* Timmerman 1975. (Used with permission.)

Illegal moose harvest can be substantial, especially in areas where other species such as elk are also hunted. Ritchie (1978) reported that illegal kills accounted for 31 percent of the known mortality in eastern Idaho over a seven-year period. Often, the illegal harvest simply involves mistaken identity: moose for elk, during the elk hunting season. However, deliberate poaching of moose also occurs in areas of easy access to individuals that do not run away from human activity. In areas where such conditions prevail, illegal harvest can be a highly important form of mortality.

Table 11.26 illustrates results of several harvest strategies on a highly productive moose population with survival rates approaching those reported for an Ontario herd by Bubenik (1975). The Leslie matrix model is again used with similar assumptions as for the elk models. Without hunting, the population nears stability, increasing at a finite rate of 1.01 at ten years. Sex ratio is equal, and the cow to calf ratio of 100:51 would be judged reflective of the high female fecundity. A harvest of 75 percent of the bulls results in a highly skewed sex ratio of 8:100 at ten years, with 12 percent of the herd harvested at that time. The population has, in the intervening decade, decreased and then begun to increase as with the red deer population exhibited in Table 11.22. A 25-percent bull harvest results in a sex ratio of 43:100 at year 10 (Table 11.26), indicating that relatively light harvests of bulls will reduce the proportion of bulls drastically. It is to be remembered that fecundity rates are

**TABLE 11.26  Age Structure and Population Changes under Various Harvest Strategies for a Highly Productive Moose Population**

| Age (years) | Survival Rate (percent)[a] ♂ | ♀ | Fecundity Rate (percent) | Initial Population ♂ | ♀ | No Harvest ♂ | ♀ | 75% Bulls Harvested ♂ | ♀ | 25% Bulls Harvested ♂ | ♀ |
|---|---|---|---|---|---|---|---|---|---|---|---|
| | | | | | | | | | | | |
| Calf | 73 | 70 | 0 | 230 | 231 | 290 | 290 | 290 | 290 | 290 | 290 |
| 1 | 79 | 78 | 20 | 180 | 173 | 209 | 200 | 209 | 200 | 209 | 200 |
| 2 | 75 | 77 | 110 | 142 | 135 | 163 | 154 | 41 | 154 | 122 | 154 |
| 3 | 81 | 78 | 110 | 107 | 104 | 121 | 117 | 8 | 117 | 68 | 117 |
| 4 | 82 | 77 | 110 | 87 | 81 | 97 | 90 | 2 | 90 | 41 | 90 |
| 5 | 76 | 77 | 110 | 71 | 62 | 78 | 69 | <1 | 69 | 25 | 69 |
| 6 | 76 | 83 | 110 | 54 | 48 | 59 | 52 | <1 | 52 | 14 | 52 |
| 7 | 71 | 88 | 110 | 41 | 40 | 44 | 43 | 0 | 43 | 8 | 43 |
| 8 | 72 | 83 | 110 | 29 | 35 | 31 | 38 | 0 | 38 | 4 | 38 |
| 9 | 76 | 79 | 110 | 21 | 29 | 23 | 31 | 0 | 31 | 2 | 31 |
| 10 | 69 | 78 | 110 | 16 | 23 | 15 | 22 | 0 | 22 | 1 | 22 |
| 11 | 55 | 67 | 110 | 11 | 18 | 11 | 13 | 0 | 13 | <1 | 13 |
| 12 | 50 | 42 | 104 | 6 | 12 | 6 | 7 | 0 | 7 | <1 | 7 |
| 13 | 66 | 50 | 104 | 3 | 5 | 3 | 3 | 0 | 3 | <1 | 3 |
| 14 | 50 | 50 | 104 | 2 | 2 | 2 | 2 | 0 | 2 | <1 | 2 |
| 15 | 0 | 0 | 104 | 1 | 1 | 0 | 0 | 0 | 0 | 0 | 0 |
| Total by sex | | | | 1000 | 999 | 1150 | 1143 | 549 | 1143 | 784 | 1143 |
| | | | | | | | | | | | |
| Population total | | | | 1999 | | 2293 | | 1692 | | 1927 | |
| Bull:cow:calf ratios | | | | 100:100:45 | | 101:100:51 | | 8:100:51 | | 43:100:51 | |
| Annual rate of increase (λ) | | | | — | | 1.01 | | 1.01 | | 1.01 | |
| Percent of population harvested in 10th year | | | | — | | 0 | | 11.5 | | 4 | |
| | | | | | | | | | | | |
| Number killed in the 10th year | | | | | | | | | | | |
| Bulls | | | | | | | | 194.2 | | 123 | |
| Cows | | | | | | | | 0 | | 0 | |
| Calves | | | | | | | | 0 | | 0 | |
| Total | | | | | | | | 194 | | 123 | |

[a]Survival rates approximate those of Bubenik (1975). The survival rates could be influenced by wolf predation.

fixed during the ten-year period, which allows examination of the effects of different harvest strategies without the confounding influences of weather or other factors.

When survival rates of this population are increased to approximate those reported by Wolfe (1977) for moose on Isle Royale, the population exhibits a finite rate of increase at year 10 of 1.08 when no hunter harvest occurs (Table 11.27). A 60-percent bull harvest reduces the sex ratio to 11:100 without affecting the rate of increase at year 10. If a harvest of 50 percent bulls, 10 percent cows, and 5 percent calves is applied to the population, it declines at year 10 when 14 percent of the total population is taken. Sex ratio has increased over the population from which only bulls have been taken, but to a level that may not be readily detectable in the field. The slight increase in the cow to calf ratio would probably not be detectable, and is noted to occur in a declining population.

When calf survival is changed from 50 to 60 percent, and the same level of harvest of both sexes is applied, the population increases at 1.075 at ten years. The relatively slight change in calf survival illustrates how sensitive the population is to such changes, which are difficult to detect in the field. The cow to calf ratio has increased from 100:45 to 100:50 with the change in calf survival with the same hunting strategy.

Heavy calf harvest of 50 percent, minimal cow harvest of 5 percent, and a bull harvest of 50 percent results in a relatively stable population but the highest yield (25 percent) from the population of the four strategies examined. The postseason cow to calf ratio is reduced as expected even though fecundity is high.

As with elk, our ability to judge moose population trends and effects of harvest in the field is not at the level where slight changes in fecundity or survival can be readily detected. Since slight changes can cause dramatic differences in trend, a conservative approach to harvest, especially of adult cows is indicated. As moose populations receive more intensive exploitation, the need to regulate harvest levels with permitted hunts, especially for cows, is needed. Examination of the age structure of the harvested sample is an obvious need, to detect changes in survival rates which may help anticipate population trend. Use of such gross indices as sex and age ratios will inevitably prove inadequate under such conditions.

**Caribou.**  Caribou management represents a juggling act between harvests by competing predators, most especially humans and wolves. Management also involves an effort to understand factors that naturally regulate caribou since the ecosystems in which they occur are among those that humans have had least effect on. Wildfires burn extensively across the taiga winter ranges and affect the abundance, kind, and distribution of forage. Wolves, grizzly bears, wolverines, and golden eagles frequent the herds, especially the calving areas. Natives and whites both obtain a subsistence living from poorly regulated harvests of caribou in some areas. The severe weather of the arctic and subartic ranges has an effect on production and survival. However, the question of which factors serve to limit, and how human exploitation interacts with each, is a major issue.

**TABLE 11.27  Changes in Moose Populations Shown in Table 11.26 When Survival Rates are Increased to Resemble Those Reported by Wolfe (1977)**

| | | | | | | | | | | Population after Ten Years of Strategy | | | | |
| Age (years) | Survival Rates (percent) | | Initial Population | | No Harvest | | 60% Bulls Harvested | | 50% Bulls, 10% Cows, and 5% Calves Harvested | | 50% Bulls, 10% Cows, and 5% Calves Harvested with Calf Survival Raised to 60% | | 50% Bulls, 5% Cows, and 50% Calves Harvested with Calf Survival at 60% | |
| | ♂ | ♀ | ♂ | ♀ | ♂ | ♀ | ♂ | ♀ | ♂ | ♀ | ♂ | ♀ | ♂ | ♀ |
|---|---|---|---|---|---|---|---|---|---|---|---|---|---|---|
| Calf | 50 | 50[a] | 230 | 231 | 644 | 644 | 644 | 644 | 242 | 242 | 313 | 313 | 308 | 308 |
| 1 | 95 | 93 | 180 | 173 | 298 | 298 | 298 | 298 | 117 | 117 | 176 | 176 | 123 | 123 |
| 2 | 95 | 93 | 142 | 135 | 261 | 255 | 104 | 255 | 56 | 99 | 82 | 145 | 70 | 109 |
| 3 | 95 | 93 | 107 | 104 | 228 | 219 | 37 | 219 | 27 | 84 | 38 | 119 | 40 | 96 |
| 4 | 95 | 93 | 87 | 81 | 201 | 188 | 13 | 188 | 13 | 72 | 18 | 98 | 23 | 85 |
| 5 | 95 | 93 | 71 | 62 | 176 | 162 | 5 | 162 | 6 | 61 | 8 | 81 | 13 | 75 |
| 6 | 95 | 93 | 54 | 48 | 153 | 138 | 2 | 138 | 3 | 52 | 4 | 69 | 7 | 66 |
| 7 | 82 | 81 | 41 | 40 | 134 | 118 | <1 | 118 | 2 | 44 | 2 | 55 | 4 | 58 |
| 8 | 82 | 81 | 29 | 35 | 105 | 91 | <1 | 91 | <1 | 34 | <1 | 41 | 2 | 46 |
| 9 | 82 | 81 | 21 | 29 | 76 | 65 | 0 | 65 | <1 | 24 | <1 | 29 | 1 | 33 |
| 10 | 82 | 81 | 16 | 23 | 47 | 40 | 0 | 40 | <1 | 15 | <1 | 18 | <1 | 20 |
| 11 | 82 | 81 | 11 | 18 | 60 | 48 | 0 | 48 | <1 | 17 | <1 | 17 | <1 | 29 |
| 12 | 43 | 60 | 6 | 12 | 41 | 33 | 0 | 33 | 0 | 11 | 0 | 11 | <1 | 20 |
| 13 | 43 | 60 | 3 | 6 | 14 | 16 | 0 | 16 | 0 | 6 | 0 | 6 | <1 | 10 |
| 14 | 0 | 0 | 2 | 2 | 5 | 8 | 0 | 8 | 0 | 3 | 0 | 3 | 0 | 5 |
| Total by sex | | | 1000 | 999 | 2442 | 2323 | 1102 | 2323 | 467 | 880 | 643 | 1178 | 593 | 1081 |
| Population total | | | 1999 | | 4765 | | 3425 | | 1347 | | 1821 | | 1674 | |
| Bull:cow:calf ratio | | | 100:100:34 | | 107:100:43 | | 11:100:43 | | 20:100:45 | | 21:100:50 | | 23:100:35 | |
| Annual rate of increase (λ) | | | | | 1.08 | | 1.08 | | 0.98 | | 1.075 | | 0.999 | |
| Percent of population harvested in 10th year | | | | | | | 8.0 | | 14.4 | | 15.1 | | 25.3 | |
| Number killed in 10th year | | | | | | | | | | | | | | |
| Bulls | | | | | | | 275 | | 113 | | 165 | | 114 | |
| Cows | | | | | | | 0 | | 65 | | 86 | | 39 | |
| Calves | | | | | | | 0 | | 16 | | 24 | | 270 | |
| Total | | | | | | | 275 | | 194 | | 275 | | 423 | |

[a] Note that rate is changed to 60 percent in last two columns.

Subsistence hunting is very different from the more common, highly regulated sport hunting. Native people who are traditionally dependent upon caribou for a major portion of their diet may take animals at any time of year, and in large quantities. Kelsall (1968) calculated that a person dependent upon caribou for all domestic requirements, including food and clothing, would utilize 50 caribou per year. The need to mix fat with protein dictated that lean meat might well be discarded in favor of parts containing fat. Different sex and age classes of caribou were taken at different times of the year for different purposes. Methods of capture and of killing also deviate from present-day sport-hunting procedures. Subsistence hunters as well as the more common sport hunter, have been known to take more caribou than needed when the opportunity permits (Kelsall 1968).

Regulation of subsistence hunting conducted by natives with treaty rights is primarily up to the natives themselves (Nicholas 1979). However, the agencies that are charged with conservation of the resource itself are legally involved. Also, there are subsistence hunters not covered by treaties. Management alternatives involving caribou that are subject to extensive subsistence hunting have included restriction of sport hunting, predator control, and efforts to work with native governments and peoples. C. D. Hunt (1979) offered the following principles for dealing with natives on wildlife matters in Canada, which, because of their commonsense value, have general application:

1. Conservation of the fish and wildlife resource must receive priority. Since subsistence hunters have an obvious vested interest in maintaining the resource, this is ultimately a common ground for all involved.
2. Special native harvest rights must continue to be entrenched in law. Preservation of native culture and the subsistence life-style are among the major reasons for this.
3. Participation in management of the resource by the user, subsistence or otherwise, is needed. Simmons, Heard, and Calef (1979) emphasize that expertise of native hunters, obtained through experience and tradition, must be respected by the wildlife manager who is trained in scientific style.

Bergerud (1974) argued that a general decline of caribou across North America around the turn of the century was caused by increased hunting mortality and natural predation. Subsistence hunting was the major form of hunting mortality, and the substitution of the modern rifle for primitive weapons was the major reason that hunting became more exploitive. Today, the snowmobile and airplane augment the efficiency of the subsistence hunter.

The role of wolf predation on the population dynamics of caribou has also been addressed by Bergerud (1980). Rates of increase of 19 caribou populations coexisting with wolves at densities of 0.4 wolves per 100 km$^2$ were compared, relative to percent of hunter harvest. The 9 populations that were exploited at a level of 5 percent or more by hunters were declining, while 3 of 8 populations hunted at levels less than 5 percent were declining. Two populations not hunted were increasing. As Kelsall and Klein (1979) point out, data relating to population size and composition are of questionable accuracy, so the accuracy of the calculations of rates of increase are unknown. However, regardless of the quality of the data base and the interpretation of it, wolf predation can be an important mortality cause and thus is a source of potential conflict with hunters of caribou. F. L. Miller and Broughton (1974) stated that wolves were the most readily managed of the mortality factors affecting caribou, probably in full recognition of the difficulty of regulating subsistence hunting and other human influences. Since the relative rate of predation on caribou may increase at low population levels if wolves have not declined accordingly, management to increase caribou may well involve wolf control and more restrictive harvests. Suffice it to conclude that wolf management is an integral part of caribou population management in many areas, which further increases the complexity of caribou management.

Subsistence and sport hunting has been implicated in the decline of a number of caribou populations, including the Kaminuriak herd of the eastern Northwest Territories (Simmons et al. 1979). This herd declined from an estimated 120,000 in 1950 to 44,000 in 1977, with virtually no sport hunting involved. However, F. L. Miller and Broughton (1974) concluded that wolf predation accounted for 37 percent of the calf crop of the population in the first two months of life in 1970, and D. R. Miller (1975) documented heavy wolf predation on large caribou concentrations involving this population. A similar model developed by Bunnell et al. (1975) indicated that reduction in hunter harvest, along with calf mortality rates no greater than 60 percent were needed to maintain the population of 63,000 at the time. Hunter harvest rather than forest fires was indicated as the most important limiting factor.

Sport hunting more than subsistence hunting appeared to be a major factor in the decline of the Nelchina, Alaska, population (Bos 1975). Predation again was implicated as important. Emigration to adjacent, less dense populations may also have occurred when the population was at very high densities. Hunting has reduced the number of adult bulls and hence affected the sex ratio of the population. Estimated harvests of 7.8 percent of the population, including 4 percent of the female segment, plus the predation had reduced the population to an estimated 10,000 as of 1973. This population has increased in response to more restrictive hunter harvests.

Caribou population management primarily involves efforts to regulate losses and is destined to be highly controversial in view of its complexity. Earlier concerns over loss of habitat due to fire have largely been replaced by concern about human harvest and wolf predation (Kelsall and Klein 1979). This species occupies remote wilderness, and populations are large even when they are suppressed. Assessment of population parameters with any degree of precision is extremely difficult. Attempts to control harvest, especially the subsistence harvest, are equally difficult and even estimates of the numbers taken are inexact. However, trends can be determined with persistent field work over a number of years. While we may wish more precise information, the logistics involved and the technology available preclude this for the present. Perhaps, a more important task is for all involved to achieve mutual understanding over directions for management. Experience with the populations and good cooperation among interested parties may be a more effective and practical means of managing caribou than attempting to obtain more precise information.

**Mountain sheep.** Mountain sheep represent the opposite extreme in yield in comparison to white-tailed deer. The work on this prized game animal also serves to illustrate how important an understanding of behavior can be in formulating harvest strategies for game species. With a very few exceptions, the harvest of bighorn sheep is restricted to males with 3/4-curl horns or more. The harvest is thus restricted to adult males, in an attempt to maintain a high-quality or trophy-style hunt that minimizes exploitation of populations. Buechner (1960) described the history of exploitation of bighorn in earlier times, and the recognition by wildlife agencies in the late 1940s and early 1950s that limited closely supervised harvests could be permitted. Classic trophy-hunting concepts have been applied to bighorn harvests since. Implicit in this system is that harvests of older mature males will not affect the breeding population, will tend to replace imminent mortality of old rams to other causes, and can actually benefit the population by removing older, presumably less viable, individuals. These reasons have been advanced as justifications for trophy hunting in general and specifically for bighorn sheep hunting.

An exchange of letters in *The Wildlife Society News* in 1971 brought out a different point of view. Greenberg (1971) wrote, concerning a poaching case involving desert bighorn sheep in Mexico, that one offender claimed he was helping the bighorns by killing off old rams, a justification without legal merit but perhaps with some biological truth. Greenberg (1971) referred to the traditional view that removal of some mature rams could stimulate higher rates of reproduction or survival in stable populations of low productivity. Geist (1971a) responded to this comment succinctly stating that there is no biological merit for harvesting mature bighorn rams either. Subsequently, Geist (1971b) documented his rationale for making this statement. The argument deals primarily with rutting behavior of mountain sheep as it affects energy expenditure of ewes. First, class IV (full curl), and class III (3/4+ curl) rams, were identified as those that accomplished most of the actual breeding. The presence of these rams over six years old serves to suppress the activities of younger rams that tend and drive anestrous females and harass all ewes much more than when the older rams are present. Older rams do not tend and harass ewes as much as younger rams, and the presence of older individuals thus serves to reduce energy expenditure of the female segment of the populations. Geist (1971a) argued that hunting rams in populations of three or more home range groups of females is probably of negligible significance if populations are unmolested after hunting, but hunting of smaller populations could be damaging if changes in habitat use or undue harassment of populations occurs. Thus, the argument was advanced that the adult male does have an important role to play in maintenance of population welfare through dominance of younger rams. In addition, adult males have different habitat preferences from those of females and maintain traditions of use of habitat that are conferred to younger rams as they join the ram band. The value of the adult male to population welfare was thus established from a behavioral point of view.

Bunnell (1978) calculated that harvest of all males of 3/4 curl or greater from the Kluane Lake Dall sheep population would remove 55 to 60 percent of the male population. Harvest of all males at full curl would remove 35 to 40 percent of the male population. Horn growth of rams was strongly correlated with precipitation, which in turn implicates forage quality and quantity. Also, condition of the dam could affect horn growth of male offspring for at least five years after parturition. Thus, range condition is an important variable affecting horn growth and trophy animal production.

Hunter harvest has had an influence on age structures of the male segment. Under ten years of permitted hunts of desert bighorns on the Desert Game Range, Nevada, sex ratios decreased from equality to 23:100 (C. G. Hansen 1967). Bighorn rams may attain 3/4-curl horns as early as the second fall of life, about 18 months, although this length is more commonly attained at age four. Under 3/4-curl regulations, a majority of older rams with most impressive horns were dying of natural causes, while younger rams sustained high hunting mortality. Mandatory training of hunters to ensure recognition of trophy rams and implementation of a regulation that requires knowledge of the Boone and Crockett scoring system by specifying a minimum score has helped to reduce harvest of younger rams.

Average age at 3/4 curl for Dall sheep in eight Alaska areas ranged from 4.9 to 6.7 years, and these rams comprised between 57 and 90 percent of the 1972–1974 harvest (Heimer and Smith 1975). Full-curl horns are grown at 8 to 10 years by most Alaskan Dall sheep. Heimer and Smith (1975) reported a conservative estimate of full-curl ram production in Alaska at 1150 rams, which was equal to the current harvest under a 3/4-curl regulation. Initial consequences of establishing a full-curl regulation would be lowered harvest and hunting success, but harvests could be expected to increase after a few years, still to a lower level than the harvest under a 3/4-curl regulation.

Just as with any species where only males are taken, the female segment will undergo mortality regardless. One rationale for allowing this to progress is that mountain sheep populations are known to fluctuate rather drastically according to weather and snow conditions, competition, and a lung worm-pneumonia complex. Stelfox (1971) illustrated this for the Canadian bighorn populations of the Rocky Mountain parks (Figure 11.17). If such fluctuations cannot be stabilized, then breeding stock should be maximized. Still, (Geist 1971b) demonstrated a correlation between ewe density and size of lamb crop the following year (Figure 11.18), suggesting that some compensatory response in production to decreased density as through hunter harvest or livetrapping could occur.

Another rationale is that many populations of bighorn are small and if sport hunting is to be allowed at all, it should be directed at the male segment only. And in most populations, the number of ewes that could be taken would be small any-

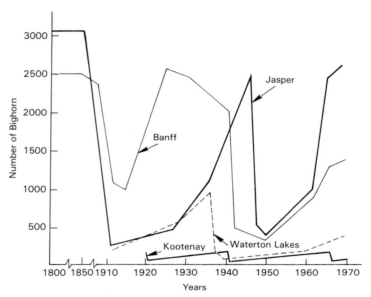

**Figure 11.7** Trends in bighorn sheep numbers in Banff, Jasper, Waterton Lake, and Kootenay National Parks, 1800 to 1970. From Stelfox 1971. (Used with permission.)

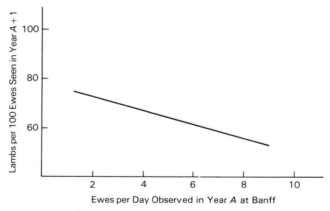

**Figure 11.18** Relationship between density of bighorn ewes in year $A$ and size of lamb crop in year $A + 1$. Source: Geist 1971b. (Used with permission.)

way. However, harvest of ewes from thriving populations in Alberta has been ongoing and is an acceptable management practice. "Harvests" of ewes by livetrapping is also a common management tool, used to reintroduce bighorn to a previously occupied range.

## Small Game

**Tree squirrels.** The two eastern tree squirrels, the gray (*Sciurus carolinensis*), and the fox (*Sciurus niger*) are among the most productive game species, thereby increasing the likelihood of significant compensatory population responses to hunter harvest. R. L. Kirkpatrick et al. (1976) reported two annual parturition periods, February-March and July-August, across the range of the gray squirrel, as is the case for the fox squirrel (L. G. Brown and Yeager 1945). Litter sizes range from 1 to 6 but average between 2.3 and 3.5 (R. L. Kirkpatrick et al. 1976). Summer litters are larger than winter litters, but survival of winter offspring is higher (Barkalow, Hamilton, and Soots 1970). Squirrels live to six or seven years (Barkalow et al. 1970; Mosby 1969), although heaviest mortality accrues to the young of the year and average life expectancy is between two and three.

Juvenile survival was positively correlated with mast crops in North Carolina by Barkalow et al. (1970), and with spring forage in Ohio by Nixon and McClain (1969). However, Mosby (1969) did not find a correlation between density and mast crops in a Virginia study in prime gray squirrel habitat. Subsequently, Montgomery, Whelan, and Mosby (1975) concluded that the gray squirrel has a very broad food base, is very efficient in utilizing it, and can attain an energy density much greater than reported for other small mammals.

The earlier work on tree squirrels by D. L. Allen (1943) in Michigan, Uhlig (1956) in West Virginia, J. M. Allen (1952) in Indiana, and others tended to emphasize the opportunity for replacing much of the natural mortality with hunter harvest. Uhlig (1956) for instance, estimated an average take of 13 percent of the gray squirrel population in West Virginia where loss to natural causes was three to four times higher. J. M. Allen (1952) reported little change in Indiana squirrel populations in heavily forested areas during the war years when hunting was minimal. Mosby, Kirkpatrick, and Newell (1977) considered hunting to be largely self-regulatory, since hunters are attracted to areas where the most squirrels occur.

However, woodlot squirrel populations are more vulnerable to hunting because of limited habitat and intensive hunting pressure. J. M. Allen (1952) reported that private woodlots sustain the heaviest hunting pressure in Indiana. While Mosby (1969) reported that about 40 percent of the fall population could be taken by hunting without reducing the breeding stock, harvests of over 58 percent of the fox squirrel population in Ohio woodlots were recorded by Nixon, Donohoe, and Nash (1974). Delays in opening of the hunting season until mid-September, after litters are weaned, were more likely to reduce harvest intensity than bag limit reduction. Uhlig (1956) reported that since 65 to 75 percent of the harvest occurs the first week of a season, length of season is relatively unimportant in affecting harvest. However, season opening dates were judged critical, since early openings tended to take lactating females and harvest would start prior to the highest fall density (Redmond 1953; Uhlig 1956). Mosby et al. (1977) concluded that squirrels' vulnerability

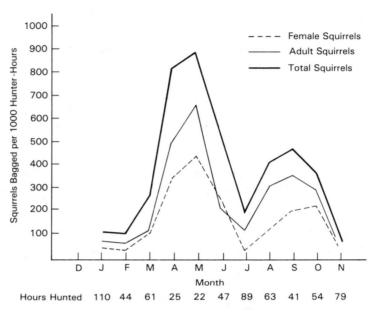

**Figure 11.19** Vulnerability of the gray squirrel to hunting, based on squirrels killed per 1000-hunter-hours in collecting 214 animals in the vicinity of Blacksburg, Virginia, 1966–1967. After Mosby, Kirkpatrick, and Newell 1977. (Used with permission.)

to sportsmen was greatest in September, and decreased progressively through the season (Figure 11.19). However, since the hunting pressure is self-regulating, dependent upon harvest success, they concluded that hunting had little effect and that variations in vulnerability of squirrels to hunters were of little consequence.

**Cottontail rabbits.** The cottontail rabbits are the most harvested game species, and rank next to deer as the most sought after by the hunter (U.S. Fish and Wildlife Service 1977a). The eastern cottontail (*Sylvilagus floridanus*) is the most commonly hunted of the eight species in the genus. The cottontail is the most prolific breeder of the game mammals. Chapman, Harman, and Samuel (1977) estimated that over 23 young were produced per female per year in Maryland and West Virginia. Litters commonly contain 2 to 6 young, and up to eight litters per year are possible (Wainwright 1969). Breeding seasons start in late January in Texas and early April in North Dakota, and run into August (Conaway, Sadler, and Hazelwood 1974). Densities of 84 rabbits per 100 acres have been reported for Michigan by Eberhardt, Peterle, and Schofield (1963) and it is notable that no decrease in productivity is found in high-density populations (R. L. Kirkpatrick and Baldwin 1974). Missouri swamp rabbits (*S. aquaticus*) live an average of 1.6 years and an age class essentially dies out at 6 years (Martinson, Holten, and Brakhage 1961), which is similar for eastern cottontails in Illinois (Lord 1961).

It is not much wonder that wildlife biologists have not been very occupied with the effects of hunting on cottontails, given the potential productivity. For instance, Wight (1959) reported that discontinuance of commercial trade in cottontails in Missouri was related to public relations reasons rather than the available population data. Payne (1964) concluded that over 75 percent of a fall population could be harvested, and that this level of harvest was quite probably impossible to achieve where dense cover exists. Pirnie (1949) concluded that hunting that removed less than 60 percent of the population could hardly be considered effective control.

The general conclusion has been that hunting removed only a portion of the available surplus of cottontails. Lord (1963) reported that hunters took only 45 percent of the known mortality of cottontails on an Illinois study area over a five-year period (Table 11.28). Over two-thirds of the midsummer populations were lost before hunting started. Hickie (1940) calculated that harvests of one rabbit per 2.4 acres could be taken in high-quality habitat, but that one rabbit per 5 to 8 acres was more typical. Such relationships are dependent upon quality and size of habitat, and to some extent hunting pressure, however.

**TABLE 11.28   Cottontail Rabbit Hunting Statistics from an Illinois Study Area**

|  | 1956–57 | 1957–58 | 1958–59 | 1959–60 | 1960–61 |
|---|---|---|---|---|---|
| Fall population | 333 | 259 | 324 | 239 | 125 |
| Late winter population | 47 | 31 | 132 | 41 | 54 |
| Gun hours | 154 | 269 | 365 | 323 | 152 |
| Number of rabbits bagged | 113 | 92 | 109 | 95 | 42 |
| Percent of fall population<br>bagged | 33.9 | 35.5 | 33.6 | 39.7 | 33.6 |
| Percent of winter mortality<br>attributed to hunting,<br>excluding crippling loss | 39.5 | 40.4 | 56.8 | 48.0 | 59.2 |

*Source:* Lord 1963. (Used with permission.)

Hunting success does vary between years and hunters, however. Applegate and Trout (1976) showed that a good relationship between rainfall and harvest exists, attributing this to the effect of precipitation on nestling mortality. Juvenile breeding in late summer may contribute substantially to the population available for hunting in fall (Kibbie and Kirkpatrick 1971). Juvenile males are more vulnerable to hunting than juvenile females, and adults of both sexes are least vulnerable (Eberhardt et al. 1963). However, a higher proportion of adults will be killed in cold weather, and juvenile vulnerability may decrease late in seasons over three months long.

If little concern about the effects of hunting on rabbit populations has been evident among biologists, as Wight (1959) indicates, concern among hunters and others has been an issue. Population fluctuations have long been the cause of the concern. McCabe (1943) postulated that a disease such as tularemia could be responsible for declines in cottontails in Wisconsin, and Hendrickson (1937) implicated a variety of factors related to habitat, weather, predation, and disease. Since harvests are so dependent upon annual production, a knowledge of limiting factors is needed regardless of controversies over the effects of hunting.

Population declines in Virginia have not been correlated with changes in quality or quantity of habitat (Jacobson, Kirkpatrick, and McGinnis 1978). Also, in a population that was at low density, seven species of parasites attained higher levels of infection and infestation than in a high-density population on similar-quality habitat. The more heavily affected population occurred in an area of higher temperatures, rainfall, and better-drained soils, which characterizes better conditions for disease and parasite development. Disease was considered the primary limiting factor, and the disease virulence theory that originated in the 1930s was considered a reasonable explanation of the population declines.

The New England cottontail (*S. transitionalis*) has declined in many parts of its original range, and habitat change from preferred forested habitat to farmland habitats preferred by the eastern cottontail has been implicated (Chapman and Morgan 1973). Additionally, the massive releases of a variety of subspecies of eastern cottontails have added diversity to the gene pool, which may in turn provide the eastern cottontail with a competitive ability to displace the New England species from its original niche. While the relationship of such work to hunting of cottontails may seem obscure, if the New England species becomes drastically reduced, conservation measures to retain it may affect hunting opportunity. Thus, a well-intentioned program of releasing cottontails into the field to enhance short-term hunting opportunity may not only pose an economical waste but could also pose a biological threat.

Long-term climatic change is ultimately involved in cottontail population density and perhaps species composition. Since warmer temperatures and higher moisture favors diseases and parasites, periods of years when these conditions occur may adversely affect cottontails. On the other hand, the New England cottontail appears to be better adapted to colder temperatures than the eastern cottontail (Chapman et al. 1977). This suggests that the competitive relationship between the two species will be a constantly fluctuating one, dependent upon current climate. These issues impinge upon the exploitation of a population, and indicate why a knowledge of limiting factors other than hunting is as important as the effect of hunting in wildlife management.

**Woodchucks.** Woodchucks (*Marmota monax*) are the third most frequently hunted small game species, after the cottontails and tree squirrels, in the eastern United States (U.S. Fish and Wildlife Service 1977a). Litter sizes of adults in south central Pennsylvania averaged about 3.4, ranging from 1 to 8 (Snyder and Christian 1960). About half of yearling females produce young at age one, but their litter sizes are smaller. Gestation periods of 31 to 32 days precede parturition, which occurs in early April.

D. E. Davis (1962) calculated the potential harvest of woodchucks on a Pennsylvania study area from populations exhibiting different percentages of adults (Table 11.29). The populations all started at 100 animals, four different rates of

TABLE 11.29  Potential Harvest of Woodchucks in Four Realistic Conditions

| | W | X | Y | Z |
|---|---|---|---|---|
| 1. Adults present | 70 | 57 | 39 | 29 |
| 2. Number of adults on May 1 | 70 | 57 | 39 | 29 |
| 3. Number of yearlings on May 1 | 30 | 43 | 61 | 71 |
| 4. Birth rate | 1.3 | 1.6 | 1.1 | 0.9 |
| 5. Number of young on May 1 | 130 | 160 | 110 | 90 |
| *Probability of survival:* | | | | |
| 6.  Adults and yearlings | 0.70 | 0.57 | 0.39 | 0.29 |
| 7.  Young | 0.23 | 0.27 | 0.515 | 0.79 |
| 8. Deaths (adults and yearlings) | 30 | 43 | 61 | 71 |
| 9. Deaths (young) | 100 | 117 | 49 | 19 |
| *When compensation is:* | | *Harvest of adults will be:* | | |
| 10.   0 | 0 | 13 | 31 | 41 |
| 11.   33% | 10 | 23 | 41 | 51 |
| 12.   67% | 20 | 33 | 51 | 61 |
| 13.   100% | 30 | 43 | 61 | 71 |
| 14. Young available to harvest | 47 | 54 | 17 | 0 |
| *When compensation is:* | | *Harvest of young will be:* | | |
| 15.   0 | 0 | 0 | 0 | 0 |
| 16.   33% | 16 | 18 | 6 | 0 |
| 17.   67% | 31 | 36 | 12 | 0 |
| 18.   100% | 47 | 54 | 17 | 0 |
| 19. Maximum harvest (lines 13 + 18) | 77 | 97 | 78 | 71 |

*Source:* After D. E. Davis 1962. (Used with permission.)

compensation for natural mortality by harvest were applied, and the populations were assumed to return to 100 animals each spring. Essentially, when woodchuck production is high, the harvest of adults is high, as in population $X$, where 43 of 57 adults and yearlings and 54 of 160 young are taken after parturition has occurred.

Young under 6 pounds weight are less vulnerable to hunting than older woodchucks (D. E. Davis, Christian, and Bronson 1964). This work suggested that the compensation for harvest was through increased survival and decreased emigration of young, although increased natality also can be expected. The calculations indicate that up to 97 woodchucks could be harvested annually from a breeding population of 100 after the breeding period was completed.

D. E. Davis and Ludwig (1981) reported a mechanism for decline in the Pennsylvania population. As habitats changed from cropland to stages of old-field succession, soil fertility decreased because fertilizers were no longer used. Accordingly, a decrease occurred in highly nutritious stands of alfalfa, clover, corn, and small grains, and an increase occurred in old-field vegetation that dried out much earlier than the crops did. Mortality rates of young woodchucks increased, attributable to less weight gain before hibernation. D. E. Davis (1981) concluded that the population was probably regulated at a level below the forage base by social factors, except for the period of the population decline.

## SUMMARY

Our understanding of the effects of exploitation has advanced considerably in the past several decades. The major conclusion to be reached may seem rather obvious, but in fact is not readily apparent: modern hunting can reduce and temporarily has reduced breeding stocks of a variety of species. Most often, these reductions have been unintentional and not anticipated. However, the reasons for these temporary reductions are much more the important lessons than the fact that reductions have occurred.

This conclusion has obvious political overtones in today's overheated society, and an elaboration is thus needed. First, most of the literature that is used for this conclusion is readily available in internationally recognized publications. Second, the data was collected by people in agencies that have a vested interest in hunting. Third, one reason for each and every study was to more effectively regulate harvest by understanding the factors that were involved. Fourth, the information is frequently used to modify harvest to achieve management goals, although it may take time to do so. Finally, there are situations where the tool of sport hunting will be used to reduce populations, and knowledge is needed about how to properly accomplish such goals, and what response can be anticipated in the population.

But the question of why we occasionally "overharvest" is more important than the fact that we do, since populations can and do recover from temporary reductions whatever the cause. First, sport hunting must be recognized as a major mortality factor for many populations, especially among the big game species. Accordingly, fluctuations in hunter harvest will be reflected in subsequent population size, especially when compensatory response in production or survival cannot override the mortality. When such cases occur, there will inevitably be years when a population is reduced below the intended long-term goal, just as there will be years when the population is less vulnerable and is maintained above the average. These kinds of fluctuations would be expected, are not unidirectional, and are indicative that management is effective.

Such populations may be considered to provide a sustained yield. However, whether they provide a long-term, maximum sustained yield or not is questionable. Larkin (1977) has pointed out fallacies of attempting to provide maximum sustained yields in fisheries that apply to wildlife as well: (1) age structures are reduced; (2) populations are less resilient in responding to adverse environmental circumstances; (3) failures in production and survival of young are more catastrophic in effect on abundance; (4) genetic variability in stocks can be reduced since subpopulations may be dramatically reduced or exterminated; and (5) the ability to precisely control the harvest, in terms of distributing it among age classes and subpopulations is poor. In short, management for maximum sustained yield is a harsh treatment of a population. Rather, optimum yields that will crop a lower proportion of a population than the maximum theoretical yield provide more flexibility and potential for population response.

Long-term harvest yields can also have genetic consequences. Ryman et al.

(1981) demonstrate that improper harvests of moose and white-tailed deer that reduce age structures and skew sex ratios have the potential of rapidly reducing genetic heterozygosity. This reduction has the potential to ultimately reduce productivity, adaptability to habitat change, and body size (M. H. Smith et al. 1976), if carried to extremes. Reductions in subpopulations as a result of intensive harvest can reduce genetic variability, even if size of adult breeding stock for the entire population remains constant.

Obviously, social pressures to maximize harvests are intense. As the human demand for a limited resource increases, game managers are hard-pressed to take the maximum number possible. As these kinds of pressures mount, maximum yield philosophy is easily espoused. Also, determination of an optimum yield, the logical alternative, involves judgment and consensus. Further, arguments involving retention of genetic heterozygosity, which might receive support in Europe, are not yet to be supported by many in North America. However, this issue should receive more professional and public attention.

Inadvertent overharvests of upland game populations appear to be the result of marginal or insufficient habitat. When populations are confined to small blocks of habitat and are persistently hunted (with well-trained dogs), populations may be reduced. This is basically an access problem related to habitat loss. The same appears to be true with woodlot squirrel populations. It is also prevalent in some areas where big game, especially elk, become more accessible due to road building for logging purposes. This problem can be corrected through restrictions in harvest, but the responsibility of the land manager to consider the consequences of increased access or reduction in habitat and to cooperate with wildlife agencies should be recognized, especially on public lands.

Regardless of the other aspects, the single most important reason for overharvest is that the ability to detect it is poor. Our ability to precisely estimate population parameters and numbers is simply inadequate, as Caughley (1976) states. The financial and technical means to detect responses is the issue. Census techniques require time and personnel to conduct in adequate fashion. Also, there are many other potentially limiting factors that interact with harvest and are difficult to assess. Thus population trend and response to a harvest regime may require a period of several years to detect, after the response has achieved a greater magnitude than would be the case if early detections were made. In many cases the technology and inability to obtain adequate sample sizes also prevents rapid assessment.

Alternative harvest management strategies will vary with species, area, and agency. One strategy is to investigate a representative population and use the information to manage across a region where apparently similar populations, habitat, and hunting conditions exist. Modifications in management under this strategy are usually a compromise between traditional patterns of harvest and what the manager would prefer to do based on data interpretations.

Another strategy is simply to set a conservative hunt that will allow a conservative harvest—an optimum yield well below the theoretical maximum sustained yield. Upland birds and small game can be managed this way with little consequence unless controversy over more intensive harvest exists. Usually, some data is available that can be considered in establishing seasons in these circumstances.

A third strategy is simply to hunt according to what people wish without regard to population data. Such a strategy usually means that the harvest will be exceedingly low unless agricultural and forest concerns over depredations are involved. In areas without much public land, owners may dictate a season they will tolerate. Rather than risk extensive land closure, wildlife agencies must cooperate or risk losing hunting opportunities.

The problem of inadequate data can also be circumvented to some extent with a simulation model for the purpose of examining various strategies. While the manager may not have a sufficient data base for a population, very often sufficient familiarization with it can produce estimates of needed population parameters that can be used to investigate efforts of a variety of harvest scenarios.

Ultimately, management efforts will inevitably drift towards exploiting populations as intensively as possible. For populations that are managed at such intensive levels (not at the maximum sustained yield but rather a high level of yield below the theoretical maximum), population response has to be adequately measured. This means that hunters must cooperate by providing specimens and information, and agencies must have adequate authority, personnel, and funds to monitor the population. The twofold bottleneck in population management involves logistics and technology. The ultimate cause is simply a lack of adequate publicity for the problem, which could aid immeasurably by gaining public support for a more professional job of management.

None of this implies rejection of any of the classic concepts involving population response to harvest. Rather, it means that sport hunters are more numerous and efficient, and that retention of habitat quality and quantity is even more important. Sport hunting depends inevitably upon recognition of the principles of fair chase and respect for the quarry. The time-tried values of common courtesy and respect towards the landowner are also at issue. The future of hunting will largely be dictated by how we treat the land, the game, and each other. In retrospect, the future of a goodly number of our institutions and traditions depends on those very same things.

# 12

# Waterfowl Management

## INTRODUCTION

Aldo Leopold (1933) recognized that waterfowl pose a unique management problem because this group (Table 12.1) comprises species that migrate across international boundaries. The impetus for any one state to manage for the needs of waterfowl was thus recognized as insufficient to meet the entire needs of waterfowl. Furthermore, as a result of their long migrations, waterfowl are subject to a wide variety of human activities that affect their populations and habitat. Eskimos may collect eggs and down on the nesting grounds in the far north. The wheat farmer in the prairie coteau region (Figure 12.1) may find ducks reproducing on the potholes within his fields and then find them depredating his grain. The Louisiana hunter sees large concentrations of wintering waterfowl that come from dispersed, distant breeding areas, a picture far different from what the hunter further north sees. The East Coast hunt clubs own valuable marshes and are politically influential, while many birders value these fascinating resources for their esthetic merits.

   Furthermore, conditions on the prairie provinces and in the upper Midwest that affect waterfowl on the Central and Mississippi flyways are different from those on the Pacific or Atlantic flyways. Ducks produced on midwestern potholes, subject to drainage and drought, do not have the same problems as coastal waterfowl whose northern breeding and nesting grounds are relatively secure but who winter on bays and estuaries that are contaminated and subject to elimination through development. Given that the waterfowl scenario is continent wide, and encompasses a wide variety of political jurisdictions, the management of these species is very complex and diverse.

   Waterfowl management has been dissected into habitat acquisition and devel-

TABLE 12.1   Common and Scientific Names of Most North American Waterfowl, Family Anatidae

| Subfamily | Tribe | Species | Common Name |
|-----------|-------|---------|-------------|
| Anserinae | Dendrocygini | *Dendrocygna bicolor* | Fulvous whistling duck |
| | | *Dendrocygna autumnalis* | Black-bellied whistling duck |
| | Cygnini | *Cygnus olor* | Mute swan |
| | | *Cygnus buccinator* | Trumpeter swan |
| | | *Cygnus cygnus* | Whooper swan |
| | | *Cygnus columbianus* | Whistling swan |
| | Anserini | *Anser albifrons frontalis* | Greater white-fronted goose |
| | | *Anser erythropus* | Lesser white-fronted goose |
| | | *Chen caerulescens* | Snow goose |
| | | *Chen rossii* | Ross's goose |
| | | *Chen canagica* | Emperor goose |
| | | *Branta canadensis* | Canada goose |
| | | *Branta leucopsis* | Barnacle goose |
| | | *Branta bernicla* | Brant |
| Anatinae | Carinini | *Aix sponsa* | Wood duck |
| | Anatini | *Anas penelope* | European wigeon |
| | | *Anas americana* | American wigeon |
| | | *Anas strepera* | Gadwall |
| | | *Anas formosa* | Baikal teal |
| | | *Anas crecca carolinensis* | American green-winged teal |
| | | *Anas crecca crecca* | Eurasian green-winged teal |
| | | *Anas platyrhynchos platyrhynchos* | Mallard |
| | | *Anas platyrhynchos diazi* | Mexican duck |
| | | *Anas fulvigula fulvigula* | Florida duck |
| | | *Anas fulvigula maculosa* | Mottled duck |
| | | *Anas rubripes* | American black duck |
| | | *Anas acuta acuta* | Northern pintail |
| | | *Anas discors* | Blue-winged teal |
| | | *Anas cyanoptera* | Cinnamon teal |
| | | *Anas clypeata* | Northern shoveler |
| | Aythyini | *Aythya valisineria* | Canvasback |
| | | *Aythya americana* | Redhead |
| | | *Aythya collaris* | Ring-necked duck |
| | | *Aythya fuligula* | Tufted duck |
| | | *Aythya marila* | Greater scaup |
| | | *Aythya affinis* | Lesser scaup |
| | Mergini | *Somateria mollissima* | Common eider |
| | | *Somateria spectabilis* | King eider |
| | | *Somateria fischeri* | Spectacled eider |
| | | *Polysticta stelleri* | Steller's eider |
| | | *Histrionicus histrionicus* | Harlequin duck |
| | | *Clangula hyemalis* | Oldsquaw |

TABLE 12.1 Common and Scientific Names of Most North American Waterfowl, Family Anatidae (*continued*)

| Subfamily | Tribe | Species | Common Name |
|---|---|---|---|
| | | *Melanitta nigra* | Black scoter |
| | | *Melanitta perspicillata* | Surf scoter |
| | | *Melanitta fusca* | White-winged scoter |
| | | *Bucephala albeola* | Bufflehead |
| | | *Bucephala islandica* | Barrow's goldeneye |
| | | *Bucephala clangula* | Common goldeneye |
| | | *Lophodytes cucullatus* | Hooded merganser |
| | | *Mergus serrator* | Red-breasted merganser |
| | | *Mergus merganser* | Common merganser |
| | Oxyurini | *Oxyura dominica* | Masked duck |
| | | *Oxyura jamaicensis rubida* | Ruddy duck |

*Source:* American Ornithologists Union, 1983.

opment, population inventory and regulation of kills, and disease control (Bellrose and Low 1978). The drastic decline in wetland habitat through drainage and contamination is a major concern. The drainage of wetlands in the Dakotas and Minnesota accelerated after World War II, prompting conservationists to amend the Duck Stamp Act in 1958 to authorize acquisition of waterfowl production areas. Destruction of wetlands in Canada has resulted in efforts by Ducks Unlimited to acquire wetlands. Over 16 percent of water area in the prime waterfowl-producing region in Minnesota was drained between 1945 and 1950, much of this with federal subsidy (Linduska 1964). Subsidized drainage occurred at the rate of 9885 acres a year from 1954 to 1961. While public laws provide for consideration of waterfowl habitat in agricultural activities that involve federal monies, the decline of habitat in the midcontinent breeding areas has been profound. This trend has stimulated interest in intensively managing areas that are specifically meant for waterfowl production, in order to make most efficient use of the available acreage. Bellrose and Low (1978) concluded that if waterfowl managers are to compete with agriculture effectively, an accelerated program of wetland acquisition coupled with more intensive management of existing wetlands will be required. The priority is for acquisition: intensive management can come as funds allow and lands are secured. Pollution and adverse alteration of wintering grounds, such as the construction of the Albemarle and Chesapeake Canal, which allowed polluted water to flow into Back Bay and Currituck Sound (Bourn 1932), has long been a source of concern.

## LAWS AND TREATIES

The laws and treaties that involve waterfowl conservation are important (see Chapter 3). The Lacey Act of 1900, which prohibits interstate shipment of illegal game, serves to involve the federal government in wildlife law enforcement. This act authorizes U.S. Department of the Interior to be involved in conservation, preservation, and restoration of game birds. The 1916 treaty with Great Britain authorizes

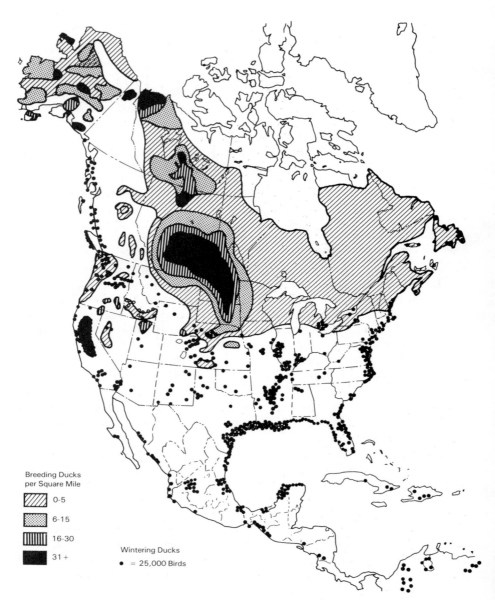

Breeding Ducks
per Square Mile

0-5

6-15

16-30

31 +

Wintering Ducks

● = 25,000 Birds

**Figure 12.1** Average distribution of North American breeding and wintering ducks. After Linduska 1964:720.

the federal government to control waterfowl because they cross into Canada, and the treaty between the United States and Mexico in 1936 expands the 1916 treaty to include Mexico. The Migratory Waterfowl Act of 1929 gives regulatory powers to the federal government on all migratory bird refuges. While these laws and treaties established that the federal government is responsible for waterfowl, the real impetus came through the Migratory Bird Hunting Stamp Act of 1934, which required hunters to buy a "duck stamp" in order to hunt waterfowl. This fund was to be used to create waterfowl refuges. The Pittman-Robertson Act of 1937, which provided for federal-state cooperation in wildlife management, enabled the states to participate more fully in waterfowl management and habitat acquisition. Subsequent acts, including the National Wildlife Refuge System Administration Act of 1966, the National Environmental Policy Act of 1969, and the Endangered and Threatened Species Act of 1969, have influenced management of the national wildlife refuge system and of waterfowl.

## THE NATIONAL WILDLIFE REFUGE SYSTEM

The most intensive U. S. program for land acquisition and management for wildlife is the Fish and Wildlife Service (FWS) Federal Refuge System. Dating back to 1903 when the Pelican Island Refuge was established in Florida to protect a colony of brown pelicans, this system provides the backbone for waterfowl habitat. Theodore Roosevelt was responsibile for establishing Pelican Island through executive order, and Franklin D. Roosevelt was responsible for greatly expanding the refuge program in the 1930s, after the great drought brought the plight of waterfowl to national attention. J. N. "Ding" Darling, the Pulitzer prize–winning cartoonist for the *Des Moines Register*, was named to a committee along with Thomas Beck and Aldo Leopold to address waterfowl problems. Then, as now, preservation of breeding grounds was identified as the first issue, and Darling, as chief of the Bureau of Biological Survey, was extremely successful in expanding the refuge system. J. Clark Salyer became chief of the Division of Wildlife Refuges within the Bureau of Sport Fisheries and Wildlife (now the FWS) and presided over the system for a 28-year period. Salyer and Gillett (1964) point out that there are bird populations that use refuges exclusively for a critical part of their life cycle, such as the greater snow goose, which winters primarily on four national wildlife refuges on the East Coast. Several refuges serve as habitat for the major share of an entire species, such as Aransas for the whooping crane and Red Rock Lakes for the trumpeter swan.

The importance of this national refuge system to waterfowl cannot be overemphasized, but at the same time state and local wildlife management areas are also important. Over 5 million acres of waterfowl management areas are available through the efforts of the several states, and many private areas such as Remington Farms in Maryland, and the famous Delta Waterfowl Research Station, Manitoba, also contribute significantly to waterfowl habitat preservation, research, and management.

While the overall purpose of national wildlife refuges has always been to protect waterfowl habitat and perpetuate waterfowl populations, the Advisory Committee on Wildlife Management appointed by Secretary of the Interior Stewart L. Udall reviewed the status and management of the federal refuge system after it became necessary to gain a clearer understanding of what the system should be. A. Starker Leopold, Clarence Cottam, Ian McT. Cowan, Ira N. Gabrielson, and T. L.

Kimball (1968) recognized that these refuges contained other important values as well: protection of endangered species; habitat for a variety of shorebirds, nongame species, and game species; recreational use (consumptive and nonconsumptive); plus a variety of educational and scientific values. Recommendations by this committee (Table 12.2) have been implemented in many ways.

This committee emphasized that refuges should be a *wildlife display* in the most comprehensive sense. Each refuge should have a primary function that re-

**TABLE 12.2   Abridged Summary of Recommendations on National Wildlife Refuges**

1. The system of 250 migratory waterfowl refuges is still inadequate to protect the resource. Breeding grounds in particular need further safeguards, and units should be preserved by purchase or lease wherever possible. State, Canadian, provincial, and private agencies should be encouraged to extend the effectiveness of the national program of breeding grounds preservation and restoration.

2. There is still need for some additional refuge units along the flyways and on the wintering grounds, though the priority is less than for breeding areas. New units should be selected to fill geographic gaps in the system or to strengthen weak units. The wintering grounds in Mexico constitute a major gap in the refuge system.

3. We recommend continuing appraisal of the existing system of refuges, with a view to perfecting the long-range plans for land acquisition and development. The national refuges constitute an open-ended system and units will doubtless be added and others deleted indefinitely into the future.

4. General refuges for nonwaterfowl—including islands, wildlife ranges, reserves for endangered species, bird rookeries, reserves for oceanic mammals, etc.—should expand too as opportunity and funds permit, with emphasis on rare and endangered species.

5. Duck stamp funds alone are inadequate to finance this program of land acquisition and development. In view of the growing recreational and educational value of refuges to the general public, we suggest that use of general funds is justified to augment the tax on waterfowl hunters in extending the refuge system.

6. There must be substantial strengthening of central administrative authority in the Division of Wildlife Refuges. The loose structure of the administrative framework in the recent past has precluded development of the system along predetermined lines of policy.

7. Insofar as possible, plans for the development and management of individual refuges should include preservation or restoration of natural ecosystems along with the primary management objective.

8. The refuge system as a whole should be designed and managed to spread migratory waterfowl as evenly as possible throughout the flyways.

9. Refuges are for people as well as animals, but patterns of public use must be rigorously controlled to protect the primary purpose of refuges, to emphasize natural values, and to minimize inappropriate activities. Wildlife-oriented uses, such as wildlife viewing, should be an important secondary objective of every refuge.

10. Hunting and fishing are appropriate uses for portions of many refuges. Keeping in mind the primary objectives of the refuges, both hunting and fishing along with other public activities should be managed to prevent undue disturbance of birds and mammals or interference with their welfare.

11. The National Wildlife Refuge should be extensively used for research and teaching by qualified scientists and naturalists. In many localities refuges are the only land units devoted solely to wildlife preservation, and thus offer unique possibilities for continuous research and ecologic education.

*Source:* A. S. Leopold et al. 1968.

ceives special attention, while at the same time providing other wildlife values. In essence, wildlife refuges should be the place where wildlife receives first priority. They also recommended that habitats should be managed as a bit of natural landscape, and urged that artificialization of the land should be minimized and done with discretion.

An environmental statement on operation of the National Wildlife Refuge System (U.S. Fish and Wildlife Service 1976) now provides overall guidance for refuge management. As of June 1974, there were 367 national wildlife refuges located in 49 states exceeding 33,800,000 acres. The specific mission of the system is to "provide, manage, and safeguard a national network of lands and waters sufficient in size, diversity, and location to make available, now and in the future, public benefits that are associated with wildlife over which the federal government has responsibility, particularly migratory birds and endangered species" (U.S. Fish and Wildlife Service 1976:I-4). Objectives implement and augment the recommendations of the Leopold committee and fall into the preservation and educational-recreational categories (Table 12.3). The objective of producing 1.6 million waterfowl in 1975 on existing refuge lands illustrates the importance of the system for waterfowl.

**TABLE 12.3   Objectives and Goals of Management of
the National Wildlife Refuge System for 1985**

1. To preserve, restore, and enhance in their natural ecosystems all species of animals and plants that are endangered or threatened with becoming endangered on lands of the National Wildlife Refuge System. The continuing annual goal is to provide 142 million use-days by threatened and endangered species.
2. To perpetuate the migratory bird resource for the benefit of people. The 1985 quantified goals on existing refuge lands are:
   a. To produce 1.6 million waterfowl
   b. To provide quality habitat which will support 1.7 billion use-days by waterfowl, and
   c. To sustain 4.2 billion use-days by other specially recognized migratory birds including hawks, owls, doves, marsh and water birds and others.
3. To preserve the natural diversity and abundance of mammals and nonmigratory birds on refuge lands. Goals are to provide 10.8 million use-days by a select group of animals including the Kodiak bear, wolverine, sea otter, desert bighorn sheep, and muskox.
4. To provide understanding and appreciation of fish and wildlife ecology and man's role in his environment, and to provide visitors at Service installations with high-quality, safe, wholesome, and enjoyable recreational experiences oriented toward wildlife. Under this objective annual goals are as follows:
   a. Provide opportunity for 780 scientific studies by college and universities
   b. Provide 288,000 activity hours of environmental education
   c. Provide 2,245,000 activity hours of wildlife interpretation
   d. Preserve and protect 191 Natural Areas, 43 Wilderness Areas and 65 special sites for their ecological, scientific and cultural values
   e. Provide 13,000 public programs and respond to 1,276,000 public inquiries
   f. Provide 45 million activity hours of wildlife oriented recreation and 16 million hours of nonwildlife oriented recreation
   g. Support 36 YCC and 2 Job Corps camps

*Source:* U.S. Fish and Wildlife Service 1976.

## MIGRATION FLYWAYS AND CORRIDORS

The flyways of Lincoln (1935) are defined as broad areas into which certain migration routes blend in a definite geographic region (Figure 12.2). They are not sharply defined north of 45° latitude, where considerable interchange of waterfowl from different flyways on the northern nesting grounds occurs. The assumption behind the use of flyways in waterfowl management is that individual birds tend to migrate

**Figure 12.2** Waterfowl flyways.

along the same routes each year. Bellrose and Crompton (1970) provided good evidence that this tends to be so with mallards and black ducks, but it is well known that geese are much more strictly traditional than are ducks. Hochbaum (1955) felt that the degree of pioneering new areas by ducks was related to the proximity of suitable areas adjacent to established nesting grounds. He felt the closer family and group bonds in geese tended to restrict pioneering and ensure faithfulness to the same home areas each year.

Lincoln (1935), J. W. Aldrich et al. (1949), and others recognized that flyways were not biologically exact, and Bellrose (1968) considered them to be primarily geographical rather than biological in nature. Bellrose (1968) reported a series of migration corridors for dabbling ducks, diving ducks, and geese east of the Rocky Mountains (Figures 12.3 through 12.7). These corridors are passageways of species and population elements that connect a series of wetland habitats from breeding to wintering areas. While hunting regulations have continued to be largely related to flyways, Bellrose (1968) predicted that identification of migration corridors provides a means to manage the kill in smaller units and by populations. An example of such management is the coordination of regulations for canvasbacks, which migrate from northwest to southeast across the Central, Mississippi, and Atlantic flyways in fall to winter on the sounds and back bays on the East Coast. However, Bellrose and Crompton (1970) felt that management of geese by corridor would be more practical than for ducks, because of the high fidelity geese show for each migration route.

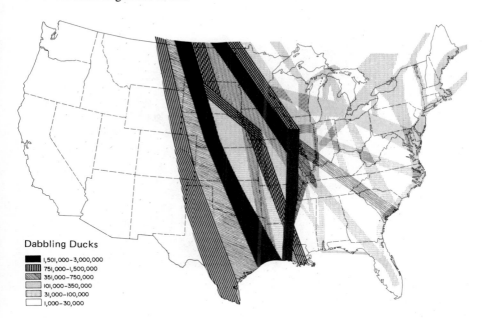

**Dabbling Ducks**

- ■ 1,501,000–3,000,000
- ▥ 751,000–1,500,000
- ▨ 351,000–750,000
- ▧ 101,000–350,000
- ▦ 31,000–100,000
- ☐ 1,000–30,000

**Figure 12.3** The migration corridors used by dabbling ducks during their fall migration. After Bellrose 1968. (Used with permission.)

Many of the migration corridors cross from the Central to the Mississippi Flyway. Prairie-nesting dabbling ducks have a more pronounced northwest-southeast fall migration than divers (Figures 12.3 and 12.4), the exception being those divers that move east along the Great Lakes to the Atlantic Coast. Flight corridors of geese are more north-south oriented than those of ducks (Figures 12.5, 12.6, and 12.7). Some blue and snow geese follow different migration routes in spring and fall.

Migration studies involve use of banded birds, direct observations, and radar. Bellrose and Crompton (1970) illustrated the high value and the biases of using banded birds for delineating migration patterns. Visual sightings, radar, and weekly census of waterfowl migrations show that the principal movement is southwest of that shown by band recoveries. The reason is that the paucity of habitat along the principal route affords little opportunity for harvest, while the eastern edge of the route does have good habitat. Therefore, a small proportion of the mallard population is subject to harvest in this eastern area although band recoveries are greater there than elsewhere along the flight route.

Bellrose (1958, 1963, 1976) discussed the orientation behavior of waterfowl. Variation in use of a number of cues to aid in navigation exists between species of waterfowl. Mallards use the sun and the landscape cues differently than blue-winged teal, for instance. Wild mallards tend to fly north when trapped and released, while Canada geese tend to fly southwest. Stars, the sun, wind, landscapes (especially lakes and rivers), and the earth's magnetic field all serve as cues. Inclement

Diving Ducks

- 251,000–500,000
- 76,000–250,000
- 26,000–75,000
- 11,000–25,000
- 1,000–10,000

Figure 12.4 The migration corridors used by diving ducks during their fall migrations. After Bellrose 1968. (Used with permission.)

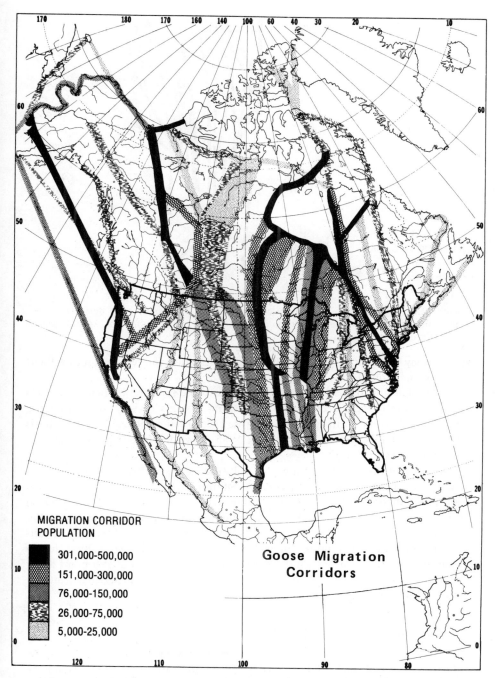

**Figure 12.5** The migration corridors used by Canada geese during their fall migrations. After Bellrose 1976. (Used with permission.)

**Figure 12.6** The migration corridors used by blue and lesser snow geese during the fall migrations from staging areas on Hudson and James bays to the Gulf Coast. After Bellrose 1968. (Used with permission.)

weather may cause flocks to overshoot their destination and require a return flight in reverse direction of the migration.

Mass fall migrations of waterfowl, such as those reported by Bellrose (1957) and Hochbaum (1955), occur when large storm systems of very low barometric pressure sweep from north to south. Bellrose (1957) estimated over 2 million birds moved from October 26 to November 4, 1955, down the Mississippi Flyway as a result of such a storm front.

*Short-stopping* by waterfowl, especially Canada geese, is a phenomenon related to the changing habitat. Hanson and Smith (1950) reported the well-known case of the Mississippi Flyway Canada geese that originally wintered primarily on the Louisiana coastal marshes. Adequate wintering areas appeared in southern Illinois after 1941, when refuges along the Mississippi River were established. The suitable wintering areas in Illinois, coupled with progressively poorer habitat due to agricultural practices further south, served to "short stop" geese at a point along their migration route that had originally been a stopover for many that wintered on the Gulf Coast.

## ESTABLISHING HUNTING SEASONS

While the basic U.S. authority for waterfowl conservation rests with the federal government in the Fish and Wildlife Service (FWS), the various states are deeply involved in population management. In fact, a system for establishing waterfowl

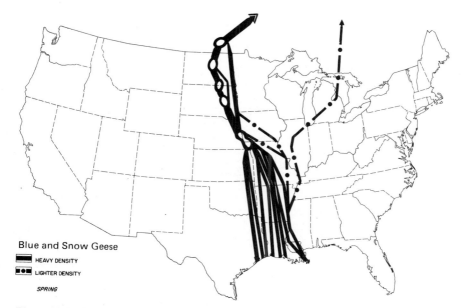

**Figure 12.7** The migration corridors used by blue and lesser snow geese during their spring migrations from the Gulf Coast to southern Canada. The areas enclosed by heavy lines between northwestern Missouri and southern Manitoba are important concentration and feeding areas. After Bellrose 1968. (Used with permission.)

hunting seasons has been devised that incorporates input from public agencies and from citizens who have been traditionally concerned with waterfowl.

Objectives of the annual regulations are as follows (U.S. Fish and Wildlife Service 1975): (1) to provide protection of migratory bird populations by regulated management of the harvest; (2) to provide outdoor recreational and harvest opportunities compatible with resource reproductive capabilities and maintenance of acceptable population levels; (3) to assist in the prevention of depredations of agricultural crops by migrating game birds; (4) to distribute hunting opportunity for migratory birds as equitably as possible among hunters along migration routes; (5) to limit the accidental taking of nontarget species where there is a reasonable possibility that hunter confusion between target and nontarget species might exist.

One conglomerate organization is important: the Flyway Council, which was established in 1952 to coordinate agencies and citizens involved in waterfowl management. Four Flyway Councils were established to represent groups within each waterfowl flyway. A National Flyway Council serves as a coordinating body. The Flyway Councils evaluate information and make recommendations to the FWS on hunting seasons and bag limits.

Figure 12.8 illustrates the schedule of regulations, meetings, and publications in the *Federal Register* that was followed in 1980. In January, the FWS Regulations Committee meets to review available data on populations and to present a preliminary set of regulations to the public for review. These proposals are pub-

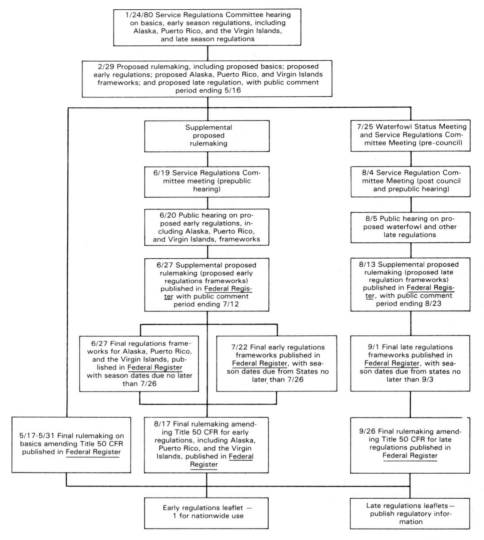

**Figure 12.8**   1980 Schedule of regulations meetings and publications in the *Federal Register*. From Federal Register, Vol. 45, No. 42, Friday, February 29, 1980.

lished in the *Federal Register* and notification of two public hearings on migratory bird regulations is included. Data to be considered will be harvest from the previous fall, information on habitat conditions, and available population data, including trends.

In late February to mid-March, the four Flyway Councils meet to review available data. Their recommendations are passed on to the FWS at a meeting held in conjunction with the North American Wildlife and Natural Resources Conference.

In June, breeding ground survey data are available for examination. At this time the FWS holds meetings and a public hearing on early seasons—those starting September 1, and in Alaska, Puerto Rico, and the Virgin Islands. In 1980, the final framework (outside limits for dates and times when shooting may begin and end, plus number of birds that may be taken and possessed) for the early seasons was published on June 27 in the *Federal Register*. These frameworks are then reviewed by the Flyway Council and individual states that recommend their seasons. The FWS publishes the final early regulations on early seasons in mid-August, and the states publish shortly thereafter. Federal regulations must appear 30 days before the season opening to provide for review and comment by Congress. In 1980, nine separate inclusions into the *Federal Register* concerning waterfowl hunting regulations were made.

Hunting seasons that begin in October or later follow a different time schedule. Meetings in late July take place to discuss breeding ground survey data. The regulation framework is published in early September, and the final federal regulations are available in late September.

If these intricate procedures for federal involvement are not enough, then the states also have public hearings, deadlines, and legal requirements to follow. Many deadlines are set early enough to preclude use of all data that will be available on the populations for that year. Some flexibility to restrict harvest pending final assessment of all data is built into the states' procedures, but state regulations cannot be more liberal than federal regulations. Waterfowl management is indeed an intricate undertaking, involving many people, agencies, and deadlines and, hopefully, lots of ducks and geese.

Procedures used to obtain the basic data for establishing hunting regulations have been reported by Geis, Martinson, and Anderson (1969). The first task involves estimating the size of the breeding population and predicting production. Subsequently, the predictions are checked against more reliable estimates when hunting season data from the previous season are available.

Breeding populations are estimated by aerial surveys of 1/8-mile strips, flying at 100–150 feet above ground between sunrise and noon. Waterfowl are recorded by species, sex, and group size. The transects have been located on a stratified random sampling basis, to give greater coverage of areas of high breeding populations. A series of ground counts to adjust for unseen birds is included. These ground routes are 5 miles in length and cover approximately 100 ponds if possible. Martinson and Kaczynski (1967) reported biases in the aerial survey, concluding that ground and aerial counts should be made on separate days, each should not be duplicated on the same day, more air-ground comparison transects were needed, and efforts to minimize observer differences were needed. The air to ground ratio, obtained by dividing birds seen from the air by those seen from the ground, is then divided into the aerial index to adjust for birds not seen.

Mallard production must be predicted for the regulations from breeding ground surveys and brood surveys, and a regression model is used (Geis, Martinson, and Anderson (1969):

$$Y = 7.926 + 1.468X_1 - 0.624X_2 - 0.028X_3 + 0.016X_4$$

where

$Y$ = predicted number of mallard young (millions)

$X_1$ = number of July ponds (millions)

$X_2$ = continental mallard breeding population (millions)

$X_3$ = % ponds remaining between May and July surveys

$X_4$ = index to number of broods (thousands) unadjusted

The importance of the prairie potholes in Canada on continental mallard production is indicated by the presence of three variables that relate to that region only. This regression model explains 92 percent ($R^2 = .92$) of the variability in mallard young for the 1955–1967 period. Confidence limits of the prediction are ±7 percent at $p = .10$, the 10 percent level of probability.

The size of the fall population is calculated by adding the size of the breeding population, minus 5 percent for mortality May–September, to the estimated production. Table 12.4 shows the prediction for the average mallard production for the 1955–1967 period, after Geis et al. (1969).

Table 12.5 shows the "check" on the prediction of the fall population, using all data available. Harvest data includes an estimate of numbers killed, listed by species, and by age and sex. Wing collections, mail questionnaries to hunters, and recoveries of banded birds apportion the kill between Canada and the United States, broken down into young and adult. Crippling losses are estimated at 25 percent of total deaths due to hunting. Geis et al. (1969) compared the predicted and "actual" production and harvest figures for the mallard and found a reasonably close fit.

The draft Environmental Statement on issuance of annual regulations permitting the sport hunting of migratory birds (U.S. Fish and Wildlife Service 1975) summarizes hunting season and waterfowl harvest statistics for the 1955–1973 period. The majority of the sport harvest of birds is derived from 11 of the 41 species: mallard, American wigeon, green-winged teal, pintail, gadwall, blue-winged

**TABLE 12.4  Predicting Mallard Production, 1955–1967**

| Factor | 1955–1967 Data | |
|---|---|---|
| | Average | Range |
| May ponds | 3.2 | 1.7–6.0 |
| July ponds ($X_1$) | 20 | 0.6–5.0 |
| Mallard breeding population in millions ($X_2$) | 9.6 | 6.1–15.5 |
| July ponds as a percent of May ponds ($X_3$) | 57 | 33–83 |
| Broods in thousands ($X_4$) | 431 | 179–1023 |
| Mallard young in millions ($Y$) | 10.1 | 6.0–18.7 |

Prediction equation: $Y = 7.926 + 1.468X_1 - 0.624X_2 - 0.028X_3 + 0.016X_4$

*Source:* Geis, Martinson, and Anderson 1969. (Used with permission.)

**TABLE 12.5**  Mallard Population and Harvest Statistics, 1963–1967
(duck numbers in thousands)

| Statistic | 1963 | 1964 | 1965 | 1966 | 1967 |
|---|---|---|---|---|---|
| Breeding population[a] | 8030 | 7930 | 6108 | 7803 | 8558 |
| Prehunting season adult population[b] | 7628 | 7534 | 5803 | 7413 | 8130 |
| Production ratio[c] | 1.0 | 0.8 | 1.6 | 1.2 | 1.2 |
| Mallard young[d] | 7628 | 6027 | 9285 | 8896 | 9756 |
| Fall population[e] | 15256 | 13561 | 15088 | 16309 | 18776 |
| U.S. harvest[f] | 2364 | 2972 | 2397 | 3749 | 4095 |
| Canadian harvest[g] | 1218 | 1214 | 932 | 1230 | 1263 |
| Total hunting kill[h] | 4775 | 5580 | 4438 | 6637 | 7142 |
| Nonhunting mortality[i] | 2947 | 2178 | 3237 | 1542 | 2952 |
| Total annual mortality rate | 0.506 | 0.572 | 0.509 | 0.501 | 0.564 |
| Rate of hunting kill | 0.313 | 0.411 | 0.294 | 0.407 | 0.399 |
| Rate of nonhunting mortality | 0.193 | 0.161 | 0.214 | 0.094 | 0.165 |

*Source:* After Geis, Martinson, and Anderson 1969. (Used with permission.)

[a]From aerial surveys in May adjusted for birds not seen by aerial crews.

[b]Calculated as 0.95 × breeding population (5% mortality of adults preseason).

[c]Wing collection data adjusted for relative vulnerability between young and adults from weighted prehunting season banding data.

[d]Calculated as pre–hunting season adult population × production ratio.

[e]Calculated as pre–hunting season adult population + mallard young.

[f]Mail questionnaire and wing collection data.

[g]Weighted distribution of band recoveries from preseason banding applied to mallard young.

[h]Calculated as (mallard young + fall population) × 1.333 to include crippling loss as 25 percent of total.

[i]Additional loss indicated to obtain subsequent preseason adult population from fall population − total hunting kill.

teal, wood duck, lesser scaup, ring-necked duck, and black duck (Table 12.6). Mallards comprise approximately one-third of the total average harvest of 10,745,000 birds in the United States over the 1955–1973 period. Black ducks constitute 21 percent of the 1.4 million birds taken annually in the Atlantic Flyway, while pintails comprise a similar percentage in the Pacific Flyway. Lesser scaup and ring-necked ducks are most commonly shot in the Mississippi Flyway, while greater scaup are taken primarily in the Atlantic Flyway. These trends in harvest by species are a reflection of their relative abundance across the continent.

Canada geese comprised approximately two-thirds of the total goose harvest of approximately 1.5 million birds, with greater and lesser snow geese, and the white-fronted goose (primarily Pacific Flyway) being next in importance. The snow goose is most prevalent in the kill in the Central Flyway. Goose harvests have increased in the 1970s from the 1960s, as a result of higher populations of Canada and snow geese. The brants are taken in coastal areas and the emperor goose is harvested only in Alaska.

A variety of different hunting seasons have been tried for purposes ranging

TABLE 12.6   Average Duck Harvest, 1961–1970 (percent)

| Species | Alaska[a] | Pacific Flyway | Central Flyway | Mississippi Flyway | Atlantic Flyway |
|---|---|---|---|---|---|
| *Dabblers* | | | | | |
| Mallard | 28.2 | 32.9 | 36.5 | 35.7 | 17.1 |
| Mallard × black | – | tr.[c] | tr. | 0.1 | 0.6 |
| Black duck | – | – | tr. | 2.5 | 20.6 |
| Mexican duck | – | tr. | tr. | – | – |
| Mottled duck | – | – | 2.9 | 1.0 | 1.5 |
| Gadwall | 1.1 | 3.1 | 9.9 | 4.7 | 1.5 |
| American wigeon | 14.9 | 12.5 | 7.0 | 5.2 | 4.3 |
| Green-winged teal | 17.4 | 13.2 | 13.2 | 8.6 | 7.7 |
| Bluewing and Cinnamon teal[b] | 0.4 | 2.1 | 6.4 | 8.0 | 2.5 |
| Shoveler | 4.8 | 6.4 | 3.9 | 2.1 | 0.8 |
| Pintail | 20.4 | 22.4 | 8.3 | 4.3 | 2.2 |
| Wood duck | – | 0.9 | 1.9 | 10.4 | 15.2 |
| *Divers* | | | | | |
| Redhead | – | 0.8 | 2.8 | 1.4 | 0.7 |
| Canvasback | 0.4 | 0.7 | 1.0 | 0.8 | 1.6 |
| Greater scaup | 2.0 | 0.5 | tr. | 0.6 | 3.2 |
| Lesser scaup | 1.7 | 1.0 | 2.9 | 6.1 | 3.5 |
| Ring-necked duck | 0.2 | 0.6 | 1.7 | 5.8 | 6.4 |
| Common goldeneye | 1.9 | 0.7 | 0.2 | 0.7 | 1.6 |
| Barrow's goldeneye | 1.5 | tr. | tr. | tr. | tr. |
| Bufflehead | 1.8 | 1.0 | 0.5 | 1.0 | 2.5 |
| Ruddy duck | – | 0.9 | 0.4 | 0.4 | 0.5 |
| Masked duck | – | – | – | – | – |
| *Mergansers* | | | | | |
| Common merganser | 0.4 | tr. | tr. | tr. | 0.1 |
| Red-breasted merganser | 0.1 | tr. | tr. | tr. | 0.6 |
| Hooded merganser | 0.1 | tr. | 0.1 | 0.5 | 1.4 |
| *Sea Ducks, etc.* | | | | | |
| Oldsquaw | 0.2 | tr. | tr. | tr. | 0.5 |
| Harlequin duck | 0.7 | tr. | – | tr. | – |
| Common eider | – | – | – | tr. | 0.4 |
| King eider | – | tr. | – | tr. | tr. |
| Common scoter | tr. | tr. | tr. | tr. | 0.5 |
| White-winged scoter | 0.7 | tr. | tr. | tr. | 1.5 |
| Surf scoter | 1.4 | tr. | tr. | tr. | 1.1 |
| Fulvous tree duck | – | tr. | tr. | tr. | tr. |
| Black-bellied tree duck | – | tr. | – | – | – |
| Hybrid (not mallard × black) | – | tr. | tr. | tr. | tr. |
| | 100.2 | 100.0 | 99.9 | 99.9 | 100.0 |

*Source:* Files, Office of Migratory Bird Management.

[a]Alaska percentages based on five-year (1966–1970) average.

[b]These two species are indistinguishable by wings.

[c]tr = trace.

from distributing hunting pressure, to increasing and decreasing the harvest. Restrictions of season starting and closing dates (the framework dates) generally reduced the kill in northern and southern states, where migrations begin and end, but not necessarily in the central states. Season starting dates may be delayed on northern breeding grounds to protect local populations. The protection comes in the form of diluting the harvest of a specific breeding population as it mixes with birds from other areas.

Season lengths affect harvest intensity more than opening and closing dates (Table 12.7). Lengths also affect species composition in the harvest, the number of hunters, and the numbers of times an individual hunts during the season.

Split seasons, designed to take advantage of different abundance peaks of waterfowl within the framework dates have also been tried. Smart (1964) reported that use of split seasons tends to increase the kill, in some cases significantly. States may opt for split seasons, especially if the framework dates are short, even though the total season length is further reduced.

Special teal and scaup seasons, outside the framework dates, have been used to increase hunting pressure on these species. Hunting pressure has been traditionally low on these species. Both are often in good supply and the teal migrate prior to the regular season. The early seasons on teal have not reduced the regular season harvest, which is comprised of later-migrating segments of this species. Illegal kill of other species constituted 2 percent of the total kill in early teal seasons and did not increase the total kill of other ducks very much. Scaup harvest may be doubled by establishing special seasons that do not coincide with regular duck hunting seasons.

Bag limits are also effective in regulating the harvest. Alterations on the number of birds allowable include the bonus bag (additional birds of certain species), restrictive bags for certain species, and the point system. In addition, harvest quotas have been set for specific goose populations where most of the harvest occurs in one or two areas, and can therefore be monitored. The Horicon Marsh in Wisconsin is an example where quotas are successfully used.

These variations have different effects in different areas. While an increase in the bag limit generally will increase the kill, there is a diminishing effect at upper levels. An increase from one to two birds may increase harvest by over 66 percent, but an increase from five to six birds may have negligible effect. Restrictions on mallard take are known to be more effective in areas where the mallard comprises a high proportion of the kill than where it does not. Harvest quotas are most effective for Canada geese, where individual populations occur in well-defined areas and are very predictable.

The point system was established to reduce the harvest of some species of ducks, particularly canvasbacks and redheads, which seem especially vulnerable to hunting. A hunter is allowed a certain number of points each day, with different values assigned to each species or sex. This system precludes the need for the hunter to identify ducks in the field since identification may be done after the duck is in hand, although ideally an identification prior to shooting is best. The daily bag limit is reached when the duck take reaches or exceeds the point limit. This en-

**TABLE 12.7  Duck Harvest by Five-Day Intervals of the Season**

| State | | | | | | | Cumulative Percent at Five-Day Intervals | | | | | |
|---|---|---|---|---|---|---|---|---|---|---|---|---|
| | 1-5 | 1-10 | 1-15 | 1-20 | 1-25 | 1-30 | 1-35 | 1-40 | 1-45 | 1-50 | 1-55 |
| Minnesota | 47.8 | 62.2 | 73.7 | 82.3 | 89.0 | 93.8 | 97.1 | 100.0 | 101.9 | – | – |
| Wisconsin | 42.0 | 57.6 | 68.5 | 78.6 | 85.7 | 91.6 | 96.2 | 100.0 | 101.3 | 102.1 | 102.9 |
| Michigan | 39.1 | 53.5 | 66.0 | 75.8 | 83.6 | 90.2 | 96.0 | 100.0 | 103.1 | 106.3 | 112.5 |
| Iowa | 39.4 | 54.7 | 67.7 | 76.8 | 83.9 | 89.8 | 95.3 | 100.0 | 105.9 | 112.2 | 116.9 |
| Illinois | 33.0 | 49.8 | 62.4 | 72.6 | 81.5 | 89.4 | 95.0 | 100.0 | 105.9 | 110.2 | 113.5 |
| Indiana | 38.2 | 53.1 | 64.5 | 75.6 | 83.6 | 90.8 | 96.2 | 100.0 | 105.0 | 109.2 | 112.2 |
| Ohio | 37.6 | 51.7 | 63.2 | 71.7 | 79.7 | 86.5 | 93.7 | 100.0 | 107.0 | 120.5 | 124.5 |
| Missouri | 25.0 | 40.5 | 54.8 | 67.3 | 77.0 | 86.3 | 94.0 | 100.0 | 104.5 | 108.5 | 111.5 |
| Kentucky | 15.6 | 25.9 | 38.0 | 48.0 | 61.8 | 74.8 | 86.4 | 100.0 | 112.5 | – | – |
| Arkansas | 25.4 | 40.1 | 51.8 | 62.2 | 71.3 | 81.2 | 90.4 | 100.0 | 108.9 | – | – |
| Tennessee | 20.7 | 32.3 | 43.3 | 53.4 | 64.2 | 76.0 | 86.3 | 100.0 | 114.7 | – | – |
| Louisiana | 27.9 | 43.5 | 56.0 | 66.6 | 76.9 | 86.1 | 92.5 | 100.0 | 107.8 | 114.2 | 118.7 |
| Mississippi | 24.8 | 38.6 | 51.2 | 63.6 | 73.5 | 84.7 | 91.8 | 100.0 | 109.7 | – | – |
| Alabama | 25.8 | 38.2 | 48.6 | 59.4 | 69.8 | 78.6 | 89.1 | 100.0 | 112.4 | 120.4 | 137.2 |

*Source:* Files, Office of Migratory Bird Management.

*Note:* Percentages are based on the total harvest during the first 40 days, based on duck wing survey data from the Mississippi Flyway, 1969–1970.

courages the hunter to emphasize low-point ducks because more of these may be bagged before the point limit is reached. Hopper et al. (1975) reported hunter acceptance of this system and a reduction in harvest of high-point birds. Violations because of bag limit excesses were noted in 3.8 to 10.6 percent of parties observed. About half of the observed violations were for shooting earlier or later than the legal period. This system was judged to be successful in directing hunting harvest toward the more abundant sex and species.

Lead poisoning of waterfowl can result when lead shot is picked up as grit or incidental to feeding. As hunting has continued over a long period and more and more lead shot has been deposited on feeding areas, the problem has become critical. Obviously, substitutes for lead shot have been considered, for which copper and steel shot are most frequently suggested. However, because of the lower specific gravity of copper and steel when compared to lead, the potential for wounding birds is increased (Cochrane 1976). Thus a judgment must be made if hunting is to be allowed when lead poisoning is a problem: will the added mortality associated with use of nonlead shot be greater than the mortality due to lead poisoning? Such judgments are difficult to make because poisoned ducks are difficult to find, and the amount of mortality is hard to determine.

The studies of Cochrane (1976) and Nicklaus (1976) provide contrasting data on the effects of lead and steel shot on waterfowl. Cochrane (1976) experimentally shot 2400 mallards with copper, steel, and lead shot, then analyzed results. Lead shot produced significantly fewer crippled birds than steel shot at ranges up to 60 m. Nicklaus (1976) evaluated 4400 mallards, 1100 of which were shot with steel and 3300 (2200 one year, 1100 the second year) with lead. These birds were from the shooting preserve on the McGraw Wildlife Foundation in Illinois. No difference in crippling rates was observed between lead and steel shot in this artificial shooting situation using semiwild birds. Thus, the variability in killing power between the two types of shot can be masked by other factors associated with the hunting situation and the skill of the hunter. Subsequent field tests on several wildlife refuges have resulted in the imposition of restrictions on use of lead shot where incidence of lead poisoning is high. Thus the trade off between lead poisoning and potentially higher crippling loss has been evaluated, and steel shot will be used more and more in place of lead shot when poisoning occurs.

## EFFECTS OF HUNTING ON MALLARDS

Waterfowl population management has received intensive research effort over the past two decades, with important changes. Up through the early 1970s, those responsible felt that shooting pressure influenced annual mortality rates of migratory game birds, for the following reasons (Geis 1963):

1. Migratory game birds are gregarious and use a specific limited type of habitat.
2. The pattern of hunting activity for waterfowl is different than for resident

species; i.e., waterfowl are exposed to a series of "opening days" over a period of at least four months.

3. Nonhunting mortality occurs in addition to, and not in place of hunting mortality.

4. Increased mortality due to hunting is not compensated for by increased productivity the following year.

Waterfowl production is primarily influenced by climatic conditions that affect water levels and temperatures in April and May on the breeding grounds in the prairie provinces (Bellrose et al. 1961). Geis (1963) argued that this precluded operation of an inverse relationship between hunting and subsequent population production. Geis (1963) based his initial argument that hunting mortality was additive on analyses by Hickey (1952) and others showing a direct relationship between band recovery rates and total annual mortality estimates. Table 12.5 illustrates the type of data used for this conclusion.

In the mid-1970s D. R. Anderson (1975) and D. R. Anderson and Burnham (1976) reexamined the available population data for the mallard. They concluded that the earlier analyses were invalid because (1) data were combined across geographic areas and averaged, which obscures the relationships on any individual area; and (2) estimates of band recovery rates and survival are subject to sampling variation that compounds the actual variation of the parameters being estimated. The traditional composite dynamic life table method of estimating survival from band recovery data was thus not considered appropriate for detecting additive hunting mortality. Band recovery rates and survival rates were found to be highly negatively correlated when both were calculated from the same data source.

D. R. Anderson and Burnham (1976), as well as others, recommended that life table analyses be discontinued in favor of better methodology. Brownie et al. (1978) recommended use of stochastic models that are based on specific, well-defined assumptions and inferences that are optimal in terms of efficiency of estimation and power of tests of hypotheses. The Maximum Likelihood estimators were used for estimating survival and band recovery rates and are discussed fully in Brownie et al. (1978).

D. R. Anderson and Burnham (1976) concluded that the annual survival rate was not significantly correlated with harvest rate for mallards, using the new approach. They analyzed records from over 683,000 mallards, banded mostly during the 1961-1971 period. The results of their analysis are further summarized as follows: (1) there are significant changes in annual survival rates; (2) there is little evidence to support the hypothesis that survival rates increase as harvest rates decrease; and (3) hunting mortality is not a completely additive form of mortality.

Implications of these findings for management are as follows: (1) since hunting takes 20 to 25 percent of the mallard population annually, or nearly half of the total mortality, the fact that this is partly compensatory implies that environmental variables are limiting the population; (2) restrictive hunting seasons are unlikely to increase the size of the breeding pouplation the following year; and (3) nonhunting mortalities are not completely compensated for, and an unknown threshold point exists at which hunting mortality does become additive. Testing of these results, estimations of the threshold point between compensatory and additive mortality, identification of environmental variables limiting the waterfowl population, and examination of ways to manage waterfowl more scientifically are needed.

D. R. Anderson and Burnham (1976, 1978) emphasize that sport hunting causes a very significant proportion of the total mallard mortality in most years, and in several years during the 1960-1971 period was additive. Further analyses (D. R. Anderson and Burnham 1978) did not demonstrate that restrictive hunting regulations that reduced harvest of mallards on all flyways resulted in increased survival. However, D. R. Anderson and Burnham (1976) recognized that the burn-out phenomenon, where local breeding populations were severely reduced or in some areas eliminated by hunting, had occurred.

The models developed by Brownie et al. (1978) to analyze band recoveries and estimate population survival are free of many of the biases involved in life table analyses. The structure of the model is as follows (Brownie et al. 1978:5):

let $f$ = annual recovery rate of banded birds

$S$ = annual survival rate

$N_i$ = number banded in year $i$

$E(R_{ij})$ = expected number of band recoveries in year $j$ from birds banded in year $i$

$\ell$ = number of years of recovery of bands

$k$ = number of years of banding

The expected number of bands recovered for year $N_i$ is

$$E(R_{ii}) = N_i f, i = 1, \ldots, k$$
$$E(R_{ij}) = N_i S^{j-i} f, i = 1, \ldots, k, j = i+1, \ldots, \ell$$

The model structure would then be

| Year Banded | Number Banded | Expected Recoveries by Hunting Season, $E(R_{ij})$ | | | |
|---|---|---|---|---|---|
| | | 1 | 2 | 3 | $\ell = 4$ |
| 1 | $N_1$ | $N_i f_i$ | $N_1 S_1 f_2$ | $N_1 S_2 S_2 f_3$ | $N_1 S_1 S_2 S_3 f_4$ |
| 2 | $N_2$ | | $N_2 f_2$ | $N_2 S_2 f_3$ | $N_2 S_2 S_3 f_4$ |
| $k = 3$ | $N_3$ | | | $N_3 f_3$ | $N_3 S_3 f_4$ |

If we then specify recovery and survival rates

| Year | $f_i$ | $S_i$ |
|------|-------|-------|
| 1 | $f_1 = 0.05$ (5%) | $S_1 = 0.50$ or 50% |
| 2 | $f_2 = 0.10$ (10%) | $S_2 = 0.50$ or 50% |
| 3 | $f_3 = 0.06$ (6%) | $S_3 = 0.70$ or 70% |
| 4 | $f_4 = 0.05$ (5%) | |

and number of birds banded, we obtain the following results:

| Year Banded | Number Banded | Expected Recoveries by Season | | | |
|-------------|---------------|---|---|---|---|
| | | 1 | 2 | 3 | 4 |
| 1 | 2000 | 100 | 100 | 30 | 18 |
| 2 | 400 | | 40 | 12 | 7 |
| $k = 3$ | 1200 | | | 72 | 42 |

Assumptions in using this model to estimate population survival are as follows:

1. Sample is representative of the population.
2. Age and sex of banded individuals are correctly determined.
3. There is no band loss.
4. Survival rates are not affected by banding or tagging itself.
5. Year of band recoveries is correctly identified.
6. The fate of each banded individual is independent of the fate of other banded individuals.
7. The fate of a banded individual is a multinomial random variable.
8. All banded individuals of an identifiable class (that is by species, sex, and age) have the same annual survival and recovery rates.
9. Annual survival and recovery rates vary by year, and/or by age and sex of individuals.

Separate models for birds banded as adults, as young and adults, and as young, subadults, and adults are developed from the basic model. Methods for placing confidence intervals on estimated parameters, and estimates of sampling precision are also available.

Evaluations of these assumptions have been made over a long period. A. Leopold (1933) obtained estimates from five sources of 5 to 80 percent of bands unreported, thus showing that the percentages of banded birds killed but unreported varied between areas. Bellrose (1955) stated that available kill figures for waterfowl at that time provided only a rough index of the harvest, because of the bias of nonreporting of bands. Attempts to improve the recovery of bands by reward were partially successful. Ratios of recovery of standard to reward ($2.00) bands ranged from 1:1.61 to 1:2.22 and averaged 1:2.12. Bellrose concluded that, allowing for some failure to report all reward bands, the kill of mallards in Illinois was 2.5 to 3.0 times greater than that indicated by unrefined data. Further analysis indicated that Canadian hunters were most zealous and those in the central zone of the United States least zealous in reporting bands. Subsequent to this, attempts to increase band recovery rates were made in an effort to obtain more accurate information from band returns.

Atwood and Geis (1960) reported on problems associated with practices that increase reported recoveries of waterfowl bands. Reliability of information based on reported banded birds bagged was dependent upon (1) the uniformity of the report ratio throughout period of interest, (2) the report ratio being similar in all parts of each area, and (3) the report ratio being known for each area of interest. Earlier work by these researchers had demonstrated that the report ratio was not constant, varying significantly by states. The variability of report ratios was found to drop when bands reported from sources other than hunters were removed from the analysis. The proportion of bands reported from all sources ranged from 48 to 62 percent for three different areas, but the range narrowed to 43 to 50 percent when only hunter reports were considered. Biases influencing band recovery rates included organized band-collecting programs such as might be done at checking stations, or by wardens in law enforcement activities. This was because such programs are of uneven intensity and hence cannot be used when comparing one area against another. Atwood and Geis concluded that the reliability of information based on banded birds bagged that are reported will be increased in proportion to the degree to which special collection practices are decreased, allowing hunters to voluntarily report their bands.

In another study, Geis and Atwood (1961) investigated the proportion of recovered waterfowl bands that were reported. A series of questionnaires (Crissey 1959) were sent annually to hunters to investigate the number of banded waterfowl each bagged. Using the assumptions that hunters responded correctly to the questionnaire, that hunters who shot a banded bird knew that they had done so, and that nonreporting hunters shot the same proportion of banded birds, Geis and Atwood (1961) concluded that two banded birds were recovered for each one reported, instead of the 2.5 to 3.0:1 ratio reported by Bellrose (1955). Atwood (1956) concluded that the characteristics of nonrespondents and respondents were similar.

Martinson (1966) was next to report the studies out of the Migratory Bird Population Station. Band recovery rates appeared to decrease from 50 percent in the 1950s to 30 percent in the 1960s, concurrent with more restrictive changes in duck hunting regulations, an increased volume of banding, and changes in the method of reporting back to the band-reporter. The use of an IBM card to report back to the hunter was highly displeasing. It could be anticipated that hunters, generally concerned with tradition, might not appreciate the intrusion of computer science by the regulating agency into their activities. Martinson concluded that band recovery rate biases should be studied further.

The time of banding waterfowl also influences the recovery rate of bands. Mallards that are banded on their nesting grounds give better mortality estimates than mallards banded during autumn migration (D. H. Thompson and Jedlicka 1948). Birds that are banded during the hunting season may have already incurred mortality and hence returns will reflect a lower mortality than that of the population from which they were banded.

Band loss by birds is a potential source of bias. Band loss may be characterized as either of the initial type, where loss occurs soon after application and prior to the first major recovery period, or of the gradual type, attributable to wear, which affects the recovery rate throughout the lifespan of the banded cohort (Martinson and Henny 1967). An analysis of the retention of extrawide bands (more resistant to wear), lock-on bands, and the regular bands suggested that no advantages of one kind over any of the others occurred. Studies of double-banded birds, however, did suggest that band loss occurs.

Another major problem in interpreting banded bird information stems from locality of banding operations. R. I. Smith and Geis (1961) have questioned whether preseason banding, which takes place primarily on national wildlife refuges, is representative of the populations. Birds associated with refuges may be subject to lower shooting pressure than nonrefuge birds. Recovery rates of birds banded on Agassiz Refuge, Minnesota, which was totally closed to hunting, were similar to those of birds banded on the adjacent Thief Lake Refuge, which was open to hunting, suggesting that protection from hunting on refuges may not be an important factor. However, Jessen (1970) reported that recovery rates from Agassiz Refuge and from a northern Ramsey County, Minnesota protected area were lower than for birds banded elsewhere, and suggested that refuge size affords some protection to local birds that would affect recovery rates on at least a local basis.

There is also the problem of differential vulnerability by sex to hunting, which Hawkins, Bellrose, and Smith (1946) did not consider significant in waterfowl. Finally, the vulnerability of hand-reared banded birds has been shown to be greater than wild-reared birds (Hickey 1952; Brakhage 1953).

Band recovery rates may vary according to time of banding, locality of banding, method of band retrieval, intensity of retrieval effort, type of hunting season, species of duck, and method of reporting information back to the hunter who collected the band and reported it. While it is desirable to obtain the highest possible reporting rates of banded ducks that are shot, the need for uniformity in reporting bands across the continent outweighs the advantages of increasing the reporting rates in local areas.

## EFFECTS OF HUNTING ON CANADA GEESE

Band recoveries for the western Canada goose occupying the Rocky Mountain region provided Krohn and Bizeau (1980) an opportunity to assess harvest effects on this population. Approximately 54,000 geese are harvested annually (crippling and other nonretrieval mortality excluded) from an estimated 113,400 fall population. Crippling rate was estimated at 15 percent of the total take. Survival rates, based on the new methods developed by Brownie et al. (1978), averaged 64.6 percent for adults and 52.8 percent for immatures from 1951 to 1973.

An examination of three factors that could serve to regulate the population (available habitat, population productivity, and sport hunting) discounted available habitat. Hunting accounts for 73 to 94 percent of the total mortality and is thus the major mortality factor. However, much mortality occurs during nesting. The question of how much compensation exists between natural and hunting mortality was unresolved, but natural mortality was considered to be less than that of mallards. Manipulation of hunting seasons and bag limits did appear to cause changes in population size. Management recommendations for these geese centered on manipulating harvest to maintain a winter population between 50,000 and 70,000 geese as measured by the nationwide winter waterfowl inventory.

## WATERFOWL HABITAT RELATIONSHIPS

The manner in which duck breeding and migratory behavior is tied into use of different habitats is of high significance (Table 12.8). Pair formation in ducks, the behavior that starts the sequence, is initiated most often on the wintering grounds, but may occur during spring migration (Johnsgard 1960; Weller 1965). O. W. Johnson (1961) reported significant spring variation in degree of sexual maturity that was related to variation in winter conditions. This could affect timing and location of pair formation as well as subsequent breeding activities. Geese and swans mate for life instead of for the single season like ducks (Bellrose 1976; Prevett and MacInnis 1980).

Dzubin and Gollop (1972) reported on effects of drought on reproduction in mallards. Emigration from drying habitats in the lower Canadian prairie to boreal habitat further north, nonbreeding, increased nest predation, lower brood sizes, and high brood mortality during interspersed movements have been observed and related to drought.

Ducks generally arrive on the breeding grounds paired. Breeding activities are centered around a pothole, which is generally less than 0.5 acre in size for dabblers

TABLE 12.8   Annual Duck Activities Related to General Habitat on Location
Where Activity Occurs

| Activity | Habitat or Location |
| --- | --- |
| Pair forming | Wintering grounds, migration routes |
| Breeding | Breeding pothole and vicinity |
| Nesting | Nesting pothole or vicinity |
| Brooding | Brood pothole(s) |
| Eclipse | Rafting on larger water bodies |
| Loafing | Specific locations at all times |

and 2 to 3 acres in size for divers in southern Manitoba (C. D. Evans, Hawkins, and Marshall 1952). Permanent potholes that are dominated by sedges, whitetop grass, or bulrush are most frequently occupied. Subsequent work shows differences between species, however. On a South Dakota area, blue-winged teal and gadwall preferred potholes over 2 acres in size (C. D. Evans and Black 1956). Potholes with very sparse cover were clearly preferred, and a tendency to use larger potholes during drought periods was noted.

Dzubin (1955) clarified the behavior of breeding pairs in the southern Manitoba pothole region. The home range includes prenesting, nesting, and incubation periods in the area where a breeding pair is most active. This area includes a territory that is defended by the drake against intrusions of others of his own species. It varies in size, and may be as small as 6 feet in diameter around the hen in the case of the canvasback. Territorialism also involves defense of a larger area, including the drake's waiting area (pothole or portion of marsh where the drake waits during egg laying and incubation). The intensity of defense of the territory will vary through time, and the size of the territory may be largest early in the breeding season. Gadwall drakes chase hens they are not paired with away from activity centers where virtually all time is spent by a breeding pair (Dwyer 1974). J. A. Cooper (1978) reported male Canada geese defended an area around the female regardless of her location and no defense of the nest occurred when the female was absent.

Nesting cover varies with availability. In general, dabbling ducks nest more on land than over water, while divers (including the ruddy duck) nest primarily on water. Among the dabblers, mallards are very adaptable and will nest over water or land. Among the divers, redheads and lesser scaup are known to nest occasionally on land (Ellig 1955), while canvasback appear to nest only over water.

While overall nest densities for any given area where several species occur may be highest where cover is heaviest (Keith 1961), there are important differences between species. Pintails can nest in sparse cover such as recent burns, heavily grazed pastures, or stubble fields. Gadwalls prefer to nest in the tallest cover and seldom nest over water (Bellrose 1976). The type of vegetation that is preferred nesting cover varies with availability. Whitetop grass and cattails in Manitoba (Hochbaum 1944; C. D. Evans et al. 1952); bulrushes, willows, and weeds at Bear River Refuge, Utah (C. S. Williams and Marshall 1938); greasewood, grass, and cattails at Freezeout Lake, Montana (Ellig 1955); and sedges in southeastern Alberta (Keith 1961) constitute important nesting habitats for the waterfowl complex in each of these areas. Tables 12.9, 12.10, and 12.11 show results of nesting studies for these different areas.

Keith (1961) reported the relative use of old and new growth for nesting cover by six species. The earliest nesters, pintail and mallard, rely primarily on previous year's growth for nesting cover, while later nesters, such as gadwall and scaup, rely principally on new growth (Table 12.12). Factors that affect nesting cover and subsequent use by the various waterfowl species are grazing, burning, and mowing. This can have management significance in situations where one species is to be favored over another.

**TABLE 12.9  Utilization of Nesting Cover by Ducks at Delta, Manitoba**

| Cover Type | Common | Casual | Rare |
|---|---|---|---|
| Bulrush islands (all emergents) | Redhead, canvasback, ruddy | Lesser scaup | Mallard, pintail |
| Bulrush (shallow water on edges) | Redhead, canvasback, ruddy | Lesser scaup | Mallard, pintail |
| Cattail (shallow water) | Redhead, ruddy | Canvasback, lesser scaup | Mallard, pintail |
| Phragmites (shallow water) | — | Redhead, ruddy | Canvasback, lesser scaup |
| Phragmites (dry ground) | Redhead | Lesser scaup | Mallard, pintail |
| Phragmites (dense stands) | — | — | Mallard |
| Phragmites (edges on dry ground) | Mallard, gadwall | Blue-winged teal, shoveler | |
| Grass-sedge-sow thistle | Gadwall, lesser scaup, blue-winged teal, shoveler, pintail | Mallard, redhead, scoter | Canvasback |
| Hay meadow | Gadwall, lesser scaup, blue-winged teal, shoveler, pintail | Mallard, scoter | Redhead |
| Lightly grazed pasture | Blue-winged teal, shoveler, pintail | Gadwall, lesser scaup | Mallard |
| Wheat or barley stubble | — | — | Pintail |
| Thickets, brush piles | — | Mallard, gadwall, pintail | — |
| Woods (lake shore, farm, bluffs) | — | Mallard | — |

*Source:* Hochbaum 1944. (Used with permission.)

**TABLE 12.10 Nesting Locations of Ducks at Bear River, Utah**

| Vegetation Type | Rating of Use by Species | | | | | | | Rating for all Species |
|---|---|---|---|---|---|---|---|---|
| | Gadwall | Cinnamon Teal | Redhead | Mallard | Pintail | Ruddy | Shoveler | |
| Hardstem bulrush | 3 | 2 | 1 | 1 | 2 | 1 | 2 | 3 |
| Alkali bulrush | 9 | 8 | 5 | 7 | 9 | 4 | 5 | 8 |
| Saltgrass | 7 | 5 | 4 | 6 | 5 | 3 | 3 | 6 |
| Cattail | 8 | 7 | 3 | 5 | 8 | 2 | — | 7 |
| Willow | 1 | 4 | — | 2 | 1 | — | 4 | 2 |
| Weeds | 2 | 1 | 2 | — | — | — | 1 | 1 |
| Cane | — | — | — | — | — | — | — | 5 |
| Foxtail | — | — | — | — | — | — | — | 5 |
| Arrowgrass | — | — | — | — | — | — | — | 6 |
| Sedges | — | — | — | — | — | — | — | 4 |

*Source:* C. S. Williams and Marshall 1938. (Used with permission.)

TABLE 12.11 Nest Location by Cover Type for 11 Species of Ducks in Three Study Areas
(percent of all nests of that species)

| Study Area & Cover Type | Mallard | Pintail | Green-Winged Teal | Blue-Winged Teal[a] | American Wigeon | Shoveler | Gadwall | Lesser Scaup | Red-head | Canvas-back | Ruddy | Average for All Species |
|---|---|---|---|---|---|---|---|---|---|---|---|---|
| **Southeastern Alberta** | | | | | | | | | | | | |
| Cattail | 17 | 2 | 5 | 1 | – | – | – | 1 | 57 | 89 | 47 | 8 |
| Rush | 70 | 42 | 86 | 51 | 81 | 41 | 58 | 86 | 43 | 5 | 53 | 62 |
| Holophytic areas | 1 | 3 | – | 10 | – | 16 | 3 | 5 | – | 5 | – | 5 |
| Mixed prairie | 11 | 35 | 9 | 36 | 14 | 43 | 13 | 6 | – | – | – | 19 |
| Burn[b] | – | 18 | – | – | – | – | – | – | – | – | – | 2 |
| Weed | 1 | – | – | 2 | 5 | – | 27 | 3 | – | – | – | 4 |
| **Freezeout Lake, Montana** | | | | | | | | | | | | |
| Greasewood | 38 | 57 | 87 | 65 | 100 | 38 | 85 | 37 | 8 | – | – | 52 |
| Islands | 25 | 26 | – | – | – | 25 | 3 | 63 | 4 | 100 | 17 | 19 |
| Emergents | 34 | – | – | – | – | – | – | – | 88 | – | 83 | 17 |
| Grass | 3 | 17 | 13 | 35 | – | 37 | 12 | – | – | – | – | 12 |
| **Grays Lake, Idaho** | | | | | | | | | | | | |
| Land | | | | | | | | | | | | |
| Island | 20 | 36 | 25 | 19 | 100 | 20 | 41 | 9 | – | – | – | 18 |
| Lakeshore | 15 | 34 | 75 | 35 | – | 20 | 38 | 23 | – | – | – | 19 |
| Field | 11 | 29 | – | 25 | – | 60 | 13 | 9 | – | – | – | 13 |
| Haystack | 5 | 1 | – | 1 | – | – | – | – | – | – | – | 2 |
| Marsh | | | | | | | | | | | | |
| Cattail island | 25 | – | – | 17 | – | – | 8 | 27 | 8 | 8 | 45 | 14 |
| Bulrush | 12 | – | – | 1 | – | – | – | 27 | 91 | 87 | 40 | 29 |
| Cattail-bulrush mixture | 2 | – | – | – | – | – | – | 5 | – | 4 | 10 | 2 |
| Muskrat house | 9 | – | – | 1 | – | – | – | – | 1 | 1 | 5 | 3 |

*Sources:* Alberta data from Keith 1961; Montana data from Ellig 1955; Idaho data from Steel, Dalke, and Bizeau 1956. (Used with permission.)

[a] Includes cinnamon teal at Gray's Lake.

[b] Mixed prairie burned in the spring prior to examination.

TABLE 12.12  Relative Use of Old and New Growth for Nesting Cover in Southeastern Alberta

| Species | Total Nests | All Old Growth | Mostly Old, Some New Growth | Mostly New, Some Old Growth | All New Growth | Average Date 50% of Clutches Started |
|---|---|---|---|---|---|---|
| | | | Cover Type (percent of total nests) | | | |
| Pintail | 88 | 64 | 20 | 8 | 8 | Apr. 29 |
| Mallard | 109 | 62 | 24 | 9 | 5 | May 9 |
| Blue-winged teal | 135 | 36 | 29 | 23 | 13 | May 28 |
| Shoveler | 41 | 24 | 41 | 15 | 20 | May 15 |
| Gadwall | 55 | 5 | 22 | 24 | 49 | June 4 |
| Scaup | 160 | 1 | 12 | 59 | 29 | June 6 |
| All species | 674 | 31 | 23 | 26 | 20 | |

*Source:* Keith 1961. (Used with permission.)

Dzubin and Gollop (1972) recognized that the distance of the nest from water had varying relationships to survival of the brood and the nesting hen. The shorter the distance of a nest from water, the shorter the trip of newly hatched ducklings would be, thus reducing risks of predation during travel over land. However, nest predation could be increased if nesting near shorelines was too prevalent, since this would raise the efficiency of predators that systematically search limited areas. Indeed, Keith (1961) reported high frequency of predation on nests in rush and cattail closest to the water, but not in other cover types.

Mean distances to water for nests are quite variable, ranging from an average 500 m in a Saskatchewan area to 50 m in a Manitoba area for mallards (Dzubin and Gollop 1972). Distances to water tended to increase during drought years. Keith (1961) reported highest nesting densities at distances over 25 feet from water. C. D. Evans and Black (1956) reported only a slight tendency of nests to cluster around potholes in the prairie pothole country of South Dakota. Steel, Dalke, and Bizeau (1956) reported that 97 percent of all nests in emergent vegetation were within 15 yards of open water in southern Idaho.

Duck broods tend to use potholes that are larger and more permanent than those used for nesting (Table 12.13). C. D. Evans et al. (1952) reported potholes over 2 acres in size were preferred in southern Manitoba and over 1 acre in size in southern Alberta (Keith 1961). Canvasback, pintail, mallard, teal, and shoveler broods are more mobile than redhead or ruddy duck broods, and tend to change potholes quite frequently. Dzubin and Gollop (1972) reported movements of mallard broods of 3 miles between potholes in one week, and 5 miles in nine days.

Loafing sites are an important part of the duck breeding habitat. The drake uses these areas to wait while the hen is laying. Muskrat houses, islands, logs, and other naturally created sites can be used, and artificially created sites are also occasionally valuable. Sugden and Benson (1970) reported no significant change in breeding population size when loafing rafts were installed on an Alberta area, while Shearer and Uhlig (1965) reported increased use of dugout ponds in Minnesota after rafts were installed. A deficiency in loafing areas has to exist before artificial sites will increase breeding densities. Stock-watering ponds and dugouts are such areas.

C. D. Evans et al. (1952) concluded that in the coteau region of the prairie provinces and the northern plains, high-quality duck breeding habitat was a well-balanced mixture of pothole types and sizes (Table 12.14). A complex of potholes, each having one or more functions in the reproductive cycle but in turn dependent on its proximity to other potholes for maximum value was necessary. This led to the development of an area concept, wherein the square mile was deemed suitable for the Lake Minnedosa region. This type of habitat complex was to be based on that size unit. Stoudt (1960) reported a hypothetical optimum production model for ducks based on a 100-square mile area as consisting of 19,300 ponds distributed in a variety of sizes and types (Table 12.15). This optimum was calculated to provide for 16,400 mallard pairs.

Many valuable waterfowl breeding areas are found outside the coteau region,

**TABLE 12.13  Summarization of Duck Breeding Habitat Preference
in the Lake Minnedosa, Manitoba Region**

| Pothole Classification | Factors Affecting Vegetation Types of Potholes | |
|---|---|---|
| A. Permanent potholes | 1. Area | 7. Muskrats |
|   1. Sedge-whitetop (grass border) | 2. Depth | 8. Mowing |
|   2. Cattail | 3. Rate of water loss | 9. Burning |
|   3. Bulrush | 4. Soils | 10. Relative age |
|   4. Zones of emergents, mixed or | 5. Ice action | 11. Origin of present |
|     denuded | 6. Grazing |     vegetation |
| B. Semipermanent potholes | | |
| C. Temporary waters | | |
| D. Artificial dugouts | | |

Breeding Pothole Preferences

| Pothole Size (acres) | Order of Preference | | Pothole Type | Percent Occupancy of Type by Breeding Pairs |
|---|---|---|---|---|
| | Dabblers | Divers | | |
| 0.00–0.49 | 1 | Not used | A1 | 78 |
| 0.50–0.99 | 3 | Not used | A2 | 20 |
| 1.00–1.49 | 2 | Not used | A3 | 100 |
| 1.50–1.99 | 4 | Not used | A4 | 71 |
| 2.00–2.99 | 6 | 1 (same) | B1 | 42 |
| 3.00–3.99 | 5 | 1 | B2 | 40 |
| | | | B3 | 0 |
| | | | B4 | 0 |
| | | | C | 67 |
| | | | D | 100 |

Use of Potholes for Diving Duck Nests

| Pothole Type | Order of Preference | | | |
|---|---|---|---|---|
| | Canvasback | Redhead | Ruddy | All |
| A1 | 4 | – | – | 6 |
| A2 | – | 1 | 1 | 2 |
| A3 | 2 | 4 | 2 | 3 |
| A4 | – | 2 | – | 4 |
| B1 | 3 | 3 | – | 5 |
| B2 | 1 | 2 | – | 1 |

Brood Pothole Preferences

| Pothole Size (acres) | Brood Days per Acre | Pothole Type | Brood Days per Acre |
|---|---|---|---|
| 0.00–0.49 | 0 | A1 | 30.4 |
| 0.50–0.99 | 21.9 | A2 | 19.4 |
| 1.00–1.49 | 18.8 | A3 | 29.4 |
| 1.50–1.99 | 14.5 | A4 | 3.6 |

TABLE 12.13  Summarization of Duck Breeding Habitat Preference
in the Lake Minnedosa, Manitoba Region (*continued*)

| Brood Pothole Preferences | | | |
|---|---|---|---|
| Pothole Size (acres) | Brood Days per Acre | Pothole Type | Brood Days per Acre |
| 2.00–2.49 | 32.5 | B1 | 1.1 |
| 2.50–2.99 | 36.3 | B2 | 0 |
| 3.00–3.49 | 20.0 | B3 | 0 |
| 3.50–3.99 | 30.4 | B4 | 0 |
| 4.00 + | 32.4 | C | 0.2 |
| | | D | 0 |

*Source:* C. D. Evans, Hawkins, and Marshall 1952.

where one or a few large marshes may be involved, centering on lakes or impoundments. Examples are Gray's Lake, Idaho, and Freezeout Lake, Montana. In these cases, broken, irregular shorelines and numerous islands and peninsulas can appreciably increase waterfowl breeding and nesting densities by breaking up the terrain and decreasing visibility. Shrubs spaced at intervals in areas of otherwise unrestricted visibility of the birds can also increase density of territorial pairs. Care should be taken, when waterfowl habitat is created, to guard against creating nesting concentrations in limited habitat. Such situations predispose broods and hens to greater rates of predation than if nesting habitat is dispersed. In addition, natural ponds, including those created by beavers, can be important waterfowl habitat (S. R. Peterson and Low 1977).

Deltas, such as those at the mouth of the Yukon and the Mackenzie rivers are also extremely valuable waterfowl breeding grounds. The Yukon-Kuskokwin Delta is primary breeding ground for cackling Canada geese, emperor geese, and black brant, and is important habitat for white-fronted geese and spectacled eider (Mickelson 1975). These deltas commonly have extensive areas of small ponds and islands, with a very high diversity and interspersion of habitat. Mickelson (1975) described a 4-square mile area near the river mouth as 5 percent ponds and sloughs, with 95 percent of it in meadow 1.5 feet above mean high tide.

Once the drakes have entered eclipse, they congregate in large rafts on the larger marshes, lakes, and reservoirs. This occurs after the hen has started incubating. Hens without broods, then flighted young and their hens subsequently congregate in these areas. Field feeding is initiated once flight feathers are regrown, and then the southward migration to winter range begins.

Wood ducks, hooded mergansers, goldeneyes, and buffleheads usually nest in hollow trees, creating a special habitat requirement not needed for other nesting waterfowl. McGilvrey (1968) reported that wood duck populations are limited over most of the range by availability of nesting cavities and that artificial nest-boxes could appreciably increase populations. Optimum height for nests was 20 to 50 feet (6 feet or higher was acceptable), with entrance size $3\frac{1}{2}$ to 12 inches in diameter (4 inches optimum). A variety of trees are desirable for cavities, but include those

**TABLE 12.14  Use of Wetland Types by Duck Broods in South Dakota, 1950–1953**

| Species | Number of Observations | Percent of Broods Using Wetland Type | | | | |
| --- | --- | --- | --- | --- | --- | --- |
| | | Intermittent Areas | Temporary Marshes | Shallow Marshes | Deep Marshes | Open-Water Areas |
| Blue-winged teal | 801 | – | 0.5 | 2.9 | 36.6 | 60.0 |
| Gadwall | 261 | – | – | – | 17.2 | 82.8 |
| Mallard | 177 | – | – | 1.1 | 44.1 | 54.8 |
| Pintail | 129 | – | 0.8 | 3.1 | 38.0 | 58.1 |
| Shoveler | 46 | – | – | 4.4 | 32.6 | 63.1 |
| Canvasback | 9 | – | – | – | 11.1 | 88.0 |
| Redhead | 54 | – | – | – | 5.6 | 94.4 |
| Lesser scaup | 15 | – | – | – | – | 100.0 |
| Ruddy duck | 116 | – | – | 0.9 | 34.5 | 64.7 |
| Other | 10 | – | – | – | 40.0 | 60.0 |
| All Species | 1618 | – | 0.3 | 2.0 | 32.6 | 65.2 |

*Source*: C. D. Evans and Black 1956.

TABLE 12.15   A Hypothetical Optimum Production Model for Waterfowl,
Based on a 100–Square Mile Study Area in Saskatchewan

| | |
|---|---:|
| Total number of ponds | 19,300 |
| Total acreage of ponds | 12,800 |
| Total number of Type 1 ponds | 1,400 |
| Total number of Type 3 ponds | 12,100 |
| Total number of Type 4 ponds | 2,400 |
| Total number of Type 5 ponds | 3,400 |
| Ponds ½ acre or less in size | 13,800 |
| Ponds ½–1 acre in size | 1,800 |
| Ponds 1–2 acres in size | 2,300 |
| Ponds 2–10 acres in size | 1,400 |
| Total pairs of mallards | 16,400 |

*Source:* Stoudt 1969:131.

that readily form and retain suitable holes. Cavities must drain and preferably have a protected entrance. McGilvrey (1968) recommended that all suitable cavity trees should be preserved in habitat managed for wood ducks, and a minimum of one usable cavity for 5 acres of timber within half a mile of water be available. Trees over water are the best nesting cavities. Nest trees for goldeneyes, buffleheads, and hooded mergansers follow similar criteria.

Canada geese prefer elevated nesting sites with solid base, nearness to open water, good visibility, suitable brood rearing areas, suitable grazing areas, and suitable aquatic feeding and loafing areas (C. W. Williams and Sooter 1940). Muskrat houses, islands in flooded meadows, haystacks, and dry ground are used (J. A. Cooper 1978; Steel et al. 1957). J. A. Cooper (1978) felt that the commensal relationship between Canada geese and the muskrat was very important. Muskrat houses on Lake Manitoba were built in most preferred cover types (cattail, bulrush, whitetop) and are natural, solid, elevated nesting platforms surrounded by water. Artificial platforms are commonly used, especially if placed in large islands on shorelines where natural nesting sites are limited (Craighead and Stockstad 1961). Preference for nesting on islands along rivers, such as the Snake River in Wyoming, is commonly noted (Dimmick 1968). Nesting densities will be increased if visibility between territorial pairs is reduced by irregular shorelines and vegetation. Canada geese are grazers, and cereal grains, bluegrasses, clovers, and alfalfa are all palatable forages. After nesting, broods and their parents will commonly concentrate near grazing areas where these species are available.

### Wetland Classifications

A number of wetland habitat classifications are available, each designated for a separate purpose, and all being useful in waterfowl habitat management. The pothole classification of C. D. Evans et al. (1952) shown in Table 12.13 is an example of a partial wetland classification that is adapted to a portion of the northern prairie pothole region. A wetland classification for this entire region by Stewart and Kantrud (1971) (Table 12.16) can be directly applied to studies of breeding duck

**TABLE 12.16  Classification of Wetlands in the Glaciated Prairie Region of North America**

| Class | Central Zone Vegetation Type | Subclasses | Cover Types[a] |
|---|---|---|---|
| I. Ephemeral ponds | Low-prairie vegetation (*Poa pratensis, Solidago altissima*, etc.) | None | 1, 2, 3, 4 |
| II. Temporary ponds | Wet-meadow vegetation (fine-stemmed grasses and sedges with associated forbs) | a. Fresh (*Poa polustris, Boltonia latisquama*, etc.)<br>b. Slightly brackish (*Hordeum jubatum, Calamagrostis inexpansa*, etc.) | 1, 2, 3, 4 |
| III. Seasonal ponds and lakes | Shallow-marsh vegetation (moderately coarse-stemmed grasses and sedges with associated forbs) | a. Fresh (*Carex atherodes, Glyceria grandis*, etc.)<br>b. Slightly brackish (*Scholochloa festucacea, Eleocharis palustris*, etc.)<br>c. Moderately brackish (*Alisma gramineum, Beckmannia syzigachne*, etc.) | 1, 2, 3, 4 |
| IV. Semipermanent ponds and lakes | Deep-marsh vegetation (coarse-stemmed emergents, or associated submerged aquatics | a. Fresh (*Scirpus heterochaetus*, etc.)<br>b. Slightly brackish (*Typha* spp., *Scirpus acutus*, etc.)<br>c. Moderately brackish (*Scirpus acutus*, etc.)<br>d. Brackish (*Scirpus paludosus, S. acutus*, etc.)<br>e. Subsaline (*Scirpus paludosus*, etc.) | 1, 2, 3, 4 |
| V. Permanent ponds and lakes | Permanent open-water zone (devoid of emergent vegetation but submerged vegetation, particularly *Ruppia occidentalis* often present. | a. Subclasses based on species composition of peripheral zones.<br>b. Slightly brackish (*Typha* spp. *Scolochloa festucacea*, etc.)<br>c. Moderately brackish (*Scirpus acutus, Hordeum jubatum*, etc.)<br>d. Brackish (*Scirpus paludosus, S. americanus*, etc.)<br>e. Subsaline (*Puccinellia nuttalliana, Salicornia rubra*, etc.) | 3, 4 |
| VI. Alkali ponds and lakes | Intermittent-alkali zone, devoid of emergent vegetation (*Ruppia maritima* often common). | None | 3, 4 |

*Source:* Stewart and Kantrud 1971.

distribution. Seasonal and some permanent ponds and lakes are known to be extremely important habitat (Stewart and Kantrud 1973).

Cowardin et al. (1979) developed a wetland classification that is broadly applicable for the entire United States. They describe wetlands as areas saturated with water, which is thus the major determinant in soil formation, plant, and animal communities using the area. They are transitional sites between terrestrial and aquatic systems. The classification of wetlands is presented in Figure 12.9. This classification is based on ecological and geomorphological attributes. The system level (Figure 12.9) in the hierarchical classification is based on substrate, including biological, geomorphological, chemical, or biological attributes. Subsystems describe whether the area is continuously or intermittently submerged. Classes define the composition of the bottom. Below classes, the system may be added on to fit the intended use and area.

Cowardin (1980) illustrated means by which the National Wetlands Classification could be useful in wildlife habitat management. The broader categories are useful in defining types of wetlands in a given area for inventory and planning purposes. Also, capability classifications are dependent upon an ecological description of the wetlands. However, knowledge of each species' habitat requirements and distributions is needed to use any classification appropriately in wildlife management.

Marshes and estuaries are environments that are created and maintained by fluctuating water levels. Kadlec (1962) reported that many of the most productive waterfowl marshes in the northern prairies and Great Lakes region are subject to natural drawdowns, which are important in retaining their productivity. Drawdowns can increase seed production of marsh plants used as food by wildlife, provide conditions suitable for emergent vegetation to establish, and increase soil fertility. At Backus Lake, Michigan, drawdowns were detrimental to invertebrate life, promoted invasion of sedges into burned communities, and reduced floating leaf species and submergents. The increase in sedges, which is important brood cover, was a benefit of the drawdown. Production of wetland plants was reduced, however, because the drawdown created very dry soil conditions. The dry soils were temporarily invaded by annuals, but species composition after reflooding was not notably different from that existing prior to the drawdown.

Development of vegetation following drawdowns is associated with seed availability, soil type and moisture, season and duration of drawdowns, and amount of stranded algal debris (S. W. Harris and Marshall 1963). On the marshes of the Agassiz National Wildlife Refuge, Minnesota, these authors recommended 1- to 2-year drawdowns at 5- to 10-year intervals to maintain emergents. Succession in relation to time of drawdown, soil type, and speed of mud flat drying can be predicted to some degree in this area (Figure 12.10).

### Botulism

Western duck sickness or avian botulism is a classic example of a serious disease, the effects of which can be reduced by habitat manipulation. The extensive mortality of waterfowl in the Salt Lake, Utah, area in 1910 first brought this

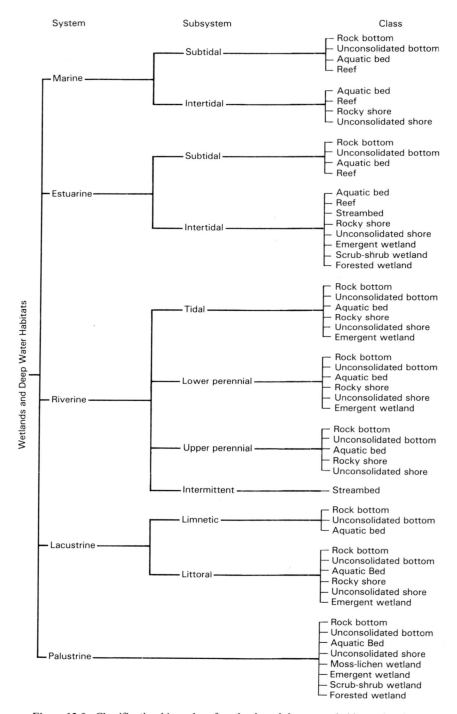

**Figure 12.9** Classification hierarchy of wetlands and deepwater habitats, showing systems, subsystems, and classes. The Palustrine System does not include deepwater habitats. From Cowardin et al. 1979.

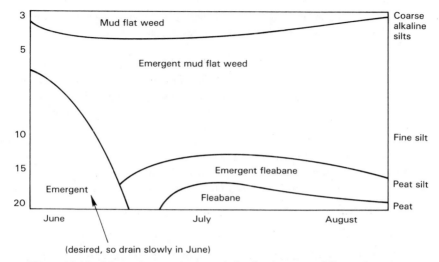

(desired, so drain slowly in June)

**Figure 12.10** Schematic presentation of the development of five major vegetation types during first year of drawdown in relation to time of drawdown, rapidity of drying, and soil type. During the second year the following changes will occur: *emergent* area; upland and shoreline weeds will invade *emergent fleabane* area; *emergent mud flat* area will change to upland weeds, except on silts, where emergents will increase; and *mud flat weed* area will change to upland weeds with some cattails. From S. W. Harris and Marshall 1963. (Used with permission.)

disease to national attention. E. R. Kalmbach was assigned to investigate the causes of this sickness in 1930, and a series of publications, most notably Kalmbach and Gunderson (1934), elucidated the causes and corrective measures. As Bellrose and Low (1978) noted, work continues on means of preventing botulism and outbreaks still occur. In 1969, an estimated 141,000 ducks died of botulism in California (Hunter 1970).

In October 1930, at a Klamath Falls laboratory, the causative agent was positively identified as *Clostridium botulinum*, type C, by L. T. Giltner (Kalmbach and Gunderson 1934). This common anaerobic bacterium thrives in decaying animal matter, most especially the carcasses of invertebrates that exist along the "feather edge" of receding alkaline waters in late summer. As water levels along the shallow shores lower, high temperatures and abundant decaying matter produce the anaerobic conditions suitable for the bacterium, of which the toxin produced as a metabolic by-product is lethal to waterfowl. Compounding the problem is the often concurrent blue-green algal blooms that also produce highly virulent toxins. Waterfowl that feed on invertebrates and algae that carry the toxin become affected.

Hunter (1970) reported that terrestrial vertebrates that die and decay where land is reflooded during warm weather also initiate botulism outbreaks. Infected maggots that feed on decaying animal matter are ingested by birds, which in turn contract the disease. No differential mortality attributable to species, sex, age, or nutritional status occurs except that geese are not as likely to feed in areas where the toxins exist. Migrating birds, which often feed heavily, seem to be especially prone to mortality, and shorebirds as well as waterfowl are vulnerable (Sciple 1953).

Kalmbach and Gunderson (1934) recognized that elimination of mud flats and shallow-water areas was a potential environmental control. Thus the capability of manipulating water tables to prevent the stranding of invertebrates and fish is needed. Also, modification of shorelines to increase the steepness and water depth is of value. When these measures are not feasible, efforts to prevent waterfowl use of infected areas through scare tactics are indicated. Infected birds can recover if they are removed from the infected area and treated with oral administration of fresh water or injection of antitoxin, depending on the severity of the disease (Bellrose 1976), but these practices are practical only on a small scale.

### Fowl Cholera

Fowl cholera can be an important cause of waterfowl mortality, especially in the Central and Pacific flyways (Strout and Cornwell 1976). The causal organism, *Pasturella multocida*, can infect a variety of other species including cattle, rats, wild boar, deer, bison, caribou, pigeons, crows, pheasants, and coots. *Pasturellosis* is the general term for the disease. The organism thrives in dead animals and feces, and can be transmitted through water and infect an animal through open wounds or by being ingested (Rosen and Bischoff 1950). The highly infectious organism will be prevalent in areas where dead and decaying animal matter exists. Gulls, which may feed on such offal and then fly over to ponds and infect the area through fecal deposits, can be carriers. Losses appear primarily in winter, with the advent of rainy weather. Efforts to keep areas frequented by waterfowl free of dead and decaying animal matter, most especially garbage dumps, are effective in reducing losses from this disease.

## TRUMPETER SWANS AND WHOOPING CRANES

The history of restoration of the trumpeter swan from endangered to viable, productive status records one of humankind's better accomplishments on behalf of wildlife. Two outstanding references that attest to this are the initial documentation by Winston E. Banko (1960) for the lower United States, and the subsequent evaluations of the species' status in Alaska by H. A. Hansen et al. (1971). This graceful species has rightfully stirred the better instincts and thoughts of many, as the quote from Henry Beston (H. A. Hansen et al. 1971): exemplifies:

> We need another and a wiser and perhaps a more mystical concept of animals. Remote from universal nature, and living by complicated artifice, man in civilization surveys the creature through the glass of his knowledge and sees thereby a feather magnified and the whole image in distortion. We patronize them for their incompleteness, for their tragic fate of having form so far below ourselves. And therein we err, and greatly err. For the animal shall not be measured by man. In a world older and more complete than ours they move

finished and complete, gifted with extensions of the senses we have lost or never attained, living by voices we shall never hear. They are not brethren, they are not underlings; they are other nations caught with ourselves in the net of life and time, fellow prisoners of the splendor and travail of the earth.

Perhaps the record of the trumpeter swan, and with luck the whooping crane, helps us to understand why our natural environment in all its diversity and complexity is so ultimately important to our future. While we have not yet ensured the survival of the whooping crane, the record of the trumpeter points the way, and shows that we can restore a species from the brink of extinction. Although the trumpeter population had been reduced to an estimated 15 birds in 1922 in the Red Rock Lakes area of Montana, Banko (1960) estimated that the carrying capacity of about 75 to 85 breeding pairs had been reached in the 1950s in that area. The total population in North America was estimated at 5390 in 1980 (Mackay 1981). H. A. Hansen et al. (1971) pointed out that in the northern areas of its range the species can yet be restored to considerable numbers. Active transplanting programs into wildlife refuges and other suitable areas are successfully in progress in the upper Midwest.

The restoration of the trumpeter in the Yellowstone region involved a time-tried sequence of actions. Establishment of the Red Rock Lakes National Wildlife Refuge in 1935 was the key action. This provided the trumpeter with a sanctuary from illegal gunning and other human interference. Winter feeding at the refuge eliminated the need for extensive migrations to winter range with the attendant and inevitable high mortality. Transplanting from this population to Jackson Hole in Wyoming and other wildlife refuges has served to establish other breeding populations.

Banko (1960) identified three U.S. regions where trumpeters were originally common breeders: (1) Yellowstone-Red Rock Lakes-Jackson Hole; (2) Flathead Valley, Montana; (3) southern Minnesota-northern Iowa. Trumpeters breed throughout Canada west of Ontario and in Alaska. Winter ranges originally included Chesapeake Bay, the Mississippi River, the San Francisco Bay area, the southern Alaska-British Columbia coast, Puget Sound, and the lower Columbia River.

The status of Alaskan trumpeter populations was virtually unknown until Gabrielson (1946) reported 300 wintering swans in the southeastern part of the state, thought to be trumpeters. H. A. Hansen et al. (1971) subsequently outlined the breeding and wintering distribution for the swans, which included interior and southern mainland Alaska below the 145- to 150-day ice-free line. Since 90 to 105 days are required for cygnets to fledge, to which must be added an average of 49 days for nest building, egg laying, and incubation, this ice-free line is the probable northern limit of trumpeter swan nesting range. Important nesting areas in Alaska include the Kenai Peninsula, the Copper River delta, Cook Inlet, Gulkana Basin, and Tanana-Kantishna Valley. Population status in these areas was judged near carrying capacity in 1968.

Opportunities to increase trumpeter swan populations are largely restricted to establishment of new populations rather than increase of existing ones. Both Banko

(1960) and H. A. Hansen et al. (1971) reported habitats they surveyed were filled. Evidence for this is that as the number of mated pairs in the Red Rock Lakes-Yellowstone region has increased, the number of cygnets per mated pair has decreased (Figure 12.11). Also, a large number of nonbreeders existed after 1950 in this region. The interpretation is that suitable breeding territories have been filled, and social interactions of a high-density breeding population are related to the decline in cygnet production. Segments of the breeding population consisting of mated pairs that fail to nest, hatching failures, and mortality of cygnets are involved in depressing productivity at high population density.

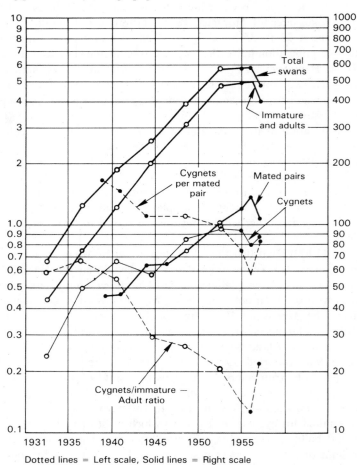

Dotted lines = Left scale, Solid lines = Right scale

**Figure 12.11** Numbers and composition of trumpeter swan population, Red Rock Lakes–Yellowstone region. Complete data was unavailable for 1931–1938, 1940, 1942–1943, and 1945; mated pair data for 1931–1957 approximate only. After Banko 1960.

Swans occupy a special position in our culture for their symbolism and beauty. The trumpeter swan record should serve as a source of inspiration and continued hope for those concerned in restoration of endangered species.

While the trumpeter swan success is a source of satisfaction, the whooping crane poses a much more difficult problem. This species, which numbered 84 individuals in 1978 on its wintering grounds in Texas and New Mexico symbolizes the current endangered species program. The whooping crane is not considered a species of waterfowl, but is included here as an important case history of management and response of a migratory bird.

The National Audubon Society brought the plight of the whooper to national attention and was instrumental in initiating restoration efforts (U.S. Fish and Wildlife Service 1980). The Aransas National Wildlife Refuge was established in 1937 to protect a wintering flock of whoopers, discovered shortly before. Their numbers reached all-time lows in the late 1930s and early 1940s at 21 (Table 12.17).

While the wintering grounds of these birds were known, it was not until 1954 that the breeding grounds were located, when a forest fire fighter in a helicopter discovered two adult whooping cranes and one juvenile in Wood Buffalo National Park (R. P. Allen 1959). These birds have suffered from habitat elimination through conversion to agricultural land and human disturbance. Shooting was considered a substantial drain on the population from 1870 to 1920, and over 309 specimens of whoopers are known to exist in museums. While few of these specimens were taken by collectors associated with the museums, the collection for scientific purposes was obviously not regulated and may have contributed substantially to the decline of the whooper. The Migratory Bird Treaty of 1961 served to legally protect the whooper and provide a basis for cooperation between Canada and the United States.

The Whooping Crane Recovery Team gives due credit to R. P. Allen of the Audubon Society, who first recorded the biology and ecology of the whooper (R. P. Allen 1959). Allen was leader of the Cooperative Whooping Crane Project (FWS and National Audubon Society cooperating). The wild population is monitored on the breeding grounds by the Canadian Wildlife Service (Kuyt 1976). Breeding ground management includes fire prevention, prohibition of public access and low-flying aircraft, and resisting commercial efforts to exploit the area. A migration monitoring program to provide protective surveillance during migration is practiced by the FWS, the National Audubon Society, and several states. Wintering grounds management includes providing agricultural crops and control of oak brush through fire to open up stands and provide mast (E. F. Johnson 1976). A moratorium on oil well drilling activity in this area when cranes are present is in force. Oil platforms are not higher than 15 feet above water to reduce disturbance and the possibility of accidents. Spills of oil and other chemicals on the intracoastal canal pose a constant threat. An extensive public relations program helps to reduce disturbance and mortality. This effort includes boat patrols that serve to alert refuge staff to hazards to the cranes. The addition of Matagordo Island to the Aransas

TABLE 12.17  Whooping Crane Wintering Populations

| Year | Texas Adult | Young of the Year | Subtotal | Louisiana | Total |
|------|-------|-----------|----------|-----------|-------|
| 1938 | 14 | 4 | 18 | 11 | 29 |
| 1939 | 15 | 7 | 22 | 13 | 35 |
| 1940 | 21 | 5 | 26 | 6 | 32 |
| 1941 | 13 | 2 | 15 | 6 | 21 |
| 1942 | 15 | 4 | 19 | 5 | 24 |
| 1943 | 16 | 5 | 21 | 4 | 25 |
| 1944 | 15 | 3 | 18 | 3 | 21 |
| 1945[a] | 14 | 3 | 17 | 2 | 19 |
| 1946 | 22 | 3 | 25 | 2 | 27 |
| 1947 | 25 | 6 | 31 | 1 | 32 |
| 1948 | 27 | 3 | 30 | 1 | 31 |
| 1949 | 30 | 4 | 34 | 0 | 34 |
| 1950 | 26 | 5 | 31 | 0 | 31 |
| 1951 | 20 | 5 | 25 | 0 | 25 |
| 1952 | 19 | 2 | 21 | 0 | 21 |
| 1953 | 21 | 3 | 24 | | 24 |
| 1954 | 21 | 0 | 21 | | 21 |
| 1955 | 20 | 8 | 28 | | 28 |
| 1956 | 22 | 2 | 24 | | 24 |
| 1957 | 22 | 4 | 26 | | 26 |
| 1958 | 23 | 9 | 32 | | 32 |
| 1959 | 31 | 2 | 33 | | 33 |

Refuge with the closing of the airbase in 1975 provides additional wintering habitat. Artificial winter feeding is not practiced because of the danger of disease associated with concentrating the birds.

One of the alternatives to relying on natural production to build populations of endangered species is to propagate young in capativity. Captive propagation of the whooping crane is now largely done at the Patuxent Wildlife Research Center. In 1978, 3 laying females produced 23 eggs, of which 12 hatched and 3 survived. Artificial insemination to increase fertility is practiced. The purpose of this effort is to built a captive flock and to provide eggs for the cross-fostering experiment at Grays Lake, Idaho. By winter 1980, only 2 of the 18 whooping cranes surviving in the cross-fostering experiment were from Patuxent eggs.

The cross-fostering experiment consists of replacing the eggs laid by wild sandhill cranes with one whooping crane egg, which is then incubated and reared by the foster sandhill crane parents. The Grays Lake area represents a prime sandhill crane habitat. Nesting success is high and nesting chronology is similar to the whooper at Wood Buffalo National Park in Canada (Drewien and Bizeau 1977). Further, the migration route for the foster-parent cranes is relatively secure, with several refuges along the route, and at the wintering areas in New Mexico. As of 1980, 18 birds constituted this population.

TABLE 12.17   Whooping Crane Wintering Population (*continued*)

| Year | Texas | | | Louisiana | | | | Total |
|------|-------|-----------------|----------|-----------|---|---|---|-------|
|      | Adult | Young of the Year | Subtotal | | | | | |
| 1960 | 30 | 6 | 36 | | | | | 36 |
| 1961 | 34 | 5 | 39 | | | | | 39 |
| 1962 | 32 | 0 | 32 | | | | | 32 |
| 1963 | 26 | 7 | 33 | | | | | 33 |
| 1964 | 32 | 10 | 42 | | | | | 42 |
| 1965 | 36 | 8 | 44 | | | | | 44 |
| 1966 | 38 | 5 | 43 | | | | | 43 |
| 1967 | 39 | 9 | 48 | | | | | 48 |
| 1968 | 44 | 6 | 50 | | | | | 50 |
| 1969 | 48 | 8 | 56 | | | | | 56 |
| 1970 | 51 | 6 | 57 | Rio Grande Valley of New Mexico | | | | 57 |
| 1971 | 54 | 5 | 59 | | | | | 59 |
| 1972 | 46 | 5 | 51 | | | | | 51 |
| 1973 | 47 | 2 | 49 | | Young of | | | 49 |
| 1974 | 47 | 2 | 49 | Subadult | the Year | Subtotal | | 49 |
| 1975 | 49 | 8 | 57 | | 4 | | | 61 |
| 1976 | 57 | 12 | 69 | 3 | 3 | 6 | | 75 |
| 1977 | 62 | 10[b] | 72 | 6 | 2 | 8 | | 80 |
| 1978 | 68 | 7 | 75[c] | 6 | 3 | 9 | | 84 |

*Source:* U.S. Fish and Wildlife Service 1980.

[a]The 1945 count of migrant population in Aransas National Wildlife Refuge environs was 14 and 3, but as 22 whoopers in adult plumage returned to the refuge in the fall of 1946, it is evident some birds were not counted in 1945.

[b]Includes one bird not spending its first winter at Aransas National Wildlife Refuge.

[c]One juvenile disappeared soon after arrival. Overwintering population peaked at 74 birds.

Minimum breeding age of whooping cranes is three years, with some pairs not nesting for the first time until much later, so progress in establishing a breeding population is slow. The stated objective of whooping crane management is to increase the Wood Buffalo-Aransas population to 40 nesting pairs, with two separate additional populations of 20 nesting pairs each (U.S. Fish and Wildlife Service 1980). Reduction of mortality, especially of juvenile birds is a high priority.

The record of numbers in Table 12.17 shows painfully slow progress, although adult numbers have doubled from 1960 to 1978. The diverse and extensive effort to restore this species to nonendangered status is a landmark episode in wildlife conservation.

## SUMMARY

The management of waterfowl can be considered overall the most comprehensive endeavor in wildlife conservation. With a large network of waterfowl management areas in place, the future of waterfowl might seem reasonably assured. However, encroachment into critical habitats, through outright elimination, as in the San Francisco Bay region, and through pollution of estuaries and lakes and drainage of potholes will still determine the size of populations in the future. As is the case with many wildlife management issues, conservationists opposed to hunting and those who advocate it engage in futile battles while the overriding problem of habitat loss continues. This issue transcends all others in importance. The extent to which those concerned with waterfowl dissipate their energies upon each other and ignore the habitat issue will without doubt one day be recognized as the major short-sighted blunder that it is. We do the cause of waterfowl conservation a serious disservice by attacking each other at the expense of addressing real issues.

It should be recognized that the current practice of population management, which involves extensive coordination between agencies over large stretches of land, represents a substantial success story in wildlife management. This is not to be construed to mean that improvement is not needed, but the evolution of management to the current level has required the cooperation of a large number of people in different organizations. There is no other management that involves more people and agencies as effectively. Criticism of public participation levels and of management direction on issues such as where to acquire habitat or to monitor populations, or over effects of hunting, has forced management agencies to continually evaluate and justify policy and procedures. Such criticism will no doubt continue and this is desirable as long as all involved retain perspective on the merits of each issue relative to the basic issue of habitat preservation.

Waterfowl population management is where many of the major advances in understanding the dynamics of vertebrate populations have been made. The early work, exemplified by the comprehensive study of J. J. Hickey (1952), involving use of life tables, certainly led the way for population studies. The subsequent work of A. Geis and W. Crissey at the Migratory Waterfowl Station continued the tradition of rigorous population analysis, and has in turn been updated through the efforts of D. R. Anderson, K. P. Burnham, and their colleagues. These investigations have been landmarks along the way toward refining our understanding of exploitation effects and regulation of waterfowl populations. It is recognized that public concern for the resource and the effects of hunting, coupled with a well-defined legal obligation, were prime motivators for this record of accomplishment.

More refinement on all aspects of waterfowl conservation is necessary, as Bellrose and Low (1978) emphasize. More attention to the needs of individual species in management is an obvious problem. While this is being addressed through modifications in the hunting regulations, it can be further enhanced. The refuge system, while extensive, can certainly be augmented. More intensive habitat management can serve to increase production. Our understanding of botulism is far greater than for other avian diseases. Continuing efforts to restore threatened and endangered species are obviously important. The status of waterfowl management can be considered the bellweather for other wildlife management, as the written record of progress shows.

# 13

# Wildlife Management in Parks and Wilderness Areas

Wildlife values in parks and wilderness areas are very high, and often are the major reasons for their establishment. Some of the best-known wildlife populations reside within the national parks, such as the elk and grizzlies of Yellowstone, the moose and wolves of Isle Royale, and the caribou, Dall sheep, and grizzlies of Denali. The first and most obvious impulse of the human being is to try to maintain and protect the wildlife in these areas. However, the parks and wilderness areas are not the same as wildlife refuges and wildlife management areas, and the misconception that they are can be a major problem for those concerned with managing them. Moreover, there are differences between parks and wilderness areas that also have implications for management of wildlife in each.

The primary purpose of national parks is twofold: (1) to conserve the scenery and history and wildlife, and (2) to provide for the enjoyment of these lands in a manner that does not impair them. In contrast, areas that are part of the National Wilderness Preservation System are managed to retain their natural values with minimal human influence, and with no additional obligation to provide the interpretive services that are part of the national parks. Wilderness areas may exist inside national parks, where access is undeveloped and conditions are near natural. Purposes for state, county, and city parks are variable but often have the goal of maintaining areas in a more or less wild state.

Areas specifically set aside for wildlife include the various wildlife management areas, wildlife preserves, wildlife refuges, and game ranges that are administered by various levels of government from the city to the federal level. On these areas, wildlife values will be given priority, and habitat management practices ranging from farming favored foods, to prescribed burning, timber management, and water management can all be used to favor habitats for the various species that use the area. While there may well be a reason to maintain habitat in conditions that are natural for the area, the wildlife involved can be favored by artificially constructed and maintained habitats. However, discretion must be used because the perception of wildness of an area is important to most who visit these areas and an implicit goal of wildlife management is to maintain populations in natural settings.

Moreover, human use of wildlife management areas may be quite intensive as long as objectives for the resources are met. Therefore, intensive hunting, bird-watching, snowmobiling, grazing, artificial feeding, and even predator control may well proceed on the wildlife management area without violating the intended values.

The situation is much different in national parks and wilderness areas. On these areas the goal is to maintain natural dynamic processes, without human influence. Obviously, this ideal will not be reached to the same degree in all federal parks and wildernesses; nevertheless, the goal is mandated and we will do what is possible to approximate it. This means that wildlife values cannot be artificially manipulated as they can on refuges and management areas. Wildlife populations ideally will fluctuate as part of the dynamic processes that occur within the wildernesses and parks.

Wildlife management in the national parks and wilderness areas thus takes on special connotations. It is to be emphasized that wildlife management and wilderness or park management are not synonymous, even though they are commonly construed as being one and the same.

The foregoing represents a strict interpretation of wildlife management appropriate to areas where natural dynamic processes will be fostered as the major objective. The ideal of allowing these processes to proceed without human intervention is likely appropriate only to the larger areas that have not been affected substantially or that can be restored if they have been. Artificial regulation of numbers of deer, wild boar, or other species that may alter vegetation in a manner detrimental to park values is one common problem. In such cases, the toleration that unhunted populations acquire to humans may be an attribute to be considered in formulating control measures. Short, well-controlled hunting seasons (not allowed in national parks), done at a time when recreational use of the area is low, may suffice. If areas of concern are small, temporary fencing to prevent access, or livetrapping and removal may also be suitable. Altering patterns of human use of the area through relocating trails or facilities either away from the area or nearer to it to reduce wild-life use may also be tried. In many wilderness areas, hunting seasons as traditionally carried out suffice to keep numbers in check. We must recognize that many so-called natural areas will be only partially natural and that human intervention either to retain their values, or because of a tradition of use, is going to occur.

Artificial habitat manipulations may also be used, such as prescribed fire or timber harvest. Prior use, especially in wilderness areas established after grazing had been ongoing, may dictate other uses not usually perceived as compatible.

## GOALS FOR MANAGING WILDLIFE

If our goals are to retain natural ecosystems, then management that maximizes production of wildlife may not be appropriate. In fact, efforts to achieve heavy, sustained yields of game species in wilderness areas are not compatible with the intent of the Wilderness Act, because human influence will be too great. Just how much hunting should be allowed inside a wilderness area will be very difficult to measure. Determining when a campsite or a meadow has deteriorated is easier than determining when a wildlife population is exploited too heavily. However, several generalizations can be used as guides. These guides are meaningful basically as ideals or goals to be concerned with. In practice, they are likely impossible to obtain very often.

First, hunting activity that alters behavior patterns of wildlife more or less permanently would not be appropriate within wilderness areas. Such behavior might be shifts in habitat use, feeding patterns, or movement patterns during hunting. This has occurred with elk where movements across drainage systems to unhunted or less hunted areas occurs in the Bob Marshall Wilderness in Montana (Knight 1970).

Second, hunting intensity that skews sex ratios, alters productivity, or otherwise produces a demonstrable population response will be too intensive. This implies that the range of fluctuation of any criterion within natural bounds will need to be known, and deviations from values that fall within that range of variation, attributable to hunting, will not be allowed.

The implications of these two generalities are that hunting intensity inside wilderness areas will need to be kept at lower levels than elsewhere, to ensure that wilderness values are retained. Very often, hunting seasons inside and adjacent to wilderness are the most liberal, on the basis of limited access providing for less intensive hunter harvest. However, if wilderness values are to be retained, wilderness areas may sustain proportionately less intensive hunting pressure and thus the less restrictive hunting seasons may prove to be unwarranted. Since the hunting interest is a major support for wilderness in many areas, the potential exists for loss of support for wilderness if hunting is reduced.

As is often the case, information on wildlife responses to natural causes of population fluctuations is lacking, and the degree of influence by humans by any means, including hunting, is therefore imperfectly understood. How do we manipulate a population at a level that does not alter its behavior or population dynamics if we do not know the range of fluctuations within which it naturally occurs? This raises the question of natural regulation of animal numbers, and the causes. If we are to judge the effects of human influence, then we must know what the uninfluenced norms and ranges are. As usual, A. Leopold (1941:300) said it first and best, in referencing the landscape: "A science of land health needs, first of all, a basedatum of normality, a picture of how healthy land maintains itself as an organism." Almost half a century later, we still lack adequate base data upon which to judge our effects on wildlife populations and the land itself. Perhaps the need to acquire this data base will become more compelling as we strive to manage our wilderness and parklands more effectively, and as pressures on resources everywhere increase to the level that we can no longer tolerate management based on opinions and scanty information.

A second goal for managing wildlife in wilderness, and in parks as well, is reestablishment of viable populations of flora and fauna that were originally native to the region, but that through human activities have been extirpated. If the species in question is innocuous and has no appreciable effect on human activities, such as the peregrine falcon, then there is no great problem. However, if the reestablishment may adversely affect other values, then controversy exists. We likely will not see the grizzly bear or the grey wolf reintroduced into many entirely suitable areas simply because of the controversy that will occur. Wolves are readily captured, highly adaptable, and rather easily controlled should they move into unwanted areas, yet fears that they will not be managed properly and that they will impair the "wilderness experience" may well prevail. And yet a strict interpretation of the 1964 Wilderness Act requires that they be reestablished in wilderness if they are indigenous. This is currently a political impossibility, but there are areas where they could be reintroduced, and should be.

Since the grizzly bear is commonly perceived as being even less compatible with human activity, chances for reestablishing it are at least as remote as for the wolf. Perhaps one of the best measures of how far we are willing to carry out the wilderness ideal lies in our efforts to reestablish these two species in the larger wilderness areas where they originally occurred. We would probably have to reduce our hunting level to accommodate the wolf. We would have to alter our camping patterns to accommodate the grizzly. Right now, the professional wildlife biologist does not have sufficient credibility to assure those interests with legitimate concerns that wolves and bears can be managed without unduly affecting others. And no one has made the point that a wilderness restored to include these species should represent a high achievement and a very great source of satisfaction to all involved, most especially those who stand to be adversely affected if it is not done right.

## "WILDERNESS SPECIES"

There has been a tendency, ever since A. Leopold (1930) classified wildlife into farm, forest, migratory, and wilderness game, to consider certain species as being "wilderness species," capable to existing only in wilderness. The assumption is that these species, which are harmed by or are harmful to humans, are best separated from humans as much as possible. This designation was once very useful because it signified species such as elk (they damage crops and compete with livestock) as well as bighorn sheep (not compatible with domestic sheep) and the large predators. Back when wilderness included many large regions sparsely populated at best, the de facto wilderness, the designation of wilderness wildlife was useful. However, with the advent of the National Wilderness Preservation System, *wilderness* took on a new meaning that included only the officially designated Wilderness, while the unofficial de facto wilderness was largely ignored. Thus wilderness wildlife became Wilderness wildlife and the land base available for these species was considerably restricted from the days when de facto wilderness was the issue.

The major objection to restricting any wildlife species to the officially designated Wilderness is that substantial nondesignated land, in multiple-use management or sometimes in dominant-use management, as on private timber lands and large ranches, is suitable for many of the original wilderness wildlife. Another objection lies with the implied assumption that the species in question cannot coexist with humans and their activities, that it needs complete isolation to survive. Finally, the assumption that a species cannot be benefited by habitat management is fostered by the designation.

In all likelihood, there should be no species classified as requiring Wilderness. Grizzly bears and wolves coexist in areas where logging occurs, without undue influence on that activity. Bighorn sheep exist in a variety of areas that will not be designated as Wilderness, and their habitats and populations can be actively managed. The issue is not one of trying to segregate wildlife from people: the issue is, rather, one of urging people to tolerate the presence of wildlife by accepting it and altering our own activities so as to make them compatible with wildlife. We have actually been altering our own behavior for ages to accommodate wildlife, albeit often in ways that were not adequate, but there are examples and there is experience to draw from. The fact remains that there is abundant habitat outside of officially designated Wilderness that is suitable for virtually all wildlife, including the large carnivora, and we need not foster the impression that only the Wilderness will suffice. Questions involving genetic interchange between populations, what constitutes a viable population, what habitat manipulations or other human interventions might be needed and on what scale, are all involved. And the human presence is virtually all-pervasive.

Perhaps the greatest concern is over the species that thrive in old-growth forests, such as the northern spotted owl, and in some areas black-tailed deer, woodland caribou, and moose. Efforts to retain habitats for these species in areas where timber will be harvested always involve direct confrontation with economic interests, so the tendency to opt for Wilderness designation as an alternative for preserving habitats for these species prevails. However, this is likely to prove to be a short-term expedient that ignores the actual purpose of Wilderness, that of preserving natural dynamic processes, and also the dynamics of old-growth forest.

Old-growth forest is an ever-changing entity, and what may be fine habitat now is likely to fall victim to an insect infestation or a forest fire. The fallacy prevails that designating a piece of old-growth as Wilderness will perpetuate it forever, and this fallacy will continue in the future.

Wilderness designation for critical habitat in effect buys time. The habitat is relatively more secure than if it is subject to intensive management. However, this does not absolve the wildlife biologist from developing habitat management plans, in conjunction with other resource managers, that provide for the wildlife that require old-growth forest. And we have an obligation, as professional biologists, to explain the issue in as much detail as possible to the wilderness advocate as well as to the timber manager and others, as we try to promote effective conservation of the wildlife resource.

## GUIDELINES FOR MANAGING WILDLIFE IN WILDERNESS

The International Association of Wildlife Administrators (1976) has developed policies and guidelines for fish and wildlife management in wilderness areas. These policies were developed as a result of the variation in activities allowed in wilderness areas in different states and federal jurisdictions. Some federal administrators used strict interpretations of the Wilderness Act, thereby preventing state wildlife agencies from pursuing activities that were allowed elsewhere. As more and more states felt constraints in managing fish and wildlife resources within wilderness, resulting from rules and policies of the land management agency, conflicts began to arise. Such conflicts included access for planting fish, marking animals, and transplanting animals in wilderness. The Wilderness Act of 1964 specifically recognizes that hunting and fishing are compatible wilderness uses and that nothing in the act will be construed as affecting jurisdiction and responsibilities of the state agencies with respect to managing fish and wildlife.

The guidelines were developed by the U.S. Forest Service, the U.S. Bureau of Land Management, and several state fish and game agencies, especially those of New Mexico and Colorado. Key points of the policy include the following:

1. Aircraft use will be allowed, but with minimum disturbance to recreationists by considering time of day, season, elevation, route, and location of landing. Aerial censuses of big game are the most common activity requiring aircraft, and are usually done at times when recreational use is low.

2. Facilities and habitat alteration for research will be permitted if such measures are necessary for continued existence or welfare of a species, especially if adversely affected by human activities in such areas. This includes clearing of debris from streams to facilitate access by spawning salmonids, an especially critical issue in the past. Such activities must be coordinated with the land management agency and approved.

3. Regarding endangered species, the importance of wilderness areas in providing habitat for some species is recognized in the policy. However, wilderness designation shall not be used solely to benefit endangered species when alternative land classification will offer equal or better protection. Transplanting of threatened and endangered species into wilderness is recognized as a useful conservation practice.

4. Wildlife studies in wilderness must be conducted within the basic concept that the natural character of the area will be preserved. Surveys, capture and marking, installation of scientific apparatus, and other activities may be allowed on a case-by-case basis. Criteria used to judge whether a study is appropriate for wilderness or not includes whether it can be accomplished equally well elsewhere. Ongoing management activities such as census and distribution surveys of big game inhabiting wilderness are obviously needed for the area. However, many investigations of a specific nature do not need wilderness to be concluded effectively, and current policy is to disallow these. There is a high demand to work in wilderness, and in order to ensure that the wilderness character is preserved, only so many investigations can be allowed. The tendency is to be conservative in allowing studies in wilderness. Often work of a basic nature, appropriate for wilderness but not of immediately perceived management signficance, will not be allowed if a more "relevant" management study is ongoing or is planned. While there is always a need to develop priorities and carefully regulate human activity of all sorts, very often a long-term investigation directed at understanding dynamic processes can be perceived as not needed, when in fact such work is most appropriate for wilderness areas. These sorts of conflicts will continue to occur but should subside as the management of the wilderness system becomes more routine as more experience is gained, and as people develop more appreciation for the value of understanding the ecosystem involved.

5. Reintroductions and supplemental transplants will be permitted in wilderness if (a) status of a threatened or endangered species would be enhanced, (b) native species that have been reduced by acts of humans could be restored or enhanced, and (c) other significant wilderness values would not be impaired. One can envision item (c) of this section of the policy as being the excuse for not reintroducing grizzly bears and wolves, which could ostensibly impair recreational use of wilderness. On the positive side, reestablishment of bighorn sheep in wilderness and elsewhere is a very positive aspect of current wildlife management in wilderness.

6. Control of problem animals may be required to reduce depredations on wildlife and livestock, to remove animals (bears) creating a public nuisance, to prevent disease and parasitic infections of wildlife and humans, and to reduce nonindigenous species, especially if in conflict with native species. All control will be approved on a case-by-case basis.

7. Visitor management to protect wildlife resources is a very critical aspect of the policy. The type and season of public use necessary to minimize conflicts with wildlife must be controlled. Access can be developed to avoid sensitive wildlife areas, and visitor use can be limited in an equitable fashion by the appropriate agency.

When all is considered, wildlife management in wilderness is to be directed primarily at minimizing conflicts with humans by controlling human use of the areas. The land management agency will ordinarily take the lead in managing use of nonhunting, nonfishing visitors by use of limited entry systems that control numbers of people in various areas. The state wildlife agency will take the lead in regulating hunting and fishing in wilderness. The cooperation of land management agencies and state wildlife agencies is very critical to assuring proper use of wilderness areas.

A variety of tools are thus available for wildlife management in wilderness areas. However, each activity must be tuned to the wilderness values involved, then justified and approved by agencies concerned on a case-by-case basis. This helps to ensure that flexibility is retained to manage wildlife populations in wilderness areas.

## CONCLUSION

Wilderness areas and national parks pose unique issues of both ethical and pragmatic nature for the wildlife manager. If we are to retain and restore the natural dynamic processes associated with these areas, we must be prepared to witness the flora and fauna kaleidoscope as the processes work their will on the landscape. As we seek to explain the value of this to others, we must rely on concepts broader than those used by the traditional resource manager in managing for maximum productivity and harvest needs. We need to keep in mind that management becomes twofold: (1) keeping human presence to a low level compatible with maintaining the resource in as natural a state as possible, and (2) monitoring the resource so we might be able to predict what change portends. And we must understand that the ultimate value of these areas is the story they will yield of the resources in their natural state and the lessons we learn for their proper management elsewhere. In this context, wildlife management in wilderness and parks may ultimately prove to be the fundamental basis of our activities elsewhere. Thus, the value of parks and wilderness areas extends beyond their boundaries. Houston (1971) stated that promotion of an environmental ethic that extends to problems such as environmental degradation is served by wilderness and parks. Wildlife management in these areas is a very important component of that contribution.

# Literature Cited

Addison, R. B., and H. R. Timmerman. 1974. Some practical problems in the analysis of the population dynamics of a moose herd. *Proc. 10th N.A. Moose Conf. and Workshop*, pp. 76–106.

Ahlen, I. 1965. Studies on the red deer, *Cervus elaphus* L., in Scandinavia. I. History of distribution. *Viltrevy* 3:1–88.

——. 1968. Research on moose-vegetation interplay in Scandinavia. In *Proc. 5th N.A. Moose Conf. and Workshop, Kenai, Alaska*, pp. 23–34.

Ahlgren, C. E. 1966. Small mammals and reforestation following prescribed burning. *J. For.* 64 (9): 614–618.

Aldous, S. E. 1941. Deer management suggestions for northern white cedar types. *J. Wildl. Manage.* 5:90–94.

——. 1952. Deer browse clipping study in the Lake States region. *J. Wildl. Manage.* 16:401–409.

Aldrich, D. F., and R. W. Mutch. 1973. *Fire management prescriptions: a model plan for wilderness ecosystems.* Missoula, Mont.: USDA Forest Serv., Northern Forest Fire Laboratory. 103 pp.

Aldrich, J. W. and others 1949. *Migration of some North American waterfowl.* USDI Fish and Wildl. Serv. Spec. Sci. Rept. Wildl. No. 1. 49 pp.

Aldrich, J. W., and A. J. Duvall. 1958. Distribution and migration of races of the mourning dove. *Condor* 60:108–128.

Allen, D. L. 1943. *Michigan fox squirrel management.* Mich. Dept. Cons. Game Div. Pub. No. 100. 404 pp.

——. 1947. Hunting as a limitation to Michigan pheasant populations. *J. Wildl. Manage.* 11:232–243.

_____ . 1973. Report of the committee on North American Wildlife Policy. *Trans. N.A. Wildl. and Nat. Res. Conf.* 38:152–181.

Allen, J. M. 1952. *Gray and fox squirrel management in Indiana.* Indiana Dept. of Cons. Pittman-Robertson Bull. No. 1. 112 pp.

Allen, R. P. 1959. Whooping cranes fight for survival. *National Geographic* 116: 650–669.

Alley, H. P. 1965. Big sagebrush control. *Univ. of Wyoming Agr. Expt. Sta. Bull.* 354:(Rev.) 16 pp.

American Ornithologists Union. 1983. Checklist of North American birds. Sixth Edition. Allen Press, Lawrence, Kansas. 877 pp.

Ammann, G. A. 1963. Status and management of sharp-tailed grouse in Michigan. *J. Wildl. Manage.* 27:802–809.

Amstrup, S. C., and J. Beecham. 1976. Activity patterns of radio-collared black bears in Idaho. *J. Wildl. Manage.* 40:340–348.

Anderson, A. E. 1969. 2, 4-D, *Sagebrush and mule deer-cattle use of upper winter range.* Colo. Div. of Game, Fish and Parks Spec. Rept. No. 21. 21 pp.

Anderson, D. R. 1975. Optimal exploitation strategies for an animal population in a Markovian environment: a theory and an example. *Ecology* 56:1281–1297.

Anderson, D. R., and K. P. Burnham. 1976. *Population ecology of the mallard. VI. The effect of exploitation on survival.* USDI Fish and Wildl. Serv. Res. Publ. No. 128. 66 pp.

_____ . 1978. Effect of restrictive and liberal hunting regulations on annual survival rates of the mallard in North America. *Trans. N. A. Wildl. and Nat. Res. Conf.* 43:181–186.

Anderson, E. W., and R. J. Scherzinger. 1975. Improving quality of winter forage for elk by cattle grazing. *J. Range Manage.* 28:120–125.

Anderson, R. C. 1965. Cerebrospinal nematodiasis (*Pneumostrongylus tenuis*) in North American cervids. *Trans. N.A. Wildl. Conf.* 30:156–167.

Anderson, R. K. 1969. Prairie chicken responses to changing booming ground cover type and height. *J. Wildl. Manage.* 33:636–643.

Applegate, J. E., and J. R. Trout. 1976. Weather and the harvest of cottontails in New Jersey. *J. Wildl. Manage.* 40:658–662.

Arno, S. F. 1976. *The historical role of fire on the Bitterroot National Forest.* USDA Forest Serv. Res. Pap. No. INT-187. 29 pp.

Arnold, D. A., and L. J. Verme. 1963. Ten years of observation of an enclosed deer herd in northern Michigan. *Trans. N.A. Wildl. Conf.* 28:422–430.

Arrington, O. N., and A. E. Edwards. 1951. Predator control as a factor in antelope management. *Trans. N.A. Wildl. Conf.* 16:179–191.

Atwood, E. L. 1956. Validity of mail survey data on bagged waterfowl. *J. Wildl. Manage.* 20:1–16.

Atwood, E. L., and A. D. Geis. 1960. Problems associated with practices that increase the reported recoveries of waterfowl bands. *J. Wildl. Manage.* 24:272–279.

Babcock, K. M., and E. L. Flickinger. 1977. Dieldrin mortality of lesser snow geese in Missouri. *J. Wildl. Manage.* 41:100–103.

Bader, H., R. Hafeli, E. Bucher, J. Neher, O. Eckel, and C. Thomas. 1954. *Snow and its metamorphism.* U.S. Army Snow, Ice and Permafrost Res. Establ. Transl. No. 14. 313 pp.

Bailey, R. W., and K. T. Rinell. 1965. *Wild turkey population trends, productivity and harvest.* Ann. P-R Project Rept., West Virginia. 15 pp.

———. 1967. Management of the eastern turkey in the northern hardwoods. In *The Wild Turkey and its management*, ed. O. H. Hewitt, pp. 261–302. Washington, D.C.: The Wildlife Society. 589 pp.

Bailey, R. W., H. G. Uhlig, and G. Breiding. 1951. *Wild turkey management in West Virginia.* W. Va. Cons. Comm. Div. of Game Manage. Bull. No. 2. 49 pp.

Baker, M. F., and N. C. Frischknecht. 1966. Small mammals increase on recently cleared and seeded juniper rangeland. *J. Range Manage.* 26:101–103.

Baker, R. A. 1975. Biological implications of a bull-only moose hunting regulation for Ontario. In *Proc. 11th N.A. Moose Conf. and Workshop*, pp. 464–476.

Balda, R. P., and N. Masters. 1980. Avian communities in the pinyon-juniper woodland: a descriptive analysis. In Workshop proceedings: management of western forests and grasslands for nongame birds, pp. 146–169. *USDA Forest Serv. Gen. Tech. Rept. No. INT-86.* 535 pp.

Balser, D. S. 1964. Management of predator populations with antifertility agents. *J. Wildl. Manage.* 28:352–358.

———. 1974. An overview of predator-livestock problems with emphasis on livestock losses. *Trans. N.A. Wildl. and Nat. Res. Conf.* 39:292–300.

Balser, D. S., H. H. Dill, and H. K. Nelson. 1968. Effect of predator reduction on waterfowl nesting success. *J. Wildl. Manage.* 32:669–682.

Banasiak, C. F. 1961. *Deer in Maine.* Maine Dept. of Island Fisheries and Game, Game Div. Bull. No. 6. 159 pp.

Bandy, P. J., and R. D. Taber. 1972. Forest and wildlife management: conflict and coordination. In *Symposium on Wildlife and Forest Management*, pp. 21–26 Corvallis: Oregon State Univ.

Banko, W. E. 1960. *The trumpeter swan, its history, habits, and population in the United States.* USDI Fish and Wildl. Serv. N.A. Fauna No. 63. 214 pp.

Barkalow, F. S., Jr., R. B. Hamilton, and R. F. Soots, Jr. 1970. The vital statistics of an unexploited gray squirrel population. *J. Wildl. Manage.* 34:489–500.

Barney, M. A., and N. C. Frischknecht. 1974. Vegetation changes following fire in the pinyon-juniper type of west-central Utah. *J. Range Manage.* 27:91–96.

Basile, J. V., and T. N. Lonner. 1970. Vehicle restrictions influence elk and hunter distribution in Montana. *J. For.* 77:155–159.

Batchelor, C. L. 1968. Compensatory response of artificially controlled mammal populations. *Proc. New Zealand Ecol. Soc.* 15:25–30.

Baumgartner, F. M. 1944. Bobwhite quail populations on hunted vs. protected areas. *J. Wildl. Manage.* 8:259–260.

Bayoumi, M. A., and A. D. Smith. 1976. Response of big game winter range vegetation to fertilization. *J. Range Manage.* 29:44–48.

Beall, R. C. 1976. Elk habitat selection in relation to thermal radiation. In *Proc. Elk-Logging-Roads Symp.*, Univ. of Idaho, pp. 97–100.

Bean, M. J. 1977. *The evolution of national wildlife law.* Washington, D.C.: U.S. Superintendent of Documents. 485 pp.

Beasom, S. L. 1974a. Relationships between predator removal and white-tailed deer net productivity. *J. Wildl. Manage.* 38:854–859.

Beasom, S. L. 1974b. Intensive short-term predator removal as a management tool. *Trans. N.A. Wildl. and Nat. Res. Conf.* 39:230–240.

Beaver, D. L. 1976. Avian populations in herbicide-treated brush fields. *Auk* 93:543–555.

Beck, A. M., and R. J. Vogl. 1972. The effects of spring burning on rodent populations in a brush prairie savannah. *J. Mamm.* 53:336–346.

Beeman, L. E., and M. R. Pelton. 1980. Seasonal food and feeding ecology of black bears in the Smokey Mountains. ed. C. J. Martinka and K. L. McArthur, pp. 142–147. In *Bears—their biology and management,* Proc. 4th Intern. Conf. on Bear Res. and Manage. Washington, D.C.: U.S. Govt. Printing Office. 375 pp.

Beer, J. R. 1943. Food habits of the blue grouse. *J. Wildl. Manage.* 7:32–44.

Behrend, D. F., and E. F. Patric. 1969. Influence of site disturbance and removal of shade on regeneration of deer browse. *J. Wildl. Manage.* 33:394–398.

Bell, R. H. V. 1971. A grazing ecosystem in the Serengeti. *Sci. Am.* 225 (1): 86–93.

Bellrose, F. C. 1955. A comparison of recoveries from reward and standard bands. *J. Wildl. Manage.* 19:71–75.

———. 1957. *A spectacular waterfowl migration through central North America.* Illinois Nat. Hist. Surv. Biol. Note No. 36. 24 pp.

———. 1958. Celestial orientation by wild mallards. *Bird-Banding* 29:75–90.

———. 1963. Orientation behavior of four species of waterfowl. *Auk* 80:257–289.

———. 1968. *Waterfowl migration corridors east of the Rocky Mountains in the United States.* Illinois Nat. Hist. Surv. Biol. Note No. 61. 24 pp.

———. 1976. *Ducks, geese and swans of North America.* Stackpole Books, Harrisburg, Pa. 544 pp.

Bellrose, F. C., and H. C. Anderson. 1943. Preferential ratings of duck food plants. *Illinois Nat. Hist. Surv. Bull.* 22 (5): 417–433.

Bellrose, F. C., T. Scott, A. S. Hawkins, and J. Low. 1961. Sex ratios and age ratios in North American ducks. *Illinois Nat. Hist. Surv. Bull.* 27:391–474.

Bellrose, F. C., and R. D. Crompton. 1970. Migration behavior of mallards and black ducks as determined from banding. *Illinois Nat. Hist. Surv. Bull.* 39:167–234.

Bellrose, F. C., and J. B. Low. 1978. Advances in waterfowl management research. *Wildl. Soc. Bull.* 6:63–72.

Bendell, J. F. 1974. Effects of fire on birds and mammals. In *Fire and Ecosystems,* ed. T. T. Kozlowski, and C. F. Ahlgren, pp. 73–138. New York: Academic Press.

Bennett, C. L., Jr., E. E. Langenau, Jr., G. E. Burgoyne, Jr., J. L. Cook, J. P. Duvendeck, E. M. Harger, R. J. Moran, and L. G. Uisser. 1980. Experimental management of Michigan's deer habitat. *Trans. N.A. Wildl. and Nat. Res. Conf.,* 45:228–306.

Bennitt, R. 1951. *Some aspects of Missouri quail and quail hunting, 1938-1948.* Missouri Cons. Comm. Tech. Bull. No. 2. 52 pp.

Benson, P. C. 1979. *Land use and wildlife with emphasis on raptors.* Prepared for USDA Forest Serv., Intermountain Region, Ogden, Utah. 32 pp.

Berg, R. T., and L. W. Elroy. 1953. Effect of 2,4-D on the nitrate content of forage crops and weeds. *Canad. J. Agr. Sci.* 33:354–358.

Bergerud, A. T. 1970. Vulnerability of willow ptarmigan to hunting. *J. Wildl. Manage.* 34:282–285.

_____ . 1971. *The population dynamics of Newfoundland caribou.* Wildl. Monogr. No. 25. 55 pp.

_____ . 1972a. Changes in the vulnerability of ptarmigan to hunting in Newfoundland. *J. Wildl. Manage.* 36:104–109.

_____ . 1972b. Food habits of Newfoundland caribou. *J. Wildl. Manage.* 36:913–923.

_____ . 1974. Decline of caribou in North America following settlement. *J. Wildl. Manage.* 38:757–770.

_____ . 1980. A review of the population dynamics of caribou and wild reindeer in North America. In *Proc. 2nd Intern. Reindeer and Caribou Symp., Norway.* ed. E. Reimers, E. Gaare, and S. Skjenneberg, pp. 556–581.

Bergerud, A. T., and H. D. Hemus. 1975. An experimental study of the behavior of blue grouse (*Dendragapus obscurus*). I. Difference between founders from three populations. *Canad. J. Zool.* 53:1222–1227.

Bergerud, A. T., and F. Manuel. 1968. Moose damage to balsam fir—white birch forests in central Newfoundland. *J. Wildl. Manage.* 32:729–746.

Bergerud, A. T., F. Manuel, and H. Whelan. 1968. The harvest reduction of a moose population in Newfoundland. *J. Wildl. Manage.* 32:722–728.

Berns, V. D., and R. J. Hensel. 1970. Radio tracking brown bears on Kodiak Island. *IUCN Publications,* n.s. 23:19–31.

Berryman, J. H. 1972. The principles of predator control. *J. Wildl. Manage.* 36:395–400.

Best, L. B. 1972. First year effects of sagebrush control on two sparrows. *J. Wildl. Manage.* 36:534–544.

Bilello, M. A. 1969. *Relationships between climate and regional variations in snow-cover density in North America.* U.S. Army Cold Regions Research and Engineering Lab. Res. Rept. No. 267. 21 pp.

Birch, L. C. 1957. The meanings of competition. *Amer. Nat.* 91:5–18.

Bishop, R. H., and R. A. Rausch. 1974. Moose population fluctuations in Alaska, 1950–1972. *Naturaliste Canadien* 101:559–593.

Biswell, H. H. 1974. Effects of fire on chaparral. In *Fire and Ecosystems,* ed. T. T. Kozlowski, and C. E. Ahlgren, pp. 321–364. New York: Academic Press.

Biswell, H. H., and J. H. Gilman. 1961. Brush management in relation to fire and other environmental factors on the Tehama deer winter range. *Calif. Fish and Game* 47:357–389.

Black, H., R. Scherzinger, and J. W. Thomas. 1976. Relationships of Rocky Mountain elk and Rocky Mountain mule deer habitat to timber management in the

Blue Mountains of Oregon and Washington. In *Proc. Elk-Logging-Roads Symp., Univ. of Idaho, Moscow,* pp. 11–31.

Blackford, J. 1955. Woodpecker concentration on a burned forest. *Condor* 57:28–30.

Blair, R. M., and E. A. Epps, Jr. 1967. Distribution of protein and phosphorus in spring growth of rusty blackhaw. *J. Wildl. Manage.* 31:188–190.

———. 1969. *Seasonal distribution of nutrients in plants of seven browse species in Louisiana.* USDA Forest Serv. Res. Pap. No. 50–51. 35 pp.

Blaisdell, J. P. 1953. *Ecological effects of planned burning of sagebrush-grass on the upper Snake River plains.* USDA Tech. Bull. No. 1075. 39 pp.

Blaisdell, J. P., and W. F. Mueggler. 1956. Effect of 2,4-D on forbs and shrubs associated with big sagebrush. *J. Range Manage.* 9:38–40.

Blaisdell, J. P., A. C. Wiese, and C. W. Hodgson. 1952. Variations in chemical composition of bluebunch wheatgrass, arrowleaf balsamroot, and associated range plants. *J. Range Manage.* 5:346–353.

Blood, D. A. 1966. *Range relationships of elk and cattle in Riding Mountain National Park, Manitoba.* Canad. Wildl. Serv. Wildl. Manage. Bull. Ser. 1, No. 19. 62 pp.

Blus, L. J., C. D. Gish, A. A. Belisle, and R. M. Prouty. 1972. Logarithmic relationship of DDE residues to eggshell thinning. *Nature* 235:376–377.

Bock, C. E., and J. F. Lynch. 1970. Breeding bird populations of burned and unburned conifer forests in the Sierra Nevada. *Condor* 72:182–189.

Boeker, E. L., and V. F. Scott. 1969. Roost tree characteristics for Merriam's turkey. *J. Wildl. Manage.* 33:121–124.

Bohmont, D. W. 1954. *Sagebrush control—good and bad!* Univ. of Wyoming Agr. Expt. Sta. Circ. No. 54. 7 pp.

Boldt, W., and G. O. Hendrickson. 1950. Mourning dove production in North Dakota shelterbelts. *J. Wildl. Manage.* 16:187–191.

Borg, K., H. Wanntorp, K. Erne, and E. Hanko. 1969. Alkyl mercury poisoning in terrestrial Swedish wildlife. *Viltrevy* 6 (4): 301–379.

Borreco, J. E., H. C. Black, and E. F. Hooven. 1972. Response of black-tailed deer to herbicide-induced habitat changes. *Proc. Ann. Conf. West. Assn. State Game and Fish Comm.* 52:437–451.

Bos, G. N. 1975. A partial analyses of the current population status of the Nelchina caribou herd. In *Proc. 1st Intern. Reindeer and Caribou Symp. Biol. Papers Univ. of Alaska, Fairbanks, Spec. Rept. No. 1,* pp. 170–180.

Bossenmaier, E. F., and W. H. Marshall. 1958. *Field feeding by waterfowl in southeastern Manitoba.* Wildl. Monogr. No. 1. 32 pp.

Botkin, D. B., P. A. Jordan, P. A. Dominski, H. Lowendorf, and G. E. Hutchinson. 1973. Sodium dynamics in a northern ecosystem. *Proc. Nat. Acad. Sci. USA* 70:2745–2748.

Bourn, W. S. 1932. Ecological and physiological studies on certain aquatic angiosperms. *Contrib. Boyce Thompson Inst.* 4:425–496.

Boyd, R. J. 1970. *Elk of the White River plateau, Colorado.* Colo. Dept. Game, Fish and Parks Tech. Publ. No. 25. 126 pp.

Brakhage, G. K. 1953. Migration and mortality of ducks hand reared and wild-trapped at Delta, Manitoba. *J. Wildl. Manage.* 17:465–477.

Braun, C. E., T. Britt, and R. O. Wallestad. 1977. Guidelines for maintenance of sage grouse habitats. *Wildl. Soc. Bull.* 5 (3): 99–106.

Brown, J. H. 1971. Mechanisms of competitive exclusion between two species of chipmunks. *Ecology* 52 (2): 305–311.

Brown, L. G., and L. E. Yeager. 1945. Fox squirrels and gray squirrels in Illinois. *Ill. Nat. Hist. Surv. Bull.* 23 (5): 449–536.

Brown, R. L. 1966. Response of sharptail breeding populations to annual changes in residual grassland cover. *Proc. Ann. Conf. West. Assn. State Game and Fish Comm.* 46:219–222.

Brownie, C., D. R. Anderson, K. P. Burnham, and D. S. Robson. 1978. *Statistical inference from band recovery data—a handbook.* USDI Fish and Wildl. Serv. Res. Publ. No. 131. 212 pp.

Browning, B. M., and E. M. Lauppe. 1964. A deer study in a redwood–Douglas fir forest type. *Calif. Fish and Game* 50 (3): 132–146.

Bryant, J. P., F. S. Chapen, III, and D. R. Klein. 1983. Carbon/nutrient balance of boreal plants in relation to vertebrate herbivory. *Oikos* 40:357–368.

Bubenik, A. B. 1971. North American moose management in light of the European experiences. In *Proc. 8th N.A. Moose Conf. and Workshop,* pp. 276–295.

——— . H. R. Timmermann, and B. Saunders. 1975. Simulation of population structure and size in moose on behalf of age-structure of harvested animals. In *Proc. 11th N.A. Moose Conf. and Workshop,* pp. 391–463.

Bue, I. G., L. Bankenship, and W. H. Marshall. 1952. The relationship of grazing practices to waterfowl breeding populations and production on stockponds in western South Dakota. *Trans. N. Am. Wildl. Conf.* 17:396–414.

Buechner, H. K. 1950. Life history, ecology, and range use of the pronghorn antelope in Trans-Pecos, Texas. *Am. Midl. Nat.* 43 (2): 257–354.

——— . 1960. *The bighorn sheep in the United States, its past, present and future.* Wildl. Monogr. No. 4, 174 pp.

Buechner, H. K., and C. V. Swanson. 1955. Increased natality resulting from lowered population density among elk in southeastern Washington. *Trans. N.A. Wildl. Conf.* 20:560–567.

Bull. E. L., and E. C. Meslow. 1977. Habitat requirements of the pileated woodpecker in northeastern Oregon. *J. For.* 75:335–337.

Bultena, C. L., and J. C. Hendee. 1972. Foresters' views of interest group positions on forest policy. *J. For.* 70 (6): 337–342.

Bump, G., R. W. Darrow, F. C. Edminster, and W. F. Crissey. 1947. *The ruffed grouse—life history—propagation—management.* Albany: New York State Cons. Dept. 915 pp.

Bunnell, F. L. 1976. The myth of the omniscient forester. *Forestry Chronicle* 52:4–6.

——— . 1978. Horn growth and quality in Dall sheep. *J. Wildl. Manage.* 42:764–775.

Bunnell, F. L., D. C. Dauphine, R. Hilborn, D. R. Miller, F. L. Miller, E. H. McEwan, G. R. Parker, R. Peterman, G. W. Scotter, and C. J. Walters. 1975. Preliminary report on computer simulation of barren ground caribou management. In *Proc. 1st Intern. Reindeer and Caribou Symp. Biol. Papers Univ. of Alaska, Fairbanks, Spec. Rept. No. 1,* pp. 189–193.

Burget, M. L. 1957. *The wild turkey in Colorado.* Wild turkey investigations, Project W39R Federal Aid in Wildlife Restoration Work Plan 1. Job No. 6, Colo. Dept. Game Fish, Denver. 68 pp.

Burkhardt, J. W., and E. W. Tisdale. 1976. Causes of juniper invasion in southwestern Idaho. *Ecology* 57 (3): 472–484.

Cade, T. J., J. L. Linar, C. M. White, D. G. Roseneau, and L. G. Schwartz. 1971. DDE residues and eggshell changes in Alaskan falcons and hawks. *Science* 172:955–957.

Cahalane, V. H. 1939. Integration of wildlife management with forestry in the central states. *J. For.* 37 (2): 162–167.

Cain, S. A., chairman. 1972. *Predator control–1971.* Report to the Council on Environmental Quality and the Department of Interior by the Advisory Committee on Predator Control, Washington, D.C. 207 pp.

Caldwell, L. D. 1964. Dove production and nest site selection in southern Michigan. *J. Wildl. Manage.* 28:732–738.

Campbell, D. L., and J. Evans. 1975. Improving wildlife habitat in young Douglas-fir plantations. *Trans. N.A. Wildl. and Nat. Res. Conf.* 40:202–208.

Campbell, H., D. K. Martin, P. E. Ferkovich, and B. K. Harris. 1973. *Effects of hunting and some other environmental factors on scaled quail in New Mexico.* Wildl. Monogr. No. 34. 49 pp.

Cartwright, B. W. 1952. A comparison of potential with actual waterfowl production. *Trans. N.A. Wildl. Conf.* 17:131–138.

Cates, R. G., and G. H. Orians. 1975. Successional status and the palatability of plants to generalized herbivores. *Ecology* 56 (2): 410–418.

Caughley, G. 1966. Mortality patterns in mammals. *Ecology* 47:906–918.

——. 1974a. Interpretation of age ratios. *J. Wildl. Manage.* 38:557–562.

——. 1974b. Productivity, offtake, and rate of increase. *J. Wildl. Manage.* 38:566–567.

——. 1976. Wildlife management and the dynamics of ungulate populations. *Applied Biology* 1:183–246.

——. 1977. Analysis of vertebrate populations. New York: John Wiley. 234 pp.

Chamrad, A. D., and J. D. Dodd. 1973. Prescribed burning and grazing for prairie chicken habitat manipulation in the Texas coastal plain. *Proc. Ann. Tall Timbers Fire Ecol. Conf.* 12:257–276.

Chapman, J. A., A. L. Harman, and D. E. Samuel. 1977. *Reproductive and physiological cycles in the cottontail complex in western Maryland and nearby West Virginia.* Wildl. Monogr. No. 56. 73 pp.

Chapman, J. A., and R. P. Morgan, II. 1973. *Systematic status of the cottontail complex in western Maryland and nearby West Virginia.* Wildl. Monogr. No. 36. 54 pp.

Chase, W. G., and D. H. Jenkins. 1962. Productivity of the George Reserve deer herd. *Proc. 1st Natl. White-Tailed Deer Disease Symp., Univ. of Georgia Center for Continuing Education, Athens*, pp. 78–88.

Chatelain, F. F. 1950. Bear-moose relationships on the Kenai Peninsula. *Trans. N.A. Wildl. Conf.* 15:224–234.

Chesness, R. A., M. M. Nelson, and W. H. Longley. 1968. The effect of predator removal on pheasant reproductive success. *J. Wildl. Manage.* 32 (4): 683–697.

Chew, R. M., B. B. Butterworth, and R. Grechman. 1959. The effects of fire on the small mammal populations of chaparral. *J. Mamm.* 40:253.

Choate, T. S. 1963. Habitat and population dynamics of white-tailed ptarmigan in Montana. *J. Wildl. Manage.* 27:684–699.

Christenson, G. C. 1970. *The chukar partridge: its introduction, life history and management.* Nev. Fish and Game Comm. Biol. Bull. No. 4. 82 pp.

Chupp, N. R., and P. D. Dalke. 1964. Waterfowl mortality in the Coeur d'Alene River Valley, Idaho. *J. Wildl. Manage.* 28:692–702.

Chura, N. J. 1961. Food availability and preferences of juvenile mallards. *Trans. N.A. Wildl. and Nat. Res. Conf.* 26:121–134.

Church, D. C. 1971. *Digestive physiology and nutrition of ruminants.* Vol. 1. Corvallis: Oregon State Univ. 316 pp.

Claar, J. J. 1973. Correlations of ungulate food habits and winter range conditions in the Idaho Primitive Area. Master's thesis, Univ. of Idaho. 85 pp.

Clark, F. W. 1972. Influence of jack rabbit density on coyote population change. *J. Wildl. Manage.* 36:343–356.

Clarke, C. H. D. 1958. Autumn thoughts of a hunter. *J. Wildl. Manage.* 22:420–427.

_____ . 1970 Wolf management in Ontario. In *Wolf management in selected areas of North America*, ed. S. E. Jorgensen, C. E. Faulkner, and L. D. Mech, pp. 19–23. Twin Cities, Minn.: USDI Fish and Wldlf. Serv.

Coburn, D. R., D. W. Metzler, and R. Treichler. 1951. A study of absorption and retention of lead in wild waterfowl in relation to clinical evidence of lead poisoning. *J. Wildl. Manage.* 15:186–192.

Cochrane, R. L. 1976. *Crippling effects of lead, steel, and copper shot on experimental mallards.* Wildl. Monogr. No. 51, pp. 8–19.

Cody, M. L. 1969. Convergent characteristics in sympatric species: a possible relation to interspecific competition and aggression. *Condor* 71:223–239.

Cody, M. L., and J. H. Brown. 1970. Character convergence in Mexican finches. *Evolution* 24:304–310.

Cole, G. F. 1958. Big game–livestock competition on Montana's mountain rangelands. *Montana Wildl.* (April), pp. 24–30.

_____ . 1972. Grizzly bear–elk relationships in Yellowstone National Park. *J. Wildl. Manage.* 36:556–561.

Colwell, R. K., and D. J. Futuyma. 1971. On the measurement of niche breadth and overlap. *Ecology* 52:567–576.

Conaway, C. H., K. C. Sadler, and D. H. Hazelwood. 1974. Geographic variation in litter size and onset of breeding in cottontails. *J. Wildl. Manage.* 38:473–481.

Conaway, C. P. 1952. The age at sexual maturity in male elk (*Cervus canadensis*). *J. Wildl. Manage.* 16:313–315.

Connelly, G. E., and W. M. Longhurst. 1975. *The effects of coyote control on coyote populations: a simulation model.* Univ. of Calif. Div. Agr. Sci. Bull. No. 1872. 37 pp.

Conney, A. H., and J. J. Burns. 1972. Metabolic interactions among environmental contaminants and drugs. *Science* 178:576–586.

Conner, R. N., and C. S. Adkisson. 1975. Effects of clearcutting on the diversity of breeding birds. *J. For.* 73:781–785.

Conover, M. R., J. G. Francik, and D. E. Miller. 1977. An experimental evaluation of aversive conditioning for controlling coyote predation. *J. Wildl. Manage.* 41:775–779.

Cook, C. W., and L. E. Harris. 1952. Nutritive value of cheatgrass and crested wheatgrass on spring ranges of Utah. *J. Range Manage.* 5:331–337.

Cook, C. W., and L. A. Stoddart. 1959. Physiological responses of big sagebrush to different types of herbage removal. *J. Range Manage.* 13:14–16.

Cook, R. S., M. White, D. O. Trainer, and W. C. Glazener. 1971. Mortality of young white-tailed deer fawns in South Texas. *J. Wildl. Manage.* 35:47–56.

Cook, S. F., Jr. 1959. The effects of fire on a population of small rodents. *Ecology* 40:102–108.

Cooper, C. F. 1961. The ecology of fire. *Sci. Am.* 204 (4): 150–160.

Cooper, J. A. 1978. *The history and breeding biology of the Canada geese of Marshy Point, Manitoba.* Wildl. Monogr. No. 61. 87 pp.

Cornelius, D. R., and C. A. Graham. 1951. Selective herbicides for improving California ranges. *J. Range Manage.* 4:95–100.

——. 1958. Sagebrush control with 2,4-D. *J. Range Manage.* 11:122–125.

Cottam, C. 1939. *Food habits of North American diving ducks.* USDA Tech. Bull. No. 643. 140 pp.

Cowan, I. M., W. S. Hoar, and J. Hatter. 1950. The effect of forest succession upon the quality and upon the nutritive values of woody plants used as food by moose. *Canad. J. Research* (D) 28:249–271.

Cowan, J. B. 1952. Life history and productivity of a population of western mourning doves in California. *Calif. Fish and Game.* 38:505–521.

Cowan, R. L., J. S. Jordan, J. L. Grimes, and J. D. Gill. 1970. Comparative nutritive values of forage species. In *Range and wildlife habitat evaluation*, ed. H. A. Paulsen, and E. H. Reid, pp. 48–56. USDA Forest Serv. Misc. Publ. No. 1147. 220 pp.

Cowardin, L. M. 1980. United States national wetland classification with possible applications to wildlife habitat. In *Proc. Workshop on Canadian Wetlands*, pp. 49–55. Ecological Land Class. Ser. No. 12. Environment Canada.

Cowardin, L. M., V. Carter, F. C. Golet, and E. T. LaRoe. 1979. *Classification of wetlands and deep water habitats of the United States.* USDI Fish and Wildl. Serv. Biol. Serv. Prog. FWS/OBS-79/31. 103 pp.

Craighead, J. J., and F. C. Craighead, Jr. 1956. *Hawks, owls and wildlife.* Washington, D.C.: Wildlife Management Institute. 443 pp.

Craighead, J. J., and D. S. Stockstad. 1961. Evaluating the use of aerial nesting platforms by Canada geese. *J. Wildl. Manage.* 25:363–372.

Craighead, J. J., J. S. Sumner, and G. B. Scaggs. 1982. *A definitive system for analyses of grizzly bear habitat and other wilderness resources.* Wildlife-Wildlands Institute Monogr. No. 1. Missoula: Univ. of Montana. 279 pp.

Crawford, H. S., J. B. Whelan, R. F. Harlow, and J. E. Skeen. 1975. *Deer range potential in selective and clearcut oak-pine stands in southwestern Virginia.* USDA Forest Serv. Res. Pap. No. SE-134. 12 pp.

Crichton, V. 1963. Autumn and winter foods of the spruce grouse in central Ontario. *J. Wildl. Manage.* 27:597.

Crissey, W. F. 1959. *Status report of waterfowl.* USDI Fish and Wildl. Serv. Spec. Sci. Rept. Wildl. No. 45. 169 pp.

Crowner, A. W., and G. W. Barrett. 1979. Effects of fire on the small mammal component of an experimental grassland community. *J. Mamm.* 60:803–813.

Cumming, H. G. 1974. Annual yield, sex and age of moose in Ontario as indices to the effects of hunting. *Naturaliste Canadien* 101:539–558.

Currie, P. O. 1975. *Grazing management of Ponderosa pine–bunchgrass ranges of the central Rocky Mountains: the status of our knowledge.* USDA Forest Serv. Res. Pap. No. RM-159. 24 pp.

Curtis, J. T. 1956. *The vegetation of Wisconsin.* Madison: Univ. of Wisconsin Press. 657 pp.

Cushwa, C. T., R. L. Downing, R. F. Harlow, and D. F. Urbston. 1970. *The importance of woody twig ends to deer in the southeast.* USDA Forest Serv. Res. Pap. No. SE-67. 12 pp.

Cypert, E. 1973. Plant succession on burned areas in Okefenokee Swamp following fires of 1954 and 1955. *Proc. Ann. Tall Timbers Fire Ecol. Conf.* 12:199–217.

Dale, F. H. 1952. Sex ratios in pheasant research and management. *J. Wildl. Manage.* 16:156–163.

———. 1955. The role of calcium in reproduction of the ring-necked pheasant. *J. Wildl. Manage.* 19:325–331.

Dalke, P. D. 1935. Food habits of young pheasants in Michigan. *American Game* 24:36, 43–46.

———. 1937. Food habits of adult pheasants in Michigan based on crop analysis method. *Ecology* 18:199–213.

Dalke, P. D., D. B. Pyrah, D. C. Stanton, J. E. Crawford, and E. F. Schlatterer. 1963. Ecology, productivity and management of sage grouse in Idaho. *J. Wildl. Manage.* 27:811–841.

Dalke, P. D., R. D. Beeman, F. J. Kindel, R. J. Robel, and T. R. Williams. 1965. Use of salt by elk in Idaho. *J. Wildl. Manage.* 29:319–332.

Darling, F. F. 1937. *A herd of red deer.* London, Oxford Univ. Press. 215 pp.

Daubenmire, R. 1968. Ecology of fire in grasslands. *Adv. Ecol. Res.* 5:209–266.

Davis, B. N. K. 1974. Advances in pesticide-wildlife studies since 1967. *J. Ent. Soc. Australia* 8:22–31.

Davis, D. E. 1962. The potential harvest of woodchucks. *J. Wildl. Manage.* 26:144–149.

_____ . 1973. Comments on *r. Bull. Ecol. Soc.* 54:14–15, 26.

Davis, D. E., J. J. Christian, and F. Bronson. 1964. Effect of exploitation on birth, mortality, and movement rates in a woodchuck population. *J. Wildl. Manage.* 28:1–9.

Davis, D. E., and J. Ludwig. 1981. Mechanism for decline in a woodchuck population. *J. Wildl. Manage.* 45:658–668.

DeBach, P. 1966. The competitive displacement and coexistence principles. *Ann. Rev. of Ent.* 11:183–212.

Decker, D. J., T. L. Brown, and W. Sarbello. 1981. Attitudes of residents in the peripheral Adirondacks toward illegally killing deer. *N.Y. Fish and Game J.* 28:73–80.

Demarchi, R. A. 1968. Chemical composition of bighorn winter forage. *J. Range Manage.* 21:385–388.

DeRose, H. R., and A. S. Newman. 1947. The comparison of the persistence of certain plant growth–regulators when applied to soil. *Soil Sci. Soc. of Am. Proc.* 12:222–226.

Des Meules, P. 1964. The influence of snow on the behavior of moose. Travaux en cours en 1963. In *Rapport No. 3*, Serv. de la faune du Quebec, Ministere de Tourisme. 30 pp.

DeVoto, B. 1947. The west against itself. *Harper's Magazine.* 194 (1160): 1–13.

DeWitt, J. B., and J. V. Derby, Jr. 1955. Changes in nutritive value of browse plants following forest fires. *J. Wildl. Manage.* 19:65–70.

Dickson, J. G., C. D. Adams, and S. H. Hanley. 1978. Response of turkey populations to habitat variables in Louisiana. *Wildl. Soc. Bull.* 6:163–165.

Diem, K. L., and S. I. Zeveloff. 1980. Ponderosa pine bird communities. In USDA Forest Serv., Work. proc.: management of western forests and grasslands for nongame birds, pp. 170–197. USDA Forest Serv. Gen. Tech. Rept. No. INT-86.

Dietz, D. R. 1970. Definition and components of forage quality. In *Range and wildlife habitat evaluation, a research symposium*, ed. H. A. Paulsen, Jr., and E. H. Reid, co-chairmen, pp. 1–9. USDA Forest Serv. Misc. Publ. No. 1147.

Dietz, D. R., R. H. Udall, and L. F. Yaeger. 1962. *Chemical composition and digestibility by mule deer of selected forage species, Cache la Poudre Range, Colorado.* Colo. Game and Fish Dept. Tech. Publ. No. 14. 89 pp.

Dills, G. G. 1970. Effects of prescribed burning on deer browse. *J. Wildl. Manage.* 34:540–545.

Dimmick, R. W. 1968. *Canada geese of Jackson Hole.* Wyoming Game and Fish Comm. Bull. No. 11. 86 pp.

_____ . 1971. The influence of controlled burning on nesting patterns of bobwhite in west Tennessee. *Proc. Ann. Conf. SE Assn. of Game and Fish Comm.* 25:149–155.

Doerr, P. D., L. B. Keith, and D. H. Rusch. 1970. Effects of fire on a ruffed grouse population. *Proc. Ann. Tall Timbers Fire Ecol. Conf.* 11:25–46.

Donohoe, R. W., and C. McKibben. 1970. *The wild turkey in Ohio.* Ohio Game Monogr. No. 3. 32 pp.

Dorrance, M. J., and L. D. Roy. 1976. Predation losses of domestic sheep in Alberta. *J. Range Manage.* 29:457–460.

Douglass, R. J. 1976. Spatial interactions and microhabitat selections of two locally sympatric voles, *Microtus montanus* and *Microtus pennsylvanicus. Ecology* 57:346–352.

Downing, R. L. 1981. Deer harvest sex ratios: a symptom, a prescription, or what? *Wildl. Soc. Bull.* 9:8–13.

Drewien, R. C., and E. G. Bizeau. 1977. Cross-fostering whooping cranes to sandhill crane foster parents. In *Endangered Birds*, ed. S. Temple, pp. 201–222. Madison: Univ. of Wisconsin Press.

Drickhamer, L. C. 1972. Experience and selection behavior in the food habits of *Peromyscus:* use of olfaction. *Behavior* 41:269–287.

_____ . 1976. Hypotheses linking food habits and habitat selection in *Peromyscus. J. Mamm.* 57:763–766.

Drolet, C. A. 1978. Use of forest clear-cuts by white-tailed deer in southern New Brunswick and central Nova Scotia. *Canad. Field-Nat.* 92:275–282.

Dubos, R. 1973. A theology of the earth. In *Western man and environmental ethics,* ed. I. G. Barbour, pp. 43–54. Reading, Mass.: Addison-Wesley.

Dunks, J. H. 1977. *Texas mourning dove band recovery analyses 1967–1974.* Texas Parks & Wildl. Dept. FA Rept. Ser. No. 14. 94 pp.

Dwyer, T. J. 1974. Social behavior of breeding gadwalls in North Dakota. *Auk* 91:375–386.

Dzubin, A. 1955. Some evidences of home range in waterfowl. *Trans. N.A. Wildl. Conf.* 20:278–297.

Dzubin, A., and J. B. Gollop. 1972. Aspects of mallard breeding ecology in Canadian parkland and grassland. In *Population ecology of migratory birds*, pp. 113–152. USDI Fish and Wildl. Serv. Res. Rept. No. 2. 278 pp.

Eberhardt, L. 1960. *Estimation of vital characteristics of Michigan deer herds.* Mich. Dept. of Cons. Game Div. Rept. No. 2282. 192 pp.

Eberhardt, L., T. J. Peterle, and R. Schofield. 1963. *Problems in a rabbit population study.* Wildl. Monogr. No. 10. 51 pp.

Edgerton, P. J. 1972. Big game use and habitat changes in a recently logged mixed conifer forest in northeastern Oregon. *Proc. Ann. Conf. West. Assn. State Game and Fish Comm.* 52 (Portland): 239–246.

Edwards, R. Y. 1954. Fire and the decline of a mountain caribou herd. *J. Wildl. Manage.* 18:521–526.

_____ . 1956. Snow depths and ungulate abundance in the mountains of western Canada. *J. Wildl. Manage.* 20:159–168.

Edwards, R. Y., and R. W. Ritcey. 1958. Reproduction in a moose population. *J. Wildl. Manage.* 22:261–268.

_____ . 1960. Foods of caribou in Wells Gray Park, British Columbia. *Canad. Field-Nat.* 74:3–7.

Ehrenfeld, D. W. 1976. The conservation of non-resources. *Am. Sci.* 64:648–656.

Einarsen, A. S. 1946a. Crude protein determination of deer food as an applied management technique. *Trans. N.A. Wildl. Conf.* 11:309–312.

_____ . 1946b. Management of black-tailed deer. *J. Wildl. Manage.* 10:54–59.

Ellig, L. J. 1955. *Waterfowl relationships to Greenfields Lake, Teton County, Montana.* Montana Fish and Game Dept. Tech. Bull. No. 1. 35 pp.

Ellis, J. E., and J. B. Lewis. 1967. Mobility and annual range of wild turkeys in Missouri. *J. Wildl. Manage.* 31:568–581.

Ellison, L. 1960. Influence of grazing on plant succession of rangelands. *The Bot. Rev.* 26:1–78.

Ellison, L. N. 1966. Seasonal foods and chemical analysis of winter diet of the Alaskan spruce grouse. *J. Wildl. Manage.* 30:729–735.

_____ . 1975. Density of Alaskan spruce grouse before and after fire. *J. Wildl. Manage.* 39:468–471.

Elton, C. S. 1958. *Ecology of invasions by animals and plants.* London: Methuen.

Emlen, J. T. 1970. Habitat selection by birds following a forest fire. *Ecology* 51:343–345.

_____ . 1973. *Ecology: an evolutionary approach.* Reading, Mass.: Addison-Wesley. 493 pp.

Enderson, J. H., and P. H. Wrege. 1973. DDE residues and eggshell thickness in prairie falcons. *J. Wildl. Manage.* 37:476–478.

Eng, R. L., and P. Schladweiler. 1972. Sage grouse winter movements and habitat use in central Montana. *J. Wildl. Manage.* 36:141–146.

Erickson, A. B., V. E. Gunvalson, D. W. Burcalow, M. H. Stenlund, and L. H. Blankenship. 1961. *The white-tailed deer of Minnesota.* Minn. Dept. Cons. Tech. Bull. No. 5. 64 pp.

Erickson, A. W. 1959. The age of self-sufficiency in the black bear. *J. Wildl. Manage.* 23:401–405.

Erickson, A. W., J. Nellor, and G. A. Petrides. 1964. *The black bear in Michigan.* Mich. State Univ. Expt. Sta. Res. Bull. No. 4. 102 pp.

Errington, P. L. 1943. An analysis of mink predation upon muskrats in north central United States. In *Iowa State College of Agr. and Mech. Arts Res. Bull. No. 320,* pp. 798–924.

_____ . 1946. Predation and vertebrate populations. *Quart. Rev. Biol.* 21:144–177, 221–245.

_____ . 1947. A question of values. *J. Wildl. Manage.* 11 (3): 267–272.

_____ . 1948. In appreciation of Aldo Leopold. *J. Wildl. Manage.* 12:341–350.

_____ . 1956. Factors limiting higher vertebrate populations. *Science* 124 (3216): 304–307.

_____ . 1963. The phenomenon of predation. *Am. Sci.* 51:180–192.

Errington, P. L., and F. N. Hamerstrom, Jr. 1935. Bobwhite winter survival on experimentally shot and unshot areas. *Iowa State College J. Sci.* 9 (4): 625–639.

Estes, R. D. 1974. Social organization of the African bovids. *IUCN Publications* n.s. 24: 166–205.

Evanko, A. N., and R. A. Peterson. 1955. Comparisons of protected and grazed mountain rangelands in southwestern Montana. *Ecology* 36:71–82.

Evans, C. D., and K. D. Black. 1956. *Duck production studies on the prairie potholes of South Dakota.* USDI Fish and Wildl. Serv. Spec. Sci. Rept. Wildl. No. 32. 59 pp.

Evans, C. D., A. S. Hawkins, and W. H. Marshall. 1952. *Movements of waterfowl broods in Manitoba.* USDI Fish and Wildl. Serv. Spec. Sci. Rept. No. 16. 47 pp.

Evans, K. E. 1968. *Characteristics and habitat requirements of the greater prairie chicken and sharptailed grouse—a review of the literature.* USDA Forest Serv. Cons. Rept. No. 12. 32 pp.

Evans, K. E., and D. L. Gilbert. 1969. A method of evaluating greater prairie chickens habitat in Colorado. *J. Wildl. Manage.* 33:643–649.

Evenden, G. F. 1969. The job outlook in the wildlife profession. *The Wildlife Society News.* 123:31–32.

Farentinas, R. C., P. J. Capretta, R. E. Kepner, and V. M. Littlefield. 1981. Selective herbivory in tassel-eared squirrels: role of monoterpenes in ponderosa pines chosen as feeding sites. *Science* 213:1273–1275.

Farmer, R. E. 1962. Aspen root sucker formation and apical dominance. *Forest Sci.* 8:403–410.

Fichter, E. 1959. Mourning dove production in four Idaho orchards and some possible implications. *J. Wildl. Manage.* 23:438–447.

Filonov, C. P., and C. D. Zykov. 1974. Dynamics of moose populations in the forest zone of the European part of the USSR and in the Urals. *Naturaliste Canadien* 101:605–613.

Flesch, R. ed. 1966. *The new book of unusual quotations.* New York: Harper & Row. 448 pp.

Flook, D. R. 1970. *A study of sex differential in the survival of wapiti.* Canad. Wildl. Serv. Rept. Ser. No. 11. 71 pp.

Follis. T. B. 1972. *Reproduction and hematology of the Cache elk herd.* Utah Div. Wildl. Res. Publ. No. 72–8. 133 pp.

Formosov, A. N. 1946. Snow cover as an integral factor of the environment and its importance in the ecology of mammals and birds. Translation from Russian by Boreal Institute, Univ. of Alberta, Edmonton, Occ. Publ. No. 1. 141 pp.

Frank, P. A., and B. H. Grigsby. 1957. Effects of herbicidal sprays on nitrate accumulation in certain weed species. *Weeds* 5:206–217.

Franklin, J. F., and D. S. DeBell. 1973. Effects of various harvesting methods on forest regeneration, pp. 29–57. In R. K. Herman and D. P. Lavender, eds., *Symposium on Even-Age Management, Oregon State Univ., Corvallis*, School of Forestry Paper 848.

Franklin, J. F., K. Cromack, Jr., W. Denison, A. McKee, C. Maser, J. Sadell, F. Swanson, and G. Juday. 1981. Ecological characteristics of old-growth Douglas-fir forests. USDA Forest Service Gen. Tech. Rept. RNW-118. 48 pp.

Franzman, A. W., J. L. Oldemeyer, P. D. Arneson, and R. K. Seemel. 1976. Pellet group count evaluation for census and habitat use of Alaskan moose. In *Proc. 12th N.A. Moose Conf. and Workshop*, pp. 127–142.

Franzreb, K. E. 1977. *Bird population changes after timber harvesting of a mixed conifer forest in Arizona.* USDA Forest Serv. Res. Pap. No. RM-184. 26 pp.

Fretwell, S. D. 1978. Competition for discrete versus continuous resources: tests for predictions from the MacArthur-Levins models. *Amer. Nat.* 112:73–81.

Fretwell, S. D., and H. L. Lucas. 1970. On territorial behaviour and other factors influencing habitat distribution in birds. *Acta Biotheoretica* 19:16–36.

Frissell, S. S., Jr. 1973. The importance of fire as a natural ecological factor in Itasca State Park, Minnesota. *Quat. Res.* 3:397–407.

Frome, M. 1975. It's time Fish and Game broadened policy. *Defenders of Wildlife.* 50:314–316.

Furubayoshi, K., K. Kirai, K. Skeda, and T. Myuguchi. 1980. Relationships between occurrence of bear damage and clearcutting in central Honshu, Japan. In *Bears— their biology and management*, ed. C. J. Martinka and K. L. McArthur, pp. 91–94. Proc. 4th Intern. Conf. on Bear Res. Manage. Washington, D.C.: U.S. Govt. Printing Office.

Gabrielson, I. N. 1946. Trumpeter swans in Alaska. *Auk* 63:102–103.

Gaffney, W. S. 1941. The effects of winter elk browsing, South Fork of the Flathead River, Montana. *J. Wildl. Manage.* 5:427–453.

Gallizioli, S. 1955. Hunting season information on the mourning and whole-winged doves of Arizona. *Proc. Ann. Conf. West. Assn. State Game and Fish Comm.* 35:226–235.

Gardarsson, A., and R. Moss. 1970. Selection of food by Icelandic ptarmigan in relation to its availability and nutritive value. In *British Ecol. Soc. Symp. 10*, pp. 47–71.

Garrison, G. 1953. Effects of clipping on some range shrubs. *J. Range Manage.* 6 (5): 309–317.

Garshelis, D. L., and M. R. Pelton. 1981. Movements of black bears in the Great Smokey Mountains National Park. *J. Wildl. Manage.* 45:912–925.

Gasaway, W. C., R. O. Stephenson, J. L. Davis, P. E. K. Shepherd, and O. E. Burris. 1983. *Interrelationships of wolves, prey, and man in interior Alaska.* Wildl. Monogr. No. 84. 50 pp.

Gashwiler, J. S. 1959. Small mammal study in west-central Oregon. *J. Mamm.* 40:128–139.

———. 1970. Plant and mammal changes on a clearcut in west-central Oregon. *Ecology* 51:1018–1026.

Geis, A. D. 1963. Role of hunting regulations in migratory bird management. *Trans. N.A. Wildl. Conf.* 28:164–172.

Geis, A. D., and E. L. Atwood. 1961. Proportion of recovered waterfowl bands reported. *J. Wildl. Manage.* 25:154–159.

Geis, A. D., R. K. Martinson, and D. R. Anderson. 1969. Establishing hunting regulations and allowable harvest of mallards in the United States. *J. Wildl. Manage.* 33:848–859.

Geist. V. 1968. On the interrelation between external appearance, social behavior, and social structure of mountain sheep. *Zeit. Tierpsychologie* 25:199–215.

———. 1971a. Bighorn sheep biology. *The Wildlife Society News* 136:61.

____ . 1971b. *Mountain sheep: a study in behavior and evolution.* Chicago: Univ. of Chicago Press. 383 pp.

Gerloff, G. C., D. G. Moore, and J. T. Curtis. 1966. Selective absorption of mineral elements by native plants in Wisconsin. *Plant and Soil* 25 (3): 393–405.

Gier, H. T. 1968. *Coyotes in Kansas.* Kansas State Univ. Agr. Expt. Sta. Bull. No. 393. 118 pp. Revised.

Gilbert, P. F., O. C. Wallmo, and R. B. Gill. 1970. Effect of snow depth on mule deer in Middle Park, Colorado. *J. Wildl. Manage.* 34:15–23.

Gill, J. D., J. W. Thomas, W. M. Healy, J. C. Pack, and H. R. Sanderson. 1975. Comparison of seven forest types for game in West Virginia. *J. Wildl. manage.* 39:762–768.

Gillman, A. P., G. A. Fox, D. B. Peakall, S. M. Teeple, T. R. Carroll, and G. T. Haymes. 1977. Reproductive parameters and egg contaminant levels of Great Lakes herring gulls. *J. Wildl. Manage.* 41:458–468.

Gjersing, F. M. 1975. Waterfowl production in relation to rest-rotation grazing. *J. Range Manage.* 23:37–42.

Glading, B., H. H. Biswell, and C. F. Smith. 1940. Studies on the food of the California quail in 1937. *Wildl. Manage.* 4:128–144.

Glading, B., and R. W. Saarni. 1944. Effect of hunting on a valley quail population. *Calif. Fish and Game* 30 (2): 71–79.

Goddard, J. 1970. Movements of moose in a heavily hunted area of Ontario. *J. Wildl. Manage.* 34:439–445.

Goodrum, P. D., V. H. Reid, and C. E. Boyd. 1971. Acorn yields, characteristics and management criteria for oaks for wildlife. *J. Wildl. Manage.* 35:520–532.

Gordon, A., and A. W. Sampson. 1939. Composition of common California foothill plants as a factor in range management. *Calif. Agr. Expt. Sta. Bull.* 627:1–95.

Gordon, F. A. 1976. Spring burning in an aspen-conifer stand for maintenance of moose habitat, West Boulder River, Montana. *Proc. Ann. Tall Timbers Fire Ecol. Conf. and Fires and Land Manage. Symp.* 14:501–538.

Gottschalk, J. S. 1972. The German hunting system, West Germany, 1968. *J. Wildl. Manage.* 36:110–118.

Graham, S. A. 1958. Results of deer exclosure experiments in the Ottawa National Forest. *Trans. N.A. Wildl. Conf.* 23:478–490.

Graham, S. A., R. P. Harrison, and C. E. Westell. 1963. *Aspens. Phoenix trees of the Great Lakes region.* Ann Arbor: Univ. of Michigan Press. 272 pp.

Grange, W. B. 1949. *The way to game abundance.* New York: Scribner's. 365 pp.

Greeley, F. 1962. Effects of calcium deficiency on laying hen pheasants. *J. Wildl. Manage.* 26:186–193.

Greenberg, R. E. 1971. The future of hunting. *The Wildlife Society News.* 134:32.

Greer, K. R. 1966. Fertility rates of the northern Yellowstone elk populations. *Proc. Ann. Conf. West. Assn. State Game and Fish Comm.* 46:123–128.

Grelen, H. E. 1975. *Vegetative response to twelve years of seasonal burning on a Louisiana longleaf pine site.* USDA Forest Serv. Res. Note No. SO-192. 4 pp.

Gross, J. E. 1969. Optimum yield in deer and elk populations. *Trans. N.A. Wildl. Conf.* 34:372–386.

Gruell, G. E., and L. L. Loope. 1974. *Relationships among aspen, fire, and ungulate browsing in Jackson Hole, Wyoming.* Jackson, Wyo.: USDA Forest Serv. and USDI Park Serv. 33 pp.

Gullion, G. W. 1966. A viewpoint concerning the significance of studies of game bird food habits. *Condor* 68:372–376.

————. 1970. Factors influencing ruffed grouse populations. *Trans. N.A. Wildl. and Nat. Res. Conf.* 35:93–105.

————. 1972. *Improving your forested lands for ruffed grouse.* Minn. Agr. Expt. Sta. Misc. J. Ser. Publ. No. 1439.

Gullion, G. W., and W. H. Marshall. 1968. Survival of ruffed grouse in a boreal forest. *The Living Bird* 7:117–167.

Gustavson, C. R., R. Garcia, W. G. Hankins, and K. W. Rusinak. 1974. Coyote predation control by aversive conditioning. *Science* 184 (4136): 581–583.

Guthery, F. S., and S. L. Beasom. 1977. Responses of game and nongame wildlife to predator control in South Texas. *J. Range Manage.* 30:404–409.

Hadley, E. B. 1970. Net productivity and burning responses of native eastern North Dakota prairie communities. *Am. Midl. Nat.* 84:121–135.

Haines, D. A., and R. W. Sando. 1969. *Climatic conditions preceding historically great fires in the North Central region.* USDA Forest Serv. Res. Pap. No. NC-34. 19 pp.

Hakala. J. B., R. K. Seemel, R. A. Richey, and J. E. Kurta. 1971. Fire effects and rehabilitation methods—Swanson-Russian Rivers fire. In *Proc. Fire in the northern environment, a symp.,* ed. C. W. Slaughter, et al., pp. 87–99. Portland: USDA Forest Serv. Pac. NW Forest and Range Expt. Sta.

Halls, L. K. 1973. Managing deer habitat in loblolly–shortleaf pine forest. *J. For.* 71:752–757.

Halls, L. K., and E. A. Epps, Jr. 1969. Browse quality influenced by tree overstory in the south. *J. Wildl. Manage.* 33:1028–1031.

Hamerstrom, F. N., Jr. 1958. Review of hawks, owls and wildlife. *J. Wildl. Manage.* 22:212–213.

————. 1963. Sharptail brood habitat in Wisconsin's northern pine barrens. *J. Wildl. Manage.* 27:793–802.

Handley, R. B., and W. R. Edwards. 1957. Mourning dove nesting studies in Mississippi. Paper presented at 11th Assn. Conf. SE Assn. Game and Fish Comm. 9 p. and 3 p. of figs.

Hansen, C. G. 1967. Bighorn sheep populations of the Desert Game Range. *J. Wildl. Manage.* 31:693–706.

Hansen, H. A., P. E. Shepherd, J. G. King, and W. A. Troyer. 1971. *The trumpeter swan in Alaska.* Wildl. Monogr. 26. 83 pp.

Hansen, H. L., and V. Kurmis. 1972. Natural succession in northcentral Minnesota. In *Aspen Symposium Proceedings,* pp. 59–66. USDA Forest Serv. Gen. Tech. Rept. No. NC-1.

Hanson, H. C., and C. W. Kossack. 1957. Weight and body-fat relationships of mourning doves in Illinois. *J. Wildl. Manage.* 21:169–181.

_____ . 1963. *The mourning dove in Illinois.* Illinois Dept. Cons. Tech. Bull. No. 2. 133 pp.

Hanson, H. C., and R. H. Smith, 1950. Canada geese of the Mississippi Flyway, with special reference to an Illinois flock. *Illinois Nat. Hist. Surv. Bull.* 25:67–210.

Hardin, G. 1960. The competitive exclusion principle. *Science* 131:1292–1297.

Harlow, R. F., B. A. Sanders, J. B. Whelan, and L. C. Chappel. 1980. Deer habitat on the Ocala National Forest: improvement through forest management. *Southern J. Appl. For.* 4:98–102.

Harniss, R. O., and R. B. Murray. 1973. 30 years of vegetal change following burning of sagebrush-grass range. *J. Range Manage.* 26:322–325.

Harper, J. A. 1970. Wolf management in Alaska. In *Wolf management in selected areas of North America*, ed. S. E. Jorgensen, C. E. Faulkner, and L. D. Mech, pp. 24–27. Twin Cities, Minn.: USDI Fish and Wildlife Serv.

_____ . 1971. *Ecology of Roosevelt elk.* Portland: Oregon State Game Comm. 44 pp.

Harper, J. A., and R. F. Labisky. 1964. The influence of calcium on the distribution of pheasants in Illinois. *J. Wildl. Manage.* 28:722–731.

Harris, A. 1967. Some competitive relationships between *Agropyron spicatum* and *Bromus tectorum. Ecol. Monogr.* 37:89–111.

Harris, C. I., and T. J. Sheets. 1965. Persistence of several herbicides in the field. *Northeastern Weed Control Conf. Proc.* 19:359.

Harris, S. W., and W. H. Marshall. 1963. Ecology of water-level manipulations on a northern marsh. *Ecology* 44:331–342.

Harris, S. W., M. A. Morse, and W. H. Longley. 1963. Nesting and production of the mourning dove in Minnesota. *Am. Midl. Nat.* 69:150–172.

Harry, J., R. Gale, and J. Hendee. 1969. Conservation: an upper-middle class social movement. *J. Leisure Research.* 1:246–254.

Hawes, M. L. 1977. Home range, territoriality and ecological separation in sympatric shrews *Sorex vagrans* and *Sorex obscurus. J. Mamm.* 58:354–367.

Hawkins, A. S., F. C. Bellrose and R. H. Smith. 1946. A waterfowl reconnaissance in the Grand Prairie region of Arkansas. *Trans. N.A. Wildl. Conf.* 11:394–401.

Hawn, L. J., and L. A. Ryel. 1969. Michigan deer harvest estimates: sample surveys versus a complete count. *J. Wildl. Manage.* 33:871–880.

Hayes, H. T. P. 1975. *The last place on earth.* New York: Stein & Day. 287 pp.

Hayne, D. W. 1975. *Experimental increase of mourning dove bag limit in eastern management unit.* Southeastern Assn. Game and Fish Comm. Tech. Bull No. 11. 56 pp.

Heady, H. F. 1973. Burning and the grasslands of California. *Proc. Ann. Tall Timbers Fire Ecol. Conf.* 12:97–107.

Heimer, W. E., and A. C. Smith, III. 1975. *Ram horn growth and population quality – their significance to Dall sheep management in Alaska.* Alaska Dept. of Fish and Game. Wildl. Tech. Bull. No. 5. 41 pp.

Heinselmann, M. L. 1973. Fire in the virgin forests of the Boundary Waters Canoe Area, Minnesota, *Quat. Res.* 3:329–382.

Heller, H. C. 1971. Altitudinal zonation of chipmunks (Eutamias): interspecific aggression. *Ecology* 52:313–319.

Hellmers, H. 1940. A study of monthly variations in the nutritive value of several natural winter deer foods. *J. Wildl. Manage.* 4:315–325.

Hendee, J. C., and R. W. Harris. 1970. Foresters' perception of wilderness-user attitudes and preferences. *J. For.* 68:750–762.

Hendee, J. C., and D. R. Potter. 1976. Hunters and hunting: management implications of research, pp. 137–161. In Proceedings of the Southern States Recreation Research, Application Workshop, USDA Forest Serv. Gen. Tech. Rept. No. SE-9.

Henderson, F. R., and E. K. Boggess. 1977. A public education program of predator damage control. *Trans. N.A. Wildl. and Nat. Res. Conf.* 42:323–328.

Hendrickson, G. O. 1937. The Mearn's cottontail in Iowa. *Trans N.A. Wildl. Conf.* 2:549–554.

Henny, C. J., M. A. Byrd, J. A. Jacobs, P. D. McLain, M. R. Todd, and B. F. Halla. 1977. Mid-Atlantic Coast osprey population: present numbers, productivity, pollutant contamination, and status. *J. Wildl. Manage.* 41:254–265.

Heptner, W. G., and A. A. Nasimowitsch. 1967. *Der elch.* Wittenberg Lutherstadt: A. Ziemsen Verlag. 231 pp.

Hess, E. H. 1966. "Imprinting" in animals. In *Psychobiology: the biological basis of behavior*, pp. 107–112. San Francisco: W. H. Freeman and Company.

Hickey, J. J. 1952. *Survival studies of banded birds.* USDI Fish and Wildl. Serv. Spec. Sci. Rept. Wildl. No. 15. 177 pp.

———. 1974. Some historical phases in wildlife conservation. *Wildl. Soc. Bull.* 2:164–170.

Hickey, J. J., and D. W. Anderson. 1968. Chlorinated hydrocarbons and eggshell changes in raptorial and fish-eating birds. *Science* 162:271–272.

Hickie, P. 1940. *Cottontails in Michigan.* Mich. Dept. Cons. 109 pp.

Hildebrand, P. R. 1971. Biology of white-tailed deer on winter ranges in the Swan Valley, Montana. Master's thesis, Univ. of Montana. 91 pp.

Hilden, O. 1965. Habitat selection in birds: a review. *Ann. Zool. Fenn.* 2:53–75.

Hill, E. P. 1972. *The cottontail rabbit in Alabama.* Alabama Agr. Expt. Sta., Auburn Univ. Bull. No. 440. 103 pp.

Hill, E. V., and H. Carlisle, 1947. Toxicity of 2,4-dichlorophenoxyacetic acid for experimental animals. *J. Ind. Hygiene and Tox.* 29:85–95.

Hines, W. W. 1973. *Blacktailed deer populations and Douglas-fir reforestation in the Tillamook Burn, Oregon.* Oregon State Game Comm. Game Res. Rept. No. 3. 59 pp.

Hines, W. W., and J. C. Lemos. 1979. *Reproduction performance by two age-classes of male Roosevelt elk in Southwestern Oregon.* Oregon Dept. Fish and Wildl. Res. Rept. No. 8. 54 pp.

Hixon, M. A. 1982. Energy maximizers and time minimizers: theory and reality. *Amer. Nat.* 119:596–599.

Hobbs, N. T., D. L. Baker, J. E. Ellis, and D. M. Swift. 1981. Composition and quality of elk winter diets in Colorado. *J. Wildl. Manage.* 45:156–171.

Hochbaum, A. 1944. The canvasback on a prairie marsh. Am. Wildl. Inst., Washington, D.C. 20 pp.

____ . 1955. *Travels and traditions of waterfowl.* Minneapolis: Univ. of Minnesota Press, 301 pp.

Hoffman, D. M. 1962. *The wild turkey in eastern Colorado.* Colo. Game and Fish Tech. Publ. No. 12. 49 pp.

____ . 1968. Roosting sites and habits of Merriam's turkeys in Colorado. *J. Wildl. Manage.* 32:859–866.

Hoffman, R. A., and P. F. Robinson. 1966. Changes in some endocrine glands of white-tailed deer as affected by season, sex, and age. *J. Mamm.* 47:266–280.

Holbrook, H. L. 1974. A system for wildlife habitat management on southern national forests. *Wildl. Soc. Bull.* 2:119–123.

Holbrook, H. L., and J. C. Lewis. 1967. Management of the eastern turkey in the southern Appalachian and Cumberland Plateau Region. In *The wild turkey and its management,* ed. O. H. Hewitt, pp. 343–370. Washington, D.C.: The Wildlife Society, 589 pp.

Holling, C. S. 1959. The components of predation as revealed by a study of small mammal predation on the European pine sawfly. *The Canad. Entomologist* 91:293–320.

____ . 1965. *The functional response of predators to prey density and its role in mimicry and population regulation.* Memoirs of the Entomological Soc. of Canada No. 45. 60 pp.

____ . 1966. *The functional response of invertebrate predators to prey density.* Memoirs of the Entomological Soc. of Canada No. 48. 86 pp.

Holmes, R. T., R. E. Bonney, Jr., and S. W. Pacala. 1979. Guild structure of the Hubbard Brook bird community: a multivariate approach. *Ecology* 60:512–520.

Holt, S. J., and L. M. Talbot. 1978. *New principles for the conservation of wild living resources.* Wildl. Monogr. No. 59. 33 pp.

Honacki, J. H., K. E. Kenman, and J. W. Koeppl. 1982. Mammal species of the world. Assoc. of Systematics Collections, Lawrence, Kansas. 694 pp.

Hooper, R. G., A. F. Robinson, Jr., and J. A. Jackson. 1980. *The red-cockaded woodpecker: notes on life history and management.* USDA Forest Serv. Gen. Rept. No. SA-GR 9. 8 pp.

Hooven, E. F., and H. C. Black. 1976. Effects of some clearcutting practices on small mammal populations in western Oregon. *NW Sci.* 50:189–208.

Hopkins, M. N., and E. P. Odum. 1953. Some aspects of the population ecology of breeding mourning doves in Georgia. *J. Wildl. Manage.* 17:132–143.

Hopper, R. M., A. D. Geis, J. R. Grieb, and L. Nelson, Jr. 1975. *Experimental duck hunting seasons, San Luis Valley, Colorado, 1963-1970.* Wildl. Monogr. No. 46. 68 pp.

Hormay, A. L. 1970. *Principles of rest-rotation grazing and multiple-use land management.* USDA Forest Serv. Training Text 4 (2200). 26 pp.

Hormay, A. L., and M. W. Talbot. 1961. *Rest-rotation grazing: a new management system for perennial bunchgrass ranges.* USDA Forest Serv. Prod. Res. Rept. No. 51. 43 pp.

Horn, H. S. 1974. The ecology of secondary succession. *Ann. Rev. Ecol. and Syst.* 5:25–37.

Hornocker, M. G. 1970. *An analysis of mountain lion predation upon mule deer and elk in the Idaho Primitive Area.* Wildl. Monogr. No. 21. 39 pp.

———. 1971. Suggestions for the management of mountain lions as trophy species in the Intermountain Region. *Proc. Ann. Conf. West. Assn. State Game and Fish Comm.* 51:399–402.

———. 1972. Predator ecology and management—what now? *J. Wildl. Manage.* 36:401–404.

Horton, K. W., and E. J. Hopkins. 1965. *Influence of fire on aspen suckering.* Canada Dept. of Forestry Publ. No. 1095. 19 pp.

Hosley, N. W. 1935. The essentials of a management plan for forest wildlife in New England. *J. For.* 33:985–989.

Hosley, N. W., Chmn. 1934. Some preliminary game management measures for New England conditions. *J. For.* 32:856–860.

Hosley, N. W., and R. K. Ziebarth. 1935. Some winter relations of the white-tailed deer to the forests in north-central Massachusetts. *Ecology* 16:535–553.

House, W. B., L. H. Goodson, H. M. Gadberry, and K. W. Dokter. 1967. *Assessment of ecological effects of extensive or repeated use of herbicides.* Report for Department of Defense Contract No. DAHCIS-68-C-0019. Kansas City, Mo.: Midwest Research Institute.

House Committee on Merchant Marine and Fisheries. 1973. *A compilation of federal laws relating to conservation and development of our nation's fish and wildlife resources, environmental quality, and oceanography.* Washington, D.C.: U.S. Govt. Printing Office. 706 pp.

Houston, D. B. 1971. Ecosystems of national parks. *Science* 172:648–651.

———. 1973. Wildfires in northern Yellowstone National Park. *Ecology* 54:1111–1117.

Howard, R. P., and M. L. Wolfe. 1976. Range improvement practices and ferruginous hawks. *J. Range Manage.* 29:33–37.

Howard, W. E. 1974. *The biology of predator control.* Module in Biology No. 11. Reading, Mass.: Addison-Wesley. 48 pp.

Hubbard, R. L., and H. R. Sanderson. 1961. Grass reduces bitterbrush production. *Calif. Fish and Game.* 47:391–398.

Huffaker, C. B., and J. E. Laing. 1972. "Competitive displacement" without a shortage of resources? *Res. on Pop. Ecol.* 14:1–17.

Hughes, R. H. 1975. *The native vegetation in south Florida related to month of burning.* USDA Forest Serv. Res. Note No. SE-222. 8 pp.

Hull, A. C., Jr., and M. K. Hull. 1974. Presettlement vegetation of Cache Valley, Utah and Idaho. *J. Range Manage.* 28:27–29.

Hull, A. C., Jr., and G. J. Klomp. 1966. Longevity of crested wheatgrass in the sagebrush-grass type in southern Idaho. *J. Range Manage.* 19:5–11.

Hull, A. C., Jr., and W. T. Vaughn. 1951. Controlling big sagebrush with 2,4-D and other chemicals. *J. Range Manage.* 4:158–164.

Humphrey, R. R. 1974. Fire in the deserts and desert grasslands of North America. In *Fire and ecosystems,* ed. T. T. Kozlowski and C. E. Ahlgren, pp. 366–400. New York: Academic Press. 542 pp.

Hundley, L. R. 1959. Available nutrients in selected deer browse species growing on different soils. *J. Wildl. Manage.* 23:81–90.

Hungerford, C. R. 1970. Response of Kaibab mule deer to management of summer range. *J. Wildl. Manage.* 34:852–862.

Hungerford, K. E. 1957. Evaluating ruffed grouse foods for habitat improvement. *Trans. N. Am. Wildl. Conf.* 22:380–395.

Hunt, C. D. 1979. A legal perspective on natives and wildlife in Canada. *Trans. N.A. Wildl. and Nat. Res. Conf.* 44:583–593.

Hunt, G. L., Jr. 1972. Influence of food distribution and human disturbance on the reproductive success of herring gulls. *Ecology* 53:1051–1061.

Hunter, B. F. 1970. Ecology of waterfowl botulism toxin production. *Trans. N.A. Wildl. and Nat. Res. Conf.* 35:64–72.

Hurd, R. M. 1955, Effect of 2,4-D on some herbaceous range shrubs. *J. Range Manage.* 8:126–128.

Hutchinson, G. F. 1948. Circular causal systems in ecology. *Ann. N.Y. Acad. Sci.* 50:221–246.

———. 1958. Concluding remarks. *Cold Spring Harbor Symp. Quant. Biol.* 22:415–427.

Hyder, D. N., and F. A. Sneva. 1956. Herbage response to sage brush spraying. *J. Range Manage.* 9:34–38.

Inman, D. L. 1973. Cellulose digestion in ruffed grouse, chukar partridge, and bobwhite quail. *J. Wildl. Manage.* 37:114–121.

International Association of Fish and Wildlife Administrators. 1976. Policies and guidelines for fish and wildlife management in wilderness and primitive areas. Washington, D.C. Mimeo.

Irby, H. D., and L. H. Blankenship. 1966. Breeding behavior of immature mourning doves. *J. Wildl. Manage.* 30:598–604.

Irwin, L. L. 1983. Deer-moose relationships on a burn in northeastern Minnesota. *J Wildl. Manage.* 39:653–662.

———. 1976. Effects of intensive silviculture on big game forage sources in northern Idaho. In *Proc. Elk-Logging-Roads Symp., Univ. of Idaho*, pp. 135–142.

Irwin, L. L. and J. M. Peek. 1983. Elk habitat use relative to forest succession in Idaho. *J. Wildl. Manage.* 47:664–672.

Jacobson, H. A., R. L, Kirkpatrick, and B. S. McGinnis. 1978. *Disease and physiologic characteristics of two cottontail populations in Virginia.* Wildl. Monogr. No. 60. 53 pp.

Jameson, D. A. 1963. Responses of individual plants to harvesting. *The Bot. Rev.* 29:532–594.

Jarman, P. J. 1974. The social organization of antelope in relation to their ecology. *Behavior* 48:216–267.

Jenkins, D., A. Watson, and G. R. Miller. 1970. Practical results of research for management of red grouse. *Biol. Cons.* 2:266–272.

Jensen, C. H., A. D. Smith, and G. W. Scotter. 1972. Guidelines for grazing sheep on rangelands used by big game in winter. *J. Range Manage.* 25:346–352.

Jessen, R. L. 1970. Mallard population trends and hunting losses in Minnesota. *J. Wildl. Manage.* 34:93–105.

Johnsgard, P. A. 1960. A quantitative study of sexual behavior of mallards and black ducks. *Wilson Bull.* 72:133–155.

Johnson, D. H. 1980. The comparison of usage and availability measurements for evaluating resource preference. *Ecology* 61:65–71.

Johnson, D. H., and A. B. Sargeant. 1977. *Impact of fox predation on the sex ratio of prairie mallards.* USDI Fish and Wildl. Serv. Wildl. Res. Rept. No. 6. 56 pp.

Johnson, E. F. 1976. Aransas whooping cranes. *Blue Jay* 34:220–228.

Johnson, J. R., and G. F. Payne. 1968. Sagebrush reinvasion as affected by some environmental influences. *J. Range Manage.* 21:209–213.

Johnson, O. W. 1961. Reproductive cycle of the mallard duck. *Condor* 63:351–364.

Johnson, W. M. 1958. Reinvasion of big sagebrush following chemical control. *J. Range Manage.* 11:169–172.

Jonas, R. J. 1966. *Merriam's turkeys in southeastern Montana.* Montana Fish and Game Tech. Bull. No. 3. 36 pp.

Jones, J. K., D. C. Carter, H. H. Genoways, R. S. Hoffmann, and D. W. Rice. 1982. *Revised checklist of North American mammals north of Mexico.* Texas Tech. Univ. Mus. Occ. Pap. No. 80. 22 pp.

Jonkel, C. J., and I. M. Cowan. 1971. *The black bear in a spruce-fir forest.* Wildl. Monogr. No. 27. 57 pp.

Jordan, J. S. 1970. Deer habitat management in eastern forests. *J. For.* 68:692–694.

Jordan, P. A., D. B. Botkin, and M. L. Wolfe. 1971. Biomass dynamics in a moose population. *Ecology* 32:147–152.

Julander, O. 1937. Utilization of browse by wildlife. *Trans. N.A. Wildl. Conf.* 2:276–287.

_____ . 1955. Deer and cattle range relations in Utah. *Forest Sci.* 1 (2): 130–139.

Julander, O., and D. E. Jeffrey. 1964. Deer elk and cattle range relations on summer range in Utah. *Trans. N.A. Wildl. Conf.* 29:404–414.

Kadlec, J. A. 1962. Effects of a drawdown on a waterfowl impoundment. *Ecology* 43:267–281.

Kaiser, P. H., S. S. Berlinger, and L. H. Frederickson. 1979. Response of blue-winged teal to range management on waterfowl production areas in southeastern South Dakota. *J. Range Manage.* 32:295–298.

Kalmbach, E. R., and M. R. Gunderson. 1934. *Western duck sickness a form of botulism.* USDA Tech. Bull. No. 411 82 pp.

Kamps, G. F. 1969. White-tailed and mule deer relationships in the Snowy Mountains of central Montana. Master's thesis, Montana State Univ. 59 pp.

Karns, P. D. 1967. *Pneumostrongylus tenuis* in deer in Minnesota and implications for moose. *J. Wildl. Manage.* 31:299–303.

Keay, J. A., and J. M. Peek. 1980. Relationships between fires and winter habitat of deer in Idaho. *J. Wildl. Manage.* 44:372–380.

Keeler, J. E., chairman. 1977. Mourning dove. In *Management of migrating shore and upland game birds*, ed. G. C. Sanderson, pp. 275–298. Washington, D.C.: Intern. Assn. Fish and Wildl. Agencies. 358 pp.

Keith, L. B. 1961. *A study of waterfowl ecology on small impoundments in south-eastern Alberta.* Wildl. Monogr. No. 6. 88 pp.

_____ . 1963. *Wildlife's ten year cycle.* Madison: Univ. of Wisconsin Press. 201 pp.

Keith, L. B., and D. C. Surrendi. 1971. Effects of fire on a snowshoe hare population. *J. Wildl. Manage.* 35:16–26.

Keith, L. B., and L. A. Windberg. 1978. *A demographic analysis of the snowshoe hare cycle.* Wildl. Monogr. No. 58. 70 pp.

Kellert, S. R. 1976. Perceptions of animals in American society. *Trans. N.A. Wildl. and Nat. Res. Conf.* 41:533–546.

_____ . 1980. Public attitudes toward critical wildlife and natural habitat issues. National Technical Information Service, Accession No. PB-80-138332. 139 pp.

Kelleyhouse, D. G. 1980. Habitat utilization by black bears in northern California. In *Bears—their biology and management,* eds. C. J. Martinka and K. L. McArthur. pp. 221–227. Proc. 4th Intern. Conf. on Bear Res. and Manage. Washington, D.C.: U.S. Govt. Printing Office.

Kelsall, J. P. 1968. *The migratory barren-ground caribou of Canada.* Canad. Wildl. Serv. Monogr. No. 3. Ottawa: Queen Printer. 340 p.

_____ . 1969. Structural adaptations of moose and deer for snow. *J. Mamm.* 50:302–310.

Kelsall, J. P., and D. R. Klein. 1979. The state of knowledge of the Porcupine caribou herd. *Trans. N.A. Wildl. and Nat. Res. Conf.* 44:508–521.

Kelsall, J. P., and W. Prescott. 1971. *Moose and deer behavior in snow.* Canad. Wildl. Serv. Rept. Ser. 15. 27 pp.

Kelsall, J. P., E. S. Telfer, and T. D. Wright. 1977. *The effects of fire on the ecology of the boreal forest, with particular reference to the Canadian north: a review and selected bibliography.* Canad. Wildl. Serv. Occ. Pap. No. 32. 58 pp.

Kennedy, J. J. 1973. Some effects of urbanization on big and small game management. *Trans. N.A. Wildl. and Nat. Res. Conf.* 38:248–255.

Kibbie, D. P., and R. L. Kirkpatrick. 1971. Systematic evaluation of late summer breeding in juvenile cottontails, *Sylvilagus floridanus. J. Mamm.* 52:465–467.

Kilgore, B. M. 1971. Response of breeding bird populations to habitat changes in a giant Sequoia forest. *Am. Midl. Nat.* 85:135–152.

_____ . 1973. The ecological role of fire in Sierran conifer forests. *Quat. Res.* 3:496–513.

Kimball, J. F., Jr., and M. L. Wolfe. 1974. Population analysis of a northern Utah elk herd. *J. Wildl. Manage.* 38:161–174.

Kirkpatrick, C. M., C. M. White, T. W. Hoekstra, F. A. Stormer, and H. P. Weeks, Jr.

1976. *White-tailed deer of U.S. Naval Ammunition Depot Crane.* Purdue Univ. Agr. Expt. Sta. Res. Bull. No. 932. 42 pp.

Kirkpatrick, R. L., and D. M. Baldwin. 1974. Population density and reproduction in penned cottontail rabbits. *J. Wildl. Manage.* 38:482–487.

Kirkpatrick, R. L., J. L. Coggin, H. S. Mosby, and J. O. Newell. 1976. Parturition times and litter sizes of gray squirrels in Virginia. *Proc. Ann. Conf. SE Assn. Fish and Wildl. Agencies* 30:541–545.

Kirsch, L. M. 1969. Waterfowl production in relation to grazing. *J. Wildl. Manage.* 33:821–828.

——. 1974. Habitat management considerations for prairie chickens. *Wildl. Soc. Bull.* 2:124–129.

Kirsch, L. M., and A. D. Kruse. 1973. Prairie fires and wildfire. *Proc. Ann. Tall Timbers Fire Ecol. Conf.* 12:289–303.

Kistchinski, A. A. 1974. The moose of north-east Siberia. *Naturaliste Canadien* 101:179–184.

Klebenow, D. A. 1969. Sage grouse nesting and brood habitat in Idaho. *J. Wildl. Manage.* 33:649–662.

——. 1972. The habitat requirements of sage grouse and the role of fire in management. *Proc. Ann. Tall Timbers Fire Ecol. Conf.* 12:305–315.

Klein, D. R. 1982. Fire, lichens and caribou. *J. Range Manage.* 35:390–395.

Klein, D. R. 1965. Ecology of deer range in Alaska. *Ecol. Monogr.* 35:259–284.

——. 1973. The ethics of hunting and the anti-hunting movement. *Trans. N.A. Wildl. and Nat. Res. Conf.* 38:256–266.

Klein, G. J., D. C. Pearce, and L. W. Gold. 1950. *Method of measuring the significant characteristics of a snow cover.* Natl. Res. Council of Canada Tech. Memo. No. 18. 60 pp.

Klemmedson, J. O., and J. G. Smith. 1964. Cheatgrass. *The Bot. Rev.* 30:226–267.

Kleppe, T. S. 1976. Federal-state coordination in managing wildlife natural resources. *Proc. Ann. Conf. West. Assn. State Game and Fish Comm.* 56:5–11.

Kline, P. D. 1965. Status and management of the white-tailed deer in Iowa, 1954–1962. *Iowa Academy of Science.* 72:207–217.

Klingman, D. L., C. H. Gordon, C. Yip, and H. P. Burchfield. 1966. Residues in the forage and in milk from cows grazing forage treated with esters of 2,4-D. *Weeds* 14:164–167.

Knight, R. R. 1970. *The Sun River elk herd.* Wildl. Monogr. No. 23. 66 pp.

Knight, R. R., and M. R. Mudge. 1967. Characteristics of some natural licks in the Sun River area, Montana. *J. Wildl. Manage.* 31:293–299.

Knowlton, F. F. 1972. Preliminary interpretations of coyote population mechanics with some management implications. *J. Wildl. Manage.* 36:369–382.

——. 1976. Potential influence of coyotes on mule deer populations. In *Mule deer decline in the West—a symposium*, pp. 111–118. Logan: Utah State Univ.

Koehler, G. M., and M. G. Hornocker. 1977. Fire effects on marten habitat in the Selway Bitterroot Wilderness. *J. Wildl. Manage.* 41:500–505.

Koehler, G. M., W. R. Moore, and A. R. Taylor. 1975. Preserving the pine marten: management guidelines for western forests. *Western Wildlands* 2:31–36.

Kohn, B. E., and J. J. Mooty. 1971. Summer habitat of white-tailed deer in north-central Minnesota. *J. Wildl. Manage.* 35:476–487.

Komarek, E. V. 1974. Effects of fire on temperate forests and related ecosystems: southeastern United States. In *Fire and Ecosystems*, ed. T. T. Kozlowski and C. E. Ahlgren, pp. 251–277. New York: Academic Press.

Kozicky, E. L., and R. Metz. 1948. The management of the wild turkey in Pennsylvania. *Pennsylvania Game News* 19:3, 20–21, 26–27, 30–31.

Kramer, A. 1973. Interspecific behavior and dispersion of two sympatric deer species. *J. Wildl. Manage.* 37:288–300.

Krebs, C. J. 1978. Ecology: the experimental analysis of distribution and abundance. New York: Harper & Row. 678 pp.

Krefting, L. W. 1951. What is the future of the Isle Royale moose herd? *Trans. N. Am. Wildl. Conf.* 16:461–472.

_____ . 1962. Use of silvicultural techniques for improving deer habitats in the Lake States. *J. For.* 60:40–42.

_____ . 1975. The effect of white-tailed deer and snowshoe hare browsing on trees and shrubs in northern Minnesota. Univ. Minnesota Agric. Exp. Sta. Tech. Bull. 302-1975. For. Ser. 18. 43 pp.

Krefting, L. W., and C. E. Ahlgren. 1974. Small mammals and vegetation changes after fire in a mixed conifer-hardwood forest. *Ecology* 55:1391–1398.

Krefting, L. W., and H. L. Hansen. 1969. Increasing browse for deer by aerial applications of 2,4-D. *J. Wildl. Manage.* 33 (4): 784–790.

Krefting, L. W., H. L. Hansen, and M. H. Stenlund. 1956. Stimulating regrowth of mountain maple for deer browse by herbicides, cutting and fire. *J. Wildl. Manage.* 20:434–441.

_____ . 1966. Effect of simulated and natural deer browsing on mountain maple. *J. Wildl. Manage.* 30:481–488.

Krefting, L. W., and R. L. Phillips. 1970. Improving deer habitat in Upper Michigan by cutting mixed conifer swamps. *J. For.* 68 (1): 701–704.

Krefting, L. W., and J. H. Stoeckeler. 1953. Effect of simulated snowshoe hare and deer damage on planted conifers in the Lake States. *J. Wildl. Manage.* 17 (4): 487–494.

Krohn, W. B., and E. G. Bizeau. 1980. *The Rocky Mountain population of the western Canada goose: its distribution, habitat, and management.* USDI Fish Wildl. Serv. Spec. Sci. Rept. Wildl. No. 229. 93 pp.

Krueger, W. C., W. A. Laycock, and D. A. Price. 1974. Relationships of taste, smell, sight and touch to forage selection. *J. Range Manage.* 27:258–262.

Krull, J. N. 1970. Response of chipmunks and red squirrels to commercial clearcut logging. *N.Y. Fish and Game J.* 17:58–59.

Kruse, W. H. 1972. *Effects of wildfire on elk and deer use of a Ponderosa pine forest.* Forest Serv. Res. Note No. RM-226. 4 pp.

Kubota, J., S. Rieger, and V. A. Lazar. 1970. Mineral composition of herbage browsed by moose in Alaska. *J. Wildl. Manage.* 34:565–569.

Kuklas, R. W. 1973. Control burn activities in Everglades National Park. *Proc. Ann. Tall Timbers Fire Ecol. Conf.* 12:397–425.

Kunz, T. H., E. L. Anthony, and W. T. Rumage. 1977. Mortality of little brown bats following multiple pesticide applications. *J. Wildl. Manage.* 41:476–483.

Kutches, A. J., D. C. Church, and F. L. Duryee. 1970. Toxicological effects of pesticides on rumen function, *in vitro. J. Agr. and Food Chem.* 18:430–433.

Kuyt, E. 1976. Whooping cranes: the long road back. *Nature Canada* 5:2–9.

Lack, D. 1949. The significance of ecological isolation. In *Genetics, paleontology and evolution,* ed. G. L. Jepson et al., pp. 299–308. Princeton: Prince. Univ. Press.

———. 1953. Darwin's finches. *Sci. Am.* 188 (4): 67–72. Offprint No. 22. 7 pp.

———. 1954. *The natural regulation of animal numbers.* London: Oxford Univ. Press. 343 pp.

———. 1966. *Population studies of birds.* London: Oxford Univ. Press. 341 pp.

Landers, J. L., R. J. Hamilton, A. S. Johnson, and R. L. Marchinton. 1979. Foods and habitat of black bears in southeastern North Carolina. *J. Wildl. Manage.* 43:143–153.

LaPerriere, A. J. 1972. Seasonal precipitation influence on mourning dove breeding populations in Iowa. *J. Wildl. Manage.* 36:979–981.

LaPointe, D. F. 1958. Mourning dove production in a central Nebraska shelterbelt. *J. Wildl. Manage.* 22:439–440.

Larcher, W. 1975. *Physiological plant ecology.* New York: Springer–Verlag. 252 pp.

Larkin, P. A. 1977. An epitaph for the concept of maximum sustained yield. *Trans. Am. Fish. Soc.* 106:1–11.

Lawrence, G. E. 1966. Ecology of vertebrate animals in relation to chaparral fire in the Sierra Nevada foothills. *Ecology* 47:278–291.

Laws, R. M. 1974. Behavior, dynamics, and management of elephant populations. In *The behavior of ungulates and its relation to management,* ed. V. Geist and F. Walther, pp. 513–529. IUCN Publ. n.s. 24. Morges, Switzerland.

Lay, D. W. 1967. Browse palatability and the effects of prescribed burning in southern pine forests. *J. For.* 65:826–828.

Laycock, W. A., and D. A. Price. 1970. Environmental influences on nutritional value of forage plants. In *Range and wildlife habitat evaluation,* ed. H. A. Paulsen, Jr., and E. H. Reid, pp. 37–47. USDA Forest Serv. Misc. Publ. No. 1147.

Leege, T. A. 1968. Prescribed burning for elk in northern Idaho. *Proc. Ann. Tall Timbers Fire Ecol. Conf.* 8:235–253.

———. 1969. Burning seral brush ranges for big game in northern Idaho. *Trans. N.A. Wildl. Conf.* 34:429–438.

———. 1976. Relationships of logging to decline of Pete King elk herd. *Proc. Elk-Logging-Roads Symp., Univ. of Idaho,* pp. 6–10.

———. 1978. The range. *Idaho Wildlife.* 1:5–7.

Leege, T. A., and W. O. Hickey. 1977. *Elk-snow-habitat relationships in the Pete King drainage, Idaho.* Idaho Fish and Game Dept. Wildl. Bull. No. 6. 23 pp.

Leopold, A. 1930. Report to the American game conference on an American game policy. *17th Am. Game Conf. Trans.*, pp. 284–309.

——. 1933. *Game management.* New York: Scribner's. 481 pp.

——. 1936. Deer and dauerwald in Germany. *J. For.* 34:366–375, 460–466.

——. 1941. Wilderness as a land laboratory. *The Living Wilderness* 6(6): 3.

——. 1945. Sex and age ratios among bobwhite quail in southern Missouri. *J. Wild. Manage.* 9:30–34.

——. 1949. *A Sand County almanac and sketches here and there.* New York: Oxford Univ. Press. 226 pp.

Leopold, A., L. K. Sowls, and D. L. Spencer. 1947. A survey of overpopulated deer ranges in the United States. *J. Wildl. Manage.* 11:162–177.

Leopold, A. S. 1964. Predator and rodent control in the United States. *Trans. N.A. Wildl. and Nat. Res. Conf.* 29:27–49.

——. 1976. Phytoestrogens: adverse effects on reproduction in California quail. *Science* 191:98–100.

Leopold, A. S., C. Cottam, I. M. Cowan, I. N. Gabrielson, and T. J. Kimball. 1968. The National Wildlife Refuge System. *Trans. N.A. Wildl. Conf.* 33:30–54.

Leopold, A. S., T. Riney, R. McCain, and L. Tevis, Jr. 1951. *The jawbone deerherd.* Calif. Div. Fish and Game. Game Bull. No. 4. 139 pp.

LeResche, R. E. 1968. Spring-fall calf mortality in an Alaskan moose population. *J. Wildl. Manage.* 32 (4): 953–956.

——. 1974. *Hunters, anti-hunters and land managers: a time for unity.* Anchorage: Alaska Dept. of Fish and Game. 8 pp.

LeResche, R. E., and J. L. Davis. 1973. Importance of nonbrowse foods to moose on the Kenai Peninsula, Alaska. *J. Wildl. Manage.* 37:279–287.

LeResche, R. E., R. H. Bishop, and J. W. Coady. 1974. Distribution and habitats of moose in Alaska. *Naturaliste Canadien* 101:143–178.

LeResche, R. E., and R. A. Rausch. 1974. Accuracy and precision of aerial moose censusing. *J. Wildl. Manage.* 38:175–182.

Leroy, D. H., and R. L. Eiguren. 1980. State takeover of federal lands—"the sagebrush rebellion." *Rangelands* 2:229–231.

Leslie, D., E. Starkey, and M. Vavra. 1984. Elk and deer diets in old-growth forests of western Washington. *J. Wildl. Manage.* 48:142–145.

Lewis, J. B. 1967. Management of the eastern turkey in the Ozarks and bottomland hardwoods. In *The wild turkey and its management*, ed. O. H. Hewitt, pp. 371–407. Washington, D.C.: The Wildlife Society. 589 pp.

Lewis, J. B., and R. P. Breitenbach. 1966. Breeding potential of subadult wild turkey gobblers. *J. Wildl. Manage.* 30:618–622.

Lincoln, F. C. 1935. *The waterfowl flyways of North America.* USDA Cir. No. 342. 12 pp.

Linduska, J. P., ed. 1964. *Waterfowl tomorrow.* Washington, D.C.: U.S. Govt. Printing Office. 770 pp.

Lindzey, F. G. 1976. Black bear population ecology. Ph.D. dissertation, Oregon State Univ. 105 pp.

Lindzey, F. G., and E. C. Meslow. 1977. Population characteristics of black bears on an island in Washington. *J. Wildl. Manage.* 41:408–412.

Linhart, S. B., H. H. Brusman, and D. S. Balser. 1968. Field evaluation of an anti-fertilty agent, stilbestrol, for inhibiting coyote reproduction. *Trans. N.A. Wildl. and Nat. Res. Conf.* 33:316–327.

Linn, J. E., and R. L. Stanley. 1965. TDE residues in Clear Lake animals. *Calif. Fish and Game* 55:164–178.

Lobdell, C. H., K. E. Case, and H. S. Mosby. 1972. Evaluation of harvest strategies for a simulated wild turkey population. *J. Wildl. Manage.* 36:493–497.

Locke, L. N., C. M. Herman, and E. S. King, Jr. 1960. The need for differentiation of trichomoniasis and pox infection in doves. *J. Wildl. Manage.* 24:348.

Longhurst, W. M., H. K. Oh, M. B. Jones, and R. E. Kepner. 1968. A basis for the palatability of deer forage plants. *Trans. N.A. Wildl. and Nat. Res. Conf.* 33:181–192.

Lord, R. D., Jr. 1961. Mortality rates of cottontail rabbits. *J. Wildl. Manage.* 25:33–40.

———. 1963. *The cottontail rabbit in Illinois*. Illinois Dept. Cons. Tech. Bull. No. 3. 94 pp.

Lorenz, K. Z. 1937. The companion in the birds' world. *Auk* 54 (3): 245–273.

Lowe, V. P. W. 1961. A discussion on the history, present status, and future con-servation of red deer *(Cervus elaphus L.)* in Scotland. *La Terre et la Vie* 1–1961:9–40.

———. 1969. Population dynamics of the red deer *(Cervus elaphus L.)* on Rhum. *J. Anim. Ecol.* 38:425–457.

Lykke, J. 1974. Moose management in Norway and Sweden. *Naturaliste Canadien* 101:723–735.

Lyon, L. J. 1971. *Vegetal development following prescribed burning of Douglas-fir in south-central Idaho*. USDA Forest Serv. Res. Pap. No. INT-105. 30 pp.

———. 1976. Elk use as related to characteristics of clearcuts in western Montana. *Proc. Elk-Logging-Roads Symp., Univ. Idaho.* pp. 69–72.

———. 1979. *Influences of logging and weather on elk distribution in western Montana*. USDA Forest Serv. Res. Pap. No. INT-236. 11 pp.

Lyon, L. J., H. S. Crawford, E. Czuhai, K. L. Fredericksen, R. R. Harlow, L. J. Metz, and H. A. Pearson. 1978. *Effects of fire on fauna*. USDA Forest Serv. Gen. Tech. Rept. No. WO-6. 22 pp.

Lyon, L. J., and C. E. Jensen. 1980. Management implications of elk and deer use of clearcuts in Montana. *J. Wildl. Manage.* 44:352–362.

MacArthur, R. H. 1958. Population ecology of some warblers of northeastern coniferous forests. *Ecology* 39:599–619.

———. 1972. Geographical ecology: patterns in the distribution of species. New York: Harper & Row. 269 pp.

MacArthur, R. H., and R. Levins. 1964. Competition, habitat selection and charac-ter displacement in a patchy environment. *Proc. Nat. Acad. Sci. USA* 51:1207–1210.

——. 1967. The limiting similarity, convergence, and divergence of coexisting species. *Amer. Nat.* 101:377–385.

MacArthur, R. H., and J. W. MacArthur. 1961. On bird species diversity. *Ecology* 42:594–599.

MacArthur, R. H., and E. R. Pianka. 1966. On optimal use of patchy environment. *Amer. Nat.* 100:603–609.

McAtee, W. L. 1918. *Food habits of the mallard ducks of the United States.* USDA Bull. No. 720. 36 pp.

McCabe, R. A. 1943. Population trends in Wisconsin cottontails. *J. Mamm.* 24:18–22.

McCabe, R. A., and E. L. Kozicky. 1972. A position on predator management. *J. Wildl. Manage.* 36:382–394.

McCaffrey, K. R., and W. A. Creed. 1969. *Significance of forest openings to deer in northern Wisconsin.* Wisconsin Dept. Nat. Res. Tech. Bull. No. 44. 104 pp.

McCall, R., R. T. Clark, and A. R. Patton. 1943. *The apparent digestibility and nutritive value of several native and introduced grasses.* Montana Agr. Expt. Sta. Techn. Bull. No. 418. 30 pp.

McClelland, B. R., S. S. Frissell, W. C. Fischer, and C. H. Halvorson. 1979. Habitat management for holenesting birds in forests of western larch and Douglas-fir. *J. For.* 77:480–483.

McClure, H. E. 1943. Ecology and management of the mourning dove, *Zenaidura macroura* (Linn.) in Cass County, Iowa. *Iowa Agr. Expt. Sta. Res. Bull.* 310:356–415.

McDowell, R. D. 1956. *Productivity of the wild turkey in Virginia.* Virginia Comm. Game and Inland Fish. Tech. Bull. No. 1. Richmond. 44 pp.

McEwen, L. C., and D. R. Dietz. 1965. Shade effects on chemical composition of herbage in the Black Hills. *J. Range Manage.* 18 (4): 184–190.

McGilvrey, F. B., compiler. 1968. *A guide to wood duck production habitat requirements.* USDI Fish and Wildl. Serv. Res. Publ. No. 60. 32 pp.

McGowan, J. D. 1975. Effect of autumn and spring hunting on ptarmigan population trends. *J. Wildl. Manage.* 39:491–495.

McIlroy, C. W. 1972. Effects of hunting on black bears in Prince William Sound. *J. Wildl. Manage.* 36:828–837.

McIvain, E. H., and D. A. Savage. 1949. Spraying 2,4-D by airplane on sand sagebrush and other plants of the other southern Great Plains. *J. Range Manage.* 2:43–52.

Mackay, R. N. 1981. The trumpeter swam—an endangered species in Canada. In *Proc. and Pap. of the 6th Trumpeter Swan Society Conf., Maple Plains, Minn.,* ed. D. K. Weaver, pp. 22–23.

Mackie, R. J. 1970. *Range ecology and relations of mule deer, elk and cattle in the Missouri River Breaks, Montana.* Wildl. Monogr. No. 20. 79 pp.

——. 1973. What we've learned about our most popular game animal. *Montana Outdoors* (Sept.–Oct.), pp. 15–21.

McLay, C. L. 1974. The species diversity of New Zealand birds: some possible consequences of modification of beech forests. *N.Z. Zool.* 1:179–196.

McLean, A., and E. W. Tisdale. 1972. Recovery rate of depleted range sites under protection from grazing. *J. Range Manage.* 25:178–184.

McMahan, C. A. 1964. Comparative food habits of deer and three classes of livestock. *J. Wildl. Manage.* 28:798–808.

Maguire, H. F., and C. W. Severinghaus. 1954. Wariness as an influence on age composition of white-tailed deer killed by hunters. *N.Y. Fish and Game J.* 1:98–109.

Mahoney, J. J., Jr. 1975. DDT and DDE effects on migratory condition in white-throated sparrows. *J. Wildl. Manage.* 39:520–527.

Marcum, C. L. 1976. Habitat selection and use during summer and fall months by a western Montana elk herd. *Proc. Elk-Logging-Roads Symp., Univ. of Idaho,* pp. 91–96.

Marion, W. R., T. E. O'Meara, and L. D. Harris. 1981. Characteristics of the mourning dove harvest in Florida. *J. Wildl. Manage.* 45:1062–1066.

Markgren, G. 1969. Reproduction of moose in Sweden. *Viltrevy* 6:129–299.

_____ . 1974. The moose in Fennoscandia. *Naturliste Canadien* 101:185–194.

_____ . 1975. Winter studies on orphaned moose calves in Sweden. *Vitrevy* 9:193–219.

Markley, M. H. 1967. Limiting factors. In *The wild turkey and its management,* ed. O. H. Hewitt, pp. 199–243. Washington, D.C.: The Wildlife Society, 589 pp.

Marsden, H. M., and T. S. Baskett, 1958. Annual mortality in a banded bobwhite population. *J. Wildl. Manage.* 22:414–419.

Marshall, W. H. 1946. Cover preferences, seasonal movements and food habits of Richardson's grouse and ruffed grouse in Idaho. *Wilson Bull.* 58:42–50.

Marshall, W. H., T. S. Shantz-Hansen, and K. E. Winsness. 1955. Effects of simulated overbrowsing on small red and white pine trees. *J. For.* 53:420–424.

Martin, A. C., H. S. Zim, and A. L. Nelson. 1951. American wildlife and plants: a guide to wildlife food habits. New York: Dover. 499 pp.

Martin, F. R., and L. W. Krefting. 1953. The Necedah Refuge deer irruption. *J. Wildl. Manage.* 17:166–176.

Martin, N. S. 1970. Sagebrush control related to habitat and sage grouse occurrence. *J. Wildl. Manage.* 34:313–320.

Martin, R. E., D. D. Robinson, and W. H. Schaeffer. 1976. Fire in the Pacific Northwest—perspectives and problems. *Proc. Ann. Tall Timbers Fire Ecol. Conf.* 15:1–24.

Martinka, C. J. 1968. Habitat relationships of white-tailed and mule deer in northern Montana. *J. Wildl. Manage.* 32:558–565.

_____ . 1972. *Habitat relationships of grizzly bears in Glacier National Park, Montana.* USDI Natl. Park Serv. Prog. Rept. 19 pp.

Martinson, R. K. 1966. Proportion of recovered duck bands that are reported. *J. Wildl. Manage.* 30:264–268.

Martinson, R. K., and C. J. Henry. 1967. *Retention of extra-wide, lock-on, and regular bands on waterfowl.* USDI Fish and Wildl. Serv. Spec. Sci. Rept. Wildl. No. 108. 19 pp.

Martinson, R. K., J. W. Holten, and G. K. Brakhage. 1961. Age criteria and population dynamics of the swamp rabbit in Missouri. *J. Wildl. Manage.* 25:271–281.

Martinson, R. K., and C. F. Kaczynski. 1967. Factors influencing waterfowl counts on aerial surveys. U.S. Fish and Wildl. Source, Spec. Sci. Rept. Wildl. No. 105. 78 pp.

May, R. M. 1973. Time-delay versus stability in population models with two and three trophic levels. *Ecology* 54:315–325.

Maykut, G. 1969. The properties of deposited snow. In *Oregon State Univ. Water Resources Research Institute Seminar, Corvallis*, pp. 7–26.

Meagher, M. 1973. *The bison of Yellowstone National Park*. Natl. Park Serv. Sci. Monogr. Ser. No. 1. 161 pp.

——. 1977. *Evaluation of bear management in Yellowstone National Park, 1976*. USDI Natl. Park Serv., Yellowstone Natl. Park Res. Note No. 7. 11 pp.

Mech, L. D. 1966. *The wolves of Isle Royale*. USDI Natl. Park Serv. Fauna Ser. No. 7. 210 pp.

——. 1970. *The wolf: ecology and management of an endangered species*. New York: The Nat. Hist. Press. 384 pp.

——. 1973. *Wolf numbers in the Superior National Forest of Minnesota*. USDA Forest Serv. Res. Pap. No. NC-97. 10 pp.

——. 1977. Productivity, mortality and population trends of wolves in northeastern Minnesota. *J. Mamm.* 58 (4): 559–574.

Mech, L. D., and L. D. Frenzel, Jr., eds. 1971. *Ecological studies of the timber wolf in northeastern Minnesota*. USDA Forest Serv. Res. Pap. No. NC-52. 62 pp.

Mech, L. D., L. D. Frenzel, Jr., and P. D. Karns. 1971. The effect of snow conditions on the vulnerability of white-tailed deer to wolf predation. In *Ecological studies of the timber wolf in northeastern Minnesota*, ed. L. D. Mech and L. D. Frenzel, Jr. pp. 51–59. USDA Forest Serv. Pap. No. NC-52.

Mech, L. D., and P. D. Karns. 1977. *Role of the wolf in a deer decline in the Superior National Forest*. USDA Forest Serv. Res. Pap. No. NC-148. 23 pp.

Mercer, W. E., and F. Manuel. 1974. Some aspects of moose management in Newfoundland. *Naturaliste Canadien* 101:657–671.

Merrill, E. H., H. F. Mayland, and J. M. Peek. 1982. Shrub responses after fire in an Idaho ponderosa pine community. *J. Wildl. Manage.* 46:496–502.

Meslow, E. C., and H. M. Wight. 1975. Avifauna and succession in Douglas-fir forests of the Pacific Northwest. In *Proc. Symp. on Manage. of Forest and Range Habitats for Nongame Birds*, pp. 266–271. USDA Forest Serv. Gen. Tech. Rept. No. WO-1.

Mickelson, P. G. 1975. *Breeding biology of cackling geese and associated species on the Yukon-Kuskokwim Delta, Alaska*. Wildl. Mongr. No. 45. 35 pp.

Miller, D. R. 1975. Observations on wolf predation on barren ground caribou in winter. In *Proc. 1st Intern. Reindeer and Caribou Symp. Biol. Pap. Univ. of Alaska, Fairbanks, Spec. Rept. No. 1*, pp. 209–220.

——. 1976. *Biology of the Kaminuriak barren ground caribou. Part 3*. Canad. Wildl. Serv. Rept. Ser. No. 36. 41 pp.

Miller, F. L., and F. Broughton. 1974. *Calf mortality on the calving ground of Kaminuriak caribou.* Canad. Wildl. Serv. Rept. Ser. No. 26. 26 pp.

Miller, G. R. 1968. Evidence for selective feeding on fertilized plots by red grouse, hares, and rabbits. *J. Wildl. Manage.* 32:849–853.

Miller, M. 1977. *Response of blue huckleberry to prescribed burns in a western Montana larch-fir forest.* USDA Forest Serv. Res. Pap. No. INT-188. 33 pp.

Mitchell, G. J., and R. H. G. Cormack. 1960. An evaluation of big game winter range in southwestern Alberta. *J. Range Manage.* 13 (5): 235–239.

Moen, A. N. 1968. Thermal energy exchange of a birch tree and a spruce tree at night. *Ecology* 49:145–147.

_____ . 1973. *Wildlife ecology.* San Francisco: W. H. Freeman and Company. 458 pp.

Mohlberg, J. M. 1960. Cautions on use of herbicides. *J. For.* 58:124.

Montgomery, M. L., and L. A. Norris. 1970. *A preliminary evaluation of the hazards of 2,4,5-T in the forest environment.* USDA Forest Serv. Res. Note No. PNW-116. 11 p.

Montgomery, S. D., J. B. Whelan, and H. S. Mosby. 1975. Bioenergetics of a woodlot gray squirrel population. *J. Wildl. Manage.* 39:709–717.

Morris, R. F. 1959. Single factor analysis in population dynamics. *Ecology* 40:580–588.

Morton, H. L., E. D. Robison, and R. E. Meyek. 1967. Persistence of 2,4-D and 2,4,5-T and dicamba in range forage grasses. *Weeds* 15:268–271.

Mosby, H. S. 1949. The present status and the future outlook of the eastern and Florida wild turkeys. *Trans. N.A. Wildl. Conf.* 14:346–358.

_____ . 1967. Population dynamics. In *The wild turkey and its management*, ed. O. H. Hewitt, pp. 113–136. Washington, D.C.: The Wildlife Society, 589 pp.

_____ . 1969. The influence of hunting on the population dynamics of a woodlot gray squirrel population. *J. Wildl. Manage.* 33:59–73.

Mosby, H. S., and C. O. Handley. 1943. *The wild turkey in Virginia.* Richmond: Virginia Comm. Game and Inland Fisheries. 281 pp.

Mosby, H. S., R. L. Kirkpatrick, and J. O. Newell. 1977. Seasonal vulnerability of gray squirrels to hunting. *J. Wildl. Manage.* 41:284–289.

Moss, R. 1967. Probable limiting nutrients in the main food of red grouse. In *Secondary productivity of terrestrial ecosystems*, ed. K. Petrusewicz, pp. 369–379. Warsaw: Polish Academy of Sciences. 879 pp.

Moss, R., A. Gardarsson, G. Olafson, and D. Brown. 1974. The *in vitro* digestibility of ptarmigan (*Lagopus mutus*) foods in relation to their chemical composition. *Ornis. Scandinavica* 5:5–11.

Moss, R., G. R. Miller, and S. E. Allen. 1972. Selection of heather by captive red grouse in relation to the age of the plant. *J. Appl. Ecol.* 9:771–781.

Moss, R., and J. A. Parkinson. 1972. The digestive of heather (*Calluna vulgaris*) by red grouse (*Lagopus lagopus scoticus*). *Brit. J. Nutr.* 27:285–298.

*Mourning dove investigations 1948-1957.* 1959. Southeastern Assn. of Game and Fish Comm. Tech. Bull. No. 1. 166 pp.

Mrak, E. M., chairman. 1969. *Report of the Secretary's Commission on Pesticides and their relationship to environmental health. Parts I and II.* U.S. Dept. HEW. 677 pp.

Mueggler, W. F. 1965a. Ecology of seral shrub communities in the cedar-hemlock zone of northern Idaho. *Ecol. Monogr.* 35: 165–185.

_____. 1965b. Cattle distribution on steep slopes. *J. Range Manage.* 18:255–257.

_____. 1966. Herbicide treatment of browse on a big game winter range in northern Idaho. *J. Wildl. Manage.* 30 (1): 141–151.

_____. 1970. *Influence of competition on the response of Idaho fescue to clipping.* USDA Forest Serv. Res. Pap. No. INT-73. 10 pp.

_____. 1975. Rate and pattern of vigor recovery in Idaho fescue and bluebunch wheatgrass. *J. Range Mange.* 28:198–204.

Mueggler, W. F., and J. P. Blaisdell. 1958. Effects on associated species of burning, rotobeating, spraying and railing sagebrush. *J. Range Manage.* 11:61–66.

Mueller-Dombois, D., and H. Ellenberg. 1974. *Aims and methods of vegetation ecology.* New York: John Wiley. 547 pgs.

Mullins, W. H., E. G. Bizeau, and W. W. Benson. 1977. Effects of phenyl mercury on captive game farm pheasants. *J. Wildl. Manage.* 41:302–308.

Mundinger, J. G. 1981. White-tailed deer reproductive biology in the Swan Valley, Montana. *J. Wildl. Manage.* 45:132–139.

Murie, A. 1948. Cattle on grizzly bear range. *J. Wildl. Manage.* 12:5772.

Murphy, D. A., and J. H. Ehrenreich. 1965. Effects of timber harvest and stand improvement on forage production. *J. Wildl. Manage.* 29:734–739.

Mussehl, T. W. 1963. Bluegrouse brood cover selection and land-use implications. *J. Wildl. Manage.* 27:547–555.

Mutch, R. W. 1970. Wildland fires and ecosystems—a hypothesis. *Ecology* 51:1046–1051.

*My Weekly Reader Eye.* 1975. Is the dangerous grizzly bear in danger? Edition 5, Vol 54 (2):9–10. Middle Lawn, Conn.: Xerox Corporation.

Nagel, W. O. 1956. Predators are like people. *Missouri Conservationist* 17:13.

Nagy, J. G., H. G. Steinhoff, and G. M. Ward. 1964. Effects of essential oils of sagebrush on deer rumen microbial function. *J. Wildl. Manage.* 28:785–790.

Nasimovich, A. A. 1955. The role of the regime of snow cover in the life of ungulates in the USSR. Translation from Russian by Canadian Wildlife Service, Ottawa, Canada. 371 pp. typed.

Nass, R. D. 1977. Mortality associated with sheep operations in Idaho. *J. Range Manage.* 30:253–258.

Negherbon, W. O. 1959. Handbook of Toxicology. Vol. 3., Insecticides. W. B. Saunders, Philadelphia. 854 pp.

Neils, G., L. Adams, and R. M. Blair. 1955. Management of white-tailed deer in ponderosa pine. *Trans. N.A. Wild. Conf.* 20:539–551.

Nellis, C. H., and R. L. Ross. 1969. Changes in mule deer food habits associated with herd reduction. *J. Wildl. Manage.* 33:191–195.

Nellis, C. H., S. P. Wetmore, and L. B. Keith. 1972. Lynx-prey interactions in central Alberta. *J. Wildl. Manage.* 36:320–329.

Nelson, B. 1969. Herbicides: order on 2,4,5-T issued at unusually high level. *Science* 166:977-979.

Nelson, D. J. 1957. Some aspects of dove hunting in Georgia. *J. Wildl. Manage.* 21:58-61.

Newton, M. 1972. Forest management for minimum conflict. In *Symposium on Wildlife and Forest Management*, pp. 233-236. Corvallis: Oregon State Univ.

Nicholas, D. 1979. Views of the National Indian Brotherhood of Canada. *Trans. N.A. Wildl. and Nat. Res. Conf.*, 44:601-603.

Nicklaus, R. H. 1976. Effects of lead and steel shot on shooting of flighted mallards. *Wildl. Monogr.* 51:22-29.

Nixon, C. M., and M. W. McClain. 1969. Squirrel population decline following a spring frost. *J. Wildl. Manage.* 33:353-357.

Nixon, C. M., R. W. Donohoe, and T. Nash. 1974. Overharvest of fox squirrels from two woodlots in western Ohio. *J. Wildl. Manage.* 38:67-80.

Norris, L. A., and D. G. Moore. 1971. The entry and fate of forest chemicals in streams. In *Symposium on forest land uses and stream environment*, pp. 138-158. Corvallis: Oregon State Univ.

Novak, M., and J. Gardner. 1975. Accuracy of moose aerial surveys. in *Proc. 11th N.A. Moose Conf. and Workshop*, pp. 154-180.

O'Gara, B. W. 1982. Let's tell the truth about predation. *Trans. N.A. Wildl. and Nat. Res. Conf.* 47:476-484.

Ohmann, L. F., and D. F. Grigal. 1979. Early revegetation and nutrient dynamics following the 1971 Little Sioux forest fire in northeastern Minnesota. *For. Sci. Monogr.* 21:80 pp.

Oldemeyer, J. L., A. W. Franzmann, A. L. Brundage, P. D. Arneson, and A. Flynn. 1977. Browse quality and the Kenai moose population. *J. Wildl. Manage.* 41:533-542.

Oleyar, C. M., and B. S. McGinnes. 1974. Field evaluation of diethystilbestrol for suppressing reproduction in foxes. *J. Wildl. Manage.* 38:101-106.

O'Roke, E. C., and F. N. Hamerstrom, Jr. 1948. Productivity and yield of the George Reserve deer herd. *J. Wildl. Manage.* 12:78-86.

Owens, T. 1982. Post burn regrowth of shrubs related to canopy mortality. *NW Sci.* 56:34-40.

Owen-Smith, N., and P. Novellie. 1982. What should a clever ungulate eat? *Amer. Nat.* 19:151-177.

Ozoga, J. J. 1968. Variations in microclimate in a conifer swamp deeryard in northern Michigan. *J. Wildl. Manage.* 32:574-585.

Palmer, W. L., and C. L. Bennett, Jr. 1963. Relation of season length to hunting harvest of ruffed grouse. *J. Wildl. Manage.* 27:634-639.

Parmalee, P. W. 1953. Hunting pressure and its effect on bobwhite quail populations in east-central Texas. *J. Wildl. Manage.* 17:341-345.

Partridge, L. 1978. Habitat selection. In *Behavioral ecology*, ed. J. R. Krebs and N. B. Davies, pp. 351-376. Sunderland, Mass.: Sinauer Associates.

Patton, D. R. 1969. *Deer and elk use of a ponderosa pine forest in Arizona before and after timber harvest.* USDA Forest Serv. Res. Note No. RM-139. 7 pp.

_____ . 1974. Patch cutting increases deer and elk use of a pine forest in Arizona. *J. For.* 72:764–766.

_____ . 1976. *Timber harvesting increases deer and elk use of a mixed conifer forest.* USDA Forest Serv. Res. Note No. RM-329. 3 pp.

Payne, N. F. 1964. The influence of hunting on rabbit populations in southeastern Virginia. Master's thesis, Virginia Polytechnic Institute, Blacksburg. 51 pp.

Pearson, A. M. 1975. *The northern interior grizzly bear,* Ursus arctos. Canad. Wildl. Serv. Rept. Ser. No. 34. 86 pp.

Pearson, H. A., J. R. Davis, and G. H. Schubert. 1972. Effects of wildfire on timber and forage production in Arizona. *J. Range Manage.* 25:250–253.

Pechanec, J. R., A. P. Plummer, J. H. Robertson, and A. C. Hull, Jr. 1965. *Sagebrush control on rangelands.* USDA Agr. Handbook No. 277. 40 pp.

Peek, J. M. 1962. Studies of moose in the Gravelly and Snowcrest Mountains, Montana. *J. Wildl. Manage.* 26:360–365.

_____ . 1966. Comparison of two mid-winter elk hunting seasons, Upper Gallatin drainage Montana. *Proc. Ann. Conf. West. Assn. State Game and Fish Comm.* 46:87–95.

_____ . 1967. *Gallatin big game studies.* Montana Fish and Game Dept. Job Compl. Rept. No. W-73-R-12. A1.1. 25 pp.

_____ . 1971. Moose-snow relationships in northeastern Minnesota. In *Proc. Snow and Ice in Relation to Wildl. and Recreation Symp.*, pp. 39–49. Ames: Iowa State Univ.

_____ . 1974a. Initial response of moose to a forest fire in northeastern Minnesota. *Am. Midl. Nat.* 91 (2): 435–438.

_____ . 1974b. On the nature of winter habits of Shiras moose. *Naturaliste Canadien* 101:131–141.

Peek, J. M., F. D. Johnson, and N. N. Pence. 1978. Successional trends in a ponderosa pine–bitterbrush community related to grazing by livestock, wildlife, and to fire. *J. Range Manage.* 31:49–53.

Peek, J. M., and A. L. Lovaas. 1968. Differential distribution of elk by sex and age on the Gallatin winter range, Montana. *J. Wildl. Manage.* 32 (3): 553–557.

Peek, J. M., A. L. Lovaas, and R. A. Rouse. 1967. Population changes within the Gallatin elk herd, 1932–1965. *J. Wildl. Manage.* 31:304–316.

Peek, J. M., R. A. Riggs, and J. L. Lauer. 1979. Evaluation of fall burning on bighorn sheep winter range. *J. Range Manage.* 32 (6): 430–432.

Peek, J. M., D. L. Urich, and R. J. Mackie. 1976. *Moose habitat selection and relationships to forest management in northeastern Minnesota.* Wildl. Monogr. No. 48. 65 pp.

Pelton, M. R., L. E. Beeman, and D. C. Eagar. 1980. Deer selection by black bears in the Smoky Mountains. In *Bears—their biology and management,* ed. C. J. Martinka and K. L. McArthur, pp. 149–151. Proc. 4th Intern. Conf. on Bear Res. and Manage. Washington, D.C.: U.S. Govt. Printing Office. 375 pp.

Pengelly, W. L. 1963. Timberlands and deer in the northern Rockies. *J. For.* 61: 734–746.

——. 1972. Clearcutting: detrimental aspects for wildlife resources. *J. Soil and Water Cons.* 27:255–258.

Penney, J. G., and E. D. Bailey. 1970. Comparison of the energy requirements of fledgling black ducks and American coots. *J. Wildl. Manage.* 34:105–114.

Perkins, C. J. 1968. Controlled burning in the management of muskrats and waterfowl in Louisiana coastal marshes. *Proc. Ann. Tall Timbers Fire Ecol. Conf.* 8: 269–280.

Perry, C., and R. Overly. 1976. Impact of roads on big game distribution in portions of the Blue Mountains of Washington. *Proc. Elk-Logging-Roads Symp., Univ. of Idaho*, pp. 62–68.

Peters, R. P., and L. D. Mech. 1975. Scent marking in wolves. *Am. Sci.* 63:628–637.

Peterson, J. G. 1970. The food habits and summer distribution of juvenile sage grouse in central Montana. *J. Wildl. Manage.* 34 (1): 147–154.

Peterson, R. L. 1955. *North American moose*. Toronto: Univ. of Toronto Press, 280 pp.

Peterson, R. O., and D. L. Allen. 1974. Snow conditions as a parameter in moose-wolf relationships. *Naturaliste Canadien* 101:481–492.

Peterson, S. R., and J. B. Low. 1977. Waterfowl use of Uinta Mountains wetlands in Utah. *J. Wildl. Manage.* 41:112–117.

Pianka, E. R. 1976. Competition and niche theory. In *Theoretical ecology: principles and applications*, ed. R. M. May, pp. 114–141. Philadelphia: Saunders.

Picton, H. D. 1961. Differential hunter harvest of elk in two Montana herds. *J. Wildl. Manage.* 25:415–421.

Picton, H. D., and R. R. Knight. 1971. A numerical index of winter conditions of use in big game management. In *Proc. Snow and Ice in Relation to Wildl. and Recreation Symp.*, pp. 29–36. Ames: Iowa State Univ.

Pimental, D. 1971. *Ecological effects of pesticides on non-target species*. Executive Office of the President, Office of Sci. and Tech. 220 pp.

Pimlott, D. H. 1953. Newfoundland moose. *Trans. N.A. Wildl. Conf.* 17:563–581.

——. 1959a. Reproduction and productivity of Newfoundland moose. *J. Wildl. Manage.* 23:381–401.

——. 1959b. Moose harvests in Newfoundland and Fennoscandian countries. *Trans. N.A. Wildl. Conf.* 24:422–448.

——. 1961. The ecology and management of moose in North America. *La Terre et la Vie* 2-1961:246–265.

——. 1963. Influence of deer and moose on boreal forest vegetation in two areas of eastern Canada. In *Trans. 4th Congress Intl. Union of Game Biologists*, pp. 105–116.

——. 1967. Wolf predation and ungulate populations. *Am Zool.* 7:267–278.

Pirnie, M. D. 1949. A test of hunting as cottontail control. *Mich. Agr. Expt. Sta. Quart. Bull.* 31:304–308.

Plummer, J. T. 1971. *Lifestyle characteristics of the hunter.* Albuquerque, N. Mex.: Am. Assn. for Cons. Infor. Feb. 22, 1971. 10 pp.

Poelker, R. J. , and H. D. Hartwell. 1973. *Black bear of Washington.* Washington State Game Dept. Biol. Bull. No. 14. 180 pp.

Poole, R. W. 1974. *An introduction to quantitative ecology.* New York: McGraw-Hill. 532 pp.

Popovich, L. 1975. The Bitterroot—remembrances of things past. *J. For.* 73:791–793.

Posados-Andrews, C., and T. J. Roper. 1983. Social transmission of food preferences in adult rats. *Anim. Behav.* 31:265–271.

Potter, D. R., J. C. Hendee, and R. H. Clark. 1973. Hunting satisfaction: game, guns or nature? *Trans. N.A. Wildl. and Nat. Res. Conf.* 38:220–229.

Prevett, J. P., and C. D. MacInnis. 1980. *Family and other social groups of snow geese.* Wildl. Monogr. No. 71. 46 pp.

Prothero, W. L., J. J. Spillett, and D. F. Balph. 1979. Rutting behavior of yearling and mature bull elk: some implications for open bull hunting. In *North American elk: ecology, behavior and management*, eds. M. S. Boyce and L. D. Hayden-Wing, pp. 160–165. Laramie: Univ. of Wyoming. 294 pp.

Pruitt, W. O., Jr. 1958. Qali, a taiga snow formation of ecological importance. *Ecology* 39:169–172.

—— . 1959. Snow as a factor in the winter ecology of the barren ground caribou. *Arctic* 12:159–179.

—— . 1960. Animals in the snow. *Sci. Am.* 202 (1): 60–68.

Pulliam, J. R. 1974. On the theory of optimal diets. *Amer. Nat.* 108 (959): 59–74.

Pyke, G. H., H. R. Pulliam, and E. L. Charnov. 1977. Optimal foraging: a selective review of theory and tests. *Quart. Rev. Biol.* 52:137–154.

Quick, H. F. 1958. Estimating the effects of exploitation with lifetables. *Trans. N.A. Wildl. Conf.* 23:241–442.

Quimby, D. C. 1966. A review of literature relating to the effects and possible effects of sagebrush control on certain game species in Montana. *Proc. Ann. Conf. West. Assn. State Game and Fish Comm.* 46:142–149.

Quirk, W. A., and D. J. Sykes. 1971. White spruce stringers in a fire-patterned landscape in interior Alaska. In *Proc. Symp. Fire in the Northern Environment*, pp. 179–198. Portland: USDA Forest Serv. Pac. NW Forest and Range Expt. Sta.

Radwan, M. A. 1969. Chemical composition of the sapwood of four tree species in relation to feeding by the black bear. *Forest Sci.* 15:11–16.

Radwan, M. A., and W. D. Ellis. 1975. Clonal variation in monoterpene hydrocarbons of vapors of Douglas fir foliage. *Forest Sci.* 21:63–67.

Ransom, A. B. 1967. Reproductive biology of white-tailed deer in Manitoba. *J. Wildl. Manage.* 31:114–123.

Rasmussen, D. I. 1941. Biotic communities of Kaibab Plateau, Arizona. *Ecol. Monogr.* 3:229–275.

Ratliff, R. D., and J. N. Reppert. 1974. Vigor of Idaho fescue grazed under rest-rotation and continuous grazing. *J. Range Manage.* 27:447–449.

Rausch, R. A. 1959. Some aspects of population dynamics of the Railbelt moose populations, Alaska. Master's thesis, Univ. of Alaska, Fairbanks. 81 pp.

Reardon, P. O., L. B. Merrill, and C. A. Taylor, Jr. 1978. White-tailed deer preference and hunter success under various grazing systems. *J. Range Manage.* 31:40–42.

Redfield, J. A. 1974. Demography and genetics in colonizing populations of blue grouse (*Dendragapus obscurus*). *Evolution* 27:576–592.

Redfield, J. A., F. C. Zwickel, and J. F. Bendell. 1970. Effects of fire on numbers of blue grouse. *Proc. Ann. Tall Timbers Fire Ecol. Conf.* 10:63–83.

Redmond, H. R. 1953. Analysis of gray squirrel breeding studies and their relation to hunting season, gunning pressure, and habitat conditions. *Trans. N.A. Wildl. Conf.* 18:378–389.

Reeves, H. M. 1979. Estimates of reporting rates for mourning dove bands. *J. Wildl. Manage.* 43:36–42.

Regelin, W. L., O. C. Wallmo, J. Nagy, and D. R. Dietz. 1974. Effect of logging on forage values for deer in Colorado. *J. For.* 72:282–285.

Reichman, O. J. 1977. Optimization of diets through food preferences by heteromyid rodents. *Ecology* 58:454–457.

Reynolds, H. G. 1966a. *Use of openings in spruce-fir forests of Arizona by elk, deer and cattle.* USDA Forest Serv. Rocky Mtn. Forest and Range Expt. Stan. Res. Note No. 66. 7 pp.

———. 1966b. *Use of ponderosa pine forest in Arizona by deer, elk, and cattle.* USDA Forest Serv. Res. Note No. RM-63. 5 pp.

Reynolds, J. G., and J. W. Bohning. 1956. Effects of burning on a desert grass-shrub range in southern Arizona. *Ecology* 37:769–777.

Reynolds, T. D. and C. H. Trost. 1979. The effect of crested wheatgrass plantings on wildlife on the Idaho National Engineering Laboratory Site, pp. 665–666. *In* G. A. Swanson, tech. coord. 1979. *The mitigation symposium: a national workshop on mitigating habitat losses of fish and wildlife habitats.* USDA Forest Service Gen. Tech. Rept. RM-65. 696 pp.

Rice, L. A., and H. Lovrien. 1974. Analyses of mourning dove banding in South Dakota. *J. Wildl. Manage.* 38:743–750.

Ricker, W. E. 1954. Stock and recruitment. *J. Fish and Res. Board Canada* 11:559–623.

Ripley, T. H. 1973. A wildlifer looks at forest resource management. *J. For.* 71:405–406.

Risebrough, R. W., and D. W. Anderson. 1975. Some effects of DEE and PCB on mallards and their eggs. *J. Wildl. Manage.* 39:508–513.

Ritchie, B. W. 1978. *Ecology of moose in Fremont County, Idaho.* Idaho Dept. Fish and Game Wildl. Bull. No. 7. 33 pp.

Robbins, C. S. 1983. Wildlife feeding and nutrition. New York: Academic Press. 343 pp.

Robel, R. J., F. R. Henderson, and W. Jackson. 1972. Some sharp-tailed grouse population statistics from South Dakota. *J. Wildl. Manage.* 36:87–98.

Robinette, W. B., and O. A. Olsen. 1944. Studies of the productivity of mule deer in central Utah. *Trans. N.A. Wildl. Conf.* 9:156–161.

Robinson, W. B. 1961. Population changes of carnivores in some coyote control areas. *J. Mamm.* 42:510–515.

Robinson, W. B., and M. W. Cummings. 1951. *Movements of coyotes from and to Yellowstone National Park.* USDI Fish and Wildl. Serv. Spec. Sci., Rept. No. 11. 17 pp.

Robinson, W. L., and G. J. Smith. 1977. Observations on recently killed wolves in upper Michigan. *Wildl. Soc. Bull.* 5:25–26.

Rogers, L. 1976. Effects of mast and berry crop failures on survival, growth and reproductive success of black bears. *Trans. N.A. Wildl. Conf.* 41:431–438.

Romesburg, H. C. 1981. Wildlife science: gaining reliable knowledge. *J. Wildl. Manage.* 45:293–313.

Root, R. B. 1967. The niche exploitation pattern of the blue-gray gnatcatcher. *Ecol. Monogr.* 37:317–349.

Roseberry, J. L. 1979. Bobwhite population responses to exploitation: real and simulated. *J. Wildl. Manage.* 43:285–305.

Rosen, M. N., and A. I. Bischoff. 1950. The epidemiology of fowl cholera as it occurs in the wild. *Trans. N.A. Wildl. Conf.* 15:147–154.

Rosene, W. 1969. *The bobwhite quail, its life and management.* New Brunswick, N.J.: Rutgers Univ. Press. 418 pp.

Rosenzweig, M. L. 1973. Evolution of the predator isocline. *Evolution* 27:84–94.

——. 1974. On the evolution of habitat selection. In *Proc. 1st Inter. Congr. of Ecol: structure, functioning and management of ecosystems*, pp. 401–404. The Hague, Netherlands. 414 pp.

Ross, B. A., J. R. Bray, and W. H. Marshall. 1970. Effects of long-term deer exclusion on a *Pinus resinosa* forest in north-central Minnesota. *Ecology* 51:1088–1093.

Rost, G. R., and J. A. Bailey. 1979. Distribution of mule deer and elk in relation to roads. *J. Wildl. Manage.* 43:634–641.

Rouse, C. H. 1954. *Antelope and sheep fences.* Prelim. Rept. USDI Fish and Wildl. Serv., Lakeview, Oregon. 22 pp.

Rowe, V. K., and T. A. Hymas. 1954. Summary of toxicological information on 2,4-D and 2,4,5-T herbicides and an evaluation of the hazards to livestock associated with their use. *Am. J. Vet. Res.* 15:622–629.

Roy, L. C., and M. J. Dorrance. 1976. *Methods of investigating predation of domestic livestock.* Edmonton: Alberta Agriculture. 54 pp.

Ruggiero, L. F., and J. B. Whelan. 1976. A comparison of *in vitro* and *in vivo* feed digestibility by white-tailed deer. *J. Range Manage.* 29:82–83.

Ruos, J. L., and D. D. Dolton. 1977. *Mourning dove status report, 1975.* USDI Fish and Wildl. Serv., Spec. Rept. Wildl. No. 207. 27 pp.

Rusch, D. H., and L. B. Keith. 1971a. Seasonal and annual trends in numbers of Alberta ruffed grouse. *J. Wildl. Manage.* 35:803–822.

_____ . 1971b. Ruffed grouse–vegetation relationships in central Alberta. *J. Wildl. Manage.* 35:417–429.

Rusch. D. H., E. C. Meslow, P. D. Doerr, and L. B. Keith. 1972. Response of great horned owl populations to changing prey densities. *J. Wildl. Manage.* 36:282–296.

Ryman, N., R. Baccus, C. Reuterwall, and M. H. Smith. 1981. Effective population size, generation interval, and potential loss of genetic variability in game species under different hunting regimes. *Oikos* 36:257–266.

Salwasser, H., S. A. Hoel, and G. A. Ashcraft. 1978. Fawn production and survival in the North Kings River deer herd. *Calif. Fish and Game* 64:38–52.

Salyer, J. C., and F. G. Gillett. 1964. Federal refuges. In *Waterfowl tomorrow*, ed. J. B. Linduska, pp. 497–508. Washington, D.C.: U.S. Government Printing Office. 770 pp.

Sampson, F. W., and W. O. Nagel. 1948. *Controlling fox and coyote damage on the farm.* Missouri Cons. Comm. Bull. No. 18. Jefferson City, Mo.

Sargeant, A. B. 1972. Red fox spatial characteristics in relation to waterfowl predation. *J. Wildl. Manage.* 36:225–236.

Satterlund, D. R., and H. F. Haupt. 1970. The disposition of snow caught by conifer crowns. *Water Resour. Res.* 6:649–652.

Saunders, B. P., and J. C. Williamson. 1972. Moose movements from ear tag returns. In *Proc. 8th N.A. Moose Conf. and Workshop*, pp. 177–184.

Schemnitz, S. D. 1961. *Ecology of the scaled quail in the Oklahoma Panhandle.* Wildl. Monogr. No. 8. 47 pp.

Schilling, E. A. 1938. Management of white-tailed deer on the Pisgah National Game Preserve (summary of five-year study). *Trans. N.A. Wildl. Conf.* 3:248–260.

Schiue, C. J., R. M. Brown, and L. W. Rees. 1958. Aspen debarking with 2,4,5-T. *J. For.* 56:503–507.

Schladweiler, P., and D. R. Stevens. 1973. Reproduction of Shiras Moose in Montana. *J. Wildl. Manage.* 37:535–544.

Schlegel, M. 1976. Factors affecting calf elk survival in northcentral Idaho. A progress report. *Proc. Ann. Conf. West. Assn. State Game and Fish Comm.* 56:342–355.

Schneegas, E. R. 1975. National Forest nongame bird management. In *Proc. Symp. on Mgmt. of Forest and Range Habitats for Nongame Birds*, pp. 314–318. USDA Forest Serv. Gen. Tech. Rept. No. WO-1.

Schnell, J. H. 1968. The limiting effects of natural predation on experimental cotton rat populations. *J. Wildl. Manage.* 32:698–711.

Schoener, T. W. 1971. Theory of feeding strategies. *Ann. Rev. Ecol. and Syst.* 2:369–404.

_____ . 1974. Some methods for calculating competition coefficients from resource utilization spectra. *Amer. Nat.* 108:332–340.

Schroeder, M. H. 1970. Mourning dove production in a Kansas osage orange planting. *J. Wildl. Manage.* 34:344–348.

Schroeder, M. H., and D. L. Sturgis. 1975. The effect on the Brewer's sparrow of spraying big sagebrush. *J. Range Manage.* 28:294–297.

Schwartz, C. C., and J. E. Ellis. 1981. Feeding ecology and niche separation in some native and domestic ungulates of the Shortgrass prairie. *J. Appl. Ecol.* 18:343–353.

Schweitzer, A. 1923. *Kultur und ethik.* Munchen: Biederstein Verlag. 280 pp.

Sciple, G. W. 1953. *Avian botulism: information on earlier research.* USDI Fish and Wildl. Serv. Spec. Sci. Rept. Wildl. No. 23. 12 pp.

Scott, V. E. 1978. Characteristics of ponderosa pine snags used by cavity nesting birds in Arizona. *J. For.* 76:26–28.

Scott, V. E., K. E. Evans, D. R. Patton, and C. P. Stone. 1977. *Cavity nesting birds of North American forests.* USDA Agr. Handbook No. 511. 112 pp.

Scotter, G. W. 1964. *Effects of forest fires on the winter range of barren-ground caribou in northern Saskatchewan.* Canad. Wildl. Serv. Wildl. Manage. Bull. Ser. 1, No. 18. 111 pp.

Segelquist, C. A., and M. J. Rogers. 1975. Response of Japanese honeysuckle to fertilization. *J. Wildl. Manage.* 39:769–775.

Seidensticker, J. C., IV, M. G. Hornocker, W. V. Wiles, and J. P. Messick. 1973. *Mountain lion social organization in the Idaho Primitive Area.* Wildl. Monogr. No. 35. 60 pp.

Severinghaus, C. W. 1947. Relationship of weather to winter mortality and population levels among deer in the Adirondack region of New York. *Trans. N.A. Wildl. Conf.* 12:212–223.

Severson, K., M. May, and W. Hepworth. 1968. *Food preferences, carrying capacities and forage competition between antelope and domestic sheep in Wyoming's Red Desert.* Univ. of Wyoming Agr. Expt. Sta. Sci. Monogr. No. 10. 51 pp.

Shaw, H. G. 1962. Seasonal habitat use by white-tailed deer in the Hatter Creek enclosure. Master's thesis, Univ. of Idaho. 52 pp.

Shaw, W. R., and D. A. King. 1980. Wildlife management and nonhunting enthusiasts. *Trans. N.A. Wildl. and Nat. Res. Conf.* 45:219–225.

Shearer, L. A., and H. G. Uhlig. 1965. The use of stock-water dugouts by ducks. *J. Wildl. Manage.* 29:200–201.

Sheppard, D. H. 1971. Competition between two chipmunk species (Eutamias). *Ecology* 52:321–329.

Short, H. L. 1970. Digestibility trials: *in vivo* techniques. In *Range and Wildlife habitat evaluation,* ed. H. A. Paulsen, Jr., and E. H. Reid, pp. 79–84. USDA Forest Serv. Misc. Publ. No. 1147.

——. 1975. Nutrition of southern deer in different seasons. *J. Wildl. Manage.* 39:321–329.

Short, H. L., D. R. Dietz, and E. E. Remmenga. 1966. Selected nutrients in the mule deer browse plants. *Ecology* 47:222–229.

Short, H. L., W. Evans, and E. L. Boeker. 1977. The use of natural and modified pinyon-pine-juniper woodlands by deer and elk. *J. Wildl. Manage.* 41:543–559.

Siderits, K. 1974. Forest diversity: an approach to forest wildlife management. *Forestry Chronicle* 51 (3): 99–103.

Silliman, R. P., and J. S. Gutsell. 1958. Experimental exploitation of fish populations. USDI Fish and Wildl. Serv. Fish Bull. No. 58 (133): 214–252.

Silver, H., N. F. Colovos, J. B. Holter, and H. H. Hayes. 1969. Fasting metabolism of white-tailed deer. *J. Wildl. Manage.* 33:490–498.

Simkin, D. W. 1965. Reproduction and productivity of moose in northwestern Ontario. *J. Wildl. Manage.* 29:740–750.

——. 1974. Reproduction and productivity of moose. *Naturaliste Canadien* 101: 517–526.

Simmons, N. M., D. C. Heard, and G. W. Calef. 1979. Kaminuriak caribou herd: interjurisdictional management problems. *Tran. N.A. Wildl. and Nat. Res. Conf.* 44:102–113.

Singer, F. J. 1979. Habitat partitioning and wildfire relationships of cervids in Glacier National Park, Montana. *J. Wildl. Manage.* 43:437–444.

Singleton, J. R. 1951. Production and utilization of waterfowl food plants on the east Texas gulf coast. *J. Wildl. Manage.* 15:46–56.

Skovlin, J. M., P. J. Edgerton, and R. W. Harris. 1968. The influence of cattle management on deer and elk. *Trans. N.A. Wildl. and Nat. Res. Conf.* 33:169–181.

Smart, G. 1964. *Evaluation of the 10 percent penalty assesses for selecting split duck hunting seasons.* USDI Fish and Wildl. Serv. Admin. Rept. No. 67. 2 pp.

Smith, A. D., and D. D. Doell. 1968. *Guides to allocating forage between cattle and big game on big game winter range.* Utah State Div. of Fish and Game Publ. No. 68-11. 32 pp.

Smith, J. G., and O. Julander. 1953. Deer and sheep competition in Utah. *J. Wildl. Manage.* 17:101–112.

Smith, J. M., and M. Slatkin. 1973. The stability of predator-prey systems. *Ecology* 54:384–391.

Smith, M. A., and J. C. M. Malechek, and K. O. Fulgham. 1979. Forage selection by mule deer on winter range grazed by sheep in spring. *J. Range Manage.* 32:40–45.

Smith, M. H., H. O. Hillestad, M. N. Mantove, and R. L. Marchinton. 1976. Use of population genetics data for the management of fish and wildlife populations. *Trans. N.A. Wildl. and Nat. Res. Conf.* 41:119–133.

Smith, R. I., and A. D. Geis. 1961. *Pre-hunting season banding of mallards and black ducks.* USDI Fish and Wildl. Serv. Spec. Sci. Rept. Wildl. No. 60. 29 pp.

Smith, R. H. 1953. A study of waterfowl production on artificial reservoirs in eastern Montana. *J. Wildl. Manage.* 17:276–291.

Snyder, R. L., and J. J. Christian. 1960. Reproductive cycle and litter size of the woodchuck. *Ecology* 41:647–656.

Solomon, M. E. 1949. The natural control of animal population. *J. Anim. Ecol.* 18:1–35.

Sommerfeld, R. A., and E. LaChappelle. 1970. The classification of snow metamorphism. *J. Glaciology* 9:3–17.

Soutiere, E. C., 1979. Effects of timber harvesting on marten in Maine. *J. Wildl. Manage.* 43:850–860.

Spalding, D. J. 1966. Twinning in bighorn sheep. *J. Wildl. Manage.* 30:207.

Spellman, R. J. 1963. Legal aspects of hunting on public lands. *J. Range Manage.* 16:105–109.

Spencer, D. L., and J. B. Hakala. 1964. Moose and fire on the Kenai. *Proc. Ann. Tall Timbers Fire Ecol. Conf.* 3:10–33.

Stankey, G. H. 1976. *Wilderness fire policy: an investigation of visitor knowledge and beliefs.* USDA Forest Serv. Res. Pap. No. INT-180. 17 pp.

Steel, P. E., P. D. Dalke, and E. G. Bizeau. 1956. Duck production at Gray's Lake, Idaho, 1949–1951. *J. Wildl. Manage.* 20:279–285.

Stelfox, J. G. 1971. Bighorn sheep in the Canadian Rockies: a history 1800–1970. *Can. Field Nat.* 85:101–122.

Stendell, R. C., E. Cromartie, S. N. Wiemeyer, and J. R. Longcore. 1977. Organo-chlorine and mercury residues in canvasback duck eggs, 1972–1973. *J. Wildl. Manage.* 41 (3): 453–457.

Stenlund, M. H. 1955. *A field study of the timber wolf* (Canis lupus) *on the Superior National Forest, Minnesota.* Minn. Dept. Cons. Tech. Bull. No. 4. 55 pp.

Stevens, D. R. 1966. Range relationships of elk and livestock, Crow Creek drainage, Montana. *J. Wildl. Manage.* 30:349–363.

Stewart, R. E., and H. A. Kantrud. 1971. *Classification of natural ponds and lakes in the glaciated prairie region.* USDI Fish and Wildl. Serv. Res. Publ. No. 92. 57 pp.

――――. 1973. Ecological distribution of breeding waterfowl populations in North Dakota. *J. Wildl. Manage.* 37:39–50.

Stiven, A. E. 1961. Food energy available for and required by the blue grouse chick. *Ecology* 43:547–553.

Stoddard, H. L. 1963. *Maintenance and increase of the eastern wild turkey on private lands of the coastal plains of the deep southeast.* Tall Timbers Res. Sta. Bull. No. 3. 49 pp.

――――. 1931. *The bobwhite quail; its habits, preservation and increase.* New York: Scribner's. 559 pp.

――――. 1935. Use of controlled fire in southeastern upland game management. *J. For.* 33:346–351.

――――. 1956. Coordinated forestry, farming and wildlife programs for family-sized farms of the coastal plain of the deep southeast. In *Proc. Soc. of Am. Foresters, Memphis, Tenn.*, pp. 186–189.

Stoddart, L. A., A. D. Smith, and T. W. Box. 1975. *Range management.* 3rd ed. New York: McGraw-Hill. 532 pp.

Stoddart, L. C. 1970. A telemetric method for detecting jackrabbit mortality. *J. Wildl. Manage.* 34:501–507.

Stoddart, L. C., and R. D. Anderson. 1972. *Biomass density of lagomorphs.* U.S. Int. Biol. Prog. Curlew Valley Validation Site Rep. No. RM72-1. 188 pp.

Stokes, A. W. 1952. Pheasant survival studies on Pelee Island, Ontario, 1946–1950. *Trans. N.A. Wildl. Conf.* 17:285–293.

Stormer, F. A., C. M. Kirkpatrick, and T. W. Hockstra. 1979. Hunter inflicted wounding of white-tailed deer. *Wildl. Soc. Bull.* 7:10–16.

Stoudt, J. H. 1969. Relationships between waterfowl and water areas in the Redvers Waterfowl Study Area. In *Saskatoon Wetlands Seminar*, pp. 123–131. Canad. Wildl. Serv. Rept. Ser. No. 6.

Strickler, G. S. 1975. *DDT residue and accumulation and decline in kidney fat of lambs grazing sprayed forest range*. USDA Forest Serv. Res. Note No. PNW-256. 6 p.

Strout, I. J., and G. M. Cornwell. 1976. Nonhunting mortality of fledged N.A. waterfowl. *J. Wildl. Manage.* 40:681–693.

Sugden, L. G., and D. A. Benson. 1970. An evaluation of loafing rafts for attracting ducks. *J. Wildl. Manage.* 34:340–343.

Sullivan, T. P. 1979. Repopulation of clear-cut habitat and conifer seed predation by deer mice. *J. Wildl. Manage.* 43:861–871.

Svoboda, F. J., and G. W. Gullion. 1972. Preferential use of aspen by ruffed grouse in northern Minnesota. *J. Wildl. Manage.* 36:1166–1180.

Swain, A. M. 1973. A history of fire and vegetation in northeastern Minnesota as recorded in lake sediments. *Quat. Res.* 3:383–396.

Swank, W. G. 1955. Nesting and production of the mourning dove in Texas. *Ecology* 36:495–505.

Swift, R. W. 1948. Deer select most nutritious forages. *J. Wildl. Manage.* 12: 109–110.

Syroechkovskiy, E. E., and E. V. Rogacheva. 1974. Moose of the Asiatic part of the USSR. *Naturaliste Canadien* 101:595–604.

Szaro, R. C., and R. P. Balda. 1979. Effects of harvesting ponderosa pine on non-game bird populations. USDA Forest Service Res. Pap. RM-212. 8 pp.

Taber, R. D., and R. F. Dasmann. 1957. The dynamics of three natural populations of the deer *Odocoileus hemionus columbianus*. *Ecology* 38:233–246.

Tande, G. F. 1979. Fire history and vegetation pattern of coniferous forests in Jasper National Park, Alberta. *Canad. J. Bot.* 57:1912–1931.

Tanner, J. T. 1975. The stability and the intrinsic growth rates of prey and predator populations. *Ecology* 56:855–867.

Teer, J. G., J. W. Thomas, and E. A. Walker. 1965. *Ecology and management of white-tailed deer in the Llano Basin of Texas*. Wildl. Monogr. No. 15. 62 pp.

Telfer, E. S. 1967. Comparison of moose and deer winter range in Nova Scotia. *J. Wildl. Manage.* 31:418–425.

——. 1974. Logging as a factor in wildlife ecology in the boreal forest. *Forestry Chronicle.* 50:186–190.

Tester, J. R., and W. H. Marshall. 1962. Minnesota prairie management techniques and their wildlife implications. *Trans. N.A. Wildl. and Nat. Res. Conf.* 27:267–287.

Tevis, L., Jr. 1956a. Effect of a slash burn on forest mice. *J. Wildl. Manage.* 20: 405–409.

——. 1956b. Responses of small mammal populations to logging of Douglas-fir. *J. Mamm.* 37:189–196.

Thiessen, J. L. 1976. Some elk-logging relationships in southern Idaho. In *Proc. Elk-logging-Roads Symp., Univ. of Idaho*, pp. 3–5.

Thilenius, J. F., and K. E. Hungerford. 1967. Browse use by cattle and deer in northern Idaho. *J. Wildl. Manage.* 31:141–145.

Thomas, D. C. 1983. Age-specific fertility of female Columbian black-tailed deer. *J. Wildl. Manage.* 47:501–506.

Thomas, J. W., R. J. Miller, H. Black, J. E. Rodiek, and C. Moser. 1976. Guildelines for maintaining and enhancing wildlife habitat in forest management in the Blue Mountains of Oregon and Washington. *Trans. N.A. Wildl. and Nat. Res. Conf.* 41:452–476.

Thompson, D. H., and J. Jedlicka. 1948. A method for correcting kill estimates from waterfowl banded during the hunting season. *J. Wildl. Manage.* 12:433–436.

Thompson, D. Q. 1965. Food preferences of the meadow vole (*Microtus pennsylvanicus*) in relation to habitat affinities. *Am. Midl. Nat.* 74:76–86.

Thompson, L. S. 1978. Species abundance and habitat relations of an insular montane avifauna. *Condor* 80:1–14.

Tierson, W. C., E. F. Patric, and D. F. Behrend. 1966. Influence of white-tailed deer on the logged northern hardwood forest. *J. For.* 64:801–805.

Tietje, W. D., and R. L. Ruff. 1980. Denning behavior of black bears in boreal forests of Alberta. *J. Wildl. Manage.* 44:858–870.

Tigner, J. R., and G. E. Larson. 1977. Sheep losses on selected ranches in southern Wyoming. *J. Range Manage.* 32:317–321.

Tilley, J. M., and R. A. Terry. 1963. A two-stage technique for *in vitro* digestion of forage crops. *J. Brit. Grassl. Soc.* 18:104–111.

Timmerman, H. R. 1975. Discrepancies in moose harvest data. *In Proc. 11th N.A. Moose Conf. and Workshop*, pp. 501–520.

Torgerson, O., and W. H. Pfander. 1971. Cellulose digestibility and chemical composition of Missouri deer foods. *J. Wildl. Manage.* 35:221–231.

Trainer, C. E. 1971. An investigation concerning the fertility of female Roosevelt elk in Oregon. *Proc. Ann. Conf. West. Assn. State Game and Fish Comm.* 51 (Aspen, Colo.): 378–385.

Trainer, C. E., and W. C. Lightfoot. 1970. Fertility of yearling male Roosevelt elk in Oregon. *Proc. Ann. Conf. West. Assn. State Game and Fish Comm.* 50 (Victoria, B.C.): 311–317.

Trainer, C. E. 1975. Direct causes of mortality in mule deer fawns during summer and winter periods on Steens Mountain, Oregon—a progress report. *Proc. Ann. Conf. West. Assn. State Game and Fish Comm.* 55:163–170.

Trautman, C. G., L. F. Fredrickson, and A. V. Carter. 1974. Relationship of red foxes and other predators to populations of ring-necked pheasants and other prey, South Dakota. *Trans. N.A. Wild. Nat. Res. Conf.* 39:241–252.

Uhlig, H. G. 1956. Effect of legal restrictions on hunting and gray squirrel populations in West Virginia. *Trans. N.A. Wildl. Conf.* 21:330–338.

Ullrey, D. E., W. G. Youatt, H. E. Johnson, L. D. Fay, and B. E. Brent. 1967. Digestibility of cedar and jack pine browse for the white-tailed deer. *J. Wildl. Manage.* 31:448–454.

Ullrey, D. E., W. G. Youatt, H. E. Johnson, P. K. Ku, and L. D. Fay. 1964. Digestibility of cedar and aspen browse for the white-tailed deer. *J. Wildl. Manage.* 28:791–797.

USDA Forest Service, 1972. *The nation's range resources.* USDA Forest Serv. Forest Res. Rept. No. 19. 147 pp.

U.S. Dept. of the Interior. 1982. *National survey of fishing, hunting, and wildlife associated recreation.* Washington, D.C.: U.S. Gov. Printing Office.

U.S. Fish and Wildlife Service. 1975. *Draft environmental statement issuance of annual regulations permitting the sport hunting of migratory birds.* Washington, D.C.: USDI Fish and Wildlife Service. 312 pp. and appendices.

_____ . 1976. *Final environmental statement operation of the National Wildlife Refuge System.* Washington: D.C. USDI Fish and Wildlife Service.

_____ . 1977a. *1975 national survey of hunting, fishing, and wildlife-associated recreation.* Washington, D.C.: USDI Fish and Wildlife Service. 91 pp.

_____ . 1977b. *Environmental assessment proposal for continuation of September hunting of mourning doves.* Washington, D.C.: U.S. Dept. Interior. 42 pp.

_____ . 1980. *Whooping crane recovery plan.* Washington, D.C.: USDI Fish and Wildlife Service. 206 pp.

U.S. Senate. 1967. Hearings before a subcommittee of the Committee on Appropriations, U.S. Senate, 90th Congress, First Session, on control of elk populations, Yellowstone National Park. 142 pp.

Uresk, D. W., D. R. Dietz, and H. F. Messner. 1975. Constituents of *in vitro* solution contribute differently to dry matter digestibility of deer food species. *J. Range Manage.* 28:419–421.

Uresk, D. W., W. H. Rickard, and J. F. Clint. 1980. Perennial grasses and their response to a wildfire in southcentral Washington. *J. Range Manage.* 33:111–114.

Urness, P. J., D. J. Neff, and R. K. Watkins. 1975. *Nutritive value of mule deer forages on ponderosa pine summer range in Arizona.* USDA Forest Serv. Res. Note No. RM-304. 6 pp.

Usher, M. B. 1972. Developments in the Leslie matrix model. In *Mathematical models in ecology*, ed. J. N. R. Jeffers, pp. 29–60. London: Blackwell Scientific Publications.

Vale, T. R. 1975. Presettlement vegetation in the sagebrush-grass area of the intermountain wash. *J. Range Manage.* 28:32–36.

Van Ballenberghe, V., A. W. Erickson, and D. Bynam. 1975. *Ecology of the timber wolf in northeastern Minnesota.* Wildl. Monogr. No. 43. 44 pp.

Van Gilder, L. D., O. Torgerson, and W. R. Porath. 1982. Factors influencing diet selection by white-tailed deer. *J. Wildl. Manage.* 46:711–718.

Vaughan, M. R., and L. B. Keith. 1981. Demographic response of experimental snowshoe hare populations to overwinter food shortage. *J. Wildl. Manage.* 45:354–380.

Verme, L. J. 1961. Late breeding in northern Michigan deer. *J. Mamm.* 42:426–427.

_____ . 1965. Swamp conifer deer yards in northern Michigan: their ecology and management. *J. For.* 63:523–529.

_____ . 1968. An index of winter weather severity for northern deer. *J. Wildl. Manage.* 32:566–574.

Verme, L. J., and J. J. Ozoga. 1971. Influence of winter weather on white-tailed deer in upper Michigan. In *Proc. Snow and Ice in Relation to Wildlife and Recreation Symp.* Iowa State Univ., Ames., pp. 16–28.

Vogl, R. J. 1967. Controlled burning for wildlife in Wisconsin. *Proc. Ann. Tall Timbers Fire Ecol. Conf.* 6:47–96.

_____ . 1974. Effects of fire on grasslands. In *Fire and Ecosystems*, ed. T. T. Kozlowski, and C. E. Ahlgren, pp. 139–194. New York: Academic Press.

Vogl, R. J., and A. M. Beck. 1970. Response of white-tailed deer to a Wisconsin wildfire. *Am. Midl. Nat.* 84:269–272.

Wagner, F. H. 1969. Ecosystem concepts in fish and game measurement. In *The ecosystem concept in natural resource management*, ed. G. M. Van Dyne, pp 259–307. New York: Academic Press.

Wagner, F. H., C. D. Besadny, and C. Kabat. 1965. *Population ecology and management of Wisconsin pheasants.* Wisconsin Dept. Nat. Res. Tech. Bull. No. 34. 168 pp.

Wagner, F. H., and L. C. Stoddart. 1972. Influence of coyote predation on black-tailed jack rabbits in Utah. *J. Wildl. Manage.* 36:329–342.

Wainwright, L. C. 1969. *A literature review on cottontail reproduction.* Colo. Div. Game, Fish and Parks. Spec. Rept. No. 19. 24 pp.

Wallestad, R. 1975. Male sage grouse responses to sagebrush treatment. *J. Wildl. Manage.* 39:482–484.

Wallestad, R., and D. Pyrah. 1974. Movement and nesting of sage grouse hens in central Montana. *J. Wildl. Manage.* 38:630–633.

Wallestad, R., and P. Schladweiler. 1974. Breeding season movements and habitat selection of male sage grouse. *J. Wildl. Manage.* 38:634–637.

Wallmo, O. C. 1969. *Response of deer to alternate-strip clearcutting of lodgepole pine and spruce-fir timber in Colorado.* USDA Forest Serv. Res. Note No. RM-141. 4 pp.

Wallmo, O. C., W. L. Regelin, and D. W. Reichert. 1972. Forage use by mule deer relative to logging in Colorado. *J. Wildl. Manage.* 36:1025–1033.

Walters, C. J., and J. E. Gross. 1972. Development of big game management plans through simulation modeling. *J. Wildl. Manage.* 36:119–128.

Ward, A. L. 1976. Elk behavior in relation to timber harvest operations and traffic on the Medicine Bow Range in south-central Wyoming. In *Proc. Elk-Logging-Roads Symp., Univ. of Idaho.,* pp. 32–43.

Ward, P. 1968. Fire in relation to waterfowl habitat of the Delta marshes. *Proc. Ann. Tall Timbers Fire Ecol. Conf.* 8:255–267.

Watt, K. E. F. 1968. *Ecology and resource management.* New York: McGraw-Hill, 450 pp.

Way, J. M. 1974. The environmental consequences of herbicide use. In *Proc. 12th Brit. Weed Control Conf.,* pp. 925–928.

Weaver, H. 1951. Fire as an ecological factor in the southwestern ponderosa pine forests. *J. For.* 49:93–98.

———. 1968. Fire and its relationships to ponderosa pine. *Proc. Ann. Tall Timbers Fire Ecol. Conf.* 7:127–149.

Webb, W. L., D. F. Behrend, and B. Saisorn. 1977. *Effect of logging on songbird populations in a northern hardwood forest.* Wildl. Monogr. No. 55. 35 pp.

Wecker, S. C. 1964. Habitat selection. *Sci. Am.* 211 (pt. 2): 109–116.

Weigand, J. P. 1980. Ecology of the Hungarian partridge in north-central Montana. Wildl. Monogr. 74. 106 pp.

Weller, M. W. 1965. Chronology of pair formation in some of the neoarctic Aythya (Anatidae). *Auk* 82:227–235.

Wells, R. W. 1968. *Fire at Peshtigo.* Englewood Cliffs, N.J.: Prentice-Hall, Inc., 243 pp.

Westoby, M. 1974. An analysis of diet selection by large generalist herbivores. *Amer. Nat.* 108:290–304.

———. 1980. Black-tailed jackrabbit diets in Curlew Valley, northern Utah. *J. Wild. Manage.* 44:942–947.

Westoby, M., and F. H. Wagner. 1973. Use of a crested wheatgrass seeding by blacktailed jackrabbits. *J. Range Manage.* 26 (5): 349–352.

Wetzel, J. F. 1972. Winter food habits and habitat preference of deer in northeastern Minnesota. Master's thesis, Univ. of Minnesota. 106 pp.

Wetzel, J. F., J. R. Wambaugh, and J. M. Peek. 1975. Appraisal of white-tailed deer winter habits in northeastern Minnesota. *J. Wildl. Manage.* 39:59–66.

White, L., Jr. 1967. The historical roots of our ecologic crisis. *Science* 155: 1203–1207.

Whittaker, R. H., S. A. Levin, and R. B. Root. 1973. Niche, habitat and ecotype. *Amer. Nat.* 107 (955): 321–338.

Wiens, J. A. 1973. Pattern and process in grassland bird communities. *Ecol. Monogr.* 43:237–270.

———. 1977. On competition and variable environments. *Am. Sci.* 65:590–597.

Wight, H. 1959. Eleven years of rabbit-population data in Missouri. *J. Wildl. Manage.* 23:34–39.

Wilbert, D. E. 1963. Some effects of chemical sagebrush control on elk distribution. *J. Range Manage.* 16:74–78.

Wildlife Society, The. 1982. *Conservation policies of the Wildlife Society.* Washington, D.C. 23 pp.

Will, G. C. 1973. Population characteristics of northern Idaho white-tailed deer, 1969–1971. *NW Sci.* 47:114–122.

Willey, C. H. 1971. *Vulnerability of Vermont's black bear population.* NE Fish and Wildl. Conf., Portland, Maine, May 25, 1971. 40 pp.

Williams, C. E., and A. L. Caskey. 1965. Soil fertility and cottontail fecundity in southeastern Missouri. *Am. Midl. Nat.* 74:211–224.

Williams, C. S., and W. H. Marshall. 1938. Duck nesting studies, Bear River Migratory Bird Refuge, Utah, 1937. *J. Wildl. Manage.* 2:29–48.

Williams, C. S., and C. A. Sooter. 1940. Canada goose habitats in Utah and Oregon. *Trans. N.A. Wildl. Conf.* 5:383–387.

Willms, W., A. McLean, R. Tucker, and R. Ritcey. 1979. Interactions between mule deer and cattle on big sagebrush range in British Columbia. *J. Range Manage.* 32:299–304.

Willson, M. F. 1974. Avian community organization and habitat structure. *Ecology* 55:1017–1029.

Wilson, E. O. 1975. *Sociobiology, the new synthesis.* Cambridge, Mass. Harvard Univ. Press. 697 pp.

Wilson, E. O., and W. H. Bossert. 1971. *A primer of population biology.* Sinauer Associates. Sunderland, Mass.: 192 pp.

Windberg, L. A., and L. B. Keith. 1976. Snowshoe hare population response to artificial high densities. *J. Mamm.* 57:523–553.

Witter, D. J., and W. W. Shaw. 1979. Beliefs of birders, hunting and wildlife professionals about wildlife management. *Trans. N.A. Wildl. and Nat. Res. Conf.* 44:298–305.

Wittinger, W. T., W. L. Pengelly, L. L. Irwin and J. M. Peek. 1977. A 20-year record of shrub succession in logged areas in the cedar-hemlock zone of northern Idaho. *NW Science* 31:161–171.

Wolfe, M. L., Jr. 1970. The history of German game administration. *Forest History* 14:7–16.

_____ . 1977. Mortality patterns in the Isle Royale moose population. *Am. Midl. Nat.* 97:267–279.

Wolff, J. O. 1980. The role of habitat patchiness in the population dynamics of snowshoe hares. *Ecol. Monogr.* 50:111–130.

Wolff, J. O., and J. C. Zazada. 1975. *Red squirrel response to clearcut and shelterwood systems in interior Alaska.* USDA Forest Serv. Res. Note No. PNW-255. 7 pp.

Woodwell, G. M. 1967. Toxic substances and ecological cycles. *Sci. Am.* 216 (3): 24–31.

Woodwell, G. M., C. F. Wurster, Jr., and P. A. Isaacson. 1967. DDT residues in an east coast estuary: a case of biological concentration of a persistent pesticide. *Science* 156:821–824.

Wright, H. A. 1973. Fire as a tool to manage tobosa grasslands. *Proc. Ann. Tall Timbers Fire Ecol. Conf.* 12:153–167.

Wright, H. A., L. F. Neuenschwander, and C. M. Britton. 1979. *The role and use of fire in sagebrush-grass and pinyon-juniper plant communities.* USDA Forest Serv. Gen. Tech. Rept. No. INT-58. 48 pp.

Wright, H. E. 1974. Landscape development, forest fires, and wilderness management. *Science* 186:487–495.

Young, J. A., and R. A. Evans. 1978. Population dynamics after wildfire in sagebrush grasslands. *J. Range Manage.* 31:283–289.

Young, V. A., and G. F. Payne. 1948. Utilization of "key" browse species in relation to proper grazing practices in cutover western white pine lands in northern Idaho. *J. For.* 46:35–49.

Young, V. A., and W. L. Robinette. 1939. *A study of the range habits of elk on the Selway Game Preserve.* Univ. of Idaho Bull. No. 34. 48 pp.

Zackrisson, O. 1977. Influence of forest fires on the north Swedish boreal forest. *Oikos* 29:22–32.

Zedler, J., and O. L. Loucks. 1969. Differential burning response of *Poa preatensis* fields and *Andropogon scoparius* prairies in central Wisconsin. *Am. Midl. Nat.* 81:341–352.

Zepp, R. L., Jr., and R. L. Kirkpatrick. 1976. Reproduction in cottontails fed diets containing a PCB. *J. Wildl. Manage.* 40:491–495.

Zielinski, W. L., Jr., and L. Fishbein. 1967. Gas chromatographic measurement of disappearance rates of 2,4-D and 2,4,5-T acids and 2,4-D esters in mice. *J. Agr. and Food Chem.* 15:841–844.

Zwickel, F. C. 1972. Some effects of grazing on blue grouse during summer. *J. Wildl. Manage.* 36:631–634.

Zwickel, F. C., J. A. Redfield, and J. Kristensen. 1977. Demography, behavior, and genetics of a colonizing population of blue grouse. *Canad. J. Zool.* 55:1945–1957.

# Index